BULGARIA

Kárdžali

Edirne

MACEDONIA AND THRACE

Xánthi   Komotiní

TURKEY

Keşan

İstanbul

Marmara Denizi

Kavála

Liménas

Thássos

Alexandroúpoli

Kavakköy

Strymonikós Kólpos

Samothráki

Ierissos

Áthos 2033

Fengári 1611

Thrakikón Pélagos

Thermá (Loutrá)

Gökçeada

Bandırma

Bursa

Sithonía

Çanakkale

Abide

Mýrina

Límnos

Ágios Evstrátios

Kyrá Panagiá   Gioúra

Pipéri

THE NORTHEAST AEGEAN

Mólyvos

WITHDRAWN

Balıkesir

Edremit

Ayvacık

TURKEY

Sporádes

Alónissos

Mitilíni

Lésvos

Plomári

Kými

Skýros

DES AND VIA

Skyros

Akhisar

Paralía Kýmis

A E G E A N   S E A

Psará

Híos

Híos

AND Í

Karystos

Pýrgi

Çeşme

Urla

İzmir

Ándros

Ándros

Kéa

Giáros

THE GULF

Kýthnos

Ermoúpoli   Síros

Tínos

Tínos

Mýkonos

Karlóvassi

Súmos

Vathý (Sámos)

Ikaría

Ág. Kírykos

Foúrni

Agathónisi

Aydın

Milás

Muğla

Sérifos

Paros

Páros

Naxos

Náxos

Pátmos

Arkí

Lipsí

Léros

Bodrum

THE CYCLADES

Sífnos

Kímolos

Andíparos

Síkinos

Íos

Amorgós

Kálymnos

Kós   Kós

Kófalos

Bodrum

Milos

Folégandros

Astypálea

Anáfi

Santoríni (Thíra)

Sýrna

THE DODECANESE

D o d e c a n e s e

Tílos

Hálki

Ródos

Mt Atávyros 1215

RHODES

Líndos

Ródos (Rhodes)

Kárpathos

Krítikó Pélagos

Kásos

CRETE

Haniá

Réthymno (Rethimno)

Iráklio (Heráklion)

Kríti (Crete)

Samariá Gorge

Arkádi

Plakiás

Ida (Psiloritis) 2456

Knossos

Ágios Nikólaos

Sitía

2452

Hóra Sfakíon

Ag. Galíni

Zakros

Ierapetra

Gávdos

INSIGHT GUIDES

GREECE

APA PUBLICATIONS L

Part of the Langenscheidt Publishing Group

The first Insight Guide pioneered the use of creative full-colour photography in travel guides in 1970. Since then, we have expanded our range to cater to our readers' need not only for reliable information about their chosen destination but also for a real understanding of the culture and workings of that destination. Now, when the internet can supply inexhaustible (but not always reliable) facts, our books marry text and pictures to provide those much more elusive qualities: knowledge and discernment. To achieve this, they rely heavily on the authority of locally based writers and photographers.

How to use this book

Insight Guide: Greece is structured to convey an understanding of the country and its people as well as to guide readers through its attractions:

The **Best of Greece** section at the front of the guide helps you to prioritise what you want to do.

The **Features** section, indicated by a pink bar at the top of each page, covers the historical and cultural background of the country, including illuminating essays on the religions, architectural traditions and outdoor adventures to be found in Greece.

The main **Places** section, indicated by a blue bar, is a complete guide to all the sights and areas worth visiting. Places of special interest are coordinated by number with the maps. Margin notes provide background information and tips on special places and events.

The **Travel Tips** listings section, with a yellow bar, provides full information on transport, hotels, places to eat, activities from shopping to sports, an A–Z section of essential practical information and a guide to the language.

A special section of photographic features showcases what makes Greece unique; from its religious festivals and flora to the treasure trove that is the National Archaeological Museum.

Photographs are chosen not only to illustrate the landscape and buildings, but also to convey the moods of the country and the life of its people.

The contributors

This thoroughly updated edition was managed by **Carine Tracanelli** and copy-edited by **Siân Lezard**.

Marc Dubin, a well-travelled Londoner who has a house in Sámos, was the main updater for this new edition. As well as thoroughly revising the Features chapters, Dubin also wrote the brand new essay on Coping with the Economic Crisis. The chapters on Thessaloníki, Macedonia and Thrace as well as the Ionian Islands were updated by fellow Greek expert **Nick Edwards**.

This version builds on the invaluable work of earlier editors and writers including: **Maria Lord, Jeffrey Pike, Professor Richard Clogg, Dr David Sutton, Professor Gail Holst-Warhaft, Aglaia Kremezi, Dr John Lord, Danny Aeberhard, John Chapple, Lance Chilton, Paul Hellander** and **Jeffrey Carson**.

The stunning photographs in this latest edition are the output of Insight regulars **Britta Jaschinski, Glyn Genin** and **Richard Nowitz**. The book was proofread by **Darren Longley**.

Map Legend

— ·· —	International Boundary
——	Regional Boundary
— — — —	Province Boundary
— · —	National Park/Reserve
– – – –	Ferry Route
⊖	Border Crossing
✈ ✈	Airport: International/Regional
🚌	Bus Station
Ⓜ	Metro
❶	Tourist Information
∴	Archaeological Site
✝ ✝ ✝	Church/Ruins
✝	Monastry
☾	Mosque
✡	Synagogue
♨	Cave
𝟏	Statue/Monument
★	Place of Interest
⌐	Beach
⁑	Lighthouse
▟ ▦	Castle (ruins)
☀	Viewpoint

The main places of interest in the Places section are coordinated by number with a full-colour map (eg ❶), and a symbol at the top of every right-hand page tells you where to find the map.

Contents

THE BEST OF GREECE: TOP ATTRACTIONS

From ancient sites steeped in history and sun-bleached islands or cool mountain villages to Venetian forts and cliffside monasteries.

△ **The Parthenon, Athens.** Although still partly covered in scaffolding and studded with cranes, this treasure of the Classical city never fails to impress. See page 141.

△ **Kérkyra Old Town, Corfu.** Venetian flair, domesticity and town planning at the far end of the Adriatic, bracketed by two imposing castles with eye-popping views. See page 323.

△ **Haniá Venetian quarter.** Touristy and plenty of touts, yet exquisite and unbeatable for strolling, popping into small museums, in old buildings or just having a drink. See page 268.

◁ **Metéora, Thessaly.** Half-a-dozen-plus frescoed monasteries and convents perch bizarrely on sheer rock pinnacles in the Píndos foothills. See page 190.

△ **Zagorohória.** Two score or so of handsome, stone-built villages in the shadow of lofty Mount Gamíla, with top-notch lodging and all adventure sports to hand in the canyons nearby. See page 201.

▷ **Mt Pílio (Pelion).** The surprise of mainland Greece, with dense forests, cobbled hiking paths, tottering old villages and Caribbean-quality beaches all in one package. See page 189.

◁ **Delphi Sanctuary.** With its striking setting at the base of Mount Parnassós, the ancients reckoned this oracle the centre of the world. See page 183.

△ **Ýdra port town.** No cars, meticulously preserved architecture, cool marble flagstones under foot and compulsive people-watching make this a winner. See page 235.

◁ **Mystrás.** At the base of Mount Taýgettos, the capital of the Morea Despotate – with frescoed palaces and monasteries – saw out the Byzantine twilight until 1460. See page 171.

▽ **Santoríni caldera view.** Commercialised to within an inch of its life but still a must-see, especially at sunset or sunrise from a bar terrace in Firostefáni, Fira or Ía. See page 254.

THE BEST OF GREECE: EDITOR'S CHOICE

Blonde crescent beaches, stunning monasteries, a castle or two, hikes through river gorges, food, music and folklore – here, at a glance, are our recommendations to help you plan your journey.

Byzantine mosaic inside Ósios Loukás monastery, Híos.

BEST MONASTERIES

Ósios Loukás monastery. Some of the best 11th-century mosaics on view in Greece. See page 183.
Néa Moní monastery. And the rest of the best 11th-century mosaics are here, on the distant island of Híos. See page 307.

Hozoviótissa monastery. The setting on Amorgós intrigued Le Corbusier on his 1911 visit. See page 254.
Loúsios gorge monasteries. Several cliffside eyries with gorgeous medieval frescoes. See page 169.
Panagía Parigorítissa, Árta. Fine dome mosaic and Renaissance-influenced architecture. See page 197.
Hóra and Monastery of St John, Pátmos. When the cruise-ship groups have left, enjoy this stunningly atmospheric hilltop village set around a labyrinthine monastery. See page 293.

The improbably perched Hozoviótissa monastery, Amorgós.

BEST CASTLES

Acrocorinth, Peloponnese. A soaring rock with an ancient acropolis stippled with Ottoman monuments, wrapped in Byzantine, Frankish and Venetian walls. See page 163.
Methóni, Peloponnese. Venetian stronghold and way-station for pilgrims, with a moat, gates, and a causeway to the remote Boúrtzi tower. See page 176.
Palamídi, Návplio. Venetian citadel critical in the War of Independence and reached via hundreds of steps. See page 166.
Knights of St John Castle, Kós Town. Well preserved, easy to visit example of the crusading order's Dodecanese strongholds. See page 289.

The watchtower at Methóni castle, surrounded by the sea.

Mólyvos, Lesvos. Medieval castle with great views over town and to Turkey. See page 303.
Monemvasiá, Peloponnese. First a Byzantine, later a Venetian, stronghold washed by the sea on three sides, and its lower town still inhabited. See page 172.

Hiking through the pristine Víkos Gorge, Zagória.

BEST BEACHES

Karavostási. The best on the Epirot coast, with views to Corfu and thick fluffy sand. See page 195.

Símos, Elafoníssi. Really broad sands at the easternmost tip of the Peloponnese. See page 269.

Hrysí (Gaïdouronísi) islet. Enact Crusoe fantasies on this day-trip islet reached from Ierápetra. See page 265.

Seïtáni beaches. Small pebble beaches and huge sandy bays are monk-seal refuges on Sámos. See page 311.

Levkáda, southwest coast Pórto Katsíki, Egremni and Gialós. Fabulous beaches all in a row. See page 330.

Velanió. Cleanest, longest, nudest beach on Skópelos. See page 317.

Stunning Pórto Katsíki beach, Levkáda.

BEST HIKES

Northern Kárpathos. A maintained network of trails links local settlements – the route from Trístomo to Diafáni is the most stunning. See page 282.

Ascent of Mt Ólympos, Macedonia. Challenging climb of Greece's highest point, and home of the ancient gods. See page 218.

Hiking in the Píndos, Epirus. From day walks to five-day hiking loops, the North Píndos offers fabulous scenery for the adventurous. See page 204.

Víkos Gorge, Zagóri. Beats Crete's Samarian Gorge for its unspoilt, riverine environment and the height of its cliffs. See page 201.

Dimosári Gorge, southern Évvia. Another canyon walk, mostly along an old and shady cobbled trail, emerging at a beach hamlet where pickup transport should be arranged. See page 321.

Mount Áthos, southern tip. The route through the "hermit's desert", between Megístis Lávras and Osíou Grigoríou monasteries on the Holy Mountain, will hopefully survive the bulldozers. See page 221.

Mount Pílio trails. Partly cobbled paths, from Xouríhti to Kalá Nerá via Miliés, descend from forested glades to seaside olive groves. See page 189.

Egiáli to Hóra, Amorgós. Trekkers come to this island specially for this spectacular five-hour traverse with the sea on both sides. See page 254.

BEST OLD TOWNS AND VILLAGES

Mastic villages, Híos. Fortified settlements with gates, arcaded passageways, keep-towers and sombre-hued houses. See page 305.

Rhodes Old Town. Among the best preserved medieval townscapes in the Mediterranean, a legacy of the crusading Knights of St John and the Ottomans. See page 273.

Tower-house villages, the Máni. Stone-built mini-fortresses pierce the sky in the Peloponnese's extreme, wild south cape. See page 173.

Réthymno Old Town. A delightful confection of Venetian and Ottoman architecture, overawed by a huge fortress. See page 266.

Thessaloníki upper town. Surrounded by massive walls and crammed full of old houses and places to eat. See page 212.

The medieval Street of the Knights, Rhodes Old Town.

12

BEST WINES

Límnos, Ároma Ínou Drýinos. Oak-aged, smokey-dry white.
Sámos, Samos Nectar or Anthemis. Best in a series of fortified, muscat-based dessert wines.
Thessaly/Macedonia border, Tsantali Rapsáni. Easy-drinking red from foot hills of Mt Ólympos.
Lésvos, Methymneos red. Velvety red born of a volcanic terrain.
Epirus, Zítsa Cooperative white wines. Reliably light, dry, semi-sparkling.
Dráma region, Château Lazaridi. Red or white high-quality blends.
Neméa, Ktima Papaïoannou. Rich dark red, a medium-priced taverna staple.

Grapes for easy-drinking wines.

BEST MUSEUMS

Acropolis Museum, Athens. Though functionally designed, it does justice to its extraordinary exhibits. See page 142.
Sámos Archaeological Museum, Vathý. One of the country's best collections of the Archaic era, with exquisite small objects from the Hera sanctuary, culminating in an enormous kouros (statue of a man). See page 310.
Theophilos and Theriade Museums, Variá, Lésvos. Two galleries in an olive grove: the first with over 50 works by naïve local artist Theophilos (1873–1934); the second, a fine modern art collection amassed by Theriade, Theophilos' patron. See page 303.
Asian Art Museum, Corfu. Highly eclectic but never less than top-drawer collection assembled by two keen Greek diplomats – everything from Gandhara reliefs to Chinese vases. See page 325.
Benáki Museum, Athens. Arguably Athens' best museum, spanning the whole of Greek history. See page 151.
Delphi Museum. The best of everything supplicants brought to the oracle here, in revamped premises. See page 185.
Olympia Museum. Superb statuary and a fine collection of Archaic bronzes make this a must. See page 178.

Fascinating finds at the Acropolis Museum.

OFF THE BEATEN TRACK

Préspa Lakes, west Macedonia. Eerily scenic upland basin on the borders with Macedonia and Albania, with sleepy villages and good birdwatching. See page 216.
Mathráki. Most vegetated but depopulated of the isolated Diapóndia islets northwest of Corfu, with a fine, long beach and basic facilities. See page 327.
Mt Smólikas. Greece's second highest mountain range, separating Epirus and Macedonia, with two small lakes and excellent hiking. See page 204.
Néda Gorge, Peloponnese. From the modern village of Figalía, below the temple of Vassae, a track threads through ancient Phigaleia to the River Néda where it thunders underground. See page 170.
Gomáti dunes, Límnos. Protected environment in the far north of the island with shallow waters, September sea lilies… and a proliferation of sun-loungers. See page 300.

Hellenic Festival performance at Herod Atticus theatre.

The sandy Gomáti dunes, Límnos.

BEST LOCAL SPECIALITIES

Pickled caper greens, Níssyros, Léros, Angístri. The "national shrub" of these islands gets the vinegar treatment, thorns and all.
Soumáda, Levkáda. A white syrup from bitter almonds, drunk diluted with cold water – this island's is the best.
Lakérda, Aegean-wide. Bonito fillet slices soaked, pressed, then cured in salt – the finest oúzo partner.
Tsípouro, Thessaly or Sporades. If you find oúzo too cloying, try this clean grape-mash spirit.
Kalatháki féta, Límnos. Small drum-shaped sheep-milk cheese.
Genuine thyme honey. Bare islands like Kálymnos make for the purest honey – dark and strongly aromatic.
Tsitsiravla, Pílio or Sporades. Pickled wild pistachio shoots, gathered in spring, are good on their own or as a salad topping.

BEST FESTIVALS

See page 392 of Travel Tips.
Hellenic (Athens) Festival. Going for well over half a century now, with big-name international artists from June to August. Most performances at Herodeio and Epidauros theatres.
Pátra Carnival. The liveliest and most organised of Greece's pre-Lenten events: floats, outrageous costumes and parades.
Easter on Ýdra or Corfu. Fishermen at Ýdra carry the Epitáfios (shrine) into the water to bless the boats and ensure calm seas; on Corfu, brass bands leave not a dry eye with their funeral hymns, and showers of old crockery thrown from windows bring luck.
Thessaloníki Film Festival. This star-studded November event, premiering both Greek and foreign works, is one of the most prestigious in Europe.
Levkáda International Folklore Festival. The largest folk-dance festival in Greece, with troupes from all over the world. Last full week of August.
Sani Festival. The best provincial mainland festival, July–August, with jazz, classical and world acts.

Fun in the water, Benítses.

Rustic tavern, Crete.

A traditional Greek Orthodox wedding on the island of Síkinos.

The Church of Christ, a Skópelos landmark.

AN ANCIENT STORY

A heady mix of sun, sea and ancient sites bathed in brilliant Aegean light, Greece has enchanted travellers for centuries.

Minoan fresco, Crete.

Modern Greece, which emerged during the 19th century from 500 years of Ottoman rule, occupies a rocky pile of peninsulas and islands at the bottom of the Balkans in the eastern Mediterranean, with a language and landscape redolent of its pre-eminent place in the development of the western world. History, drama, politics, philosophy: the words as well as the concepts have their roots here. Around its rugged terrain are the names of the city-states which vied for supremacy in this region 2,000 years ago: Corinth, Sparta, Mycenae, Rhodes, Athens. And here too are Delphi, the Parthenon and Mount Olympos, forever associated with the ancient gods.

Whether you arrive in Greece by boat, plane or overland, your first impression as you stretch your legs is likely to be of the sun. Glimmering on the water, reflecting off metal and glass, casting shadows, the Mediterranean sun is omnipresent. Like the flash of a hidden camera, the brilliant light catches you unawares and transfixes you.

The Fishermen's Memorial, Sámi.

From that minute, you seem effortlessly to become a part of the Greek landscape – blue sky above, white sand below, ancient ruins, olive groves, a hillside vineyard… It is easy to fall in love with this radiant country, not least because so many of its over 11 million people are emotionally open, unafraid of shedding a tear, either in sorrow or in joy. Many travellers first experience this passion in the warmth of the welcome they receive, and they may even feel a little uneasy at the exuberance of their hosts. Yet those travellers tend to return time after time – for the mirror-smooth Aegean Sea shimmering in the still of the morning, for the *kafenía* with their wooden, thatched chairs and rickety tables offering some shade from the blistering afternoon heat, and for the silvery green olive groves where the cicadas drone at evening time.

The country's membership of the European Union and its capital's hosting of the 2004 Olympic Games have done much to accelerate modernisation. But modern is less a synonym for homogeneous than it is in many other rapidly changing countries. A sense of history and a respect for tradition remain powerful, and most Greeks are proud to share their culture with visitors. The Greek word *xénos* means not only "stranger" or "foreigner" but also "guest", and a fortunate *xénos* will be invited into a Greek family's house to be lavishly supplied with food and drink and questioned with genuine curiosity. The aim of this book is both to guide visitors around Greece and its islands and to preview what is likely to be an entirely captivating experience.

The rugged, unspoilt coastline of Ýdra.

A DIVERSE LAND

Mountains and caves, salt marshes and cloud-forest,
blazing summers and snow in winter – few countries
have such varied landscape and climate.

People perceive Greece as a land where people eat oranges and the sun shines all the time, but it is equally accurate (if not more so) to describe it as a place where it rains buckets and apples figure largely in the diet. Greece is actually the most varied country in the Mediterranean, with habitats ranging from near-deserts to temperate cloud-forests, from salt marshes to alpine peaks.

The splintered outline of the southeastern Balkan peninsula is the result of the flooding of the Mediterranean basin, which occurred when a debris dam at the future Strait of Gibraltar gave way. Waters from the Atlantic surged in and gradually submerged the mountain ranges, which segmented the deep, hot depression – a process completed only after the last Ice Age, and probably the basis of the Biblical flood account. Isolated, exposed summits became the Greek islands, Crete being the highest and largest. If the Mediterranean could be re-drained, the coastal ranges of former Yugoslavia, the Albano-Greek Píndos, the Peloponnesian mountains, Crete and the Turkish Toros would form one unbroken system. This mountainous arc has a core of karstic limestone, sensitive to erosion by rain and thus peppered with caves, sinkholes and subterranean rivers. Glaciers of the last Ice Age also had a role in shaping the mountains as far south as the present-day Gulf of Corinth.

Earthquake zone

Greece remains an active subduction zone, where the African tectonic plate burrows under the European plate. This means numerous faults, frequent – often destructive – earthquakes and a significant level of geothermal activity. Over 100 thermal spas are scattered across both the mainland and the islands. This geothermalism is predictably accompanied by

The sprawling olive groves of Lésvos.

vulcanism: you can trace the boundary of the plate collision zone by "joining up" the extinct or dormant volcanic islands of Méthana (now a peninsula), Póros, the submerged calderas of Mílos and Santoríni, and Nísyros, which has erupted within historical memory. In the northeast Aegean, Lésvos, Límnos and Aï Strátis islands are also of volcanic origin.

Only about one quarter of Greece's surface area is cultivable, principally in Thessaly and Macedonia. Much of the farmland occupies low-lying plains or upland plateaux, often the beds of former lakes drained to reclaim the land for agriculture or eliminate malarial mosquitoes. Only a few perennial freshwater lakes survive on the mainland north of the Gulf of Corinth:

they tend to be shallow and murky, more suited to irrigation, fishing and wildlife conservation than recreation. The largest and most scenic is Lake Trihonída in Étolo-Akarnanía; runners-up include Vegorítída, Mikrí Préspa and Kastoriá in western Macedonia, plus Pamvótida in Epirus. The Epirote Píndos Mountains have a few glacial tarns, but lakes are almost entirely absent from the large islands owing to overly porous rock strata; Koúrna, near Haniá on Crete, is the largest.

Stony or partly forested mountains make up three-quarters of the country – and as Henry Miller put it, nowhere has God been so lavish

> Greece has long made a modest profit from its minerals – bauxite, nickel and chromite on the central mainland, assorted volcanic substances on Mílos and Nísyros – and is set to become Europe's largest gold producer by 2016.

coast of the Pílio peninsula with its lush "jungle" – in general precipitation is highest in the Ionian Islands (particularly Corfu and Zákynthos) and the western mainland, where the Píndos mountain range forces moisture-laden air from the

High-perched villages in central Greece witness harsh winters.

with rocks as in Greece. The hills are often bonily naked; the country's forests have been under steady attack since ancient times, and the rate of deforestation has accelerated alarmingly since World War I. Fires, usually deliberately started, are the main cause: under current climatic conditions, it takes a Greek pine wood more than 50 years to recover completely from a blaze.

Hot summers, cold winters

Greece's stereotypical "Mediterranean" climate and vegetation is in fact limited to the coastal areas; "modified continental" is a more accurate tag for the weather elsewhere, with hot, muggy summers and cold winters. Although there are numerous microclimates – such as the northeast

Ionian Sea to disgorge its load as rain or snow.

The rest of the country lies effectively in a "rain shadow", although the directional pattern is reversed at Mt Olympos near Thessaloníki, rising 2,917 metres (9,568ft) in the space of a few kilometres inland from the moist Thermaic Gulf, which sends wet air masses west to be trapped on the summit of the ancient gods. Olympos is the highest of a score of peaks over 2,300 metres (7,550ft), home to about a dozen ski resorts. While nobody is likely to fly in from northern Europe especially to ski – snowfall patterns are too unreliable – the resorts have long been popular with the Greeks themselves.

Greece's fabled, convoluted coast is claimed to cover a distance equal to that of France, a country four times larger. But, despite figuring prominently on tourist posters, beaches are the exception rather than the rule. Much of the shoreline is inhospitable cliff, providing neither satisfaction for sand-seekers, nor anchorage for mariners. In fact, the most likely visitors are birds, as Greece lies under major migratory paths linking north-central Europe and Africa. When it is not cliff or beach, the Greek littoral is peppered with lagoons, estuaries and salt marshes that serve as important wildlife refuges. Some of the most important of these are at Kalógria near Pátra, Kalloní on Lésvos, the delta of the Évros river in Thrace, the Korissíon

been dammed, usually for irrigation and flood control rather than for hydroelectric power. Such projects, evidence of a non-accountable, central-planning mentality which has waned almost everywhere else in Europe, remain highly controversial – none more so than the Mesohóra dam on the Ahelóös, which has been declared illegal by the Greek Council of State, and had its funding revoked by the European Union. If ever filled, this massive reservoir – intended to irrigate the Thessalian plain – would doom already threatened fisheries and wetlands at the Ahelóös delta. A more positive outcome of damming is the

The bridge at Árta, on coastal Epirus.

lagoon on Corfu, the Alykí marsh on Kós and the vast lagoon complex at Mesolóngi.

Controversial dams

No point in Greece is more than 100km (62 miles) from the sea, so the numerous rivers are not only short, but swift, as they lose altitude quickly, to the delight of local kayakers and rafters. The only major rivers to flow lazily along as in northern Europe, in their lower reaches anyway, are the Aliákmonas, the Píníos, the Ahelóös and the Árakhthos; the Áxios and Strymónas and Évros in Macedonia and Thrace also conform to people's idea of a continental river, but have their sources in other Balkan states. Since World War II, most rivers north of the Gulf of Corinth have

artificial wetland at Kerkíni on the Strymónas, a mecca for birds.

Greece's rugged terrain, and its high proportion of territory as islands, have since the time of the ancient city-states encouraged separate regional development. For such a small country, there are numerous dialects, in contrast to, say, far vaster Russia, which has little variation in its speech. Land communications were late in coming; well into the 20th century, it was easier to sail from Athens to the eastern Peloponnesian coast, or from Haniá to Crete's southern shore, than to go overland. Geographical determinism is an easy trap to fall into, but the mutual isolation of the provinces has undoubtedly been a dominant factor in shaping Greek identity, for better or worse.

Settentrion

DALMATIA

ALBANIA PARS ILLYRIDIS

MACEDONIA

Migdonia

Sintica

Orbeli

Iori

Pelagonia

Astraei

Linchos

Ematia

Bottiaia

Pieria

Amphaxitis

Iamboli

Paraxia

Golfo di Salonichi

Comenolitari

Neuriopes

Macedonia

PARTE DEL GOLFO DI VENETIA detto Adriatico

Tamoriza

Eordei

Dassaretii

Elymiotæ

Parthini

Stymphalis

ALBANIA

Orestae

Atintani

Canina

Elyma

Chimera ol'Chaonia

Chimera et Ceraunii

Paroræi

Pindus M.

Poneska

Tympha

Pelagonia Tripolitis

TESSALIA

Estiæos

Iannalia

Pelasgiotis

Magnesia

EPIRO

Tymphæa

Hellopes

Larta

Dolopes

Dryopes

Thessaliotis

Pindus M.

Phtiotis

Thesproti

Molossi

Apraratij

Elatria

Cassiopæi

Amphilochi

Athamanes

Perrhæ

Doris

Phocis

Locris

Livadia

Beotia

Corfu I. ol'Corcyra

Paxus

Pachsu I. ol'Paxus

Paxus altera ol'Antipachsu I.

Agræi

Acarnania

MARE IONIO

Santa Maura I. et Leucas Insula

A Despotato

Ætolia

Locri Ozolæ

Ducato di At

Eugia I. et Ægina

Golfo di Lepanto ol'Cirreus, et Corynthiacus sinus

Dardanelli

Cefalonia I. ol'Cophalenia

Val di Compare ol'Ithacâ Ins.

Golfo di Patrasso

Achaia

Clarenza

ARCADIA

PELOPONNESUS

MOREA

Zante I. ol'Zacynthus

Golfo d'Arcadia ol'Sinus Choleatus

Elis

Belvedere

Tzacconia

Braccio di Mainax

Messenia

Laconia

Striuali I. ol'Strophades Insulæ

LA GRECIA
VNIVERSALE ANTICA
Paragonata con la Moderna da
Giacomo Cantelli da Vignola
Con le direttioni delle Carte Migliori e de piu accreditati Scrittori di Geografia. data in luce da Gio.
Giacomo Rossi in Roma alla Pace l'anno 1682.
con Priu. del S. Pont.

Sapienza I. ol'Sphagia

MARE DI SAPIENZA

Cerigo I. ol'Cythera

O DI GRECIA

MARE IONIO

Mezzogior

Giorgio Widman Sculp.

THRACIÆ PARS oggi ROMANIA

Bistones

Niceopoli
Nessetia

Braca

Beryga Asperos et Abdera

Doriscus campus

Eno et Enge

Maronea S.P.S.

Cico.

Maximianopoli

CONSTANTINCPOLI
Bizantium
olim Stambul

Scutari

Calcedona

Nicomedia
Comidia
Nicor.
et Inngimidet
Ischunt

MARE DI MARMARA
olim PROPONTIS

Gallipoli

Li Dardanelli
Sesto

Abido

Marmor a I. et Proconnesus
Neuros et Elaphoneus

Chirico I. et Cyzicus

Mysia Minor

ANATOLIA

Mysia Maior

Troia

Lembro I. et Imbria

Stalimene I. et Lennos

Tasso I. et Thassus et Asrie

Samandrachi I.
et Samothrace

Metelino I.
olim Lesbos

ARCIPELAGO

oggi

MAR BIANCO

anticamente

ÆGÆVM MARE

Sciro I. et Syrus

Pelagnesi I. et Meneus

ISCARIOM MARE

Nicaria I.
et Scaria

Samo I. et Samos

Andro I. et Andros

Tino I. et Tenos

Rocho I.

Stapodia I.

Mandria I.

Delos grande et Rhene

Micolo I. et Miconus

Caura et Anscopolis

Dragonisi

Insulæ Cyclades

Thermia
et Cythnia

Nicsia I. et Naxus

Zea I. et Cia

Palmosa et Patino
et Patmos

Lero I. et Leria

Mandria I.

Fermaco I.

Molaca et Miletus

Cariar

Doris

Isola di Rodi et Rhodus

Parini et Pares

Copra I. et Clarus

Morgo I. et Amorgus

Zinara I.

Capra I.

Lango I.

Serfino I.
et Seriphus

Rachis I.

Pirai

Leuita I. et Lebinthus

Nisari
et Nisyros

Carchi o Chalcia I.

Sporades Insulæ

MAR. MIRTOVM

Nio I. et Ios

Sicandro I.

Camena I.

Gierra I.

Serpe I.

Policandro I.
et Cithnus

Namfio I. et Anaphe

Stampalia I. et Astypalea

Ferulli I.

Sife no I. et Siphnus

Milo I. et Melos

Tiresia I. et
Therasia

Santorini o S. Erini
et Thera Insula

Planu I.

Levo I.

Scarpanto I. et Carpathus

MARE DI SCARPANTO olim Carpathium Mare

Cassio I. et Cassus

MARE DI CANDIA ol CRETICVM Mare

Standia I. et Dia

Candia

CANDIA olim CRETA

Scala
Miglia d'Italia
Leghe comuni di Francia
Leghe comuni di Germania
Leghe d'un hora di comune

DECISIVE DATES

Cycladic and Early Bronze Ages: c.3000–1450 BC

3000–2100 BC
Cyclades settled from Asia Minor; colonists introduce metal-working to these islands and to the mainland.

2100–1500 BC
Minoan culture, noted for its great cities and palaces, and sophisticated art, reaches its zenith on Crete.

c.1650–1610 BC
The settlement at Santoríni Akrotiri on Thera is annihilated by a volcanic eruption.

c.1450 BC
Most Minoan centres on Crete are devastated by fire, possibly during a revolt caused by social and environmental instability following the Thera cataclysm.

Mycenaean and Dorian Period: 1400–750 BC

1400 BC
A Peloponnesian tribe, the Myceneans, rise to prominence, building grand citadels at Mycenae and Tiryns.

c.1150 BC
"Sea Peoples" from Eurasian steppes, later dubbed the Dorians, invade large areas of Greece.

776 BC
The Dorians hold the first Olympic games, in honour of Zeus and Hera.

Archaic Period: 750–500 BC

750 BC onwards
City-states, including Athens, Sparta, Thebes and Corinth, compete for supremacy.

550 BC
Sparta forms Peloponnesian League with neighbouring states. Rivalry with Athens increases.

500 BC
The Greek city-states control large parts of the Mediterranean and Black Sea coast.

Classical Period: 500–338 BC

490 BC
The Persian king, Darius, attempts to conquer Greece but is convincingly defeated by the Athenian army at Marathon.

481–479 BC
Xerxes, Darius's son, invades. Athens is captured, but then in a surprise attack, Greek boats sink the Persian fleet off Salamis.

Minoan figurine, Iráklio Archaeological Museum, Crete.

431–404 BC

The Peloponnesian Wars, with Sparta and Athens the main protagonists. Athens capitulates; Sparta takes control of much of Greece.

338 BC

Philip II of Macedonia defeats Athens and Thebes at the Battle of Chaironeia and unites all Greek cities except Sparta.

Hellenistic and Roman Period: 338 BC–AD 395

336 BC

Philip II of Macedonia assassinated. His son, Alexander the Great, develops Greece (or rather, Macedonia) into an imperial power.

323 BC

Alexander's huge empire is divided on his death amongst his successors, the Diadokhi; centres of political power consequently shift from

Count Ioannis Kapodistrias, Greek president from 1827 until his assassination in 1831.

Greece to the Middle East and Egypt.

320–275 BC

The Diadokhi war among themselves; Rome emerges as a major power.

146 BC

Rome annexes Greece as a province of the Roman republic, and subsequently empire.

Byzantine Period: AD 395–1453

395

The Roman Empire is divided into East and West, with Greek-speakers dominant in the East.

1204

The Fourth Crusade, directed by the Venetians, attacks, plunders and briefly occupies Constantinople. Frankish Crusaders and Venetians divide Greek territory among themselves. Fortified harbours and land fortresses are built across the mainland, especially on the Peloponnese, and on many islands, particularly Rhodes, the east Aegean ones and Crete.

Bishop Germanos blessing the flag, by Theodoros Vryzakis, (1865), National Gallery, Athens.

1453

Ottomans Turks under Sultan Mehmet II capture Constantinople; final disappearance of Byzantine Empire.

Ottoman Period: 1453–1821

1453

Communal administration of the Greek Orthodox population left to its own clergy, upon payment of taxes.

1500–1600s

Life in rural Greek territories is not congenial, with arbitrary taxation and venal governors.

Late 1700s

Living conditions improve throughout the Ottoman Empire; a wealthy, often educated Greek Orthodox gentry emerges in places like Mount Pílio, Zagóri, Lésvos, Híos and Pátmos.

1821

The Greek War of Independence breaks out almost simultaneously on the islands and the Peloponnese, where Archbishop Germanos blesses the revolutionary

standard at Agía Lávra monastery.

The Emerging State: 1821–1922

1821–31

Three major European powers intervene in the Greek War of Independence. Their military assistance and diplomatic pressure ensure the emergence of an autonomous Greek state.

1832–33

Russia, France and Great Britain stipulate "final" borders of Greece and install Prince Otto of Bavaria as first king of Greece.

1863–64

Danish prince King George I succeeds the ousted Otto. Ionian Islands ceded to Greece.

1910

The Liberal Party under Eleftherios Venizelos comes to power and governs until 1920.

1912–13

The Balkan Wars erupt. Greece wrests southern Macedonia, Epirus, Crete and the east

Aegean Islands from the Ottomans.

1916–17

Greece enters World War I on the Allied side after bitter wrangles between republicans and monarchists.

1919–22

Encouraged by the Allies, Greek troops land at Smyrna, attempt to occupy much of Anatolia, but are defeated by Atatürk's Turkey. King Constantine I goes into exile; a republic is established.

Refugees, Occupation, Civil War: 1923–49

1923

The borders between Greece and Turkey are settled and in a traumatic population exchange, 1.2 million Orthodox Greeks quit Asia Minor and 380,000 Muslims leave Greece for Turkey.

1928–33

Venizelos returns to office after alternating parliamentary and military rule.

1935

The monarchy is restored after an unsuccessful republican coup.

1936–41

Quasi-fascist dictatorship under General Ioannis Metaxas. When World War II is declared, Greece is initially neutral.

1940

Mussolini's invasion repulsed.

1941–44

Joint German, Bulgarian and Italian occupation of Greece.

German troops fighting the Greek Resistance in the mountains during World War II.

Resistance groups base themselves in the mountains.

1944–49

Germans and Bulgarians retreat; Allies attempt to reimpose royalist regime, prompting a three-year civil war between conservative forces and Communist rebels.

Postwar Politics: 1950–Present

1950s

Conservative parties rule, mostly under Constantine Karamanlis; Communist Party is outlawed.

1963–64

First free post-war elections return centrist governments under Georgios Papandreou.

1967

A junta of army officers under Georgios Papadopoulos seize control of the country.

1974

The junta attempts to take over Cyprus, fails and collapses. A referendum abolishes the monarchy; Greece is again a republic, with Communists legalised.

1981–89

The Greek Socialist Party, PASOK, governs with Andreas Papandreou as prime minister until brought down by scandals.

1989–1993

Néa Dimokratía (Conservative) party regime until PASOK regains power.

1996–2004

Kostas Simitis succeeds Andreas Papandreou as PASOK prime minister.

2002

Greece adopts the euro as its currency.

2004

Néa Dimokratía wins elections under Kostas Karamanlis, nephew of Constantine. Athens hosts the Olympic Games.

2007

Criticised over its handling of devastating forest fires, Néa Dimokratía still wins snap elections.

2009

George Papandreou, son of Andreas, leads PASOK to electoral victory.

2010–11

Greece's finances revealed as insolvent after decades of Néa Dimokratía and PASOK mismanagement. Papandreou resigns in favour of unelected "unity" government. Two bailout packages offered by a troïka of international lenders, at the cost of harsh austerity measures and civil unrest.

2012

Two successive, inconclusive elections produce a three-party coalition mandated to negotiate better aid terms with the troïka. Neo-fascist Golden Dawn party becomes prominent. Continued use of euro doubted.

Thessaloníki demonstrates against the austerity measures in 2011.

The famous Phaistos Disc, a highlight of Iráklio's Archaeological Museum.

ANCIENT GREECE

The rich civilisations that rose and fell in the Aegean have left a precious inheritance that is still relevant today.

The basis for the modern way of life in Greece was laid around 5500 BC, when settlers moved down from the north to the plains of Thessaly, then on to rockier land in the Peloponnese (Pelopónnisos), and began to cultivate olives and vines, as well as the cereals they had originally grown. Seaborne trade with the islands – particularly for obsidian from Melos, vital for weaponry – also commenced. Some three millennia later, a prosperous Bronze Age civilisation arose on Crete (Kríti), and influenced the entire Aegean.

Minoan and Mycenaean cultures

The Minoans, whose rituals have filtered down to us through the legend of Theseus and his labyrinthine struggle with the Minotaur, left proof of their architectural genius in the ruined palaces of Knossos and Phaistos (Festós). Adventurous sailors, they preferred commerce to agriculture. The 5th-century BC historian Thucydides reports that King Minos of Crete established his sons as governors in the Cyclades and cleared the Aegean of pirates. The Minoans also established a number of outposts in the Peloponnese and made contact with the Egyptians.

By 1550 BC, their civilisation had reached its zenith. Yet barely a century later, for reasons that remain unexplained, most Minoan settlements were destroyed by fire and abandoned. Akrotíri, on Thera (Santoríni), had been annihilated by a volcanic eruption in about 1630 BC, which also damaged Crete. But the causes of the wider disintegration of Minoan control remain a mystery. Only Knossos continued to be inhabited as Cretan dominance in the Aegean ended.

An ancient inscription, Líndos, Rhodes.

The Minoans' place was taken by Mycenaeans, inhabitants of Mycenae (Mykínes), a bleak citadel in the Peloponnese. We do not know whether the rulers of Mycenae exerted direct power over the remainder of the mainland. But in the *Iliad,* Homer portrays their king, Agamemnon, as the most powerful figure in the Greek forces, which suggests that Mycenae had achieved some sort of overall authority.

In its heyday, the Mycenaean world contained men rich enough to commission massive stone tombs and delicate gold work. Rulers were served by a complex array of palace scribes and administrators who controlled the economic life of the state, exacting tribute, collecting taxes and allocating rations of scarce metals.

Invasion of the Sea Peoples

Starting in the 12th century BC, this society, like the Cretan one before it, began to wither away. Classical myth connects the end of the Mycenaean age with the arrival of Dorian tribes, more properly known as the "Sea Peoples". In fact, there was no clear connection between the two events. Mycenaean power had declined irreversibly by the time the Sea Peoples entered Greece. These invaders, like later ones, entered Greece from the north and northeast. They were probably nomads from beyond the Black Sea, which would explain their inclination

suffered. Trade dwindled and communities became isolated from one another. Building in stone seems to have been too great an effort for the small pastoral settlements that had replaced the Mycenaean centres. Homer's *Odyssey* is set in a simple society where even the rulers busy themselves with menial tasks, and where wealth is measured in flocks and herds.

The Geometric Period

In the 8th century BC, there were signs of revival as trade expanded. There were contacts with civilised peoples such as the Etruscans in

Minoan vase.

to travel and account for their lower level of culture.

They also brought their own form of the Greek language. In areas where they settled densely, we find West Greek dialects, while Attica, the Aegean Islands and the Ionian colonies continued to use East Greek forms. The hostility, at a later date, between Athens and Sparta (Spárti) was based in part on this division between Ionian and Dorian peoples.

The Dorian migration, from about 1120 BC onwards, shortly preceded the onset of the Iron Age, and that of the Geometric period (named after its pottery decoration). Historical evidence for the period between the 11th and 9th centuries BC is patchy, but evidently civilised life

> By the 13th century BC, the Mycenaeans had adapted the Minoan Linear B script into the first written Greek. However, a proper alphabet only emerged with the modification of the Phoenician script during the 9th century BC.

the west, and the Phoenicians and Egyptians in the east. Artistic influence from the east was increasingly evident in metalwork and pottery. With the adoption of the Phoenician alphabet, writing revived among a much larger circle than before.

Another, equally important Greek concept was borrowed from the Phoenicians; the notion of the *polis* (city-state). In the Geometric era, small, isolated settlements were loosely grouped into large kingdoms. This system survived in both western and northern Greece into Classical times when Thucydides described how "the Aetolian nation, although numerous and warlike, yet dwell in unwalled villages scattered far apart".

Elsewhere, however, a network of small independent states grew up. At first, these were based around clusters of villages rather than one large urban centre. But with the population explosion of the mid-8th century, large on a population of slaves who were excluded from power, such as Sparta, a major *polis*, and Thessaly, an *ethnos*. Other states, such as Athens, although not unfamiliar with slavery, had a more broadly based citizen body that included Greeks from outside the city.

Kings, aristocrats and tyrants

In general, Homer's kings must have surrendered power towards the end of the Geometric period and beginning of the Archaic era, giving way to an aristocratic form of rule. But this too became entrenched in power and increasingly

The theatre at Epidauros.

conurbations evolved and expanded as surplus population moved from the country to the town. Land became more intensively cultivated and highly priced. In the early Geometric era, the slump in population had caused arable land to fall into disuse. Farmers turned from sowing cereals to stock-breeding; now this process was reversed. Available land could not support such a rapidly growing population. (There is a clear parallel with the Peloponnese in the 19th century, and in both cases the outcome was the same: emigration on a massive scale.)

Together with the division between the new *polis* and the older *ethnos* (kingdom), there was now a further distinction. Some states, mostly in the Dorian parts of the country, were reliant resistant to change. As commoners settled on land and amassed wealth, pressure grew for constitutional reform. Aristotle correctly identified the connection between the demand for reform and changes in military technique, saying "when states began to increase in size, and infantry forces acquired a greater degree of strength, more persons were admitted to the enjoyment of political rights". Just as the shift from monarchy to aristocracy had been reflected in the move from chariots to horseback fighting, the emphasis now switched from cavalry to infantry; aristocracy lost ground to democratic pressure. Men would only fight in the new larger armies if the aristocrats granted them political rights.

Military power swung away from the traditional horse-breeding aristocracies of Chalkis, Eretria and Thessaly to new powers: Corinth, Argos and, above all, Sparta, where the state was protected by an army of heavily armed foot-soldiers known as hoplites, whose core was a body of citizens trained as infantrymen from birth.

Often the demand for radical reform met with resistance from the upper classes, but some individuals, more far-sighted, recognised the need for change. One such was Solon, nick-named "the Law-Giver", who was elected in

it. In the 6th century, tyrants seized power in a number of states. Usually they were dissident aristocrats, who gained the support of the lower classes with promises of radical change – promises which were often kept, as it was in the new ruler's interest to weaken the power of his peers. In the mid-7th century, for example, Kypselos of Corinth was supposed to have redistributed land belonging to his fellow aristocrats.

But it would be wrong to regard the tyrants as great innovators. They were symptoms of social change rather than causes of it. Conscious of

Theseus and Prokrustes portrayed on a vase painting from around 470 BC.

early 6th-century Athens to introduce sweeping constitutional changes. Realising that the city's strength would depend upon the organisation of the citizen body, he opened up the Assembly to the poorest citizens and in other ways loosened the grip of the aristocracy.

Inevitably, these changes were attacked from both sides, as Solon himself complains in a number of his poems. But they did lay the foundations for the tremendous expansion of Athenian power throughout the next century.

Another result of these political tensions was tyranny. For the ancient Greeks, "tyrant" was not a pejorative; it simply meant a ruler who had usurped power instead of inheriting

their own vulnerability, they resorted to various propaganda expedients to stay in power. The most potent of these was the religious cult, and it is from the time of the tyrants that religion came directly to serve state purposes.

Religion was not only important to the state as propaganda; it was also a major economic factor. While the popular religious festivals and games earned revenues – enormous in some cases – for the city that staged them, temples, sacrifices and other rituals were very costly. Apart from waging wars, temple-building was probably the greatest drain on a city-state's resources. Thus the scale of its religious activities provided some measure of the wealth of a community.

Greeks versus the Persian Empire

Alongside the rise of an artistic culture shared across state boundaries, a process of political unification began. People in different cities started to become aware of a common Hellenic culture. The historian Herodotos was a keen promoter of the idea of one Greece, and asserted that the Greeks were "a single race because of common blood, common customs, common language and common religion". This shared cultural identity was reinforced by increasing numbers of religious festivals and athletic competitions that attracted participants from numerous Greek states.

But the sharpest spur to unity was an outside threat: the rise of the Persian Empire. Midway through the 6th century, King Cyrus had conquered the Ionian Greek cities on the Asia Minor coast, and Persian aspirations were further encouraged by his son Darius (521–486 BC) who conquered Thrace, subdued Macedonia and, after quashing an Ionian revolt in Asia Minor, sent a massive expeditionary force westwards into Greece. Athens appealed for help from Sparta, militarily the strongest Greek city, but succeeded in defeating the Persians at Marathon in 490 BC before the Spartan forces actually arrived.

This victory did more than save Attica; it also confirmed Athens as the standard-bearer for the Greek military effort against the Persians. This explains why a frieze displaying the warriors killed at Marathon (situated just over 23km/15 miles from Athens) was placed in a prominent and highly unusual position around the Parthenon in the 440s BC. Only then was Athens becoming a power to be reckoned with. The silver mines at Laurion (modern Lávrion) in Attica began producing enough wealth to finance a major shipbuilding programme from early in the 5th century. Even so, for two generations after that, Aegina (Égina) remained superior to Athens as a Saronic Gulf trading force.

The Siphian frieze inside the Delphi Museum depicts scenes from the Trojan War.

Athens and Sparta

A decade after the battle of Marathon, when Darius's son Xerxes organised a second attack on Greece, the city-states rallied around Sparta. Spartan king Leonidas and his Three Hundred (actually 2,300, including Thespians, Thebans and Spartan helots) valiantly sacrificed themselves trying to halt the Persian advance at Thermopylae. While Athens had the largest navy, the Spartans controlled the Peloponnesian League, with its considerable combined land forces. Both the crucial naval victory at Salamis in 480 BC and the land victory at Plataea the following year were won under Spartan leadership.

But no sooner had the Persian menace been banished than the Greek alliance broke up. There was intense suspicion among the rival city-states, especially between Sparta and Athens. Thucydides described how, as soon as the Persians withdrew, the Athenians rebuilt their city walls for fear that the Spartans would try to stop them.

The development of a Classical "cold war" became obvious as Athens extended its control over the Aegean with the help of the

of Pericles, its most influential leader, Athens refused to back down. Diplomatic efforts to resolve the dispute failed. Finally, in the spring of 431 BC, a Spartan ally, Thebes, attacked an Athenian ally, Plataea, and open war broke out between the two superpowers.

The Second Peloponnesian War dragged on for years since neither side was able to deal a deathblow to the other. The Peace of Nikias in 421 BC gave both sides breathing space, but lasted just six years.

The uncertain peace was finally shattered when the Athenians launched a massive assault

The Caryatids of the Erechtheion, built on the Acropolis at the peak of Athens' glory.

Delian League. Significantly, the Persian threat had receded long before peace was officially declared in 449 BC. Moreover, between 460 and 446 BC, Athens warred with its neighbours in an effort to assert its supremacy. Naval rivals such as Aegina were singled out for attack. There was even small-scale fighting between Athens and Sparta (the First Peloponnesian War), until the so-called "Thirty Years' Treaty" brought an uneasy truce in 445 BC.

In 433 BC, Athens allied itself with Corcyra, a strategically important colony of Corinth. Fighting ensued, and the Athenians took steps that explicitly violated the Thirty Years' Treaty. Sparta and its allies accused Athens of aggression and threatened war. On the advice

THE RISE OF ATHENS

The Athenian Empire owed much to the Delian League, a naval alliance formed in 478 BC to liberate the Asia Minor Greeks and continue the struggle against the Persians. It was also underpinned by much anti-Spartan sentiment. Sparta's own version of the alliance, the Peloponnesian League, consisted of land forces, requiring minimum financing. But the creation of a navy called for long-term planning and central coordination – a crucial difference. Athens' smaller allies found it increasingly difficult to equip their own ships, and instead sent money to the Athenians. Thus Athens grew in strength as its allies became impoverished.

against Syracuse in Sicily. Aided by a force of Spartans, Syracuse was able to break an Athenian blockade. Even after gaining reinforcements in 413 BC, the Athenian army was defeated again. Soon afterward, the navy was also beaten, and the Athenians were utterly destroyed as they tried to retreat.

But even the Sicilian disaster did not end hostilities – although it had a huge impact on Athenian domestic politics. By 411 BC Athens was in political turmoil: democracy was overthrown by an oligarchical party, which was in turn replaced by the more moderate regime of

Alexander the Great's campaigns dramatically extended the boundaries of the Greek world.

the Five Thousand. At the end of 411 BC the rebuilt Athenian navy, fresh from several victories, acted to restore democratic rule. But the democratic leaders refused Spartan peace offerings, and the war continued at sea, with the Spartan and Athenian fleets exchanging costly victories. The end came in 405 BC when the Athenian navy was destroyed at Aegospotami by the Spartan fleet under Lysander, who had received much aid from the Persians. The next year, starved by an impenetrable blockade, Athens capitulated. Athens' defeat was perhaps the worst casualty in a war that crippled Greek military strength. The most culturally advanced Greek state had been sent into final eclipse.

Civic breakdown

Literature and art both flourished even during these incessant periods of fighting, but economic activity did not. A world where each tiny *polis* was determined to safeguard its independence at any cost carried within it the seeds of its own destruction.

The paradox was that city-states with imperial pretensions chose not to take the steps that might have brought success. Unlike Rome, Greek city-states did not extend citizenship to their subject territories. Nor could the military strength of Athens keep pace with its imperial

> One reason the Greek city-states failed as imperial powers, the Roman Emperor Claudius observed, was because they "treated their subjects as foreigners".

commitments, which explains the permanent cycle of conquest and revolt. The Spartans had the additional headache of a large slave population, the helots, often prone to revolt in their own province.

The first half of the 4th century continued this pattern. On the one hand, there were long wars between cities; on the other, evidence of prolonged economic difficulties as Corinth fell into irreversible decline, and Athens struggled in vain to recapture its previous prominence. Spartan power remained supreme until 371 BC when Thebes defeated the Spartan army at Leuktra.

The city-state system was gradually starting to fall apart. The old model of a citizen army was superseded by a more professional force, relying upon trained mercenaries. Aristotle noted that "when the Spartans were alone in their strenuous military discipline they were superior to everybody, but now they are beaten by everybody; the reason is that in former times they trained and others did not".

The spread of mercenaries, in fact, reflects the economic problems of the 4th century. Mercenary service, like emigration or piracy, was a demographic safety valve, and whereas in Archaic Greece of the 8th to the 6th centuries mercenaries had come from just a few backward areas, during the 4th century they were increasingly recruited from major cities as well. This points to economic difficulties over an increasingly wide area.

As in earlier times, military changes were connected with political ones. The decline of the citizen armies coincided with a trend away from democracy in favour of more autocratic government. Power shifted from the city-states towards Thessaly, an *ethnos* regime, and later still, towards Macedonia, which had been another old-fashioned kingdom.

Both regions had the advantage over Attica in that they were fertile and not short of land.

The temple of Olympian Zeus in Athens was completed by the Roman emperor Hadrian.

More rural than the city-states to their south, they managed to avoid the domestic political turmoil that periodically erupted in the latter. The military successes of the Thessalian tyrant, Jason of Pherae, in the early 4th century, indicated the confidence of these newcomers.

A little later, King Philip II of Macedonia moved southwards, secured the vital Thermopylae (Thermopýles) Pass and, after gaining control of Thessaly, defeated an alliance of Thebes and Athens at Chaeroneia in 338 BC. Banded together in the League of Corinth, the Greek city-states were compelled to recognise a new centre of power, Macedonia.

Alexander's Empire

In the *Republic*, Plato writes: "We shall speak of war when Greeks fight with barbarians, whom we may call their natural enemies. But Greeks are by nature friends of Greeks, and when they fight, it means that Hellas is afflicted by dissension which ought to be called civil strife".

This passage reflects three sentiments that were becoming widespread in the 4th century: first, that the Greeks were all of one race; second, that warfare between city-states was undesirable; third, that it was natural for the Greeks to fight their enemies in the east. It is ironic in this regard that a successful concerted effort against the Persians was made only under the leadership of Macedonia, traditionally a marginal power in the Greek world.

Philip's son Alexander mopped up any remaining resistance in Greece, then led a Greek-Macedonian army on a brilliant rampaging campaign to the east and south. In just over 10 years, he systematically swallowed up the ancient Persian Empire, reaching as far as the Indus Valley (in modern Pakistan). He even found time to conquer Egypt, where he founded Alexandria.

Alexander the Great's overseas empire drastically altered the boundaries of the Greek world. The city-states of mainland Greece no longer occupied centre stage. The mainland was drained of manpower as soldiers, settlers and administrators moved eastwards to consolidate Greek rule. At the same time, the intellectual and religious world of the Greeks opened up to new influences.

ALEXANDER'S RULE

The Greek-speaking world not only expanded, it was also coming together: under the rule of Alexander the Great, inhabitants began to speak the same language, as *koine* or "common" Greek replaced local dialects in most areas. In 3rd-century Macedonia, for example, local culture was "Hellenised", and the native gods were replaced by Olympian deities. For the first time, coinage became widely used in trade – something which had been impossible so long as each city had its own currency. Now the Attic drachma became acceptable in an area ranging from Athens to the Black Sea, from Cappadocia to Italy.

But there were limits to this process, for although the city-states gave up their political freedom, they clung to self-determination in other spheres such as local taxation and customs duties. Likewise the calendar: in Athens, the year began in July, in Sparta in October, on the island of Delos, January.

Philosophers were debating ideas of communal loyalties that transcended the old civic boundaries. Perhaps this reflected the way in which these were being absorbed within larger units, such as the Hellenistic kingdoms, the Greek federal leagues and, eventually, the Roman Empire. Whatever the cause, the most influential philosophical school, Stoicism, emphasised the concept of universal brotherhood and talked of a world state ruled by one supreme power.

Roman expansion

Gradually but inexorably, Macedonian expansion curtailed the political autonomy of the city-states. In the 3rd century, they formed federations, and tried to exploit disputes between the Diadokhi, or successor-generals, who had inherited Alexander's empire. This policy had only limited success, mainly because of the paltry military resources available to the Greek leagues.

Early in the 2nd century, disputes among the city-states brought about Roman intervention for the first time in Greek history. Within 20 years, Rome had defeated first Macedonia, and then the Achaean League which had organised a desperate Greek resistance to Roman rule. The Roman consul Lucius Mummius marked his victory over the League by razing Corinth in 146 BC, killing the entire male population, and selling its women and children into slavery. As a deterrent to further resistance, this was brutal but effective. Conservative factions were confirmed in power in the cities and Greece became a Roman protectorate. In 27 BC, when the Roman Empire was proclaimed, the protectorate became the province of Achaea.

Greece – a Roman backwater?

By the 1st century AD, Greece was no longer the centre of the civilised world. Athens and Corinth could not rival Alexandria or Antioch, let alone Rome. The main routes to the east went overland through Macedonia; to the south, by sea to Egypt. But while Greece was certainly a commercial backwater, its decline was only relative: along the coast, cities flourished. The *polis* remained much as it had been

in Hellenistic times, and the Roman authorities permitted a degree of political self-rule. Philhellenic emperors such as Hadrian even encouraged groups of cities to federate in an effort to encourage a pan-Hellenic spirit.

But the *polis* was no longer a political force. Hellenistic rulers had feared the Greek cities' power; the Roman and later the Byzantine emperors feared their weakness and did what they could to keep them alive. They were vital administrative cogs in the imperial machine; if they failed, the machine would not function.

Two centuries of relative tranquillity were

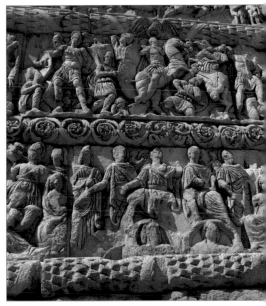

The Arch of Galerius, Thessaloníki, completed in AD 303.

shattered by the invasions of the Goths in AD 255–270. They were successfully repelled, but the shock led to a loss of confidence and economic deterioration. Civic building programmes continued on a much reduced scale. The wealthy classes became increasingly reluctant benefactors, and two centuries passed before imperial authorities and the church revived the demand for architectural skills.

By that time, much had changed. In AD 330, Emperor Constantine had designated Constantinople an imperial co-capital on a par with Rome. By the late 4th century, Christianity had been made the official religion of the empire. The transition from Rome to Byzantium had begun.

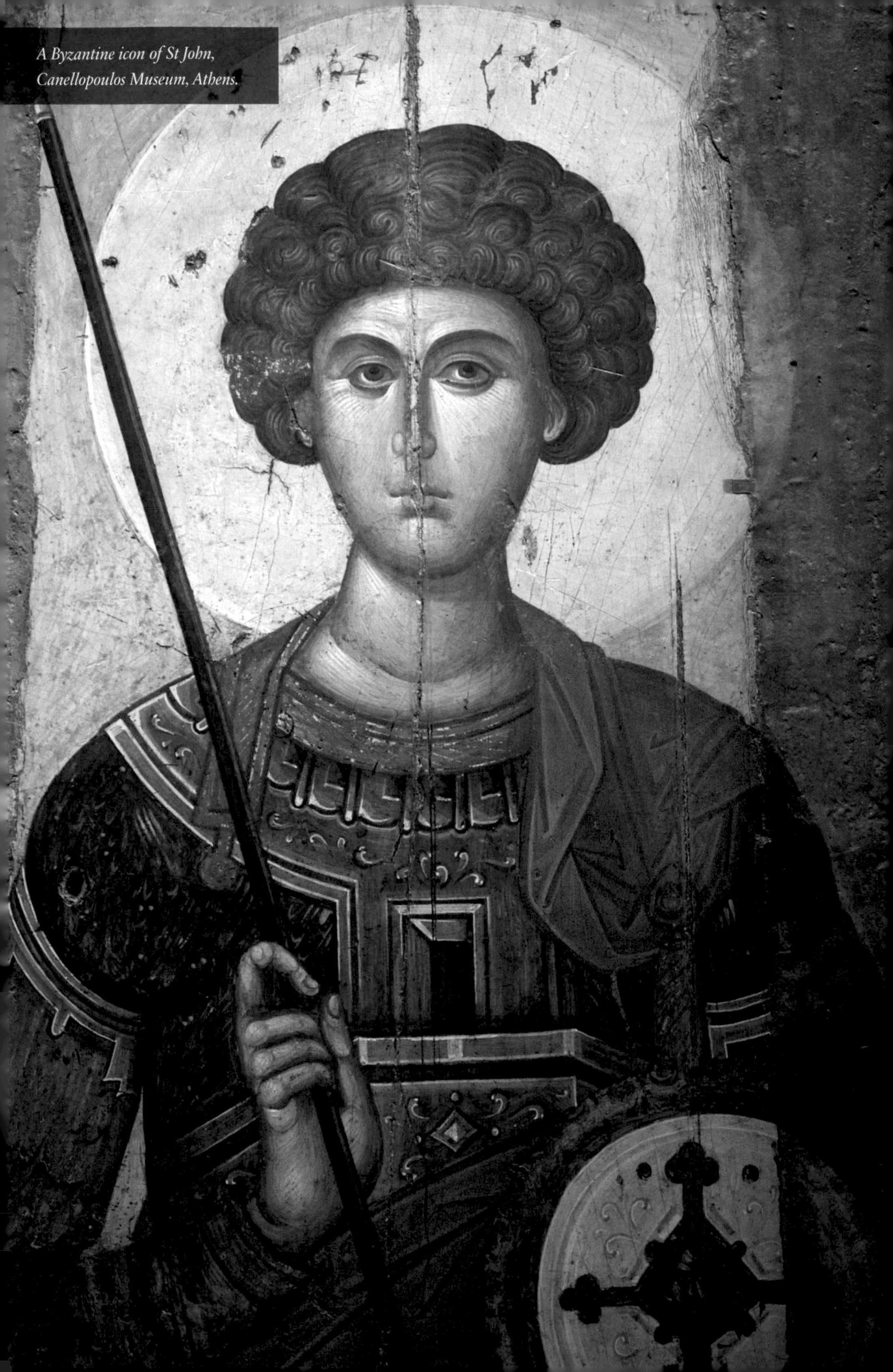

A Byzantine icon of St John, Canellopoulos Museum, Athens.

BYZANTINE GREECE

The legendary wealth of Rome's eastern empire
attracted many potential invaders, from the Franks
and Venetians to the Ottomans.

The Byzantine Empire was established with the foundation of Constantinople, but the final separation of the eastern and western empires was not complete until the late 5th century, when Rome was taken by the Ostrogoths. With its political structure anchored in Roman tradition and a new religion triumphant over paganism, the Byzantine Empire survived a millennium of triumphs and declines until Constantinople fell to the Ottoman Turks in 1453.

A revealing incident occurred in the capital Constantinople in AD 968. Legates from the western Holy Roman Empire brought a letter for Nikephoros Phokas, the Byzantine Emperor, in which he was simply addressed as "Emperor of the Greeks" while the Holy Roman Emperor, Otto, was termed "august Emperor of the Romans". The Byzantine courtiers were scandalised. The audacity of it – to call the universal emperor of the Romans, the one and only Nikephoros Phokas, the great, the august, "Emperor of the Greeks" and to style a poor barbaric creature "Emperor of the Romans!"

The well-restored medieval monastery of Filérimos, Rhodes.

Greek and Byzantine identity

Behind this reaction lies the curious cultural fusion which made up Byzantine identity. From the Hellenistic era came the belief in the superiority of the Greek world, and the summary dismissal of outsiders as barbarians. From Rome came a strong sense of loyalty to empire and emperor. And in the fervour that marked their belief in the moral superiority of *their empire* – which they regarded not as the "Eastern Roman Empire" but as the only true empire – is the stamp of evangelical Christianity.

The inhabitants of this empire did not call themselves Greeks or Byzantines: they were Romans, "Roméï". But the mark of a *Roméos* was

that he spoke Greek and followed the rite of the Orthodox Church. Thus three elements of identity – Greek culture and language, Roman laws and regulations, and Christian morality – became intermingled.

Invasions by barbarian Huns, Visigoths and Ostrogoths during the 5th century helped shape the Greek part of the empire. Constantinople avoided the fate of Rome, which fell to similar onslaughts, by a combination of skilful bribery and a strong army. Thus, as the West was carved into minor kingdoms, the East remained largely intact, and the balance of power in the former Roman Empire moved conclusively to the East.

The Emperor Justinian (ruled AD 527–65) laid the foundations on which the Byzantine

Empire would rest for nearly a century. An ambitious and dynamic leader, he greatly expanded the empire's territory by conquering the southern Levant, northern Africa and Italy, in an effort to re-create the old Roman Empire. Justinian's administrative reforms created a centralised bureaucracy, a new fiscal system, and a provincial administration. The codes of Roman law were revised and unified in the Corpus Iuris Civilis, which remains to this day a cornerstone of European jurisprudence. These reforms greatly advanced the unification of the diverse peoples of the empire in a Hellenic context. In

northward and westward, taking Egypt, Syria, Iraq, Iran and Afghanistan. Portions of Asia Minor were wrested from the Byzantine Empire, and twice between AD 668 and 725, Constantinople was nearly overrun by Muslim forces.

The real break with Greek antiquity came late in the 6th century when Greece was first attacked and then settled by Slavic-speaking tribes from the north. Major cities such as Athens, Thebes and Thessaloníki were safe behind defensible walls. But much of the indigenous population of the Balkans, Greeks included, fled, especially to Calabria on the

The road to Maráthi's ancient quarries, Páros.

the end, Justinian's institutional reforms proved far more lasting than his military conquests.

The end of antiquity

Justinian's wars brought the empire to the verge of bankruptcy and left it militarily vulnerable. Threats from both East and West plunged the empire into a spiral of decline that lasted for nearly 300 years. The first menace to the Empire from the East came from the Persian Sassanid Empire. Zoroastrian Sassanid forces took control of Palestine, Syria and Egypt, and even threatened the capital, Constantinople, at one point. A more serious threat soon developed with the advent of Islamic expansionism. Erupting out of the Arabian Peninsula, Muslim forces swept

southern tip of Italy, or relocated their settlements to higher, more secure regions of the Balkans. The invasions marked the end of the Classical tradition in Greece, destroying the urban civilisation of the *polis*, and with it Roman and Greek culture.

But the Slavic arrivals failed to preserve their own distinct cultural identities, and quickly became Hellenised. Greek remained the mother tongue of the region, and Christianity remained the dominant faith. Although the Slavic invasions and Islamic conquests of the 7th and 8th centuries reduced the extent of the Byzantine state, it survived as a recognisable entity grounded more firmly than ever in the Balkans and Asia Minor.

In AD 841, Greece's most famous ancient temple, the Parthenon, became the Orthodox cathedral church of Our Lady of Athens.

The Greek language may have survived, but the old urban culture did not. The disappearance of the city-states is shown by the way in which the word *pólis* came to refer exclusively to Constantinople as though there were no other cities. A small urban elite studied and wrote in *koine* Greek but had little impact on the mass of

The military gains of the Macedonian dynasty initiated a period of economic growth and prosperity and a cultural renaissance. Agriculture flourished as conditions stabilised and, as emperors increasingly used land grants to reward military service, the area under cultivation expanded. The prosperity of improved agricultural conditions and the export of woven silk and other craft articles allowed the population to grow. Expanding commercial opportunities increased the influence of the nearby Italian maritime republics of Venice, Genoa and Amalfi, which even-

Mosaic of Byzantine Emperor Justinian.

the population; their books were probably read by less than 300 people at any one time. Ancient monuments were avoided because peasants thought that they were inhabited by demons.

Byzantine revival

When a new dynasty, which came to be called Macedonian, took the throne of the Byzantine Empire in 867 in the person of Basil I, its forces began to roll back the tide of Islamic expansion. Antioch, Syria, Georgia and Armenia were reconquered. The Byzantine fleet regained Crete in 961 and drove Muslim pirates from the Aegean Sea, reopening it to commercial traffic. Consolidation of the Balkans was completed with the defeat of the First Bulgarian Empire by Basil II in 1018.

tually gained control of the Mediterranean trade routes into Greece.

But Byzantium's period of renewed glory was short-lived, lasting from the mid-9th to mid-11th centuries. The empire lacked the resources to maintain tight control over its territories. It was beset on all sides – by the Italian city-states to the west, the Slav kingdoms to the north, the Persians and Arabs in the east. The Greek peninsular and island provinces, being less vital than Anatolia, which supplied Constantinople with corn, were ceded more readily to other powers.

In 1071, a new enemy, the Seljuk Turks from central Asia, crushed a Byzantine army at Manzikert in Anatolia, capturing the emperor. In the late 11th century, a Norman army, allied with the Pope and commanded by Robert Guiscard, arrived from the west to ravage parts of Greece, including Thebes and Corinth. Civil war among rival military factions impaired the empire's ability to respond to such incursions, so Byzantium gave Venice trading rights in Greece in return for protection against the Normans. But before long, the Byzantines needed to counter Venetian power by encouraging the Genoese.

Crusaders and Venetians

When the Muslims seized Jerusalem, some European kings, claiming Christian ideology

de la Roche, the west coast and various islands by Italians – particularly the Venetians.

Venice was a powerful naval power, with boundless ambition for trade and territory. As a pay-off for the assistance given to the Crusaders, after the sack of Constantinople Venetians were allowed to take control of many of the Greek islands that had been part of the Byzantine Empire. The Ionian Islands were divided into fiefdoms among noble Venetian families (and remained under Venetian control until 1797); other Venetian aristocrats helped themselves to islands in the Aegean – notably Marco

Seventeenth-century iconostasis, Zákynthos Museum.

as their motive, but in fact seeing political and commercial advantages too, sailed east to recover the Christian holy places from Muslim control. In the process, they gained footholds in territories that had been part of the Byzantine Empire – Cyprus, for example, taken by Richard I of England during the Third Crusade.

This was only a foretaste of still worse misfortune. In 1204, Constantinople itself was sacked by the Crusader forces en route to the Holy Land for the Fourth Crusade – diverted there by the Venetians under Doge Enrico Dandolo. The empire was fragmented. Successor states arose in Epirus, Nicaea and Trebizond. Greece itself was divided into small kingdoms ruled by Western princes – the Duchy of Athens under the Burgundian Othon

Sanudo, a nephew of the Doge, who claimed Náxos, founded a duchy and effectively ruled the whole of the Cyclades from there. Even Crete, "the Great Island", became a Venetian territory, sold to Venice for a nominal sum by Prince Boniface of Montferrat, the titular leader of the Fourth Crusade, in return for its assistance in the conquest of Constantinople. Thus by the mid-13th century, Venice had control of the shipping routes to the Black Sea and Asian Minor, Egypt and North Africa.

Byzantium fights back

Only the resolute resistance of the Palaeologos Dynasty (1261–1453) prevented the Byzantine Empire from collapsing completely. The

Palaeologi fought back into mainland Greece, recaptured Constantinople and most of the southern Balkans. But there was considerable confusion in western Greece, which briefly came under Serbian control, and in Thessaly, where the Vlachs established a separate principality.

Southern Greece and the islands remained under the control of the Venetians, the Genoese, various other Italian adventurers and, in the case of Rhodes and most of its surrounding islands, the Knights of St John, a military order which had arisen during the Crusades – although in the 14th century the Palaeologi re-established

– if he could seize and hold it – in Bithynia, facing the Byzantine strongholds at Bursa, Nicomedia (Izmit) and Nicea. Leadership subsequently passed to his son, Osman I, the eponymous founder of a dynasty – the Osmanlı, better known in the West as the Ottomans – that was to endure for 600 years.

Towards the end of the 14th century, Asia Minor and the Balkans had fallen to the Ottoman Turks, and by 1400 the Byzantine Empire had shrunk to just Constantinople, eastern Thrace, Thessaloníki, Trebizond and part of the Peloponnese. In April 1453, Mehmet II ("the Conqueror") besieged Constantinople

Mystrás on the Peloponnese.

a Byzantine presence at Mystrás. One of the results of this political confusion was ethnically and religiously mixed populations.

A threat from the east

According to semi-legendary accounts, Ertuğrul, khan of the Kayı tribe of the Öğüz Turks, fled from Persia in the mid-13th century to escape Genghis Khan's Mongol hordes. He was granted territory

> *The Venetian-, Genoese- or Crusader-held Aegean islands resisted longest against the Ottomans. Tínos only fell in 1715 – over 250 years after the Greek mainland.*

and took it within two months. Eight years later, Trebizond and Mystrás had succumbed, too.

The fall of "The City" reverberated throughout Europe: with it had fallen the last descendants of the Roman Empire itself. Before long, Constantinople would again be the capital of a Mediterranean empire stretching from Budapest to the Caspian Sea and from the Persian Gulf to Algeria – but now it would be a Muslim city in the Ottoman Empire. The great Greek Byzantine Empire had come to an end. Although in the West this seemed the inevitable result of Byzantine decline, to the Greeks it was a more traumatic moment. They had passed under the rule of an alien creed, which however was preferable for many to domination by Catholic powers.

Ali Pasha, tyrant of Ioánnina.

OTTOMAN GREECE

Greek nationalism grew slowly as the Ottoman
Empire declined – until in the 19th century a bloody
struggle for independence was launched.

The Ottoman Turks who now controlled the Balkans were the latest in a series of nomadic tribes who had moved westwards from central Asia. They were highly mobile, and their devotion to conquest made up for their initially scant numbers.

News of the fall of Constantinople was received with horror in Europe, but as an isolated military action it did not critically affect European security. To the Ottoman Empire, however, the capture of the imperial capital was of supreme symbolic importance. Sultan Mehmet II, a man of culture and learning as well as a superb warrior, regarded himself as the direct successor of the Byzantine emperors. He made Constantinople the capital of the Ottoman Empire as it had been of the Byzantine Empire and he set about rebuilding and repopulating the city. The cathedral of Agia Sofia was converted to a mosque, and Constantinople – which the Turks called Istanbul (from the Greek phrase *eis tin pólin*, "at/in the city") – replaced Baghdad as the centre of Sunni Islam.

But Constantinople also remained the ecclesiastical centre of the Greek church. Ottoman religious tolerance was reflected in the imperial government system. The sultan recognised minority religions, and permitted each *millet*, or religious community, a measure of self-government. Thus Mehmet II proclaimed himself the protector of the Greek Orthodox Church, and appointed a new patriarch after the custom of the Byzantine emperors. Patriarch Gennadios II Skholarios guaranteed loyalty and taxes to the Turks, in return for a degree of self-government for the Greeks. The church came to exert both religious and civil powers over Ottoman Greeks.

Under their new masters, the Greeks lived much as they had done earlier. Their houses,

Ottoman inscription on a Muslim tomb in Ioánnina.

like those of the Muslims, tended to be miniature fortresses, built on two or three floors around a central courtyard. The restored merchant's mansions in Kastoriá give a good idea of the effect. However, under Ottoman influence, Greek cuisine changed for the better – *garum* (fermented fish sauce) on everything was out, while *moussakás*, elaborate pastries and thick "oriental" coffee – which Ali Pasha, the "Lion of Ioánnina", found helpful in poisoning his rival, the Pasha of Vallona – was in.

Restricted rights

Although the Orthodox Greeks were allowed to conduct their religious affairs without too much interference from the Ottoman hierarchy, they nevertheless suffered several disabilities that did not apply to Muslims. Christians were not allowed to bear arms and were thus exempt from military service. But in return, they had to pay a special head tax, the *haratçh*.

In a court of law, a Muslim's word was always taken over that of a Christian, although disputes between Greeks were usually settled in Greek religious courts. A Christian man could not marry a Muslim woman without converting, though the opposite configuration was common, with the wife keeping her

home villages, but the levy was still resented. It was formally abandoned by the late 17th century – largely because of rampant success by Muslims in enrolling their children.

A long-drawn-out conquest

Although the Turks had firm control of Constantinople/Istanbul after 1453, it took more than two centuries for them to establish control over Albania, and all of Balkan Greece and its islands (indeed, except for Levkáda, the Ionian Islands, with the Venetians well entrenched, never succumbed

A water colour of Thessaloníki by the great traveller and artist Edward Lear, clearly showing the city's minarets.

religion. Christians who adopted Islam but then reverted to Christianity were invariably punished for such apostasy by death. These "neomartyrs", however, helped to sustain the faith of the Orthodox populations under the Ottoman rule.

The most feared imposition on (mostly Slavic) Orthodox Christians was the janissary levy or *devşirme*: Christian villages were required, at irregular intervals, to surrender a quota of their fittest, most intelligent male children to the Ottomans. These conscripts were forcibly converted to Islam and trained to serve as praetorian guards (janissaries) or civil servants. Some janissaries rose to high office and were sometimes able to help their relatives or

to the Ottomans). Albania, resisting under Skanderberg, was only pacified late in the 15th century.

Lésvos, for example, fell to the Turks in 1462, but it was not until the conquest of Genoese Híos in 1566 that all the islands of the northeast Aegean were under Ottoman control. Similarly, the Dodecanese, with its motley population of Greeks, Jews, pirates and Latin adventurers, resisted until late 1522, when the Knights of St John on Rhodes finally yielded to an imperial force numbering 100,000 after a six-month siege. With the fall of Rhodes, the position of neighbouring islands became untenable, and within five years they had all surrendered as well.

Crete took even longer to subdue. Since the early 13th century, the "Great Island" had been Venice's stronghold in the eastern Mediterranean, and its strategic value encouraged the Venetians to reinforce the major cities – Iráklio, Haniá and Réthymno – with solid fortresses that can still be seen today. An attack on an Ottoman convoy in 1645 provided the excuse for an assault on Crete. The Turks took Haniá after a bloody battle, then Réthymno, and soon had control over the whole island except the capital, Iráklio. It was not until 1669, after a gruelling 22-year siege, that the Ottomans took

Athens, controlled by Crusaders and their descendants since 1204, had declined to a minor provincial town when the Ottomans arrived in 1456, and remained so until the 1830s.

powers – which provided opportunities for Greeks to stage optimistic but vain uprisings against the empire. In the aftermath of the defeat inflicted on the Ottoman navy at Lepanto by the Catholic Holy League in 1571, revolts broke out

the city and finally ruled all of Crete (except for three Venetian-fortified offshore islets: Spinalónga, Soúda and Gramvoúsa).

Attempts at revolt

Powerful enemies continually threatened the sultans' grip on Greece. The Venetians (and later the Russians) were thorns in the Ottoman flesh. The resulting conflicts left Greece much weaker. In 1537, for instance, an Ottoman fleet carried off half the population of Corfu after an attack on the Venetian garrison there, leaving the island with barely one-sixth of the numbers it had had in antiquity.

The expansionist ambitions of the Ottomans brought them into conflict with other European

on the Greek mainland and the Aegean Islands, but were promptly crushed by the Ottomans. A similar fate befell the short-lived revolt launched by Dionysios Skylosofos in Epirus in 1611.

The Peloponnese was also caught in a bloody tug-of-war between Ottomans and their enemies. During the Russo-Turkish war of 1768–74, Greeks in the Máni region attempted to revolt, with devastating results. Their uprising was initially supported by Alexei and Fyodor Grigoryevich Orlov, members of an aristocratic Russian family, who brought their fleet to Greece in 1770 and raided the Peloponnese with little permanent outcome other than exposing the Greeks to Ottoman reprisals. They were more successful in the Aegean, destroying the Turkish fleet at Çeşme and occupying many islands until 1774.

Resistance to the Ottomans

In truth, the Ottomans never established total control over the Greek mainland; in the mountains, groups of brigands known as *kléftes* (klephts) had formed. They were essentially bandits, equally likely to plunder a Greek village as a Muslim estate but, thanks to their attacks on Ottoman officials such as tax collectors, in folklore they came to symbolise the spirit of Greek resistance to the Ottoman authorities. They are

merchant community. Commercial links with Europe introduced wealthy Greeks to European lifestyles, and also to European cultural and political ideas. This mercantile middle class funded the intellectual revival which characterised the late 18th century in Greece, endowing schools and libraries, and sponsoring higher education.

The struggle for independence

In 1814, three Greek merchants in Odessa formed a secret organisation called "The Friendly Society" (*Filikí Etería*) devoted to "the betterment

Ermoúpoli on Sýros.

certainly viewed in this light in the klephtic ballads that emerged, extolling the bravery and military prowess of the *kléftes* and their heroic resistance to the Turkish oppressors.

In an effort to counter klephtic depredations and to control the mountain passes, the Ottomans established a militia of *armatolí*. Like the *kléftes*, these were Christians – and the distinction between *kléftes* and *armatolí* was highly fluid, with roles easily exchanged. However, the existence of these armed bands meant that, when the struggle for Greek independence broke out in the early 19th century, there was a record of military experience.

More important for the development of Greek nationalism was the growth of a Greek

GREEK SCHOLARS IN THE WEST

Economic success in 18th-century Greece was a significant factor in the development of its culture and identity. Large numbers of school teachers, with the backing of rich merchant benefactors, studied in the universities of Europe, notably in Italy and Germany. There they encountered the heady nationalist doctrines inspired by the French Revolution – and also discovered the reverence in which the language and culture of Ancient Greece were held throughout Europe. By the end of the 18th century, nationalism had found a fertile ground among young educated Greeks.

of the nation", which rapidly acquired a network of sympathisers throughout the Ottoman lands. A number of vain attempts to secure themselves powerful backing were finally rewarded when their members organised an uprising against Ottoman rule in 1821.

Scattered violent incidents merged into a major revolt in the Peloponnese. The Ottomans found themselves initially outnumbered and were forced to retreat to their coastal fortresses, while atrocities were committed by both sides. Greeks slaughtered Turkish and Jewish civilians in Trípoli; Turks slaughtered the Greek inhabitants of Híos. Later, Egyptian troops, under Ibrahim Ali, laid waste most of the Peloponnese.

The struggle for Greek independence, which lasted from 1821 to 1832, was not a straightforward affair. Opposing the Ottomans was an ill-assorted band of *kléftes*, *armatolí*, merchants, landowners, intellectual theorists and aristocratic families known as Phanariots – all as keen to further their own interests as to advance the cause of Greek nationalism. When they were not fighting their Muslim opponents – mostly Egyptian or Albanian troops rather than "Turks" – they turned on each other.

Soon after the 1821 uprising, no fewer than three provisional Greek governments proclaimed themselves, each poised to take control of the liberated territories. A democratic constitution was drawn up in 1822, then revised in 1823, by which time the three factions were unified in a central authority. But the following year, feuding between rival groups culminated in outright civil war (prompting one chieftain, Makrygiannis, to protest that he had not taken up arms against the Turks to end up fighting Greeks).

Foreign support

Ironically, the belief that this was a national struggle was held with greatest conviction by the foreign philhellenes – Lord Byron among them – who came to help the Greeks. These men were influential in getting Western public opinion behind Greece. Thus Britain, France and Russia, all initially unsympathetic to the Hellenic dream, eventually put military and diplomatic pressure on the Ottomans to acknowledge Greek independence – a policy of "peaceful interference", as the British Prime Minister Stratford Canning described it. The turning point came with the almost accidental destruction of the Ottoman fleet by an allied armada at Navarino in 1827. This intervention by the three Great Powers ensured that some form of independent Greece came into being, although its precise borders took several years to negotiate.

Count Ioannis Kapodistrias, a Greek diplomat formerly in the service of the Russian tsar, was elected the first president of independent Greece by a National Assembly in 1827. He encouraged Greek forces to push north into the central mainland, and his efforts were

Ioannis Kapodistrias, who some feared was aiming for dictatorship, was assassinated.

rewarded when the 1830 Protocol of London fixed the new state's northern boundary to run roughly from Árta to Vólos, including the Sporades.

Although well liked by the peasantry, the more traditional Greek elites (whom Kapodistrias loathed) were alarmed by his high-handed administrative style, suspecting him of aiming at one-man rule. On 9 October 1831, he was shot by two chieftains of the Máni as he entered a church at Návplio. With the threat of anarchy and renewed civil war looming, Britain, France and Russia set about finding another suitable candidate to lead the new country.

INDEPENDENT GREECE

Independence did not guarantee peace and stability: enemy occupation, civil war and a military junta have all marked the path to today's democracy.

The new state was desperately poor, overrun by armed brigands and beset by political factionalism. In 1834, Maniot rebels defeated government troops and sent them home stripped of their equipment. There were few good harbours or roads; Athens remained a poor, dusty, provincial town. Internally, conditions were worse than they had been under Ottoman rule.

Bavarian absolutism was partly to blame. Some months after Kapodistrias's death, Greece was declared a kingdom and the crown given to Otto, son of Ludwig I of Bavaria, who arrived at Návplio in 1833 on a British man-of-war.

Widespread calls for a constitution were ignored until, in 1843, a bloodless coup in Athens forced Otto to accept constitutional rule and parliamentary government for Greece. Consecutive 1844 and 1864 constitutions endowed the country with democratic trappings, especially after Otto was deposed by a more forceful coup in 1862.

The "Great Idea"

The new kingdom was home to less than one-third of the Greeks around the Aegean. The prospect of "liberating" those Greeks still under Ottoman rule, of creating a new Byzantium by recapturing Constantinople and avenging the humiliation of 1453, was known as the "Great Idea" (*Megáli Idéa* in Greek) and aroused enormous enthusiasm. When King George I succeeded King Otto in 1863, he tellingly assumed the title of "King of the Hellenes" rather than simply "King of Greece". But irredentism (the annexation of a neighbouring state on the grounds of ethnicity or prior historical possession) was never a realistic policy since, without allies, the Greek army was no match for the Ottomans; yet the *Megáli Idéa* survived repeated

The Corinth Canal, completed in 1893, separates the Peloponnesian peninsula from the Greek mainland.

setbacks. Only after the catastrophic 1922 defeat at the hands of the Turkish nationalists did this irredentist vision finally collapse.

The prominent late-19th century populist Theodoros Deligiannis encouraged foolhardy irredentist expeditions to Thessaly and Crete. His more far-sighted rival, Harilaos Trikoupis, realised that such adventures were unwise so long as Greece was dependent on foreign loans, which gave its creditors veto power over foreign policy initiatives. Trikoupis set out to reduce this dependency by development. Roads were improved, railways constructed, Piraeus became Greece's busiest port, and the Corinth Canal dug.

But despite the appearance of a few textile and food-processing factories, industry remained rudimentary; Greece was a rural nation of peasant smallholders. The lack of large estates (except in Thessaly) minimised social inequalities but it also meant that most farmers remained too miserably poor to adopt modern farming methods. The export of currants brought brief prosperity, but the global 1893 depression hit the entire economy. Greece went bankrupt, and hunger drove many peasants to emigrate.

A new government

Domestic problems only increased enthusiasm for the Great Idea. Thessaly and southeastern

A naïve depiction of Eleftherios Venizelos.

Epirus had been acquired in 1881, without any fighting, through the Congress of Berlin. When troubles on Ottoman Crete in 1897 provoked a wave of sympathy on the mainland, Greek naval forces were sent to the island while the army marched northwards – only to be humiliatingly defeated by Ottoman forces.

On Crete and in Macedonia, Ottoman rule was steadily crumbling. But the emergence of the new Balkan nations Bulgaria and Serbia complicated Greek foreign policy, for both countries shared Greece's aspiration for territory in Macedonia.

A precedent for military intervention in politics had been set with the coups of 1843 and 1862. In 1909, junior army officers revolted and invited a radical new politician, Eleftherios

Venizelos, to come over from Crete and form a government in 1910. A consummate tactician, Venizelos channelled the energies of the Greek middle class into his own Liberal Party, a dominant force in politics for the next 25 years.

A decade of wars

When the Balkan Wars erupted in 1912–13, Greece was strong enough to first wrest Epirus and southern Macedonia from the Ottoman forces and then to defend its gains, in alliance with Serbia and Romania, from a hostile Bulgaria. The full gains from the fighting

The notorious Dillesi gang who terrorised central Greece.

included – in addition to Macedonia – Epirus, Crete and the east Aegean Islands. Greece's area and population were nearly doubled at a stroke.

There was barely time to assimilate these new territories before the country was embroiled in World War I. Venizelos and the new king, Constantine I, quarrelled over whether to bring Greece into the conflict. The prime minister wanted Greece to give the Entente active support, while Constantine, brother-in-law of Germany's Kaiser Wilhelm II, insisted on keeping the country neutral. Who would have the final say over foreign policy – the king or parliament? The dispute attained the pitch of civil war by 1916, when Venizelist Corfu violated neutrality by hosting the Serbian army and government in exile, and Thessaloníki served as the "rebel" capital. In June 1917, Constantine was forced to leave the country and Greece entered the war on the side of the Entente, helping precipitate the final Central collapse in autumn 1918 with attacks across the Macedonian front.

Venizelos hoped that the Entente powers would reward Greece for its support with new territories. The annexation by Greece of Smyrna (Izmir), with its rich hinterland and large ethnic Greek population, had long been a basic tenet of the Great Idea. When, in May 1919, the British, French and Americans approved the landing

changing to a "neutralist" position and refusing to sell them arms – and even selling some to the Turks. Kemal gradually forced the Greek army back behind long defensive lines ever closer to the coast. After a year-long stalemate, Kemal overran the Greek positions in late August 1922; the Greek army abandoned Smyrna a few days later. The Turkish army entered the city on 9 September, burning both the Armenian and Greek quarters and killing an estimated 30,000 of the Christian inhabitants in the process.

The 1923 Treaty of Lausanne, which definitively ended the Greco-Turkish war, fixed the

Victorious troops returning from Bulgaria during World War I.

of Greek troops in Smyrna, it began to look as though the dream might at last be realised.

The Asia Minor Disaster

In late 1920, the pendulum of Greek political sentiment swung back, removing Venizelos from office and returning King Constantine I from exile. Army morale was damaged by politically motivated changes in command, but the revival of Turkish national fervour sparked by the Greek advance and galvanised by the emerging Turkish leader, Mustafa Kemal (subsequently Atatürk), was far more dangerous. Greek forces advanced to within 80km (50 miles) of Ankara in August 1921, but were hampered by their former European allies

two countries' boundaries which hold today (with the exception of the Dodecanese islands, occupied by the Italians until after World War II). In addition, a massive population transfer, based on religion rather than language, was stipulated: 380,000 Muslim inhabitants of Greece moved to Turkey in exchange for 1.3 million Orthodox Christians (in fact 1 million of these had already left Anatolia since 1914). Except for a dwindling population in Istanbul and on the islands of Imbros and Tenedos, this ended a 2,500-year Hellenic presence in Asia Minor. The Greeks refer to these events as "the Asia Minor Disaster", and they remain a defining factor in the Greek perception of both themselves and of the Turks.

In the early 20th century, many Greek villages depended heavily on money sent home by young men who had emigrated, particularly to the United States.

Republican interlude

Exhausted by 10 years of war, the Greek state now faced the huge problem of absorbing indigent newcomers into a country that had difficulty in sustaining its existing population. The economy benefited from the cheap labour, and Greece

finally began to industrialise. But the refugees also increased social tensions. Almost a million of them settled in squalid shanty towns outside the city centres.

After the disaster, King Constantine was forced to abdicate for good after a military coup, six high-ranking officers and royalist ministers were court-martialed and executed, and a parliamentary republic was established. It lasted only 13 years and was characterised by political intrigues and a brief military dictatorship under Theodoros Pangalos. The only period of stability – Venizelos's return to power from 1928 to 1932 – was terminated by the shock of international economic depression. In 1933, the Liberals were succeeded by the royalist People's Party, whose leaders only half-heartedly supported the republic. An abortive Venizelist coup in 1935 resulted in Venizelos himself going into exile in Paris.

Return of the monarchy

The politicians' feuding rendered parliamentary government vulnerable to military pressure. The failed 1935 coup quickly resulted in a renewed mandate for the People's Party, and shortly after, the army backed restoration of the king, Constantine's son George II. In 1936, he offered the premiership to an extreme right-wing politician, Ioannis Metaxas, a former senior army officer and fervent royalist – despite his party having few parliamentary seats – to avoid more numerous Communist MPs exercising the balance of power. Soon afterwards, Metaxas responded to a wave of Communist-inspired strikes by declaring martial law and abolishing parliament. But self-styled "First Peasant" Metaxas never managed to firmly implement his so-called "Third Hellenic Civilisation". Despite imitating some of the characteristics of Fascist regimes, he regarded Britain as Greece's traditional patron in foreign affairs. But Germany's increasing dominance in the Balkans, as against Britain's naval strength in the Mediterranean, dictated a stance of neutrality.

But Germany was not the only power with designs on the Balkans. In April 1939, Mussolini invaded Albania and in October 1940 he prepared to cross the Albanian border into Greece. Metaxas could no longer hope to keep Greece neutral. Receiving the Italian ambassador in his dressing gown early on 28 October, he listened to a recital of trumped-up charges and responded to the ultimatum for free passage of Italian troops into Greece with a curt "This means war". *Óhi* or "No" Day is now a national holiday.

World War II and the Occupation

Fighting alone in the mountains of Epirus, the Greek forces surprised onlookers by pushing the Makaronádes ("Spaghetti Eaters", as the Italians were quickly dubbed) deep back into Albania. But in the spring of 1941, Hitler sent German troops south to pacify the Balkans in preparation for his attack on the Soviet Union. Victory was swift: the Nazi invasion of Greece began on 6 April, and by the end of the month they had appointed General Georgios Tsolakoglou as the first quisling prime minister.

Greece was occupied by German, Italian and Bulgarian forces, each with their designated zones. While their hold over the countryside was often tenuous, it was firm in the towns, which suffered most from food shortages, notably in the terrible famine of winter 1941–42 when over 100,000 perished. From the towns also the Germans deported and exterminated Greece's long-established Jewish communities during 1943–44. King George and the legal government had left the country in 1941 and

German officers on top of the Acropolis, Athens.

passed the war in British Egypt.

Yet in the mountains, organised resistance emerged, drawing on the klephtic tradition and making forays down into the plains. Much the largest of these groups was the Greek Popular Liberation Army (the Greek initials being ELAS), organised by the Communist-dominated National Liberation Front (Greek acronym EAM), but commanding broad support. Clashes between the three main rival resistance groups – there were also royalist EDES and centrist-Venizelist EKKA – were common, while the Germans and their new stooge, Greek Prime Minister Ioannis Rallis, established the collaborationist Security Battalions.

The dominance of EAM meant that when the British first contacted resistance groups in 1942, they found that military considerations collided with political ones. ELAS, with perhaps 60,000 fighters, was well placed to pin down German troops. But the British, suspecting that EAM intended to set up a Communist state in Greece after the war, also armed the other groups as a counterweight. EAM/ELAS, for its part, was annoyed that Churchill wished to restore the monarchy without consulting the Greek people. In turn, Churchill had little sympathy for ELAS guerrillas, whom he described as "miserable banditti".

Into the Cold War

In October 1944, the German forces abandoned Greece, replaced by Greek and British troops. In December 1944, bitter fighting erupted in Athens between ELAS fighters and British troops. Inflation continued to soar, the black market still flourished and violence erupted country-wide between the Security Batallions and their opponents.

The December 1944 fighting marked a decisive turning point in the slide towards the civil war that subsequently broke out between the national government and Communist insurgents, raging from October 1946 until October 1949. King George had returned to Greece in September 1946 following an apparently rigged plebiscite on the monarchy.

Greece during the late 1940s became a key battleground in the developing Cold War. In March 1947, the United States took over from Britain as Greece's principal external

IMPERIALISM IN ACTION

Italy occupied Rhodes and the Dodecanese from 1912 to 1943. During the years of Mussolini's rule, the islanders lived under the strictures of a totalitarian regime intent on "Italianising" the islands. A secret police network guarded against nationalist activity; the supremacy of Roman Catholicism was mandated; the blue and white colours of the Greek flag were prohibited in public; all shop signs had to be in Italian, with slogans such as "*Viva il Duce, viva la nuova Italia imperiale!*" daubed on the walls of recalcitrant shopkeepers. During the 1930s, under the harsh governorship of ardent Fascist Cesare Maria de Vecchi, many islanders emigrated.

patron. American military and economic aid flooded in, enabling the central government, at times very hard-pressed, to defeat the rebel Democratic Army in the mountains of north-west Greece by October 1949. But the victory entailed the incarceration of suspected left-wingers on desolate prison-islands like Makrónisos, Gyáros and Paleó Tríkeri and the forcible evacuation of entire villages.

Violation of civil rights and the emergence of a powerful security apparatus did not end in 1950. Politics continued to be polarised, although the royalist-republican divide had

Greece had joined NATO in 1951, and the pro-Western orientation of its foreign policy secured continued support from the United States. However, the relationship was not straightforward: when the Cyprus dispute flared up in 1954, Greece refused to take part in NATO manoeuvres, and relations with putative ally Turkey soured. This foreshadowed problems later governments would have defining Greece's role in Europe. Nonetheless, the Cyprus issue was resolved – temporarily – when that island became an independent republic in 1960.

British troops liberate Athens in 1944.

become one between the royalist Right and the far Left; the banned Communists participated in the electoral system behind a front party, United Democratic Left (UDL).

Greece looks West

Democracy had weathered the civil war – but only just, with women finally granted the vote in 1952. In the following decade, a degree of stability was achieved, with only two conservative prime ministers in power between 1952 and 1963 – from 1955, the redoubtable Constantine Karamanlis. Yet this stability was precarious, relying as it did on restricted civil liberties, and a first-past-the-post electoral system designed to exclude small parties from parliament.

The "economic miracle"

During the 1950s and 1960s, Greece, like Italy and Spain, experienced an "economic miracle" which transformed the country. Malaria was wiped out through anti-mosquito spraying, electric power reached many remote areas and communications improved. Athens mushroomed until it contained more than one-third of the country's entire population – as it still does.

Old forms of political control, which had operated best in small rural communities, began to erode. A new urban middle class arose which regarded the conservative elite as lacking a vision of Greece as a modern state.

The bitterly fought 1961 elections saw the resurgence of the political centre under the leadership of former Venizelist Georgios Papandreou. When the results were announced in favour of Karamanlis and his National Radical Union, Papandreou alleged that they were fraudulent.

Public disquiet at possible links between the palace, the ruling party and extreme right-wing violence increased in May 1963 when a prominent UDL deputy, Grigoris Lambrakis, was assassinated at a rally in Thessaloníki. Shortly afterwards, Karamanlis resigned and in the two

hold elections in May 1967, Constantine was faced with the prospect of a third Centre Union victory.

However, schemes hatched between the king and senior army officers for military intervention were dramatically pre-empted when a group of junior army officers, working according to a NATO contingency plan, executed a swift coup d'état early on the morning of 21 April 1967. Martial law was proclaimed; all political parties were dissolved. The so-called Colonels (only two junta officers actually held this rank) were in power.

Women fought with the Resistance during the civil war.

successive elections that followed, Papandreou's Centre Union Party won power, the first centrist ruling party in Greece for over a decade. With conservative politicians prepared to surrender power – and Karamanlis gone into voluntary exile in Paris – an extended period of centrist rule now seemed possible, although right-wingers in the military and the palace saw this as a threat.

When Papandreou demanded a reshuffle of senior army officers, he found himself opposed by his defence minister and the new young king, Constantine II. The king tried clumsily to bring down the Centre Union government, but when Papandreou agreed with the main conservative opposition to

The military junta

The military junta was motivated by self-interest, anti-Communism and ultra-nationalism. This combination was certainly not new: on various occasions in the interwar period, army officers had used the rhetoric of national salvation to avert being dismissed in politically motivated purges. In their attitudes, too, the new junta's officers drew on earlier examples. They claimed that they wanted the country to "radiate civilisation in all directions" by establishing a "Greece of the Christian Greeks" which would make it once again "a pole of ideological and spiritual attraction". This was an old dream, an escape from the modern world into a chimaeric fusion of classical Athens and Byzantium.

The first signs of widespread discontent coincided with the 1973 economic downturn. The protest leaders were students, whose occupations of university buildings in March and November were brutally broken up. After the November student occupation of the Athens Polytechnic, Colonel Georgios Papadopoulos, the regime's figurehead, was replaced by the even more sinister Brigadier Dimitrios Ioannides, previously commander of the military police.

In the end, the Cyprus problem toppled the junta. A foolhardy Greek nationalist coup,

prompted by Athens, against Cypriot president Archbishop Makarios led the Turks to invade northern Cyprus. Ioannides ordered Greek forces to retaliate by invading Turkey, but mobilisation was so chaotic and the disparity of forces so obvious that local commanders mutinied. On 24 July 1974, Constantine Karamanlis made a triumphant return from exile to supervise the restoration of parliamentary democracy.

Karamanlis's "New Democracy"

The transition to democracy proceeded remarkably smoothly considering the enormous problems that Karamanlis faced. Aware of his own vulnerability, he moved slowly in dismissing junta collaborators, and for some time never slept in the same quarters two nights running to forestall attempts by junta diehards to abduct him. At the elections held in November 1974, Karamanlis's New Democracy (Néa Dimokratía or ND) party won an overwhelming victory, though many people seemed to have voted for ND simply as a guarantor of stability.

Karamanlis was in theory able to proceed with necessary reforms, since a December 1974 referendum produced a decisive vote for the abolition of the monarchy, compromised by the king's actions before and during the junta. To replace it, Karamanlis created a presidency with sweeping powers. In the event of a swing to the Left, Karamanlis could simply resign his parliamentary seat and become president.

A move to the Left

Signs of such a swing were evident after the 1977 elections in which Andreas Papandreou's Panhellenic Socialist Movement (PASOK) made large gains. The younger Papandreou, Georgios's son, represented a new post-war generation; with his background as a professor of economics in the US, he seemed the ideal candidate to lead a technocratic party. Yet he still cultivated his 1960s reputation as a radical, vehemently attacking Karamanlis's policies, taking a belligerent stand over relations with Turkey, and threatening that a PASOK government would take Greece out of both NATO and the EEC, subject to a referendum. Support for PASOK grew, until, in 1980, Karamanlis resigned as prime minister and was voted in as president by parliament.

A TOTALITARIAN APPROACH

With their peasant or lower-middle-class backgrounds, the junta officers symbolised a provincial reaction to the new world of urban consumers brought about by Greece's economic "miracle" of the 1950s and 1960s. They stressed the need for a return to traditional morality and religion, and set about this with a fanatical attention to detail. Not only did they close the frontiers to bearded or mini-skirted foreigners (at least until the tourist trade was hit), they also prevented Greeks from reading "subversive" literature – much ancient drama included. This grim period of Greek history was marked by torture and internal exile of opponents.

Papandreou and PASOK

After PASOK's victory in the October 1981 elections, based on the simple campaign slogan of *Allagí* ("Change"), Papandreou formed Greece's first notionally socialist government. His significance lies not in his socialism – though the regime was manifestly anti-big-business – but in his remarkable success in articulating populist views, and engaging in no- or low-cost gestures such as instituting civil marriage and recognising the ELAS wartime resistance for the first time.

PASOK rhetoric carried the party until the three successive elections of 1989 and 1990,

Tank patrols Athens' streets during the failed military coup by King Constantine against Greece's junta, December 1967.

when accumulated scandals returned the New Democracy party to power. This proved to be only a short interregnum, for – helped by a fatal split within ND – PASOK won early elections in October 1993, returning Andreas Papandreou to office until ill health forced him to step down two years later. PASOK chose as his successor the relatively uncharismatic Kostas Simitis, who contrasted markedly with the flamboyant style of his predecessor.

As prime minister, Simitis had to oblige a population long accustomed to government largesse to accept economic reality. After Andreas Papandreou's death in June 1996, the government followed a tighter economic policy so as

to allow Greece to join the European Monetary Union (EMU). This was not easy, since many PASOK deputies and labour unions strenuously opposed such attempts.

FYROM and Turkey

In foreign affairs, the emergence of an independent Macedonian state from the ruins of ex-Yugoslavia in 1991 acted as a red flag before a bull to the more nationalist fringe of Greeks. In 1993, Antonis Samaras pulled the plug on the ND government by defecting with other deputies to form the short-lived Politikí Ánixi party, whose main platform was intransigence on the Macedonia issue. But by the late 1990s, Greece was reconciled to the existence of an independent Macedonian state on her northern border, although agreement has yet to be reached on its name – Former Yugoslav Republic of Macedonia (FYROM), or the more disparaging Ta Skópia (The Skopje Things), are the only labels permitted in Greek public discourse.

Traditionally poor relations with Turkey improved markedly late in 1999 when there was an upsurge of public sympathy in each country for the other when both were afflicted by severe earthquakes. Helped by good personal rapport between the Greek and Turkish foreign ministers, one result was Greece dropping opposition to Turkish EU candidacy.

On the domestic front, Simitis secured a very narrow victory over nephew-of-Constantine Kostas Karamanlis's ND party in spring 2000 elections. Simitis continued with austerity measures aimed at controlling public expenditure and curbing inflation. These enabled Greece to join the eurozone in 2001 and it adopted the euro in early 2002 – abandoning Europe's oldest currency, the drachma. Despite Simitis' nickname of *O Logistís* (The Accountant), it eventually became evident that the books had been cooked under his watch to allow Greece to join the EMU, so Simitis now languishes in enforced retirement, persona non grata for any sinecure post with the EU.

The visit of Pope John Paul II to Athens in May 2002 demonstrated how long historical memories are in Greece when the Pope formally apologised for the sack of Constantinople following the diversion of the Fourth Crusade in 1204.

Just two months later, *Dekaeftá Noemvríou* ("17 November"), Europe's longest lived far-left terrorist group, which had operated with seeming impunity (and 23 fatalities) since 1974, was abruptly liquidated. By late 2003, trials saw most of its members convicted and jailed.

The 2004 Olympics

Simitis resigned before the elections of March 2004, leaving his polished foreign minister, George Papandreou (son of Andreas), as PASOK party leader. Despite 17 November having been wound up during PASOK's term, a decisive victory was won by ND under Kostas Karamanlis. He appointed himself minister of culture as well as premier to oversee the behind-schedule construction of the Olympic Games venues. Basic urban infrastructure, such as the new international airport at Spáta and the Athens metro, had been in place since 2001. In the event, Greece staged memorable games that confounded the most cynical critics – but left huge cost overruns and crumbling facilities with no compelling future role.

In 2007, despite major scandals concerning crooked investments and missing contributions for the national pension scheme, and widespread criticism of ND's handling of August's forest fires – the worst in living memory – Karamanlis called early elections for September and won almost as handily as in 2004.

The new parliament only sat for half its statutory term of four years; "Kostakis" ("Charlie" or "Chuck" approximately), as the younger Karamanlis was derisively dubbed, unwisely called another snap election in October 2009, resulting in a resounding defeat for his party; and "Georgakis" ("Georgie" as George Papandreou the younger was equally disparagingly nicknamed) finally realised his dream of becoming prime minister.

The crisis unfolds

Although PASOK had clearly benefitted from public disgust at ND inaction and corruption since 2004, there was to be no honeymoon period for them. State finances turned out to be in far worse condition than anticipated, such that Greece's ability to pay its public payroll and meet its periodic obligations for bond maturities and debts to both domestic and foreign lenders was in doubt. Total debt, with little hope of ever paying it off, eventually approached 400 billion euros. Greece was

obliged to beg for a bailout from international lending agencies.

In May 2010, a €110 billion loan was offered by the so-called troïka, comprising the IMF, the European Union and the European Central Bank, subject to conditions. These were the implementation of the harshest austerity measures ever imposed by any civilian government: the privatisation of most government assets and enterprises, whether profitable or not; an effective crackdown on rampant tax evasion by freelance professionals, depriving state coffers of half their expected revenue, along with

Andreas Papandreou in 1994 in Washington, DC, during an official visit to the US.

sharp hikes in taxes; and the implementation of so-called structural reforms, to make the Greek economy more competitive and spur growth. Some of Greece's public debt was to be written off in order to reduce the Greek debt-to-GDP ratio from a shocking level of nearly 200 percent to 120 percent by 2020 – still nothing to boast about, given that normal levels in other countries are well down into two figures.

These proposals sparked vehement opposition from those worst affected within Greece, up to and including repeated civil disturbances in Athens which merely frightened off potential tourists, clients of Greece's only reliably functioning enterprise. The economy instead shrunk so precipitously that a second bailout of €130 billion had to be secured in late 2011, with a two-year extension on the implementation of reforms negotiated in late 2012. Aid tranches were often held back by lenders, pending passage of key austerity measures in an increasingly restive Greek parliament.

The street-level effects of all these measures have been massive unemployment, in particular the dismissal of many civil servants and the cutting of most salaries and pensions to Third World levels. Many businesses, small and large, have failed, evident in the vast number of

George Papandreou addresses the ruling Socialist PASOK party in 2004.

boarded-up shop fronts in Athens, Thessaloníki and other large towns, and the growing number of homeless. No improvement or growth is foreseen until at least 2016, and public patience with austerity has been stretched to breaking point; Óhi állo sósimo, "No More Rescue", is a common graffito.

Political meltdown

Politically, the effects of the crisis have been equally cataclysmic, effectively disintegrating the party duopoly which had run Greece since 1974. Papandreou resigned as prime minister in November 2011, deferring to a unity government led by European banker Lucas Papademos, whose brief was to negotiate effectively with the troika. Despite appreciable headway in this, and widespread feeling that he, albeit unelected, should be left in place longer, inexorable pressure built up for spring 2012 elections.

These, on 6 May, returned a hung, unprecedentedly splintered parliament, with seven parties taking seats, and support for both PASOK and ND plunging below 20 percent nationwide. After futile negotiations to form a viable coalition, further elections took place on 17 June. Their results were broadly similar, with the same seven parties represented, and ND again the top poller, this time at 29.66 percent, fractionally ahead of SYRIZA at 26.9 percent. Even with 50 bonus seats for the front-running party, ND had to cobble together a coalition with all-but-extinguished PASOK and DIMAR (Democratic Left). SYRIZA, originally a leftist umbrella for old PASOK cadres, assorted activists and MPs expelled from other parties for failing to vote for austerity measures, benefitted mightily from the evaporation of both the PASOK and the hardline Communist vote, as noncooperative Communist behaviour since May convinced many that another ballot cast for them would be wasted. But SYRIZA, poised in the wings to be the next governing entity should the current coalition stumble, remains an unknown quantity despite becoming a unitary party in December 2012.

The worst surprise from both balloting rounds was the emergence of the neo-Nazi, violently xenophobic Hrysí Avgí (Golden Dawn), which fed on the collapse of rival far-right party LAOS – and the public's disgust with dynastic-dinosaur politics. Despite gaining barely seven percent of the vote and only 18 MPs, they make plenty of noise, courting publicity with regular outrages. A noxious stew of ex-military commandos, Orthodox fanatics, common criminals, black-clad body-builders, heavy metal fans and bikers, their symbol is a swastika-like adaptation of the ancient Greek meander. Assailed for performing Nazi-style salutes in public, party members retorted, "These hands may salute but they do not steal". They function as Greece's id, doing and saying things that "respectable" burghers only think about. Were elections to be held today, they would likely finish third after SYRIZA and ND, and members openly predict they will become a governing party.

Coping with the Crisis

Greeks have been coping with their extended economic crisis in a number of creative ways.

Not a month goes by in Greece without a "back to the land" newspaper feature – young people, not just retirees, re-occupying old family property, rent-free, in their ancestral village. Here they can grow their own food, raise children in a bucolic environment, and perhaps even ply the trade they did back in town, if they weren't unemployed. Young people who can't leave the cities move back in with their parents (many never left) or occupy a spare flat owned by the family.

Failing internal migration, there's outright emigration; Australia, Canada, the UK, Germany and the Netherlands are favourite destinations. There are simply no well-paying jobs for recent graduates in Greece, with thousands applying for any vacancy; engineers in particular are fairly sure of positions overseas.

Greek banks, thanks to huge portfolios of non-performing loans, are dangerously undercapitalised. Since 2010, they have lost nearly 40 percent of their deposits as customers, fearful of a sudden changeover to a rapidly devaluating "new" drachma, withdraw euros as banknotes for keeping under mattresses.

Many small businesses have shut down. Others vacate commercial premises but continue to operate out of sitting rooms or converted garages at home. Pawnshops are burgeoning, as "we buy gold" signs and flyers in every town indicate. House calls are available for those not wanting to publically parade their circumstances.

As insurance, fuel and road tax costs soar, up to 40 percent of vehicles circulate without insurance coverage, and many cars are for sale, or abandoned illegally, sans number plates, on public thoroughfares. Bicycling as a means of transport is big, and cycling shops are one of the few flourishing retail sectors.

Winter heating has become a major issue, with massive conversion to energy-efficient wood stoves (especially to avoid punitive new taxes on heating oil). With unfiltered chimneys puffing everywhere, it's become a major air-quality issue and the government is being urged to rescind the taxes.

Make do and Mend

Second-hand goods, including formerly disdained clothing, are now socially acceptable, as is rubbish and roadside-scavenging. Anybody involved in fixing things – eg, tailors, seamstresses, shoe repairmen, auto mechanics – has a huge backlog of work.

Little is bought new unless heavily discounted, so shops hold sales continually. Middleman-free street markets are emerging, with farmers selling produce direct to consumers. Barter networks (using websites and/or open-air markets) have appeared in Athens, Vólos and other towns. One accrues credits through jobs done or voucher systems.

Seeing the state as effectively useless, people take far more independent initiative. Parents may hire a whole island bar for a benefit party to fix the local,

Farmers selling potato sacks at cost price in Thessaloníki in March 2012. Similar 'solidarity' actions take place throughout the country.

structurally unsafe school. Or taverna owners in a seaside resort sponsor divers at summer's end to retrieve all the junk submerged in the adjacent picturesque fishing harbour, knowing that the local *limenikó sóma* (harbour corps) will never do anything.

Leisure spending is way down – people eat out perhaps once a week, not two or three times as before. Many *tavérnes* only open on certain peak nights in winter. Those that offer real value or *prix fixe* menus (a recent novelty) are full to bursting, while fancy places struggle. Smarter live-music venues, recognising that some money is better than none, have moderated cover prices to attract customers, say from a formerly untenable €30 down to €15.

GREEKS TODAY

In many ways, Greece has become a modern
European country. But there are other facets
of the national character that have not
changed in centuries.

I s the phrase "modern Greece" an oxymoron?
A Greek might well pose this question to
Western visitors, given the history of the past
200 years: to claim a place among the Western
European family of nations, Greeks have been
obliged to prove themselves more like their
2,500-year-old forebears than their peasant
grandparents. Which is perhaps to say that
notions of "modernity" are always in the eye of
the beholder, and that contemporary Greece,
more so than many parts of the world, is shot
through with contradictions.

The spread of Westernisation

Anyone who has been a regular visitor to Greece
over the past 40 years cannot help but be aware
of the rampant Westernisation of consumption
and behaviour patterns – not just in Athens but
also in small villages. During the 1970s, most
Greek young women were, to not put too fine
a point on it, dumpy, spotty, cultivating lank-
and-greasy hairdos, and dressed in such styles
(or lack thereof) as to make East Germans of the
time look positively glamorous. Fast forward to
the Naughties and the look is quite different –
women in their twenties dressed to the nines
and expensively quiffed even in the throes of
the current crisis, and a good head taller than
their peers of three decades before. In a country
that until recently associated thinness with illness or meanness, one can now find ubiquitous
slimming centres and beauty salons hawking
the latest dietary and depilation secrets to anx-
ious young women. Gyms, runners and cyclists
have multiplied too, especially after the 2004
Olympics, surfing a wave of shame provoked by
the sight of sleek, fit athletes – Greeks of both
genders have long been among the most obese
in the EU, along with the British and the Maltese.

*General Confederation of Greek Workers demonstrate against
yet more job cuts and tax hikes, September 2012.*

Striking changes are also manifest in national
politics, as election campaigns – the subject of
tremendous passion throughout the 1970s and
1980s – have been met increasingly with contempt
reflected in a startlingly high abstention rate (over
one-third) for a country where violators of the com-
pulsory-voting law were until recently punished
with fines. Politicians as a class now enjoy an esti-
mation on a par with heinous criminals, regarded
as universally corrupt and self-serving. Many Greeks
now prefer to make their views known on the
street, in demonstrations peaceful or otherwise.

A strong national identity

Yet there is another side to contemporary
Greece that stands firm against the tide of

Westernisation and homogenisation, epitomised by the public protest over a proposed law in the mid-1990s which would have forced tavernas and bars to close at 2am rather than 4am. This was supposedly to increase worker efficiency. The widespread and continued outcry over this proposal eventually led to it being shelved, or at worst applied week nights only. An attempt to re-introduce the measure more recently met with near-identical results. Amidst the often acrimonious exchange of abuse between Germany and Greece during the current crisis, mediated in great part by

Localism and homeland

Another facet of contemporary Greece that stresses the local can also be found in the unusual relationship that exists between villages and the large urban centres of Athens and Thessaloníki. While certainly not free of the snobbery that urban dwellers commonly express for the "backwardness" of their rural cousins, most of Greece is somewhat unusual in having a comparatively short urban memory. There are few Athenians whose grandparents were born in that city. Thus, a Greek who answers the question "Where are you from?"

Celebrating the anniversary of the victory over invading Italian troops in 1940.

each country's gutter press, a recurrent motif by Greek partisans was "they (the dreary northern Europeans) envy us our lifestyle.

Greece's working day, with its ostensibly inefficient split every Tuesday, Thursday and Friday into morning and early-evening work shifts (producing two sets of daily commutes in towns as people go to and from a siesta at home – or the beach), has also come under heavy attack from overseas creditors and eurocrats. The compromise solution, for many shops in Athens at least, is north-European style *synéhies óres* (a single shift) from October to April. But come summer, the *mikrós ypnos* or siesta again reigns supreme as shops revert to the only rhythm sensible in the roasting heat.

with "Athens" will invariably be asked "Yes, but where is your village?"

What seems an unusual query for anyone from a city such as London, Paris or New York makes perfect sense to the Athenian. These rural loyalties are manifested in the enormous flows of people out of the cities for Easter, most of August, and at election times, when many who have grown up in the largest towns still retain voting privileges in their family's ancestral village – where, indeed, their vote will numerically have more effect. Many city-dwellers – a rapidly increasing proportion of the population – will wax lyrical about the virtues of the food, the air and the water in their village; about an uncle's freshly pressed olive oil, a grandmother's cheese, an aunt's fig or pomegranate tree.

The population of Greece is currently around 11,300,000, of whom almost 4 million live in Athens. Thanks to a century of emigration, there are also around 6 million Greeks living overseas.

Regional pride is often more a matter of friendly rivalries, with differences in traditional costumes and wedding rituals, or whether Easter lamb (or goat) is prepared on a spit or in a clay oven, becoming topics of lengthy dis-

The hip crowd at a café in Ermoúpoli in Sýros.

cussion. Such localism should not be surprising given that, in Greek, the word "homeland" (*patrída*) is used to refer as equally to one's country and to one's village or region of birth. Hence the condition of *xenitiá*, or "longing for homeland", experienced by many in the far-flung Greek diaspora is inherently equivocal: is one primarily nostalgic for the sight of the Parthenon or for the view across the valley to the mountains?

The women's sphere

Perhaps nowhere are the paradoxes of contemporary Greece more evident than in shifting gender relations. Gender in Greece has always been more complicated than the stereotype of Mediterranean male dominance. Men have certainly dominated the public sphere of politics, but women have always dominated in their own public sphere of the church and religious life (this in spite of the all-male church leadership).

In many parts of Greece, particularly the Aegean Islands, dowry and house ownership have given women resources not available to their husbands (although there is also property passed down through the male line). With the tourist boom, many of these houses have been turned into lodgings, providing women with a source of ready cash as well. This meant that despite the rhetoric of male power, women have often been able to control things from behind the scenes.

As one woman from the island of Kálymnos put it: "Women would make the pretence of consulting their husbands, but more often they would simply make decisions for the family in their husbands' absence. My mother sold the family house while my father was away fishing for several months and then found ways to sugar-coat the news to him when he returned". This notion of female power is perhaps best captured by Lainie Kazan in the Hollywood film *My Big, Fat Greek Wedding* (2002): "Yes the man is the head of the family, but the woman is the neck – she can turn him in any direction she wants". All this, mind, in a culture where "Re Kopeliá! (Hey girlie!)" is still considered an acceptable form of public address in shops or tavernas by certain older men to younger women.

The early 1980s coming to power of the first PASOK government brought legal changes

KÓS VERSUS KÁLYMNOS

What Greece may have, until recently, lacked in ethnic diversity, it certainly made up for in the multitude of claims to regional diversity. Residents of villages, towns and cities are eager to discuss the myriad differences in manners and customs of their nearby neighbours. Often this may lead to hyperbole: "The Kalymniots are all crazy!" insisted a taxi driver on the neighbouring island of Kós. "The Koans are all lazy", a Kalymniot shoots back, calling them – for good measure – kótes (a pun on the island-name Kós, and extreme insult in Greek, meaning "hens", reserved usually for frivolous women).

improving women's position in relation to property ownership and pensions, as well as mandating civil marriage – a church ceremony by itself was no longer sufficient. And women moved into national politics in increasing numbers. The two Greek Communist parties have been led by women in recent years (Aleka Papariga and, briefly, Maria Damanaki before she became an EU Maritime Affairs and Fisheries Commissioner), and ex-Prime Minister Constantine Mitsotakis' daughter Dora Bakogianni has long been a figure to be reckoned with in the centre-right ND party, having served as foreign minister and mayor of Athens. Women, however, remain under-represented in the Greek Parliament as a whole, at fewer than 20 percent of the 300 MPs.

Loosened family bonds

While these changes in the public sphere have been substantial, in everyday life it might be more accurate to think less in terms of a shift in power from men to women than as a shift from the older to the younger generation. As Greece has moved away from agriculture and other "traditional" occupations into a more anonymous urban society, parents and other relatives no longer have the crucial technical knowledge that will determine their children's future work lives. Their control over the personal lives of the younger generation has also largely withered away. No longer can parents "keep their daughters locked up in their houses", as many claimed to do in the old days – most parents cease trying when the girl is about 15. It is now common, even in smaller towns, for couples to cohabit for extended periods in Holy Bedlock rather than get married, and even have children out of wedlock – something unheard of in the 1980s. Perhaps the most prominent example of this is Alexis Tsipras, currently head of the opposition centre-left SYRIZA party, who has neither married his long-term partner nor had their two children baptised.

Women in the men's world

The traditional Greek *kafeníon*, serving just Greek coffee, brandy and *oúzo* to an all-male clientele, is an increasingly endangered species. Such establishments are now vastly outnumbered by the so-called frappádika, which serve cold or hot cappuccino and espresso, *Nes-frappé*

and other exotic drinks to a young, mixed-sex crowd glued to their mobiles or tapping on tablet devices. Ironically, recent years have seen the simultaneous increase in coffee shops that pride themselves on making Greek coffee the old-fashioned way, heated ever-so-slowly over a bed of ember-heated sand: kafés sti hóvoli.

In late-night bars, it is no longer uncommon to see women engaged in dances that were once the sole preserve of men, like the *zeïbékiko*, the swaying, eagle-like solo dance which had long been a particular expression of Greek male passion and pain. And the dowry,

Generations old and new in Náousa on Páros.

a source of economic security to an older generation of women, is shunned by the daughters of these women as an insult to ideas about romantic love.

While older Greeks tend to see a struggle for power between the sexes, many younger people embrace at least a notion of "equality". Fathers now take a large share of childcare, and that extends to pushing the pram and changing the odd nappy – something unthinkable four decades ago. Also, in a marked contrast to Anglo-Saxon practice, if the parents go their separate ways, unless the father has behaved monstrously towards them, it is considered normal and expected that he will continue to have a close relationship with any offspring.

Fresh fish from the back of the truck, Lésvos.

Olive farmer from Páros.

PEOPLE AND IDENTITIES

The population of Greece is more diverse today
than it has been for centuries, but Greek character
is still defined by ancient traditions.

Until the early 1990s, Greece was unusual in the remarkable homogeneity of the ethnic and religious identifications of its population. This apparent homogeneity was itself a historically recent development – the preceding Byzantine and Ottoman empires were remarkably multicultural by today's standards – and was due in large part to events such as the population exchanges between Greece and Turkey in 1923 and the near-total extermination of Greek Jewry by the Nazis during World War II. This relative homogeneity has meant that Greek citizenship and "Greek" ethnicity have been seen as almost synonymous.

Post-war populations

In the post-war period, upwards of 97 percent of the population identified themselves by ethnicity as Greek and by religion as members of the Greek Orthodox Church. This still left room for some different identifications, including a sizeable Muslim Turkish minority in Thrace, plus much smaller ones on Rhodes and Kos; a Slav/Macedonian minority in Greek Macedonia; small Vlach villages throughout west-central Greece; the Pomaks, a separate Muslim group which claims ancestry from the aboriginal Thracians; the remaining Jewish population in Thessaloníki, Lárissa, Ioánnina, Corfu, Halkída, Vólos and Rhodes; Greek Catholics largely on the islands of Tínos and Sýros; Roma and Jehovah's Witnesses throughout the country. However, all of these minorities are regarded with varying degrees of suspicion or outright dislike by "mainstream" Greeks.

There are also ethnically identified Greeks who distinguish themselves in terms of origins, including the Greeks from the Pontic region and Caucausus around the Black Sea, Greeks from northern Epirus (today in Albania), Asia

Waiting for custom in Líndos.

Minor Greeks from west/central Anatolia, ethnic Greeks from Bulgaria or Romania, plus Arvanites, whose ancestors migrated to Greece in the Middle Ages and who spoke until recently a medieval dialect of Albanian.

Asia Minor refugees

An interesting case of borderline "ethnic" difference is the Greek refugees from Asia Minor who came to Greece during the Greek-Turkish population exchange of 1922 (in fact, the majority had arrived gradually, beginning in 1914, when the Ottomans moved against many Anatolian Greek Orthodox communities in revenge for the sufferings inflicted on Muslim communities in the Balkans by the victors of the two Balkan wars). Although relatively indistinguishable from mainland Greeks in physical features and religion, the refugees, most of whom settled around Piraeus, Athens and Thessaloníki, still hold onto a separate identity several generations after their uprooting.

So what set this group apart from mainland Greeks? They brought with them a shared heritage and historical experience distinct from that of metropolitan Greece, a cosmopolitan outlook, a sense of grievance and dispossession (many refugees joined the Greek Communist Party in the 1930s), and a distinctive tradition in food and music – indeed,

deep in the Asia Minor interior, didn't speak a word of Greek upon arrival; Turkish was their first language, written somewhat awkwardly in the Greek alphabet. Many of these karaman-lídiki manuscripts and books still exist. Such "Turkish" habits earned them contempt from "real" Greeks who called them tourkóspori (seeds of the Turk) and giaourtovaptisméni (baptised in yoghurt, after that foodstuff hitherto little known in metropolitan Greece).

Coastal Asia Minor Greeks also brought with them a sense of class superiority: many of them had been well educated or were wildly successful

Classroom on the beach in Páros.

the once underground, now popular *rebétika* music traces its roots to the Asia Minor refugees.

Being under the Ottoman Empire for a century longer than Greece proper, they felt a particular tie to Byzantium and the legacy of Constantinople. Their experience of major cosmopolitan cities, particularly Smyrna and Istanbul (or Constantinople as they refer to it), gave a sense of multiculturalism and high culture which didn't exist on the Greek mainland. Indeed, most Asia Minor refugees have positive memories of Greek-Turkish relations, claiming that it was the machinations of politicians and the "Great Powers" which caused problems between them. Thousands of such refugees from Cappadocia and Karamania,

merchants (or both) and felt themselves superior to what they saw as the "peasants" of Balkan Greece, even if they no longer enjoyed the financial advantages they once had. As refugees, the only possessions most were able to bring with them were the skulls of ancestors, a handful of earth from home and religious icons sewn into clothing. These icons were closely guarded, and passed down to children and grandchildren.

Often completely overlooked in the fixation on Asia Minor Greeks are the 300,000-plus ethnic Greeks who arrived, mostly from Bulgaria, but also Romania and what today is FYROM (former Yugoslav Republic of Macedonia. Because they came gradually over a long period (1913–28), they were able to bring considerable wealth with them, usually selling their real property and not just abandoning it as the Anatolian Orthodox did. This migration, though mediated by treaties, was effectively voluntary – all the Greeks of the Black Sea had to do to stay in their home countries was espouse that nationality and adhere to the national church. A surprising number did, and these days many Bulgarians are happy to admit to an ethnic Greek grandparent (or even two).

Food for thought

A Greek saying goes: "Eat, in order to remember!" In this straightforward, Proustian injunction lies a whole social and moral philosophy. Indeed, if anything unites all the diverse regions, classes, rural and urban dwellers, ethnic groups and both genders that make up modern Greece, it is perhaps best found in an attitude towards food as an embodiment of the good life, in which friends, family and community are all blended. It is striking to the outsider that Greek food, which does not rank among the world's haute cuisines, can be such a focus of everyday life, conversation and memory.

So what makes Greek food Greek? No doubt a cookbook writer will speak of ingredients and preparations. But equally key is the context of eating, that food be shared among friends, neighbours, even strangers and fortunate tourists, that people dip their forks into collective bowls, with one man spearing a particularly juicy tomato or nicely done bit of fish and force-feeding it to his friend; that there be music and boisterous conversation. That one should always have a full plate: there is no clearer symbol of the good life in Greece. At the same time, convention dictates that glasses are only to be filled two-thirds full at most; topping up is considered boorish.

Eating with the dead

Kóllyva made from boiled, sugared winter wheat kernels, supplemented by some or all of the following ingredients – pomegranate seeds, sesame seeds, almonds, sugared almonds, walnuts, parsley, breadcrumbs, currants, pistachios and raisins – is the food that living women offer in memory of the dead, or that the dead symbolically consume as part of their ongoing participation in the community of the Greek Orthodox faithful. It is obligatorily prepared for the two annual *Psyhosávvata* (Soul Saturdays, one before Lenten Sunday, the other preceding Pentecost Sunday), when the dead are collectively remembered.

When preparing this dish, the entire family gathers and sprinkles a handful of it into a plate in the shape of a cross, asking God to forgive the deceased (indeed, the standard polite way to refer to a departed person is o *synhoriménos/i synhoriméni*, the "forgiven one"). Once the *kóllyva* is ready, the female head-of-house takes it to the church to be blessed. After the service, the priest reads each family's list of the named dead relatives who they wish to be remembered. Once the liturgy is over, the women retrieve their lists and plates and, on the steps of the church, feed spoonfuls of *kóllyva* to each

Cretan shepherds.

HOME FROM HOME

The refugees were not able to bring much to Greece, but they did carry their memories with them, and often preserved their spatial maps of life in Asia Minor by renaming their new Athenian neighbourhoods or towns after the places they had known (invariably prefixed by "Néa/Néos" (new), for example Néos Marmarás). One man in his twenties, whose grandparents were refugees, notes: "It's hard to forget about Asia Minor, they are always reminding us. My grandmother has made me promise to go back to her home village just to see it, and to bring back some water and some soil. Even if she is no longer alive, she wants me to pour it onto her grave".

New Immigrants – and Extremist Reactions

Since 1990, over a million immigrants have entered Greece, producing a huge ratio (1:10) of foreign-born to native in a once-homogeneous culture.

In 2005, an Athens newspaper ran a cartoon encapsulating Greece's demographics. An elderly man

Golden Dawn supporter.

stops a little boy and asks, "Can you help me find the Kafenio Orea Ellas (Café Beautiful Greece)?" The boy replies, "Sure! Go straight past the Kurdish Culture Club, turn right at the Bengali halal butcher, it's between the African cheap-call shop and the bar with the Russian floozies, you can't miss it!" Most new arrivals are Albanian or central European, but also come from a dozen other states. Racist (re-) actions are now commonplace; as one NGO leaflet put it, "Our grandfathers refugees, our parents emigrants, and we – xenophobes and racists?"

Greece has responded to its refugee crisis in substandard fashion, contravening various UN and EU rules (except the Dublin Regulation, which requires refugees to remain in the first European state of landfall – a hosting Greece can ill afford). As part of the Schengen Group, it sees itself, as in past ages, as first line of defence against barbarian hordes. Barbed-wire fencing on the Greek-Turkish land frontier helps stem traffic approaching 80,000 persons annually; east Aegean islands are also prime landing spots. After brief detention, most refugees disappear into the immigrant underground.

In 2001, legal status was offered to the (then) 500,000 illegals who could prove two years' residency and make social insurance contributions. But barely 350,000 applied, and irksome red tape meant that subsequent amnesties netted scarcely any more applicants.

Until recently, immigrants did the tedious, dirty and/or dangerous work locals disdained, at half the price. Albanians in particular are notable stonemasons, a skill nearly extinct among Greeks; hotel staff were often Russian, Ukrainian, Bulgarian or Romanian. They helped support the local social insurance system – like Spain and Italy, Greece has a dwindling, ageing native population.

The rise of Golden Dawn

But since the crisis began, migrants found themselves surplus to employment requirements. Many took their savings and headed home. Others, unable or unwilling to leave, are targeted for attack by the overtly nationalist, neo-Nazi Hrysí Avgí (Golden Dawn) Party. Widespread resentment of immigrants – especially after violent crimes committed by Pakistanis and Afghans – was instrumental in GD's recent rise.

Golden Dawn thugs frequently undertake vigilante action against immigrants legal or otherwise: raiding street markets, demanding trading licenses from "obviously" non-Greek sellers, and trashing their stalls where none were forthcoming. Motorcycle-riding GD activists have smashed the windows of cars driven by foreigners in Athens, and three Asians have been killed to date. Cadres have also set up soup kitchens for the numerous new poor, but only serve food to "real" Greeks with identity documents. The police stand accused of actively cooperating with Golden Dawn, and of casting up to half their votes for them.

Accordingly, immigrants who complain about abuse often suffer sustained beatings and torture at police stations. The government panders to anti-immigrant sentiment lest it lose more votes to Golden Dawn. During late 2012, repeat roundups of immigrants were conducted by the Athens police, in an operation ironically named Zeus Xenios (Hospitable Zeus). Of 60,000 people detained, nearly 5,000 were deported after their documents were found to be wanting.

other, in a true moment of reciprocity and shared memory.

Any *kóllyva* left over from this communal act is offered to passers-by, perhaps even to tourists, as the women make their way home. But the ritual is not definitively over until that evening, when a plate of *kóllyva* is left out on the dining room table, with the front door open, so that the dead can also come and partake.

Honouring the departed

Kóllyva plays a key role not just in the two annual collective rituals of eating with/ remembering the dead, but at the regular memorial ceremonies that must be held for each deceased person three, nine and 40 days after death, and then three, six and nine months after, and finally every year on the anniversary of the death. These memorials begin in church with a liturgy in honour of the dead, and are followed by a reception, sometimes in the church courtyard, sometimes in a nearby reception hall, or, more intimately, in people's homes. Coffee and assorted baked goods are served, but *kóllyva* is the centrepiece. A photograph of the deceased is often placed near the plate of

Christmas family dinner, Athens.

GREECE AND FETA CHEESE

Féta (the word just means "slice") as a national symbol? It is certainly true that this pungent, delicately textured cheese has been embraced by tourists ever since they discovered slices of it sprinkled with olive oil and oregano complementing the motley flavours and colours of a Greek salad. *Féta* is made from variable mixes of goat's and ewe's milk (*egopróvio* says the label in Greek), and variations are found across the lower Balkans and Turkey. But in the mid-1990s, in the wake of challenges by Denmark to the EU calling for the right to produce a cheese called "feta", this humble staple took on new ethnic significance. In this case, it was the whiteness of *féta* produced from

egopróvio milk, compared to what Greeks claimed was the yellower Danish "feta" produced predominantly from cow's milk, which seemed to stand for the purity of Greek *féta* – a tasty reflection of the whiteness of those eternal symbols of Greekness themselves, the Parthenon Marbles.

But if *féta* seems simple from the outside, that is not the experience of the Greeks themselves who will discuss the fine distinctions of taste, smell, texture and provenance between different types of tomato, olive oil, fig, or spring water. In talking about food, Greeks are not wallowing in the mundane, but rather recognising the key role that it plays in creating social/family relations.

kóllyva, as if he or she were offering it to the assembled mourners. Indeed, the living are not just offering *kóllyva* to the dead, but on behalf of the dead; in other words, the soul of the dead person will be relieved of its sins by these acts of generosity on their behalf.

The custom of preparing *kóllyva* has a long history, resembling practices carried out in ancient Athens of *panspermia* – offerings of boiled grains to the dead or to Hermes, the god who guided the dead down to the underworld. The use of pomegranate seeds is another link to the ancient Greek symbolism of death.

members to faithfully observe the fast. If they prove unable to keep it up, the women will at least fast in their place during the 40 days of Lent that culminate in the Easter feast and other fasts throughout the year, including the "Little Lents" before Christmas and 15 August.

If you attend a Greek liturgy, you will notice the predominance of women and children inside the church. Men, when they come to church, tend to sit outside and talk with their friends. It is not that Greek men are not religious, but they do tend to have a long-standing distrust of priests and of women's spaces –

Al fresco lunch in Ýdra.

In the Christian tradition (the practice was proclaimed canonical by the patriarch of Alexandria in the 7th century), the symbolism is clearly one of death and rebirth, as the grain or seed which falls to the ground must rot before it yields new life.

Food and faith

Food plays an important role in Greek Orthodox Christianity, most notably in the cycle of fasting and feasting throughout the year that sets the daily and seasonal rhythms of life for numbers of Greek rural and urban dwellers. As in many aspects of Greek religion, women are the caretakers of the observance, coaxing husbands, children and other family

some even refer to the church as the woman's coffee shop. Absence from church is further mitigated for men by the fact that women bring consecrated bread, incense, basil and other items associated with the church home with them.

Women also prepare the appropriate foods for the different saints' days celebrations, which function like birthdays in Greece. This religious devotion gives women a particular power within the family. As one woman noted when her husband half-jokingly threatened to leave her and move back to his village for some peace and quiet, "If you leave, you won't have anyone to light a candle for you in church. If you leave, who will tend to your soul then?"

Name days

The great majority of Greeks are named after Orthodox saints, according to a system in which parents name children typically after the children's grandparents. A special bond tends to exist between a child and their eponymous grandparent, and in some cases that child will be favoured in property inheritance from that grandparent. Exceptions to this rule include naming a child after a recently deceased relative, after a protector saint (especially if the pregnancy or birth was difficult) or after an ancient Greek name – but even people with a resolutely "pagan" name will also have an alternate baptismal name (eg, a woman named Kyveli, the savage oriental goddess Cybele, may officially be Maria Kyveli). But this basic pattern ensures that there are relatively few names circulating through the system at any one time.

Everyone named Katerina will celebrate their name-day on 25 November, the date associated with the martyrdom of Agía Ekateríni of Alexandria. Name-day celebrations do not involve receiving presents or throwing a party, but rather opening one's house to family and neighbours who wish to come by and give you their good wishes, while you provide them with sweets and coffee. Name days thus have a collec-

> Traditionally, Greeks did not celebrate on their birthdays (birthday parties for children are a recent Western importation), but rather on the feast-day of the saint after whom they are named.

tive aspect absent in birthdays, tying individual Greeks to their community, to grandparents and ancestors who have shared that name, and to the history of Greek Orthodoxy.

A common act of religious devotion in Greece is to build a chapel for one's saint (or for a miracle-working saint who helped you) and to hold liturgies in the saint's honour. Saints are protectors and intercessors between humans and God and are seen as responding to people's prayers if they show proper devotion.

Ritual as sensory experience

Entering a church or chapel in Greece can be an overpowering sensory experience. From the scents of myrrh and frankincense which are spread by priests, swinging censers rhythmically back and forth, to the flicker of candles which each person lights and places in a sand-filled brazier when entering, or again to the reverberating pitch of the liturgy being sung by the psáltes (cantors), often projected via loudspeaker throughout the town or village. And of course there is the sight of the multicoloured icons, illustrating key stories from the Bible, and the taste of communion bread and wine mixed to the consistency of gruel and presented by the priest on a spoon. This sensory aspect of Greek Orthodoxy is part of official doctrine as well, an expression of the notion of the "deifica-

Boarding the ferry at Skiáthos.

tion of matter", the idea that humans manifest the spiritual not in opposition to the material but in and through the material world.

Explosive Easter

Local differences come in many hues, from the typical colours used for house-painting, to the different dialects – such as Cretan, where the sound "k" is replaced by a more ancient "tch" found also in Cyprus – to the matrilineal inheritance patterns that characterise many of the Aegean Islands. On the island of Kálymnos, difference takes the form of a sonic assault every Easter.

In most of Greece, Easter is celebrated with the setting off of fireworks, an index of the heavenly activity that Easter commemorates. On

Kálymnos, fireworks are replaced by dynamite – several thousand euros' worth, formed into projectiles and hurled from the courtyards of churches, from the two clifftops that bracket the harbour town, or in a "friendly" exchange across neighbouring back yards. No mere firecracker barrage can quite compare to the sound of dynamite going off around you, and Kálymnos's Easter celebrations have been known to both attract some stout-hearted tourists and to send others scurrying for the next boat out.

The practice of dynamite-throwing from the island's heights can be traced back to the Italian

Women have a prominent role in Greek religious life.

occupation of the Dodecanese in the early 20th century. Legend has it that one Easter, Kalymniots set off dynamite from one mountain and, while the Italian authorities were hurrying to investigate, then set off charges on the opposite mountain. As one man put it, it was a way of saying "We're alive" to the colonisers. Why has this "tradition" persisted, with the Italian occupation now a distant memory? Perhaps as a reminder, not only to neighbouring Turks but to Athenians and other Greeks, that Kálymnos is not to be trifled with.

Hospitality and honour

Local loyalties run high in Greece. One aspect of localism that tourists may find themselves on the receiving end of is local claims to being more "hospitable" (*filóxeni*) than their neighbours. "Neighbours" is a relative term: people will claim that Southern Europeans are more *filóxeni* than Northern Europeans, Greeks more than Italians, their town or village more than Athenians, and they themselves more than the person across the street. Greeks often buy in bulk – 2kg of cheese, a couple of watermelons – in order to always have food on hand to offer guests, invited and uninvited alike.

If you think you detect a competitive nature to hospitality in Greece, you are not far off the mark, as generosity is closely tied to Greek notions of honour. Acts of generosity are part of building one's reputation. They also, as noted by anthropologists, make claims to the higher status of the giver than the receiver.

This often has a faint feel of role reversal in cases where the receiver of hospitality comes from a Northern European country or the United States: Greeks are well aware that their country's voice is routinely ignored in international contexts, especially since the advent of the economic crisis, and so by being generous they are in a sense also subtly communicating the message: "You may be from a powerful country with the whip hand over us, but for the moment you are dependent on me".

All this is in no way to deny the genuineness of generous offers, nor the curiosity they may express about life in other countries over a proffered cup of coffee. A generous appreciation of your host's hospitality and, in some cases, a postcard, text message or email from abroad is all that is usually expected in return.

A SONG OF THE MOUNTAINS

Throughout the centuries, the Greeks have used their landscape – rugged mountains, rolling plains – as a metaphor to describe the different natures of the people living there, a convention this old Cretan folk song (composed by hill-dwellers, one presumes) cunningly exploits:

Fie on the young men down on the plains
Who taste the good things in life,
The choicest foods,
And are base to look at, like creeping lizards.
Joy to the young men up in the hills
Who eat the snow and the dew-fresh air
And are fine to look at, like the orange-tree.

Ýdra greengrocer.

LITERATURE

Greece was the cradle of European poetry and drama; modern writers keep the tradition alive with outstanding novels, drama and especially poetry.

When someone asked Greece's most famous composer, Mikis Theodorakis, where he got his inspiration for the hundreds of songs he had written in his lifetime, he said: "It's perfectly simple. I never thought of my music as anything but a way of clothing Greek poetry".

Perhaps only a Greek would have given such an answer. Relative to the size of its population, more poetry is published in Greece than in any other European country except Slovenia, and it is still common for Greeks to present their friends with slim volumes of verse they have written and self-published. Poetry is something people still revere and read for pleasure, and the marriage of poetry and music, familiar from the folk-song tradition, still endures.

Folk songs and the oral tradition

Both Greeks and non-Greeks have sought traces of continuity between ancient and modern Greece, and found it – if sometimes only in their imagination – in the folk songs and dances of rural Greece. In the 19th century, philhellenes and early Greek nationalists viewed the folk tradition as a way of establishing Greece's legitimate claim to liberation from the Turks. Certainly the country's folk songs are remarkable in their rich variety of imagery and metaphor, and it is not surprising that the first poets of modern Greece used them as a source of inspiration.

Although the tradition is dying out, it is still possible, in a village in the mountains of Epirus or the Peloponnese, to come upon a festival or a wedding where the night is filled with songs like this:

Now the birds, now the swallows,
now, now the partridges,
now the partridges chatter and speak:

Dionysios Solomos, writer of the lyrics to the Greek national anthem.

– Wake, my lord, wake my good lord
wake, embrace a body like a cypress,
a white throat, breasts like lemons…

Some of the most memorable folk lyrics of Greece are the laments for the dead. In these powerful songs, usually performed by women, Death is addressed in the person of Charos (from the ancient Charon), a sinister figure on a black horse:

Why are the mountains black, why so heavy with clouds
is the wind fighting them, is rain lashing them?
The wind doesn't fight, nor the rain lash.
Only Death crosses them, carrying off the dead.
He drags the young in front of him, the old behind

and the tender children are lined up on his saddle. You will have to search hard for such songs in the tourist-laden landscape of the Aegean Islands, once the source of an astonishing variety of music, song and dance. Yet even on Skópelos you just might overhear men in a taverna conversing in mandinádes (rhyming couplets), ordinarily set to music on the island of Crete. Crete is in fact exceptional in preserving a lively, traditional music scene where song lyrics are still improvised by local performers, but do not expect to hear the old island songs of Mýkonos, Santoríni or Rhodes when you visit.

no clear answer. Most of Greece was untouched by the Renaissance, but a notable exception was the island of Crete, which had been under Venetian rule until its conquest by the Ottomans in the mid-17th century. Some argue that the plays and poems produced on that island from the 15th to the 17th centuries mark the beginning of modern Greek literature. The most famous of these works is the *Erotókritos*, a long romance in verse by Vitsentzos Kornaros. Remarkably, this written text became part of the oral tradition of the island, all 10,000 lines of it being sung as if it were a folk song until

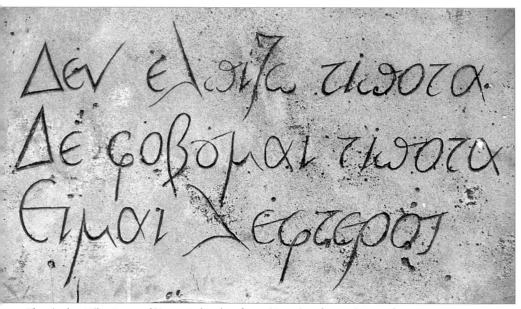

The epitaph on Nikos Kazantzakis' grave: "I don't hope for anything, I don't fear anything, I'm free".

Fortunately, until recently, there existed an exceptionally active recording industry in Greece, and among the best sources of folk-song texts are the booklets accompanying CDs of same, some with translations supplied. Recording notes will also provide the serious Greek music fan with lyrics to the popular urban songs of Greece, the *rebétika*, though English versions are often merely summaries. Risqué and laced with slang referring to hashish smoking, they open an interesting window onto the shady life of Piraeus in the early to mid-20th century.

What is modern Greek literature?

The question of where Ancient Greek literature ends and modern Greek literature begins has

THE GREEK DOSTOYEVSKY

The Murderess, by Papadiamantis, may well be one of the most daring stories of its day. It tells the story of an old woman who, having witnessed the misery of local women's lives, begins to murder infant girls rather than let them grow up. At the end of the story, she drowns while being pursued by the police, her guilt punished by divine rather than human justice; but Papadiamantis's sympathetic treatment of her character brings many assumptions of traditional Greek behaviour into question. "Once married, she was her husband's slave... when she had children, she served them, and when they had children, she became their slave".

the 20th century. It is rare to hear more than a small section of the poem sung today, but it is an exhilarating experience to listen to even a handful of these verses performed in a Cretan nightclub, preserved since the Renaissance in popular memory.

Another contender for the source of modern Greek poetry is the Ionian island of Zákynthos. Like Corfu, the other Ionian Islands had been part of the Venetian Empire from the late 14th to early 15th century. The aristocracy were Italians, often married to local women, and the poet who is often referred to as Greece's

difficult for the non-Greek reader to discover the prose of 19th-century Greece. Only lately have the works of two other remarkable prose writers begun to appear in English: Alexandros Papadiamantis and Georgios Vizyenos Papadiamantis (1851–1911) was the son of a village priest from Skiáthos and most of his fiction is set on that small Aegean island. The 200 stories he produced in his lifetime, including the novella *The Murderess*, offer a vivid, unsentimental portrait of Greek island life. They are written in a combination of formal Greek and village dialect reminiscent of Dickens or Hardy.

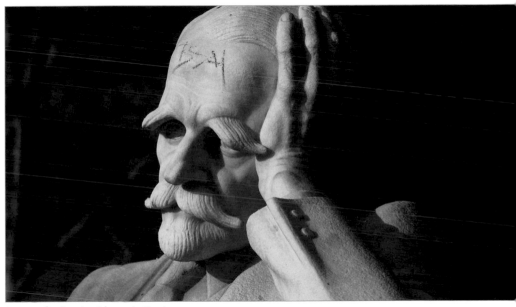

A statue of early writer Adamantios Korais.

"national" poet was the child of such a union. Born on Zákynthos in 1798, Dionysios Solomos was educated in Italian but, fired by the spirit of the Greek revolution, he began to write in Greek. His most famous poem is the *Hymn to Liberty*, which became the lyrics of the new nation's anthem. Solomos's co-islander Andreas Kalvos, who spent most of his life in Italy, also achieved national recognition as a poet. Between them, the two poets inspired the national school of Romantic poets.

The 19th century

Emmanuel Roïdis's wickedly satiric novel *Pope Joan* has achieved a deservedly wide readership in several languages, but it is otherwise

Translations of the half-dozen stories of Georgios Vizyenos (1849–96) have only recently become available in English. Enigmatic and sophisticated, his short stories are, like Papadiamantis's, preoccupied with questions of guilt and traditional Greek mores.

The early 20th century

Poetry flourished during the 20th century in Greece, a period dominated by four tragedies: the Greco-Turkish War of 1919–22 that resulted in the loss of an ethnic Greek presence in Asia Minor; World War II, when Italian, Bulgarian and German troops occupied the country; the 1946–49 civil war; and the military dictatorship of 1967–74, which put a temporary end to the

Greeks' struggle for democracy and freedom of expression. Poetry, often sung poetry, gave a voice to people's suffering during these periods. The banning of poetry and song during these crises was a reflection of how powerful such expression was.

With the restoration of democracy in 1974, Greece's entrance into the European Community and the galloping urbanisation of the post-dictatorship era, tastes in literature changed. Songs and poems no longer talked about the heroism of the people or the beauty of Greek nature, but about the disillusionment the new urban reality of a country whose population had increased by over 25 percent as a result of the Asia Minor war. More daring than their rural contemporaries, they experimented with Modernist techniques. The most original of these writers were Nikos Pentzikis, Giannis Skaribas and Giannis Beratis.

Prize-winning poets

Those poets who matured in the early to mid-20th century are best known outside of Greece. In 1963 and 1979 respectively, two Greek poets, George Seferis (pseudonym of Georgios

Odysseus Elytis, Nobel Prize winner in 1979.

of urban life or private concerns. Prose, which had occupied a secondary position to poetry, proliferated in the last half of the 20th century. With few exceptions, the better early-modern Greek prose writers had favoured the short story over the novel; but in the aftermath of the Asia Minor defeat, a group of novelists emerged who chronicled the events of the period and became known as the Aeolian School. Two were refugees from Asia Minor (Stratos Doukas and Ilias Venezis, and the third from the island of Lésvos, a few miles off the Turkish coast. All three began their literary careers on Lésvos; their prose was realistic and the Greece they depicted was rural.

Meanwhile, in Athens and Thessaloníki, a number of young writers began writing about

A NON-CONFORMIST LIFE

Thanks to his unorthodox views and writings, Nikos Kazantzakis was to court controversy not only throughout his life, but even after his death in 1957. When his book *The Last Temptation of Christ* was first published, the Orthodox Church sought to prosecute him, then excommunicated him. When it was made into a film in 1988, Athenian priests together with Orthodox parishioners marched on the cinemas, and projection screens were slashed in anger. Today, admirers can make for the Kazantzakis Museum in the village of Myrtiá, 24km (15 miles) due south of Iráklio, where well-arranged displays illustrate an extraordinary literary and political life.

Seferiadis) and Odysseus Elytis (born Odysseas Alepoudelis), won the Nobel Prize for Literature, drawing attention to the extraordinary flourishing of poetry in a country that was considered a cultural backwater by many western Europeans. A third poet, Constantine Cavafy (Konstantinos Kavafis; 1863–1933), was admired by E.M. Forster and W.H. Auden and became one of the most influential poets of the 20th century.

Living and writing his whole life outside modern Greece, in Alexandria, Cavafy removed himself still further from his contemporaries by setting most of his poems in the past.

as Homer's original. These figures tower over modern Greek literature like a formidable Dead Poets' Society, their works overshadowing those of their contemporaries and followers. Kazantzakis, of course, was also a novelist, and if English-speakers have read any modern Greek novels, they are probably his *Alexis Zorba, Christ Recrucified* or *Freedom and Death*.

Poetry out of conflict

Scarcely known outside Greece are the Greek poets who were Cavafy's near-contemporaries – Kostas Karyotakis, Kostis Palamas, Angelos

George Seferis, Nobel Prize winner in 1963.

Like Cavafy, the characters that inhabit his elegant, ironic poems are Greeks of the eastern Mediterranean whose Hellenism is based on language and a common respect for Greek culture. His poem, Ithaka, may be the most often quoted modern Greek poem of all:
Ithaka has given you your lovely voyage
Without Ithaka you would not have set out.
Ithaka has no more to give you now.

Two other poets who benefitted from international attention and foreign translations were Nikos Kazantzakis and Giannis Ritsos. Kazantzakis's modern sequel to *The Odyssey* (1938), in Kimon Friar's fine translation, was probably read by more English-speakers than Greeks, despite the fact that it is twice as long

Sikelianos and Kostas Varnalis. It was left to the somewhat younger poets who came of age in the 1930s to bring modern Greek poetry into the mainstream of European writing. Despite their political differences, these poets drew on what they saw as the enduring virtues of the Greek spirit as a way to confront the evils and privations of the war years. For Seferis, Ritsos, Kazantzakis, Andreas Embirikos, Elytis, Nikos Kavadias and many others, the war was a devastating experience that initially united Greeks against a common enemy and then tore them into two bitterly opposed camps who fought one another in a civil war lasting until 1949. During this period, many writers and intellectuals were persecuted by right-wing forces and imprisoned on Aegean Islands. Giannis Ritsos was among those who spent years in prison and exile. Others, like Seferis, spent the war years outside Greece. But no Greek writer was left unscathed, and these dark years inspired some of the greatest works of modern Greek poetry.

Elytis, whose long poem *To Áxion Estí* (*Worthy it is*), memorably set to music by Mikis Theodorakis, drew on all the traditional resources of the Greek language – ancient, Byzantine, folk song – to create a modern secular liturgy. Beginning with the poet's childhood on Crete, *To Áxion Estí* spares the

outside the country, you have to be translated; and even then the chances of being recognised are small unless you are discovered, like Cavafy, by an E.M. Forster, or recognised by a Nobel Prize. Since the 1960s, tourism has helped create a market for Greek literature, especially if it fits the traveller's ideas of what Greece is all about. Writers who instead concentrate on the less attractive themes of modern urban life are less likely to appeal to non-Greek readers. One brilliant exception is the Istanbul-born writer Petros Markaris (1937–), who has made a name for himself with his ingenious crime nov-

A Karagiózis shadow puppet show.

reader none of the horrors of the war – including a long passage from a soldier's diary on the Albanian front – but ends in a redeeming "Gloria", praising the beauty of the Greek island and its lovely women:

Sífnos, Amorgós, Alónisos
Thásos, Itháki, Santoríni
Kós, Íos, Síkinos.
Praised be Myrto standing
on the stone wall facing the sea
like a beautiful eight or a jug
with a straw hat in her hand.

The post-war writers

The central challenge to Greek literature is that so few people read Greek. To become known

els set in Istanbul or Athens, featuring Detective Costas Haritos.

Greek writers, many of them women who began publishing in the 1950s and 1960s, were mostly born in Athens or Thessaloníki. They matured in a period of tentative democracy that was rudely interrupted by seven years of stultifying dictatorship (1967–74). Reluctant to adopt the themes of earlier generations, they wrote about personal relationships, disillusionment and Athenian life. Among the contemporary women Greek poets whose works exist in English translation are Katerina Angelaki-Rooke, Kiki Dimoula, Jenny Mastoraki, Maria Laina and Rhea Galanaki (now better known as a novelist). This is necessarily a brief list, not intended to diminish the brilliance of their male contemporaries, among whom Manolis Anagnostakis (died 2005), Titos Patrikios, Nasos Vagenas, Tassos Denegris (died 2009), Yannis Kondos and Mihalis Ganas stand out.

Of this generation, Katerina Anghelaki-Rooke (born 1939) is probably the poet who has been most widely translated and therefore the most instrumental for the reception of Greek poetry abroad. Anghelaki-Rooke is brilliantly articulate in French, English and Russian and has translated the works of many of the most "untranslatable" writers from those languages into Greek – including Dylan Thomas and Pushkin. Her old red house on Égina has long been a mecca for foreign writers and scholars of Greek literature, many of whom have relied on Anghelaki's sharp insights into her country's literature as their guide to reading and translation. Her own poems are characterised by a combination of frank, lyrical sexuality and ironic self-criticism. As she writes in *Penelope Says*:

The body keeps remaking itself
getting up and falling into bed
as if it had been chopped down,
sometimes sick and sometimes in love hoping
that what it loses in touch it gains in essence.

In prose as in poetry, women writers have emerged since 1950, to rival their male counterparts. Novels about Greek society may be the traveller's best guide to the changing mores and manners of Greek life. And since many Greek writers have chosen their own recent history as a subject for their fiction, novels and short stories may also be a good introduction to the vicissitudes of the period. Alki Zei's *Achilles' Fiancée*, for example, is a gripping *roman-à-clef* about the period of the civil war and its aftermath, when Leftist guerrilla fighters took refuge in the Soviet Union. Among the other outstanding contemporary Greek novelists whose works have been translated into English are Costas Taktsis, Thanasis Valtinos, Margarita Liberaki, Maro Douka, Eugenia Fakinou, Menis Koumandareas, Apostolos Doxiadis and Vangelis Hatziyannidis.

Drama

Modern Greek dramatists have not, as yet, achieved the international recognition of their poetry- and fiction-writing colleagues. Despite a lively national theatrical scene that began promisingly in the 19th century and continues to satisfy the tastes of a large local audience, only a handful of Greek plays have been translated. Surprisingly, women dramatists were among the first to compose original plays, notably Evanthia Kairi, whose *Nikiratos* was produced in 1826.

Many writers better known in other fields turned their hand to writing plays, among them Kazantzakis, Palamas and Sikelianos; but in the post-war period, the theatre has been dominated by a group of writers whose primary concern is the theatre. The most outstanding

Poet Katerina Anghelaki-Rooke.

of these was the prolific Iakovos Kambanelis (1922–2011).

Another delight for those who have some knowledge of Greek is the shadow puppet theatre. The hero of these charming, ribald, satiric performances, Karagiózis, is an anti-hero with whom Greeks have always identified. Set in the Ottoman period, the comic puppet plays, once watched by open-mouthed children and their guffawing parents in the village square, have always been tailored to fit each new political crisis and allowed Greeks to laugh at themselves, even in the harshest periods of their history. As the song-writer, Dionysios Savvopoulos, put it:

What consumes me, what saves me
Is that I dream like Karagiózis…

MUSIC AND DANCE

Music in Greece goes far beyond Zorba's Dance
played on a bouzouki and reflects the country's
complex political and cultural history.

The sounds of Greece: the whine of motor-scooters; the thrumming of ferry-boat engines; passengers and taxi-drivers shouting at one another; the clang of church bells; sheep and goats bleating, their bells tinkling, donkeys braying, and music – loud music blaring from nightclubs, cars, cafés. The Greeks do not seem to need or desire quiet; they fill any silence with noise. They also love music, and even if it has to compete with ambient noise, they listen to it constantly.

What may surprise the visitor is that nearly all of the music they play is distinctively Greek. It may be influenced by American, Spanish or Brazilian music, but more often than not it is Greek in instrumentation or rhythm. Anyone who came to Greece 40 years ago must lament the steady erosion of Greece's traditional folk music; however, despite globalisation and modernisation, Greek music is still flourishing and full of surprises.

A continuous tradition?

Anyone who has attended the famous Dora Stratou folk-dance performances in Athens, or any other presentation of Greek music for tourists, will have been told that modern Greek music and dance preserve some of the features of their ancient Greek origin. These claims are hard to substantiate, since we have almost no idea what ancient Greek music sounded like. We know its instruments and its famous system of modes (such as Dorian, Lydian, Aeolian), but only a few tantalising fragments of notation have survived. Greek vases show dancing figures, accompanied by lyre, flute and tambourine, who could as well be dancing at a modern Greek wedding, but neither these line-dances nor their instrumentation are unique to Greece.

What was unique about Greece was the desire of 19th-century western philhellenes and early

These ceramic figurines show that the Minoan people also enjoyed dancing.

Greek nationalists to see, in modern Greece, traces of continuity with the mythical world of antiquity. The claims that early folklorists made for a continuous tradition were not only slim, but they were based almost entirely on the poetry of Greek songs, ignoring both the astonishing variety and richness of the music, and also the ritual context in which it was performed. Like all folk music, Greek songs and dances were not originally performed for entertainment but were associated with religious festivals, weddings, funerals or seasonal work.

Music of the mainland

While there is some overlap between these categories, Greeks usually make a distinction between regional folk music (*dimotikí mousikí*) and popular or city music (*laïkí*). In the case of regional folk music, they also distinguish between music from the mainland (*steriani*) and music from the islands and coastline (*nisiótika, paraliaki*). Mainland Greece is further divided into regions that have their own musical traditions: Epirus, in the northwest, Macedonia, Roúmeli, Thrace and the Peloponnese.

The most common rhythms of the mainland are the threes of the *tsamikós* (taking its name from the Albanian Cham tribe), the sevens of the *kalamatianós* (named after the town of Kalamáta

the Peloponnese, you are these days more likely to find recorded music at such events.

The islands and Asia Minor

The islands once boasted an amazing variety of musical traditions. West of the Greek mainland in the Ionian Islands, which had for centuries been under Venetian control, people sang songs in four-part harmony. Called *kantádes*, these songs, usually accompanied by a guitar, were clearly influenced by Neapolitan folk song. Partly because of their western European character and partly because they were songs that could be sung in a restaurant or tavern,

Street parade musicians.

in the Peloponnese but common throughout central and southern Greece) and the slow double and triple time of the *syrtós* and *sta tría*. Once, it was common to hear music performed outdoors by classic pairs of instruments, either a large drum (*daoúli*) and folk oboe (*zourná*), or a bagpipe (*gáida*) and tambourine (*daïrés, défi*); nowadays it is more common to hear an ensemble that includes clarinet, violin, drum and perhaps an accordion or a hammered dulcimer (*sandoúri*).

In addition to Epirus, other areas of mainland Greece where the traveller may still be lucky enough to find live music at a summer *panigýri* (religious festival) are Thrace and Macedonia, both of which have a wide variety of local songs and dances. In central Greece and

THE MUSIC OF EPIRUS

A well-known Greek singer hailing from the Aegean once said, "When I die I want to be born again as an Epirot". The music of Epirus is certainly among the most beautiful of any Greek region.

Epirus is famed for its skilled clarinet players, who improvise like jazz masters on the folk clarinet (actually a B-flat Albert clarinet, still played by many musicians in Central Europe).

It is also one of the regions of Greece where you are still likely to encounter live music being played at a festival or a wedding, especially in the mountain villages.

kantádes became very popular in Athens where they were still sung by groups of men and women until the 1960s. The island of Zákynthos remains famous for its *arékia*, the local variant of *kantádes* and, although the genre is slowly dying out, it is not uncommon to hear the islanders perform these light and charming songs. The Ionian Islands were also, in the 19th and early 20th centuries, a regional centre for Italian opera, which was performed in opera houses on both Corfu and Kefaloniá.

In the Aegean, music is usually somewhat arbitrarily divided into groups conforming to the grouping of islands. Here, the dance rhythms are mostly double, with the most common dance being some variety of *syrtós*. The exceptions are the nine-beat rhythms of the *zeïbekikó* and *karsilámas*, plus the four-beat couples' dance, the *bállos*, found in the Aegean islands and off the coast of Asia Minor, particularly Lésvos, and the Dodecanese. The traditional local instruments were the *lýra* (not to be confused with the ancient Greek lyre)

> Improvised rhymed couplets in 15-syllable metre (*mandinádes*) are a common feature of Aegean island music and persist to this day, especially on the islands of Crete, Kárpathos and Kálymnos.

or bowed viol, and the *tsamboúna*, or island bagpipe. As with the mainland instruments, there has been a shift in instrumentation, with the violin replacing the *lýra* on most islands, accompanied by the *laoúto*, akin to a mandolin, often with the addition of accordion, hand-drum or clarinet.

Whereas live music has all but disappeared from many Aegean islands, Crete is something of an exception. Any traveller wanting to discover more about Greek folk music might well begin his or her journey in Crete. Still performed on the classic combination of the Cretan *lýra* and *laoúto*, Cretan music continues to flourish and is being performed by young as well as older players. Not only is the tradition of improvised poetic couplets still preserved, but sections of the long poem *Erotókritos*, a 17th-century verse play, are still performed as part of many singers' repertoires. Cretan dancing is spectacular, and the combination of music and dance, whether it is performed in a noisy nightclub or at a village wedding (sometimes lasting for three days), is still awe-inspiring.

The islands of the central Aegean, especially the Cyclades, have become so overwhelmed by tourists that these days it is difficult, on most of them, to hear live music. Those lucky enough to encounter it at some special occasion like a wedding will discover the vanishing beauty of the *nisiótika*, songs and dances performed by a violin-led ensemble. The islands near the Turkish mainland, especially Lésvos, once had a very different musical tradition, one strongly influenced by the cosmopolitan cities of Smyrna (modern Izmir) and Aïvali (Ayvalık), both of which had large Greek populations until the

A traditional wedding on Ýdra.

1920s. On Lésvos, there were many local varieties of the Asia Minor songs and dances, some only found in a particular village, and it was through its principal town, Mytilíni, that many of the features of Asia Minor music found their way into the popular music of Greece.

One type of music that the tourist is unlikely to encounter – in part because it is considered bad luck to perform them outside their proper context – but which is rich in its lyrics and striking in its emotional style of performance, is the *miróloï* (funeral lament). It is rare for women to perform such songs at funerals in urban centres, but in the remote countryside, no funeral is complete without its chorus of women lament-singers. In most regions of Greece, laments are distinguished from songs. They are a genre apart, and yet they have melodies that may be performed as separate instrumental pieces in other contexts – even at weddings, strangely enough. It is through these songs that women communicate with the other world, addressing the dead directly and often berating them for leaving the living behind.

While these laments are performed in the context of a Christian ritual, they are remarkable in their lack of Christian references and in their striking pagan imagery. Despite repeated clashes with the Orthodox Church, village women have

basis of all Byzantine chant, was not a system of modes like those of ancient Greece, but based on such a collection of songs. What was important was the association of a set of melodic formulas with their liturgical function: certain tunes came to have a symbolic function in the Church and were incorporated into the hymns.

By far the greatest composer of Byzantine hymns was Romanos O Melodos (Romanos the Melodist), born in Syria in the late 5th century and probably active at the height of the Emperor Justinian's reign. His combination of dramatic poetry with melody has never been surpassed

A tsamboúna, the island bagpipe.

been permitted to continue improvising these laments as part of the funeral service, with priest and female chorus taking turns to articulate conflicting messages about the afterlife.

Religious music

Greeks often refer to the music of the Orthodox Church simply as Byzantine music. This is only partly true. While some of the music heard in the Orthodox services dates to the Byzantine period, much of it was composed later. Early Byzantine music was influenced by the chant of Syria and Palestine rather than Greece or Rome, and was probably based on melodies already familiar to the congregation from the local folk tradition. The *okotíhos*, which forms the

in the Eastern Christian tradition and his hymns still form part of the Orthodox liturgy.

There is now a considerable variety of music performed in Greek churches, some of it accompanied by an organ, and some including polyphonic arrangements, although many churches still retain the earlier style of monophonic singing (without harmonies) by a chorus, with a drone supplied. The richest music of the Church calendar can be heard at Easter week, particularly the Thursday evening Crucifixion service, and at the Epitáfios, or Good Friday evening liturgy. Don't miss a chance to hear young Nektaria Karantzi, the only student of the great Thracian singer Khronis Aïdonidis, performing Byzantine music in either a secular or church setting.

The sound of the city

For many visitors to Greece, one of the attractions is the "Zorba factor". That dance of Anthony Quinn and Alan Bates on a Greek beach in the 1964 movie *Zorba the Greek*, accompanied by the rapid twanging of the *bouzoúki*, spells a particular exuberance and excitement regarded as quintessentially Greek. Granted, the two men are dancing on a Cretan beach, but they are not dancing a Cretan dance. They are dancing urban music composed by Greece's most famous modern composer, Mikis Theodorakis. It is music and

The Asia Minor style was generally performed in cafés known as *cafés-aman* in the towns of the Anatolian coast, where the ensembles were made up of a violin, guitar, *oud, sandoúri or kanun* (zither) and perhaps an accordion. Non-Muslim women and men both performed in these venues and their repertoire of songs often included rather daring and humorous underworld songs about hashish, drinking, prison and prostitutes. Leading female performers in this genre were Rita Abatzi and Roza Eskenazi.

With the arrival of the refugees, cafés-aman sprang up in Piraeus and Athens, and the taste

Musicians on guitar and mandolin, Skiáthos Town

dancing derived from a particular style of Greek music called *rebétika*, a style that still forms the basis of much of modern Greece's popular music and is played by revival groups all over Greece.

Rebétika is a music associated with certain ports of Asia Minor and Greece from the beginning of the 20th century onwards, though it probably existed around the east Aegean coast and the Black Sea for decades before that.

Rebétika is often, but not always, divided into two types: the Piraeus-style *rebétika*, and the Asia Minor music brought into Greece through the islands and by the flood of refugees who arrived in the mainland following the Greco-Turkish War of 1919–22.

for this music in the Greek communities of the US led to a burgeoning recording industry. Refugees, many of them poor and unemployed, also joined local musicians in the back streets of Piraeus, where a new sort of music began to grow in popularity. This was performed not by the traditional café instruments, but on the *bouzoúki*, a long-necked, lute-like instrument that had already been observed in the Cyclades being used for folk music by the great traveller James Theodore Bent early in the 1880s.

By the 1930s, the *bouzoúki* and the songs it accompanied were all the rage in Greece. Rather like the urban blues of the US, or the tango of Argentina, the songs of the prewar *rebétika* were daring in their lyrics and appealed to an audience that revelled in hearing about the shady milieu they depicted.

Markos Vamvakaris, the central member of the "Piraeus Quartet", is often regarded as the "father" of *rebétika*. Other outstanding figures were Stratos Pagioumtzis, Giannis Papaïoannou, the prolific songwriter Vassilis Tsitsanis and his singers Sotiria Bellou, Ioanna Georgakopoulou and Stella Haskil, whose recordings are as fine an introduction as one could wish to *rebétika*.

The heyday of the *rebétika* lasted from the 1930s to the 1950s, but the songs were revived

deliberately set out to provide the public with a new sort of popular music that would elevate and inspire. They both recognised *rebétika* as the only musical form that could reach a broad public, but as classically trained musicians, they wanted to extend the boundaries of popular song and combine it with the poetry of the country's leading poets.

Beginning in the late 1950s, the two composers transformed Greek music and produced some of the most exciting popular music in Europe by joining the rhythms of the *rebétika* (particularly the dramatic 9/8 of the solo male

Mikis Theodrakis, who won international fame.

in the 1970s, beginning in the years of the dictatorship (1967–74) when the music of Theodorakis was banned by the colonels and other composers either refused to compose or found their lyrics censored. References to smoking hashish also appealed to a generation of young Greeks who identified with the streetwise, social outcasts of *rebétika*.

Popular music of the 1960s–1970s

Mikis Theodorakis and his fellow-composer Manos Hatzidakis were the leaders of an extraordinary experiment in Greek popular music. After the terrible years of World War II and the civil war, Greeks were demoralised and emotionally exhausted. The two composers

dance, the *zeïbekikó*) with the poetry of Seferis, Ritsos, Nikos Gatsos and Elytis. In the case of Mikis Theodorakis, this music acquired a strong political dimension because of his commitment to the freedom of the persecuted Greek Left. During the dictatorship, his music was banned and he was imprisoned for years, making his music still more popular among the population at large. Gatsos was just one of a group of lyricists such as Manos Eleftheriou and Kostas Virvos, who were not "straight" poets but nonetheless of critical importance for Greek song.

Theodorakis and Hatzidakis's music has had a lasting effect on Greek music. Not only are their songs still popular (Theodorakis's music is still likely to be played at the latest Athens street demonstration), but they inspired a younger group of composers to follow in their footsteps, writing music for the theatre and cinema as well as song cycles. Among the best known of these composers, who belong to what is loosely termed the New Wave or more specifically *éntkhno* (folk-influenced orchestral music), are Dionysios Savvopoulos, Giannis Markopoulos, Manos Loïzos and Stavros Xarhakos.

The contemporary music scene

Some of the best-known figures of the Greek musical scene are singers rather than compos-

of a movement called Ta Paradosiaká (The Traditional), concentrating on the rediscovery of Ottoman and Asia Minor traditions in Greek music, with Turkish musicians joining performances. Leading figures were Irishman Ross Daly, a virtuoso musician resident on Crete, and Sokratis Sinopoulos, a master of the *polítiki* (Constantinople) *lýra* and *laoúto*.

As a direct outgrowth of this, the hottest contemporary music is apt to feature collaborations between Greeks and Turks, for example the long-running shared appearances of Glykeria and Thessaloníki-resident Dilek Koç,

Island wedding in full swing.

ers, though some do write their own material. Maria Farandouri, George Dalaras (Giorgos Dalaras), Mariza Koch, Alkinoös Ioannides, Dimitris Mystakidis, Sokratis Malamas, Haris Alexiou, Nena Venetsanou, Glykeria, Eleftheria Arvanitaki, Dimitra Galani, and most recently Savina Giannatou plus Martha Frintzila, have all become internationally popular. The phenomenon of World Music has created a demand for certain types of Greek sounds, both folk and urban, and these singers have represented Greek music to a broad audience.

Composers who came of age during the 1980s, like Stamatis Kraounakis the late Nikos Papazoglou and Nikos Xydakis, are less widely known. The same decade saw the emergence

or the concert tour of multinational musicians which accompanied the release of *My Sweet Canary*, an Israeli-produced documentary on the life and career of Roza Eskenazi. Top musical venues are widely dispersed around central Athens and the outer suburbs, from Votanikós, Gázi or Psyrrí to Exárhia and Neápoli. Athens by night is still full of music that lifts the spirits and lasts till morning. And for those fortunate enough to catch a concert by a star performer, discover a good if little-known *rebétika* group performing in a small club, or stumble on a wedding in the mountains of Crete, the splendid, haunting music that once filled the air of Greece may still set the night on fire.

MIXING PIETY WITH PLEASURE

Greek religious festivals – and there are many – celebrate saints' days and other events in the religious calendar with devotion and high spirits.

Greek island life is punctuated throughout the year by saints' days and religious festivals or *panigýria*. As there are around 300 saints in the Orthodox calendar, there is an excuse for a party most days of the year.

Easter is the most important festival of the year. It's a great time to visit, with traditional services marking the Resurrection everywhere from humble chapels to mighty monasteries. Colourful, noisy and potentially dangerous – on Kálymnos they throw dynamite to ensure Christ has truly risen – it's like Firework Night and Christmas rolled into one.

During Holy Week, or *Megáli Evdomáda*, churches are festooned in purple ribbons and velvet. On Maundy Thursday, monks on Pátmos re-enact the washing of Christ's feet at the Last Supper, while that evening sees the moving Crucifixion liturgy. On Good Friday, the *Epitáfios*, or bier of Christ, is decorated by the women and paraded through the streets as sombre hymns are chanted.

On Easter Saturday evening, the church livery changes from purple to red-and-white. At midnight, everything is plunged in darkness as the priest lights the first candle from the holy flame, to represent the light of the world, and intones: "*Hristós anésti*" (Christ has risen). This is the signal for the congregation to light their candles. Families then break the Lenten fast with Easter soup made from the lamb's viscera and later play conkers with red-dyed eggs.

On Easter Sunday, there is great rejoicing as a lamb or kid is barbecued outdoors over charcoal, with the usual music and dancing. There are often parties on Easter Monday, and on some islands (especially Crete) an effigy of Judas is filled with fireworks and burned.

Saints' days are celebrated by panigýria (festivals) at hundreds of small chapels throughout the islands.

"Clean Monday" is the end of the pre-Lenten carnival, with exuberant celebrations on some islands, including kite-flying and flour fights.

Bishops lead the procession of Saint Gerasimos's silver casket to the monastery, Kefaloniá. The parade is accompanied by the singing of religious songs

An Orthodox believer venerates the Holy icons at Skopje Cathedral during the Good Friday processions. On Good Friday the Orthodox church remembers the passions and the crucifixion of Jesus Christ. The following evening, believers gather in front of the churches around the country waiting for midnight, when the priests proclaim that "Christ is risen". The Macedonian Orthodox Church celebrates Easter according to the Julian calendar.

Altar boys escort the procession of the Epitáfios in Thessaloníki.

Priest blessing the bread, Síkinos.

CELEBRATING ALL YEAR ROUND

Greeks mix piety and pleasure with gusto for all their festivals, from the most important to the smallest fair. The biggest religious festival after Easter, the Dormition of the Virgin *(Kímisis tis Panagías)* on 15 August, draws Greeks home from all over the world.

Following a liturgy on the evening of the 14th, the icon of the deceased Virgin is solemnly processed through the streets, possibly while accompanying brass bands play dirges. There are communal celebrations afterwards, particularly spectacular in Kárpathos, with dazzling costumes, special dances and traditional songs.

Every month, there are festivals on the islands for everything from sponges to snakes, and national holidays like *Óhi* or "No Day" (28 October), with patriotic parades to mark the Greeks' emphatic refusal of Mussolini's surrender ultimatum.

Celebrations begin the night before feast days and everyone in the community takes part, from babies to grannies. Patron saints are honoured with services followed by barbecues, music and dance.

In Ólympos, the remote mountain village on Kárpathos, the eldest daughter, or kanakára, wears her traditional costume and dowry of gold coins for major festivals.

FOOD AND DRINK

**Simple recipes using seasonal, local ingredients
is the key to Greek cuisine – but food for the Greeks
is about more than just cooking and eating.**

*The cook sets before you a large tray on which
are five small plates. One of these holds garlic,
another a pair of sea-urchins, another a sweet
wine soup, another ten cockles, the last a small piece
of sturgeon. While I'm eating this, another is eating
that; and while he is eating that, I have made away
with this. What I want, good sir, is both the one
and the other, but my wish is impossible. For I have
neither five mouths nor five hands…*
   – Athenaeus: The Deipnosophists

The scene conjured up by Athenaeus in the
quote describes the frustration Greeks, as well
as tourists, often feel when they fail to taste all
the dishes that are part of a *mezédes* spread. It is
obviously an age-old problem, as the passage
comes from a semi-ficticious Greek work of the
3rd century BC. Although pizza, hamburgers,
gýros and the ubiquitous Greek salad can render
modern Greek food banal, the age-old tradition
of sharing many small dishes – as prelude to a
meal or the meal itself – lives on.

Greeks were essentially vegetarian until about
the mid-20th century, not by choice but because
it was not possible to pasture large herds and
provide meat for everybody. The traditional
Greek diet, frugal yet delicious, was based on
the agricultural produce of each region: vegetables, weeds and leafy greens – foraged from
the hills or cultivated – and grains, mainly in
the form of home-made bread. Olive oil was
the principal fat used, while olives, beans and
other legumes, local cheeses and yogurt were
everyday staples.

Only occasionally was the diet enriched
with some fresh or cured fish, or with meat.
Meat was a rare, festive dish, consumed on
Sundays, at the major festivals of Easter and
Christmas, as well as on important family
feasts. But after the mid-1960s, as the country

*Starters of féta cheese and fava, which is made from puréed
yellow peas and similar to pease pudding.*

became more affluent, meat gradually took on
a significant role at the Greek table. Around
that time, the Greek demographic structure
also changed.

Some four out of 10 middle-aged Greeks
now living in big cities originally came from
agricultural areas. They relocated in the last
50 years or so, bringing with them the cooking and culinary habits of their mothers and
grandmothers. Although well settled in the
urban environment, most of them have kept
their ancestors' village homes and visit them on
long weekends, during the summer holidays, as
well as at Christmas and Easter. Many have also
kept much of their land, so it is still common
for Greek families to produce the olive oil they

consume; about 18kg (40lb) per person each year. People who do not produce it themselves buy it from friends who have a surplus.

Along with olive oil, *psomí* (bread) was the basic staple food up until the mid-1960s, as it used to be in ancient and Byzantine times. Although Greeks can now afford a great variety of foods, they still consume enormous quantities of bread. Traditional breads are often made with a combination of wheat, barley and sometimes maize flour, using sour old-dough starter. Barley grows easily with only spring rainfall in mountainous southern

well for many months, they are easy to carry in the field and are the ideal food for sailors. Moreover, baked every two or three months, they made efficient use of oven heat, as wood is scarce on most islands.

Outside influences

In its long history, Greece has been subjected to many culinary influences. The Venetians and Genoese, who ruled much of the country during the Middle Ages, and later the Ottoman Turks, who ruled northern Greece and Crete up until the early 1900s, have all left their marks

For a taste of real Greek cooking, follow the locals to backstreet tavernas.

An indication that Greeks still take their religious fasts seriously can be found in the branches of McDonald's in Greece, where special Lenten menus are offered during these periods.

Greece and on the islands, so it has been a staple for centuries. Today, in Crete and other islands *paximádia* (rusks) – slices of twice-baked and completely dry barley bread which only need to be briefly soaked in water to soften – are still very popular. *Paximádia* are perfectly suited to traditional lifestyles: they keep

on Greek cooking; since then, the cuisine brought by Asia Minor refugees has been of paramount importance. But the most important factor in shaping people's eating habits was the rules of the Greek Orthodox Church. Even non-religious Greeks sometimes abstain from foods deriving from animals – meat, dairy products and eggs – during the fasting periods that precede Easter, Christmas and 15 August. This is the reason why many traditional dishes such as *gemistá* (stuffed vegetables), *yaprákia* or *dolmádes* (stuffed grape or cabbage leaves), *píttes* (filo-wrapped pies) come in two versions: one with meat and/or cheese, and one without, often called *gialantzí* ("liar's" *dolmádes*, ie fake, meatless) for fasting days.

Festival food

Numerous religious holidays are scattered throughout the year. Many have evolved from ancient celebrations and are often closely related to the seasons and the lunar calendar. Easter, Greece's most important feast, seems to have its roots in the agricultural spring festivals of antiquity. Celebrated in the open country, amid fragrant herbs and multicoloured flowers, the Easter table features succulent spit-roasted baby lamb or kid – at the right age for slaughter in spring – and salads of wild greens, tender raw artichokes

The informal tavern is the most common form of eatery.

and fresh fava beans. *Magirítsa*, a delicious soup made with chopped lamb's innards, spring onions and dill, with a tart egg-and-lemon sauce, is eaten during the small hours of Easter Sunday, after the midnight Resurrection Mass. Traditional Easter sweets are stuffed with *myzíthra*, a generic name for the various regional creamy fresh cheeses of the season, usually made with a combination of goat's and sheep's milk.

Pork is associated with Christmas and New Year, as pig slaughtering and curing is done from October onwards. Fish is consumed on 25 March, and always at meals that follow funerals. Despite its many islands, fish and seafood

has never been plentiful enough to become an everyday food in Greece, not even for those who live by the sea. The fish and seafood of the Aegean is delicious but scarce, and the best fish islanders manage to catch is sold to the big cities for much-needed cash.

Dining out

Despite its rich culinary heritage, Greece has a very recent restaurant tradition and the finest *magirevtá* (cooked dishes) are still best savoured in the home. People eat lunch at around 3pm and dinner at around 9pm – in the summer at around 10pm or even later. Breakfast is usually just a cup of coffee and a biscuit. Wine accompanies the meals, especially dinner, and a salad of fresh, raw or blanched seasonal vegetables or greens is always part of the everyday menu. Seasonal fruits are the most common dessert. Sweets were originally part of the festive table but now tend to be eaten daily, while meat (until the recent economic crisis) had also become an almost everyday staple.

Traditionally, two kinds of restaurants attract the Greeks when they want to entertain their families and friends. A *psistariá* (grill house) offers charcoal-grilled meat (baby lamb, kid, pork, veal and chicken), often by weight. *Psarotavérnes* (fish taverns) are scattered all over the shoreline, on the islands and the mainland. Fresh fish and seafood, the catch of the day, is grilled or fried according to the customer's choice. Both meat and fish taverns offer a few appetisers and seasonal salads.

Frugal, ingenious Greek cooks have learned to complement a few simple ingredients with rice, potatoes, some cheese and a few pieces of meat to create dishes that dieticians now hold up as models of the famously healthy Mediterranean diet. The irony is that modern Greeks, in their quest to distance themselves from their poverty-stricken past, have enthusiastically forsaken this traditional fare and adopted the unhealthy eating habits of northern Europeans and Americans.

Local foods

Many traditional foods had nearly disappeared when, in the mid-1990s, a trend towards updated homestyle cooking began to emerge in Athens and gradually all over the country. Visitors should ask for regional specialities – for example, *píttes* (cheese- or herb-stuffed turnovers) in Epirus; *trahanás* soup (pasta made with yogurt and sourdough) all over the mainland; *lahano dolmádes* (stuffed cabbage leaves) or local *loukánika* (sausages) almost everywhere; and *loúza* or *lóza* (pork loin macerated in wine and air-dried or smoked) in the Cyclades. Look out, too, for thyme honey on small, unforested islands, and *pastéli* (a sesame seed and honey sweet), home-cured caper greens, and wonderful local shepherd's cheeses, often just called *tyráki* (small cheese).

> Greek food traditionally follows the seasons. Cooks do not make gemistá (stuffed tomatoes and peppers) or melitzanosaláta (aubergine dip) in the winter, even though these vegetables are now available all year round.

In the Cyclades and the Dodecanese, goat's and sheep's milk cheeses are a real treat, but they seldom travel further than their island of origin. Greece is finally beginning to capitalise on its delicious artisan foods, with fancy delis in the largest cities and speciality boutiques on many tourist islands. There are now even a few truffle (*troúfa*) reserves scattered across the mainland – Greek beech and oak forests are perfect for their culture.

Greek wines

Some of the most admired wines in antiquity were produced in Greece. Oar-powered cargo ships carried clay amphoras filled with the precious liquid to ports and markets all over the Mediterranean. Yet if we were to try these wines today, we would probably find them undrinkable. They were mainly sweet, and contained flavourings and herbs such as thyme, mint and even cinnamon. Seawater and pieces of pine bark were also added as preservatives, to keep the wine from turning sour.

The Byzantines continued to add resin to some wines. A more refined legacy of this is modern *retsína*, a white wine laced with Aleppo pine resin. *Retsína* was widely consumed until the mid-1970s. But as the new generation of quality Greek wines gradually spread, its consumption declined sharply. Today, many medium-sized and small wineries, employing

modern techniques and talented oenologists, combine indigenous and imported grape varieties to produce quality wines.

Greek vineyards are diverse, following the contours of the country's morphology. Omnipresent hills and mountains divide the land into small regions, each with its own microclimate. Many indigenous grape varieties – many of which existed also in antiquity – are grown, which acquire different characteristics in each region. According to EU regulations and Greek law, the system of controlled appellations of origin (AOC) matches the Greek varieties to

Grilled octopus makes for an affordable seafood meal.

the areas where the best of their kind is traditionally produced. But you will also find exceptional regional wines outside of these AOC classifications.

Northern Greece

Macedonia, perhaps the most rewarding mainland wine region, is the home of the *xinómavro* grape, which produces well-loved, robust red wines. Naoussa is the best-known example, while Amyndeon, made from the same grape, is a lighter red and can also be a pleasant still or sparkling rosé. *Xinómavro* combined with the *negóska* variety – another Macedonian native – makes Goumenissa, a meaty red. By itself, *negóska* yields a soft red. Extensive vineyards on the central peninsula of Halkidikí produce the Côtes de Meliton wines, both white and red, from a combination of French (Cabernet Sauvignon and Cabernet Franc) and Greek varieties. The Dráma region is not yet an AOC, but the two Lazaridi wineries make upmarket wines based on Sauvignon Blanc and Sémillon for whites, and Cabernet Sauvignon plus Merlot for reds.

In Epirus, the most isolated, mountainous region of northwestern Greece, Zitsa, a fresh, fruity, often sparkling white is produced from the *débina* variety. In the valley below Métsovo,

traditionally used for the production of *retsína*. Matsa in Kántza is one of the best Attic vineyards, known for fine white wines based on *malagouziá* grapes, native to western Greece.

In the northeastern Peloponnese, Nemea, made from *aigiorgítiko* grapes, is one of the most versatile Greek reds. Mantineia, a delicate aromatic white wine, is produced at vineyards north of Trípoli, mostly from *moskhofílero* grapes. The Pátra area yields dry and sweet white and red wines. Muscat of Patras and Muscat of Rio as well as the dark Mavrodáfni (Mavrodaphne) are three well-loved sweet dessert wines.

Greek wine producers use both indigenous and imported grape varieties.

Katöï, a fine, rich red, is made from imported Cabernet Sauvignon vines. For maps and details of all northern-Greek Wine Roads, visit www.wineroads.gr.

Thessaly produces two distinguished wines. Rapsani vintners make a red with a fine bouquet, from *xinómavro*, *stavrotó* and *krasáto* grapes grown on the southeastern slopes of Mount Olympos. Anhiálos, on the shores of Pagasitikos, has a fresh white wine, made from a blend of *savatianó* and *rodítis* grapes.

Central Greece and Peloponnese

Attica, the region around Athens (not an AOC region), nonetheless produces very interesting wines. The main variety here is *savatianó*,

Some scholars believe that medieval Monemvasiá used to be where malmsey wine (called also malvasia or malvoisie) was made. Others claim that this wine, mentioned by Shakespeare, was actually produced in Crete, with the boats transporting it merely stopping at Monemvasiá on their way north. This magnificent sweet white is no longer made in Greece, but apparently resembled madeira.

The islands

On the island of Límnos, a quaffable white wine is produced from Alexandrian Muscat grapes, while the *limnió* variety, mentioned by Aristotle, produces light, fragrant red wines. Lésvos boasts the all-organic Methymeos winery in the remote village of Hídira, producing superior reds and whites from a local heirloom type of grape, grown in a volcanic caldera. In northeastern Híos, the Ariousos winery has recently revived the ancient red grape varieties *krasséro* and *agianítis* in a line of quality reds, as well as more conventional whites. Vineyards on Sámos, a mountainous island, are planted on terraced hills, rising to 800 metres (2,625ft); Ageri is the best-value label of dry white wine here, made from *moskháto* grapes, *fokianós* and *rítinos* grapes are the source of easy-drinking rosé, while the local fortified dessert wines,

The ubiquitous oúzo.

in four grades, are world famous. Rhodes produces dry whites mainly from *athíri* grapes, and dry reds made chiefly from *mandilariá* grapes, as well as sparkling wines of middling quality.

Crete produces 20 percent of Greek wines. Although far to the south, the cool etesian winds never let the temperature rise much, and lofty Mt Psilorítis keeps hot African winds from reaching the northern slopes where most vines are cultivated. Arhánes and Pezá are two apellations of dry red made from *kotsifáli* and *mandilariá* grapes. Another red, Dafnés, is made from the ancient grape liátiko. A dry red made from *liátiko* and *mandilariá*, and a very popular fruity white mostly from *vilána* grapes, comprise the AOC of Sitía.

Santoríni, the spectacular volcanic island, produces lovely white wines made from *asýrtiko* or aidáni grapes, as well as good reds from the *mandilariá* and *mavrotrágano* varieties. To guard their vines from the strong etesian winds, local growers shape their branches into intricate basket shapes, inside which the grapes grow. *Vi(n)sánto* is a marvellous fortified sweet wine made from partly sun-dried white grapes. Similar sweet wines, often called *liastó*, are produced throughout the Cyclades. On Páros, sprawling vines produce a red with dark colour and a characteristic bouquet, made from *mandilariá*, *savatianó* and *monemvasiá* grapes (the latter unrelated to the medieval malmsey-producing grape).

Corfu, Zákynthos and Levkáda produce interesting wines, but only Robóla from Kefalloniá, a dry white from the eponymous grapes, is an AOC.

FIRE WATER; OÚZO AND OTHER SPIRITS

The most popular Greek drink, traditionally served with *mezédes* is *oúzo*, produced across the country. When absinthe fell into disfavour in the early 20th century, *oúzo*'s popularity rose. Many people enjoy it so much on holiday they take a bottle home, only to find the pleasure doesn't travel well; it's not the same without the fierce Greek sunshine, a beautiful beach and a plate of Greek olives.

Only *oúzo* that is made in Greece can bear that name according to EU regulations. *Oúzo* is made from distilled grape-pressings left after the wine-making process, and takes its flavour from anise, fennel seeds and other spices.

Some people say the best *oúzo* is from Lésvos; others will insist that the *oúzo* of Tyrnávos, Thessaly, or that of Híos, is superior. In Híos, there also exists *mastíha*, a sweeter version of *oúzo* flavoured exclusively with mastic, the aromatic sap of the mastic bushes that grow on the island.

Another popular strong alcoholic drink, akin to Italian *grappa*, is made from the distillation of grape-skins and stems. This is called *tsípouro* in central and northern Greece and *rakí* or *tsikoudiá* in Crete, where it is recommended as a universal panacea. On Rhodes and Sámos, a nearly identical distilled clear spirit is called *soúma*.

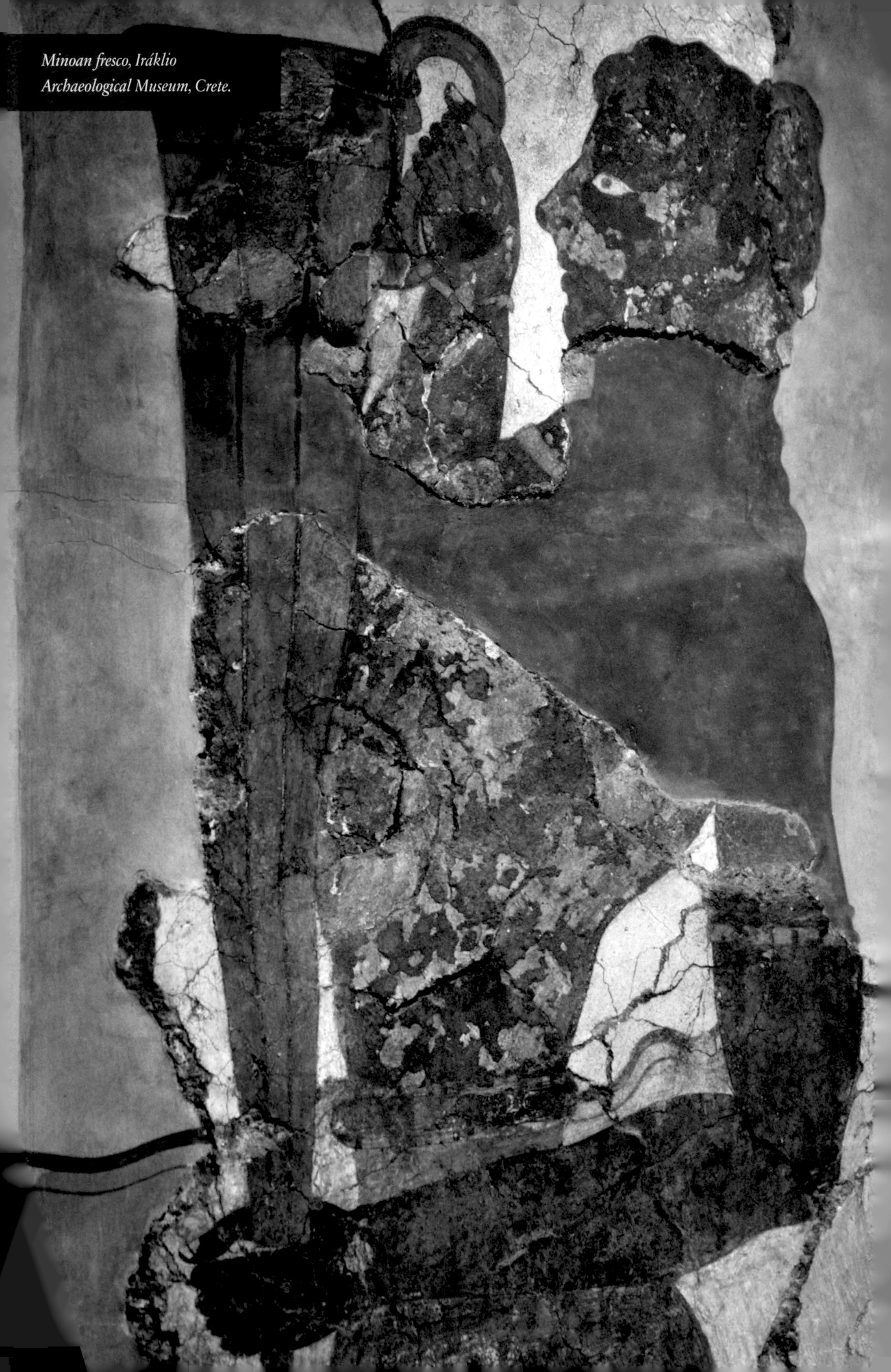

Minoan fresco, Iráklio Archaeological Museum, Crete.

ART AND ARCHITECTURE

The Classical, Hellenistic, Roman and Byzantine eras,
left Greece with an artistic heritage that has
inspired later artists and architects.

Few countries have influenced Western art more than Ancient Greece. But because of its geographical position, Greece itself has been subjected to many influences. The origins of Greek art lay in Neolithic Anatolia, the Middle East and Egypt. Greece, in turn, influenced Rome, and thus Western Europe and the Byzantine world. Absorbed into the Turkish Ottoman Empire for 500 years, on liberation Greece was on the receiving end of Western influences, often mixed with its Byzantine heritage. The region's fine marbles, good clays and early exploitation of Cypriot copper ensured an enduring artistic gift.

The Bronze Age

The earliest art is that of the Cyclades. Neolithic and Bronze Age cultures developed complex settlements, but the most characteristic artefacts are the Cycladic idols, placed for unknown purposes with early burials. Here, the Greek love of idealised, perfect forms is already apparent. Facial details, save for relief noses, were probably painted on.

By 2300 BC, Minoan civilisation had emerged fully in Crete and on neighbouring Santoríni, characterised by palace complexes such as Knossos and Phaistos, and the town at Akrotíri. Architecture was labyrinthine, of stone with plastered and frescoed walls, and looked inwards onto courtyards which were venues for elaborate games, including bull-leaping as represented in paint and ivory figures.

The sacred bull – suggested by the twin horn symbol – was represented in terracotta, and as rhytons (drinking vessels) of gold or soapstone. The frescoed composite plants and chariots pulled by winged beasts, and the sculpted flounced dress of the snake goddess, a

The Lion Gate, Mycenae.

protective deity, demonstrated Mesopotamian influence. Sea and land creatures – shells, octopuses, bees – inspired vase decoration and jewellery. The double-headed axe, used as a motif, was a sacred symbol.

The peaceable, sophisticated Minoan culture declined around 1450 BC as the Myceneans of the mainland gained ascendancy. Warlike and great sea traders, they adopted Minoan motifs such as wasp-waisted costumes and the downward tapering column seen on the Lion Gate at Mycenae (c.1600 BC). This entry to the citadel/palace is the first large-scale European sculpture, relying on a corbelled arch technique also used for the Cyclopean-scale vaulted chambers at Tiryns, and more adventurously for tholos ("beehive") tombs, the most impressive of which is the Treasury of Atreus (c.1375 BC) at Mycenae, a 15-metre (49-ft) span dome with side chamber. Earlier shaft graves have revealed elaborate niello-inlaid bronze daggers, lion and bull-head rhytons, and the remarkable, haunting and somewhat heraldic gold masks placed over the faces of the dead.

Geometric and Archaic art

Iron Age peoples entered Greece c.1120 BC: Mycenaean society finished and the so-called

figures were carved, perhaps as personifications of gods, as grave markers, or as worshipper figures. Early *kouroi* demonstrated Egyptian influence in their stance and braided hair. Over time, the males become less anatomically stylised and the girls' clothing become looser; smiles were depicted, and the feel was for naturalism. These statues represented ideal figures shown in the prime of life: in time, the depiction of the ideal came closer to reality, but the sense of idealisation was never lost.

Central to this concept was harmonic proportion. In the evolution of the temple, a

Sphinx, Kerameikos Cemetery museum, 6th century BC.

Dark Ages, preceding the Geometric period, ensued until about 900 BC. Few Geometric artefacts except pottery vessels survive. Decorated with geometric horizontal banding, including spirals akin to Minoan and Mycenaean work, and also the "Greek key" (properly known as the meander pattern), these were often associated with burials. Some depict funerary processions with geometrised figures; others assumed anthropomorphic shapes. From c.850 BC, small figurines of seated goddesses, charioteers, animals and warriors appeared in bronze, ivory and ceramic.

The Archaic period, c.750–490 BC, was one of rapid development. In sculpture, large *kouroi* (nude male) and *korai* (draped female) standing

perfectly balanced system of horizontals and verticals developed. Archaic temples followed the Doric form: it was sturdy (likened to a man), with sharply fluted columns that had simple capitals and no base. These carried an entablature featuring square metope panels between vertical triglyph mouldings. The form of a colonnaded, box-like structure as a "home" for the deity, often sited on a hilltop, created a perfect backdrop for the open-air ceremonies.

Classical art

The subsequent Classical period, 490–336 BC, saw further rapid developments. Although known by report, scarcely any early Greek paintings survive: ceramic decoration gives some clues to its qualities. Archaic vase-painting had been dominated initially by a Corinthian "orientalising" style of fabulous beasts, and then by a vigorous Athenian style of figurative ware in which black figures were placed against the red of the pot (black-figure ware). Around 500 BC, a reversal of the process yielded red-figure ware, in which a finer linearism captured greater detail and movement, enhanced by the development of foreshortening and eventually rudimentary perspective.

The greater structural strength of bronze when cast hollow led to more adventurous

> Early writers tell of panel paintings of exact mimicry of nature by the masters Zeuxis and Apelles. In sculpture, too, much has been lost, and many works are now known only through Roman marble copies of lost bronzes.

poses of movement, as with the *Poseidon* (or Zeus) recovered from the sea off Évia in 1928. The sculptor Polykleitos's *Doryphoros* (Javelin thrower) was originally in bronze. In this, he realised *controposto* – the establishment of convincing weight distribution in a figure.

Late Classical sculpture saw the emergence of a more private attitude to the figure, particularly in portraiture and the self-involved statues of Praxiteles; notably his *Knidian Aphrodite* and the *Hermes with the infant Dionysos*. The former introduced the nude female figure, previously rare. A feminine architectural theme was provided by the more slender and elegant Ionic style of temple, where the spiral volutes of the capitals were equated to a girl's curling hair. In these temples, the entablature rejects the Doric metopes and triglyphs, but might include a continuously sculpted frieze section. After 370 BC, a more forceful sculptural manner emerged with Skopas of Paros. His active military reliefs foreshadowed the dynamic work of Alexander the Great's favoured sculptor, Lykippos, whose *Apoxyomenos* (Sweat-scraper) was given a tight muscularity and the smaller proportioned head of an aggressive figure.

Hellenistic art

Alexander's accession in 336 BC, marking the beginning of the Hellenistic era, was followed by the rapid expansion of the Greek Empire: his capital was established at Babylon, and the centres of artistic production tended to move eastwards, particularly to Anatolia. Pergamon was especially important sculpturally during the period 250–160 BC. In sculpture, emphasis was put on movement, as in the *Nike of Samothrace* (now in the Louvre in Paris), realism, the display of emotion and more complex poses. From this period survive many mass-produced ceramic figures of gods, dancing figures and satyrs, often known as Tanagra figures after the town in Boeotia. During

Vase excavated at Elefsína.

this luxury-loving age, the continuance of refined goldwork for jewellery, and filigree and leaf diadems was matched by the remarkable Derveni krater, a copper-alloy *repoussée* wine vase used as a cinerary urn despite its Dionysiac scenes.

In architecture, a new, complex quality was introduced with the foliate Corinthian column capital, first used at the Choragic monument to Lysikratos, Athens, in 336 BC . The Corinthian order was often used on a gigantic scale, as in the Temple of Olympian Zeus, Athens, c.170 BC. Houses appear to have been simple structures, judging from painted Thracian tomb chests preserved in the Thessaloníki Archaeological Museum.

The absorption of Greece by Rome after 146 BC reaffirmed Roman admiration and development of Greek forms of art and architecture. Indeed, apart from sculptures, a few larger episodes such as the mosaic *Battle of Isos* (Pompeii, *c.*50 BC) are known through their Roman copies. The practical bent of the Romans emphasised physically truthful portraiture and its use as propaganda (see the *Augustus* from Athens's Roman agora), and hero worship as with the bust of *Antinoös* from Pátra. Roman forms of arched architecture were adopted, as was a preference for sumptuous palaces. The surviving is known as Byzantine art. Christianity led to an art of symbolism, and because of a fear of idolatry, sculpture in the round became rare, as did the nude; figures thus became defined by their drapery. Many artefacts of this mystic art were produced in Byzantium and exported to the Balkans. Levantine motifs, particularly from silks, were mixed with Roman ones in an art that emphasised richness and sophistication, religiosity and secularity, although little survives of the latter type.

Architecturally, two forms of church emerged alongside the Roman basilica form of nave,

Mosaic depicting the arrival of Asklepios, god of healing, on Kós, with Hippocrates to the left; Kós Archaeological Museum.

Corinthian columns on the Temple of Olympian Zeus, Athens.

Galerius Gateway, AD 298–303, at Thessaloníki conveys something of their splendour: its reliefs reflect the Roman-Hellenic interest in illusionism and narrative.

Christianity and Byzantium

That Christian communities were quickly established in Greece is demonstrated by St Paul's letters to the Corinthians and Thessalonians. Constantine the Great's decision to make Byzantium (modern İstanbul) his capital in 330, coupled with his advocacy of Christianity (though he himself did not convert until on his deathbed), determined the future direction of Greek religion and what

PHEIDIAS THE GREAT

From 447 to 432 BC, Pheidias mastered the depiction of narrative schemes and vigorous action in his reliefs and statues for the Temple of Zeus at Olympia and the Parthenon in Athens. The Parthenon reliefs were brightly painted. For both temples, Pheidias created gigantic divine statues of ivory and gold, now lost. A perfect blend of naturalism with idealism had been achieved, well seen in the *Nike adjusting her sandal* (Temple of Nike Apteros, Athens Acropolis). The narrative interest had a parallel in dramas and the creation of semicircular theatres moulded from the contours of the land.

aisles and apse: one, the central domed space, sometimes over an octagon (as at Ósios Loukás), and the other a cruciform domed space (such as Ágii Apóstoli, Athens). In these, the dome was often emphasised by the image of almighty Christ giving his blessing (the Pandokrátor), a fitting symbol as one took communion below.

Many paintings were destroyed during the Iconoclastic crisis of 726–843, when the validity of figural imagery was challenged. However, Néa Móni on Híos has good mosaics from c.1050, and Mystrás has fine 13th- and 14th-century paintings. Other devotional works were

> Surviving decoration is often mosaics of pigmented glass tesserae, usually implanted with gold leaf, that were set at slight angles so that in the flickering candlelight the images shimmered.

relief-carved ivory codex (book) covers, boxes and *pyxes*; but most characteristic were icons (tempera- or occasionally encaustic-painted panels of saints). These were initially domestic and often for women at home, but were later placed on pillars flanking the space to the altar. In turn, more icons were added to the *témblon* or barrier before the altar, and in time they multiplied to create an iconostasis or screen separating nave from chancel and congregation from clergy (as with the fine example found in Megálou Meteórou monastery). An arrangement of a central Christ flanked by Mary and St John the Baptist, Saints Peter and Paul and other apostles and saints in order of importance became known as the Great Deisis. Such screens greatly enhanced the mysticism of the Orthodox Church, which formally dates from the Great Schism of 1054.

Byzantine culture was increasingly under threat, first from Islam but also from the West, particularly its former allies, Venice and Genoa. However, it did experience an artistic revival in manuscripts and the paintings at Mystrás, which show a greater interest in plasticity, under the Palaeologos dynasty (1261–1453).

The capture of Byzantium by the Ottoman Turks in 1453 meant Greece became nominally part of the Islamic world, although from as early as 1204, the Ionian and some of the Aegean Islands, the Dodecanese, Crete

and several mainland cities were ruled by Venice, Genoa and other Western powers (see page 50). In consequence, Venetian and Frankish influence was felt in architecture, notably on the Peloponnese, the northeast Aegean islands, the Cyclades and on Crete, in both military and domestic architecture. After 1453, many refugee painters emigrated to the Venetian-held Ionian Islands, Crete or Venice itself, so Venetian influence is evident in the 16th- and 17th-century icon-painting of Mihaïl Damaskinos, Emmanuel Tzanes and Theodoros Poulakis.

Mosaic from the Monastery of the Panagía, Ýdra.

Art under the Ottomans

Ottoman rule in Greece allowed religious tolerance, but the Islamic scepticism of figurative imagery was nevertheless felt, particularly in larger public works. Although icon-painting persisted, more emphasis was put on the decorative arts in which Eastern and Western influences are found, especially in textiles – including kilims – jewellery and metalwork (lamps, platters and other domestic utensils). Often distinct, lively regional and island vernacular styles are apparent, particularly in embroidery.

Domestic architecture favoured timber-panelled rooms which stylistically linked traditions from İstanbul with European precedents. The emigration of many Greeks in all directions, known as the diaspora, helped fuse many influences into Greek art. One notable example is that of Greek craftsmen working at İznik on ceramic ware with Grecian subject matter. Many domed Ottoman civic buildings have been destroyed, but numerous others survive, especially in regions united with Greece after 1881. These include the *bezesténi* (covered bazaar), two baths and several mosques in Thessaloníki, a hammam and three mosques in Rhodes, plus scattered mosques, baths and ornate fountains

Crete's most famous painter is Domenikos Theotokopoulos, whose Adoration of the Magi (Benáki Museum, Athens) shows his work as an icon painter before his move to Venice and later to Spain – where he was known as El Greco.

of 1821–28 and full independence in 1830. A Bavarian prince was appointed king and it is therefore Germanic influence, particularly from Karl Friedrich Schinkel, that dominates

The Italian-style Governor's House in Rhodes New Town.

The Mosque Murad Reis, an Ottoman legacy on Rhodes.

in Ioánnina, Tríkala, Lárissa, Návplio, Halkída, Véria, Kós, Crete, Lésvos and Híos. In the last three locales, hammams and mosques have been restored for use as event venues.

Neoclassicism

Roman Pompeii, discovered in 1763, provoked a renewed interest in antiquity, and the German scholar Johann Joachim Winckelmann suggested that Greek art was superior to Roman. Consequently, a pro-Hellenic movement arose in Western Europe which, allied to growing nationalist aspirations, led to a resurgence of interest in Classical Greece (often known as neoclassicism) which dominated the arts during and after the War of Independence

neoclassical architecture – especially in Athens, the capital from 1834.

Monumental, largely Ionic structures that reflect mainstream European neoclassicism are Friedrich Von Gärtner's Royal Palace (1835–43), and the work of two Danish architects, Christian Hansen's National Capodistrian University (1837) and Theophilus Hansen's National Library (1888–91) and Academy (1856–85), the Observatory (1842) and the Záppio (1874–88). Ernst Ziller, though belonging to the next wave of immigrant architects, contributed the Numismatic Museum (originally the Schliemann residence: 1878–80), the Presidential Mansion (1891–97) and many other landmark buildings across Greece.

Native architects adopted the style, notably Lysandros Kaftantzoglou (Athens Technical University) and Stamatis Kleanthis, Schinkel's student. The latter built the neoclassical Wortheim house (Athens, 1843) and also the Renaissance-revival-style mansion of the Duchess of Plaisance, now part of the Byzantine Museum (Athens, 1840–48). This eclectic attitude gained pace and, unsurprisingly, Byzantine adaptations found favour, as with Kaftantzoglou's Athens Eye Clinic, and as late as 1933 with the church of Ágios Konstandínos, by Aristotelis Zahos, at Vólos.

Plato (1815), or Leonidas Drosis's Penelope (1873, both in the National Gallery in Athens). Given the dominance of German tutors at the Royal School of Fine Arts, Teutonic concepts affected students like the Tiniot Lazaros Fytalis, whose Shepherd (1856, National Gallery) owes something to Schadow. Ioannis Vitsaris's Pavlopoulos Tomb (1890, Athens Próto Nekrotafío) demonstrated interest in western Baroque, while Kostas Demetriades's Male Figure (1910, National Gallery) picked up contemporary naturalist tendencies.

Hansen's neoclassical Academy, Athens.

Scores of houses composed as assemblages of geometric forms with classical detailing and an overall symmetry show the popularity of the neoclassical style.

Just as architecture paralleled the mainstream European patterns, so too did painting and sculpture. Sculpture, marginalised during the Byzantine and Ottoman years, was revived, initially in the Classical taste, especially at Tínos where a school of decorative carving flourished. The greatest exponent of this school was Yannoulis Chalepas, celebrated for his Oréa Kimoméni (Sleeping Beauty) Grave Monument (1877) in Athens' Próto Nekrotafío (First Cemetery). Other examples are the Corfiot Pavlos Prosalentis's

In painting, portraiture – at first somewhat naïve – and subject painting took off following independence, thus supplementing the Venetian-influenced religious works that had been popular in the Ionian Islands in the 18th century, such as Panagiotis Doxaras' Birth of the Virgin (Zákynthos Museum), as well as his painted ceiling for the Ágios Spyrídon church in Corfu.

Events of the 1821–28 battles provided many dramatic paintings with a romantic flavour and occasional religious overtones, such as Theodoros Vryzakis's Exodus from Mesolóngi (1853, National Gallery). Greek life was also celebrated, as in the Munich-trained Nikolaos Gyzis's Children's Betrothal (1877, National

> *A key figure in post-war architecture was Emmanouel Vourekas, responsible for the landmark Hilton Hotel on Vassilís Sofías, which Conrad Hilton considered the most beautiful of the 53 in his chain.*

Gallery) or Nikiforos Lytras's *The Dirge on the Isle of Psará* (pre-1888). Both artists were also attracted to Orientalist subjects, while Gyzis (1842–1901) had a marked predilection in later years for symbolism and mysticism. By the late 19th century, other artists were picking up on new subjects, landscape and portraiture (Polychronis Lembesis) and still life (Périclès Pantazis), while others fell under the spell of Impressionism and its offshoots – for example, Symeon Savvides's Boats on the Bosphorus (1903, National Gallery).

The 20th century

Greek artists of the 20th century broadly followed major European trends and readily accepted modernism, not least because many studied in Paris or Germany. (An important exception was the neo-Byzantinist Photis Kontoglou, who, although well-travelled in Europe and Africa, remained rooted in Orthodox tradition.) However, where most progressive Western developments occurred before 1930, Greek modernist artists were latecomers; consequently, in international terms much appears derivative.

Elements of Cubism appear in the paintings of Kostantinos Parthenis, and of Nikos Hadjikyriakos-Gikas, for example *Athenian Houses* (1927–28); in *Sky* of 1966, Gikas touches on futurism (both pictures are in the National Gallery). Surrealist imagery akin to Giorgio de Chirico surfaced with Nikos Engonopoulos (*Poet and Muse*, 1938, National Gallery), and persisted in later artists such as Christos Karas (*Three Graces*, 1974, National Gallery). Perhaps more successful was Ioannis Tsarouhis's interpretation of Matisse's linearism, as in Youth in an Overcoat (1937, National Gallery), also seen in Yiannis Moralis's figurative work of the 1940s and 1950s (as in *Figure*, 1951, National Gallery). Moralis's classicist realism was typical of much painting produced during the dictatorship; sometimes painterly as with Panagiotis

Tetsis, or linear with Giorgos Mavroïdis. Such work can feel more truly Greek than the experiments with abstraction and recent conceptual and post-modernist art.

Sculptors of the early 20th century were likewise often trained in Paris. Consequently, the impact of Maillol is felt in Michael Tombros's *Fat Woman* (1926, National Gallery), and Despiau in Bella Raftopoulou's *Sculpture* (1932, National Gallery). These matched an interwar concern for the figure while embracing some abstraction, a trend that lingered into the 1950s and 1960s with Georgios Kastriotis's enchant-

Farewell at Sounio, Theodoros Vryzakis.

ing *Dance* (1953, National Gallery), and Yannis Pappas's *Male Figure* (1965, artist's collection). But generally, from 1949, abstraction and the international style tended to prevail. Kostas Koulentianos's *Tree* (1988, Athens, Portalakes collection) reflected the spirit of Chadwick; Takis's *Light Signals* (1985, Paris, private collection) revealed a dull post-modernist wit; and Hrysa Vardea's *New York Landscape* (1971–74, Athens, Mihalarias collection) used light intriguingly but in a formally predictable presentation.

In architecture the eclecticism that persisted into the 1930s extended to vernacular forms. Not just with Zahos, who drew inspiration from Macedonian and Aegean traditional building, but also Dimitris Pikionis who, with a greater eye for functionalism, came closer to modernism in his Pefkákia School (1933, Athens), and as a landscape architect designed the approach zone to the Acropolis during the 1950s. Zahos was also in part responsible for the rebuilding of Thessaloníki following the fire of 1917. True modernism was introduced with buildings on Híos by the Bauhaus-trained Ioannis Despotopoulos, aka Jan Despo; P Mihaïlidis, who worked with Le Corbusier; and Patroklos Karantinos who studied under French pioneer Auguste Perret,

(completed 1991); the Athens School of Music (1976); the Museum of Cycladic Art by Yiannis Vikelas (1986) with its serene interior; the solar-powered Mytaras house by Mihalis Souvatzidis (1985); the round Ágios Dimítrios School by Takis Zenetos (1976); and the sculptural Emmanouíl Benáki Street apartments by Atelier 66 (1972). These and others parallel the best architecture in any modern city.

Across the country, Aris Konstantinidis designed most of the Bauhaus-y late-1950s hotels of the government-owned Xenia chain, though surviving specimens are looking

Icon painter in his studio showroom.

and then worked on the ambitious ministry-led programme of new school buildings in the 1930s. Many Athenian blocks of flats were in the modernist manner, examples being those by Kyriakos Panagiotakos on Themistokléous (on the corner with Arahóvis), or those by Mihaïlidis and his colleague Thoukidydis Valentis on nearby Zaïmi (on the corner with Stournára).

The 1950s and 1960s rebuilding of the rapidly expanding cities saw, as in most countries, much shoddy and uninspired concrete building, both public and private. Nevertheless, certain structures, essentially to internationalist patterns, are particularly distinguished, especially around Athens: the Mégaro Mousikís

rather dated (if not derelict) unless privatised and revamped.

Into the 21st century

Nothing of comparable merit has emerged indigenously since the millennium; "facadism" – whereby buildings from the 1920s or 1930s are gutted and rebuilt inside, preserving only their original street profile – is big on Athens' main boulevards. The most iconic structures of the 2004 Olympic Games – the new roof of the OAKA stadium in Maroúsi, suspended by cables from giant swooping arches, and a couple of pedestrian suspension bridges relying on his trademark leaning single pylon – were the work of Spanish architect Santiago Calatrava.

Loggerhead turtles have lost their
nesting beaches to mass tourism.

FLORA AND FAUNA

As befits its wide variety of habitats, Greece contains a great diversity of wildlife – including some of Europe's last bears, wolves and jackals.

G reece is a land of tremendous ecological diversity, second in Europe, in this respect, only to the Iberian Peninsula. Biomes range from the temperate forests of the Píndos and Rodópi mountains in the north to the arid semi-desert of eastern Crete, or from the alpine vegetation on the bald, rocky upper slopes of mountains like Smólikas and Ólympos to the delta marshlands of Évros or even the dunes of islands such as Rhodes and Límnos. The current mosaic of landscapes and habitats is due to a combination of geography and the hand of man. Sited in the region where Europe butts up against Asia Minor, and only a short hop from Africa, Greece lies at an ecological crossroads.

Since Neolithic times (12,000 to 3,000 BC), man has wrought enormous changes on the landscape, clearing the primeval forests that once covered much of the country for fuel, shipbuilding, pasture and agriculture.

Habitats

Somewhat less than a quarter of Greece is now forested, with the largest tracts being in the north of the country, in the Rodópi Mountains and the Píndos ranges. Here you have a variety of oak, chestnut, beech and other broadleaf woodlands, with tracts of fir and pine forest more related to the Scandinavian north than to the Mediterranean south of Europe. Drive inland, north from Amfípolis on the coast of Central Macedonia, and you will pass through three of Europe's major vegetation zones in the space of 150km (90 miles): Mediterranean, Central European and Northern conifer, typified by trees like birch, Scots pine and Norway spruce.

Pastureland covers some 40 percent of the country, while around 30 percent is cultivated land. Areas where traditional agriculture is still

Olive groves on Lésvos.

practised are often rich in wildlife but, as elsewhere in Europe, labour-intensive traditional practices are declining. Terrain unsuited to modern agriculture is being abandoned to scrub, which means a decline in the diversity of habitat; where intensive modern agriculture has taken over, the use of herbicides, insecticides and fertilisers degrades the land from a wildlife perspective. There are, however, still plenty of mature olive groves which provide a good habitat for birds and insects.

One of Greece's most emblematic habitats is Mediterranean *maquis* – scrubby, drought-resistant vegetation that covers much of the mainland and islands. This consists of low trees like the glossy-leaved kermes oak (*Quercus coccifera*) and the holm oak (*Quercus suber*), with its thinner, tapering leaves; hardy shrubs like myrtle, arbutus, strawberry tree and bay; and the fragrant under layer of phrygana – plants like wild rosemary, oregano, lavender and thyme.

On river banks, you will notice trees like willows, oleanders, plane trees and poplars; species such as Australian eucalyptus have also been widely introduced. Eucalyptus thrives in the dry climate, but ecologists view the species with circumspection or downright hostility due to the amount of water these trees suck out from the soil and the damaging effects that has on the soil's pH value. Seaside tamarisks, which tolerate saline soil, are nearly as disdained by purists.

Wetlands are one of the most threatened habitats in Greece – three-quarters of the country's original wetlands have been lost, and many others are under extreme pressure, what with the heavy demands for water for agriculture and tourist usage as well as targeted drainage for construction. Nevertheless, Greece still possesses various wetlands of great importance, including many protected under the international Ramsar Convention: Pórto Lágos and lakes ranges Vistonís and Ismáris; the Néstos Delta; Lake Mikrí Préspa; the Misolóngi lagoons; Amvrakikós Gulf; lakes Vólvi and Korónia; Lake Kerkíni; the contiguous deltas of the Aliákmon, Axiós and Loudías rivers; Évros Delta; and the Kotýhi lagoons. These encompass a variety of habitats from river deltas, shallow lagoons, salt-marsh, swamps, reed beds and lakes.

Elusive mammals

Man's impact on the wildlife of Greece has been as significant as his impact on the land's habitats. The Barbary lions and Anatolian leopards known to the Ancient Greeks are long gone, hunted to extinction. And many of the most famous species that have survived are scarce and elusive – only the luckiest or most patient visitors will glimpse them in the wild.

In the mountains of northern Greece, you can still find areas of real wilderness, where some of the country's rarest land mammals are to be found. First among these are the continent's most southerly population of European brown bears (*Ursos arctos*), found in the North Píndos range along the border with Albania and FYROM, and also in the Rodópi Mountains of Eastern Macedonia and Thrace, close to the border with Bulgaria.

The conservation body ARCTUROS (www. arcturos.gr) – which has an information centre in Aktós, near Flórina – sets out to protect both the 150-odd animals that survive and the habitat they live in. Bears have been protected by law since 1969, but still suffer from illegal hunting and habitat destruction.

Wolves

The wolf is officially listed as "vulnerable": population estimates range from a few hundred to low thousands, mainly in the Rodópi Mountains along the border with Bulgaria, but

The profusion of flowers and plants provides food for an equal profusion of insects.

also along the borders with FYROM and Turkey, the Píndos mountains of west-central Greece, Kerkíni, Falakró and the Évros region. Wolves died out in the Peloponnese some time between 1940 and 1970, and their survival elsewhere is precarious: they are threatened principally by habitat loss through logging, illegal hunting, road kills, hybridisation with dogs, and habitat disturbance through recreational tourism.

ARCTUROS works to protect Greece's population of wolves (*Canis lupus*) who have a sanctuary at Agrapídia. It is only fairly recently that wolves have enjoyed protected status – official bounties were paid until 1980 and, until 1991, they were still considered "vermin", which meant they could be hunted to protect livestock.

Although wolves do take sheep from time to time, other ungulates – mainly red deer (*Cervus elaphus*), fallow deer (*Dama dama*) and roe deer (*Capreolus capreolus*) – form the preferred diet.

Wild sheep, otters, lynx

Other notable mountain mammals include three species of wild sheep: the nimble chamois (*Rupicapra rupicapra*), the European mouflon (*Ovis musimon*) and the Cretan wild goat/ibex (also known as the *agrími* or *krí-krí; Capra aegagrus cretica*), with its bearded chin and curved horns, most dramatic on the large males. This latter species, worshipped in antiquity, is now endangered, largely due to hunting. It is mainly found in the Gorge of Samariá national park in western Crete, but during the 1960s, breeding colonies were established on nearby islands like Día and Ágii Pándes in an effort to save it from extinction.

Otters (*Lutra lutra*) can still be found but are scarce, and your best chance of seeing them is in river-rich areas like Thessaly, Préspa or Víkos-Aóös in Epirus. Similarly elusive are members of the cat family – the endangered lynx (*Lynx lynx*), with its characteristic ear tufts, which survives in the Víkos-Aóös National Park; and the much smaller wild cat (*Felix sylvestris*) – resembling a large grey domestic cat, with black

> A type of very small wild horse has lived on the island of Skýros since ancient times. There are fewer than 150 surviving pure-bred members of this unique breed.

stripes and a bushy tail – which are found in a variety of habitats on the mainland and as part of a small, threatened population on Crete, only confirmed to exist in the late 1990s.

Common mammals

Other woodland mammals include the wild boar (*Sus scrofa*) and the common Eurasian badger (*Meles meles*); the former is found on larger wooded islands as well as the mainland. In northern conifer forests, look out for the red squirrel (*Sciurus vulgaris*) with its bushy tail, white underbelly and ear tufts (a subspecies is also endemic to Lésvos). The pine marten (*Martes martes*) is distinguished from its more widespread cousin, the beech or stone marten (*Martes foina*), by its creamy, yellowish throat

patch, as compared with the latter's which is pure white. In addition to these two types of martens, you might see other members of the mustelid family, including the weasel (*Mustela nivalis*) and the European polecat (*Mustela putorius*). The most common nocturnal mammals you are likely to see are the country's numerous species of bat.

The red fox (*Vulpes vulpes*) is common and widespread, unlike a similar-looking animal more commonly associated with Africa and western Asia: the golden jackal (*Canis aureus*). Greece is the northwesternmost limit of the jackal's

Brown bears in the Rodópi Mountains.

range, but populations have collapsed since the 1980s. Now under a thousand remain, mainly in wetlands and *maquis* regions of Fokída, the Peloponnese, Halkidikí and the island of Sámos, as confirmed by a 2008–09 WWF survey (www. wwf.gr). Hunting jackals was forbidden in 1990, but they are still persecuted for stealing sheep and chickens, frequently taking the blame for kills by stray dogs. In fact, 50 percent of their diet is vegetarian, and the rest comes from carrion and hunting live reptiles, frogs, insects, small rodents and the ubiquitous rabbits.

Reptiles and amphibians

Not all of Greece's wildlife is elusive, and nor does tracking it down always demand time and effort.

Basking in the sun or making a dash for it, geckos can often be seen in rocks and along paths.

Other curious lizards of Greece include the Mediterranean chameleon (*Chamaeleo chamaeleo*), growing up to 30cm (1ft) long, and unmistakable with its prehensile tail, wedge-shaped head and bulbous eyes, now found only on Sámos, plus its cousin the African chameleon (Chamaeleo africanus), confined to Pýlos in the Peloponnese. The large, rough-scaled agama lizard (*Laudakia stellio*) lives in parts of northern Greece, and on Corfu, Paxí, the Cyclades, Dodecanese and the eastern Aegean islands. The Aegean Islands in fact have numerous reptilian endemics: six species of lizards and three types of snake are not found anywhere else in Europe.

Greece's snake species include Europe's most venomous, the nose-horned viper (*Vipera ammodytes*), with distinctive zigzags on its back; but most – like the grass snake (*Natrix natrix*) or the fast-moving Dahl's whip snake (*Columber najadum*) – are harmless.

One of Greece's most famous reptiles is the yellowish Hermann's tortoise (*Testudo hermanni*), once heavily exploited for the pet trade, but now protected. It lives in scrubby land in coastal regions throughout the country; keep an eye out for it when looking around ruins. A related species found nearly as widely is the spur-thighed tortoise (*Testudo graeca*); its cousin, *Testudo marginata*, is mostly restricted to the north of the country, and the Sporades.

Greece is home to two species of toads and 11 kinds of frogs, including tiny tree frogs and the highly endangered *Pelophylax cerigensis*, restricted to just a few hundred individuals on Kárpathos and Rhodes.

Marine life

Greece has more coastline than any other Mediterranean country – some 15,000km (9,300 miles) of it. The benign temperature of the Aegean and its relatively small tides make it good snorkelling territory. Look out for two types of octopuses – the common (*Octopus vulgaris*), with double rows of suckers, and the curled (*Eledone cirrhosa*), with single rows of suckers – plus cuttlefish, sea urchins, starfish, sea cucumbers, gorgonian and anemones. You may also spot pipefish (*Sygnathus acus*) and seahorses (*Hippocampus*).

At local harbours, you will primarily see various species of breams, parrotfish, hake, swordfish,

mackerel and dogfish-type shark among the fishermen's catch. The Mediterranean is heavily overfished, with industrial fleets being particularly to blame; one prestige species that bears the brunt of this is the bluefin tuna (*Thunnus thynnus*).

Loggerhead and hawksbill turtles

Among the most vulnerable marine species is the loggerhead turtle (*Caretta caretta*). Many die each year, entangled and drowned by fishing nets, but the real threat to their continued survival is the status of their ancestral nesting

The Mediterranean chameleon is now only found on Sámos island.

FAVOURITE LIZARDS

While the majority of wild animals are eager to keep away from people, some species actually visit you, in what might be called the wildlife equivalent of room service. Perhaps the most enchanting of these are the country's three species of geckos (commonest the orangey-tan *Hemidactylus turcicus*) – the most keen-sighted of all lizards, whose large eyes are perfect for hunting insects at night or in darkened rooms. Not only do they look cute, but their ability to run along vertical and even upside-down surfaces thanks to the adhesive pads on their feet inspired the development of Velcro fasteners.

sites. Many of the beaches turtles once chose to nest on have lost out over the years to tourism developments; the only significant remaining nesting sites are on Zákynthos, the Peloponnese and Crete. Natural hazards have always meant that only a tiny proportion of eggs laid make it to adulthood: animals like foxes predate on the eggs (laid between the end of May and August), and birds eat hatchlings (which emerge from July to the end of October) as they make their way to the sea. But human disturbance has even more devastating effects. Noise and curious tourists can cause adult turtles to abandon

Dolphins and whales

On boat trips, keep your eyes peeled for one of the cetaceans that can be found in Greek waters: the common dolphin (*Delphinus delphis*), frequently seen playing in schools in the bow wave of boats; its larger, darker cousin, the bottlenose dolphin (*Tursiops truncatus*), the dolphin most commonly seen in aquariums; the striped dolphin (*Stenella coeruleoalba*); a long-finned pilot whale (*Globicephala caretta*); a sperm whale (*Physeter catadon*); or a fin whale (*Balaenoptera physalus*).

Mediterranean monk seals are a protected species.

nests, and light pollution disorientates hatchlings, causing them to head inland, where they die, rather than out to sea. Similar problems afflict the hawksbill turtle (*Eretomochelys imbricata*), which occasionally is found around the Ionian islands.

If you are keen on turtle protection, stay away from nesting beaches at night and think of joining ARCHELON, the Sea Turtle Protection Society of Greece (www.archelon. gr). They have set up protected zones and rescue stations on Crete, the Peloponnese and Zákynthos, where the National Marine Park established for the turtles is finally overcoming past mismanagement and hostility from tourist concerns at Laganás.

The monk seal

Perhaps Greece's most important marine mammal, however, is the predominantly brown or grey Mediterranean monk seal (*Monachus monachus*), unusual among seals because it lives in warm waters. It eats mainly fish, squid and octopus, and· can grow to over two metres (6ft) in length and weigh more than 300kg (660lbs). In ancient times, monk seals were common – they figured on Greek coins from as far back as 500 BC and featured in the writings of Homer, Plutarch and Aristotle. Now, however, they are one of the most endangered mammals in the world. Between 300 and 500 individuals survive, with Greece, Dalmatia and Morocco having the

> *Greater flamingos (Phoenicopterus ruber) used to overwinter from Africa at salt marshes on Kós, Sámos, Lésvos and Límnos, but for unknown reasons they ceased arriving in about 2007.*

only significant populations, and it is a battle to save them.

Whereas in ancient Greek times they were trusting, they are now shy of man and confined to the most isolated coasts. During Roman times and the Middle Ages, they were hunted assiduously for their pelts, meat and oil, but they have also been hard hit in the last hundred years by pollution, disease and a steep decline in fish stocks. Until very recently, they were persecuted by fishermen who viewed them as competition for fish stocks and who resented them for damaging fishing nets. Now one of the reasons for their continued vulnerability is disturbance through tourism – often unwittingly, as when yachts seek out the type of deserted coves where the caves in which the seals live and breed are located.

Among their last remaining strongholds are Sámos and northern Kárpathos, where perhaps 30 individuals live, and the National Marine Park of the Northern Sporades, created in 1992, which has a population of about 55 seals. The main society fighting for their protection is the Hellenic Society for the Study and Protection of the Monk Seal (www.mom.gr). It is based on Alónisos, where it runs an exhibition centre in Patitíri and the Seal Treatment and Rehabilitation Centre for sick and orphaned seal pups at Stení Vála; there is also an information centre in Diafáni, Kárpathos. MOM's work has helped bring about some small encouraging signs: local attitudes towards the animals have shifted, so that they are rarely intentionally killed; and scientists believe that local seal birth rates – about eight annually – have stabilised. More information on this fascinating creature can be found at www.monachus-guardian.org.

Birds

Sited on important avian migration routes, Greece is an excellent destination for bird-watchers, especially in spring and autumn, but also in winter, when many northern European

birds come to avoid the cold. Enthusiasts should contact the Hellenic Ornithological Society (www.ornithologiki.gr/index.php?loc=en).

One of the best wetland sites in the country is the Préspa National Park, on a mountainous plateau in western Macedonia, comprising the almost all-Greek Lake Mikrí (Little) Préspa, and Lake Megáli (Great) Préspa, its waters and shoreline shared with Albania and FYROM. Here you can find breeding colonies of both great white pelican (*Pelecanus onocrotalus*) and Dalmatian pelicans (*Pelecanus crispus*), as well as the threatened pygmy cormorant (*Phalacrocorax*

Both black and white storks migrate through Greece, nesting on the way.

pygmaeus), which also breeds on lakes Kerkíni and Petrón.

Another critical site is the Évros Delta, where you can see wetland and pastureland birds like the lesser white-fronted goose (*Anser erythropus*), the crane (*Grus grus*), the Eurasian spoonbill (*Platalea leucorodia*), the glossy ibis (*Plegadis falcinellus*), the purple heron (*Ardea purpurea*) and the white stork (*Ciconia ciconia*), which is also highly visible across central mainland Greece in summer, nesting on church belfries and utility poles.

As for seabirds, one of the most important is the Audouin's gull (*Larus audouinii*), which is endangered but still found across the

Aegean, while great cormorants (*Phalacrocorax carbo*) and smaller shags are widespread in the Sporades, Cyclades and east Aegean.

Short-toed larks (*Calandrella brachydactyla*) and calandra larks (*Melanocorypha calandra*) are common on open agricultural land. Your eye might also be caught by the vivid hues of the turquoise-coloured European roller (*Coracias garrulus*), not to mention the smaller bee-eater (*Merops apiaster*), both of which you may see perched on fence or telegraph wires.

Other glamorously coloured birds include the golden oriole (*Oriolus oriolus*), which is country, but, like most birds of prey, they are vulnerable to hunting and poisoned bait, often put down to kill foxes or – illegally – wolves. The lammergeier (*Gypaetus barbatus*), a type of vulture famous for its habit of dropping bones from a great height to smash them so that it can extract the marrow, has vanished from Crete but may just still hang on in the mainland mountains. Three other vultures are more commonly seen in Greece – the griffon vulture (*Gyps fulvus*), the black vulture (*Aegypius monachus*) and the white-and-black Egyptian vulture (*Neophron percnopterus*). Other major birds of

The endangered imperial eagle.

frequently found in woodland and orchards; and the kingfisher (*Alcedo atthis*), found near streams and waterways, as well as hiding in sea-level rock formations. In olive groves and open country, watch out for the ground-feeding hoopoe (*Upupa epops*), with its unmistakable pinkish head and crest and a long curved bill.

Birds of prey

The Dadiá Forest in Thrace is one of the best places in Europe to see birds of prey, including three highly endangered birds: the imperial eagle (*Aquila heliaca*), the white-tailed or sea eagle (*Haliaetus albicilla*) and the golden eagle (*Aquila chrysaetos*). The latter still exists elsewhere in remote mountainous regions of the prey include the fish-eating osprey (*Pandion haliaetus*) and numerous types of kites, harriers, hawks, buzzards and falcons.

Perhaps the most famous of Greece's falcons is the Eleonora's falcon (*Falco eleonorae*). Similar to a peregrine but with a longer tail and more slender wings, it is often seen in groups hunting off coastal cliffs in the Aegean. Over two-thirds of the entire world population of this threatened bird species spend their summer months in Greece, hunting insects during spring and early summer, and delaying their breeding season so that they can raise their fledglings on migrant birds heading to Africa in the autumn, before they too head off on their long annual migration to overwinter on Madagascar.

The gloriously clear waters at Ladikó Bay, on the east coast of Rhodes.

Líndos acropolis, Rhodes.

A refreshingly shady lunch option on Corfu.

The blue balconies and tall, white houses of Mandráki, Nísyros.

INTRODUCTION

A detailed guide to the entire country, with principal
sites clearly cross-referenced by number to the maps.

Mandráki church.

As Henry Miller wrote in *The Colossus of Maroussi*, "marvellous things happen to one in Greece – marvellous *good* things which can happen to one nowhere else on earth. Somehow, almost as if He were nodding, Greece still remains under the protection of the Creator. Men may go about their puny, ineffectual bedevilment, even in Greece, but God's magic is still at work and, no matter what the race of men may do or try to do, Greece is still a sacred precinct – and my belief is it will remain so until the end of time".

Another quotation, this time from a dictionary, defines the Greek word "chaos" as "disordered, formless matter said to have existed before the ordered universe". Chaotic is certainly one way of describing the physical geography of a country characterised by heaps of rocks, furrowed mountain ranges and a jagged coastline. Flat, fertile areas such as the Thessalian plain are the exception.

Palaiokarya bridge and waterfall, Thessaly, Central Greece.

The extensive Pindos mountain range in the west forms the country's backbone, while in the east, the peaks of Mount Olympos, at nearly 3,000 metres (10,000ft), are the highest in Greece. The coast is a series of so many coves and inlets that it runs to a length of 15,000km (9,300 miles). The 60-odd inhabited islands that spill out into the seas surrounding Greece are divided into distinct groups: the Ionian islands to the west, the Sporádes to the east, and the Cyclades and Dodecanese trailing out southeast from Athens. The three largest islands are Crete, Lésvos and Évia, the latter little known outside of Greece.

In this section, our expert writers will take you on 15 individual journeys. Starting with the capital, Athens, we take a clockwise loop through the mainland and then set sail for the many islands, finishing in the westerly Ionian archipelago. En route, you will find the history, geography and local culture of each area covered in detail. The opening hours given for sites and museums are for summer only (May–September), unless otherwise stated; different hours usually apply from October to April. Tourist facilities on the islands in particular tend to close abruptly once the summer season has finished – which varies from early September when school starts, to late October for Rhodes, and the southerly "Great Island" of Crete.

The chapters have been loosely designed as two-week itineraries, but of course the longer you stay, the better. Perhaps, like Lord Byron, you will one day be able to declare: "It is the only place I ever was contented in".

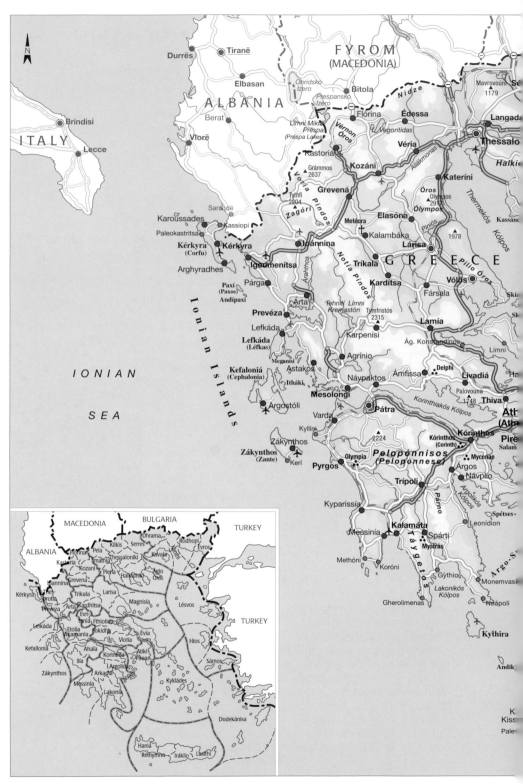

BULGARIA Kárdžali Edirne BLACK SEA

TURKEY

Dráma Xánthi Komotiní İstanbul

Kavála Keşan Marmara Denizi

Liménas Alexandroúpoli

Thássos Kavákköy

monikós
Kólpos

ssos Samothráki

Áthos Fengári Thermá
1611 (Loutrá) Bandırma Bursa

Áthos
2033 Thrakikón Pélagos

Sithonía Çanakkale

Gökçeada Abide

Mýrina Ayvacık Edremit Balıkesir

Límnos

Ágios
Evstrátios

á Gioúra Mólyvos

ziá Pipéri Akhisar TURKEY

issos Mytilíni

Sporádes Lésvos
Plomári

Skýros

ia Skyros Psará

noea)

Paralía Kymis İzmir

Hios Urla
Híos Çeşme
Karystos Pyrgi

Ándros Aydın Denizli

AEGEAN SEA

Ándros

Kéa Tínos Sámos Vathy
Karlóvassi (Sámos)

Giáros Ikaría
Tínos Ág. Foúrni
Kírykos Agathónísi

Ermoúpoli Arkí
Kýthnos Sýros Mýkonos Milâs Muğla
Lipsí

Cycládes Pátmos

Sérifos Léros

Páros Náxos Bodrum

Náxos

Sífnos Kálymnos Fethiye
Kímolos Andíparos
Amorgós Kós
Síkinos Íos Kós

Milos Kéfalos

Folégandros Níssyros Sými Ródos Kaş

Astypálea Tílos
Anáfi Mt Atávyros Megisti
Sýrna Hálki 1215 (Kastellórizo)

Santorini Líndos
(Thíra)

Dodecanese Ródos
(Rhodes)

Kritikó Pélagos

Kárpathos

Réthymno Iráklio Kríti (Crete)
(Rethimno) (Heraklion)
Ida Ágios Kásos
Arkádi (Psiloritis) Nikólaos
Plakiás 2456 Sitía
Horá Knossos Zakros
Sfakion Ag.
Galini Ierapetra

Gávdos

Greece

0   50 km
0   50 miles

The Kesarianí Monastery offers sweeping views of Attica below.

THE MAINLAND

The mainland of Greece contains a wealth
of historical monuments, in landscapes
that are often breathtaking.

*Woodland surrounding
Mýtikas peak*

Many visitors to Greece head straight for the islands – of which there are of course dozens to choose from, offering everything from sybaritic nightlife to serene tranquillity, from historical marvels to stunning natural beauty. Naturally, this book explores Greece's offshore assets in great detail later on (see page 229). But to bypass the Greek mainland is to overlook the heart of the country, to miss its range of dramatic scenery, and to neglect some spectacular ruins recalling the grandeur of ancient civilisations.

The six chapters that follow explore this rich and varied land, starting in Athens, birthplace of democracy and home to the most impressive remains from the Classical period to be found in Greece. However, relics of ancient civilisations can be seen throughout the mainland – the ancient strongholds of Mycenae and Tiryns, predating the Trojan War; the holy site of Delphi, regarded by the ancients as the centre of the world; the stadium and temples of Olympia, where the Olympic Games began; and wonderfully preserved theatres at Epidauros, Argos, Dodona and elsewhere.

*The Temple of Poseidon at
Sounion.*

Monuments from the Byzantine period include elegant churches and monasteries decorated with glorious mosaics or frescoes. Thessaloníki, the second city of the Byzantine Empire, has a rich heritage of these stylish churches, and the monasteries of Dafní and Ósios Loukás are world famous for their art treasures. Venetian and Frankish occupation enriched Greece's coastline with picturesque castles and walled cities such as Monemvasía, Návplio and Koróni. Throughout the country, archaeological museums are treasure-houses of beautiful and intriguing relics of Greece's complex past.

But the Greek mainland is not just about history: its timeless landscapes are often captivating. The rugged mountain ranges of central and southern Greece, snowcapped for four months of the year, descend through craggy ridges to sea-girt peninsulas and promontories. Deep gulfs and inlets penetrate the land, bounded by mountains cradling tiny harbours and fishing villages, or bordered by pine slopes. Elsewhere, a narrow coastal plain meets the sea in a fretwork of bays, some of them inaccessible overland.

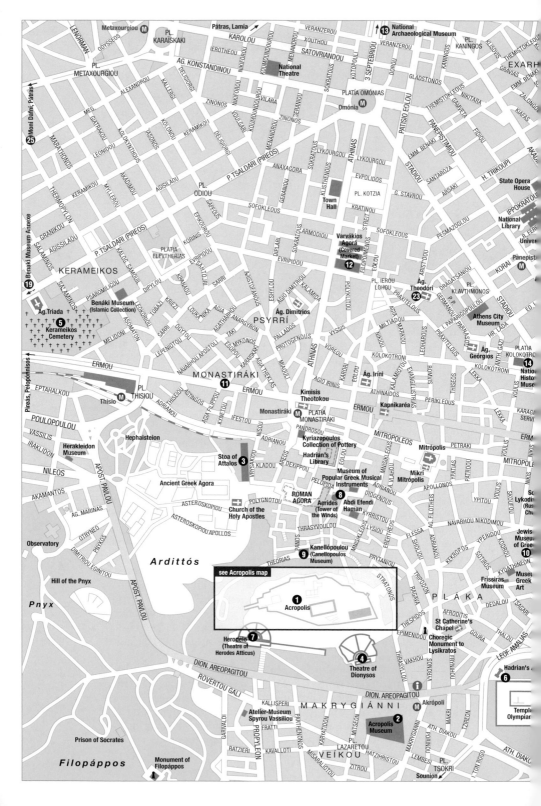

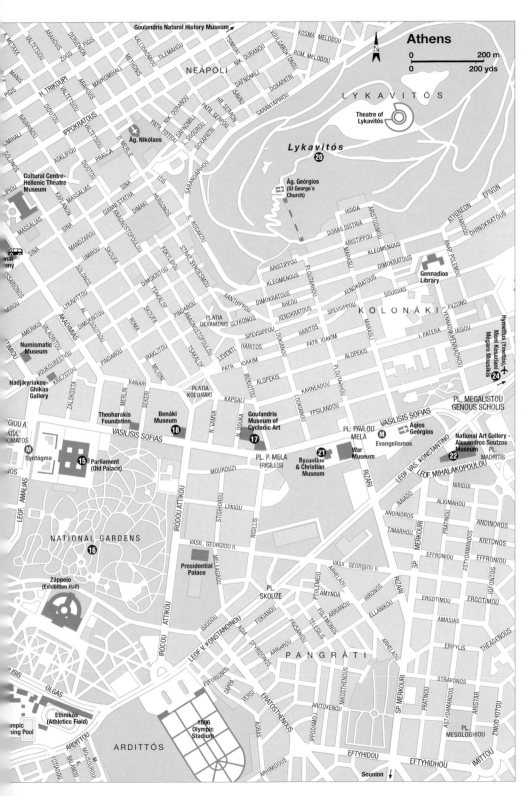

The Acropolis at dusk.

ATHENS

Both East and West converge in this vibrant
metropolis, lively and brimming over, just like its
inhabitants. The city is also home to some of the
country's finest, cutting-edge museums.

f there is one quality for which Athens (Athína in Greek) should be credited, it is elasticity. Throughout its long history, the city has by turns been obscure, triumphant and, now, the capital of the modern Greek state. Athens is barely mentioned in Homer, but emerged as a growing power in the 6th century BC. During the Periclean "golden age", Athens became a great centre of art and literature, commerce and industry. With Macedonian expansion came the first shrinkage, though Athens remained a prestigious intellectual centre with particular emphasis on philosophy and oratory.

During the Hellenistic period, Athens was overshadowed by the great kingdoms founded by Alexander's successors – but not obliterated. The rulers of Egypt, Syria and Pergamum courted the old city with gifts of buildings and works of art. Yet it was already beginning to rest on its laurels, to turn into a museum-city, a "cultural commodity" rather than an active, living organism. Besieged and sacked by Lucius Cornelius Sulla in 86 BC, restored and pampered under two phil-Athenian Roman emperors, Augustus and Hadrian, sacked again by the Herulians in AD 267 and Alaric the Goth in AD 395, Athens entered the Byzantine era as a small provincial backwater, shorn of all its glory. The edict of the Byzantine emperor

Évzone guards outside the Parliament.

Justinian forbidding the study of philosophy there (AD 529) rang down the curtain on the ancient city.

From broken city to capital

Under Latin rule (1204–1456), invaded, occupied and fought over by the French, Catalans, Florentines and Venetians, Athens shrank even more. It was only after the Ottoman conquest in the 15th century that it began to expand again, but still falling far short of its ancient limits. There were more setbacks, including a devastating Venetian incursion

Main Attractions

THE ACROPOLIS
NEW ACROPOLIS MUSEUM
STROLLING IN PLÁKA
VARVÁKIOS AGORÁ
SUNDAY/EASTER SERVICES AT
  AGÍAS IRÍNIS
NATIONAL ARCHAEOLOGICAL
  MUSEUM
BENÁKI MUSEUM
HADJIKYRIAKOS-GHIKAS
  GALLERY
DÁFNI MOSAICS
POSEIDON TEMPLE, SOÚNIO

FACT

One thing to be prepared
for, on a visual level, is
the ubiquitous graffiti;
Athens must be one of
the most heavily
"decorated" of all
European cities. Luridly
colourful or often
supremely witty, it
ranges aesthetically from
the crudest tags to high
art, sometimes
apparently
commissioned or at least
tolerated (as at the
trolley depot near
Kerameikos cemetery).
As Greece undergoes
more social travail under
austerity, it can only
proliferate further.

in 1687. Athens finally rose from its ruins after the War of Independence, an "exhausted city", as Christopher Wordsworth noted in 1832, that was suddenly raised, unprepared, to the status of capital of the new Greek state.

Athens is thus a town that has grown haphazardly since then, and too fast. It never had a chance to mellow into venerable old age. Old and new have not blended too well; you can still sense the small, pre-1940s city pushing through the huge sprawl of today's modern capital, like the proverbial thin man struggling to get out of every fat man. Occasionally, you come across what must have once been a suburban villa, ensconced between tall office buildings, its owner still fighting with hermetically closed windows against building-site dust and the roar of the traffic.

Congestion in Athens can be unbelievable, particularly when there is some work stoppage or demonstration underway and traffic is forced off the main streets, or it increases because the metro or buses are on strike. When it works, however, public transport makes journeys to, and through, the heart of the city, in a matter of minutes. Fairly thorough pedestrianisation of central Athens has made it more liveable and inviting, palpably less polluted.

In addition, branching off from the manic central arteries are the minor veins of the city, relatively traffic-free. Most apartment blocks have balconies and verandas, and there you can see the Athenians in summer emerging from their afternoon siesta in underpants and nighties, reading the paper, watching the neighbours, watering their plants, eating their evening meal.

Later on after dark, younger Athenians head out for nightlife, still fairly lively and long despite the economic pinch. The original district for this was Psyrrí, just beyond Monastiráki (with which it shares a metro station). Accounts of hip Psyrrí's demise in popular lore are greatly exaggerated, but it is true that the margin of trendiness and gentrification spreads steadily outward and further northwest, encompassing the formerly dismal neighbourhoods of Gázi, Rouf, Keramikós, Metaxourgío and Votanikós. Hot venues, for

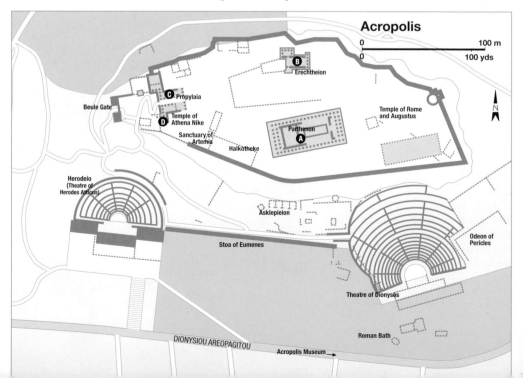

Acropolis

0   100 m
0   100 yds

B Erechtheion

C Propylaia

Beule Gate

Temple of Rome and Augustus

D Temple of Athena Nike

Sanctuary of Artemis

Parthenon

A

Halkotheke

Herodeio (Theatre of Herodes Atticus)

Asklepieion

Odeon of Pericles

Stoa of Eumenes

Theatre of Dionysós

N

Roman Bath

DIONYSIOU AREOPAGITOU

Acropolis Museum →

cutting-edge arts events as well, change regularly – consult a listings website or ask a friendly local.

The Acropolis

Seen from the right angle driving east on the **Ierá Odós** (the Sacred Way), especially at night, or looking up at its rocky bulk from the Pláka, the **Acropolis ❶** (Apr–Sept daily 8am–6.30pm, Oct–Mar Mon–Sat 8am–4.30pm, Sun 8am–2.30pm; the Acropolis ticket is also valid within four days for the ancient Greek Agora, the Theatre of Dionysos, the Roman Agora, Hadrian's Library, the Kerameikos Cemetery and the Temple of Olympian Zeus) still has a presence that makes the grimy concrete of modern Athens fade into insignificance. Climb up in early morning in summer or early afternoon in winter, when the crowds are thinnest, and a strip of blue sea edged with grey hills marks the horizon. On a wet or windy day, walking across its uneven limestone surface feels like being on a ship's deck in a gale.

The Acropolis nowadays looks like a stonemason's workshop, much as it must have done in the 440s BC when the **Parthenon ❷** was under construction as the crowning glory of Pericles' giant public works programme. Some of his contemporaries thought it extravagant: Pericles was accused of dressing his city up like a harlot. In fact, the Parthenon celebrates Athena as a virgin goddess and the city's protector. Her statue, 11 metres (37ft) tall and constructed of ivory and gold plate to Pheidias's design, once gleamed in its dim interior; in late antiquity, it was taken to Constantinople, where it disappeared.

Conservators have taken down hundreds of blocks of marble masonry from the Parthenon to replace the rusting iron clamps inserted in the 1920s with non-corrosive titanium (rust made the clamps expand, cracking the stone, while acid rain turned carved marble surfaces into soft plaster). The restorers also succeeded in identifying and collecting about 1,600 chunks of Parthenon marble scattered over the hilltop, many blown off in the 1687 explosion caused by a Venetian mortar igniting Ottoman munitions stored

The previously traffic-clogged road of Dionysíou Areopagítou around the base of the Acropolis has been pedestrianised, part of a plan to link the ancient sites with a car-free promenade. This, and its continuation Apostólou Pávlou, are now popular places for evening strolling.

Acropolis Museum exhibits.

THE PARTHENON FRIEZE

The Parthenon Marbles are a 76-sq-m (500-sq-ft) stretch of sculpted figures – mostly from the frieze – carved under the direction of the master-sculptor and architect Pheidias. By 1799, when Lord Elgin was appointed British ambassador to the Ottoman Empire, the Parthenon was in a sorry state, having been practically destroyed and then plundered by the invading Venetians in 1687. Elgin negotiated a permit from the sultan to remove "some blocks of stone with inscriptions and figures", which he did between 1801 and 1812. He then shipped the marbles back to Britain, and in 1816 sold them to the British Museum, where they remain today.

The marbles are an integral part of one of the most beautiful buildings that still survives from antiquity, say the Greeks, and can be better appreciated in the city that made them. A key aim in building the **Acropolis Museum** was to reunite the surviving sculptures that once adorned the Parthenon: with its controlled environment, there were hopes that the museum would overcome what had ostensibly been the main objection to the return of the marbles, namely Athens' lack of a suitable location in which to display them. So far, however, the world's major museums claim that to return the marbles would set a disastrous precedent.

In Ottoman times, the Turkish military commander housed his harem in the Erechtheion.

The impressive Acropolis Museum.

inside the temple. When they are replaced, about 15 percent more building will be on view. New blocks cut from near the ancient quarries on Mount Pendéli (14km/9 miles north of Athens), which supplied the 5th-century BC constructors, will fill the gaps.

The **Erechtheion** ⓑ, an elegant architecturally complex repository of ancient cults going back to the Bronze Age, is already restored. The Caryatids now supporting a porch over the tomb of King Kekrops, a mythical founder of the ancient Athenian royal family, are modern copies. The surviving originals were moved to the Acropolis Museum to prevent further damage from the *néfos*, the ochre summer blanket of pollution, now thankfully less frequent, that hangs over Athens.

Completed in 395 BC, a generation later than the Parthenon, the Erechtheion also housed an early wooden statue of Athena, along with the legendary olive tree that she conjured out of the rock to defeat Poseidon the sea-god in their contest for sovereignty over Attica.

The **Propylaia** ⓒ, the battered official entrance to the Acropolis built by Mnesikles in the 430s BC, was cleverly designed with imposing outside columns to awe people coming up the hill. Parts of its coffered stone ceiling, once painted and gilded, are still visible as you walk through. Only reassembled recently, the exquisite square temple of **Athena Nike** ⓓ (finished in 421 BC) stands on what was once the citadel's southern bastion. It supposedly occupies one of the spots – the other is Cape Sounion – where Theseus's father, King Aegeus, is said to have thrown himself to his death on seeing a black-sailed ship approaching the harbour. Theseus had promised to hoist a white sail for the return voyage if he had succeeded in killing the Minotaur on Crete, but carelessly forgot.

Acropolis Museum

The sculptures that Lord Elgin left behind are in the **Acropolis Museum**

2, below the Parthenon by Akrópoli metro station (Tue–Sun 8am–8pm, Fri until 10pm; www.theacropolismuseum.gr). Opened in 2009, the Acropolis Museum is the result of a competition won by New York-based Swiss architect Bernard Tschumi. From outside, the concrete-and-glass building, with its retro, mid-20th-century feel, is starkly antipathetic, in contrast to two neighbouring, listed apartment blocks on Dionysíou Areopagítou, threatened with demolition but ultimately saved by public outcry; no. 17, of 1930s vintage, ranks as Athens' best surviving example of Art Deco.

Once inside, however, the building works much better, effectively harnessing natural light for the optimum presentation of sculptural objects (a different proposition from the kind of light called into play when displaying paintings or drawings). From the entry on Dionysíou Areopagítou, a glass walkway leads over excavated sections of ancient Athens, including dwellings, wells, water and sewage works, an olive press, and even a Classical symposium hall with mosaic flooring. The excavations extend well under the museum which hovers above, supported by 100 massive anti-seismic columns, and muted natural light filters through the glass panels that make up much of the flooring.

From the ground floor, the upper levels are reached by a ramp, simulating the approach to the Acropolis and watched over by the six scarred but still impressively female Caryatids (one of them a copy, as the sixth original resides in the British Museum in London). On the first floor, the Archaic exhibition features the famous "Calf-bearer" or Moschophoros, and various coquettish *korai* (sculptures of women) revealing the Archaic ideal of beauty – look closely and you can make out their make-up, earrings and the patterns of their crinkled, close-fitting dresses.

Then up past the second-floor restaurant and shop to the top floor and the pièce de résistance: a glass gallery holding a reconstruction of the Parthenon pediments, of the same size and compass orientation as the real Parthenon looming just outside the wrap-around windows. The friezes, including the triangular western aetoma, are mounted at eye level – unlike the originals, which sat overshadowed by the eaves so that the ancient Athenians couldn't really appreciate them. The authentic fragments which Greece retains have been mounted; everything else is a plaster cast, pointedly awaiting the return of their prototypes, the so-called Elgin Marbles, from the British Museum.

The Agora and Theatre of Dionysos

Just to the north of the Acropolis lies the **Ancient Greek Agora** (daily summer 8am–6.30pm, winter 8am–2.40pm). The main entrance to this site is on Adrianoú Street, but there is an alternative way in behind the church of the Holy Apostles. While the Acropolis was mainly a religious site, the Agora was used for all public

Sculpture in the Stoa of Attalos, in the ancient Greek Agora.

The Tower of the Winds.

The well-preserved Hephaesteion temple.

kneeling *kouros* (a statue of a nude youth). The *Hephaisteion* (also known as the Theseion), the temple opposite, is the most complete surviving Doric order temple and gives some idea of what the intact Parthenon looked like – though the vaulted ceiling dates from its time as a church.

On the south side of the Acropolis lies the **Theatre of Dionysos** ❹. The marble seating tiers date from around 320 BC and later, but scholars generally agree that plays by playwrights such as Aeschylos, Sophokles, Euripides and Aristophanes were first staged here at religious festivals during the 5th century BC. A state subsidy for theatre-goers meant that every Athenian citizen could take time off to attend (entrance on Dionysíou Areopagítou; summer daily 8am–6.30pm, winter Mon–Fri 8am–4.30pm, Sat–Sun 8am–2.30pm).

Just east of the theatre, in Pláka's Platía Lysikrátous, stands the **Choregic Monument to Lysikratos**, the earliest example of the use of external Corinthian columns (the last and most ornate order of ancient Greek architecture). The inscription commemorates the victory of Lysikratos in 334 BC in a drama contest; the elegant monument was originally crowned by a tripod. During medieval times, a Capuchin monastery, which hosted Lord Byron during his second stay in Athens, incorporated the monument.

Cemetery and Islamic art

Beyond modern Thisío district, the **Kerameikos Cemetery** ❺ (daily summer 8am–6.30pm, winter 8am–2.40pm) in the potters' district of the city was a burial place for prominent ancient Athenians. An extraordinary variety of sculptured monuments – tall stone urns, a prancing bull, winged sphinxes and melancholy scenes of farewell – overlooked the Sacred Gate, from which the paved Sacred Way led to Eleusis, where the mysteries were held. In the site museum (summer Tue–Sun 8am–6.30pm, Mon

purposes: commercial, religious, political, civic, educational, theatrical, athletic. Today, it looks like a cluttered field of ruins.

The reconstructed **Stoa of Attalos** ❸, a 2nd-century BC line of shops, contains a wonderful, small archaeological museum (summer Tue–Sun 8am–6.30pm, Mon 11am–6.30pm, winter Tue–Sun 8am–2.40pm, Mon 11am–2.40pm); top marks go to a small perfume vial in the form of a

1.30–6.30pm, winter Tue–Sun 8am–2.40pm) is a collection of grave goods, an excellent guide to Greek vase-painting, from a squat geometric urn with a rusting iron sword twisted around its neck to the white *lekythoi* (oil or perfume flask) of Classical Athens, and self-consciously sophisticated Hellenistic pottery.

Nearby, on the corner of Agíon Asomáton and Dipýlou Streets, an annexe of the Benáki Museum houses an **Islamic Art Collection** (summer Tue–Sun 9am–3pm, Wed 9am–9pm, winter Thur–Sun 9am–5pm; www. benaki.gr), which ranks among the best in the world. More than 8,000 artefacts chart the evolution of Islamic art and civilisation up to the 19th century. The superb displays include a 16th-century velvet saddle from Bursa and the marble-faced interior of a 17th-century Cairo reception room.

Roman Athens

A few Roman monuments recall a time when Athens was revered, but stripped of its movable artworks. The 2nd-century Emperor Hadrian,

a fervent admirer of Classical Greek culture, erected an ornate arch, known as **Hadrian's Arch ❻**, marking the spot where the Classical city ended and the provincial Roman university town began. On the side facing the Acropolis is the inscription "This is Athens, the ancient city of Theseus", on the side facing the Olympieion it reads "This is the city of Hadrian and not of Theseus".

Little of this Roman city can be seen beneath the green of the **Záppio Park** and the archaeological area behind the towering columns of the **Temple of Olympian Zeus** (Stilés Olympíou Diós; daily summer 8am–6.30pm, winter 8am–2.40pm). Work on the temple had been abandoned in around 520 BC when funds ran out, but Hadrian finished the construction and dedicated the temple to himself.

Later in the century, Herodes Atticus, a wealthy Greek landowner who served in the Roman senate, built the steeply raked theatre on the south slope of the Acropolis (the **Herodeio** or **Iródio Theatre ❼**, now used for Athens Festival performances)

The towering columns of the Temple of Olympian Zeus.

as a memorial to his wife Regilla. A 1st-century BC Syrian, Andronikos of Kyrrhos, was responsible for the picturesque **Tower of the Winds** ❽ (**Aérides**; daily summer 8.30am–6.30pm, winter 8am–2.40pm), in the **Roman Agora**, a well-preserved marble octagon that is a highlight. It is decorated with eight relief figures, each depicting a different wind direction, and once contained a water-clock. Later, it served as a *tekke* (ceremonial hall) for Ottoman dervishes. The other standout of the forum is **Hadrian's Library** (daily 9am–2.40pm), an enormous colonnaded-courtyard building subsequently adapted to accommodate a four-apsed Byzantine basilica, from which mosaic flooring survives.

Pláka

Pláka, the old quarter clustering at the foot of the Acropolis, has been restored to its former condition (or rather to a fairly good reproduction of it), cars prohibited (for the most part), derelict houses rescued and streets tidied up. It has become a delightful, sheltered place to meander in; you might almost imagine yourself in a village, particularly in the winding narrow streets of the Anafiótika district that nestles below the Acropolis.

Pláka is also the best place to track down Athens' Ottoman past. The 15th-century **Fethiye Mosque** beside the Roman Agora is one of the finest, and oldest, examples of Muslim architecture in the city; it is unfortunately closed to visitors. However, nearby on Platía Monastiráki the Tsizdarákis Mosque (1759) now houses the **Kyriazopoulos Collection of Pottery** (Wed–Mon 9am–2.30pm). The mosque's interior has been sensitively conserved and is well worth a look, especially the brightly painted *mihrab*. Perhaps the most fascinating remnant of Turkish life, however, is the 16th-century **Abdi Efendi Hamam** (Wed–Mon 9am–4pm) on Kyrrístou. This *hammam* (Turkish bath) with its warren of atmospheric rooms has been beautifully restored; a well-produced guide gives background on the building and the place of bathing in Greek and Turkish culture.

Just uphill from the hammam at the eclectic **Canellopoulos (Kanellopoulou) Museum** ❾ (Tue–Sun 9am–4pm; free), a new wing shelters exquisite ancient objects like Archaic ceramic birds in flight and relief sphinxes on a *pithos*; the original 19th-century mansion is now devoted to early Christian and Byzantine displays, like several Fayyum portraits, Coptic textiles and rare icons. Nearby, at Pános 22, the well-labelled Man and Tools annexe of the Greek Folk Art Museum (Tue–Sun 9am–4pm), showcases extinct or vanishing craft-trades and their implements – some truly bizarre, like a *kataïfi* dough-extruder.

A few steps from Aérides, also housed in a neoclassical mansion, is the excellent **Museum of Popular Greek Musical Instruments** (Tue, Thur–Sun 10am–2pm, Wed noon–6pm; free; www.instruments-museum.gr), showcasing the collection of Fivos Anoyanakis. On two floors are

Pláka is full of tourist souvenirs.

documented and displayed every instrument ever played in Greece, their sounds to be heard at the adjacent listening posts. The shop, a branch of the premier record store Xylouris, stocks (of course) plenty of Greek traditional music CDs, while the lovely garden often hosts summer-evening concerts by top contemporary Greek musicians – check the posters out front.

At the eastern edge of Pláka is another pair of worthwhile museums. Highlight of the **Museum of Greek Folk Art** at Kydathinéon 17 (Tue–Sun 9am–4pm) is a completely reconstructed room of murals by the naïve artist Theophilos of Lésvos (1868–1934). At the end of Kydathinéon, at Níkis 39, the **Jewish Museum of Greece** ❿ (Mon–Fri 9am–2.30pm, Sun 10am–2pm; www.jewishmuseum.gr) records the long presence of Jews in the territory of modern Greece through documents, costumes and liturgical items, with frequent special exhibits and events.

Monastiráki

This entire area, essentially Athens' central bazaar, is a vast sprawl of shops, which get more upmarket towards Platía Syndágmatos. **Monastiráki** ⓫ brings to mind the market described in a 4th-century BC comedy by Euboulos: "Everything will be for sale together in the same place at Athens, figs, summoners, bunches of grapes, turnips, pears, apples, witnesses, roses, medlars, honeycombs, chickpeas, lawsuits, beestings-puddings, myrtleberries, allotment machines, irises, lambs, waterclocks, laws, indictments". Kitsch-collectors will find much to interest them: Greek kitsch is arguably the most orgiastically hideous in the world. Monastiráki Square, by the eponymous metro station, emerged from the throes of an overhaul completely pedestrianised and more inviting; the little central monastery-church of the name, originally 11th-century, is usually open.

Retaining a traditional pattern, similar shops still tend to cluster together, as can be seen from those around the **Mitrópolis** (Athens' cathedral), specialising in ecclesiastical articles. The cathedral itself dates from the mid-19th century and is as large as it is undistinguished. However, next door the small "**old cathedral**" (formally known as Panagía Gorgoepikóös or Ágios Eleftheríos) dates from the 12th century, although its masonry is a

The kombológi – a small chain of stone or wooden "worry-beads" – is good for relieving tension.

A slice of Athenian nightlife.

Relief in the National Archaeological Museum.

The National Archaeological Museum.

hotchpotch of materials reused from earlier churches. Above the door arch is a 2nd-century relief showing the calendar of Attic festivals.

Robustly vulgar **Pandrósou Street** bills itself as the **Flea Market**, though the genuine article(s) – liveliest at weekends – is/are at **Platía Avyssinías**, crammed with old furniture dealers. In the lanes all around are daily shops selling everything from old engravings to superannuated light fixtures. Head north up Athinás or its side-streets from Monastiráki square and you find the shops get more practical: wood stoves, handtools, screws, chainsaws, irrigation systems, hats, camping gear, knobs and knockers – truly a serendipitous accumulation.

Equally so are the goods in the **Varvákios Agorá ⓬**, a 19th-century gem roughly halfway between Monastiráki and Omónia squares on the east side of Athinás Street, originally endowed by Ioannis Varvakis, hero of Yiannis Smaragdis' 2012 film *God Loves Caviar*. This is the city's main covered meat-and-fish market, where shoppers mill between open stands displaying fish, seafood and any type and part of animal you can imagine. Near the base of Eólou is the flower market on **Platía Agías Irínis**, flanked by the eponymous church which features the finest Sunday-morning and Easter chanting in the city, courtesy of the Lykourgos Angelopoulos choir.

Omónia to Sýndagma

The city's heart, now largely pedestrianised, lies within an almost equilateral triangle defined by **Platía Omónias** in the north, Monastiráki in the south and **Platía Syndágmatos** to the southeast.

North of Omónia (also close to Viktória metro station) and crammed with treasures from every period of antiquity is the **National Archaeological Museum ⓭** (Mon 1.30–7.45pm, Tue–Sun 8am–6.45pm; www.namuseum.gr; for full description see page 158). It emerged from a

five-year refit in 2008 and retains its rank as one of the world's great galleries.

Omónia itself went in for a facelift at the millennium. However, it remains traffic-plagued and the rather bleak concrete piazza that now covers the centre of the square is drearily unimaginative. The parallel streets of Stadíou and Panepistimíou run southeast from Omónia to Platía Syndágmatos. Halfway down Panepistimíou is Christian and Theophilus Hansen's neoclassical trilogy of the **National Library, University and Academy**. Erected between 1837 and 1891, they are built of Pentelic marble and draw heavily on ancient Greek architectural forms. Startlingly bright painting and gilding gives some idea of how the now-stark marble of ancient monuments may have first appeared.

Further along is the house of Heinrich Schliemann, designed by Ernst Ziller (1878), now home to the **Numismatic Museum** (Tue–Sun 9am–4pm). Of greater interest is the **National Historical Museum** ⓮ (Tue–Sun 9am–2pm),

which occupies the prominent Old Parliament Building on Stadíou. Arranged thematically as much as chronologically, the museum covers episodes like the War of Independence to the Balkan Wars by way of a folklore collection and foreign philhellenes.

Sýndagma Square (Platía Syndágmatos, or Constitution Square) is the de facto centre of the city, dominated by the **Parliament Building** ⓯, which was originally the Royal Palace, built in 1836–42 for King Otto. The changing of the *Évzone* Guard, a favourite tourist spectacle, takes place hourly in front of the Parliament.

Ermoú, running west from the square, is now a long pedestrian walkway with fashion outlets, enlivened by pavement buskers. Improved lighting makes this an attractive area to wander in the evening in search of a taverna or café – of which there are many in the perpendicular lanes. Also on Ermoú is the attractive Byzantine

The Benáki Museum contains treasures from all periods of Athens' history.

Busy Monastiráki.

Athens is a treasury of Byzantine art.

The Parliament.

church of **Kapnikaréa**, thought to date from the 11th century; inside are frescoes executed by the neo-Byzantinist Photis Kontoglou.

The **National Gardens** (sunrise to sunset; free), much the coolest spot downtown during summer, are just behind the parliament building. Full of tangled bowers and ponds alive with terrapins, ducks or fish, there are also constant rivulets of water running along recessed troughs and numbers of escaped parrots or budgies in the trees. It was laid out by Queen Amalia as the palace gardens during the 19th century. She used the new Greek navy to bring back botanical specimens from their voyages around the world. Sadly, the single café is grossly overpriced – you'll have better luck at the popular Aigli, just outside the gardens proper, next to the 1888-vintage **Zappeio hall**, another Theophilus Hansen work, which hosts regular conferences and is often surrounded by nocturnal book fairs.

Kolonáki

Chic Kolonáki is the city's upmarket shopping district – though half its shops have closed down thanks to the crisis – as well as being the location of many diplomatic missions and some highly desirable apartments. It is not, however, devoid of culture; Kolonáki – or rather its southerly margins – has some of the finest museums in the city.

Going back to 3000 BC, the two-wing **Museum of Cycladic Art** (Mon, Wed, Fri 10am–4pm, Thur 10am–8pm, Sat 10am–3pm; entrance fee; www.cycladic.gr) features a unique collection of slim, stylised Cycladic statuettes in white marble, beautifully mounted. These figures, mostly of the third millennium BC, were scorned by 19th-century art critics as hopelessly primitive, but their smooth, simple lines attracted Picasso, Brancusi and Modigliani. Mostly female, the figures hail from graves scattered throughout the Cyclades islands; to this day, scholars are still uncertain of their true purpose. The museum is also renowned for frequent special exhibits with un-Cycladic themes.

The **Benáki Museum** ⓱ (Wed, Fri, Sat 9am–5pm, Thur 9am–midnight, Sun 9am–3pm; www.benaki.gr), together with its two annexes and fantastic temporary exhibits, easily counts as the best all-round museum in Athens. Its wonderfully eclectic permanent collection of treasures from all periods of Greek history includes jewellery, costumes, and two icons attributed to El Greco. Among the most impressive exhibits are the collection of traditional costume, mostly bridal and festival dresses, and the reconstructed reception rooms of a mid-18th-century Kozáni mansion. Also compelling are the displays of gold on the ground floor, and the collections relating to the Greek struggle for independence. The museum has a gift shop and a pleasant if pricey terrace restaurant. For information on the **Benáki Museum annexe** ⓳, see feature on page 154.

Mount Lykavitós ⓴ (Lycabettus; 215 metres/704ft) rises above Kolonáki, crowned by the tiny chapel of Ágios Geórgios. The easiest way to get to the summit is by the funicular railway that starts from the top of Ploutárhou Street (every 30 minutes, in summer 9am–2.30am). From the top, the views over the city are spectacular.

While not strictly speaking in Kolonáki (being on the far side of Vassilísis Sofías), three other nearby museums merit a visit. The **Byzantine and Christian Museum** ㉑ (summer Tue–Sun 8am–8pm, winter 9am–4pm; www.byzantinemuseum.gr) was originally housed in a mock-Tuscan villa, commissioned by the 19th-century philhellene Duchesse de Plaisance (who has a suburban metro station named for her). Most exhibits, dating from the early Christian period to 13th-century Attica, now reside in an impressive modern underground wing. Despite being subterranean, the galleries are light and spacious, and the artefacts (including the 7th-century Hoard of Mytilene) well-displayed and informatively labelled; what was once a specialist collection has been transformed into one of Athens' major museums.

Icons and church relics on display at the Byzantine Museum.

Right next door is the **War Museum** (Tue–Sun 9am–2pm), established during the 1967–74 dictatorship and thus usually disdained or overlooked. Outside stand assorted 20th-century artillery and aeroplanes, while the interior offers a surprisingly absorbing collection of uniforms, weaponry and documents (scantily labelled in English), particularly good on Greece's tribulations during World War II.

Near the Hilton hotel hulks the modern **National Art Gallery** ㉒ (Mon, Wed, Thur, Fri, Sat 9am–4pm, Sun 10am–2pm). The core collection of Greek art from just before independence to recent years does a good job of placing it in social context and as part of international trends. Few artists here except Nikos-Hadjikyriakos Ghikas – who gets a room to himself – are household names overseas, but that's no reflection on their merit. Best modern piece has to be Photis Kontoglou's mural, which adorned his own house. Again, there are frequent, popular temporary shows which often rope in Greek and foreign masterpieces.

Inside the National Gallery.

Byzantine Athens

Of the city's Byzantine past little remains, but a dozen or so churches, many dating from the 11th century and most in Pláka, can be tracked down. One of the best – and one of the few normally open – is **Ágii Theodóri** ㉓ just off Platía Klavthmónos, built in the 11th century in characteristic cruciform shape with a tiled dome. The masonry is picked out with slabs of brick and decorated with a terracotta frieze of animals and plants.

On Athens's eastern and western limits lie two famous monasteries: Kesarianí and Dafní. **Kesarianí** ㉔ (Tue–Sun 8am–3pm) on Mount Hymettus, surrounded by high stone walls, is named after a spring which fed an aqueduct constructed on Hadrian's orders. Its waters, once sacred to love goddess Aphrodite, were long credited with healing powers (and encouraging child-bearing), though sadly are no longer potable. The monastery church dates to the 11th century but the frescoed figures who gaze out of a blue-black ground were painted mostly in 1682. Highlights include, in the conch,

the Virgin Enthroned flanked by the Communion of the Apostles; the vaulting contains scenes from the life of Christ, while the narthex displays assorted miracles.

Dafní ㉕ is 11km (7 miles) out of town on the road to Eleusis (bus from Platía Eleftherías, near Psyrrí; Tue–Fri 9am–2pm; free). This small monastery is a curious architectural combination of Gothic and Byzantine, occupying the site of an ancient sanctuary of Apollo. The church is decorated with magnificent 11th-century mosaics, most famously a fierce-looking Christ Pandokrátor, staring down from the vault of the dome, surrounded by Old Testament prophets. The building dates from 1080 but the Gothic porch was added in the 13th century when Dafní belonged to Burgundian Cistercian monks and served as the burial place of the Frankish Dukes of Athens.

Piraeus

Athens' port is a city in its own right but most people merely pass through on their way to the islands. From

central Athens it is most easily reached by metro (line 1; 40 minutes journey time); alternatively, express bus X96 runs to Piraeus (Pireás) from Athens airport via the coastal suburbs, with stops near the hydrofoil quay, Platía Karaïskáki, the metro station and the northeast quay.

Piraeus Archaeological Museum (Tue–Sun 9am–4pm) has various wonderful bronzes. On the first floor is a graceful, Archaic Apollo *kouros*, pulled from the sea in 1959; made in 530–20 BC, this is the earliest known life-sized bronze statue. Two other bronze statues, of Athena and Artemis and both dating to the 5th century BC, were found shortly after in Piraeus when new sewers were being dug.

The hills of Athens

Central Athens is said to have eight hills (*lófi*). As well as Lykavitós and the equally conspicuous rock of the Acropolis, flanked by the **Pnyx** on one side, and **Philopappou** (Filopáppou) on

Christ Pandokrátor is surrounded by gold on the dome of Dafní monastery.

Taking in the fabulous view from the top of the hill of Philoppappus.

GETTING TO THE ISLANDS

If you want to catch a ferry to one of the islands, your ticket agent should tell you which quay/gate (numbered E1–E10 going clockwise around the port) your boat departs from. Gates E1 to E3 are too far to walk to in the heat; a free shuttle bus (every 10min), from gate E5, takes you there. As a general guide, boats to the Cyclades depart from E5–E7 opposite the metro station, or E10; slow boats to the Argo-Saronic from E8 on the far side of Platía Karaïskáki, southwest of the metro; direct boats to Crete leave from E3–E4, on the north side of the port; hydrofoils and catamarans to Argo-Saronic islands leave from E9 on Aktí Miaoúli; Dodecanese-bound boats leave from all the way around the port at E1; while those for the northeast Aegean go from E2.

Athens Private Art Museums

Beginning before the millennium and continuing through challenging economic circumstances, Athens has added an impressive roster of mostly private art museums to its portfolio of galleries.

The best known is the **Benáki Museum annexe** (Thur & Sun 10am–6pm, Fri–Sat 10am–10pm), housed in Greece's former main Lada showroom (nearest metro is Thisío). As many as five separate exhibits may be going on at any one time, showcasing 20th-century art or architecture; recent highlights have included retrospectives of Greek photographers Voula Papaioannou and Kostas Balafas, the Czech Josef Koudelka, the Greek architect Emmanouel Vourekas and the Belgian expressionist-surrealist James Ensor. There's also a tempting shop and popular café-restaurant.

Just about walking distance away is the **Herakleidon** (Iraklidón 16 in Thisío; Fri 1–9pm,

Modern European Art at the Frissiras Museum.

Sat–Sun 11am–7pm; www.herakleidon-art.gr), with large permanent collections of M.C. Escher and Victor Vasarely prints plus always-stellar temporary exhibits (eg Toulouse Lautrec); again, the well-stocked shop is hazardous to your wallet.

A slightly longer walk south, along pedestrianised Apostólou Pávlou, leads to the **Atelier-Museum Spyros Vassiliou** at Webster 5a (summer Tue 10am–4pm, Wed noon–6pm, Thurs–Sat 10am–4pm, winter Tue–Sat 10am–6pm; www.spryosvassiliou.org), exhibiting some 40 works of this versatile artist (1902–1985) in his former studio and family dwelling. Vassiliou's long career encompassed stage design, posters and a later preponderance of acrylics on canvas.

From here, you can continue easily on foot, across Dionysíou Areopagítou, to the Frissiras Museum (Monís Asteríou 3 and 7; Wed–Fri 10am–5pm, Sat–Sun 11am–5pm; www.frissiras-museum.com), the largest collection in town devoted to modern European art, mostly portraiture, of the last 50 years; the permanent holdings at no. 7 (may close owing to staff shortages) feature familiar names like Paula Rego, R.B. Kitaj and David Hockney, while the no. 3 premises have non-stop temporary shows.

Across Sýndagma, next to the French embassy at Vasillís Sofiás 9, the galleries of the elegant **Theoharakis Foundation** (Mon, Tue, Wed, Sat, Sun 10am–6pm, Thur–Fri 10am–8pm; www.thf.gr) are another reliable bet for blockbuster temporary exhibits – recent ones have featured modern Russian painters and the seminal late 1800s Greek painter Nikolaos Gyzis.

Just a block or so behind, at Kriezótou 3, is perhaps the best small Athens art museum for the uninitiated: the **Hadjikyriakos-Ghikas Gallery** (Wed–Sun 10am–6pm), technically yet another annexe of the Benáki. It's somewhat misnamed – while indeed installed in the former home of the great painter, with his top-floor residence and atelier preserved as at his death in 1994, most of the many galleries honour (with intelligent labelling) just about everybody who was anybody in 20th-century Greek cultural life. To name just a few: the archaeologist (and neo-Byzantine architect) Athanasios Orlandos, architects Dimitris Pikionis and Aris Konstantinidis, the photographers Nelly's (sic), Takis Tloupas and Spyros Meletzis, the caricaturist Bost, painters Yiannis Moralis and Yorgos Manousakis – a painless if not so quick (allow 2 hours to visit) introduction to intellectual currents in the modern nation.

the other, where Athenians fly kites on the first day of Lent, there are: the hill of **Ardittós**, next to the marble horseshoe **stadium**, built by Herodes Atticus in AD 143 and totally reconstructed in 1896 (the first modern Olympic Games were held there – it is now a popular concert venue); the **Hill of the Nymphs**, capped by the grey 19th-century, Hansen-designed **Observatory**; the barren, windblown **Tourkovoúnia**; and **Lófos Stréfi**, something of a "needle park" for local down-and-outs.

For a real escape, you have to go further afield, up one of the three mountains that encircle Athens. The road-accessible summit of **Mount Hymettus** (Ymittós), 5km (3 miles) east of Athens, beloved of honey-bees, glowing violet at sunset, makes a tranquil vantage point from which to contemplate the whole of Attica. **Mount Párnitha**, just over an hour northwest, was sadly burnt to a crisp in August 2007, losing all of its thick fir forest.

Below Mount Pendéli on the northeast is Athens' most exclusive suburb, **Kifisiá**, populated, like Kolonáki, with the city's great and sometimes not so good, who reside in often whimsical early 20th-century villas. Kifisiá's only specific attraction is the **Goulandris Natural History Museum** (Tue–Fri 9am–2.30pm, Sat 10am–4.30pm, Sun 10am–2pm), devoted to the flora, fauna and geology of Greece.

Excursion to Attica

Outside Athens, a 69km (43-mile) drive to **Cape Sounion** on the windy tip of the Attica peninsula takes you to the Doric **Temple of Poseidon** (daily 9.30am–20mins before sunset). Completed in 440 BC, its slender, salt-white columns, fetchingly illuminated by night, are still a landmark for ships sailing to/from Piraeus. Lord Byron set a bad, much imitated example by carving his name on a column on the north side. Today, the grounds swarm with introduced guinea fowl (*frangókotes*), effectively mascots of the site. Down the hillside, you can see the remains of ancient ship sheds in the bay below; a sandy beach northwest of the temple, with its pricey tavernas, is more likely to appeal.

Just 10km (5 miles) north of Soúnio on the Attic east-coast road is

Zéa Marina.

TIP

If you're craving a swim near Athens, the best beaches are some distance away, most easily accessible by rented car. On the west Attic coast, sandy Mávro Lithári, just before Paleá Fókia, is a good choice, while sandy Ágios Spyrídon cove at Pórto Ráfti is very popular. Skhínia, near ancient Marathon and Rhamnous, is another sand beach, part of a protected area.

Lávrio, the industrial hub of Attica before the rise of Piraeus, with an explosives plant and metalworks. Mining was still practised locally from the 19th century until 1989 by French and Greek companies, extracting arsenic, silver, lead, iron, and ferromanganese; the ancient silver-mine tunnels, between Soúnio and Lávrio in Keramíza district, can be toured (follow signs to Keramíza, and take old clothes). The town itself, mostly passed through en route for its ferry boats to Kéa and the north Aegean, deserves a halt. The partly neoclassical centre has been gentrified and pedestrianised, the harbour front has charm, though conventional attractions are limited to a good, central archaeological museum and – at the north entrance of Lávrio – the rehabilitated French mining company buildings which you can visit (ask at the nearby café-restaurant).

Excursion to Brauron

From Lávrio, it's easy to continue to the **Sanctuary of Artemis** at **Brauron** (modern Vravróna) on the east coast of Attica, 35km (22 miles) directly from Athens. A 5th-century BC colonnade visited by owls at twilight is flanked by a 16th-century chapel, built on the site of an altar to Artemis. Nearby is the still-flowing sacred spring, an arm of the Erásinos River running past the site. In Classical times, well-born female children aged from seven to twelve ("little bears") performed a ritual dance at the quadrennial Arkteia festival honouring Artemis as the goddess of childbirth and virgins. Their plump statues – dressed like miniature adults, often clutching birds as offerings – are now in Room 3 of the much-improved site museum (Tue–Sun 8am–2.40pm; site closed for repairs until late 2013), while in Room 2 are several fine stelae of the goddess, flanked by some of her totemic animals (stags, lions, dogs), facing groups of worshippers approaching with bulls to sacrifice in her honour. Room 1 helps you make sense of the sanctuary before visiting it.

Excursion to Marathon

The battle of **Marathon** in 490 BC was fought on a seaside plain 42km (26 miles) northeast of Athens, between the modern villages of Néa Mákri and Marathónas. What can be seen today are the presumed burial mounds of the Athenians and of the Plataeans, and the Archaeological Museum (all Tue–Sun 8.30am–2.40pm).

The burial mound of the Athenians, a circular tumulus 9 metres (30ft) high, 50 metres (164ft) in diameter, and 185 metres (600ft) in circumference, has a modern copy of the ancient stele on the top (the original is in the National Archaeological Museum). The mound is impressive, but nothing compared to the victory it symbolises. The mighty Persian Empire, the largest on earth, had sent its army against Athens, and approximately 9,000 Athenian soldiers were joined before the battle by 1,000 soldiers from Plataea in Boeotia. A runner was sent to ask the Spartans for help, but the Spartans did not arrive until after the battle. The Athenians

View of Athens from Mount Hymettus.

won despite being outnumbered by a factor of three, with the Persians losing 6,400 men and the Athenians 192. The Athenians were cremated and buried together in the mound. The mound of the Plataeans is near the archaeological museum, about 3km (2 miles) to the west. Nothing marks the Persian graves, but they seem to have been buried to the northeast, around the small church of the Panagía Mesosporítissa.

Excursion to Rhamnous

Rhamnous (summer daily 8.30am–3pm, winter Mon–Sat 8am–3pm), the site of an ancient fortress town on the northern borders of Attica with a sanctuary of Nemesis, lies 53km (33 miles) from Athens and 13km (8 miles) from Marathon. The sanctuary contains two temples, today merely foundations. The older, built after Xerxes' defeat in 480 BC, was dedicated to Nemesis and also to Themis, the god of justice. The slightly larger Doric temple of Nemesis, built in 436–32 BC, almost touches the older temple. The fortified garrison, its walls roughly 800 metres down from

the sanctuary towards the shore, flourished in the 5th and 4th centuries BC.

Excursion to the Sanctuary of Amphiareion

The city-state that built the **Sanctuary of Amphiareion** (daily 8.30am–2.40pm) late in the 5th century BC was ancient Oropos, now buried beneath modern Skála Oropós, known for its Évia-bound ferries. The sanctuary, 37km (23 miles) north of Athens, had its acme during the Hellenistic period, much patronised by those in search of advice or medical help. The supplicant sacrificed a ram to Argive hero Amphiaraos, after which a dream would either cure the illness or answer a question. The surviving remains, in a lovely valley overlooked by pines, comprise a temple of the cult hero, a Roman theatre with many seats and a stage building, a long stoa, plus a small museum.

Stunning Ágios Spyrídon cove at Pórto Ráfti.

The Temple of Poseidon.

A NATIONAL TREASURE TROVE

The National Archaeological Museum in Athens houses a fabulous collection of ancient art and artefacts.

The museum provides an unrivalled survey of ancient Greek art. Don't be intimidated by the collection's size, but plan carefully, using the ground plan available from the ticket booth. During tourist season, avoid midday, when coach tours march through the galleries.

The first gallery in from the foyer is the confusingly named Prehistoric Collection, devoted to artefacts from the Mycenaean period (1600–1100 BC). The so-called Mask of Agamemnon is just one of three hammered-gold death masks on display, along with bronze items and octopus-motif pottery. In flanking rooms which completely circle the ground-floor perimeter, you'll find numerous examples of ancient Greek sculpture, from the Archaic era (750–490 BC) to the Classical (490–336 BC), Hellenistic (336–146 BC) and Roman (146 BC–AD 330) periods. Note the fine Eleusinian cult relief of the goddess Demeter offering grain to Triptolemos, watched by Persephone. In the far south gallery is the famous Roman group of Aphrodite, watched by Eros, about to whack a dirty old Pan with her sandal.

Two outstanding bronze statues are the 2nd-century BC Little Jockey from the Artemísion wreck, beyond the Myceneaean room, and the Ephebe of Antikythera. The small bronze objects collection, towards the rear left of the building, has exquisite statuettes, helmets and griffon heads. Just behind is the well-selected Egyptian exhibit, a fast gallop through that civilisation, with the eclectic Stathatos collection around the corner.

The upper floor is principally ancient Greek pottery, including finely detailed Tanagra figurines, near rooms of glass, precious metalwork and jewellery. The famous Thera frescoes are just a small portion of the displays in the Minoan Akrotíri room.

Herakles defeating king Vousiris and his servants in Egypt, c.470 BC.

The northeasterly galleries by the ticket booth house splendid Archaic kouroi and kourai (standing statues of men and women respectively), most of them from atop graves. The exceptional kore of Merenda is featured in the orientation leaflet, while this 7th century kouros was found in the Sanctuary of Poseidon at Sounion.

Bronze Horse and Jockey of Artemesium (2nd century BC).

The range of exhibits in the museum is huge; it has one of the world's largest collections of carved reliefs.

Minoan fresco depicting blue cavorting monkeys on the island of Santoríni.

FABULOUS FRESCOES

In the middle of the 2nd millennium BC the Cycladic island of Thera (today Santoríni), was much influenced – probably even ruled – by the Minoan civilisation of Crete. A Minoan settlement at Akrotíri on Santoríni, dating to approximately 1630 BC, was excavated by Spyridon Marinatos between 1967 and 1974. The most beautiful finds from Akrotíri are its frescoes. Just two, of boxers and antelopes, are kept in the National Archaeological Museum, while the rest remain on Santoríni.

Late in the 17th century BC, Thera's volcano erupted in a tremendous explosion. The entire settlement of Akrotíri, including buildings up to three storeys high, was beautifully preserved beneath volcanic ash. The frescoes decorated the interior walls of houses in the ancient town. Most of them show everyday scenes, such as a naked fisherman carrying home a bountiful catch, elegant ladies, blue cavorting monkeys, graceful antelopes, but there is also a 5.5-metre- (18.5-ft-) long detailed fresco of a naval campaign.

Also from the Artemision wreck is a mid-5th-century BC bronze Zeus (or possibly Poseidon), in the act of hurling a now-vanished thunderbolt or trident.

This gold death mask found by Heinrich Schliemann at Mycenae and dating to the 16th century BC has become famous as the "Mask of Agamemnon". In fact, the Trojan Wars occurred much later.

The Apollo Temple with its seven standing Doric columns.

THE PELOPONNESE

Steeped in ancient history – from Agamemnon's Mycenae to the first Olympic stadium – this giant peninsula also offers fine beaches, turquoise-coloured bays, and the wild and unspoilt Máni.

The Peloponnese (Pelopónnisos) takes its name from the legendary hero Pelops, plus the Greek for island, *nísos*, although it is seldom considered an island. Driving over from Attica (Attikí), it's easy to miss the little isthmus – riven by the Corinth Canal, lending some credence to the "island" tag – that joins the Peloponnese to the mainland. The area's medieval name was the Moreás, now rarely used; it derives either from an abundance of mulberry trees (*mouriés*) or more probably from the mulberry-leaf shape of the peninsula.

Korinthía province

By an administrative quirk, Korinthía province in the northeast includes a bit of the central mainland northeast of the canal; 13km (8 miles) beyond the spa resort of Loutráki lies the **Perahora Heraion ❶**, with an Archaic **Hera temple** and a *stoa*. Another important ancient sanctuary, the venue for the quadrennial Isthmian games, can be found at **Isthmia** on the southwest side of the canal; the Roman baths here contain extensive floor mosaics of sea creatures real and imaginary, while the well-arranged if one-room site **museum** (Tue–Sun 8.30am–2.40pm) features vivid *opus sectile* panels from

AD 375 portraying harbour scenes, sea creatures, Nile bird life and revered ancient personalities, as well as finds from the local shrines to Poseidon and Palaimon.

The canal itself, dug between 1882 and 1893, is obsolete in our era of mega-container ships, but a few freighters and yachts still squeeze through its 23-metre-wide (75-ft) channel, to the delight of spectators up on the pedestrian bridge – who can also watch the antics of the bungy-jumpers who practise here. At

Main Attractions
NEMEA ZEUS TEMPLE
ANCIENT MYCENAE
NÁVPLIO
EPIDAUROS THEATRE
LOÚSIOS GORGE REGION
MYSTRÁS
MONEMVASIÁ
ANCIENT MESSENE
ANCIENT OLYMPIA MUSEUM
VOURAÏKÓS RACK-AND-PINION
  TRAIN

Aphrodite and pastoral mosaic at the Ancient Corinth Museum.

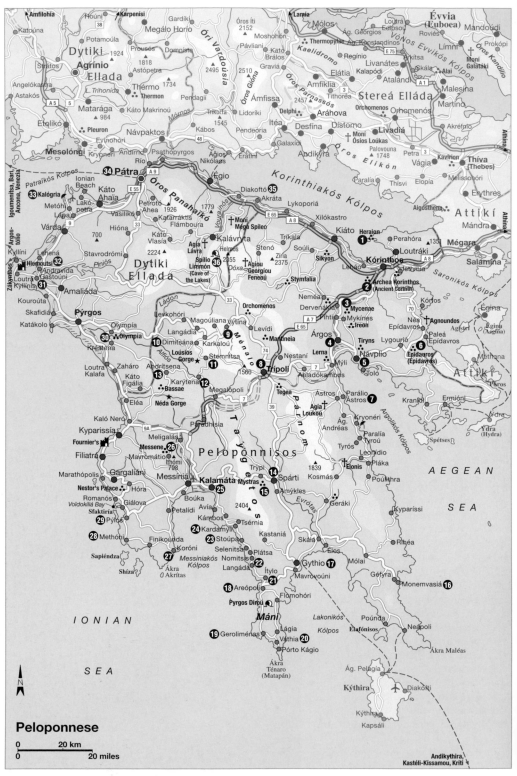

Peloponnese

0   20 km

0   20 miles

the Saronic Gulf end of the canal, two flanking cafés provide vantage points to watch the workings of the submersible bridge on the old highway to Athens – taking a dive whenever ships pass.

If you're intent on reaching ancient Epidauros directly, especially for a performance, carry on south of Isthmía along the fast, partly coastal road via confusingly named Paleá Epídavros, once the harbour for the ancient sanctuary. On the way, pause at the 11th-century monastery of Agnoúndos, where the tall, narrow katholokón (the church of the monastery) has fine frescoes from the 11th to the 18th centuries (the highest being the oldest).

Ancient **Corinth** ❷, 4km (2½ miles) southwest of modern **Kórinthos**, could not help but prosper through domination of trans-Isthmian haulage in pre-canal days. The Hellenistic city was razed by the Romans in 146 BC in reprisal for resistance, but refounded a century later as capital of Greece. What remains (daily summer 8am–7.30pm, winter 8am–5pm), despite devastating earthquakes in AD 375 and 521, is the most complete imperial Roman town plan in Greece. Corinth's well-deserved reputation for vice and luxury predictably exercised Saint Paul when he arrived in AD 52 for an 18-month sojourn.

A typically Roman obsession with plumbing is evident: there are the graphically obvious latrines off the marble-paved **Lehaion Way**, the still-functioning **Lower Peirene Fountain** at its end, and the ingenious **Glauke Fountain**, its four cisterns hewn from a monolith and filled by an aqueduct. Of the earlier Greek city, only seven columns of a Doric **Apollo Temple** still stand, though the site **museum** (same hours as site) retains a generous collection of late Archaic pottery and some intricate Roman-villa mosaics from Corinth's glory years.

Rather more evocative, however, is the nearly impregnable hilltop fortress of **Acrocorinth** (Akrokórinthos; summer daily 8am–7pm, winter Tue–Sun 8.30am–3pm; free), long the military key to the peninsula and necessarily

FACT

The word "currant" derives from the word "Corinth" – a reference to the city's long-established trade in dried grapes, still one of Greece's most successful exports.

The Corinth Canal was completed in 1893.

held by every occupying power. Enter via the gentler west slope through a set of triple fortifications to find yourself amid weedy desolation; little is left of the Ottoman town here, evacuated after Greek rebels took it in 1822. Most sieges, however, were successfully resisted thanks to the **Upper Peirene Fountain**, a subterranean structure near the southeast corner of the ramparts. At the very summit stand foundations of an **Aphrodite Temple**, reputedly once attended by 1,000 sacred prostitutes; the view all around is quite marvellous, stretching up to 60km (40 miles) in every direction.

Nemea and Stymfalía

The toll motorway to Kalamáta forges southwest from modern Kórinthos. Near **Dervenákia**, an exit leads west 8km (5 miles) to ancient **Nemea**, yet another shrine with its own biennial games. You can see the **stadium** where these events – supposedly inaugurated by Herakles, slayer of the Nemean lion – were held, but the most striking landmarks are nine Doric columns and two architraves of a 4th-century BC **Zeus Temple**, mostly re-erected since 1995; its fellows, toppled by Byzantine vandals, lie all about like many sausage slices. The dispersed site (summer daily 8am–7.30pm, winter Tue–Sun 8.30am–3pm), including a well preserved baths and worthwhile museum, occupies the floor of a bucolic valley; surrounding vineyards produce the grapes for the full-bodied Nemea red wines, some of Greece's best, with several roadside vintners in Arhéa Neméa village open for tasting and purchase.

From Neméa, it's easy to continue west to the valley and shallow, reedy lake of **Stymfalía**, site of yet another of Herakles' labours (dispatching the Stymphalian birds), closed to the northwest by often snowcapped Mount Zíria (2375m). Highlight of the area is the excellent roadside Environment Museum of Stymfalia (Wed–Mon summer 10am–6pm, winter 10am–5pm; www.piop.gr), which ably documents all rural local activities, from lake-fishing to bee-keeping, and provides a viewing

Návplio waterfront and the fortress-island of Boúrtzi.

platform for the ducks, grebes and coots who gather on the water. The way continues west via Kastaniá village to the eerie upland of Feneós; at its north edge there's a namesake village, the scenic Dóxa lake and Agíou Georgíou Feneoú **monastery**, offering exceptionally vivid 18th-century frescoes and friendly monks. Return to the Corinth gulf coast via **Tríkala** village on the north flank of Zíria, divided into three districts; this was the first mountain resort in Greece, owing to easy access from Athens since the 1920s.

Argolída province

The twisty old highway enters the Argolid plain at modern **Mykínes**, a village devoted to citrus and tourism; nearby stands ancient **Mycenae ❸**, a fortified palace complex covering an easily defendable, ravine-flanked ridge. Mycenae gave its name to an entire late Bronze-Age era – and made the reputation of a German self-taught Classical scholar (and self-made millionaire), Heinrich Schliemann. From 1874 to 1876, he excavated here, relying on little other than intuition and a belief in the literal accuracy of Homer's epics. Greek archaeologists had already revealed the imposing **Lion Gate** of the citadel, but the rich tomb finds Schliemann made, now in the National Museum of Athens, amply corroborate Mycenae's Homeric epithet "rich in gold". Later revisionists point to Schliemann's sloppy excavating techniques and economy with the truth – the gold death mask which prompted his boast "I have gazed upon the face of Agamemnon" is now dated to 300 years before Troy – but the dedicated amateur did beat the experts to the greatest archaeological find of that century.

At the site itself (daily summer 8am–7.40pm, winter 8.30am–2.40pm), little remains above waist height inside the perimeter walls of the palace, though a rather alarming secret stairway descends to a siege-proof cistern in the northeast corner. Outside, however, are two burial chambers of unsurpassed ingenuity: the tholos tombs dubbed, very speculatively, the **Treasury of Atreus** and the **Tomb of Clytemnestra**, also known as "beehive" tombs after the manner of their construction.

Ancient Argos

The onward road divides at **Árgos ❹**, capital of Argolída province and a major agricultural centre. Tomatoes and citrus – the latter introduced by American advisers after World War II – are grown extensively; the modern town itself is of little interest apart from its **Archaeological Museum** (Tue–Sun 8.30am–2.40pm). But just south, beside the Trípoli-bound road, sprawl the ruins of **ancient Árgos** (same hours as museum); most notable is the huge, steeply raked theatre. From the opposite end of town, drivers can reach the Frankish castle atop

Mycenae's treasures were uncovered by the archaeologist Heinrich Schliemann.

Inside the Treasury of Atreus at Mycenae.

Lárissa hill, site of the ancient **acropolis**, for a view nearly on a par with that of Acrocorinth, extending from Mt Zíria to Návplio (Nauplion), by way of the low hillock of ancient Tiryns.

Just over halfway to Návplio from Árgos loom the 13th-century BC ruins of Homer's "wall-girt" **Tiryns** (daily summer 9am–7.30pm, winter 8.30am–2.40pm), another royal palace complex. The site, an 18-metre (60-ft) bluff rising from an ancient marsh, was not as naturally defensible as Mycenae, so the man-made fortifications – originally twice their present height – wcre necessarily more involved. Massive masonry blocks reaching 3 cubic metres (100 cu. ft) each were joined in mortar-less walls termed "Cyclopean", after the only beings thought capable of manoeuvring them. No heraldic lions over the entry-gate here, and no beehive tombs; but Tiryns intrigues with a **secret stairway** (off-limits) to the westerly postern gate and, near the southeast corner, a corbel-ceilinged **gallery** (viewable past a barrier), its

High-perched Karýtena.

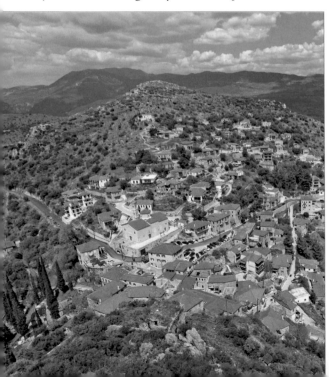

walls polished smooth by the millennial rubbings of sheltering sheep.

Návplio and Epidaurus

Návplio ❺, rising in tiers at the southeast corner of the plain, is more than a little mirage-like, for the well-preserved old town retains an elegance a world away from utilitarian Árgos just 12km (7 miles) to the northwest. The neoclassical architecture, pedestrian-friendly marble streets and interlocking fortresses date mostly from the second Venetian occupation of 1686–1715, and subsequent Ottoman reconquest; the fortified rock here had been a pivotal point in their struggles for control of the Aegean from the 15th century onward. Between 1829 and 1834 Návplio served as the country's first capital, but today it's a laid-back place, despite playing a role as an upmarket resort; it stays busy year round, thanks to Athenian weekenders.

Návplio is overawed by **Akronavpliá**, four separate fortresses of various ages just overhead, plus, on an easterly hill, the sprawling, early 18th-century castle of **Palamídi** (daily 8am–7pm, shut 6pm winter), whose meandering curtain wall encloses seven self-contained bastions designed to withstand the strongest artillery of the era. Yet its Venetian garrison capitulated with barely a fight in 1715 to the Ottomans, who in turn surrendered to the Greek rebels after a more protracted siege in 1822. Just under 900 steps (or a road) lead up from the Old Town to the summit – and to more eyefuls of the Argolid.

Down in town, excellent museums include the Archaeological Museum (Tue–Sun 8.30am–2.40pm), in a restored Venetian barracks, where pride of place goes to a complete set of Mycenean armour; the Peloponnesian Folklore Foundation Museum (Wed–Mon 9am–3pm); and, in the new quarter, an annexe of Athens' National Gallery (Mon, Wed, Thur–Sat 10am–3pm, Wed, Fri also 5–8pm, Sun

10am–2pm), always with stellar temporary exhibits.

Some 27km (17 miles) east of Návplio, **Epidauros** (**Epídavros**) ❻ is visited mainly for the sake of its magnificent 4th-century BC **theatre**, whose perfect acoustics tour guides perpetually demonstrate with coins dropped on the orchestra floor. Because it lay buried until the late 19th century, the theatre masonry survived the ages relatively unscathed, and restoration has been minimal. It is now the venue for sell-out performances of ancient drama during July, as part of the Hellenic Festival; special buses from Athens are laid on, as are boats from Aegina to nearby Paleá Epídavros port.

The theatre is just one part of a vast sanctuary (daily 8am–7.30pm, until 5pm in winter) to the healing demi-god Asklepios, extending northwest, and steadily being excavated and re-erected. Standing tall already are the propylon of the Hestiatoria, the Enkimitirion colonnade, and the Tholos of Polykleitos, a circular, once-domed structure with a concentric maze in the foundations thought to originally contain serpents (sacred to Asklepios), and centre of the god's cult. The site museum is, by contrast, of specialist interest.

Arkadía province

Heading west from Návplio along the Argolid gulf coast road, past Lerna (modern Mýli), where Hercules slew the many-headed Hydra, you enter Arkadía – specifically, its easterly sub-region of Kynouría – just before **Parálio Ástros** ❼ an established beach resort whose older houses back against a headland crowned with a medieval fortress built atop a Mycenean acropolis. Ástros, 5km (3miles) inland, has a worthwhile archaeological museum and 5km further west, adjacent to medieval Loukoú monastery with fine 16th-century frescoes being steadily cleaned and rather worldly nuns, the fascinating remains of an arcaded

Roman aqueduct so encrusted with lime stalactites as to form a Dalí-esque sculpture.

The road south from Ástros passes fine beaches like Kryonéri and Poulíthra before turning inland at sizeable Leonídio, homeland of Tsakonian – a relict Dorian dialect being revived in writing on local signage. Now your way creeps up through a spectacular, Wild-West type gorge, past the convent of Elonís, to the "hill station" of **Kosmás**, high amidst fir trees on the flank of Mt Párnom and the best base to explore this range, blessed with good walking and one of the starriest night skies in Greece. From Kosmás, it's easy to cross the mountain (in your own car) to either Mystrás or Monemvasiá.

Both the old highway from Mýli and the inland expressway converge on the pear- and apple-planted uplands around dull **Trípoli** ❽, capital of Arkadía province. This has little to offer aside from a good **archaeological museum** (Tue–Sun 8.30am–2.40pm) with finds from Trípoli's ancient nearby predecessors: Tegea,

Sheep on the road near Trípoli.

Loánnou Prodrómou is one of Greece's most spectacular monasteries.

with a tumbled Athena temple, and Mantineia, now amidst a major wine-growing district.

Exiting the motorway at Nestáni, passing close by the freakish neo-Byzantine wedding-cake church of Agía Fotiní at Mandínia, the main westbound road skirts the base of fir-cloaked, blade-like **Mount Ménalo** with its ski resort (the closest to Athens), via the handsome villages of **Levídi** and **Vytína ❾**, the latter a popular weekend base for Greeks. Beyond Vytína, towards Ilía province, the most logical and compelling halt is

Langádia, its famous masons responsible for sturdy stone houses teetering on a slope above the local gorge.

But the main attraction of montane Arkadía resides along the Loúsios valley, reached by a turning south between Vytína and Langádia. Near the head of the Loúsios valley, **Dimitsána ❿** sprawls engagingly over a saddle demarcated by the river, its skyline graced by four belfries. The imposing mansions here date from its mercantile golden age, the 1700s. Specific local sights include the **Open Air Water Power Museum** (summer Wed–Mon 10am–6pm, winter 10am–5pm), with mill workings in situ, and further down the same side road, cliffside **Emyalón Monastery** (closed 1–5pm), with four resident monks, and frescoes from 1608.

Stemnítsa ⓫ 11km (6.5 miles) south of Dimitsána along the east flank of the Loúsios, has been officially renamed Ypsoúnda, but the Slavic toponym remains more popular; it's an atmospheric, introverted place in a hidden cirque, with imposing mansions looking only at each

other. A single jewellery shop recalls the former silver-smithing industry, while a Folklore Museum (Mon–Fri 10am–1pm, Sat–Sun 10am–2pm, Tue closed) highlights pan-Hellenic items, local dress and (best of all) fascinating publicity posters for a local karagiózis (shadow-puppet) player.

Hyperbolically dubbed the "Toledo of Greece", thanks to its evocative castle and houses overlooking a kink in the **Alfiós River**, the sleepy demeanour of **Karýtena** ⓬, 16km (10 miles) beyond Stemnítsa, belies a tumultuous history. Established as the seat of a Frankish barony during the 13th century, it was later retaken by the Byzantines, who endowed Karýtena with three churches (Ágios Nikólaos has fine 18th-century frescoes) and an arched bridge over the Alfiós. Both bridge and town figured on one side of the old 5,000-drachma note; the beturbanned Independence War chieftain Kolokotrónis glared out from the other, for he successfully resisted a long Ottoman siege here in 1826.

All of these hill towns serve as gateways to different parts of the **Loúsios** Gorge, which in its relatively short extent has a lot to offer. Canoeing and kayaking on the two local rivers are offered locally by several outfitters, while a marked hiking trail threads the canyon from just below Dimitsána to the Atsíholos bridge. The first significant stop, also reached by road from Dimitsána, is the restored Néa Filosófou monastery on the west bank, home to two monks, with late 17th-century frescoes including Jesus walking on the Sea of Galilee; a little beyond, the 10th-century Paleá Filosófou monastery is largely ruined and almost indistinguishable from its cliff-side surroundings.

Further downstream, also accessible by narrow roads from Stemnítsa or **Ellinikó** village, awaits the spectacular 11th-century monastery of Agíou Ioánnou Prodrómou (St John the Baptist; closed 1–5pm), one of those swallow's-nest-type monasteries which the Orthodox Church loves to tuck into cliff faces. It has just three monks, frescoes and a well-stocked ossuary. The west-bank trail (and a branch of the road) continues

Chapel overlooking the Loúsios Gorge.

Shepherds' crooks in Langádia village.

Mount Taÿgetos on a fine spring day.

to the medieval Kokkorás bridge, the Byzantine chapel of **Ágios Andréas** and excavated ancient **Gortys**, an *asklipeion* or therapeutic centre; the architectural highlight here is a peculiar round structure, thought to be a bathhouse. Finally, a minor road from Karýtena descends to the two-arched Atsíholos bridge and then the eponymous village, beyond which awaits Kalamioú monastery, new and old. A caretaker monk at the newer foundation will unlock the 1713-vintage church, covered with superb, rare frescoes such as two Christs Emmanuel in the vaults, and a visualisation of the Byzantine hymn Epi Soi Haire. A short stair-path leads to cliff-clinging old Kalamioú, mostly ruined except for a rock-cut church sheltering slightly older, moderately well preserved frescoes of the Life of Christ.

From Karýtena, the main road west follows the Alfiós, past its co-mingling with the Loúsios, to **Andrítsena** ⓭, actually over the border in Ilía province. Sadly, shuttered traditional shops along the main street recall the village's past as a major entrepôt with 3,000 souls; today's permanent population is a tenth of that. A steady trickle of summer tourist traffic passes through to the 5th-century temple of **Apollo Epikourios** at **Bassae** (Vásses), 14km (9 miles) south. Although the most intact ancient shrine in Greece and a Unesco World Heritage site, it's unlikely to enchant, concealed as it is by a colossal, guy-wired permanent tent to protect it from winter frosts.

More rewarding for many is the **gorge of the River Néda** 18km (11 miles) south, just below modern Figália village and ruins of ancient Phigaleia, whose citizens originally built the temple in gratitude for Apollo having lifted a plague. A marked, 90-minute trail loop (or a steep road, just passable to ordinary cars) descends past the ruins – best of these a temple of Athena, whose altar glimpses the sea – to the lushly vegetated north bank of the river, where a spur path goes briefly west to the *stómio* or tunnel-cave, through which the Néda runs underground for 10km

(6 miles). Photogenic waterfalls on the Marathónios tributary stream feed the main river just before it disappears from view.

Lakonía

As you descend the 64-km (40-mile) road from Trípoli to modern Spárti, the long ridge of **Mount Taýgetos** with its striated limestone bands looms into sight on the right. Ahead stretches the olive-and-citrus-rich floodplain of the Evrótas River, belying the stereotypical image of ancient Sparta as a harsh, "spartan" place (the province's name, Lakonía, also lives on abroad as "laconic" – supposedly the distinguishing characteristic of the Classical natives).

Spárti ⓮, the modern successor to ancient Sparta, is an unexciting place redeemed only by some attractive squares and neoclassical facades, vestiges of Bavarian town planning in 1834. The archaeological museum (Mon–Sat 8.30am–2.40pm, Sun 9.30am–2pm) is particularly rich in late Roman floor-mosaics from local villas, and eerie votive offerings from the **sanctuaries of Apollo** at Amýkles and **Artemis Orthia** on the acropolis – where youths were flogged until bloody to honour the goddess. At the acropolis itself, however, 700 metres northwest of town, not much remains aside from a badly eroded theatre and the sparse remains of the Byzantine church of **Ágios Níkon**.

What little the Spartans built was appropriated for the construction of Byzantine **Mystrás** ⓯ 6km (4 miles) west (daily summer 8am–8pm, winter 8am–2pm). A romantically ruined walled town, clinging to a conical crag and topped by a castle, Mystrás is a corruption of mezythrás, the Greek for "cream-cheese maker" – thought to be a reference to this cheese's traditional conical shape.

Originally founded by the Franks in 1249, Mystrás grew to a city of 20,000 souls under the Byzantines,

becoming the capital of the Morean despots after 1348.

The church of **Perívleptos monastery** contains a complete cycle of frescoes depicting the *Dodekaeorton* or 12 major church feasts, with such light touches as children up a tree in the Entry to Jerusalem. Nearby **Pandánassa** convent, the newest church built in 1428 and now home to nuns, has a typically Gothic exterior as well as vivid frescoes within, the best of these neck-craningly high. By contrast, the oldest church, the **Mitrópolis** or cathedral of Ágios Dimítrios, is resolutely conservative in structure, notwithstanding awkward domes added later; here frescoes include a complete cycle of Christ's Miracles. The **Vrondóhion** monastic complex harbours yet another 14th-century church, the more daring **Afendikó**, the weight of its six domes borne by a system of piers below and colonnaded gallery above. Sea monsters bob in the Baptism fresco, while above the altar, apostles marvel at Christ ascending in a mandorla.

FACT

In March 1821, Germanos, the local Archbishop of Pátra, gave his blessing to an uprising against the Ottomans, which led to the liberation of all Arkadía.

Mystrás's Perívleptos church has some superb frescoes.

Monemvasiá's fortifications cling to a crag by the sea.

Monemvasiá and Gýthio

Originally the port of Mystrás, **Monemvasiá** ⓰, lies 94km (58 miles) southeast of Spárti. Like Mystrás, it's a fortified double town, clinging to a limestone plug rising 350 metres (1,150ft) from the sea and inevitably nicknamed the "Gibraltar of Greece" – although the "Dubrovnik of Greece" would be an equally apt term for the tile-roofed, wall-encased lower town on the south slope. Supporting a population of 50,000 in its heyday as a semi-autonomous city-state, Monemvasiá prospered by virtue of its fleets and handy location, halfway between Italy and the Black Sea. Never taken by force, it did surrender on occasion through prolonged siege – no food could grow on the rock, though enormous cisterns provided water.

Mystrás church bell tower.

The lower town, within its 900-metre three-sided circuit of Venetian walls, is invisible as you cross the causeway until the massive west gate (closed to vehicles) suddenly appears. Immediately above the gate perches the house in which prominent poet Giannis Ritsos was born in 1909; one wonders what the conservative locals made of his forthright Marxism and bisexuality. On his death in 1990, he was buried in the nearby cemetery, with one of his poems chiselled on the gravestone in lieu of religious sentiment.

Linked by a maze of tunnels, arcades and cul-de-sacs at the end of steep, cobbled lanes, many of the lower-town houses have been bought up and restored by wealthy Athenians and foreigners. Masoned steps zigzag up the cliff face overhead to the older, upper town, first settled and fortified in the 6th century AD but abandoned since the early 1900s and now utterly ruined. The sole exception to the desolation is the 14th-century **Agía Sofía** church with its 16-sided dome, poised at the edge of the northerly cliff and the first point in Monemvasiá to catch the sunrise.

THE BYZANTINE GEM

Until the Ottomans took over in 1460, the court at Mystrás flourished as a major cultural centre, attracting scholars and artists from Serbia, Constantinople and Italy. The latter's influence is evident in the brilliantly coloured (and remarkably well-preserved) frescoes which adorn Mystrás's churches – these are as crammed with extraneous figures, buildings and landscapes as any Italian painting of the time. Architecturally, the churches are a composite of three-aisled-basilica ground plan and domed cross-in-square gallery, making them airily well lit by Byzantine standards. Proto-Renaissance sensibilities (and the Frankish wives of most of the despots) inspired belfries and colonnaded porticoes. It is easy to see why Mystrás is regarded as the last great Byzantine architectural flowering before the onset of the Ottoman era.

Overnighting at Monemvasiá is expensive, and beaches are remote; if you have transport but not the wallet, there are wonderful alternatives to either side. **Kyparíssi**, 56km (34 miles) north with the final approach along a one-lane corniche, is an idyllic Shangri-La grouped in three neighbourhoods, with a good pebble beach and fish tavernas. Elafónisos, the Peloponnese's only inhabited island, 39km (24 miles) to the south towards Neápoli via Poúnda jetty, has a single town with all amenities but some of the best beaches around at Símos (south of town) and Panagítsa (west).

Gýthio ⑰, 65km (40 miles) west of Monemvasiá, is a port town on the ferry routes to Kýthira and Crete, a holiday resort in its own right, and a deceptively congenial gateway to the austere Máni. The quay is lined by tiled vernacular houses and pricey seafood tavernas; across the Lakonian Gulf the sun rises over **Cape Maléa**, and Mount Taýgetos is glimpsed one last time on the north. In ancient times, Gýthio served as Sparta's port, and more recently exported acorns for use in tanning. There are few sights, apart from a Roman theatre and the Museum of the Mani (Tue–Sun 9.30am–3pm) on **Marathonísi** islet (ancient Kranae), tied to the mainland by a causeway.

The best nearby sandy beach – and weirdest sight – is 5km north at Selinítsa, where an enormous, derelict smugglers' freighter, the Dimitrios, has been grounded in a few feet of water since 1981.

The Máni

An arid, isolated region protected by Taýgetos' southerly outriders, the **Máni** was the last part of Greece to espouse Christianity (in the 9th century), but made up for lost time by erecting dozens of small country chapels. Little grows except stunted olive trees, though in late summer an extra dash of colour is lent by hedges of fruiting prickly pears. "Outer" or **Éxo Máni** (Ítylo northwest to Kalamáta) is more tourist-friendly, fertile and

Cherries for sale, in Monemvasiá lower town. In medieval times, food supplies were the rock-city's weak point; everything had to be imported from the mainland.

A view towards Monemvasiá.

Gýthio waterfront.

better watered; "Inner" or **Mésa Máni**, south of a line connecting Ítylo with Gýthio, has the more noteworthy churches on the west shore, and tower-studded villages sprouting from the east-coast settlements. But extreme conditions have prompted wholesale depopulation, and the villages here only fill during the autumn hunting season.

From Gýthio, the main road into the Máni passes the castles of **Passavá** and **Kelefá**, the only Ottoman attempts at imposing order locally, before reaching **Areópol** ⓲, main market town and tourist base of the Inner Máni. Formerly Tsímova, stronghold of the Mavromihális clan, it was renamed after independence for Ares the god of war, in recognition of its contribution to the independence struggle. Two churches, both 18th-century, distinguish it: **Taxiárhis** with its campanile and zodiacal apse reliefs, and frescoed **Ágios Ioánnis**, near which is a worthwhile museum of Christianity in the Máni, located inside the Pikoulakis Towerhouse (Tue–Sun 8.30am–2.40pm; charge).

Some 8km (5 miles) south, just off the west-coast road towards **Cape Mátapan** (Ténaro), the caverns at **Pýrgos Diroú** are the sole organised tourist attraction in the Máni (daily summer 8.30am–5.30pm, winter 8.30am–3pm); visits are partly by boat along a subterranean river, and queues can be long.

Between here and Geroliménas stand various frescoed Byzantine churches; sadly, most are permanently locked, and hunting for the warden can be futile. Two of the best, at Áno Boularí, are also the easiest to access. Apply in the Geroliménas post office for the keys to **Ágios Stratigós**, with extensive frescoes from the 12th to the 18th centuries; and to nearby **Ágios Pandelímon** which has the earliest (10th-century) frescoes around, depicting saints Pandelímon and Nikitas in the apse. **Geroliménas** ⓳ itself, 20km (12 miles) from Areópoli, can offer tavernas and accommodation, but not much else – it dates only from 1870. The 35 ridgetop tower-houses of dramatic, deserted **Váthia** ⓴, 10km

(6 miles) further east, have become photogenic synonyms for the Máni.

The main tarred road out of Geroliménas loops along the eastern shore via **Lágia** (famed for its broad-based, tapering towers and purple-marble quarries) and **Flomohóri** (with the highest towers and pebbly **Kótronas** beach below) before re-emerging at Areópoli. Just across the ravine dividing Inner Máni and Areópoli from Outer is bluff-top **Ítylo** ㉑ lushly set and – unlike so many of its neighbours – relatively prosperous; below the village lie the frescoed monastery of **Dekoúlou** and the beach resort of **Néo Ítylo**.

The pride of **Langáda** ㉒ village 14km (9 miles) north, is the central 11th-century church of **Metamórfosi tou Sotíra**, whose frescoes still await uncovering and restoration; contiguous **Plátsa** and **Nomitsís** have four more Byzantine chapels. Mass tourism takes over at the picturesque fishing port of **Ágios Nikólaos** (Selenítsa); nearby **Stoúpa** ㉓ has two sandy bays and plenty of facilities as well. **Kardamýli** ㉔ ranks as the premier resort before Kalamáta, offering a long pebble beach, a late-medieval citadel and some good walking just inland.

Messinía province

Kalamáta can also be approached directly from Spárti via the spectacular 60-km (37-mile) road which crosses Mount Taýgetos. **Kalamáta** ㉕ itself suffered a devastating 1986 earthquake which left half the population homeless; despite subsequent emigration, it's still the biggest town hereabouts (40,000 people), with an attractive seafront and some lively untouristy tavernas to recommend it.

The worthiest nearby target is ancient **Messene** ㉖, 27km (16 miles) north, the Peloponnese's most up-and-coming archaeological site (summer Tue–Fri 8.30am–6.40pm, Sat–Sun 8.30am–4.40pm, winter Tue–Sun 8.30am–3pm; free; www.ancientmessene. gr), at modern Mavromáti village. Already excavated and commendably labelled are the enormous stadium, the biggest in Greece, an intact tomb at its far end, extensive colonnades, an *ekklesiastirion* (type of theatre), and

WHERE

It was on **Marathonísi** that Paris and Helen legendarily spent their first night together, and so launched a thousand ships.

Váthia in the Máni.

the hulking Arcadia Gate in the walls (raised against the Spartans, Messene's deadly enemy) of the ancient city, which flourished into Roman times, and was supplied with water from the still-gushing spring in the centre of the modern village.

Most visitors to Messinía province, however, have their sights set on the low southwesterly promontory ending in **Cape Akrítas**, with its fine beaches and balmy climate. Prime destination is **Koróni** ㉗, founded by Venice in 1206 to guard the sea lanes between the Adriatic and Crete. The castle here still shelters a few houses, orchards and pine groves, but a convent occupies most of it. The town outside the walls (built since 1830) has weathered tourism well, its vernacular houses with their wooden balconies still lining the steep stair-streets. **Zánga beach**, one of the best in the Peloponnese, extends for 3km (2 miles) west.

Methóni ㉘, another "eye of Venice" lying 35km (22 miles) west, grew wealthy after 1209 from the pilgrim trade to Palestine. Its sprawling castle (daily 8.30am–3pm; free),

Sturdy tower-house typical of the Máni region.

washed on three sides by the sea, combines military architecture of various eras: beyond the Venetian sea-gate, a Turkish octagonal tower – the Boúrtzi – overlooks two islets, while a French arched bridge of 1828 spans the Venetian moat. Little remains of the medieval town inside, however, and the modern village outside the walls is not nearly as attractive as Koróni's, and nor is the beach.

Pýlos ㉙, 13km (8 miles) north, is another rather sleepy town; despite its pleasant setting on huge, landlocked **Navaríno Bay**, what life there is seems confined to the immediate environs of **Platía Tríon Navárhon**, the main square. The bay has seen two momentous naval battles: in 425 BC, when the Athenians bested the Spartans off **Sfaktiría island**, and in October 1827, when a combined French, Russian and English armada sank Ibrahim Pasha's Ottoman fleet, thus guaranteeing Greek independence. The three allied admirals are honoured by an obelisk in their namesake square. The huge Venetian-Ottoman fortress of **Niókastro** (Tue–Sun 8.30am–2.40pm)

FEUDS IN THE MÁNI

While there may be some truth to Maniot claims that they are descended from the ancient Spartans, more crucial to the region's history was the arrival, during the 13th to the 15th centuries, of refugee Byzantine nobility. These established a local aristocracy, the Nyklians, which formed competing clans; only they had the right to erect tower-mansions.

Poor farmland and a fast-growing population spurred not just piracy and banditry, but complex vendettas between clans. Blood feuds could last for years, with sporadic truces to tend crops; women, who delivered supplies, were inviolate, as were doctors, who treated the wounded impartially. Combatants fired at each other from neighbouring towers, raising them as high as five storeys so as to lob rocks onto their opponents' flat roofs. The vendettas generally ended either with the annihilation or utter submission of the losing clan. Rather than rule the Máni directly, the Ottomans encouraged the feuding in the hopes of weakening any concerted rebellions, appointing a Nyklian chieftain as bey to represent the sultan.

The office passed between rival clans, but under the last bey, Petros Mavromihalis, the clans united, participating in the Greek independence uprising as of 17 March 1821. Rather less illustriously, the brother and son of "Petrobey" assassinated first president Ioannis Kapdistrias on 9 October 1831, for perceived insults to the Mavromihalis clan.

dominating Pýlos contains a huge mosque-church, being restored, and a collection of fine historical or ethnographic engravings installed inside the French barracks of 1828.

For beaches, you'll have to head for the north end of the bay beyond Giálova, where perfectly half-circular Voïdokiliá bay is both beach and wildlife refuge, featuring on every poster and postcard of Messinía. About 11km (6 miles) north of Giálova lies the Bronze Age Palace of **Nestor** (summer Tue–Fri 8am–7.30pm, Sat–Sun & winter daily 8.30am–2.40pm), discovered in 1939, excavated more recently and now protected by a synthetic roof. The elderly museum at Hóra Trifylías (Tue–Sun 8.30am–2.40pm) desperately needs a refit, but a huge trove of gold tomb finds from Peristéria manages to shine through.

On your way out of Messinía, stop – halfway between Filiatrá and pretty Kyparissía – at Agrílis for Fournier's **Castle** (always viewable), the brainchild of a returned Greek-American. This four-storey, crenellated, turretted folly with pseudo-heraldry is flanked by outsized figures of the Trojan horse, Helen and Hector – a monster of kitsch unequalled (given stiff competition) in Greece, but hugely enjoyable.

Olympia and the Cape of Kyllíni

From **Kyparissía** it's a pleasant coastal drive to ancient **Olympia** ㉚, where the Kládeos River meets the Alfiós. The sanctuary here served for two millennia as a religious and athletic centre; of all the Hellenic competitions associated with shrines, the Olympic Games, held every four years at the late-summer full moon, were the most prestigious, and the pan-Hellenic truce declared for their duration was honoured by the various city-states on pain of stiff fines. Although the first verified games were held in 776 BC, the Altis, a sacred forest at the base of the hill of Kronos, was consecrated to pre-Olympian deities as early as the second millennium BC. Recent fires have stripped the hill's pines, but the site is still liberally planted with Zeus' oaks, and in early spring, judas trees provide vivid flashes of colour.

Methoní's Baírtzi, a fine example of Ottoman military architecture.

TIP

To see the best examples of the distinctive Maniot tower-houses, head for the villages of Váthia, Kítta, Nómia and Flomohóri.

The most salient monuments at the Olympia site (summer Mon–Sat 8am–8pm, Sun 8am–3pm, spring/fall Mon–Sat 8am–7pm, Sun 8am–3pm, winter Mon–Fri 8am–5pm, Sat 8.30am–3pm) are the **Palaestra** training centre, whose courtyard colonnade has been re-erected; the **workshop of Pheidias**, the celebrated sculptor (identified by a cup found with his name inscribed); the Leonidaion guesthouse, with its lobular central pool; the Archaic **Hera temple** with its dissimilar columns; the enormous **Zeus temple**, now reduced to column sections; and the **stadium** with its 192-metre (630-ft) running course and surviving vaulted entrance.

In the newer **Olympia Museum** (summer Tue–Sat 8am–7.40pm, Sun–Mon 9am–4pm, spring/autumn Tue–Sat 8am–7pm, Sun–Mon 9am–4pm, winter Mon 10.30am–5pm, Tue–Fri 8.00am–5pm, Sat–Sun 8.30am–3pm), among the best half-dozen in Greece, pride of place goes to the pediment reliefs recovered from the Zeus temple debris, now on display in the central hall, depicting the battle between the Lapiths and the Centaurs, with the god Apollo at the centre of the composition. Other unmissable items include the Hermes and baby Dionysos of Praxiteles, showcased in Room 8 at the right rear; the Geometric and Archaic bronze gallery (Room 2), offering a gorgon shield ornament, a hammered relief of a mother griffon, various helmets, griffon heads as cauldron ornaments; and the painted terracotta of Zeus with Ganymede in Room 4, near the heavily damaged Nike of Paionios. If time permits, the old museum nearby (Mon–Fri 9am–4pm) offers a fine late Roman mosaic, a statue of Hadrian's lover Antinoös, a stele of Herakles wrestling with the Nemean lion, and a bronze miniature of two human wrestlers.

The closest beaches to Olympia (modern Olymbía) are southeast of the picturesque cruise-ship port of Katákolo, full of converted old warehouses. More edifying targets lie northwest along the main highway, in **Gastoúni** ㉛ where the 12th-century church of Panagía Katholikó at the southwest edge of town offers narthex frescoes, recently cleaned, nearly on a par with those at Mystrás, including a wonderful bestiary amongst apocalyptic scenes.

Further into the cape ending at Kyllíni, **Hlemoutsi** ㉜ (Tue–Sun 8.30am–2.40pm) – visible from a great distance away, the name a corruption of Clermont – was the strongest purpose-built Frankish castle in the western Peloponnese, erected in 1220–23 by Geoffrey de Villehardouin to survey the straits with Zákynthos. Restoration of the hexagonal citadel inside the huge, fan-shaped bailey is ongoing, which means the rooftop viewpoint and some of the vaulted halls may be closed, but it's still well worth the trip. The adjacent modern village of Kástro is functional enough for an overnight or a meal, and the beaches just downhill, opposite Zákynthos, are excellent.

Pátra is awash with colour at Carnival.

Aháïa province

Continuing deeper into Aháïa province along the coast north of **Kyllíni**, sample the enormous, 7-km (4-mile) beach of **Kalogriá** ③ and the swamps (plus umbrella-pine dune forest) just behind. This, one of the largest wetlands in the Balkans, has finally gained protected status as a national park; get the full story from the information office in Lápa, the village where you leave the main highway for the beach.

Pátra ③, 38km (24 miles) further, is Greece's third-largest city, and the principal port for ferries to Italy and some of the Ionian Islands. With its fearsome traffic, anonymous post-war architecture and lack of beaches, it's hardly the ideal spot for a quiet holiday retreat; only the ancient **acropolis** (with an originally Byzantine castle) seems peaceful. But linger at Carnival time to witness Greece's best observance, with parades, floats and conspicuous attendance by students and the gay community.

Some 44km (27 miles) east along the motorway toward Athens, **Diakoftó** ③ is the start/end point of the famous rack-and-pinion (odondotós) railway up the precipitous **Vouraïkós Gorge**. Long one of the most popular train-rides in Greece, its future – like the entire railway system – is threatened by troïka demands for closure, but while it lasts, take advantage (current news on www.odontotos. com). Because of the grade, it takes well over an hour to cover the mere 22km (14 miles) to Kalávryta,

Kalamáta is best known for its prosperous export trade in large, shiny purplish-grey olives. They are excellent eaten with oúzo.

terminus of the line and victim of a fierce Nazi reprisal in December 1943 when the town was burned and all the men shot. Today it is busiest in winter, thanks to the Mt Helmós ski resort overhead, but you can also use it as a base to visit the **Spílio Limnón/ Cave of the Lakes** ③ (daily 9.30am– 4.30pm, may open longer at holidays; www.kastriacave.gr), 17km (11 miles) south near Kastriá village, where tours take in the first 500m of a series of small lakes formed by natural dams.

Voïdokiliá beach, near Pýlos.

CENTRAL GREECE

A region rich in temples and monasteries, from Delphi – mythical centre of the ancient world – to the Monastery of Ósios Loukás and the dramatic Metéora peaks.

Roúmeli, the poetic medieval term for south-central Greece, encompasses the present-day provinces of Étolo-Akarnanía, Evrytanía, Fokída, Viotía and Fthiótida – even more ancient place-names revived by the modern Greek state. Few contemporary visitors concern themselves much with these tongue-twisting toponyms as they rush headlong towards the main attraction of the region, the Classical site at Delphi. Their single-mindedness is forgiveable, since Delphi uniquely combines a wealth of monuments with a breathtaking setting.

The drive from Athens takes anywhere from 2.5 to 3.5 hours depending on your route; the most historic, scenic one follows a steep but well-paved road over the pine-covered mountains from near dreary **Elefsína** – perhaps detouring for a pebble-beach swim and a fish lunch or – with a late start out of Athens – even an overnight at **Pórto Germenó** ❶ on the Gulf of Corinth – to **Thíva** (**Thebes**) ❷. The modern town has been built on top of the ancient one, so little is visible of the ancient Thebes so prominent in Greek myth and history. A small ancient palace has, however, been excavated and the excellent archaeological museum (closed for complete reconstruction until late 2013) contains tomb and sanctuary finds from Bronze Age to Classical Boeotia, especially the painted sarcophagi from Tanagra.

Livadiá and Aráhova

The next main town, **Livadiá** ❸, was a major power base for the Frankish Crusader fiefdoms during the 13th and 14th centuries. In the gorge of the River Érkyna yawns the entrance to the ancient Oracle of Trophonios, near a graceful Ottoman bridge and below the Catalan-built castle. Springs nurture a dense colony of plane trees,

Main Attractions

PÓRTO GERMENÓ
ÓSIOS LOUKÁS
ANCIENT DELPHI SITE
DELPHI MUSEUM
GALAXÍDI
NÁVPAKTOS
KARPENISIÓTIS VALLEY
MAKRYNÍTSA, ON PÍLIO
TSANGARÁDA & ITS BEACHES, PÍLIO
AGÍOU NIKOLÁOU ANÁPAVSA, METÉORA

Ósios Loukás monastery.

Central Greece

0   20 km
0   20 miles

a pleasing backdrop to the handful of tavernas on the pedestrianised banks.

Beyond **Livadiá**, the road west begins to climb into the foothills of **Mt Parnassós**. The left turn for Dístomo village and the **Monastery of Ósios Loukás** ❹ (May–mid-Sept 8am–2pm, 4–7pm, otherwise 8am–5pm), dedicated to a local 10th-century ascetic named Luke, is clearly marked. The monastery commands a wonderful view over a secluded valley in the shadow of Mt Elikónas. The smaller chapel of the Virgin (on the left) dates from the 10th century; the 11th-century *katholikón*, or main church, contains superb mosaics, survivors of a 1659 earthquake. The best and easiest to view, including a *Resurrection* and *Washing of the Apostles' Feet*, are in the narthex.

The village of **Aráhova** ❺ clings to the toes of Parnassós; formerly a bastion of pastoral culture, it has now adopted a new role as a ski resort, with Athenian-weekender chalets sprouting rapidly on the outskirts. Tourist souvenirs, including various types of pasta and the almost-purple local wine, are pitched more at Greeks than foreigners.

Delphi

The ancient site of **Delphi** ❻ is 11km (7 miles) further along, built on terraces at the base of sheer cliffs, the whole poised to topple over into the Plístos Gorge. One of the major religious centres – indeed, reckoned the geographical centre – of the ancient world, a much-consulted oracle functioned here for over a millennium until the proscription of paganism in AD 391. Since its excavation by the French towards the end of the 19th century, Delphi has ranked as the most popular, memorable ruin on the mainland, attended as well by gliding birds of prey launching themselves from the palisades. A visit involves steep climbs rewarded by ever-changing viewpoints and new monumental treasures.

The first locale, on the south side of the road, is the so-called **Marmaria** (daily same hours as main site below; free), comprising a gymnasium (complete with a straight track and a round bath) and the sanctuary of Athena Pronaia. Pronaia means "guardian of the temple" and ancient visitors passed first through this shrine. The original 7th-century BC temple was destroyed by the Persians, and replaced by the present complex; the most interesting structure here is the 4th-century *tholos* (a circular building with a vaulted or conical roof), whose purpose remains unknown.

On the north side of the road gushes the Castalian Spring (fenced off). Parts of the older, rectangular fountain right next to the road date to the 6th-century BC, although thin marble slabs on the floor are Hellenistic or early Roman. All pilgrims had to perform ritual ablutions here.

The main sacred precinct at Delphi is the **Sanctuary of Apollo** (daily summer 8am–8pm, winter 8.30am–3pm), above the road past the Castalian Spring. Many of the ruins exposed

The Sanctuary of Athena Pronaia, Delphi.

today date from Roman times, but just as many monuments, including the stadium and main temple, are earlier. For the casual visitor, highlights include the Athenian Treasury, the Athenian stoa and the Temple of Apollo.

The top sights at Delphi

The Doric-order **Athenian Treasury** (late 6th- or early 5th-century) was pieced together by French archaeologists in 1904–06, using the inscriptions covering its surface as a guide. The late-6th-century **Athenian stoa,** today retaining three complete Ionic columns before a polygonal wall, was a roofed area protecting trophies from various Athenian naval victories, including the defeat of the Persians at Salamis in 480 BC. An inscription reads: "The Athenians have dedicated this portico with the arms and bow ornaments taken from their enemies at sea".

Plays were performed at Delphi's theatre during the Pythian Festival, held every four years.

The **Temple of Apollo** just above the Athenian stoa is the third confirmed temple to have stood here, and there are literary rumours of three even earlier ones; two 7th- and 6th-century predecessors were done for by fire and earthquake respectively. What you see dates from 369–329 BC, and is impressive enough, measuring 66 by 26 metres (215 by 85 ft): six columns were re-erected by the French. The god Apollo was associated, among other things, with prophecy, his main function here. His oracle resided under the temple flooring in the *adyton* chamber, where a chasm in the earth belched forth noxious and possibly mind-altering vapours. Consulting the oracle of Delphi consisted of several stages. The petitioner's question would be relayed to the god Apollo by a priestess known as the Pythia, who could hear the answer only when she was in a trance – induced, conveniently enough, by residing in the vapour-filled adyton. Her ravings, in turn, could be understood only by the sanctuary's priests, who interpreted them for the supplicant – often ambiguously – for a suitable fee. One of the oracle's more memorable pronouncements was that Oedipus would kill his father and marry his mother – thereby

giving the world its most tragic hero and Freud his Oedipus complex.

The small **theatre** above the temple, originally 4th-century but thoroughly restored during the Roman era, seats 5,000 people and has marvellous acoustics. The **stadium**, a long narrow oval, is well worth the somewhat steep walk beyond the theatre. It retains 12 rows of seats on the north side and six rows of seats, now mostly tumbled, on the south (sadly, off-limits). You will easily find the starting and finishing lines, the limestone blocks complete with grooves for the runners' toes.

The **Delphi Museum** (summer Mon 12.30–6.30pm, Tue–Sun 7.30am–7.30pm, winter daily 8.30am–2.45pm; entrance included in site ticket) underwent a comprehensive refit in the run-up to the 2004 Athens Olympics, further highlighting its magnificent collection. The bronze charioteer of 470 BC with his onyx eyes is the most famous denizen, but look out also for two huge 6th-century *kouroi* (standing statues of men), the votive, life-sized bull made from hammered silver sheets, the Ionic Sphinx

of the Naxians, dating from 565 BC, and the Siphian frieze with scenes from the Trojan War and a battle between the gods and the titans.

The coast of Fokída

Below Delphi and its namesake modern, touristic village, a vast plain of olive trees stretches south towards the Gulf of Corinth. Literally gritty **Itéa** was once the ancient port of Delphi and still ships out the odd cargo of purple-red bauxite, strip-mined from the flanks of Mt Gióna to the west. But the real star of this often bleak coast is little **Galaxídi** ❼. With its Venetian-influenced mansions, the place seems closer in style to Koróni or Návpaktos than the rough-hewn village houses of Fokída.

Local shipowners prospered during the 18th and 19th centuries when Galaxídi was, amazingly, the fourth-busiest harbour in Greece – thus the elaborate housing. But captains refused to convert to steam after the

The Naxian sphinx, now at the Delphi Museum, stood on a tall Ionic column below the Apollo Temple terrace.

Galaxídi, a popular weekend retreat for wealthy Athenians.

The Venetian castle at Návpaktos extends down to ramparts guarding the harbour.

The Rio Andirrio bridge in the Gulf of Corinth.

1890s, and the place sank into obscurity until being rediscovered by wealthy Athenians looking for a pleasant weekend bolt-hole. Foreign tourists are thus few, but there are plenty of comfortable lodgings and expensive restaurants along the south harbour quay, where yachts congregate.

The coastal road of Fokída heads west, passing **Ágios Nikólaos** (regular ferries to Égio on the Peloponnese) and **Trizónia**, the only inhabited island in the Gulf of Corinth, before arriving at **Návpaktos** ❽, just inside Étolo-Akarnanía.

Walk or drive up from the little egg-shaped Venetian harbour to the sprawling, pine-tufted castle above. Much the largest place on the gulf's north shore, today Návpaktos gracefully combines the functions of low-key resort and market town. The better hotels and most restaurants stand behind plane-tree-shaded Grímbovo beach, although bathing there is dubious;

retire instead to westerly Psáni beach.

Étolo-Akarnanía

Continuing further west into Étolo-Akarnanía from Návpaktos, the landscape becomes flatter and less dramatic; the main sight en route is the earthquake-proof **suspension bridge** at the **Río-Andírrio straits**, the longest in the world (2,880m/ 9,449ft) and clearly visible from jets 10,500 metres (35,000ft) up. The road veers inland briefly before arriving at **Mesolóngi** ❾, where Lord Byron died on 19 April 1824. The Ottomans had been trying to take the town since 1822; in April 1825, the final attack was mounted by 30,000 troops against 5,000 active insurgents. After a year of close siege, about half the population of 20,000 – combatants and civilians alike – broke out but were ambushed, with only about 1,600 surviving. Those remaining in town fired their own powder magazines, killing themselves, several thousand children and the elderly, plus many Turkish attackers.

The northeast entrance to the town through the Venetian wall is known as the **Gate of the Sortie**, built by King Otto where the inhabitants defied the siege. To the west lies the **Garden of Heroes** (signposted "Heroes' Tombs"), with a tumulus covering the bodies of the anonymous defenders; the tomb of the Greek commander, Markos Botsaris; and a statue of Byron. Today, Mesolóngi is, more on sentimental than practical grounds, the capital of Étolo-Akarnanía, and lives mostly from the products of the vast and sometimes whiffy lagoons which surround the town on three sides: salt, *avgotáraho* (compressed grey-mullet roe), and smoked eels. The latter two items can be sampled at several tavernas on and around Athanasíou Razikótsika, at the heart of the old quarter, or at Tourlída, out on the lagoon.

Beyond Mesolóngi, and the enormous walls of ancient **Pleuron** on the mountain side, the road splits near **Etolikó ❿**, a strange place built as a medieval refuge on an island in a lagoon. The more popular highway goes through the **Klisoúra Gorge** past unsightly **Agrínio**, commercial capital of the province, and on through tobacco fields to **Amfilohía** at the southernmost tip of the Amvrakikós Gulf.

A more interesting route to western Epirus veers off at Etolikó and mostly follows the coast all the way. Once across the mighty Ahelóös River and over the hills of the **Lesíni ash forest,** you emerge at **Ástakos,** a minor ferry port with services to Itháki but also a major yacht anchorage. The onward road offers spectacular views over small and large members of the Ionian archipelago before cruising through **Mýtikas** and **Páleros,** two little resorts in the lee of Lefkáda which make excellent meal stops or overnight halts. At the end of the journey is **Vónitsa**, with its little castle, gulf-front tavernas and, as usual hereabouts, a merely functional beach; from here you are poised to head either southwest to Lefkáda or northwest through a tunnel under the mouth of the Amvrakikós Gulf to Préveza.

FACT

Spanish novelist Miguel de Cervantes, of Don Quixote fame, then a naval marine on a Spanish ship, lost the use of his left hand at the battle of Lepanto, fought off Návpaktos in 1571.

Welcoming Lord Byron at Mesolóngi by Theodoros Vryzakis, 1861.

THE BATTLE OF LEPANTO

The Ottomans used Návpaktos as a base before sailing out to their defeat in the naval battle of Lepanto (the Venetian name for Návpaktos), crushed by an allied Christian armada commanded by John of Austria in 1571. An Ottoman chronicler lamented, "The Imperial fleet encountered the fleet of the wretched infidels and the will of Allah turned another way".

Notably, Lepanto was the last major naval battle in the Mediterranean fought entirely between galleys. For all its resonance in the West, however, the battle – gleefully celebrated as the first major bloodying of the "Terrible Turk" – had little local effect, since the Ottomans had already taken Cyprus that summer, and they quickly rebuilt their navies and went on to conquer Crete within a century.

Willows, planes and laurels border the Piniós River which cuts through the Vale of Témbi, making it a delightful place to hike. You can also take a canoe or kayak trip through the gorge.

Karpenisiótis valley, nicknamed the "Greek Switzerland".

North into Evrytanía

From Návpaktos, a little-used but highly scenic road goes northeast into the valley of the Évinos River, beloved of rafters, and then climbs again to the basin of Lake Trihonída, the largest natural body of fresh water in Greece. On a plateau out of sight to the northeast lies the lively town of **Thérmo** and its predecessor, ancient **Thermon** ⓫ (Tue–Sun 8.30am–3pm; free), the main religious centre of the ancient Aetolians.

Beyond Thérmo, the gradient steepens as you head north through the forest to Evrytanía province. First up are **Prousós** ⓬ village and monastery, poised on the precipitous, landslide-prone north slopes of Mt Panetolikó; its isolation made the area a haunt of revolutionary hero Karaïskakis. Some spectacular gorges bring you to the main **Karpenisiótis valley,** heart of Evrytanía and nicknamed the "Greek Switzerland". Helvetic indeed are the green slopes and fir trees, matched by Swiss-style

stratospheric accommodation prices. The ski centre on Mt Veloúhi, north of the provincial capital of **Karpenísi** ⓭ is a popular target, as are day-walks up Mounts Kaliakoúda and Helidóna, the valley's 2,000-metre (6,200-ft) flanking peaks. The main villages just outside Karpenísi (which was ravaged by World War II and the civil war), more appealing for a stay or a meal, are Megálo Horió, Mikró Horió, Voutýro, Gávros and Koryskhádes.

North from Fokída to Thessaly

From the Delphi area, it is also possible to head straight north between mounts Parnassus and Gióna towards **Lamía** ⓮, capital of its own province and a pleasant lunch stop. On the way, you pass near to a hallowed site of Ancient Greek heroism. In antiquity, **Thermopylae** ⓯ was a narrow passage between the cliffs and the sea, although today silt from a nearby river has displaced the coastline by almost 5km (3 miles). In 480 BC, the Spartan general Leonidas held the pass for three days against a vastly

larger Persian army, until the Persians, tipped off by the traitor Ephialtes, outflanked the defenders by using a higher pass. Leonidas ordered most of the Greek army to retreat, but covered their flight by fighting to the end with his hand-picked guard of 2,300 men. A monumental statue of Leonidas now marks the spot, across the road from the grave mound for the Greek dead. Just beyond are the still-popular hot sulphur springs (Thermopylae means "hot gates") after which the pass is named.

Less than one hour's drive along the motorway from Lamía, **Vólos** ⑯, capital of the Thessalian province of Magnisía – is certainly not the most photogenic of towns. Destroyed by several earthquakes between 1947 and 1957, it is a busy, modern port, a sort of compressed version of Thessaloníki and Piraeus. That said, it is also a spirited town, with (like most of Thessaly) a tradition of leftist politics, a university, and arguably the densest Greek concentration of *ouzerís* along its waterfront. This gets leafier and more Aegean as you head east towards the

excellent **archaeological museum** (Tue–Sun 8am–8pm, Mon 1.30–8pm), which houses finds dating back to Neolithic times and Vólos' early days as ancient Iolkos.

Mount Pílio

The great Thessalian plain, once the bed of an inland sea, is ringed by mountains; the only natural outlet is where the Piniós River exits through the fabled **Vale of Témbi**, a 10-km (6-mile) gorge between **Mount Olympos** (Ólymbos) and **Mount Óssa.** Looming above Vólos is **Mount Pílio** (Pelion), legendary home of the centaurs. These fantastic beings had the legs and bodies of horses, the arms and heads of men, and – well-versed in magic and herbology – served as the wise tutors of several ancient heroes, including Achilles. Probably the centaurs were a mythologisation of an aboriginal tribe who, hiding in the dense Pílio forests, preserved the lore of pre-Hellenic ages.

Intriguingly, the entire region was a prominent centre of learning in Greece during the 17th and 18th

FACT

Jason, who set out in his ship Argo to find the Golden Fleece, began his journey in Iolkos, an ancient site on the outskirts of Vólos.

Picturesque Damoúhari port.

Orchards of cherry and apple spread out on the terraced hillsides below Mount Pílio. You'll find cherry jam for sale in the local village shops, as well as candied nuts and jars of tsitsíravla (pickled terebinth shoots).

centuries. Many important officials of the Austro-Hungarian Empire, of the sultan's inner circle and even of the Russian court, were educated on Mount Pílio. The peninsula probably became such a nursery of Greek erudition owing to its timber-based wealth and distance from grasping Ottoman officials.

The Pílio Peninsula (www.pelionet. co.uk) has two faces: the damp, shaggy northeast flank dropping to the Aegean, with excellent sand beaches of near-Caribbean hue; and the balmy, olive-covered slopes fringed with pebble shores lapped by the Pagasitic Gulf. Even if you fly to Vólos' airport at Néa Anhíalos and pick up a hire car, a week is realistically needed to tour it. The obvious, over-subscribed target is **Makrynítsa** ⓱, 17km (11 miles) north of Vólos, with its large concentration of 18th-century mansions and a fountain-and-church-flanked square. But **Vyzítsa** ⓲ to the east is quieter, with nearly as many grand houses.

Zagorá ⓳ and **Tsangaráda** in the northeast each comprise four villages in one, their several parishes strung

Postcard-perfect Mylopótamos beach.

out along kilometres of road: because of abundant water, few Pílio communities form dense clusters as on the islands. Tsangaráda is also a major hiking trailhead, for example down to the beach at Damoúhari or inland along an old trail once used by the locals to reach the rail station at Miliés.

The main developed coastal resorts are **Ágios Ioánnis** ⓴, near Zagorá, **Plataniá** in the far south and **Áfyssos** closer to Vólos. For contrast, try to stop at relatively unfrequented villages like **Láfkos, Sykí** and **Promýri** in the south. **Tríkeri** ㉑ and its port Agía Kyriakí, at the crab-claw southwest tip, lead a largely separate existence, with a strong maritime tradition. Beaches are too numerous to list, although the postcard stars tend to be of **Mylopótamos** with its natural arch, and **Damoúhari** port with its tiny Venetian castle, both below Tsangaráda.

The Metéora

Heading up to the Metéora, you may want to detour to **Ambelákia** ㉒, some 30km (20 miles) north of Lárisa. The village's outstanding architectural heritage includes the mansion of George Schwartz (Tue–Sun 9am–2.30pm), whose painted rooms evoke domestic interiors of the Ottoman bourgeoisie.

As you approach **Kalambáka** from Tríkala, towering rock formations – the **Metéora** ㉓ – rise before you in one of the great spectacles of mainland Greece. Some of the most extraordinary monasteries in the world cling to these massive pinnacles, whose name derives from the verb *meteorízo,* "to suspend in the air". These cones, cylinders and rounded buttresses, flecked with vegetation and caves like so many unbrushed, carious molars, are remnants of river sediment deposited at the margins of the prehistoric sea covering the plain of Thessaly some 25 million years ago. Tectonic-plate pressure and erosion by the young Piniós River are jointly responsible for their present shape.

Heading north out of Kalambáka through the village of **Kastráki**, set unimprovably in the shadow of the rocks, you encounter monasteries in the following order. **Agíou Nikoláou Anápavsa** (Sat–Thur 9am–3.30pm, winter until 3pm), built around 1388, has well-cleaned frescoes by the monk Theofanes of the Cretan School (*c.*1527), including a stylite (column-dwelling) hermit being supplied by winch-hoist, as would have been done locally. **Megálou Meteórou** (summer Wed–Mon 9am–5pm, winter Thur–Mon 9am–4pm) is the largest and highest monastery, although its church is overshadowed by a collection of rare icons and manuscripts in the refectory. **Varlaám** (summer daily 9am–4pm, winter Sat–Wed 9am–3pm), founded in 1517, offers 16th-century frescoes by Franco Catellano (partly retouched in 1870), including an Ascension and a *Pandokrátor* in the two domes respectively. It is also the last monastery to preserve in situ its old windlass mechanism, formerly used for elevating monks and supplies; a new electric pulley lifts the latter now.

Beautiful little **Roussánou** (summer daily 9am–6pm, winter Thur–Tue 9am–2pm), completely occupying a knife-edge summit, was built in 1545 for monks, later abandoned, and re-occupied by nuns in the 1970s. It too has vividly gory 17th-century frescoes dwelling on martyrdom by various unpleasant means. **Agías Triádos** (Fri–Wed, summer 9am–5pm, winter 9am–12.30pm, 3–5pm), with a final approach of 130 steps tunnelled through a rock, has frescoes in its *katholikón* (main church) which were thoroughly cleaned during the 1990s. Like other monastic churches here, this was built in two phases, resulting in two domes, two *Pandokrátors* and two complete sets of Evangelists. **Agíou Stefánou** (Tues–Sun, summer 9am–1.30pm, 3.30–5.30pm, winter 9am–1pm, 3–5pm), like Roussánou, is run as a convent but, heavily damaged by bombs during World War II, is the obvious one to skip if time is running short.

The Megálou Meteórou monastery contains 16th-century frescoes by Franco Catellano.

The Varlaám monastery as seen from Megálou Meteórou.

ROCK-TOP MONASTERIES

Religious hermits were already colonising the caves in this region by the 10th century, but legend attributes the first rock-top monastery (Megálou Meteórou) to the Athonite monk Athanasios, midway through the 14th century. Progress was slow as materials were transported first by rope ladder, then by winches and baskets, and it took nearly three centuries to finish Megálou Meteórou, by which time it was just one of 24 religious communities that were flourishing on the summits. After the 17th century, the monastic impetus slowed, and the more flimsily erected structures began to crumble on their exposed perches; the vicissitudes of modern Greek history since independence further hastened decline, and today only eight of these extraordinary buildings survive, of which just six are inhabited and open to pilgrims.

Sunset over the Víkos Gorge.

EPIRUS

A spectacular mountain region of limestone peaks, wooded valleys and traditional stone villages, the northwest also offers a pristine national park where bears and wolves still roam.

nland Epirus (Ípiros in Greek) is a world apart from the azure, sun-bleached Greece of the coasts. Its character is determined by the limestone peaks and deep river gorges of the Píndos range, which attains its greatest height just before the Albanian border in mounts Smólikas (2,637 metres/8,645ft) and Grámmos (2,520 metres/8,270ft). The winter precipitation, the highest in mainland Greece, ensures that forests are shaggy and rivers foaming.

An isolation enforced by both mountains and climate fostered the growth of medieval semi-autonomous villages built by traders and craftsmen returning from abroad. Local stone and wood has been transformed into imposing houses, with street cobbles, walls and roof slates blending in a uniform grey which, far from being depressing, is a classic example of harmonious adaptation to environment.

In antiquity, this was considered the limit of the civilised world; few ruins have been unearthed besides shadowy oracles at Dodona (Dodóni) and Acheron, and the planned Roman town of Nikopolis. The Byzantines had scarcely more time for this rugged terrain south of the Vía Egnatía, even though during the 13th and 14th centuries, the Despotate of Epirus extended from the Ionian Sea

to Thessaloníki. This mini-state sheltered members of the Byzantine nobility who had fled the imperial capital when it was sacked by the Fourth Crusade in 1204. They left behind intriguing churches around Árta, joining earlier masterpieces at Kastoriá in western Macedonia.

Like the rest of northern Greece, Epirus was not incorporated into the modern state until March 1913, during the First Balkan War and some 80 years after the end of the initial Greek War of Independence.

Main Attractions

KARAVOSTÁSI BEACH
PÁRGA
ANCIENT KASSOPE
NIKOPOLIS MOSAICS
ÁRTA BYANTINE CHURCHES
IOÁNNINA LAKEFRONT
ANCIENT DODONA THEATRE
WESTERN ZAGOROHÓRIA
OLD BRIDGES NEAR KÍPI, ZAGÓRI
HIKING THE ZAGORIAN PÍNDOS

The coast at Párga.

FACT

Low-impact, high-quality tourism has been successfully promoted in Zagóri, particularly in the gateway villages where the inhabitants sided with the conservationists to protect the national park.

Low impact tourism in Zagóri

The area suffered from neglect and mass emigration, but archaeological initiatives and financial incentives have boosted the economy, and many buildings have been restored. This is most notable in the Zagóri district of Epirus, where entire villages are now preserved as homogeneous traditional settlements. Simultaneously, old roads have been widened and paved, and new ones bulldozed, giving access to the tiniest hamlets. Because of the nature of tourism here, Zagóri is one of the few places in Greece where more than lip service is paid to the idea of quality trekking routes – although trails off the most popular itineraries can be haphazardly marked

and maintained at best, and facilities in the villages where you finish a day's hike can be rudimentary.

As in the whole of Greece, a touristic plum as lucrative as Zagóri has inevitably become the focus of ongoing battles between conservationists, developers and entrepreneurs. Dirt roads serving timber tracts and the high pastures scar the landscape, as does the national power corporation's reservoir at the sources of the Aöös River. Cuttings and tunnellings for the Vía Egnatía have a significant visual impact, especially near Métsovo. Yet during the late 1980s and early 1990s, not a few shepherds and villagers allied themselves with urban mountaineers, local tourism personnel, international ecologists

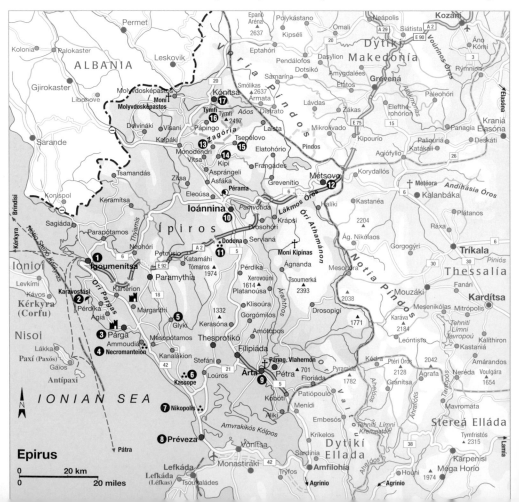

Epirus

0   20 km

0   20 miles

and even the European Kayaking Federation to halt a scheme promoted by Ioánnina-based interests for a second dam on the lower Aóös, plus various ski lifts and roads which would have ruined the national park at the heart of Zagóri.

From Igoumenítsa to Párga

The modern port of **Igoumenítsa ❶**, at the very northwestern corner of mainland Greece, is the third busiest in the country after Pátra and Piraeus (Pireás), a turnstile sort of a place where an enforced halt should be avoided at all costs. Far more rewarding is the coastal road south, which after 33km (20 miles) reaches the side road for **Karavostási ❷**, indisputably the finest beach in Thesprotía province. Two rivers at each end of the long strand are responsible for the ample sand, and since it is an archaeologically protected area, development is still limited. Just up the hill from the side-turning sits the village of **Pérdika,** whose pedestrianised centre offers a range of tavernas and a surprisingly lively night scene, courtesy

The Víkos Gorge.

of Athenians and Greeks returned from overseas.

From the Karavostási-Pérdika junction, a few more kilometres – via the well-preserved castle of **Agiá** (daily all day; free) – bring you to **Párga ❸**, Epirus's main coastal resort and deservedly so for its fine beaches, tiered houses and dominant Norman-Venetian castle. From the 14th to the late 18th centuries, this was the Serene Republic's lone stronghold in Epirus, peopled by Souliot Orthodox Christians in constant conflict with

Boats moored in the bay of Párga.

EMIGRATION AND REVIVAL

During the 20th century, the remoteness that once protected this region undermined its continued vigour. The ravages of World War II and the subsequent civil war, along with poor communications, the non-sustainability of traditional livelihoods and apparently punitive government neglect, spurred massive emigration, particularly to North America, Germany and Australia. By the 1970s, many Epirot villages were in an advanced state of physical and social decline. Numerous houses were left to decay (or shoddily repaired), while others sheltered an ever-dwindling population of the economically inactive elderly.

But matters have slowly changed. The government has acted to integrate the region into the national economy, most obviously with frequent flights to Ioánnina and good roads, including the Vía Egnatía expressway and its ambitious tunnels through the Píndos, plus the pending Ionian Highway up from Mesolóngi. Emigration has slowed down and just occasionally – thanks to tourism, subsidies for logging or grazing, and better infrastructure – even halted. Attitudes towards village life have softened, with traditional architecture and methods now viewed less as stumbling blocks to economic prosperity and more as cultural heritage to be preserved.

their Muslim neighbours, as well as a small community of Jews who lived from the export of citrons to Europe for Jewish liturgical use. The British acquired it in 1814 and soon ceded it to the rapacious Ali Pasha of Ioánnina; the townspeople collected their holy relics and moved to Corfu and Paxí. Párga now enjoys 100 percent hotel occupancy (mostly from package tours) from early July through to early September, although out of season it still makes an atmospheric stop.

Oracle of the dead

Some 22km (14 miles) southeast, beside **Mesopótamos** village, lies the **Necromanteion** ❹ (Nekromándio; daily 8.30am–3pm) of Acheron, the venerable oracle of the dead described by Circe in *The Odyssey*. Today, the Ahérondas River (one of the legendary rivers swirling around Hades) has silted up the surrounding agricultural plain, but in Homeric times the oracle was a suitably mysterious, tree-fringed island in a lagoon. Suppliants entered the sanctuary via a maze of corridors and were then lowered by a pulley into a vaulted underground chamber to experience whatever spectral hoax the resident priests had concocted.

The Ahérondas enters the sea at **Ammoudiá** just 5km (3 miles) to the west. The river makes bathing at the beach here cold, and should you choose to stay the night, the mosquitoes are out in force after dark. But lunching at the row of tavernas on the pedestrianised quay, where tour boats for hire to the Necromanteion bob at anchor, is exceedingly pleasant; and a small but excellent visitor information centre (Mon–Sat erratic hours; free) at the town entrance covers the natural history and ethnology of the area.

Inland from the Necromanteion, closer to its source, the Ahérondas squeezes through a spectacular gorge. From the village of **Glykí** ❺, a side track signposted for the "Skála Dzavélenas" dead-ends at the start of the *skála*: a spectacular 90-minute path down to the river bed and up into the realm of the Souliots, a Christian tribe never completely subdued by the Ottomans. From Glykí, continue south another 30km (19 miles) to the combined side turning for **Zálongo** and ancient Kassope. The former, a mountain top monastery of little intrinsic interest, was witness to a dramatic incident in 1803 which has since become a staple of Greek nationalist legend known by every schoolchild: trapped by Ali Pasha's forces, several dozen Souliot women fled to a nearby pinnacle, where – rather than submit to the enemy – they danced off the edge into thin air clutching their children. A hideous 1961 sculpture by aptly named Georgios Zongolopoulos celebrates their defiance.

Kassope, Nikopolis and Préveza

Nearby, **Kassope** ❻ (daily 8.30am–3pm, may be open other times) is less visited and eminently rewarding: a minor Hellenistic city whose jumbled

Nikopolis, "City of Victory", was founded by the emperor Augustus.

ruins are matched by a fine view over the Ionian Sea and Lefkáda island. No views are to be had from the artificial Roman city of **Nikopolis** ❼, some 15km (9 miles) south and 600 metres (2,000ft) below, but in recent years the site has been tidied up and made more comprehensible, especially the theatre, and three superb floor mosaics in the Dometios basilica. A site museum (daily summer 8am–8.30pm, winter 8.30am–3pm), 2km south towards Préveza, ably documents Roman and early Christian life here with statuary, coins, household implements and grave goods.

Préveza ❽, once a sleepy, shabby provincial capital, has also been spruced up, partly to cater for package tourists in transit between Áktio airport and the fine beaches to the north or Lefkáda. In its old bazaar, with rather more character than Párga's, a clutch of restaurants still offer the gulf's famous sardines, and summer nightlife is loud and varied. A few years ago, a tunnel under the gulf finally replaced the old RO-RO ferry ride across to Áktio.

Artá and Byzantine churches

Some 50km (31 miles) over on the far side of the gulf lies **Árta** ❾, the ancient Ambracia and capital of King Pyrrhus (he of the original pyrrhic victory). It later became the seat of the Despotate of Epirus, and retains a legacy of churches from that era. Most notable is the enormous, cubic **Panagía Parigorítissa** (Tue–Sun 8.30am–3pm), which dates from the late 13th century and betrays Italian influences in its palazzo-like exterior. High in the dome, supported by a gravity-defying cantilever system, floats a magnificent mosaic of the Pandokrátor (Christ in Majesty); it's the finest on the mainland after Dafní near Athens, despite damage from World War II bombing by the Italians.

In the citrus groves around the town lie other late Byzantine churches and monasteries, the most beautiful of which is **Panagía Vlahernón** in the village of **Vlahérna**, 6km (4 miles) to the north. Despot Michael II added the domes in the 13th century, and is thought to be entombed

FACT

Áktio, the promontory dovetailing with Préveza at the mouth of the Amvrakikós Gulf, was Roman Actium, also the name of the naval battle in which Octavian defeated Anthony and Cleopatra's forces in 31 BC. Octavian then named himself Emperor Augustus and established Nikopolis, "Victory City", nearby.

Church of Panagía Parigorítissa.

The Aslan Pasha Mosque, now the Municipal Museum, has fascinating relics of Ioánnina's colourful past.

Across Lake Pamvótis to the city of Ioánnina.

inside. A magnificent floor mosaic is on view under glass near the altar.

Ioánnina

Lining the shores of **Lake Pamvótis** (Pamvótida), spread below the stark face of Mount Mitsikéli, **Ioánnina**  has been one of Greece's great cities for nearly 1,000 years: a beacon of Hellenic culture, a traders' *entrepôt* and, in the 19th century (its last glorious epoch), the capital of the infamous Ali Pasha. Today the town remains one of Greece's liveliest provincial centres.

Ioánnina's layout is testimony to Ali's dubious legacy. While he left behind the city's most distinctive monuments (its mosques, and the redoubtable Kástro in its present form), he also had much of the city burned to deny it to a besieging Ottoman army, sent by the sultan to put down his unruly vassal in 1820. This, along with a 1960s penchant for

large apartment blocks, has resulted in the relentlessly modern Ioánnina which lies outside the old town.

The wide expanse of central **Platía Pýrrou**, joined to the plazas of Akadimías and Dimokratías and lined by various public buildings, makes an obvious starting-point for a city tour. Just east of Dimokratías stands the archaeological museum (Tue–Sun 9am–4pm), home to a fine collection of bronzes and tablets inscribed with questions for the Dodona oracle.

Except for a couple of cinemas with good first-run fare, this area is no longer the main nocturnal hub of Ioánnina. That has shifted downhill along Avérof towards the Kástro to take better advantage of the town's setting, past two shop fronts selling the famous local bougátsa (custard or cheese pie) at Dimokratías 2 and Avérof 3 respectively. State-of-the-art late-night bars cluster at the far end of Ethnikís Andístasis, in a former tradesmen's bazaar by the lake, and around Platía Mavíli, on the opposite side of the citadel. On summer nights, the latter – better known as Mólos – throbs

ALI PASHA IN IOÁNNINA

Unlike most large Greek centres, Ioánnina's history does not predate early Christian times, when an earthquake blocked the natural drainages of the surrounding plain and thus created the lake. Its name derives from an early church of St John the Baptist, long since vanished. After the Latin conquest of Constantinople in 1204 and the establishment of the Despotate of Epirus, Ioánnina grew in size and importance as refugees from "The City" swelled its population. It surrendered to the Ottomans in the 15th century; in 1788, Ali Pasha designated this town of 35,000 inhabitants (large for that time) his headquarters. Nicknamed "the Lion of Ioánnina", this maverick Albanian Muslim tyrant paid only minimal allegiance to the Ottoman sultan while establishing an autonomous fiefdom.

with townspeople taking an evening stroll along the waterfront, which is lined with vendors selling roast corn, halvás and bootleg CDs of local clarinet music from gas-lit pushcarts.

Kástro, the five-gated, walled precinct of various Epirot rulers including Ali Pasha himself, best conjures up Ioánnina's colourful past. A tangle of alleyways rises to a fortified promontory jutting out into the lake; at the lower corner looms the **Aslan Pasha Mosque,** now home to the Municipal Ethnographic Museum (daily summer 8am–8pm, winter 9am–4pm), with its diverse collection of Epirot costumes, jewellery and donations from the city's once-large Jewish community.

One of Ali Pasha's most infamous exploits – involving Kyra Frosini, the beautiful Greek mistress of Ali's eldest son – is supposed to have taken place near the mosque-museum. In the most common variant of the tale, Ali punished the girl for resisting his advances by having her and 17 female companions tied up in weighted sacks and drowned in the lake. Islamophobic-kitsch postcards of the incident are still sold, depicting wild-eyed "barbarians" and swooning Greek maidens in the clutches of their tormentors.

At the summit of the citadel looms the **Fethiye Tzami** (Victory Mosque) and one of Ali's heavily restored palaces – today an indifferent Byzantine Museum (summer Mon 12.30–7pm, Tue–Sun 8am–7pm, winter Tue–Sun 8am–5pm). The former treasury nearby makes an appropriate showcase for displays on the city's traditional silver industry.

After defying the sultan for three decades, Ali finally met his end on the islet of **Nisí,** on the far side of the visibly polluted lake (bus-boats make the trip from Mólos all day until 11pm). A small house in the grounds of Ágios Pandelímon monastery was his last hide-out; here, trapped on the upper storey by a Turkish assassin, Ali was shot through the floorboards then decapitated.

Monasteries with more peaceful histories, and a fine island loop walk, lie in the opposite direction. The nearest to Nisí village, **Agíou Nikoláou Filanthropinón,** contains vivid

Ioánnina's lake and Aslan Pasha Mosque.

The monastery of Agíou Nikoláou Filanthropinón, near the island-village of Nissí, is worth a visit for its vivid frescoes.

Dodona's theatre.

late-Byzantine frescoes; some depict unusually gruesome martyrdoms, while others, by the entrance, depict ancient sages such as Plutarch, Aristotle and Thucydides.

Diversions around Ioánnina

Some 20km (12 miles) south of Ioánnina lies **Dodona** ⑪ (Dodóni), Epirus's main archaeological site (daily June–Aug 8.30am–5pm, Sept–May 8.30am–3pm), nestling in a valley at the foot of Mount Tómaros. According to Herodotus, its oracle (the oldest in Greece and, until the 4th century BC, the most important) was established by a priestess abducted from a similar one in Egyptian Thebes. Zeus – considered resident in the trunk of a holy oak tree – was worshipped here, priests and priestesses deciphering the rustlings of the leaves which were the god's sacred pronouncements. The carefully restored **theatre,** dating from the 3rd-century reign of King Pyrrhus, has a capacity of 17,000 spectators – always far too large for the needs of the little town that existed here from 1000 BC until early Byzantine times. It is now, sadly, roped off; foundations of the Zeus sanctuary lie beyond it.

Though now superseded by the Vía Egnatía expressway south of town, the old highway east into Thessaly curls clockwise around the lake. This road passes **Pérama** (daily summer 8am–8pm, winter 8am–sunset), one of Greece's most spectacular cave systems, on the outskirts of Ioánnina. Then, after a long, twisting ascent, the village of **Métsovo** ⑫, 58km (36 miles) from Ioánnina, appears in a ravine below. It ranks as the "capital" of the Vlach, famous for its imposing houses, handicrafts, cheeses and the traditional costumes still worn by some of the older inhabitants.

Apart from the wonderful frescoes covering the interior of the medieval monastery of Ágios Nikólaos, a short walk below town, the only other recognised sight is the **Arhondikó Tosítsa Museum** (Fri–Wed 9am–1.30pm, 4–6pm, winter 3–5pm; guided tours only), its reconstructed interior displaying fine woodwork and textiles.

Unlike so many Greek mountain villages, Métsovo is thriving: local worthies who made their fortunes abroad have set up endowments to encourage local industry, such as the nearby ski resort whose clients periodically fill the dozen or so hotels – of a better standard than most in Ioánnina.

East of Métsovo towards the Metéora in Thessalía (Thessaly), the Katára Pass ("Curse Pass", 1,694m/5,557ft) for decades accommodated the highest paved road in the country, but this is now abandoned and absolutely impassable since the Vía Egnatía opened.

The Zagorohória

The road northwest out of Ioánnina leads to the region of **Zagóri** which forms a culturally and geographically distinct region of Epirus. Its 46 villages – called the Zagorohória – lie in an area bounded by the Métsovo–Ioánnina–Kónitsa highway and the Aóös River. Because of the region's infertile soil, local men emigrated to major commercial centres in Eastern Europe during the Ottoman era, subsequently returning to their homeland with considerable wealth. This allowed locals to hire a representative to send taxes to the sultan directly rather than suffer from tax-farmers, securing a large measure of autonomy.

Central Zagóri is best reached by the side road some 14km (9 miles) out of Ioánnina, prominently marked for the **Víkos Gorge. Vítsa** village has fine traditional houses, a shaded central square, one of the oldest churches in the region (Ágios Nikólaos), and the easiest trail access to the floor of the gorge, the intricately engineered Skála Vítsas. Just up the road, more frequented **Monodéndri** ⓭ supports a taverna offering local cuisine on its lower plaza, near the photogenic basilica of Ágios Athanásios flanking the classic path descending to the gorge. For the less committed, either the 1990s-vintage, rather tasteless *kalderími* (cobbled path) to the eyrie of Agía Paraskeví monastery, or the 7-km

(4-mile) drive up to the Oxiá overlook, will afford breathtaking views.

From the junction below Vítsa, the easterly main road passes the turning for exquisite **Dílofo** on its way to the major villages of Kípi, Kapésovo and Tsepélovo. **Kípi** ⓮ stands nearest to a much-photographed cluster of 18th- and 19th-century packhorse bridges, the most famous of which is the three-arched Plakída span. East of Kípi, **Negádes** has a frescoed basilica, one of the best examples of the Zagorian style, while above and to the north perches Kapésovo, with a rural museum in its enormous old school.

Vradéto

Kapésovo also marks the start of a one-hour path incorporating the most amazingly sinuous of all Zagorian *kalderímia* (paths) ending at **Vradéto,** the highest (1,340 metres/4,400ft) – and formerly most desolate – village in the area, now enjoying a mild renaissance (although the winter population is still only seven). Continue on foot for about 40 minutes and you will

EAT

Alas, Nisí's tavernas are touristy and poor in quality; if Ioanninans want a lakeside meal, they patronise the half-dozen restaurants which line **Pamvotídas,** the shoreline street heading northwest from Mólos.

Inside the caves at Pérama.

Pápingo Trail

The four-to-five-day hiking loop outlined below begins and ends in the Pápingo villages where there is plentiful accommodation, as well as reliable tavernas.

Be prepared to hike into and out of Pápingo, along the trail linking it to Klidoniá village on the Ioánnina–Kónitsa highway, if you happen not to coincide with the bus service. The alpine refuge on Astráka col, just visible from Megálo Pápingo, is open from May to October (www.astrakarefuge. com or tel: 6973 223100 to reserve bunks). It is a 900-metre (2,950-ft) ascent of at least three hours, with water available at regular intervals. If the refuge is full, camp near the spring at the north end of the seasonal **Xiróloutsa pond** (15-minute path descent east from the col). Spend the balance of the day with a short walk (1 hr each way) up to **Drakólimni,** an alpine tarn at

Pápingo peaks.

2,050 metres (6,725ft) altitude, ideal for views and picnics, just northwest of the 2,500-metre (8,200-ft) Gamíla peak.

A five-to-seven-hour hike the next day takes you between mounts Astráka and Gamíla, through alpine meadows grazed by cattle, and past the head of the Mégas Lákkos Gorge to Tsepélovo (steep final descent; net altitude loss of 850 metres/2,800ft). Water is scarce, so plan accordingly. You should have a comfortable overnight stay in one of Tsepélovo's dozen hotels and smaller inns, although reservations are advisable during July and August.

From the ravine flanking Tsepélovo to the west, a crumbled but discernible *kalderími* climbs the cliff to the uplands towards Vradéto; after about 90 minutes you are forced onto a paved road for the final 45 minutes. From Vradéto (café serving drinks only), descend the amazing *skála* to Kapésovo (45 minutes), then use the old dirt track (not the asphalt highway) to arrive in **Koukoúli** within the next 45 minutes and in time for lunch. You can stay overnight here at the single inn, or carry on eastwards to Kípi (another 45 minutes), which has another taverna as well as several inns.

From either Koukoúli or Kípi, there are marked routes into the upper end of the Víkos Gorge, crossing it by the Misíou bridge and ascending the stair-*kalderími* to Vítsa (2 hrs), with abundant accommodation and a taverna or two. A three-hour track partly shortcuts the road up to Monodéndri, 300 metres (985ft) above Kípi, with several more inns and tavernas.

A signposted, well-renovated *kalderími* takes you down to the usually dry bed of the Víkos Gorge (45 minutes). A fairly strenuous path marked as the O3 route negotiates the length of the canyon, on its true left bank after the first few minutes. At the intersection of the gorge and the Mégas Lákkos side canyon (2.5 hrs), a potable spring flows (unreliable after July). Continue through thick forest, then open pasture, before reaching the movable sources of the Voïdomátis River (4.5 hrs from Monodéndri), which well out of the base of the Pýrgi formations.

Bearing left on an obvious cobbled path leads to **Vitsikó** (Víkos) village, 45 minutes away, where you will find two inns; the O3 route crosses the river, heading up and right, reaching either of the Pápingos within two hours, for a day's total of 6.5 hours. About 90 minutes along, there is a divide in the path where you cross a stream on the left to head up to Megálo Pápingo, rather than continue straight to Mikró Pápingo.

reach Belói viewpoint, more or less opposite Oxiá. Twelve kilometres (7 miles) further, the paved road arrives at **Tsepélovo** ⑮, flanked by rural monasteries and crammed with more mansions. Frescoed Rangóvou monastery stands just below.

Back on the Ioánnina-Kónitsa highway, you pass through **Kalpáki,** where, in the early winter of 1940–41, the Greeks halted the Italian invasion, rolling Fascist troops back into the snowy Albanian Mountains for a season of hell; a small roadside museum (summer daily 9.30am–1pm & 5.30–8pm, winter 9.30am–3pm) tells the tale in full. Just beyond, a 19-km (12-mile) side road heads east to the focus of most Zagorian tourism, the paired villages of **Pápingo** ⑯, **Megálo** and **Mikró.** They have become quite fashionable, especially during peak holiday seasons, but there is no denying their superlative setting at the foot of the 600-metre (1,970-ft) Pýrgi, the sheer outriders of Mount Gamíla. This massif (the heart of the national park) offers fine hiking, most notably to newt-filled **Drakólimni** (Dragon Lake).

The icy **Voïdomátis River,** popular with kayakers, drains out of the lower Víkos canyon at Klidoniá, where a lovely old bridge marks the edge of the national park a few hundred metres in from the busy highway. An even bigger one spans the Aóös River some 10km (6 miles) north, where it exits some narrows to a vast floodplain. A 90-minute walk along the southern bank of the Aóös Gorge leads below steep, forested slopes to the **Stomíou monastery,** magnificently perched on a cliff.

Kónitsa ⑰ itself offers a fine view of the floodplain, but an earthquake in 1996 and massive shelling during the civil war put paid to any real architectural distinction here. For that, head 23km (14 miles) west to the monastery and namesake village of **Molyvdosképastos,** just where the Aóös enters Albania. The monastery's early 14th-century church betrays a Serbian influence with its high, stovepipe dome. Early in the 1990s, it was reinhabited by rather zealous monks, who encourage your conversion on the spot.

Exhibits in the Arhondikó Tosítsa Museum, Métsovo.

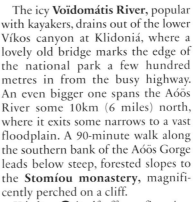

Métsovo elders.

ZAGORIAN PEOPLE AND LANDSCAPE

Zagóri's villages differ markedly: the east is populated largely by Vlachs (more properly, Arouman), a people rooted in Greece since antiquity, speaking a Romance language and living as caravan-drovers and shepherds driving their flocks from summer to winter pastures. Early in 1944, the occupying Germans retaliated against local resistance by burning most of the eastern villages, which were later rebuilt haphazardly. The western and central Zagorohória show more of a Slav/Albanian influence in place names and architecture; happily, most survived the war unscathed and today constitute one of Greece's showpieces.

The Zagorian landscape embraces sheer rock faces, limestone dells, dense forests, upland pasture and deep canyons. The national park at its core, comprising the Víkos Gorge plus the Voïdomátis and Aóös rivers, was established partly to protect a threatened population of bears, lynx, wolves and birds of prey. Yet even in the remotest corners there are signs of man: a post-Byzantine monastery with belfry, or a graceful, slender-arched bridge from the Ottoman period. Unfortunately, the pastoral culture that used to feature prominently is in sharp decline; EU subsidy policy means that few shepherds now occupy the high pastures, and unattended cattle herds have mostly replaced the tenanted sheepfolds of the past.

Due east of Kónitsa looms 2,637-metre (8,650-ft) **Mount Smólikas**, roof of the Píndos and second summit of Greece after Mount Olympos. From several of the Vlach villages along the Aóös north bank, trails lead up towards the peak and yet another "Dragon Lake", and then onward to either Kerásovo village on the northern toes of the mountain, or to Samarína at the eastern end of the range.

The 105-km (65-mile) road from Kónitsa to **Neápolis** is the main paved connection between Epirus and western Macedonia. It follows the valley of the Sarandáporos River upstream, between Smólikas and Mount Grámmos, site of the final battles of the civil war, passing faded blue-painted graffiti "Elefthería Gia Vória Ípiros!" ("Freedom for Northern Epirus!") – an expression of lingering irredentist sentiment for the Albanian portion of Epirus, home to perhaps 70,000 remaining Greek Orthodox.

Hiking in the Píndos

The North Píndos offer many rewarding hiking routes, from strenuous, multiday, high-level treks to various interconnected day hikes. Landscapes vary from the limestone dells of the Gamíla uplands to the forested Víkos Gorge floor. In these days of global warming, the best seasons are no longer high summer but from mid-May to mid-June, and September to early October. Although the local trail system is extensive on paper, it is unevenly maintained and often badly waymarked; the usual method is multicoloured paint splodges or, for the long-distance O3 route, metal diamond-shaped symbols nailed to trees.

The 1:50,000 *Pindus Zagori* topographic map issued by Anavasi cartographers (available in Greece and the UK) is essential if not infallible, as is a keen sense of direction, an ability to double-check trail information from villagers, and a good sense of humour. In any month, the Píndos weather can change rapidly with little warning, so rain gear and a light tent are essential – the latter also because indoor accommodation can fill up suddenly.

Kónitsa bridge over the Aóös river.

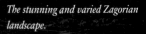
The stunning and varied Zagorian landscape.

THESSALONÍKI

Greece's second city does not live in the shadow of Athens. It has its own distinctive character, with more Balkan influences and a host of splendid Byzantine churches.

To a visitor approaching by sea, contemporary **Thessaloníki** ❶ presents the uniform facade of modern apartment blocks characteristic of so many Mediterranean seaside cities. At the beginning of this century, the same view was marked by minarets rising elegantly from a tile-roofed town picturesquely climbing between medieval ramparts to an upper quarter, with vast cemeteries outside the walls. When more than half the town was destroyed by the Great Fire of August 1917, British and French architects (who were accompanying Allied expeditionary forces at the time) were promptly commissioned to produce a new town plan.

Surviving Art Deco buildings enhance the wide, sea-facing boulevards they designed, although their advice to ban high-rises was disregarded. But the fire spared much, including the old hillside quarter of **Kástra**. Roman ruins, Byzantine churches, Ottoman public and domestic buildings, and displaced Jewish tombstones lie encircled by Roman and Byzantine walls, or scattered alongside asphalt boulevards and pedestrian lanes. And after years of neglect, this great architectural heritage has been signposted and selectively renovated.

One of Greece's liveliest and most interesting cities, Thessaloníki was

founded in 316–315 BC by the Macedonian king, Kassander, who named it after his wife, and it rose into prominence under the Romans, boosted by their **Via Egnatia** "trunk road", which stretched from the Adriatic to the Hellespont (Dardanelles). Saint Paul visited twice, and wrote two Epistles to the Thessalonians; Christianity (and the city) got further boosts from the Byzantine emperors, especially Theodosius (who issued his edict here, banning paganism) and Justinian, who

Main Attractions

PLATÍA ARISTOTÉLOUS
MUSEUM OF BYZANTINE CULTURE
ROTUNDA OF ÁGIOS GEÓRGIOS
ÁGIOS DIMÍTRIOS
KÁSTRA
LEFKÓS PÝRGOS (WHITE TOWER)
EPTAPYRGÍO
MODIÁNO MARKET

The Arch of Galerius.

began new churches to supplement those adapted from Roman structures. Despite Slavic and Arab raids, frequent earthquakes, fires, adjacent malarial swamps and a spotty water supply, resilient Thessaloníki prospered. Even in temporary decline, it made a rich prize for the Ottomans in 1430.

Sephardic settlers

After 1500, large numbers of Sephardic Jewish refugees from Spain and Portugal settled here, giving Salonica – as they called it – its most distinctive trait for the next four centuries. On the eve of the Balkan Wars, they accounted for just over half the population of 140,000, making it the largest Jewish city of that era. In 1943, 70,000 remained to be deported to the Nazi death camps, and fewer than 1,000 remain today.

Following the three wars leading up to 1923, the city came to epitomise a Greek refugee town: in absolute numbers, Athens may have had more, but by proportion of population, Thessaloníki contains more

citizens with Anatolian ancestry than anywhere else in Greece. There are abundant Turkish surnames (such as Dereli and Mumtzis) and spicy cuisine rarely found elsewhere in Greece; indeed, the city has some of the best places to eat in the country. Its own self-deprecating nicknames have long been I *Protévousa tón Prosfigón* (The Refugee Capital), after the ring of 1920s settlements, all prefixed "Néa" (New), across eastern Macedonia, and *Ftohomána* (Mother of the Poor).

But 21st-century Thessaloníki is not all changing demographics. After years in Athens' shadow, it has come into its own. The International Fair held every October in permanent grounds by the university promotes the city as a Balkan trade centre and the natural gateway to the upper Balkans. Thessaloníki is confidently on the move, with innovative restaurants and clubs occupying historic buildings, its native musicians (such as Sokratis Malamas) frequently at the forefront of Greek song.

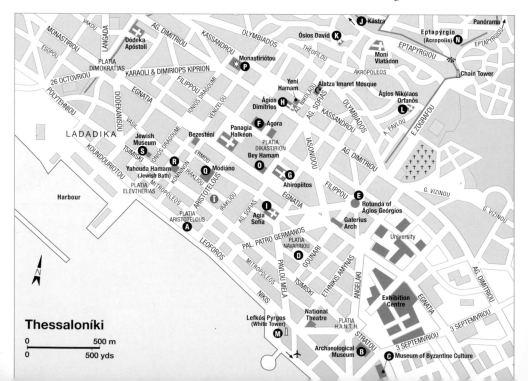

Thessaloníki

A tour of the city

Platía Aristotélous  is the hub of the downtown city, stretching up from the waterfront towards the Roman Agora and the dominant church of Ágios Dimítrios. The sunny cafés and bars are popular here, especially in the early evening, while morning shoppers enjoy the daily market to the west, and lunchtime and evening diners fill the pavement tables of market restaurants to the east. Leofóros Níkis follows the seafront and is a good place for a stroll or a fashionable bar-hop from the port to the White Tower, with views across the wide blue bay to Mount Ólympos.

The city has, unsurprisingly, been as hard hit by the financial crisis and austerity measures as anywhere in Greece, so plans for an underground metro system, following the line of Egnatía, and for the seafront road to be sunk below ground to leave the zone free for pedestrians and the bar clientele to enjoy, have both suffered delays and are not expected to be completed for some years.

At the eastern end of the seafront, behind the White Tower (more on this later), is the **archaeological museum** (summer Mon 10.30am–8pm, Tue–Sun 8am–8pm, winter Tue–Sun 8.30am–3pm; entrance fee; www.amth.gr), which displays Macedonian, Hellenistic and Roman finds from the entire region, including the notable **Síndos** collections. Sumptuous jewellery and household effects in gold, silver and bronze vie for your attention. Just beyond the Archaeological Museum is the **Museum of Byzantine Culture** (summer Mon 10.30am–8pm, winter Mon 8.30am–5pm, Tue–Sun 8.30am–3pm; combined tickets recommended; www.mbp.gr), with artefacts from the Early Christian period (4th–7th century) through to the Middle Byzantine period (8th–12th century). The exhibits in this modern building are beautifully displayed and clearly explained; among the most impressive pieces are a 5th-century mosaic floor, wall paintings from a local house, and some extraordinary early textiles.

On the waterfront.

During Ottoman rule, most Byzantine churches were converted into mosques, and their interiors coated in whitewash. This fresco, from Ágios Dimítrios in Thessaloníki, is one that survived.

Great people-watching on the waterfront.

Roman Thessaloníki can be seen in **Platía Navarínou** in the shape of the excavated remains of the Hippodrome and the **Palace of Galerius Caesar,** the Christian-hating Emperor who martyred the city's patron saint, Demetrius, in AD 305. And on the inland side of Via Egnatia survives the western part of **Galerius's** triumphal **arch**, erected over this highway in AD 297 to celebrate a victory over the Persians. The reliefs on the arch repay close inspection, showing, as well as Galerius himself, Diocletian and Julius Caesar.

The other remaining building in this Roman complex is the **Rotunda of Ágios Geórgios** (Tue–Sun 8.30am–3pm; free), just northwest of the arch. Perhaps intended as Galerius's mausoleum, this is one of the few remaining examples of circular Roman architecture, enduring largely through conversion into a church, then a mosque. Glorious 4th-century wall mosaics partially survive, high up inside the dome and recesses; the truncated minaret is the city's last surviving one.

The largest Greco-Roman site is the **Agora** or forum (AD 32–138) on Platía Dikastiríon, uncovered in 1966, which was the social and religious centre of ancient Thessaloníki. Its theatre provides a summer concert space.

Byzantine Thessaloníki

More fine and important Byzantine churches survive in Thessaloníki than in any other Greek city. The earliest examples are clear adaptations of the colonnaded Roman basilica, in turn descended from Greek temples, with the outermost columns replaced by walls. The most significant are near the Agora: 5th-century **Ahiropíitos** (hunt for fine mosaic patches under the arches, between ornate columns) and its heavily restored contemporary, **Ágios Dimítrios** (Mon 12.30–7pm, Tue–Sat 8am–8pm, Sun 10.30am–8pm), the largest church in Greece. Both are double-aisled basilicas with a central nave.

Ágios Dimítrios is the city's main church. It was founded shortly after the saint's demise, on the site of his martyrdom and was almost entirely rebuilt after the 1917 fire, which spared only the apse and the colonnades. Six small mosaics of the 5th to 7th century, featuring the saint, survive mostly above the columns standing on either side of the altar. The fire was responsible for the rediscovery of the crypt (Sun 10.30am–8pm, Mon 12.30–7pm, Tue–Sat 8am–8pm; free), which is thought to be partly constructed from the Roman baths where the saint was imprisoned; a reliquary found on the site supports this. Also here are the attractive remains of a fountain that previously fed a fishpond.

Below the Agora to the west of Ahiropíetos is **Panagía Halkéon** (daily 7.30am–12 noon), founded in 1028. The brick-built church is in the shape of a cross and contains a cycle of frescoes dating back to the 11th century. During the Ottoman occupation, it served as the mosque of the local coppersmiths.

South of Ahiropíetos is the 8th-century **Agía Sofía** ❶ (Holy Wisdom; daily 7am–1pm, 5–6.30pm; free), built in conscious imitation of its namesake in Constantinople. This one, 10 metres (33ft) wide, has a vivid Ascension, with the Apostles watching Christ borne heavenward by angels, rather than the *Pandokrátor* (Christ Enthroned) that became the rule later. In the apse and the *ikonostásis*, you can detect traces of an earlier mosaic of the Cross behind the Virgin Enthroned. It was one of a pair, and the other figural cross survives in the adjacent vault.

The steep alleys of **Kástra** ❿ are about a 20-minute walk from the seafront. Since the late 1980s, this neighbourhood of dilapidated half-timbered houses below the acropolis (citadel) has been transformed from poor and despised to renovated and trendy, with scattered tavernas and cafés.

Tiny 5th- or 6th-century **Ósios Davíd** ⓚ (Mon–Sat 9am–12 noon and 4–6pm), all that's left of the **Látomos Monastery**, is tucked away in this district. The west end of this church has vanished, but visit for the sake of an outstanding early mosaic in the apse, revealed in 1921 when Ottoman whitewash was removed. It depicts the vision of the Prophet Ezekiel of Christ Emmanuel, shown as a beardless youth seated on the arc of heaven, surrounded by the symbols of the Evangelists. Together, the mosaics of Ósios Davíd and Ágios Dimítrios rank as the best pre-Iconoclastic sacred art in Greece, and predate the more famous work at Ravenna in Italy.

Another batch of churches all well uphill from the Via Egnatia date from the 13th and 14th centuries – examples of a cultural "golden age" at odds with the Byzantine Empire's political decline and the numerous disasters visited on Thessaloníki from the 10th to the 12th century. Financial constraints meant that frescoes, rather than mosaics, were the preferred ornamentation in these churches, most of them attached to now-extinct monasteries. By far the best of these is **Ágios Nikólaos Orfanós** ❶ (Tue–Sun 8.30am–2.45pm; free), at the northeast edge of Kástra. Among the

FACT

Churches often fly flags showing a two-headed eagle on a yellow background. This is the symbol of Byzantium. The Patriarch of the Greek Orthodox Church still resides in the ancient Byzantine capital of Constantinople, today's Istanbul.

The Roman Rotunda, built in the 4th century AD, is now the church of Ágios Geórgios.

better-preserved and more unusual frescoes are *Christ Mounting the Cross* and *Pilate Sitting in Judgment*, the very image of a Byzantine scribe; in *Washing of the Feet*, it seems the talented painter inserted an image of himself on horseback, wearing a turban.

At the nearby monastery of **Vlatadon**, the only one among the city's 20-odd to still be occupied by monks, you may hear peacocks cry. The monastery was founded in around 1360 by the Empress Anna Paleologina, but 11th-century wall paintings survive in the small church, which is open during services.

The city walls

Thessaloníki's seafront **Lefkós Pýrgos** (**Thessaloníki**)  (White Tower; Tue–Sun 8.30am–3pm; www.lpth.gr), effectively the city's logo, was built during the brief Venetian occupation as an addition to the Roman-Byzantine walls. The Ottomans used it as a prison; that, and the massacre of unruly Janissaries here in 1826, earned it the epithet "Bloody Tower". The Greeks whitewashed it

Panagía Halkéon, one of the city's many Byzantine churches.

post-1912 – thus the new alias – and then removed the pigment in 1985. A spiral staircase, with small windows, emerges at a lovely café and then the crenellated roof terrace, affording fine views over the seafront and bay, and up to Kástra.

The vanished curtain wall leading inland from here past the university linked the White Tower with the **Chain Tower**, the northeastern corner of the fortifications; beyond it lies the **Eptapýrgio**  (Yedi Küle in Turkish), the Seven Towers Fortress, on the northeastern corner of the old walled **acropolis**. The seven towers on the northern side of the Eptapýrgio incorporate part of the Early Christian acropolis walls, and the six towers on the southern side were built during the Middle Byzantine period. The Ottomans made considerable additions to the fortress, transforming it into a jail in the late 19th century, and it continued to function as a jail until the 1980s. It is now sometimes used as an exhibition space.

Ottoman and Jewish Thessaloníki

Thessaloníki was taken by the Ottomans in 1430, 23 years before the fall of Constantinople. The new overlords converted most churches into mosques during the first century of their rule, tacking on minarets and whitewashing over mosaics and frescoes. As a result, there are few purpose-built Ottoman mosques, though there are other interesting civic buildings. Worthy 15th-century specimens include the graceful Ishak Pasha or **Alatza Imaret Mosque** at the base of Kástra – around the corner from the **Yeni Hamam**, or bathhouse, engagingly restored as a bistro, concert hall and summer outdoor cinema – and the dilapidated **Hamza Bey Mosque** on the Via Egnatia, last used as the Alcazar cinema. It has yet to get the same treatment as the nearby **Bezesténi**, a refurbished six-domed covered market now tenanted by luxury shops. The nearby **Bey Hamam O** (Mon–Fri 11am–8pm, Sat noon–5pm), dating from 1444, has intact stalactite vaulting over the entrance and inside.

At the rear of the Turkish consulate, at 7 Apostolou Pavlou, stands the wooden house where Mustafa Kemal (Atatürk), founder of the Turkish republic, was born in 1881 (daily 10am–5pm; free). And a few hundred metres east of the archaeological museum, at the edge of the 19th-century "New Town", is the **Yeni Cami** or "New Mosque" – an Art Nouveau folly erected by the influential Ma'min (Dönme). This so-called crypto-Jewish sect followed the 17th-century self-proclaimed Messiah, Shabbetai Zvi, into Islam. In the mass exchange of populations between Greece and Turkey in 1923, most of the Ma'min were among the 100,000 Muslims who left the city.

By contrast, there are few tangible traces of Thessaloníki's Jewish past, owing to the 1917 fire and the Nazi desecration of cemeteries and synagogues in 1943. Only the Art Deco **Monastiriótou synagogue P**, near the Ministry of Northern Greece, survived the war. Centrepiece of the vast central market – which extends to either side of Aristotélous, selling everything from wooden furniture to live poultry – is the covered **Modiáno Q**, a fish, meat and produce-hall named after the Jewish family that established it. Their former mansion, out beyond the Yeni Cami, now houses the Folk and Ethnological Museum of Macedonia (Mon–Sat 9am–3pm, until 9pm on Weds), which has informative displays on housing, costumes and handicrafts. Though only half-occupied today, the Modiáno still supports several authentic, atmospheric *ouzerí* in the west arcade.

Close by, the Louloudádika Hamam or Flower-Market Bath was also known as the **Yahouda Hamam** or Jewish Bath **R**; the Jewish clientele is gone, but the flowers are still outside. In the same area, on Agíou Miná, is the

Jewish Museum of Thessaloníki S (Tue, Fri, Sun 11am–2pm, Wed, Thur 11am–2pm, 5pm–8pm; www.jmth.gr). This two-storey museum presents the history of the Jewish community in Thessaloníki and contains interesting material from the ancient, destroyed, Jewish cemetery.

Outside the city

For an escape from the city, try a half-day excursion to **Panórama**, an affluent village 11km (7 miles) to the east whose views justify its name; several *zaharoplastía* sell such Anatolian specialities as *salépi* (orchid-root drink), *dódurma* (Turkish ice cream) and *trígona*, triangular cream pastries. **Hortiátis**, 10km (6 miles) north of here, has since ancient times supplied Thessaloníki with water. It also retains some pines spared by arsonists, plus good tavernas. From either point, you can on a clear day look southwest across the Thermaïc Gulf to glimpse the bulk of **Mount Olympos** (Ólymbos) to the southwest, the traditional separation point between Macedonia and Thessaly.

EAT

For atmospheric bars, restaurants and clubs, head for Ladádika, the former red-light district and port quarter behind the passenger ferry terminal.

The view from the city walls.

MACEDONIA AND THRACE

Along with a landscape of fertile plains and forbidding mountains, you'll find a wondrous mix of peoples here – as well as the major holiday playground of Halkidikí.

Main Attractions
KASTORIÁ
PRÉSPA LAKES
DION
VERGÍNA
MOUNT ÁTHOS
KAVÁLA
PHILIPPI
XÁNTHI
DADIÁ FOREST RESERVE

Thessaloníki ❶ (see page 207), first city of northern Greece and "capital" of Macedonia and Thrace, stands halfway between Albania to the west and Turkey to the east, and scarcely 100km (60 miles) south of FYROM (the Former Yugoslav Republic of Macedonia) and Bulgaria – a boundary settled after World War I. Bordering so many Balkan states, into which ancient Macedonia (Makedonía) and ancient Thrace (Thráki) spread, has given the region great ethnic variety and

cultural richness. Northern Greece does not possess the magnificent archaeology and stunning temples of the centre and the south and its latitude spells a short summer season. But it does have some key sites, a large number of Byzantine churches and some handsome Ottoman-era domestic architecture; as well as varied and dramatic landscapes and exceptional areas of wildlife, from snow-capped mountains to broad, fertile plains. Dominating the southern part of this region is Mount Olympos, the highest mountain in Greece, which you can climb from Litóhoro (see page 218).

Northwest Macedonia

Coming from Epirus, you officially enter Macedonia just before **Pendálofos** ❷, the only place of any importance or appeal en route. Its fine stone houses – still in the Epirot style – straggle across the ravines which give the town its name ("Five-hills"). At **Neápolis** ❸, the road divides: north to Kastoriá, southeast to **Siátista** ❹. Perched on a bleak ridge some 20km (12 miles) from the fork, this small town is noted for its fine 18th-century mansions or *arhondiká* – the residences of the *árhons*, or leading citizens – offering a glimpse into the self-contained society that flourished here during late Ottoman times. Then a wealthy centre for fur-trading,

A fresco from Agíou Dionysíou, Áthos.

tanning, wine-making and a stopping point for caravans on the trade route to Vienna, Siátista declined when commercial networks changed after Greek independence.

Start with the **Nerandzópoulos mansion** on Platía Horí, whose warden has the keys to other interesting structures such as the **Manoúsi**, **Kanatsoúli** and **Poulikídou residences**. Visiting these will give you a good background for nearby Kastoriá, another town which prospered from the fur trade.

Returning north, the road follows the upper valley of the **Aliákmonas River**, the longest in Greece, whose 300-km (185-mile) course arcs from the Albanian border to the Thermaic Gulf. Soon you reach the **lake of Orestiáda**, or Kastoriá, almost divided in half by the eponymous town built on a peninsula. On the town's southern outskirts lies a significant military cemetery, the last resting place of government troops who were killed during the battle for Grámmos-Vítsi, which brought an end to the civil war. In the town itself, a lakeside plaza named after General James Van Fleet serves as a reminder that American equipment and advisers guaranteed a royalist victory over communist insurgency.

Kastoriá

Kastoriá **5** is one of northern Greece's more appealing spots, a peaceful mountain town on a peninsula jutting into a large tranquil lake, with a popular promenade of restaurants and bars. Its 54 surviving medieval churches indicate its importance in Byzantine times. Many were erected as private chapels by rich furrier families, and shops still sell myriad furry items, mostly made from mink. (*Kastóri* is the Greek for beaver, now extinct.)

The Byzantine art and architecture here is among Greece's finest, showing strong folk and Slav influences. You can see the best in a single morning, starting with the fine icon collection at

the **Byzantine Museum** (Tue–Sun 8.30am–3pm; free; the warden here also has control of the keys to most of the churches), and working your way south to the **Karyádis quarter**, with its fine old mansions.

Triple-aisled **Ágii Anárgyri** – built in 1018 by Emperor Basil II – sits at the northeast edge of town, overlooking the lake. Nearby **Ágios Stéfanos** is the second-oldest church in town (10th-century), again with intricately geometric masonry and an unusual women's gallery inside. South of the museum, tiny **Panagía Koumbelidíki** is unmistakable with its disproportionately tall, drum-shaped dome, the only one in town, painstakingly rebuilt after Italian bombing in 1940. There are some fine frescoes inside and a highly unusual Holy Trinity, complete with bearded God, in the barrel vault.

Continuing south and downhill, the extensive frescoes of the single-aisled basilica **Ágios Nikólaos Kasnítsi** are

Panagíaki Koumpelidíki is one of 54 medieval churches in Kastoriá.

Waterfall at Édessa.

The village of Ágios Germanós and the Préspa Lakes.

the best-preserved in Kastoriá; female saints predominate in the narthex, which long served as the women's section, while the image of the Virgin in the Assumption on the west wall is curiously reversed right-to-left. Finally, the **Taxiárhis tis Mitropóleos** is the oldest surviving church (9th-century), with a later (14th-century) fresco of the Virgin Platýtera adored by archangels in the apse.

In the low-lying Karyádis (Dóltso) district, inland from the southern lakefront, stand the restored **Natzís** and **Immanouíl arhondiká** (residences of the *árhons*, or leading citizens) of the same style and era (18th century) as those in Siátista. The **Folklore Museum** (Mon–Sat 9.30am–1pm, 4–7pm, Sun 11am–1pm, 4–7pm) is lodged in the Mansion of Nerantziz Aïvazís on nearby Kapetán Lázou. The refurbished mansion dates from the late 17th century when it stood on the lake shore, and it shows how the wealthy Christian and merchant Aïvazís family lived. From here, a narrow lake-shore

lane heads 2.5km (1.5 miles) east to **Panagía Mavriótissa** monastery, now in ruins apart from two Siamese-twin churches – one 11th-century, the other 14th, both with fine frescoes. Peacocks strut, providing a fine view for the diners who patronise the adjacent lake-view restaurant.

To the Préspa Lakes

Some 36km (22 miles) north of Kastoriá, following a branch of the Aliákmonas, is the side road to the **Préspa Lakes** ❻ basin. This atmospheric backwater, where the northwestern borders of Greece meet those of FYROM and Albania, was designated a Balkan Park by the governments of the three countries in 2000. There are two lakes: **Mikrí Préspa**, shallow and reedy, lying mostly in Greece, and deeper, reed-free **Megáli Préspa**, shared by Albania, FYROM and Greece.

MikríPréspa is the nesting ground for some extraordinary bird life, notably two endangered species of pelicans and pygmy cormorants, but also for a unique trout and a hardy breed

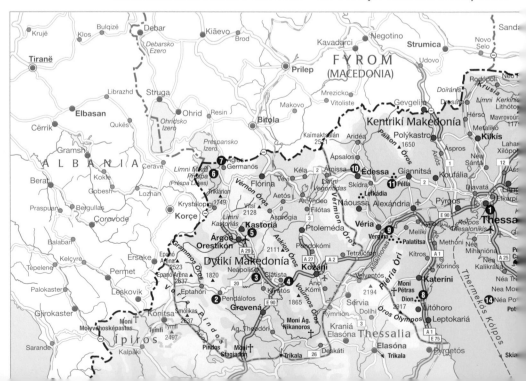

of small cattle. The bird life is most active in the spring. The cattle are in the surrounding hills, also a haven for bears and wolves, although you will be lucky to spot any of them.

The best single target in the region is **Ágios Germanós** ❼, which has a visitor centre, good lodging and two frescoed Byzantine churches. **Psarádes**, the only Greek village on **Megáli Préspa**, also has an information centre and more tourist facilities, and offers the opportunity to take a highly worthwhile boat excursion to the painted cave-church of **Panagía Eleoússa**. Mikrí's islet of **Ágios Ahíllios** has an evocatively ruined 10th-century basilica and is connected to the mainland by a 1-km (0.5-mile) long pontoon. The main road leading east passes through nondescript **Flórina**, worth a stop only for its wonderful Museum of Modern Art (daily summer 6–9pm, winter 5–8pm; free), then on towards Thessaloníki.

On the northern horizon, you will notice snowy **Mount Vóras** (Kaïmaktsalán). This area saw little

peace during the first half of the 20th century, with the Macedonian Struggles (1903–08), the Balkan Wars (1912–13), and a two-year battle in World War I between Serbs and Greeks on one side, Germans and Bulgarians on the other. World War II and subsequent civil war strife add to a narrative equalled in few parts of the globe.

Vergína, Véria and Pella

Traces of Phillip II of Macedonia (382–336 BC) who united the Greek people, and of his son Alexander the Great (356–323 BC), whose empire stretched as far as India, are scattered in a broad arc west to southwest of Thessaloníki, at the edges of the current flood plains of the Axiós and Aliákmonas rivers. In ancient times, the Thermaïc Gulf covered this plain, but the silt-bearing rivers have pushed the shoreline east. All of these sites can be toured with your own transport in a full day out of Thessaloníki.

Dion ❽, northeast of Mount Olympus (Ólympos), was founded by Macedonian kings both as a military mobilisation ground and a precinct

Pella's Lion Hunt mosaic.

closed). However, pride of place in the museum goes to a 1st-century BC hydraulis or water organ, a type of pipe organ and the oldest to be found in the world.

Vergína 9, on the south bank of the Aliákmonas, was formerly **Aigai**, the first Macedonian capital, and remained the royal necropolis. It got its modern name after the exchange of populations in 1923, when incoming Greeks called it after a fairytale queen. Now a Unesco World Heritage Site, the subterranean chamber tombs of Philip II and three others lay undiscovered until Manolis Andronikos of the Aristotle University of Thessaloníki broke through to the tombs on 8 November 1977. It was one of the most important archaeological discoveries of the 20th century. The dazzling treasures of the chamber tombs (summer Mon noon–7.30pm, Tue–Sun 8am–7.30pm, winter daily 8.30am–3pm), including gold artefacts, ivory carvings and vivid paintings, are impressively displayed as Andronikos found them. Lesser tombs (same hours) and a summer palace, the **Palatítsa** (closed for renovations), lie just up the hill.

holy to the Olympian gods; its ruins, dating largely from the Roman and Byzantine eras, were buried by an earthquake-triggered mudslide in the 5th century AD (daily summer 8am–7pm, winter 8.30am–3pm). Since 1990, well-preserved mosaics have been found here, the best – of Medusa – transferred to safekeeping in the completely modernised village museum (same hours except Mon summer 12.30–7pm, winter

Some 18km (11 miles) northwest, **Véria** sits at one end of an escarpment running north to Édessa. Extensive Ottoman neighbourhoods of vernacular houses have been preserved, and more than 35 Byzantine churches are open to the public. Begin at the Véria Byzantine Museum (Tue–Sun 8.30am–3pm), wonderfully housed in a restored 19th-century flour mill at Thomedoú 1, but don't miss the 14th-century wall paintings in the Hristós Monastery (Tue–Sun 8.30am– 2pm).

North of Véria, in the Mieza suburb of **Náoussa** (about 2km/under a mile from the centre), there are substantial and attractive grass-covered remains of the school of Aristotle (open access), and imposing Macedonian tombs can be visited at **Lefkádia** (Tue–Sun 8:30am–3pm).

Some 43km (27 miles) from Véria, **Édessa** 10 is unlike any other Greek

MOUNT OLYMPOS

The imposing bulk of Mt Olympos (Ólympos) – Greece's highest mountain at 2,917 metres (9,568ft) – dominates the horizon southwest of Thessaloníki. The ancient Greeks believed the mountain was the home of the gods, presided over by Zeus. Its summit defied climbers for years, not least because of the numerous bandits who lurked in the surrounding region. Sultan Mehmet IV is supposed to have attempted the mountain in 1669, but it was not until 1913 that two Swiss mountaineers with their Greek guide managed to scale the highest peak, Mýtikas ("the needle").

The climb is usually tackled from the village of Litóhoro, south of Kateríni, with an overnight stay in either the Giósos Apostolídis or Spílios Agápitos mountain refuge (book in advance during the summer through the SEO or EOS mountaineering clubs respectively, both of which have an office in Litóhoro). The climb itself is not technically difficult: the initial part is just a walk in, but the last section is steep and very exposed. You will need a good sense of balance and a head for heights, particularly when taking what is known as the Kakí Skála ("evil stairway") for the final few hundred metres. This overlooks the Kazánia chasm, a sheer drop of 500 metres (1,650ft).

town because of the numerous rivulets that wind through it heading for its waterfalls. A path leads down the ravine, through cascade mist, past a cave in the cliffside; upstream, on top of the bluff, is a medieval bridge serving the Via Egnatia. Offering further reasons to linger, the attractive 19th-century Városi quarter at the precipitous edge of town has a Folklore Museum (Tue–Sun 10am–6pm), with a nice collection of household items and traditional objects, and an Open-Air Water Museum (daily 10am–10pm), in a complex that includes the mills and the old hemp factory, now a café and occasional performance space.

Pella ⓫, a third of the way back to Thessaloníki, was the Macedonian capital after the mid-4th century BC. From here, Philip II ruled a united Greece after 338 BC, and here also his son Alexander studied under Aristotle – and trained for his fabled campaigns in the Orient. Most of the imperial capital is yet to be unearthed, but the superb mosaics of a lion hunt, Dionysos riding a panther, and other mythological scenes, more than justify a visit to the site and the museum (both summer Mon 1.30–8pm, Tue–Sun 8am–8pm, winter daily 8.30am–3pm).

East to Halkidikí

Many roads lead east out of Thessaloníki. One heads initially north to the town of **Kilkís** and the Greek shore of **Lake Doïránis**, then into the Strimónas river valley towards the road crossing into Bulgaria at **Promahónas**. On the way you can dip slightly south to the Límni Kerkinis wetlands, home to 300 species of birds at various times of year and a developing eco-tourism centre.

A more direct, northeasterly road leads to **Sérres** ⓬, important since Byzantine times and still a prosperous town. It was burned down by the retreating Bulgarians in 1913 and has been largely rebuilt, but two Byzantine churches remain, much altered by war and restoration: 11th-century **Ágii Theodóri** and 14th-century **Ágios Nikólaos**. A domed Ottoman building, called Bezesten, in the central

Mount Ólympos.

FACT

Porto Karrás is a gated community created by Greek ship-owner Yiannis Karrás in 1973. The Grand Resort has two massive 5-star hotels and the biggest private marina in northern Greece.

Ouranoúpoli on Halkidikí.

square serves as a museum (Tue–Sun 8am–2.30pm).

In a wooded mountain valley 19km (12 miles) north is another, more venerable foundation: the monastery of **Tímiou Prodrómou**, where Gennadius Scholarios, first patriarch of Constantinople after the city was captured by the Ottomans in 1453, elected to retire and is entombed.

The busiest road east of Thessaloníki skirts the lakes of **Korónia** and **Vólvi** en route to Thrace, but a slightly less travelled one veers southeast towards **Halkidikí**, a hand-like peninsula dangling three fingers out into the Aegean. Long a favoured weekend playground of Thessalonians, since the 1980s it has also seen ever-increasing foreign patronage, especially Hungarians, Czechs, and Bulgarians in search of sun, sand and sea on a cheap sunny package or on a few tanks of fuel. Little is left to suggest the area's important role in classical times, when local colonies of various southern Greek cities served as battlefields during the first decade of the Peloponnesian War between Athens and Sparta. However, fossils and a half-million-year-old skull have been discovered in the **Petrálona Cave** (daily 9am–7pm in summer; closes 5pm in winter), 50km (31 miles) southeast of Thessaloníki, revealing the existence of prehistoric settlement.

The tips of Halkidikí

At **Stágira** on the way to Áthos, a modern statue of Aristotle overlooks the Ierissós Gulf and the philosopher's birthplace, ancient Stageira. **Xerxes's Canal**, now silted up, was built around 482 BC across the neck of Áthos peninsula to help the Persians avoid the fate suffered in their previous campaign, when their fleet was wrecked sailing round Áthos cape. This and Xerxes's floating bridge over the Hellespont were considered by the Greeks to be products of Persian megalomania – "marching over the sea and sailing ships through the land". The medieval **Potídea Canal** still separates the **Kassándra** peninsula from the rest of the mainland and serves as a mooring ground for fishing boats. The nearby site of ancient Olynthos (Tue–Sun 8.30am–3pm) is surprisingly rewarding, with extensive remains.

The beautifully forested slopes of Mount Holomóndas cover the centre of rolling hills (the palm of **Halkidikí's three-fingered hand**); **Polýgyros**, with a dull archaeological museum, is the provincial capital, but **Arnéa** ⓭ sees more tourists for the sake of its woven goods and well-preserved old houses. Kassándra, the westernmost "finger", had little life before tourism – most inhabitants were slaughtered in 1821 for participating in the independence rebellion, and the land lay deserted until resettlement by post-1923 refugees from the Sea of Marmara. **Néa Potídea** ⓮, by the canal, and **Haniótis,** near the tip, are probably your best bets for human-scale

development on a generally oversubscribed bit of real estate.

Sithonía, the middle finger, is greener, less flat and less developed; the **Mount Áthos** monasteries owned much of it before 1923, so again there are few old villages, apart from rustic **Parthenónas**, just under Mount Ítamos. The adjacent clutter of **Néos Marmarás** ⑮ and the mega-resort of **Pórto Karrás** are exceptions to the rule of ex-fishing villages converted slowly for tourism, with ample campsites, low-rise accommodation and beautiful sandy beaches. **Toróni** on the west coast is still relatively unspoiled, while nearby **Pórto Koufós**, landlocked inside bare promontories, is a yachter's haven. **Kalamítsi beach** on the east coast has an idyllic double bay, although **Sárti** further north is the main package venue.

Following the coast north past **Pyrgadíkia** fishing hamlet brings you to the base of Áthos, the easterly finger, whose pyramidal summit rises in solitary magnificence across the gulf to the east. Several resorts, including the beach-fringed islet of **Ammoulianí**

and cosmopolitan **Ouranoúpoli** ⑯, grace Áthos, but most people come here for the Holy Mountain because Ouranópoli is the entrance to Mount Áthos. For people not entering Mount Áthos, tour boats from Ouranópoli go around the peninsula, making it possible for these impressive monasteries to be seen from a respectful distance.

Mount Áthos

The fame of **Áthos** ⑰ (www.inathos. gr) derives from its large monastic community, today nearly 2,000 strong. In past ages, these monks earned it the epithet "holy", now an intrinsic part of the Greek name: **Ágion Óros**, the Holy Mountain. Its Christian history begins with the arrival of hermits in the mid-9th century, roughly 100 years before the foundation of the first monastery. Peter the Athonite, the most famous of the early saints, is said to have lived in a cave here for 50 years.

The first monastery, **Megístis Lávras**, was founded in AD 963 by St Athanasios, a friend of the Byzantine emperor, Nikiforos Fokas. Thereafter,

Dionysíou monastery, built on a rock high above the sea.

THE MONASTERY TRAIL

Megistis Lavras is still the most important and imposing of the twenty surviving monasteries, which are spread throughout the peninsula and vary greatly in size, opulence and cultural interest. An increasing number of roads are being bulldozed, but the network of paths that link the monasteries is still the best way to get between them. Roads (and boats) extend down the Athonite northeast coast as far as Megístis Lávras, beyond which an often spectacular trail system rounds the end of the peninsula, taking in all monasteries and skítes (dependencies) as far as Osíou Grigoríou, keeping clear of the road system for the most part.

As the length of stay is restricted by the requisite permit (see www.mounta thosinfos.gr), it is best to choose a cluster of monasteries in one area and reserve accommodation months in advance.

foundations multiplied under the patronage of Byzantine emperors who supported them with money, land and treasures; in return, these donors are prayed for, and imperial charters zealously guarded in the monastery libraries.

The 20 surviving monasteries are all coenobitic, a rule in which monks keep to strict regulations under the direction of an abbot, or *igoúmenos*. Property is communal; meals are eaten together in the *trapezaría* or refectory. All monasteries observe a Greek liturgy except for the Russian **Pandelímonos**, the Serbian **Hilandaríou** and the Bulgarian **Zográfou**; all adhere to the Julian calendar, 13 days behind the Gregorian, and all (except for **Vatopedíou**) keep Byzantine time, reckoned from the hour of sunrise or sunset. Many monks prefer to live in smaller, less regimented monastic communities, the *skítes* and *kelliá* which are dotted around the peninsula but still dependent on the main monasteries. A few choose to live like hermits in an *isyhastírion*, a rough, unadorned hut or a cave, perched precipitously on a cliff edge.

In the 1970s, Áthos was perhaps at its nadir, with barely a thousand monks – many of limited educational and moral attainment – dwelling in dilapidated monasteries. Since then, a renaissance has been effected. The Holy Mountain's claims to be a commonwealth pursuing the highest form of spiritual life known in the Orthodox Christian tradition appear to have struck a chord, and the quality and quantity of novices from every corner of the globe (especially Russia, following the collapse of Communism) is on the rise.

The number of pilgrims to Áthos has grown, too, even though the appropriately Byzantine process of obtaining an entry permit is expressly designed to discourage the frivolous and the gawkers (and women are not allowed entry). Only genuine religious pilgrims need apply; or at least that is the ideal. Political if not doctrinal strife is never far from the Holy Mountain. Most monks are born Greek, and prefer Greek predominance. Slavic novices and pilgrims have complained, since 1990, that they are discriminated against vis-à-vis Greeks. But divisions among Greek monks are well known, involving entire bodies of monks moving from one monastery to another in stormy disputes with abbots or civil authorities.

If you are a man and you want to visit Áthos (no women allowed), you must phone or fax (no email) most monasteries to reserve space in guest quarters often bursting with as many as 100 men a night in full season and, once there, put up with the squealing of other guests' mobile phones. Accommodation and food are free, but taxi rides from one monastery to another can be costly. Walking is the best way to visit the monasteries, but the distances can be great and you will only get to visit a handful of monasteries anyway in your limited allotted time. Only time will tell if the

ÁTHOS – NO WOMEN ALLOWED

Áthos is probably most famous for the *ávaton* edict, promulgated in 1060 by Emperor Constantine Monomahos, which forbids access to the Holy Mountain to all females more evolved than a chicken (although an exception seems to have been made for female cats, which are kept to control the rodent population).

How did this come about? Revisionists point to prior chronic hanky-panky between monks and shepherdesses, while the religious claim that the Virgin, in numerous visions, has consecrated lush Áthos as Her private garden – and women would simply be an unnecessary temptation. Over the years, many women have tried to gatecrash in disguise, only to be ignominiously ejected; a variety of women's groups in Greece and abroad have now taken up the issue.

A more serious challenge was posed in 1998 when the (female) foreign ministers of Sweden and Finland threatened to refuse to sign a decree upholding the Mount's "special status", since it contravenes one of the European Union's most cherished laws: freedom of movement (Greece is one of 11 EU states that signed the Schengen Accord abolishing border controls among member states in 2000). The Athonite authorities have, nonetheless, vowed to resist all attempts to change the Holy Mountain's single-gender character.

Mountain can defend itself against the world.

Kavála

North of Áthos, the coast road threads through several resorts on the Strymonic Gulf, popular with Thessalonians and Serrans, before crossing the Strimónas itself at ancient **Amphipolis**. Scant ruins remain of this city, a Thracian settlement colonised by Athens in 438 BC, atop a bluff protected on three sides by the river. Most passers-by content themselves with a glimpse from the river bridge of the **Lion of Amphipolis**, a colossal statue reassembled from fragments from the 4th and 3rd century BC. On the east bank, the road forks: a faster but less scenic coastal highway, or the inland road along the base of Mount Pangéo via **Elevtheroúpoli**, threading through picturesque, slate-roofed villages.

Both routes converge on the port of **Kavála** ⑱, Macedonia's second city; as Neápolis, it was an important stop on the Via Egnatia, and a port for ancient Philippi. Well into the 1920s, Kavála was a major tobacco-curing and export centre, though today the harbour sees more passenger ferries en route to Thásos and the north Aegean than it does commercial traffic. A mansion from the tobacco boom days houses the Folk and Modern Art Museum (Mon–Fri 8am–2pm, Sat 9am–2.30pm; entrance fee), featuring the Thásos-born sculptor, Polygnotos Vagis. The treasures in the modern archaeological museum (Tue–Fri 8am–7pm, Sat–Sun 8am–2.30pm; entrance fee) include tomb finds from both Avdira and Amphipolis.

The medieval walled **Panagía** quarter, southeast of the harbour, merits a leisurely stroll up to the hilltop citadel, tethered to the modern town by a 16th-century aqueduct. Start along **Poulídou**, passing a clutch of restaurants favoured by locals, arriving soon at the gate of the **Imaret** – a sprawling domed compound, allegedly the

largest Islamic public building in the Balkans. Originally an almshouse and hostel, it is now an atmospheric hotel.

Philippi

Some 14km (8.5 miles) northwest, ancient **Philippi** ⑲ – although named after Philip II – contains little that is Macedonian. From the acropolis, where three medieval towers rise on the ruins of Macedonian walls, you have extensive views of the battlefield which made Philippi famous. Here, in 42 BC, the fate of the Romans hung in the balance as the republican forces of Brutus and Cassius, participants in the assassination of Julius Caesar in 44 BC, confronted the armies of Caesar's avengers, Antony and Octavius. Upon their defeat, both Cassius and Brutus committed suicide; the Battle of Actium in 32 BC ended the struggle between the two victors.

The **Roman ruins** (Tue–Sun summer 8am–7pm, winter 8.30am–3pm), mainly to the south of the highway, include foundations of both the forum and palaestra, plus a well-preserved public latrine in the southwest corner of the

TIP

The northeast has hotter summers and cooler winters than the rest of Greece. The best time to visit Halkidikí is in June or early July, when the land is still green and the hills still covered in flowers.

Xánthi New Town.

DRINK

In Xánthi, the numerous, modern bars and cafés along **Vasilísis Sofías** do a roaring trade, thanks to students from the University of Thrace, which has a campus here.

grounds. Philippi is reputedly the first place in Europe where St Paul preached the gospel. He arrived in AD 49, but offended the local pagans and was thrown into prison (a frescoed Roman crypt now marks the site). In AD 55, however, he got a better reception from the congregation later addressed in his **Epistle to the Philippians**. By the 6th century, Christianity was thriving here, as the remains of several early basilica-churches testify.

Driving east from Kavála, you soon cross the Néstos River, the boundary between Macedonia and Thrace, at the apex of its alluvial plain, a vast expanse of corn and tobacco fields. Some beautiful scenery along the Néstos Gorge can best be seen by train, or from the old highway, between Dráma and Xánthi.

Thrace

Ancient Thrace covered much of present-day Bulgaria and European Turkey, as well as the Greek coastal strip between the Néstos and Évros rivers. Greek colonisation of the coast from 800 BC onwards often led to conflict with the native Thracian

The Lion of Amphipolis.

tribes. The Via Egnatia spanned the area, leaving scattered Roman and, later, Byzantine fortifications. Later, Thrace was overrun and settled by both Slavs and Ottomans. It was eventually and messily divided between Bulgaria, Turkey and Greece, between 1913 and 1923, following various wars. Although a traumatic population exchange between Turkey and Greece occurred in 1923, the Muslim inhabitants of the Greek part of Thrace were allowed to remain in return for protection granted to 125,000 Greek Orthodox living in Istanbul. (Today, the Greeks in Istanbul have been reduced to barely 2,000, whereas the population of Muslims of Thrace has increased slightly to about 130,000.)

An ethnic Turkish minority dwells principally in Xánthi, Komotiní and the plains southeast of the two cities; gypsies who adopted Islam and the Turkish language are also settled here. Another Muslim minority, the Pomaks, live in the Rodópi range above Xánthi and Komotiní; descended from medieval Bogomil heretics, they speak a Slavic language and traditionally cultivate tobacco on mountain terraces. The best base for exploration of this area and trekking is Stavroupoli.

The open-air Saturday market at **Xánthi ㉑**, just 53km (33 miles) from Kavála, makes a good introduction to the region's Muslim demographics. The call to prayer rings out over the town five times a day. Turkish and Pomak women favour long, dark overcoats and plain-coloured yashmaks (head-scarves), now gradually being replaced by more stylish grey or brown coats and printed scarves. The gypsy women stand out in their colourful shalvar bloomers, their scarves tied behind the ears. Many men still wear burgundy-coloured velvet or felt fezzes, or white skullcaps.

Xánthi became a prosperous commercial and administrative centre in the 19th century, thanks to tobacco. Renowned masons were brought from Epirus to build merchants' mansions, tobacco warehouses and *hans* (inns). The *hans*, large square buildings around a central courtyard, were resting spots and trade centres near the marketplace. One of the handsome 19th-century mansions at the base of the old town has become a Folk Museum (Tue–Sun 9am–2.30pm). Further uphill lie the minarets and houses of the Turkish quarter, with numerous satellite dishes for tuning into Turkish-language TV.

At **Komotiní** ㉑, 56km (35 miles) east of Xánthi via the bird-stalked lagoon of **Vistonída** and the water-girt monastery of **Ágios Nikólaos**, Muslims constitute nearly half the population. The Democritus University of Thrace is based here and though it is less immediately attractive than Xánthi, there is an old bazaar of cobbled lanes (Tuesday is the busiest day), with tiny shops, 14 functioning mosques and many old-fashioned coffee houses. A **Folk Museum** (Mon–Fri 10.30am–1pm) just off the central park displays local embroidery, costumes and metalwork); the **archaeological museum** (daily 8.30am–6pm; free) keeps finds from such Thracian sites as **Avdira**, south of Xánthi, and **Maroneia**, south of Komotiní.

Avdira itself does not repay a visit in its bedraggled state, although it is famed for nurturing two major philosophers: Democritus (*c*.460–370 BC), who first expounded atomic theory, and the sophist Protagoras (c.490–420 BC). Odysseus legendarily called at Maroneia after leaving Troy on his return to Ithaca, procuring a sweet red wine which later saved him and his companions from the cyclops Polyphemus. A cave north of the sparse cliff-top site retains the name of **Polyphemus's Cave**.

Alexandroúpoli

The old road from Komotiní zigzags 65km (40 miles) through barren hills before coming down to the rather drab port of **Alexandroúpoli** ㉒, gateway to Samothráki island.

It's wisest to press on into the valley of the Évros River, especially if you're a birdwatcher. The delta, east of the Roman spa of Traianopolis, is excellent for waterfowl, while the **Dadiá Forest Reserve**, a successful World Wide Fund for Nature (WWF) venture, shelters black and griffin vultures. In between, you can pause at **Féres** for the sake of its 12th-century church, **Panagía Kosmosótira**, whose lofty, five-domed interior is generally open to visitors.

North of the turning for Dadiá, the first town of any size is **Souflí** ㉓, once famous for silk production. Corn fields have now replaced the mulberry trees whose leaves once nourished the silkworms, and only a small museum commemorates the vanished industry. **Didymótiho**, 30km (18 1/2 miles) further upstream, has a Byzantine fortress at the old town's summit and an abandoned mosque on the square, whose features speak of Seljuk (and earlier) prototypes.

From here, most traffic is bound for Turkish **Edirne**, whose graceful minarets are just visible from the Greek border town of Kastaniés.

Xánthi at carnival time.

Sými harbour.

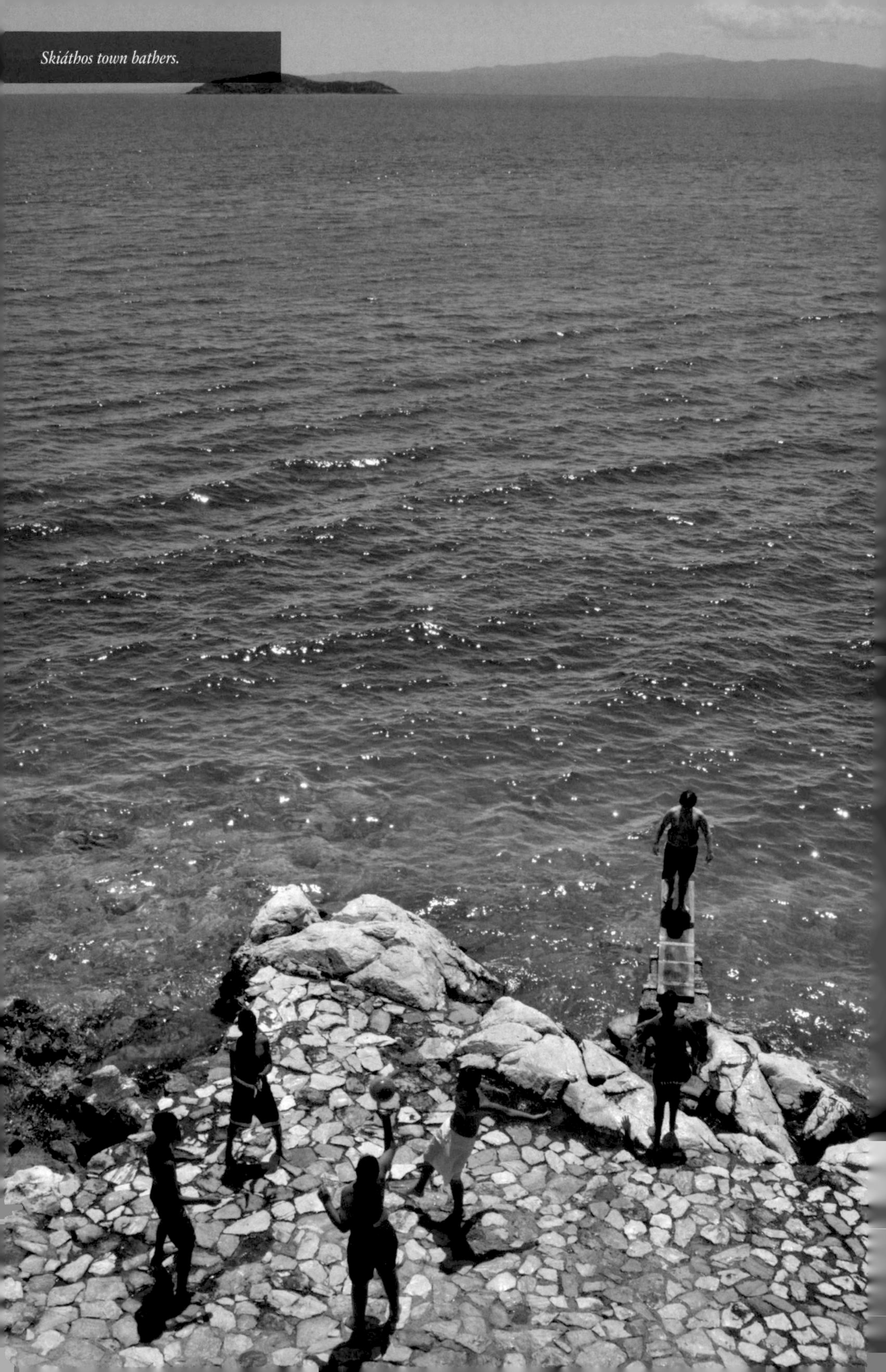

Skiáthos town bathers.

THE ISLANDS

Greece has more inhabited islands than any
other European country – but it's anyone's
guess how many there are.

Island windmill.

The poet Odysseus Elytis once said: "Greece rests on the sea". It's an observation that few countries could claim with such confidence. Some 25,000 sq km (10,000 sq miles) of the Aegean and Ionian seas are covered by islands. And, in characteristic Greek fashion, the exact number of them has been the topic of discussion and dispute. There may be 3,000 islands and islets, of which 167 are inhabited. Or, according to someone else's calculations, there may be only 1,000, of which fewer than 70 are populated.

The criterion that defines a populated place is open to interpretation. Does a tiny outcrop, bare save for one goatherd and six goats, constitute an inhabited island? Can an island that is totally deserted except for annual pilgrimages to a small chapel at its summit claim to be inhabited?

The arithmetic matters far more to foreigners than to the Greeks, who are interested in sea and sky, in food and festivals, rather than in facts and figures. What is indisputable, however, is the sheer variety of landscape and experience to be found lurking behind the familiar images.

This is what we attempt to show in this section – islands with an ancient past and a modern outlook, an array of choices juxtaposed against pure, simple pleasures. In order to accommodate everything that is encompassed in the phrase "a Greek island", we have devoted space to tiny islands such as Kímolos and Lipsí, as well as the well-known giants like

The perfect horseshoe harbour of Ásos.

Crete and Rhodes and the holiday favourites such as Mýkonos and Corfu. We do not ignore the familiar, popular islands, of course, but we explore them to seek out the true heart of the place behind the tourist clichés.

The best way to enjoy the islands is to arrive with a certain attitude of mind. By all means, begin by uncritically enjoying the cluster of blazing white buildings against a shimmering sea, donkeys set against a backdrop of olive groves, and so on – the images seared into the senses by holiday brochures. But, when the novelty wears off, or perhaps earlier, examine each island as if it were an onion and start stripping off the skins. How to strip the onion is a large part of what this book is about.

So, welcome aboard the ferry and prepare for a cruise around Europe's most fascinating and welcoming islands – however many of them there might be.

ISLANDS OF THE SARONIC GULF

Salamína, Aegina, Angístri, Póros, Ýdra and Spétses
are all within easy reach of the mainland and
popular with day-trippers. But they are distinctive,
rich in history and remarkably attractive.

Athens and the islands of the Saronic Gulf are often lumped together in guidebooks. There is some sense in this, since many Athenians frequent these islands at weekends, while during the summer they become veritable extensions of the more fashionable Athenian neighbourhoods. Yet this view of the Argo-Saronic islands doesn't take into account their separate identities. They are islands, not suburbs, each with their own character.

Salamína (Salamis)

Salamína is best known for an ancient naval battle (480 BC) in which outnumbered Athenian ships routed the enormous Persian fleet – the ships being the "wooden walls" that the Delphic oracle had predicted would save the Greeks. Pride of the island is **Fanéroméni Monastery ❶** (typical midday closure) on the Voudóro peninsula, just 6km (4 miles) from the capital, **Salamína Town;** it's now a tenanted nunnery, with brilliant 17th-century frescoes, while its boathouse served as a retreat of the great poet Angelos Sikelianós.

The island is decidedly not push but it is relatively undeveloped and can be reached quickly, just a few minutes' ride across from Pérama, through the waters which saw the battle, to the port of **Paloúkia ❷**. Most

Heading for Paloúkia.

of the inhabitants live in **Salamína** (also called **Kouloúri**), which has an archaeological museum (Tue–Sun 8.30am–2.40pm) and a Folk Museum (Mon–Fri 9am–4pm), plus decent tavernas. Cyclists will find Salamína's back roads uncrowded and untaxing on the stamina. The best beaches are on the south coast at Peráni and Peristéria.

Aegina (Egina)

Aegina (www.aegina-com.gr) is close enough to be within easy reach of

Aegina beach.

The 5th-century temple of Aphaea on Aegina.

the mainland and far enough away to retain its island identity. About an hour and a half by ferry from Piraeus – or 45 minutes by hydrofoil or catamaran – it has little trouble attracting visitors. The island remains more popular with Athenians seeking a retreat from the city than with foreign tourists or other Greeks. The main local produce is pistachio nuts, sold all along the harbour street.

Shaped on the map like an upside-down triangle, the island's southern point is marked by the magnificent cone of **Mount Óros,** the highest peak in the Argo-Saronic islands, visible on a clear day from Athens's Acropolis. The island's centre and eastern side is mountainous; a gently sloping fertile plain runs down to the northwestern corner where **Aegina (Egina) Town** ❸ overlays in part the ancient capital of the island.

The town has numerous 19th-century mansions constructed when the first Greek president, Ioannis Kapodistrias (1776–1831), lived and worked here, as well as an enormous disused jail (being restored) that

began life as a Kapodistrias-funded orphanage. Some 3km (2 miles) north of town is the **Christos Kapralos Museum** (June–Oct Tue–Sun 10am–2pm, 6–8pm, Nov–May Fri–Sun 10am–2pm), dedicated to this prominent Greek sculptor and painter, occupying his former studios.

The modern harbour, crowded with yachts and fishing boats, adjoins the ancient harbour, which is now the shallow town beach north of the main quay. The little beach ends at the ancient site of *Kolóna*, meaning "column", after the single conspicuously standing column of the **Temple of Apollo**. This Doric temple, built in 520–500 BC, was superseded by a late Roman fortress, fragments of which survive on the seaward side. Although from the sea the temple looks unimpressive, the view from its promontory is very fine. A small **museum** (Tue–Sun 8.30am–3pm) on the site features finds from 2,500 years of local settlement.

The island's most famous ancient monument is the **Temple of Aphaea** ❹ (summer daily 8am–7pm, winter

Tue–Sun until 5pm), in the north-east, above the summer resort of **Agía Marína**. The temple crowns a hilltop in a pine grove commanding a splendid view of the Aegean. Built in about 490 BC, it is the only surviving Greek temple with a second row of small superimposed columns in the interior of the sanctuary.

On the way to the temple, you will pass the modern **Monastery of Ágios Nektários** (daily except for midday break), the newest (and very popular) Orthodox saint, canonised in 1961. Across the ravine from the monastery is ghostly **Paleohóra** ("old town"), established inland during the 9th century as protection against piracy. Abandoned after Greek independence, most of the surviving 38 churches are in utter disrepair, but you can still see the fragments of brilliant post-Byzantine frescoes in several unlocked chapels.

The west coast of the island is quite gentle, with passable sandy beaches at **Marathónas** and **Eginítissa,** but better reasons to head out here are to enjoy a meal in one of the many fish tavernas along the harbour at **Pérdika** ❺, or to take a boat from there to swim at the clean and sheltered bay on the uninhabited islet of **Moní.**

Angístri and Méthana

Angístri (Agístri) ❻, the small island facing Aegina Town, has become very much a destination in its own right, especially with trendy Athenians who guarantee a surprisingly lively nightlife. It is lapped by the cleanest, most aquamarine waters in this part of the gulf, and has considerable appeal inland with its dense pine forests. **Skála,** where conventional ferries call, is the main resort with the only sandy beach, though **Mýlos,** 1,500m west where hydrofoils stop, has more character, with a church, old houses, shops and again plenty of places to stay and eat. A bus links the two, and also plies to the two southerly hamlets of **Metóhi** and **Limenária,** both with tavernas. The most attractive, and famous, beach is pebbly **Halikiáda** south of Skála, supposedly Greece's oldest naturist cove; its 125-metre extent is colonised

FACT

Between the 7th and 5th centuries BC, Aegina was a leading maritime power and main rival of Athens; its silver coins – with a relief tortoise on one side, a dolphin on the other – became common currency in the Dorian city-states.

Póros Town harbour.

FACT

Póros' Poseidon sanctuary was the headquarters of the Kalaureian League, an association that included Athens. Athenian orator Demosthenes, who had opposed Macedonian domination of his city, sought refuge here in 31 BC after an Athenian revolt was quelled by Antipater. Surrounded by Macedonians sent to arrest him, Demosthenes took poison but stepped outside the sanctuary before dying so as not to defile holy ground.

Fisherman's catch, Ýdra harbour.

by a semi-permanent tent colony. Dragonéra cove on the west coast, looking west to the Peloponnese, is the runner-up.

Although linked to the Peloponnese via a road along a slender isthmus, **Méthana** ❼ is far easier reached by sea as a regular stop on the line to Póros, and so ranks as an honorary Argo-Saronic island. It is in fact a dormant volcano, with lush vegetation and basalt-built cottages. Low-key Méthana port is distinguished only by its hot springs; a better destination, in the far northwest, is **Kaméni Hóra** hamlet; from here, a marked path leads 15 minutes through a chaos of solidified lava to a volcanic cavern, with fine views en route towards Angístri and Aegina.

Póros

The island of Póros is separated from the Argolid mainland by a narrow passage of water – *póros* in Greek means "passage" or "ford". As your boat turns into the ford from its northern entrance, the channel opens out and the white houses, tiled rooftops and

hilltop clocktower of lovely **Póros Town** ❽ appear. Almost landlocked, it provides one of the most protected anchorages in the Aegean. Póros can also be reached (with considerably more effort) by driving via the **Isthmus of Corinth** to **Paleá Epídavros** and then further down the coast to little **Galatás**, just across the channel.

Although Póros has numerous hotels, and Athenians have owned vacation houses here for decades, the island has never been as fashionable as Ýdra or Spétses, but during summer it gets every bit as crowded. Póros Town itself almost completely covers the sub-island of Sferiá, southwest of the small channel separating it from the larger part of the island, Kalávria.

North of the channel, you can still see the ruins of a Russian naval station established in the 1780s, but the most venerable building on Kalávria is the **Monastery of Zoödóhou Pigís** (Virgin of the Life-Giving Spring; daily 8am–1.30pm, 4.30pm–sunset), beautifully situated on a wooded hillside east of town and still home

to a few monks. Below extends Monastiríou beach, perhaps the best on an island not known for stellar ones.

Above the monastery, a road climbs through pines to the ruins of the **Sanctuary of Poseidon ⑨**, in a saddle between the highest hills of the island. The temple was excavated by the Swedish Archaeological School during the 19th century, and they are digging again, so much is roped off, but its setting is rewarding.

Ancient **Troezen ⑩** is about 8km (5 miles) from Galatás on the Peloponnese. The mythological hero Theseus is said to have grown up here before he went off to become king of Athens. Theseus also supposedly returned later to Troezen, providing Euripides and Racine with the plots for their famous plays about the young queen Phaedra who unjustly accused Theseus's son Hippolytos of having violated her. The most obvious ruins of Troezen are of a shrine to Hippolytos (only foundations remain) and a Byzantine basilica in a perilous state. Nearby, the **Diavologéfyro**

(Devil's Bridge) may disappoint, being a small natural rock span once used as an aqueduct.

Ýdra (Hydra)

The island of **Ýdra ⑪** – in antiquity Ydrea, "the well watered" – now appears as a long, barren rock. But the harbour, with its fine old stone buildings, is still lovely; the town has attracted the artistic and the fashionable since the 1950s and the masses ever since.

The heart of the island is its harbour-town, also called **Ýdra**. All around the picturesque bay, white, tile-roofed vernacular houses climb the slope, interspersed with massive grey *arhondiká* (mansions of the shipping families who made fortunes in the 18th and 19th centuries), many of them designed by architects from Venice and Genoa. Along the quay are tourist shops and cafés, with the clock tower of the 18th-century **Monastery of the Panagía** in the centre; much of the masonry used to build it was taken from the ancient Sanctuary of Poseidon on Póros. The U-shaped

The Monastery of the Panagía, Ýdra.

View from the Póros rooftops across to Galatás.

Donkeys carrying marble slabs, Ýdra.

Kamíni port, southwest Ýdra

harbour itself is girded by a little thread of a breakwater, and flanked by l9th-century cannons.

The town has many good back-street tavernas, as well as extremely popular bars and clubs. Yet the higher reaches and the hills beyond remain surprisingly untouched; narrow alleys and steep staircases lead from one quarter to the next. The uniformity of white walls is broken again and again by a century-old doorway, a bright blue window frame, a flight of striking scarlet steps, or a green garden fence. One stair-path ultimately climbs to **Agía Evpraxía,** the only inhabited (by nuns) and visitable (except at midday rest) rural monastery on the island.

Mandráki, northeast of town, has the only sandy beach, but heading southwest is more rewarding. A wide coastal path goes to **Kamíni** and **Vlyhós,** with its early 19th-century arched stone bridge. There are good tavernas in both places. Water taxis are the only way to reach **Ágios Nikólaos** and **Bísti** ⑫ beaches, the island's best,

at the southwest tip, unless you undertake an arduous cross-country hike, equipped with a good map. An easier path-walk leads southeast and within 80 minutes to the equally good, pine-shaded pebble beach at **Limnióniza.**

Spétses

Spétses ⑬ is the southwesternmost of the Argo-Saronic Gulf islands, though just off the Argolid coast with which it has short-hop seagoing links. In antiquity, it was called Pityousa, "pine tree" island, and, despite huge fires in 1990 and 2001, it is still the most wooded of the group after Angístri. Tourist development here is more extensive than on Ýdra but less than on either Póros or Aegina, and in recent years, responsible planning has helped preserve the island's charm.

Although **Spétses Town** has its share of bars and fast-food places, the **Paleó Limáni** (Old Harbour) area still radiates a gentle grace. The 18th-century *arhondiká* (merchants' houses) you see in this part of the town now belong to wealthy Athenian families who return every summer.

Like Ýdra, Spétses' heyday was the late 18th century, when seagoing trade made it prosperous. Also like Ýdra, it became a hive of activity during the Greek War of Independence, offering its merchant fleet of over 50 ships for the Greek cause. The island is distinguished for being the first in the archipelago to revolt against Ottoman rule in April 1821, and the fortified main harbour of **Dápia**, still bristling with cannon, forms one of the town's focal points.

Laskarina Bouboulina, a great heroine of the Greek War of Independence, was from Spetses, and her great victory is celebrated every 8 September by a *panigýri* (religious festival, see page 98) focused on the church of the **Panagía Armáta** on the lighthouse headland close to the Old Harbour. A mock battle is staged and a model Turkish flagship is burned in the harbour amidst a fireworks display.

Although after the War of Independence Spétses' fleet declined, shipbuilding traditions continue unabated. The small **museum** (Tue–Sun 8.30am– 2.30pm), in the imposing 18th-century

arhondikó of shipowner Hatzigianni Mexi, contains polychrome prows of ships from the revolutionary fleet and an ossuary holding the bones of Bouboulína. Her own family mansion, also a museum (guided tours only; consult the sign outside for schedule) stands behind the Dápia.

Outside of town to the northwest is the **Anargýrios and Korgialénios College,** a Greek version of an English public school. John Fowles taught here and portrayed both school and island in his 1966 novel *The Magus.* The school has closed, though the buildings are sporadically used as a conference centre.

The town beach of **Ágios Mámas,** busy **Agía Marína** a bit beyond, and amenitied **Ligonéri** east of town, can't compare to the beautiful beaches of **Zogeriá, Agía Paraskeví,** Agía Anárgyri and **Xylokériza** (going around the island's perimeter in an anticlockwise direction). **Ágii Anárgyri** is ⑭ is the most developed and sandiest, with proper tavernas and watersports.

Sandals for sale in Spétses.

Genteel Spétses Town.

NATIONAL HEROINE

Laskarina Bouboulina, Greece's national heroine of the Greek War of Independence, was a Spetsiot woman who took command of her second husband's fleet after he was killed by Algerian corsairs. She contributed eight of the 22 Spetsiot ships that blockaded the Ottomans in Návplio (Nauplion) for more than a year until the garrison surrendered in December 1822.

In the September before Návplio surrendered, an Ottoman fleet attempted to lift the blockade by threatening Spétses. The fighting was indecisive but the imperial fleet eventually withdrew, frightened by a ruse. Fezes were placed on the asphodel plants growing densely along the shore; from a distance these, swaying in the wind, looked like men – presumably armed.

Marble taken from the Temple of Apollo, Páros Old Town.

THE CYCLADES

From the hectic nightlife of Mýkonos and Íos to the rugged beauty of Mílos and Sérifos, and the unspoilt seclusion of Síkinos and Anáfi, there is something for all tastes among these islands.

For many people, the Cyclades are Greece; other island chains are mere distractions from this blue Aegean essence. They were inhabited by 5000 BC; by the third millennium, a fascinating island culture flourished here, with fine arts and crafts and lively commerce – as anyon e who visits the excellent Museum of Cycladic Art in Athens will appreciate (see page 150).

Of the 56 islands, 24 are inhabited. There are three basic ferry routes from either Piraeus or Rafína ports: the easternmost takes in bucolic Ándros, religious Tínos, metropolitan Sýros, and cosmopolitan Mýkonos. The central line joins popular Páros, Náxos and Amorgós, concluding at spectacular Santoríni or remote Anáfi. The most western itinerary calls at Kýthnos, Sérifos, Sífnos and Mílos, usually extending to Folégandros and Síkinos. Especially in high season, links are possible between the basic routes. With scant links to other Cyclades, Kéa attracts Athenian weekenders.

Ándros

Ándros ❶ was settled centuries ago by Orthodox Albanians; their stone dwellings in the north contrast with the whitewash and red tile of the other villages. The port town, **Gávrio**, does have ample tourist infrastructure,

though more visitors bases themselves at **Batsí**, 6km (4 miles) south, a pleasant Cycladic fishing town with a long beach. On the east coast, **Ándros Town (Hóra)** ❷ remains remarkably unspoiled. Because so many rich Athenians have weekend houses here, tourism has not been assiduously pursued. The prize exhibit in the **archaeological museum** (Tue–Sun 8.30am–3pm) is the famous Hermes of Ándros, a 4th-century AD copy of Praxiteles' 4th-century BC statue at ancient Olympia. Nearby, the

Map on page 240

Main Attractions

CONTEMPORARY ART MUSEUM, ÁNDROS
ERMOÚPOLIS TOWNSCAPE, SÝROS
ANCIENT DELOS
THE CAVE, ANDÍPAROS
NÁXOS OLD TOWN
HOZOVIÓTISSA MONASTERY, AMORGÓS
SOUTH COAST BEACHES, MÍLOS
VIEW OVER CALDERA, SANTORÍNI
MUSEUM OF PREHISTORIC THERA, SANTORÍNI
CLIMB TO PANAGÍA KALAMIÓTISSA, ANÁFI

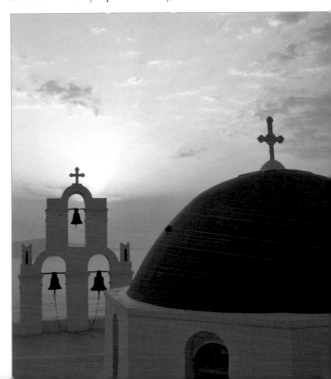

Santoríni, famous for its whitewashed villages and blue-domed churches.

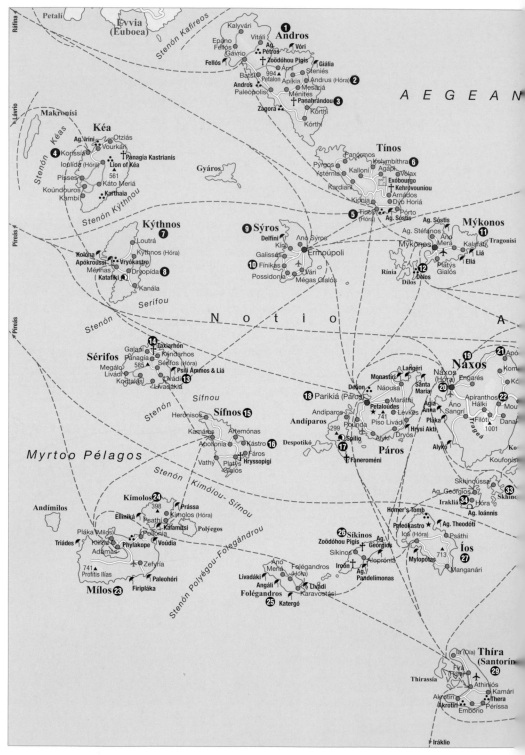

Petalí

Ráfina

Évvia
(Euboea)

Stenón Kafíreos

Kalyvári

Andros ❶

Epáno
Fellós
Gávrio

Vitáli

Ag.
Pétros
✝ Zoödóhou Pigis

Vóri

Fellós

994 ▲

Giália

Batsí

Andros

Petalón

Arní

Steniés

Apíkia

Andros (Hóra) ❷

Mesariá

Paleópolis

Ménites

Dyó Horiá

✝ Panahrándou ❸

Zágora

Kórthi

Lávrio

Makronísi

Kórthi

Kéa

Kéas

Ag. Iríni

Otziás

Vourkári

Kotissiá

Tínos ❻

Pireás

Panórmos

Ioulída (Hóra)

Stenón Kéas

561

✝ Panagía Kastrianís

Lion of Kéa

▲

Pýrgos
Ystérnia

Kolymbíthra

Agápi

Kalloní

Vólax

Pisses

Káto Meriá

Kardianí

Exóbourgo

Koúndouros

Kambí

Karthaía ▲

Gyáros

Kiónia

✝ Kehrovouníou

Arnádos

Dyó Horiá

Tínos
(Hóra)

Pórto

Stenón Kýthnou

❺

Ag. Sóstis

Ag. Sóstis

Ag. Stéfanos

Mýkonos ❶❶

Áno
Merá

Kalafáti

Tragonísi

Kýthnos ❼

Loutrá

Sýros ❾

Delfíni

Áno Sýros

Kíni

Mýkonos

Liá

Eliá

Pireás

Kolóna
Apókroussi

Kýthnos (Hóra)

Mérihas

✝ Vryókastro

Galissás

Ermoúpoli

Rínia

Platýs
Gialós ❶❷

Dílos

Katafíki

Dryopída ❽

Fínikas ❶❿

Vári

Díloş

Kanála

Possidonía

Mégas Gialós

Serífou

N o t i o   A

Stenón

Galaní

Sérifos

Taxiárhon ❶❹

Panagía
585 ▲

Kéndarhos

Serifos (Hóra)

Langéri ❶❾

Monastíri

Náxos ❶❾

Apó ❷❶

Kom

Megálo
Livádi

Koútalas

Livádi ❶❸

Livadákia

Psili Ámmos & Liá

Delion

Náxos
(Hóra)

Sánta
Maria

Engarés

Kó

Síle

Parikiá (Páros) ❶❽

Petaloúdes

Áno
Sangrí

Náousa

Maráthi

★ 741

Apíranthos ❷❷

Hálki

Mou

Sífnou

Herónisos

Andíparos

Andíparos

Píso Livádi

Lévkes

Filóti

1001

Danaé

Kamáres

Artemónas

299

Poúnda

Hrysí Aktí

Pláka

Kó

Sífnos ❶❺

Apollonía

Kástro ❶❻

Despotikó

Spília ❶❼

Aliko

Koufoní

Vathý

Platýs
Gialós

Fáros

✝ Faneroméni

Páros

Dryós

Ag. Geórgios

Skhinoússa

Iraklía ❸❹

Skhin

Hryssopigí

Dryós

Hóra

Myrtoo Pélagos

Stenón Kimólou- Sífnou

Homer's Tomb

Ag. Ioánnis

Skhinoússa ❸❸

Andímilos

Kímolos ❷❹

398 ▲

Prássa

Paleókastro ★

Ag. Theodóti

Elliniká

Psáthi

Kímolos (Hóra)

Síkinos ❷❻

Ios (Hóra)

Psáthi

Kafamítsi

Polýegos

Zoödóhou Pigis

Ag.
Geórgios

✝

Íos

713

Pláka

Mílos

Pollónia

Triádes

Kímos

Phylakopé

Voúdia

Síkinos

Mylopótas ❷❼

Adámas

Stenón Polyégou-Folegándrou

Alopronía

Iroón ✝

Ag.
Pandelímonas

741 ▲
Profítis Ilías

Zefyría

Áno
Merá

Folégandros
(Hóra)

Manganári

Mílos ❷❸

Firipláka

Paleohóri

Livadáki

Angáli

Folégandros ❷❺

Livádi

Karavostási

Katergó

Ia (Oia)

Thíra
(Santoríni)

Thirassía

Firá
Hóra ❷❾

Thirassía

Athiniós

Kamári

Akrotíri

Thera

Akrotíri

Périssa

Emborió

Iráklio

A E G E A N

Rínia

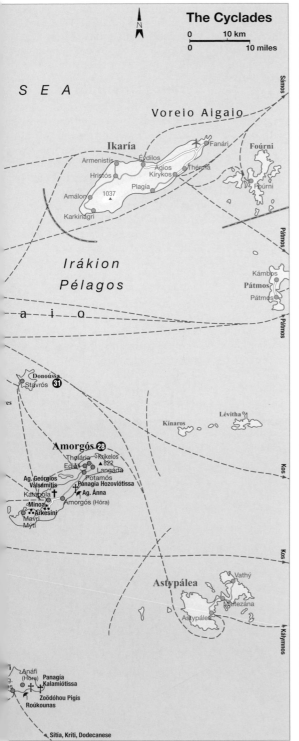

The Cyclades

Goulandris Museum of Contemporary Art (summer Wed–Mon 10am–2pm, winter Sat–Mon 10am–2pm; www.moca–andros. gr) has a fine permanent collection by both Greek and foreign artists, plus renowned temporary exhibits. South of the Batsí–Hóra road is the most spectacular of Ándros's 13 monasteries, **Panahrándou ❸** (9am–1pm, 4.30pm–sunset); over 1,000 years old, but home to just one monk.

Ándros has many beaches – the best on the west coast, either side of Batsí, are **Hryssí Ámmos, Kyprí, Agía Marína** and **Delavóyas**. The east shore is more exposed to the meltémi, but try **Giália** north of Hóira, and **Kórthi** bay in the far south, popular with windsurfers.

Kéa (Tziá)

Kéa-bound boats leave from the mainland port of Lávrio, some 50km (30 miles) from Athens, and land at **Korissía ❹**. The main town, **Ioulída**, huddles below a rounded ridge overlooking the island's northern flank, a site chosen for its inaccessibility from pirates. The famous **Lion of Kéa**, a smiling, maneless beast almost 6 metres (20ft) long, is a 15-minute walk northeast of Ioulída. Carved from grey granite, it is probably early Archaic.

In the 19th century, there were a million oak trees on well-watered Kéa, and many still provide shade. Olive trees, however, are absent; since ancient times, the island has been noted for its almonds. The jagged west coast has many sandy coves, some accessible by boat only. **Písses**, with a square, Hellenistic watchtower at **Agía Marína** just inland, and **Koúndouros**, are two of the more developed beaches. Close to Korissía is Vourkári, with yachts at anchor and pricy tavernas, plus **Agía Iríni**, a Minoan excavation. Walkers are well served by a network of numbered trails, intelligently rehabilitated and marked thanks to EU funds.

Tínos

Tínos receives many thousands of tourists – but they are mostly Greek Orthodox here for the church, the **Panagía Evangelístria** or "Annunciated Virgin". In 1822, local nun Pelagía dreamt of an icon; it was duly unearthed and the church was built to house it. The icon's healing powers have made **Tínos Hóra** ❺ the Lourdes of Greece. Women fall to their knees upon arrival, and crawl painfully to the church (less painfully since a carpeted lane for that purpose was installed on the main approach). Healing miracles often occur. Despite all the foregoing, Tínos is about half Catholic in population, with most of them out in the rural villages.

For a reminder of the Ottoman conquest, visit the peak of **Exóbourgo**, 643 metres (2,110ft), with its ruined fortress (Tínos was the last Cyclade to fall to the Turks, in 1715). A bus ride to Exóbourgo and beyond will also reveal some weird, mushroom-shaped, wind-sculpted rocks, especially above **Vólax** village, known for its basket-weaving.

Kolymbíthra ❻ in the north is Tínos's best beach. **Ágios Sóstis**, near Pórto on the south coast, is also a decent stretch of sand. Of the monasteries to see, the abandoned **Katapolianí**, near **Ystérnia**, is exceptional. **Kardianí**, the village southeast of Ystérnia, is Tínos's most

spectacularly set – though arcaded **Arnádos** and adjacent **Dýo Horiá** give it stiff competition. As on Kéa, a prepared network of trails appeals to walkers during the cooler months.

Kýthnos (Thermiá)

After iron-mining operations ceased, **Kýthnos** ❼ lost its prime source of income. Foreign tourism has not supplemented it, but Athenian visitors have helped. **Mérihas** on the west coast has the biggest choice of accommodation. In summer, a "taxi-boat" runs from Mérihas to **Episkopí**, **Apókroussi** and Kolóna beaches to the north, the best on the island. **Hóra**, 6km (4 miles) northeast of Mérihas, is exquisite: its streets are spanned by wood-beamed arches joining facing houses, while rock pavements are decorated with white-painted fish, stylised ships and flowers.

The island's alias of Thermiá derives from thermal baths at Loutrá, on the northeast coast, 5km (3 miles) north of Hóra. The recent advent of posh lodgings is helping to banish Loutrá's somewhat fusty reputation. Above

Ermoúpoli harbour.

Loutrá, at Maroúla, excavations have revealed the earliest known Cycladic settlement, dating from before 4500 BC. A ravine splits tile-roofed **Dryopída** ❽ (the medieval capital) into two; the chambered **Katafíki cave** here is linked in legend with the Nereids (sea nymphs in Greek mythology).

Sýros

Sýros ❾ remains the Cyclades' capital, but when Piraeus (Pireás) overtook it as a trade centre in the late 1800s, its port went into decline. However, it retains excellent inter-island ferry links and useful facilities. The capital, **Ermoúpoli**, has been "discovered", with the renovation of grand buildings, public and private, and multiplication of tourist facilities. The area called **Vapória** ("the ships"), uphill from the shopping streets, is where you'll find many 19th-century neoclassical mansions (a few doubling as hotels). The elegant, marble-paved main square, Platía Miaoúlis, is flanked by an imposing Town Hall, just behind which the restored Apollon Theatre was originally modelled on La Scala in Milan. The entire Belle Epoque townscape is under Unesco protection. Like Tínos, Sýros is about half Catholic, with most of them residing in the hill village of **Áno Sýros** above Ermoúpoli.

Fínikas ❿, a beachside town in the southwest, is possibly named after the Phoenicians, probably Sýros's first inhabitants – or more likely after a palm tree (**fínikas** in Greek). The island's south is rounder and greener than the rugged, thinly populated north and has good beaches at **Possidonía** and **Vári** as well as Fínikas. Up the west coast, **Galissás** and **Kíni**, with the best beaches (and sunsets), are popular resorts. During Roman times, and again from 1948 until 1974, political prisoners were interned on **Gyáros**, the exceedingly bleak desert island to the northwest.

Mýkonos

Mýkonos ⓫ has become glamorous and prosperous by turning its

Most of the Cyclades islands that grew their own grain have windmills, but the majority have fallen into disuse.

Galissás beach resort.

Freshly-caught octopus is served in most of the Cycladic islands.

Mýkonos nightlife.

domed chapels and whitewashed surfaces. The odd-shaped **Paraportianí** (Our Lady of the Postern Gate; closed to the public) is probably Greece's most photographed church.

Little Venice, a row of buildings hanging over the sea on the west, is the least frenetic part of town, with atmospheric café-bars thronged at sunset. The **Folklore Museum** (Mon–Sat 4.30–8.30pm; free) and the **archaeological museum** (Tue–Sun 9am–3pm), at different ends of Mýkonos's quay, are full of interesting objects. Caïques also depart from here for **Delos** ⑫, the sacred island that is the centre of the Cyclades (in myth, Mýkonos was Delian Apollo's grandson – see also page 257). Or you can strike inland to **Áno Merá**, 7km (4 miles) east, the only other village, and visit the red-domed Tourlianí monastery (9am–1pm, 2pm–sunset), which houses some fine 16th-century icons.

rocky, treeless ruggedness into a tourist-pleasing package that works – making it more expensive than any other Greek island except Santoríni. Summer draws thousands of tourists to **Mýkonos Town** to sample its celebrated bars, August–September gay scene, cozy restaurants, and the clothes and jewellery shops. Despite the glitz, the portside Hóra is among the most solicitously preserved in the Cyclades, with its wooden balconies loaded with flowers, multicoloured

Among Mýkonos beaches, **Paradise** is half straight nude, **Super Paradise** half gay nude, and both are stunning; below Áno Merá, **Kalafáti** is popular

with windsurfers, and Eliá exclusively gay; **Platýs Gialós** and **Psaroú** in the west are popular with families.

Sérifos

A long easterly promontory encloses **Livádi** ⓭, Sérifos's harbour. With a half-dozen each of tavernas, hotels and café-bars, this is a pleasant place to stay, with good beaches on either side at **Livadákia** (where there's more prime accommodation) and **Ágios Sóstis**. **Sérifos Hóra** spills precipitously from a crag above; regular buses make the ascent, but the old stair-path (a 40-minute climb) makes for a more authentic approach.

Hóra has two parts, a somewhat neglected lower neighbourhood and the architecturally protected **Kástro**, with a scenic church at its east end. Kástro's central plaza with its trendy cafés, gaily coloured town hall and church of Ágios Athanásios provides a focus. The view from the edge of Hóra east over the gleaming bay and the other islands is spectacular.

From Hóra, numbered trails head north to either Kállitsos village, or Panagía plus Galaní villages, the latter two accessible also by road and very occasional seasonal bus. Between Kállitsos and Galaní stands the fortified medieval **Taxiárhon Monastery** ⓮, only open when the local parish priest is inside.

Sérifos abounds in little bays, many still unspoiled and very quiet outside of summer. Beyond Livadákia, Karávi is scenic and usually naturist; in the far southwest, **Megálo Livádi** and Gánema coves once hosted mines, whereas today there are handy tavernas.

Sífnos

Sífnos ⓯ was, and to a reduced extent still is, a potter's isle. In the narrow, pretty harbour, **Kamáres**, and at Platýs Gialós and isolated Hersónisos, potters still set out racks of earthenware to dry in the sun. Weaving and jewellery-making were the other crafts; there are fine examples of these in the **Folklore Museum** (summer only daily 9.30am–2pm, 6–10pm) of the capital, **Apollonía**. Contiguous to Apollonía, **Artemónas** is Sífnos's

Lévkes countryside.

The Cycladic Bronze Age

Early Cycladic peoples left behind beautiful artefacts arising out of an organised and flourishing culture, most famously the mysterious, stylised marble sculptures which have been found in tombs.

Bronze Age settlements and cemeteries excavated on a number of islands are generally considered to be the first complex, organised, settled communities in Europe. The Early Cycladic Bronze Age began about 3200 BC and is thought to have lasted until around 2500 BC. The later Bronze Age (2500–2000 BC) is divided by scholars into Middle and Late Cycladic. These latter periods increasingly

Cycladic bronze figurine.

display the influence of the Minoan culture of Crete, and show a move towards urban settlement. In general, the term Cycladic Culture refers to the Early Cycladic, and it is during this period that the individuality of the culture of the Cycladic islands is most evident.

The settlements of the Early Cycladic were small, of around 50 people, comprising densely packed stone-built housing, usually only of one storey. Accompanying the settlements, outside the residential area, were cemeteries of small cist graves (rectangular graves lined with stone) and chamber tombs, clustered in family groups. The dead were inhumed in a contracted (foetal) position along with everyday objects. Much of the evidence we have of how Early Cycladic society functioned comes from these cemeteries.

The often stark difference in grave goods between tombs provides evidence of a stratified society. While some graves contain a very rich variety of artefacts, including gold and silver jewellery, others have very little, often only a single marble figure. How these differences between rich and poor played out is a matter of conjecture, but many artefacts display a high degree of skill in their manufacture, indicating a class of skilled craft workers. Hunting, fishing, animal husbandry and agriculture provided food. The islanders were practised traders, pointing to the existence of a merchant class, presumably, among the wealthier members of society. Skilled sailors, they had contact with the Greek mainland, Crete, Turkey and even the distant Danube Basin.

White marble figurines

Of all the items left by these peoples, the marble figurines are perhaps both the most beautiful and enigmatic. Their different typologies are used by scholars to differentiate the various Cycladic eras. The predominately female figures are generally around 20cm (8ins) in length (a few near life-sized sculptures have been discovered) and are made of white marble. Almost two-dimensional in their execution, they have flattened oval heads, schematic breasts and folded arms; many features would have been painted on the marble (on the face, only the nose is rendered in relief). It is conjectured from the position of the feet that they were intended to lie horizontally, but there is no conclusive evidence for this, just as there is no evidence for their function. Explanations from scholars range from their being apotropaic (warding off evil), to divinities, symbolic after-death companions or ancestors.

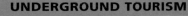

wealthiest town, with mansions and old churches.

The oldest community, however, is **Kástro** ⓰, the medieval capital, perched 100 metres (330ft) above the sea and 3km (2 miles) to the east of Apollonía. Catalans and Venetians once ruled the island; the walls they built are still in evidence, as are some remains of an ancient acropolis. Most of the buildings are from the 14th century. The big Venetian building in the centre of Kástro is the **archaeological museum** (Tue–Sun 9am–3pm; free).

Sífnos's southerly coastal settlements make tranquil bases. A marked footpath leads from **Katavatí** just south of Apollonía to **Vathý**, a hamlet on a deep inlet also linked by road to Platýs Gialós. Vathý's most visually stunning feature is the **Taxiárhis** (Archangel) Monastery (open only for service on the feast day), poised as though ready to set sail onto the sands. But Sífnos's most famous postcard/poster subject is **Hryssopigís** (Golden Wellspring) **Monastery** (open only on the feast day), built in 1653 on an islet now reached by a small footbridge.

Andíparos

Until the end of the last glacial period 10,000 years ago, the small, pretty island of Andíparos (www.antiparos.info) was joined to Páros. A narrow channel now separates them, plied by short-hop ferries from Poúnda bringing visitors to its famous **Spílio** ⓱ (**cavern;** summer daily 10am–4pm; spring/autumn 10am–3pm, closed Nov–May). Although only the topmost levels are accessible, and the impact is reduced somewhat by concrete steps down and a constant bilingual narration soundtrack, stalactite/stalagmite formations – 45 million years in the making – still impress. Arhilohos of ancient Páros was the first recorded visitor, the Marquis de Nointel the most flamboyant one, celebrating Christmas Mass here in 1673.

Andíparos Hóra itself is engaging, first put on people's radar by serving as location for the 1960 film Mantalena, which boosted Greek starlet Aliki Vougiouklaki's career – and subsequently made the little island an obligatory stop for alternative types transiting between Ibiza and India.

Páros church.

UNDERGROUND TOURISM

The **Cave of the Stalactites** (summer daily 10.45am–3.45pm; charge), the principal sight on Andíparos, was discovered during the reign of Alexander the Great, around 330 BC, and has been attracting visitors ever since. Despite the depredations of souvenir-hunters, who have broken and removed stalactites and stalagmites for centuries, it is still a fantastically spooky chamber, full of weird shapes and shadows.

Almost as impressive as the formations are the inscriptions left by past visitors, including King Otto of Greece and Lord Byron. The oldest piece of graffiti has sadly been lost – a note from several individuals stating that they were hiding in the cave from Alexander the Great, who suspected them of plotting his assassination. Another inscription (in Latin) records the Christmas Mass celebrated here by the French Marquis de Nointel in 1673, for an audience of 500.

In summer, buses and boats run to the cave from Andíparos Town, or else it's a two-hour walk. Then you descend more than 70 metres (230ft) from the cave entrance to the vaulted main chamber. There are concrete steps now, and electric lighting, making the descent easier, but the effect is still breathtaking. The entire cave is actually twice as deep as the part to which you are allowed access, but the rest has been closed because it would be too dangerous.

Páros is famous for the world's most translucent marble.

The snug little harbour of Náousa.

Its now barely inhabited **kástro** (medieval Venetian town plan where the houses are arranged in a defensive compound), complete with central cistern and chapel, is of a type seen elsewhere only at Síkinos and Kímolos. The island measures just 11km by 5km (7 miles by 3 miles), so there are no impossible distances, especially if you bring a scooter over from Páros. Lively nightlife and good sand have lured much trade to Andíparos from its larger neighbour. Tamarisk-shaded **Psaralíki**, within walking distance of town, is decent enough, but with your own transport (or the seasonal bus), **Sorós** 9km (5.5 miles) away on the southeast coast is Andíparos' best beach, with two tavernas.

Páros

The capital and main port of **Parikiá** (**Páros**) ⑱ resembles Mýkonos in appearance and in nightlife, but is gentler in spirit. The main sights here are the beautiful 4th-to-6th-century **Ekatondapyliarí church** (Our Lady of a Hundred Doors; daily 7am–9pm), the **archaeological museum** (Tue–Sun 9am–3.45pm) just behind, and the Venetian kástro overlooking the southwest waterfront, built largely of ancient masonry. Páros is famous for the world's most translucent marble; you can still visit the ancient quarries at **Maráthi** and pick up a chip, though the tunnels themselves are off-limits. Finally, Parikiá has one of the better town beaches in the Cyclades just northeast at **Livádia**, where tiny children confidently learn to sail at the Nautical Club.

Lévkes, the medieval capital, is the largest inland village. There are several 17th-century churches, and a lovely lower **platía** (square) flanked by cafés. Beyond Lévkes, best of the east coast beaches are Logarás and Hrysí Aktí, both with plenty of facilities and the latter a mecca for windsurfers. At the beautiful northerly port-resort of **Náousa**, the old harbour's colourful boats seem to nudge up right against the fishermen's houses, and the old quarter forms a quasi-**kástro**. With

upmarket boutiques and restaurants, it proves more exclusive (and expensive) than Parikiá. Nearby beaches, some served by caïque, tend to be crowded; best head northeast to sandy **Lángeri** or **Sánta María**, or northwest to the lighthouse peninsula and **monastery of Ágios Ioánnis Détis** (always locked), giving its name to the **natural reserve** just behind, car-free and criss-crossed with marked hiking trails, the best ones converging on the lighthouse.

Southern Páros is comparatively little frequented; the standouts here are the workaday fishing port (with beaches and tavernas) of **Alykí**, and the so-called **Valley of the Butterflies** (**Petaloúdes; daily May–Sept 9am–8pm**), a walled oasis of huge trees. The black and yellow butterflies – actually Jersey Tiger moths – abound in early summer.

Náxos

Náxos ❶ is the largest, loftiest and most magnificent of the Cyclades, replete with high, windswept ridges, long beaches, remote villages, ancient ruins, medieval monasteries or towers and a fascinating history. Central **Hóra** (**Náxos Town**) ❷ forms a labyrinth of Venetian-era mansions and fortifications, post-Byzantine churches, arcaded lanes and secluded restaurants. Hóra is divided into sections whose Latinate place names reflect the island's long Venetian occupation. The former French School, built into the ramparts, now houses the **archaeological museum** (Tue–Sun 8.30am–2.30pm). On Palátia islet (accessible by causeway) north of Hóra's ferry dock, the colossal free-standing marble doorframe called **Portára** is all that remains vertical of a never-completed Apollo Temple dating 530 BC.

Near the northern tip of Náxos is the small resort of **Apóllonas** ❸, with two beaches. A huge 6th-century BC *kouros* (statue of a man) lies on the hillside above the settlement,

abandoned in the quarry when the marble cracked. There are two other small, but better defined **kouri** near Mélanes in the centre of the island.

Náxos, oddly, is famed for its baby potatoes, while vegetable gardens and fruit trees grow densely around the many inland settlements, next to Byzantine churches and crumbling Venetian manors. Three villages on the road from Hóra to Apóllonas are particularly worthy of attention: Koronída, Apíranthos and Halkí.

Koronída (alias **Komiakí**), the highest village on the island, is extremely attractive, has wonderful views over the surrounding vineyards, and is the original home of the local *kitrón* liqueur. **Apíranthos** ❷ (aka Aperáthou) was originally settled by Cretan refugees in the 17th and 18th centuries. The town, whose streets are paved in marble, even looks Cretan. There are three small museums (Natural History, Geology, Archaeology; all Tue–Sun 8.30am–2pm) in the maze of lanes, plus cafés and tavernas from which to enjoy the view.

The unfinished Temple of Delian Apollo on Náxos.

At the foot of Mount Zás – the highest (1001m/3097ft) mountain in the Cyclades – sprawls the Trageá, a vast plateau covered mostly in olive trees. **Halkí**, the Trageá's main town, has several fine churches, the best (on the road north to Moní) being **Panagía Drosianí** (The Dewy Virgin; daily 10am–4pm), built in stages between the 4th and 12th centuries and retaining some of the oldest, albeit battered, frescoes in Greece.

From Áno Sangrí just southwest of the Trageá, a paved road descends 5km (3 miles) through a beautiful valley to the well-reconstructed Temple of Demeter (grounds always unlocked; *c.*530 BC).

Some of the Cyclades' best beaches line the southwest coast, facing Páros. **Agíos Prokópios** and **Agía Ánna** are the most popular; **Pláka, Glyfáda** and **Alykó** are less developed and more scenic, with naturist areas.

Mílos and Kímolos

Lying to the southeast, volcanic Mílos ㉓ is a geologist's paradise. Snaking streams of lava formed much of the island's coastline, thrusting up weirdly shaped rock formations. The island has always been extensively quarried, once for obsidian, now for bentonite, perlite, pozzolana and kaolin.

Mílos has graciously adapted to its growing stream of tourism, concentrated in **Adámas**, the port, and Pollónia, a fishing village in the northeast. Inside **Agía Triáda** church (Mon–Sat 9.15am–1.15pm, 6.15–10.15pm) in Adamás, Cretan-style icons dominate; Cretan refugees founded the town in 1853. The island's capital, **Pláka** (alias **Mílos**), has both an **archaeological museum** (Tue–Sun 8.30am–3pm) and a **Folklore Museum** (Tue–Sat 10am–2pm, 6–9pm, Sun 10am–2pm). A sunset hike to the **Panagía Thalassítra** (Mariner Virgin), the chapel above Pláka, and the old **Kástro** walls gives splendid views of Mílos and, on a clear day, as far as Páros.

Southwest of Pláka lies the **Vale of Klíma**, on whose seaside slope the ancient Milians built their city. Excavations undertaken in the late 19th century uncovered a Dionysian

MINERALS AND MINING

Mílos is, in reality, a far older, cooled-down version of Santoríni – at some point in the distant past a volcano collapsed, leaving a caldera, which became today's huge central bay. Its volcanic mineral wealth has always been extensively mined: in prehistory for obsidian, nowadays for bentonite, perlite, barite, gypsum, sulphur, kaolin and china clay. Gaping quarries disfigure the landscape, especially in the east, and the local mining companies still provide employment for a quarter of the islanders. Kímolos has quarries from which Fuller's earth and, to a lesser extent, bentonite, are extracted. The latter has a number of uses (it even turns up as an ingredient in Nivea cream). Ironically, the chalk which gave the island its name (kimoliá in Greek) is no longer extracted locally.

altar, and remains of an ancient gymnasium. The theatre is very well preserved, probably because of its Roman renovation. Nearby, a marble plaque marks the spot where a farmer unearthed the Aphrodite of Mílos (Venus de Milo) in 1820. Below the theatre lies one of the island's prettiest villages, **Klíma**, with brightly painted boathouses lining the shore, as well as the only **Christian catacombs** (Tue–Sun 8am–2.30pm; group tours only) in Greece. Carved into the hillside, they are the earliest evidence of Christian worship in the country. A 200-metre corridor is lined by tombs (all looted) which held around 5,000 bodies.

The island's best beaches lie along the southern limb of Mílos, at **Paleohóri** (with volcanic steam vents on the shore), **Agía Kyriakí**, **Firipláka** and **Provatás**. You'll need your own vehicle to reach them.

Ten km (6 miles) northeast from Adamás lies the rubble of the ancient city of **Phylakope** (Tue–Sun 8.30am–2.40pm; free), whose script and art resemble the Minoan. It flourished for a thousand years after 2600 BC.

Pollónia is a popular resort with a tamarisk-fringed if windy beach – making it a major windsurfing centre.

The tiny island of **Kímolos** ❷❹ – 36 sq km (14 sq miles), with a population of under 800 – is an irresistible presence for anyone who is staying in Pollónia. The small ferry takes just 20 minutes to cross the narrow channel to Kímolos's only landing, **Psathí**. Kímolos, once a pirates' hideout, today provides refuge from the more crowded islands. Although it is seriously undeveloped, it has several reasonable south-coast beaches, like **Skála** and **Kalamítsi**, within feasible walking distance of the port. **Hóra**, the single town, is a 20-minute walk up from Psathí port. The core of Hóra is the gated, 16th-century Venetian **Kástro**, its perimeter houses still inhabited.

Folégandros and Síkinos

Despite its tiny size – 32 sq km (12 sq miles) populated by under 700 people – **Folégandros** ❷❺ has played a not insignificant role in

Náxos harbour and town.

recent history: many Greeks were exiled here during both the 1930s' dictatorship and then the colonels' junta, following a precedent set by the Romans. Today, it is increasingly trendy for Greeks, French and Italians in particular, with a predictable effect on prices and retail-therapy opportunities.

Hóra is a magnificently sited medieval town with an inner **kástro** high above the sea. **Hryssospiliá** (Golden Cave) near Hóra, gapes in the cliff behind; a place of ancient worship and medieval refuge, it is closed for archaeological investigations. The island's "trunk road" continues beyond Hóra, threading the scattered ridge-line houses of **Áno Meriá**; paths and tracks lead southwest down to sheltered sandy beaches, the best of these being **Angáli**.

Although on the same ferry services as neighbouring Folégandros, rocky Síkinos ㉖ (population 240) so far seems to have shrugged off most tourism – unsurprisingly, as it's an austere island with few obvious diversions – and also escapes mention in the history books for long periods. The main rural monument, the **Iroön** at Episkopí, once identified as a temple to Apollo, is more likely to have been an elaborate Roman tomb, incorporated into a church during medieval times.

The three southeasterly beaches, **Aloprónia** (also the port and main resort), **Ágios Nikólaos** and **Ágios Geórgios**, face Íos. From Aloprónia harbour, it is an hour's hike (or regular bus ride) to Hóra, comprising the double village of Horió and **Kástro**, with its wonderful medieval defensive square. The abandoned convent of **Zoödóhou Pigí** looms above.

Íos

A tiny island with limited historic attractions, **Íos** ㉗ is not devoid of natural beauty or charm. The harbour of **Gialós** is one of the Aegean's prettiest, while the hilltop Hóra (aka Íos), capped by a windmill, blazes with the blue domes of two medieval churches. Its layout and flanking palm trees look almost Levantine. But ever since the 1960s, Íos has drawn

The brightly painted boathouses of Klíma.

the young and footloose, and despite local efforts to diversify, in summer at least this remains its defining characteristic. Íos nightlife resembles a downmarket, younger Mýkonos, with the crowds returning by bus from the beach or Gialós and filling clubs of all sizes until the small hours. Once ensconced inside a bar, they could be anywhere in the Western world, with few older Greeks in sight.

However, Íos also has many good swimming beaches, especially on the southwest coast, where the main developed resort is **Mylopótas**. Occasional buses run to superior **Manganári bay** in the far south, or Agía Theodóti on the east coast. For (relative) seclusion, head under your own steam beyond the latter to **Psáthi** beach.

On the way to Psáthi are the remains of **Paleokástro**, a Venetian fortress containing the marble ruins of what was the medieval capital. At a lonely spot toward the northern cape, behind the cove of **Plakotós**, is a series of **tombs**, probably Roman, yet one of these the islanders believe belongs to Homer, supposedly buried here while en route from Sámos to Athens.

Amorgós

A spine of mountains on **Amorgós** ㉘ – the tallest being Kríkellos in the northeast, at 822 metres (2,696ft) – precludes expansive views here unless you're on top of them. The southwesterly port-resort of **Katápola** occupies a small coastal plain, while the elevated **Hóra**, accessible by a regular bus service or a fine old trail, centres on a crumbled 13th-century Venetian castle. Hóra has no fewer than 40 churches and chapels – including one that holds only two people, the smallest church in Greece – as well as stepped plazas where cafés set out their tables.

The island's two most famous churches are outside Hóra. **Ágios Geórgios Valsamítis** (rarely open), 4km (2 miles) southwest, is built over a sacred spring; this church's pagan oracle was only cemented over after World War II, but you can still

Urn from Akrotiri on Santoríni. The largest Minoan city outside Crete, it was destroyed in a volcanic eruption in 1625 BC – at first, archaeologists thought they'd found Atlantis.

Tholária, traditional taverna, Amorgós.

hear it trickling below while fine frescoes stare at you from above. Half an hour east of Hóra, clinging limpet-like to tawny cliffs, the 11th-century Byzantine monastery of the **Hozoviótissa** (daily 8.30am–1pm, 5–7pm) – one of the most beautiful in Greece – is home to a revered icon of the Virgin from Palestine, three friendly monks, and a treasury-museum (same opening times as monastery).

Beaches in the northeast of Amorgós, around the second port-resort of **Egiáli**, are most alluring, especially the trio reached by the trail that runs northwest from the main beach. **Langáda** and **Tholária** are exquisite villages up the hillside, reached by well-marked paths, with tavernas and lodging. Indeed, hiking is the main reason to come to Amorgós – the premier trail (a 5-hour hike) goes from Potamós, above Egiáli, to Hozoviótissa.

Santoríni (Thíra)

Entering the bay of **Santoríni** ㉙ on a boat is one of Greece's great experiences. Broken pieces of a volcano's rim – Santoríni and its attendant islets – form a multicoloured circle around a seemingly bottomless lagoon that, before the volcano's eruption (*c*.1625 BC), was a hummocky volcanic plateau. Thíra, or Thera, are the island's official and ancient name respectively. Foreigners and most Greeks, however, prefer its medieval name, Santoríni, possibly after St Irene, one of three sisters martyred by Diocletian in 304. **Firá**, the capital, sits high on the rim along with its northern suburbs Firostefáni and Imerovígli, their white houses (many antiseismically barrel-vaulted) much rebuilt after a catastrophic 1956 earthquake. East of Firá, the land drops more gradually, with fertile fields leading to the east coast and dark-sand beaches. A few bare cliffs rise again in the southeast. On one of them sits 9th century BC **Ancient Thera** (Tue–Sun 8.30am–2.45pm), a most evocative setting even if little remains standing. **Akrotiri** in the far south, a large Minoan town preserved in volcanic ash like Pompeii, is fully excavated

Firá, Santoríni.

and visitable (Tue–Sun 8am–5pm). But many of its best artefacts – pots and original frescoes – are in Firá's **Museum of Prehistoric Thera** (Tue–Sun 9am–4pm).

Though Firá, Firostefáni and Imerovígli are highly developed, many other places offer plentiful accommodation, with less density and/or tackiness. **Ía** (**Oia**), on the island's northernmost peninsula, is perhaps Greece's most photographed village. As at Imerovígli, **skaftá** ("dug-out") houses in the volcanic cliffs converted into highly sought-after accommodation, are a local speciality. More conventional accommodation beckons at **Kamári** and **Périssa**, busy resorts on the east coast. Both have roasting hot black pebble beaches; either make a good starting point from which to climb up to Ancient Thera, then down the other side, with boats available to shuttle you back.

Cruise ships put in below Firá at **Skála Firá**, from where you ascend by donkey, by funicular or by foot up the stone stairway. Big ferries anchor at **Athiniós**, 10km (6 miles)

further south. The most popular boat excursions offered are to **Thirassía**, Santoríni's sleepy and beachless satellite islet opposite Ía; and to the volcanic islets of **Paleá** and **Néa Kaméni** in the middle of the submerged caldera, where passengers have the opportunity to bathe in marine hot springs or clamber over a still-steaming cinder cone.

Anáfi

About 250 people live on **Anáfi** ➌⓪ in winter, surviving mainly by fishing and subsistence farming. Summer tourism has boosted the economy, but development is slow despite the island figuring regularly on ferry lines between Santoríni, Crete and the Dodecanese.

The south-facing harbour, **Ágios Nikólaos**, has few amenities – best walk briefly east to palm-tree-tufted Klisídi beach, with rooms and tavernas. A short bus ride or half-hour walk up, the **Hóra** offers a wider choice of both, and life in the streets is still fairly untouristy. Both a road (seasonal bus) and maintained path

Food with a view, Santoríni.

head east via the south coast to **Zoödóhou Pigís Monastery** (daily 11am–1pm, 4–6pm), erected over the ancient shrine to Apollo. Extensive courses of marble masonry in its walls are believed to be remnants of the old temple. Above the monastery soars the massive pinnacle, claimed larger than Gibraltar, that is Anáfi's most distinctive feature. Under an hour's climb from the lower monastery brings you to smaller, blindingly white **Panagía Kalamiótissa** on the summit, a popular sunrise vantage for those prepared to sleep out here. The church is not open, but you can get water from the cistern outside. Between the pinnacle and Klisídi are various outstanding beaches, best of these **Katsoúni** and **Roúkounas**.

The Back Islands (Little Cyclades)

The so-called "Back Islands" or Little Cyclades beyond Náxos – **Donoússa**, **Irakliá**, **Skhinoússa** and **Koufonísi** – have permanent populations of 100 to 200 each. They're hardly secret (or cheap) destinations now, with ample tourist facilities including bank ATMs on each one.

Hilly **Donoússa** ㉛ has lovely south-coast beaches popular with campers, and some walking opportunities; views southwest from the port village take in the barren Makáres islets and the grand profile of Náxos. **Koufonísi** ㉜ (technically Áno Koufonísi) is the flattest of the quartet, and the busiest with a Páros-Mýkonos-type clientele, thanks to excellent beaches and a charming main village. The entire south coast looks across to Káto Koufonísi (day-trip accessible, with another beach and taverna) and hulking Kéros (off-limits), which was a third-millennium BC burial site and source of much of the Cycladic material in Greek museums. **Skhinoússa** ㉝ has no less than 16 beaches, few with facilities, fringing the coast, while its hilltop Hóra has an adjacent medieval fortress. **Irakliá** ㉞ has two settlements: the harbour, Ágios Geórgios, and Hóra, just over an hour's hike above, plus a visitable cave, but the fewest beaches of the group.

Small fishing boats still play their part in the economy of the Cyclades.

Ancient Delos

Extensive Greco-Roman ruins occupying much of minuscule Delos (Dílos), southwest of Mýkonos, make the four-square-kilometre (1.5-sq-mile) islet the near-equal of Delphi and Olympia.

If you suffer from seasickness, be forewarned: the island occupies one of the most turbulent reaches of the Aegean. The boat trip takes about 40 minutes; in windy conditions (the norm), breakfast should be a dry bread-roll or two, nothing more. In summer, there are also daily trips to Delos from Tínos.

Delos became a shrine because Leto, a nymph pregnant by Zeus, gave birth there first to Artemis and then, clutching a palm tree, to Apollo. A floating rock, Delos was rewarded for braving Hera's jealous wrath by four diamond pillars that anchored it to the seabed.

Most of the ruins occupy a broad area on the island's west coast. To the south is the theatre quarter, with various domestic buildings. On the north of the site are the sanctuaries to which pilgrims from all over the Mediterranean came with votive offerings and sacrificial animals.

For nearly a thousand years, Delos was the political and religious centre of the Aegean, and host to the Delian Festival, held every four years and, until the 4th century BC, Greece's greatest religious gathering. The Romans turned it into a grand trade fair, and made Delos a free port. It also became Greece's main slave market, where as many as 10,000 slaves (as against 25,000 local residents) were said to be sold daily. In 88 BC, Mithridates, king of Pontus, sacked Delos, followed by the pirate Athenodoros in 69 BC; it never recovered, and fell into disuse.

The Sanctuaries of Apollo and Dionysos

Follow the pilgrim route from the Sacred Harbour to a ruined, monumental gateway leading into the Sanctuary of Apollo. Within are three temples dedicated to Apollo and one to Artemis, and the remains of a colossal marble statue of the god. Close by is the Sanctuary of Dionysus, with several Dionysic friezes and outsized phalli standing on pedestals – including a marble phallic bird, symbolising the

body's immortality. Continue to the stunning Lion Terrace, where five Archaic lions squat. (These are copies; the weathered originals, carved from Naxian marble, are in the museum.) Below this is the Sacred Lake, and a palm tree which marks the spot of Apollo's birth.

Most visitors delight in the residential portion of Delos, occupied by merchants rather than gods. Their houses, close to the commercial port, form a warren separated by narrow lanes equipped with Roman drains and niches for oil-burning street-lamps. The main street leads to the modest theatre, which seated 5,500, with superb views from the uppermost of its 43 rows. Either side of the theatre are grander mansions named for the subjects of their still-exquisite courtyard mosaics: Dionysos, Trident, Dolphin, Masks.

From the theatre quarter, a gentle stroll leads to the summit of Mount Kýnthos (110 metres/360ft), offering memorable views of the ruins and the Cyclades. Finish off your tour by descending first past the Hellenistic grotto of Hercules, and then stopping at the terrace of shrines to the Foreign Gods. During the town's prime, practically the entire Levant traded here, under the tutelage of shrines erected to their own divinities.

One of the lean lions, carved in the 7th century BC, which guard Delos' Sacred Lake.

The aquamarine waters of the Gulf of Mirabello.

CRETE

Greece's largest and southernmost island is characterised by soaring mountains, Venetian townscapes, a proudly independent people and unique remains of Europe's first great civilisation.

Megalónisos (Great Island) is what Cretans call their home, and "great" refers to far more than size. It certainly applies to the Minoan civilisation, the first in Europe and the core of Cretan history. Visitors by the thousands pour into the ruins of Knossos, Phaistos, Malia and Agía Triáda, before heading towards one of the scores of excellent beaches. With two major international airports, Crete cannot be classified as undis covered, but through its sheer scale it manages to contain the crowds and to please visitors with widely divergent tastes. While a car is essential for discovering the best of the island, car hire is, unfortunately, comparatively expensive unless you book well in advance on-line.

For four months of the year, snow lies on the highest peaks which provide a dramatic backdrop to verdant spring meadows ablaze with flowers. This, as botanists and ornithologists know well, is by far the best time to visit. The former arrive to view more than 150 species which are unique to the island, while the latter are thrilled by more than 250 types of bird heading north. In spring, the island is redolent with sage, savory, thyme, oregano – and dittany, the endemic Cretan herb. It has long been reputed to be aphrodisiac – the

dialect name for the plant is *érondas*, as in erotic.

Crete, much more than other Greek islands, is a place both for sightseeing and for being on the beach. Minoan ruins are the major magnets, but there are also Greek, Roman and Venetian remains, and a score of museums. There are hundreds of Byzantine churches, many with rare and precious frescoes. If the church is locked, enquire at the nearest café. Even if you don't track down the key, you will enjoy the encounter with local people.

Minoan bull at the Iráklio Archaeological Museum.

FACT

Walk Iráklio's Venetian walls and you will reach the tomb of local author Nikos Kazantzakis, of Zorba the Greek fame. His epitaph reads: "I believe in nothing, I hope for nothing, I am free".

Iráklio (Heráklion)

Crete's capital since 1971, **Iráklio ❶** has nearly a third of the island's population and is Greece's fifth-largest city. Once among the wealthiest Greek towns, it – like most of the country – has fallen on hard times since 2008, with unemployment above the national average. Extensive World War II damage was compounded by poor (or rather, no) urban planning choices thereafter. Despite this, attempts are ongoing to remedy a scruffy civic infrastructure, with the old quarter and Venetian monuments getting as much conservationist attention as scarce funds allow.

Most tourists head first for the Minoan site of **Knossos ❷** (daily Apr–Sept 8am–8pm, Oct–Mar 8.30am–3pm; see also page 270). To fully appreciate the site, this should be combined with a visit to Iráklio's outstanding **archaeological museum ❹** (Tue–Sat 8am–8pm, Sun–Mon 9am–4pm); although largely closed for works since 2006, two galleries opened in late 2012, displaying the "greatest hits" from a collection of more than 5,000 objects, including the famous Phaistos Disc and the delicate bee pendant from Malia. The tourist office is just opposite, and both are moments from the cafés of **Platía Eleftherías ❸** (Freedom Square).

Iráklio's other major attractions date from the Venetian era, Crete's most prosperous period in historical times. Head seawards towards the old harbour, guarded by the **Koulés fortress ❸** (closed for restoration until 2014), whose three external reliefs of the Lion of St Mark confirm its provenance. From here, stroll westwards along shorefront Sofokéous Venizélou to the excellent **Historical Museum ❹** (Mon–Sat 9am–5pm; www.historical-museum.gr), which covers Cretan history and ethnography from the Byzantine Empire to the present. Inside are fine icons and fresco fragments, stone relief carvings, documentation of the local Jewish, Muslim and Armenian communities, folk textiles and a recreation of a traditional Cretan home. Models and prints across the centuries show how Iráklio has developed, as does

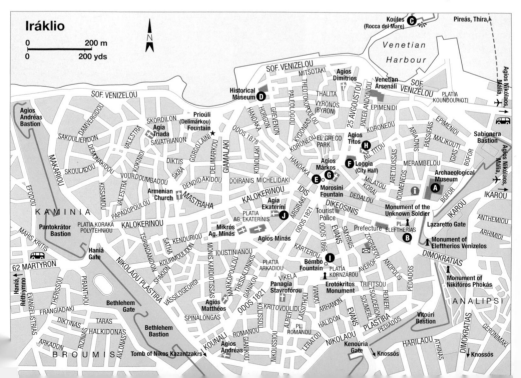

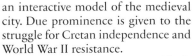
an interactive model of the medieval city. Due prominence is given to the struggle for Cretan independence and World War II resistance.

Return to the city centre at **Platía Venizélou** (Lion or Fountain Square), which takes its popular names from the stylish 17th-century **Morosíni fountain ❸** and guardian marble lions 300 years older. Overlooking the square is the handsome Venetian *loggia* ❹ (now the city hall), flanked by the churches of **Ágios Márkos ❺** (today the municipal art gallery; Mon–Fri 9am–1.30pm, 6–9pm, Sat 9am–1pm) and **Ágios Títos ❻** (irregular opening). Since 1966, when it was returned from Venice, the skull of St Titus, St Paul's apostle to Crete and its first bishop, has been housed in Ágios Títos.

Walk south along noisy Odós 1866, "market street", redolent with tantalising smells, jammed with people but now very touristy. Admire the Venetian **Bembo Fountain ❼** and the adjacent Turkish pumphouse (now a café) at the far end before turning west towards the **Icon and Sacred Art Museum** (daily 9.30am–3.30pm), inside 15th-century **Agía Ekateríni ❽** church. Stars of the collection are six icons by 16th-century master Mihaïl Damaskinos.

Finally, walk along the 15th-century **city walls,** in their day the most formidable in the Mediterranean, once besieged for 21 years. They stretch for nearly 4km (2.5 miles) and in parts are 29 metres (95ft) thick. En route, pause a moment at the tomb of the great Cretan author and iconoclast **Nikos Kazantzakis** and enjoy the spectacular views.

Around Iráklio

In and around the village of **Arhánes ❸**, 12km (8 miles) south of Knossos, are two churches with interesting frescoes, a good archaeological museum and three Minoan sites the Anemospilia sanctuary, the Gioukhtas peak sanctuary and the caves. Evidence suggests that when the **Anemospiliá** temple was destroyed by an earthquake, a priest was in the ritual act of sacrificing a youth. This conjecture has outraged

The Venetian church of Ágios Títos.

Morosíni fountain.

The mountainous interior.

some scholars as much as Nikos Kazantzakis's books outraged the established Orthodox Church.

A drivable track from Arhánes leads up **Mount Gioúkhtas** (811 metres/2,660ft), from where you can admire the panorama while griffin vultures soar overhead. Resembling a recumbent figure, said to be Zeus, the mountain top has a Minoan peak sanctuary and inaccessible caves in which Zeus is supposedly buried. Perhaps this proves the truth of the aphorism that "all Cretans are liars" because to most ancient Greeks, Zeus was, after all, immortal.

Týlissos ❹, 13km (8 miles) southwest of Iráklio, one of the few modern villages to retain its original pre-Hellenic name, offers three well-preserved Minoan manor houses (daily 8.30am–2.40pm). Twenty km (13 miles) further along the same road, **Anógia** ❺ is a weaving and embroidery centre. Many locals wear native dress but this is not touristic folklore: Anógia has a long tradition of resistance – the village was razed and the menfolk massacred in 1944 – and its people are among the proudest and most musical in Crete.

From Anógia, another road climbs to the magnificent **Nída plateau,** from where it is a 20-minute uphill stroll to the **Ideon Cave,** which was the nursery, if not the birthplace, of Zeus. Here, the infant god was hidden by the Kouretes, who clashed their weapons to drown the sound of his cries, while the nymph Amalthea fed him goat's milk. Strong walkers might wish to push on along the marked E4 path to the summit of **Mount Psilorítis,** at 2,456 metres (8,060ft) the highest point on Crete.

Return to Iráklio and continue eastwards along the coastal highway for 24km (15 miles) to the so-called Cretan Riviera – reminiscent of Blackpool or Coney Island – and its resorts of **Hersónisos, Stalída** (Stalís) and **Mália**. These are neither elegant nor ethnic: bars, loud music, and fast-food outlets abound. Beaches are not always brilliant, and development is best explained by proximity to Iráklio airport.

The palace at **ancient Mália** ❻ (Tue–Sun 8.30am–2.40pm), traditionally associated with King Sarpedon, brother of Minos, is contemporary with Knossos. The ruins are not as extensive as Knossos or Phaistos, but even without reconstruction, they are more comprehensible. Recent excavations have unearthed the **Hrysólakkos** (Golden Pit) from the proto-Palatial period (2000–1700 BC), an enormous necropolis with numerous gold artefacts.

Lasíthi province

From the "Riviera", a twisting mountain road leads up to the **Lasíthi Plain**, 840 metres (2,750ft) above sea level and 57km (36 miles) from Iráklio. This fertile upland used to produce abundant crops of potatoes, grain, apples and pears, but depopulation and unusual rains hampering spring planting has meant agricultural decline. The fabled 10,000 windmills here, now derelict, no longer pump up water from the limestone below, having been replaced by diesel pumps. **Psyhró** ❼ village is closest to the

giant **Dikteo** (**Diktian**) **Cave,** another birthplace of Zeus.

Back on the coast (reached by the scenic Lasíthi–Neápoli road), **Ágios Nikólaos** ❽, 69km (43 miles) from Iráklio, is invariably abbreviated by tourists to "Ag Nik". Magnificently situated on the Gulf of Mirabello and overlooked by mountains to the east, this is also the capital of Lasíthi district. Between here and **Eloúnda** (10km/6 miles away) are some of the island's best and most expensive hotels, despite Ag Nik lacking a decent beach, though adequate ones lie a short distance southeast. Tourist facilities cluster around Ag Nik's little harbour and adjacent **Lake Voulisméni,** 64 metres (210ft) deep but once believed to be bottomless. Eloúnda's **Spinalónga** island ❾ (summer daily 9am–6.45pm, winter by arrangement), an isolated leper colony until 1957 (the last in Europe), with a massive Venetian fortress and poignant memories, is readily reached from Eloúnda or much closer Pláka by boat.

Clinging to the hillside 12km (7 miles) south of Ag Nik, **Kritsá** ❿ is

FACT

The island of **Spinalónga** was immortalised in Victoria Hislop's eponymous novel, and the successful Greek TV series based on it – Greek tourists appear here in droves now.

Váï's palm-fringed beach.

Minoan vases at the Iráklio Archaeological Museum.

Some 19km (12 miles) southeast of Ag Nik, is **Gournia** ⓫ (Tue–Sun 8.30am–2.40pm), a Minoan town rather than a palace, complete with streets and houses, spread over a ridge that overlooks the sea. In spring, when the site is covered with a riot of wild-flowers, even those bored with old stones will appreciate it.

Sitía ⓬, 70km (44 miles) from Ag Nik, looks set to remain a backwater since works for expanding the tiny local airport to accept jets have been suspended indefinitely. Mostly a place to just hang out behind the sandy beach, its specific attractions are few – chiefly the **archaeological museum** (Tue–Sun 8.30am–2.40pm), full of finds from Minoan Zakros. After 16km (10 miles), you reach fortified Toploú Monastery (daily 9am–1pm, 2–6pm, Oct–Mar closes 4pm), with its famously intricate icon Lord Thou Art Great, though most of the premises are off-limits. About 8km (5 miles) further along, you arrive at **Váï** ⓭, renowned for its myriad palm trees, large sandy beach and tropical ambience. The

claimed to be the home of Crete's best weavers. Their brilliantly coloured work hangs everywhere – for sale – complementing the flowers and contrasting with the white-washed homes that line the narrow village alleyways. Below stands the 13th–15th-century church of **Panagía Kyrá** (Tue–Sun 8.30am–5.30pm), Crete's greatest Byzantine treasure. Although many frescoes are damaged or still uncleaned, the *Presentation of the Virgin* and Last Supper appear in full glory.

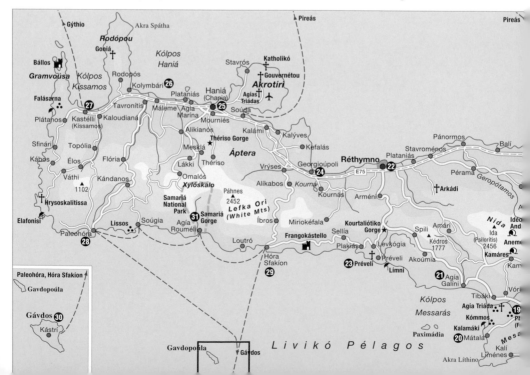

palm trees are native to Crete, and the beach is usually crowded.

Zakros  (July–Oct daily 8am– 5pm, Nov–June 8am–3pm), 43km (27 miles) from Sitía, is another great Minoan site, situated below the spectacular **Valley of the Dead,** where caves were used for Minoan burials; the best approach is via the marked path down through the gorge, starting at inland **Zákros** village. The palace-town has the customary central courtyard with royal, religious and domestic buildings and workshops radiating outwards; most date from 1900–1600 BC, the apogee of Minoan civilisation. You may then dine, swim or even stay at adjacent **Káto Zákros** beach hamlet.

Another road from Sitía leads initially south to the low-key resort of **Makrý Gialós** ⓮, with a long, gently shelving sand beach. Some 29km (18 miles) west, past sheltered coves like Agía Fotiá and Ahliá, lies **Ierápetra** ⓰, the south coast's only real town, and Crete's fourth largest. With little to offer besides a tiny Venetian fort (daily summer 8.30am–7.30pm) and

a small but interesting archaeological "collection" (Tue–Sun 8.30am–3pm) inside a former Koranic school, Ierápetra has mostly devoted itself to greenhouse agriculture. The prime local targets are offshore **Hrysí** (**Gaïdouronísi**), graced by idyllic beaches, or the village resort of **Mýrtos**, 15km (9 miles) west, with an enduring "alternative" ambience and more excellent sand.

South from Iráklio

Head south from Iráklio over the island's spine and you reach a breathtaking view of the **Plain of Mesará,** whose rich soil and benign climate make it an agricultural cornucopia. At the edge of the plain, the main enclosed site of **Gortys** ⓱ (modern Górtyna; daily summer 8am–7pm, winter 8am–5pm) is 41km (26 miles) from Iráklio. This was the capital of the Romans, who came to Crete in 67 BC to settle feuds but who stayed and annexed the island. Outstanding are the Roman *odeon* and a triple-naved

The minaret of Ierápetra's Ottoman mosque.

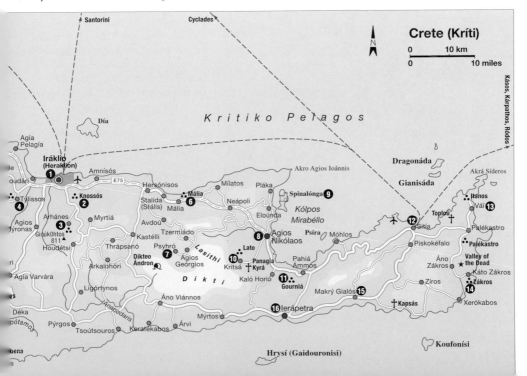

Crete (Kríti)

basilica of Ágios Títos, the latter by far the best-preserved early church in Crete. But the most renowned artefacts are some stone blocks incorporated into the *odeon*. About 2,500 years ago, a 17,000 character text, the Law Code of Gortys, was incised on these. The script is written in ox-plough manner – reading left to right along one line, then right to left along the next.

It's a brief drive south to the long beach at **Léndas** ⓲ (72km/45 miles from Iráklio); nearby **ancient Lebena** was the port for Gortys, and its therapeutic springs made it a renowned sanctuary with a temple to Asklepios, the god of healing. Only traces of this, notably a Hellenistic mosaic, can be seen.

Phaistos ⓳ (modern Festós; daily 8am–7pm summer, 8am–5pm winter), Crete's second great Minoan palace, occupies a magnificent location 16km (10 miles) west of Gortys. Staterooms, religious quarters, workshops, storerooms and functional plumbing can all be identified; those purists who bristle at Knossos's reconstruction will find this site more satisfying, as they

will **Agía Triáda** 3km (2 miles) west (daily 10am–4.30pm), a combination of Minoan summer villa and later Dorian town.

The closest beaches are at **Mátala** ⓴, 70km (44 miles) from Iráklio. The resort first gained renown when the caves in the sandstone cliffs flanking the small sandy beach became home to 1960s hippies.

The scenic 30-minute walk south to Red Beach is highly recommended, though **Kómmos** beach to the north is much larger and has a Minoan site, the old port of Phaistos, still being excavated. The larger south-coast resort of **Agía Galíni** ㉑ also lies on the Gulf of Mesará, though a little further west. The harbour, with a short wide quay and a tiny main street jammed with tavernas and bars, is enclosed within a crescent of steep hills covered with modest hotels.

Réthymno and around

From Iráklio, the new coastal road runs west towards Réthymno. Leave the expressway 25km (16 miles) from the capital for **Fódele,** a small village rich in orange trees and locally made embroidery. A restored house (May–Oct Tue–Sun 9am–7pm) here is said to be the 1541 birthplace of Domenikos Theotokopoulos, better known as **El Greco.** Fódele's fame may be fleeting, for the latest word is that El Greco was probably born in Iráklio.

At Stavroménos, turn southeast for the beautifully situated **Arkádi Monastery** (80km/50 miles from Iráklio; daily 9am–8pm), Crete's most sacred shrine to its suicidal 1866 resistance to the Turks. The elaborate 16th-century western facade of the church figured on the retired 100-drachma note.

Réthymno ㉒ (Réthimno), which prides itself on being Crete's intellectual capital (reflected in an internationally respected university), has a well-preserved old town with a small, picturesque Venetian harbour; the quayside – choc-a-bloc with

Busy Réthymno street.

restaurants – is guarded by an elegant lighthouse.

On the west, the immense ruined **Fortétsa of 1580** (daily mid-March–mid-Nov dawn–dusk) is claimed to be the largest extant Venetian castle, with excellent views. Inside, almost the only intact structure is the 1647-built Ibrahim Han Mosque, the largest domed structure in Greece.

The town's other main attractions – the **Rimóndi Fountain,** the **archaeological museum** (Tue–Sun 8.30am–2.40pm) with a fine collection of painted clay sarcophagi, the **Historical and Folklore** Museum (April–Oct Mon–Sat 9.30am–2.30pm, 6–9pm), with a wealth of rural impedimenta, and the **Nerantzés Mosque** (a converted Venetian church) – all lie between the fortress and the long town beach which starts just past the old port. Venetian and Ottoman houses with unexpected architectural delights line the narrow streets linking these sights, while minarets and wall fountains with ornate calligraphy recall the long Ottoman tenure (and an urban population almost half Muslim before 1898).

Due south from Réthymno, the main road towards Agía Galíni first passes the turnings for **Préveli Monastery** ㉓ (daily Apr–May 9am–7pm, June–Oct 9am–1.30pm, 3.30–7pm), famously active in helping to evacuate stranded Allied servicemen after the fall of Crete in 1941, and **Plakiás**, with its five distinct beaches and spectacular mountain backdrop, 43km (27 miles) from Réthymno.

The busy E75 coastal expressway continues west from Réthymno towards Haniá, crossing the provincial boundary just before **Georgioú-poli** ㉔ at the mouth of the River Armyrós, which meets the sea at one end of a good long beach. Some, however, may prefer the novelty of nearby Lake Kourná, the only freshwater lake in Crete, with tavernas, idyllic swimming and pedaloes or kayaks to rent.

Arkádi Monastery, Crete's most sacred shrine.

Haniá's Venetian-built waterfront.

ICONS AND EL GRECO

The artist El Greco (1541–1614), a Cretan native who studied under Titian, is best known for his portraits and religious pictures painted in Rome and Toledo. His highly distinctive style anticipated modern impressionism by his use of cold white, blue and grey colour schemes, and by his sacrifice of realism to emotional effect. His work also strikingly fuses Byzantine and Renaissance influences, a legacy of his early training as an icon-painter in Iráklio.

These icons were not objects of idolatrous worship, but this was precisely the indictment of the so-called Iconoclasts during the 7th and 8th centuries. In an effort to purify the religion, they proceeded to literally deface thousands of icons throughout Byzantium. Intact pre-9th-century icons are consequently very rare. Iráklio's church of Agía Ekateríni here has a fine collection of icons, including six by Mihaïl Damaskinos, a contemporary of El Greco. Both artists are thought to have studied at the church, all that remains of the Mount Sinai Monastery School, founded by exiles from Constantinople after the fall of "the City".

Two works by El Greco can be viewed on Crete – *View of Mount Sinai and the Monastery of St Catherine and Baptism of Christ*, in Iráklio's Historical Museum.

The "Iron Gates" in the Samariá Gorge.

Agía Rouméli.

Haniá and around

Haniá ㉕ (Chaniá), 59km (37 miles) from Réthymno, is Crete's second city and claims to be one of the oldest continuously inhabited places in the world. One of the most vibrant towns in Greece, it has drawn a large population of foreigners and Greeks from elsewhere. At its heart is a delightful old town arrayed around the two Venetian harbours, replete with exquisite Venetian and Ottoman buildings, many of them home to museums. The best two are the **archaeological museum** (April–Oct Tue–Sun 8am–8pm, Mon 2–8pm, Nov–March Tue–Sun 8.30am–3pm), inside a former Venetian monastery, with a collection strongest on painted Minoan larnakes (sarcophagi), Cretan coins with local motifs, Roman statuettes, and Hellenistic mosaics, and the well-designed **Byzantine Museum** (Tue–Sun 8.30am–3pm) inside San Salvatore church, with icons, jewellery, coins, a floor mosaic and fresco fragments rescued from country chapels. A surviving synagogue, **Etz Hayyim** (Mon–Fri 10am–5pm; Sat eve services; www.etz-hayyim-hania.

org), has been restored for visits, although 99 percent of Haniá's Jews were deported by the Germans in 1944. Just south of the old-town walls, the **Agorá**, or covered market, was opened in 1913, a copy of Marseille's halles. One of Crete's shopping highlights, its cross-shaped arcades offer shade, a few tavernas and a variety of edible souvenirs.

The closest escape is to the **Akrotíri Peninsula** just east, with several small villages and beaches, plus three important monasteries. Seventeenth-century **Agía Triáda** (alias Zangarolón; daily 9am–7pm) is now essentially a museum, with an imposing Venetian facade. **Gouvernétou Monastery** 4km north is a functioning monastery not open to non-Orthodox, but marks the start of a strenuous, two-hour (round trip) hike down to the evocative remains of 11th-century **Katholikó**, Crete's oldest monastery.

The road west from Haniá hugs the coast, passing several busy small, contiguous resorts, before arriving at **Kolymbári** ㉖, gateway to **Goniá Monastery** (Sun–Fri 8am–12.30pm, 4–8pm, Sat pm only, winter

afternoon hours 3.30–5.30pm) with Ottoman cannonballs stuck in its walls. Beyond, there are memorable views of the plain of Kastéli and the Bay of Kísamos cradled by the peninsulas of Rodopoú and Gramvoúsa. The pleasant but rather characterless town of **Kastéli-Kissámos** ㉗ (42 km/26 miles from Haniá) has an outstanding museum (Tue–Sun 8.30am–2.40pm) with Crete's best Roman mosaics. Excursions can be made from here to the "Blue Lagoon" and Venetian island fortress at **Bállos**, at the tip of Gramvoúsa, or to spectacular **Falásarna** beach at the base of the peninsula, complete with ancient city.

From **Plátanos** village above Falásarna, a twisting corniche road leads to Váthi and the turning southwest for 10km (6 miles) more to the **Hrysoskalítissa Convent** (daily 8am–2pm). The name, meaning "Golden Stairway", reflects the legend that one of the 90 steps that lead to a viewpoint is made of solid gold, invisible to sinners. From here, the road continues 5km more to the excellent beaches

– hence very busy in season – of shallow **Elafonísi** lagoon. Símos is a highlight. Wade across to the island of the same name, and you are at westernmost Crete.

Different roads from Haniá or Kastéli, both via Kándanos with several frescoed churches on its outskirts, lead to the southwesterly resort of **Paleóhora** ㉘ (76 km/48 miles from Haniá), relatively low-key with a choice of sand and shingle beaches, or to ex-hippie-haven **Soúgia**, with a huge pebble beach and an enjoyable trail-walk to ancient Lissos. Both are linked by daily ferry to **Hóra Sfakíon** (Sfakiá) ㉙, 75km (47 miles) from Haniá, a small, picturesque coastal town with a heroic past. Its main *raison d'être* today – but don't tell this to the macho Sfakians – is as a transfer point for exhausted tourists returning by ferry from their Samariá Gorge excursion. All three resorts also have boats to the remote islet of **Gávdos** ㉚, the southernmost point in Europe (or the northernmost in Africa, as some wags put it).

The cliffs around the Samariá Gorge are the home of the rare and elusive Cretan wild goat, the agrími or krí-krí.

THE SAMARIÁ GORGE

Crete offers an exciting and spectacular walk through the **gorge of Samariá** ㉛ , claimed to be the longest (16km/10 miles) in Europe. The walk starts by descending a steep stair-path at Xylóskalo, 1,200 metres (3936ft) above the sea, at the southern end of the vast Omalós plain, itself a 45km (28 miles) tortuous drive from Haniá.

After about 6km (3.5 miles), with most of the steeper descent over, the abandoned **village of Samariá** and its church of Osía María come into view. Stop and admire the church's lovely 14th-century frescoes – an opportunity to regain your breath without loss of face. The going now gets tougher and involves criss-crossing the riverbed (be warned: flash floods can occur and wardens' warnings should be heeded). There is a lot of scree on the way, so you should wear sturdy walking shoes and take great care. As the gorge narrows, the walls soar straight upwards for 300–600 metres (1,000–2,000ft). Soon after passing the church of Aféndis Hristós, the **Sideróportes** (Iron Gates) are reached: here the gorge – scarcely penetrated by sunlight – is little more than 3.5 metres (11ft) wide.

The park is under the strict aegis of the Haniá Forest Service, which specifically forbids certain activities, including singing. While you are walking, the elusive Cretan wild goat, the *agrími*, will probably be nearby, though it is unlikely that you will see any. On the other hand, you may spot bearded vultures overhead.

There is a further 3km (2 miles) of hot and anticlimactic walking before celebrating with a longed-for swim or cold drink at new, coastal **Agía Rouméli** with its tavernas and pensions. In ancient times, this is where Cretan cypress wood, much coveted in the ancient world, was exported to Egypt. Once refreshed, the only practical exit from the gorge – other than more tough hiking east or west along the coast – is by boat eastwards to Hóra Sfakíon or westwards to Soúgia and Paleóhora. There are no roads.

The gorge is open from about May 1 until October 31, exact dates depending on weather and stream conditions (daily dawn–sunset; entrance fee). Allow four to six hours for the walk.

CENTRE OF EUROPE'S FIRST CIVILISATION

Until 1894, Crete's Minoan civilisation was little more than a myth. Now its capital is one of the largest and most thoroughly restored sites in Greece.

Knossos (pronounced Knossós in modern Greek) can be a baffling place, difficult to grasp. Some visitors find that the concrete reconstructions and repainted frescoes (often extrapolated from very small existing fragments) aid comprehension. But for many, used to other, more recent ruins that are clearly defensive or overtly religious, the site is mysterious. Can we hope to look back at fragments of a culture from 3,500 years ago and understand its imperatives and subtleties?

In legend, Knossos was the labyrinth of King Minos, where he imprisoned the minotaur, the human-taurine child of his wife Pasiphae. In reality, the place was probably not in the modern sense a palace, but rather an administrative and economic centre, unified by spiritual leadership. The 1,300 rooms of the main complex were used for both sacred and commercial purposes: lustral baths for holy ceremonies; store rooms for agricultural produce; workshops for metallurgy and stone-cutting. Nearby are the Royal Villa and the Little Palace.

Try to visit earlier or later in the day (better yet, visit out of season), to avoid the heat and the worst of the crowds. Look for subtle architectural delights – light wells to illuminate the larger rooms; hydraulic controls providing water for drinking, bathing and

flushing away sewage; drains with parabolic curves at the bends to prevent overflow. It is well worth hiring a certified guide to take you around – available ones congregate near the ticket booth.

Combine Knossos with an afternoon visit to the archaeological museum.

The Prince of Lilies or Priest-king Relief, plaster relief at the end of the Corridor of Processions, believed by Arthur Evans to be a priest-king, wearing a crown with peacock feathers and a necklace with lilies on it, leading an unseen animal to sacrifice.

The famous double horns now sitting on the south facade were once regarded as sacred symbols, though perhaps this is an overworking of the bull motif of the site.

he South Propylon has near life-size frescoes of processionary ouths, including the famous slender-waisted cup-bearers. In Iinoan art, male figures were coloured red, female white.

A (replica) fresco depicting the capture of a wild bull decorates the ramparts of the north entrance, leading to the road to Knossos' harbour at Amnisos.

The throne room, possibly a court or council room, has a gypsum throne, and frescoes of griffons. These may have symbolised the heavenly, earthly and underworldly aspects of the rulers.

Sir Arthur Evans, the English archaeologist whose reconstruction of Knossós, a significant quantity of it based on conjecture, was to prove controversial.

CONTROVERSIAL RESTORATIONS

In 1878, a local merchant, Minos Kalokairinos, uncovered part of Knossos, but the owners of the land prevented further excavation and even the wealthy German Heinrich Schliemann got entangled in unproductive negotiations for purchase of the site.

However, once Crete gained autonomy in 1898, the way was open for the English archaeologist Arthur Evans (later knighted) to buy the land and begin excavating. He worked here from 1900 until 1931, though by 1903 most of the ruins had been uncovered.

Evans' use of reinforced concrete to reconstruct long-vanished timber columns, and his completely speculative upper-storey reconstructions, have received considerable criticism. Moreover, the Minoan frescoes are not only arbitrarily placed, but (those in the Iráklio Museum as well) almost completely modern, painted from scratch by his assistants Piet de Jong and Émile Gilliéron. It's also clear that both the restoration and fresco-retouching was heavily influenced by the Art Nouveau and Art Deco styles prevalent at the time. Others have charged that Evans, a fairly typical Victorian chauvinist, manipulated evidence to fit his theory of the thalassocratic Minoans as prehistoric proto-British imperialists.

Excavation continues to this day, under subtler management.

The Palace as it would have looked in its heyday.

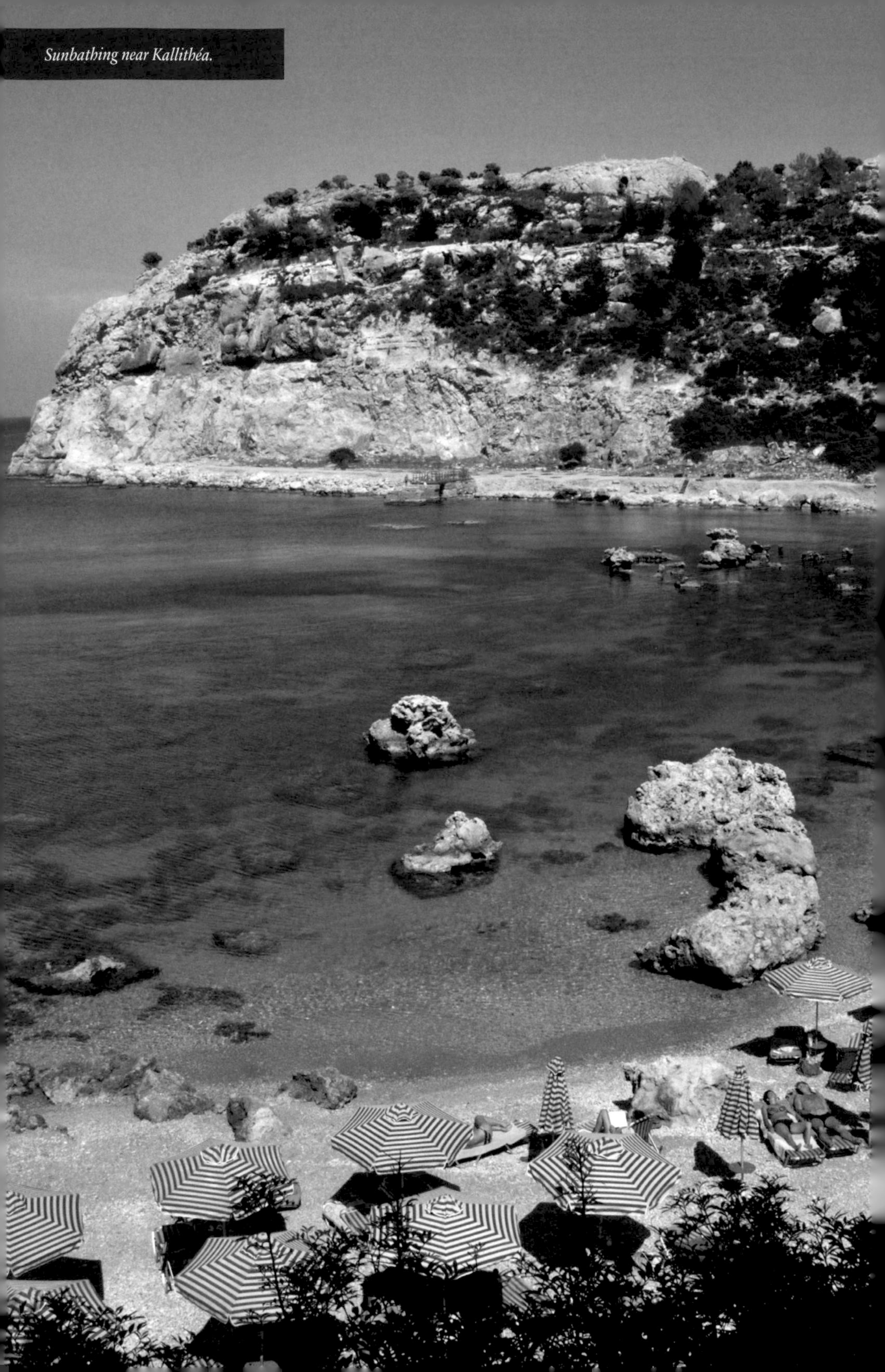
Sunbathing near Kallithéa.

RHODES

According to the ancient Greeks, Rhodes was "more beautiful than the sun". Even today's brash resorts cannot dim the appeal of its benign climate, entrancing countryside and unique history.

The largest and best-known of the Dodecanese islands, Rhodes (Ródos; www.rhodesguide.com) is endowed with a balmy climate and a wealth of monuments from many eras. Ancient Rhodes originally consisted of three city-states: Kameiros, Ialysos and Lindos. Following Athenian attacks, they decided to unite, founding the city of Rodos at the island's northeast tip, separated from Asia Minor by a strait just seven nautical miles wide. Fortifications were completed by 408 BC, and the town laid out in the popular grid plan of that era, championed by a certain Hippodamos.

Well-defended by its fleet and strategically positioned, Rhodes prospered as a trading station and led a charmed life despite fickle alliances, as the moment suited, with Athens, Sparta, Alexander the Great, or the Persians. For more on the Rhodes' colourful past, see box.

The Old City

Despite still-visible damage from Allied bombing in early 1945, the Old City of **Rhodes ❶** is one of the architectural treasures of the Mediterranean, a remarkably complete walled medieval town. The ramparts themselves (entrance from gate beside Palace of the Grand Masters) give a good

perspective over the palm-and-minaret-studded lanes. At the northwest summit stands the **Palace of the Grand Masters ❶** (summer Mon 12.30–7pm, Tue–Sun 8am–7pm, winter daily 8am–2.40pm), destroyed in 1856 by an ammunition explosion and hastily reconstructed by the Italians during the 1930s. On the ground floor are two excellent galleries detailing medieval and ancient Rhodes, with exemplary layout and labelling.

From outside, the better-restored **Street of the Knights (Odós Ippotón)**

Main Attractions

PALACE OF GRAND MASTERS, RHODES OLD TOWN
SYNAGOGUE-MUSEUM, RHODES OLD TOWN
MUSEUM OF MODERN GREEK ART, RHODES NEW TOWN
LÍNDOS ACROPOLIS
ANCIENT KAMEIROS
THÁRRI MONASTERY FRESCOES
PIGÉS KALLITHÉAS RESTORED SPA
TSAMBÍKA MONASTERY & BEACH
PARALÍA KALÁTHOU BEACH
WINDSURFING AT PRASONÍSI

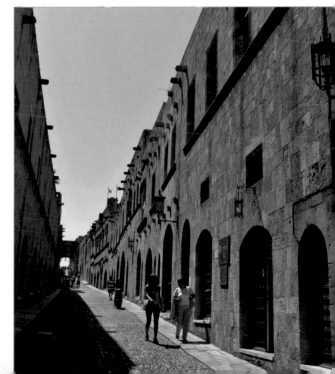

Street of the Knights (Odós Ippotón) in Rhodes Old Town.

Rhodes through the Ages

Rhodes has always played, but never directed, on the world stage – too large for outsiders to ignore, too small to be a power in its own right.

Under Alexander the Great, Rhodes forged links with the Ptolemies; consequently, the Rhodians refused to fight the Egyptians alongside King Antigonos. After Alexander's death, Antigonos sent his son, Demetrios Polyorketes, along with 40,000 men to attack the city in 305 BC; he failed after a year-long siege. The leftover bronze military hardware was melted down to make the island's most famous landmark, the Colossus of Rhodes, a representation of Apollo. A beacon to passing ships, it stood over 30 metres (100ft) tall, somewhere near the harbour entrance, for nearly 70 years before it collapsed during an earthquake in 226 BC.

The city emerged from the siege with prestige and prosperity enhanced, eclipsing Athens as the cultural beacon of the east Mediterranean. However, it got ideas above its station when it unwisely tried to reconcile the warring Romans and Macedonians. Rome retaliated in 168 BC by effectively making Rhodes a Roman vassal; involvement in Rome's civil wars a century later saw Rhodes sacked by Cassius and its fleet destroyed. After Octavius's victory in 42 BC and the establishment of imperial Rome, Rhodes regained some autonomy, and again served as a finishing school and sybaritic posting for officialdom. But its glory days were over. In late Roman and Byzantine times, the island endured second-rate status, prone to barbarian raids.

Early in the 14th century, the Knights Hospitaller of St John – expelled from Palestine and Cyprus – settled on Rhodes, ejecting the Genoese who had been holding the island on sufferance of the Byzantines. They proceeded to occupy and fortify virtually all of the Dodecanese, rebuilding Rhodes Town's rickety Byzantine city walls and acting as a major irritant to the sultan with their depredations of Ottoman shipping. Finally, in mid-1522, Süleyman the Magnificent landed an army of 200,000 on Rhodes to end the problem; Rhodes's second siege was shorter and more conclusive than the first, but only just. The Knights resisted valiantly, but finally were forced to surrender. On New Year's Day 1523, 180 survivors concluded honourable terms of surrender and sailed off to exile on Malta.

The Ottomans suitably appreciated their hard-won possession, at least initially, and instituted the regime common to fortified cities in their empire: Christians were forbidden from staying overnight within the walled old town, although Jews were tolerated in their small quarter to the east. This exclusionary edict gave rise to the *marásia* or Orthodox suburb villages which hem Rhodes Town on three sides, often bearing the names of their main parish churches. The Ottomans built a few grand mosques from scratch within the walls, but more usually appropriated small Byzantine and Crusader churches as *mescids* (the Muslim equivalent of a chapel). Even at the zenith of Ottoman power, the Muslim population of the entire island never much exceeded 15 percent. Ottoman rule became increasingly desultory and inefficient until the Italians effectively annexed Rhodes in spring 1912.

Marine Gate, Rhodes Old Town.

B, where the chivalric order once housed its members according to their native language, leads downhill to the badly labelled **archaeological museum C** (summer Tue–Sun 8am–7.10pm, winter Tue–Sun 8am–2.40pm), with its "Marine Venus", inspiration for Lawrence Durrell's travel memoir on his two years in Rhodes; the **Byzantine Museum D** (Tue–Sun 8.30am–2.40pm), opposite in the former cathedral of the Knights, with its exhibits of local icons and frescoes; and the nearby ethnographic **Decorative Arts Collection** (temporarily closed), with doors and chests salvaged from Dodecanesian village dwellings.

Despite an enduring resident Turkish minority, Ottoman monuments are not much highlighted except for the **Ottoman Library** (Mon–Sat 9.30am–4pm) and a wonderful **Turkish Bath E** (closed for renovations) on Platía Aríonos. The arcaded synagogue of **Kal Kadosh Shalom F** (summer Sun–Fri 10am–3pm; donation), in the former Jewish quarter, can also be visited, as can its adjacent museum (same hours) on the Rhodian Jewish community. The synagogue serves largely as a memorial to the more than 1,800 Jews of Rhodes and Kós who were deported to Nazi death camps in June 1944.

The New Town

Established by the Orthodox Greeks who were banished from the Old City by the Ottomans, and developed by the Italians when they took control in the early 20th century, the New Town (**Neohóri**) is the commercial centre of Rhodes and the administrative capital of the Dodecanese. Here, designer shops abound, peddling Lacoste, Benetton and Trussardi. Watch the world go by and the yachts bobbing from one of the pricey, touristy pavement cafés at **Mandráki** port. Marginally cheaper are the cafés inside the **Néa Agorá G** (covered market), though it's largely a tourist-trap of bad restaurants redeemed in part by the

Statue of Aphrodite in the Archaeological Museum of Rhodes.

The Palace of the Grand Masters.

Art Deco fish market gazebo at the centre.

Mandráki's quay buzzes night and day with caricature artists, popcorn vendors, sponge-sellers and touts hawking boat trips. Excursion boats leave by 9am for the island of Sými, calling first at Panormítis Monastery, or down the east coast to Líndos. Catamarans depart from Kolóna harbour, a 15-minute walk east, while full-sized ferries leave inconveniently from remote Akándia harbour, 1km southeast.

Mandráki, guarded by the round bastion-lighthouse of **Ágios Nikólaos ⓗ** (**St Nicholas' Fort**), is also an established port of call for the international yachting circuit, with local charters, too. By the harbour entrance stands a cluster of Italian monuments: the Governor's House with its Gothic arches, the **cathedral of St John the Evangelist ⓘ** (**Evangelismós**) next door (with fine Photis Kontoglou frescoes inside; you should be able to visit before or after a service) and, across the way, the post office, Town Hall and Municipal

Theatre. Opposite the theatre, the **Mosque of Murad Reis ⓙ** stands beside one of the island's larger Muslim graveyards. Beyond this is the **Villa Cleobolus** (not open to the public), where Lawrence Durrell lived from 1945 to 1947.

West, on Ekatón Hourmadiés (100 Date-Palms) Plaza, the **Museum of Modern Greek Art ⓚ** (Tue–Sat 9am–2pm; www.mgamuseum.gr) has the richest collection of 20th-century Greek painting outside of Athens. All the big names – semi-abstract Níkos Hadjikyriakos-Ghikas, Spyros Vassiliou, Yiannis Tsarouhis with his trademark portraits of young men, surrealist Nikos Engonopoulos, naïve artist Theophilos, neo-Byzantinist Photis Kontoglou – are well represented. Annexes around the corner and in the old town on Platía Sýmis host temporary exhibits.

Three ancient city-states

One of the original Dorian city-states, **Líndos ❷**, 44km (27 miles) south along the east coast, is the island's other big tourist magnet.

Local preserves for sale at a street market.

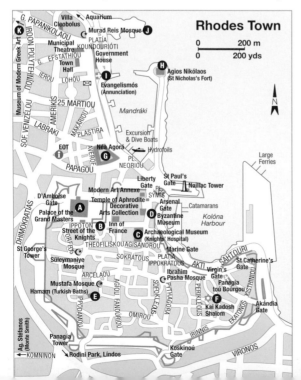

Settled early thanks to its fine natural harbour – the island's only one aside from Mandráki at Rhodes Town – its strong acropolis supports a restored Hellenistic Athena temple and another Knights' castle (summer Tue–Sun 8am–6.45pm, Mon 12.30–6.45pm, winter Tue–Sun 8am–2.40pm). Clustered below is the late-medieval village of imposing mansions built by local sea-captains; with its barren surroundings, the place has always lived from the sea. Italian, German and British bohemians first rediscovered Líndos in the 1960s, attracted by the pellucid light. But it has long since morphed from being an artists' colony to become a package-tour dormitory: midsummer visits, when you can hardly move down the narrow, cobbled streets, are not recommended.

The second of the original city-states, **Kameiros** ❸, 33km (20 miles) down the windswept west coast from Rhodes Town, merits a visit for displaying a perfectly preserved Classical townscape (summer Tue–Sun 8am–6.45pm, winter Tue–Sun

8am–2.40pm), without the usual later accretions. Unlike old Líndos, it was abandoned shortly after 408 BC. At ancient **Ialysos** ❹ (Tue–Sun 8.30am–2.40pm), 12km (7.5 miles) southwest of Rhodes Town, only a Doric fountain and some Hellenistic temple foundations are evident from the ancient city-state. Today, the site is best known for its appealing medieval monastery of **Filérimos** (same hours as Ialysos), well restored after World War II damage.

Ancient Kameiros.

Island sights

Superbly sited Knights' castles at **Kritinía** ❺ and **Monólithos** ❻, both beyond Kameiros, make suitable targets to visit, along with the villages of **Siánna** and Monólithos in between, well equipped for visitors, with numerous tavernas. The best Byzantine monuments in the interior

Knights' Castle at Kritinía.

Tsambíka monastery is a magnet for childless women. If a childless woman conceives after praying there, the child is named Tsambíkos or Tsambíka, names unique to Rhodes.

are the late Byzantine church of Ágios Nikólaos Foundouklí (always open) with smudged frescoes, just below 798-metre (2,600-ft) Profítis Ilías, and the monastery of **Thárri** ❼ (daily, all day) with its glorious, cleaned 14th-century frescoes, hidden amid partly burned pine forest between Líndos and Monólithos.

The best beaches cluster on the more sheltered east coast. The first resort travelling south from Rhodes Town is Kallithéa, which sprang up around the **Pigés Kallithéas spa** ❽ (daily summer 8am–6pm, winter 8am–4pm), established there by the Italians. Round the headland is Kallithéa Bay, one of the best beaches on the island and the most energetically exploited for tourism. On the south side of the bay is **Faliráki** ❾, one of Greece's more notorious resorts. By day, every form of water sport is available; by night, just a few surviving clubs compete with loud music and improbably alcoholic cocktails.

Pebbly **Traganoú,** at the north end of Afándou bay, has caves and overhangs, and is mostly patronised

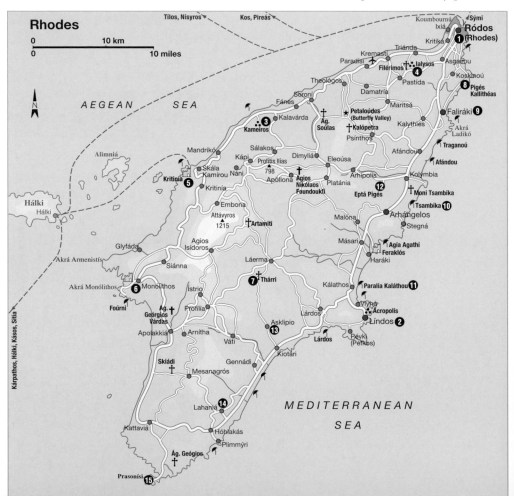

by Rhodians. **Tsambíka beach** ⑩ huddles beneath a giant promontory on which stands a tiny, eponymous monastery of the Virgin in her avatar of fertility goddess – hundreds of ex-votos testify to her successful intervention for childless couples. **Paralía Kaláthou** ⑪ is the best undeveloped beach on this coast.

Inland from Tsambíka, **Eptá Pigés** ⑫ is an enduringly popular oasis, its reservoir an Italian legacy. Northwest of there, the **Petaloúdes (Butterfly Valley)** is the seasonal home of millions of Jersey tiger moths, attracted by the Liquidambar orientalis trees in this secluded stream canyon.

Beyond the Líndos promontory, there are few specific sights aside from the wonderfully frescoed 11th-century church (daily 9am–5pm; charge) at **Asklipío** ⑬ village, just inland from the burgeoning resort of Kiotári. There are more, usually empty beaches at Gennádi; further south, the ravine-hidden, well-watered village of **Lahaniá** ⑭ for some decades attracted a second generation of drop-outs after the

Orientalised Art Deco, complete with palm trees, at Kallithéa.

original Líndos scene, who renovated traditional houses here under now-expired lease agreements. Land's End for Rhodes is the sandspit-tethered islet of **Prasonísi** ⑮, reached from Kattaviá village. Topography and winds combine to make the broad, flat beach here one of the premier venues for windsurfing and kiteboarding in Greece, with three schools operating every season.

ITALIAN ARCHITECTURE IN THE DODECANESE

The Italians, who occupied the Dodecanese from 1912 until 1943, adorned the historic centres of Rhodes and Kós towns with grandiose public buildings, constructed a huge naval base and the planned town of Porto Lago (Lakkí) on Léros, and did much to reconstruct Kós Town after it was levelled by the 1933 earthquake. Because of its associations with Fascism, any buildings linked to this period, whatever their quality, were until recently disparaged if not deliberately neglected; since the millennium, Italian monuments on all three of the islands cited have benefited from consolidation works.

In Rhodes, a new administrative centre – the Foro Italica – was created, comprising all public services, and centred on Pizza del'Impero with its all-important Fascist Party Headquarters with its tower and speaker's balcony. Beyond lay the city's purpose-built tourist area, which included La Ronda Sea Baths (today a popular bar-restaurant), the Albergo delle Rose (now the casino) and the aquarium at the northerly cape.

Art Deco style featured in the Fascist Youth Building and the football stadium; other buildings, such as the

nautical club, the aquarium and the Customs House mixed elements of Art Deco with abstract Ottoman motifs. Out in the countryside, the Pigés Kallithéas spa is the best example of orientalised Art Deco, stylishly blending with its surroundings.

The later phase of Fascist rule, from 1936, coinciding with the harsh tenure of Governor Cesare Maria de Vecchi, stressed the perceived continuity between the Knights Hospitallers and the Italians. Many monuments of the Knights were restored, and new buildings in a "neo-Crusader" style, such as the Bank of Rome, were erected. At the same time, buildings such as the Albergo delle Rose and the Courthouse were "purified" by removing the allegedly superfluous, orientalising features of Art Deco, and replacing these with a cladding of poros stone. In this final stage, Italian architecture in the Dodecanese conformed to Rationalist-Internationalist canons of the decade, with more monumental and rigidly symmetrical structures. The Puccini Theatre (now the Municipal Theatre) on the Piazza del'Impero was the best example of many such around this square.

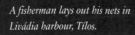
A fisherman lays out his nets in Livádia harbour, Tílos.

THE DODECANESE

Closer to Turkey than Greece, the archipelago has enormous variety, from holy Pátmos to busy Kós, from wild Kárpathos to tranquil Lipsí, from fertile Tílos to the volcano that is Nísyros.

Greek place names often reveal history, and "Dodecanese" (Dodekánisos), a new name by Greek standards, is no exception. Through four centuries of Ottoman rule, these islands were known as the Southern Sporades, a name still appearing on older maps. During this period, smaller, more barren islands here were granted considerable privileges – in effect, being invited to look after themselves – while larger, more fertile Rhodes and Kós were more strictly governed and colonised by Muslims.

After the establishment of an independent Greece in 1830, and periodic armed hostilities between it and the Ottoman Empire, such privileges were gradually withdrawn. The 12 larger islands (*dódeka nisiá* in Greek) submitted a joint objection against these infringements in 1908; it failed, but the new name stuck, despite there being – depending on how one counts – 18 or even 20 inhabited isles in this chain, extending from northwest to southeast in an arc along the Turkish coast.

In 1912, the Italians, as part of a larger war against the Turks, took this group of islands to cut the Ottoman supply lines to Libya. Despite initial promises to relinquish the archipelago once the Turks left Tripoli, the Italian annexation was consolidated by

World War I and the subsequent rise of the Fascist regime after 1923, when the group was officially renamed the "Italian Islands of the Aegean". The Fascists were busy colonialists, erecting numerous distinctive edifices (see page), planting eucalyptus to drain swamps, building roads and imposing their language, religion and political culture on public life. Repression was stepped up considerably in 1936 when governor Mario Lago was replaced by Cesare Maria de Vecchi, an ardent monarch-Fascist who

Main Attractions
EAST COAST BEACHES, KÁRPATHOS
ÓLYMPOS VILLAGE, KÁRPATHOS
SÝMI
VOLCANIC CALDERA, NÍSYROS
KNIGHTS' CASTLE, KÓS
SOUTHWESTERN BEACHES, KÓS
ARCHAEOLOGICAL MUSEUM, KÁLYMNOS
HÓRA, ASTYPÁLEA
HÓRA AND ITS MONASTERY, PÁTMOS

Attractive Mandráki, Nísyros.

Secluded Ápella beach, Kárpathos.

Emborió, Hálki.

helped depose Mussolini and was condemned to death by the Salo Republic (though he escaped to South America). In a series of bloody actions against now pro-Allied Italian forces, the Germans assumed control of the Dodecanese in late 1943, but in turn surrendered the islands to the British less than two years later.

Finally, in early 1948, after a 10-month interlude of Greek military rule imposed to weed out local collaborators with the Italians, the Dodecanese were united with Greece to become the country's southeasternmost, and most recent, territorial acquisition. Massive emigration to Australia, South Africa and North America ensued, as in chaotic post-war Greece, union with the "mother" country initially brought little other than freedom of movement. Today, the islanders live – as they always have – largely off the sea, which has brought them a catch of vital importance to the local economy: tourists.

Kárpathos, Kásos and Hálki

The most dramatic way to arrive at **Kárpathos** is by ship from Rhodes, invariably departing at or before dawn. After several hours' journey, the island appears with its imposing, often cloud-flecked summit-ridge. Boats stop at **Diafáni** ❶ (www.diafani.com), the northerly port given a jetty only in 1996. By the mid-morning light, onward passengers have an hour to get acquainted with Kárpathos. Its eastern shore drops steeply to the sea, baby pines sprouting from slopes denuded during the fierce blazes of the 1980s; occasionally, the cliffs stop at large, white, empty beaches.

After these first impressions, the main port of **Pigádia** ❷ in the east is inevitably a disappointment, with little to recommend it other than its fine setting; it dates only from the 19th century, but the islanders themselves – not invading

forces – effectively wrecked it with concrete constructions from the 1960s onwards. This lack of distinction also has something to do with Kárpathos's status as a backwater since ancient times; neither the Knights of St John nor the Ottomans bothered much with it, leaving it to the Genoese and Venetians, who called it Scarpanto.

Getting to a beach is going to be a top priority. An excellent one stretches immediately north for 3km (1.2 miles) along Vróndi Bay. More secluded ones, visible on the ferry ride in, prove close-up to have aquamarine water and white-sand or pebble shores, guarded by half-submerged rock formations. The best of these are Ápella, Aháta and Kyrá Panagiá, accessible either on small-boat excursions or overland – although some Kárpathiot roads are appalling and hire cars are expensive. The west coast is served by good roads but far more exposed, though at remote Levkós, a series of three bays tucked in between headlands, there are excellent beaches and a busy resort.

Most villages are well inland and high up, the standard medieval strategy against pirates, of whom Kárpathos had more than its fair share. The wealthiest settlements are a trio – **Apéri ❸**, Óthos and Voláda – just south of cloud-capped Mount Kalilímni, 1,215 metres (3,985ft) high, plus **Menetés** near Pigádia, all studded with a variety of traditional and contemporary villas.

Ólympos, draped over a windswept ridge in the northwest of the island, has long been something of a honeypot for anthropologists, academic and amateur, owing to its relict Dorian dialect, its colourful costumes (Easter and Assumption Day are celebrated with special verve here), music and communal ovens.

But conventional tourism here has been as distorting – and rescuing – as subsidies from abroad have been elsewhere on Kárpathos; the last of several ridgeline windmills stopped working as a real accessory to life late in the 1970s, but one was restored as a (briefly) functioning museum-piece a few years later. It now just makes for a good photo.

KARPATHIOT ARCHITECTURE AND DRESS

The source of wealth in Kárpathos seems mysterious at first, since there is little fertile lowland, no industry, and mass tourism began only in the late 1980s. In fact, Kárpathos lives largely off remittances from seamen and emigrants (mostly in the US); this economy has profoundly affected local culture, architecture and attitudes. It has deliberately slowed the development of tourism and, paradoxically, also enhanced the position of women who stayed behind. Overseas values have left their mark on house-building, although even the most vulgar modern pile may sport a date of construction, the owner's initials and a traditional emblem, perhaps a mermaid or double-headed Byzantine eagle.

In its original form, the vernacular Karpathiot house consists of a single, mud-floored space appropriately divided; to one side a raised wooden platform or *dórva*, where the bride's dowry linen, festival clothing and mattresses are kept, the latter rolled out at night. In the centre, a wooden pole – the "pillar of the house" – upholds the ceiling, and to complete the symbolism, a painting or photograph of the couple is pinned to the pole under their

wedding-wreath – a custom perhaps developed to acquaint children with chronically absent fathers. The walls are decked with shelves and plate-racks, containing hundreds of kitsch and near-kitsch ornaments: not local handicrafts, but ethnic dolls, gaudy pottery and other baubles collected by wandering Karpathiot sailors. Even modern, multi-room villas still model their *salóni* (sitting room) on this pattern.

Many Dodecanese islands are matrilineal (as opposed to matriarchal). On Kárpathos, it's merely more evident, at least in the northernmost villages of **Ólympos ❹** and **Diafáni**, where some women still wear traditional dress; the well-travelled men have worn approximations of Western garb for as long as anyone can remember. The women's waistcoats, blouses, aprons, headscarves and boots are still locally made, but this everyday costume is completed by Irish wool scarves and imported sequins and embroidery, much of it Chinese and Bulgarian. Festival dress is rather more colourful and includes a gold-coin collar, the number of coins signalling a girl's wealth to prospective suitors.

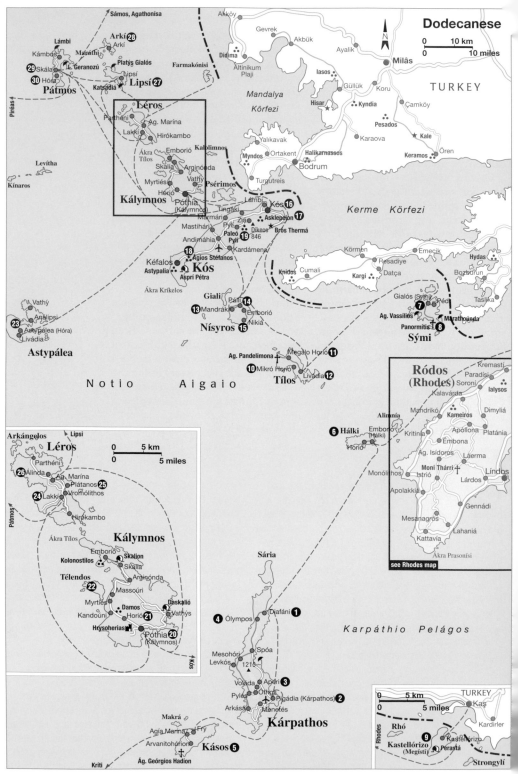

Dodecanese

0 — 10 km
0 — 10 miles

Sámos, Agathonísa

Akköy
Gevrek
Akbük
Ayalik
Didíma
Altinikum
Plaji
Milâs

Lámbi
Arkí (28)
Arkí

Kámbos
Maráthi
Platýs Gialós
Farmakónisi

(29) Skála
L. Geranozú
Lipsí
Lipsí (27)

(30) Hóra
Pátmos
Katsadiá

Iasos
Güllük
Koru

TURKEY

Hisar
Kyndia
Çamköy

Pesados
Karaova
Kale
Ören

Mandalya
Körfezi

Piréas

Léros
Parthéni
Ag. Marína
Lakkí
Hirókambo

Yalikavak
Myndos
Ortakent
Halikarnassos
Keramos

Bodrum

Levítha

Ákra
Tílos
Emborió
Skália
Arginónda
Vathý
Psérimos
Myrtiés
Hório

Kínaros

Kálymnos
Tingáki
Póthia
(Kálymnos)

Lámbi
Kós (16)
Marmári
Ziá
Asklepeíon (17)
Mastihári
Pylí
Paleó
Dikeos
(19) Pylí
846
Brós Thermá

Andimáhia
Kardámena

Kerme Körfezi

Turgutreis

Körmen
Reşadiye
Emecik
Hydas
Bozburun
Datça
Taslika

Knidos
Cumali
Kargi

Kéfalos
(18)
Agios Stéfanos
Kós
Astypalia
Áspri Pétra

Ákra Kríkelos

Giali
Páli
(14)
(13) Mandráki
Emborió
Nikiá
Nísyros (15)

Gialós (Sými)
Péd
(7)
Ag. Vassilios
Marathoúnda
Panormítis
(8)
Sými

Vathý
Análipsi
(23)
Astypálea (Hóra)
Livádia
Astypálea

Ag. Pandelimona
Megálo Horió (11)
(10) Mikró Horió
Livádia (12)
Tílos

Notio   Aigaio

(6) **Hálki**
Hório
Emborió
(Hálki)

see Rhodes map

Ródos
(Rhodes)
Kremastí
Paradísi
Soroní
Ialysos
Kalavárda
Mandrikó
Dimyliá
Kameiros
Apóllona
Platánia
Kritina
Émbona
Ág. Isidoros
Láerma
Moní Thárri
Istrió
Monólithos
Lárdos
Líndos
Apolakkiá
Gennádi
Mesanagrós
Lahaniá
Kattavía
Ákra Prasonísi

Arkángelos
Lipsi
Léros
0 — 5 km
0 — 5 miles
Parthéni
(26) Álinda
Ag. Marína
Plátanos (25)
(24) Lakkí
Vromólithos
Hirókambo
Ákra Tílos

Kálymnos
Emborió
Skalion
Kolonostilos
Skálla
Télendos
Arginónda
(22)
Massoúri
Myrtiés
Daskalió
Damos
Kandoúni
Hório (21)
Vathýs
Hrysoherias
Póthia (20)
(Kálymnos)

Kós

Pátmos

Karpáthio   Pelágos

Sária

Diafáni (1)
(4) Ólympos

Mesohóri
Spóa
Levkós
1215
Voláda
Apéri (3)
Pyles
Othos
Arkása
Menetés
Pigádia (Kárpathos) (2)
Kárpathos

Makrá
Agía Marína
Frý
Arvanitohórion
Kásos (5)
Ág. Geórgios Hadion

Kriti

0 — 5 km
0 — 5 miles
TURKEY
Kaş
Rhodes
Rhó
Kardirler
(9) Kastellórizo
Kastellórizo
(Megísti)
Perastá
Strongylí

If you stay in either Diafáni or (less comfortably) Ólympos, much the best way to spend time is to go for walks on the path network across the north of the island; Avlóna farm hamlet, the beach and ruins at Vrykoúnda, more ambitiously to Trístomo inlet, or simply down the canyons to Diafáni are popular targets. Diafáni – something of a beach resort, busy in August – is more geared up for overnight tourism, with a wide selection of facilities.

Kásos and Hálki

Just southwest of Kárpathos, **Kásos** ➎ is its bleak satellite, devastated by an Ottoman massacre in 1824 and totally dependent ever since on seafaring. Effectively protected from conventional tourism by its lack of beaches, it consequently has limited tourist facilities – especially off-season – and is thus frequented mostly by overseas-based Kassiots during the summer festival period.

Hálki ➏, just off the west coast of Rhodes, is another bare speck of limestone enlivened by the colourful port of **Emborió**. Formerly home to sponge-divers, most of it was restored and it is now packed from April to October with upmarket package tourists. Here, too, beaches are few, mostly pebbly and difficult to access.

Sými

Sými (www.symigreece.com) lies northeast of Rhodes, between the outstretched "claws" of Turkey's Datcá Peninsula. Although still retaining some conifer forest, it is waterless and dependent on cisterns or tanker-boats, which means limited tourism. Most visitors come for the day to the photogenic harbour, which at the end of the 19th century supported a greater population (25,000) than Rhodes Town. Prosperity rested on sponge-diving, for which the island long held the Ottoman monopoly, and the related caïque-building industry. Although the Italian takeover of both the Dodecanese and the Libyan coast (where the sponges were harvested) failed to break the Greek hold on the sponge industry, World War II and the rise of

Gialós greeting featuring traditional dress.

The ferry approaches the port of Gialós.

TIP

If you decide to buy a natural sponge as a souvenir of Sými, ask for one that has not been bleached. Bleach is used to make the sponge look more inviting, but it also weakens the fibres.

synthetic sponges brought down the curtain on an era. War-related privations scattered the population to Rhodes, Athens and overseas, and today fewer than 3,000 call **Gialós ❼** (the quayside settlement) and Horió (the hillside village) home. Some caïques are still fashioned in the Haráni boatyards, but the sponges sold from Gialós's souvenir-stalls are mostly imported from Florida and the Philippines.

Pédi, the valley south of Horió ridge, is the only arable patch of land on the island. There is a small waterside hamlet, too, and some scraps of sand beach, flanked on the north by a badly designed yacht marina. Emborió bay, north of Gialós, offers a pebble beach, a Byzantine mosaic floor under a protective shelter, and a small catacomb complex. Indeed, most of the island's beaches are pebbly, and accessible only by arduous hikes or boat excursions; the favourites are Ágios Vassílios, Marathoúnda (with a taverna) and Nanoú. Among rural monasteries, the most artistically distinguished

are **Mihaïl Roukouniótis,** due west of town, with its vivid 18th-century frescoes, and (even better) **Agía Marína Nerás** chapel (always open), and **Kokkimídis** monastery (always open), south along (or just off) the paved road to the gargantuan monastery of **Panormítis ❽** (8.30am– 2pm, 3–4pm). Being on the sea-lane in from Rhodes, this gets the most visitors, irrespective of merit – a small museum, a large pebble courtyard and a sombre memorial to resistance fighters executed here in 1944 are the main sights.

Kastellórizo (Megísti)

Kastellórizo ❾, some 70 nautical miles east of Rhodes in the shadow of Anatolia, has similarly come down in the world. At the turn of the 19th century, this limestone dot on the map had a population of over 10,000 thanks to the best natural harbour between Piraeus and Beirut, and a schooner fleet based here. But the fleet was sold rather than motorised; the island was heavily shelled during World War I while occupied by the French, then rocked by a 1926 earthquake and a 1944 munitions blast, which together destroyed three-quarters of the houses.

Most "Kassies" emigrated after the war to Rhodes and Western Australia, leaving a virtual ghost town barely clinging to life. The US Government even tried to convince Greece to cede the island to Turkey in 1964, in return for limited hegemony in Cyprus. Geopolitical realities still prevail: the islanders are obliged to get almost everything, from haircuts to fresh vegetables, across the way in Turkish Kaş, where a number of townspeople are of part-Kassie ancestry.

In the end, it was pleasure-yachting and an Oscar-winning film (*Mediterraneo*, filmed here in 1989–90) that probably saved Kastellórizo from desolation. A steady stream of (initially Italian) tourists has revived its fortunes, along with an airport and

Bringing in the catch in Livádia harbour, Tílos.

other government subsidies. There are no beaches and little to see other than rural monasteries, an ancient acropolis, a sea-cave entered only by boat and a tiny red-stone Crusader castle that gives the island its Italianate name. But the social scale of **Kastellórizo Town** is cosy, and the nightlife surprisingly lively.

Tílos and Nísyros

Seahorse-shaped **Tílos,** north of Hálki and west of Rhodes, is the least maritime of these islands. With fertile volcanic soil and sufficient ground water, the islanders instead made Tílos the granary of the Dodecanese. Discerning tourists are attracted by tranquillity, some fine beaches and good hiking opportunities. Historically, there were just two villages, imaginatively named **Mikró Horió ❿** (Little Village, in the centre) and **Megálo Horió ⓫** (Big Village, in the west), continually at odds with each other. Mikró was abandoned after World War II in favour of **Livádia ⓬**, the port and main tourist resort. The rivalry supposedly ended

with the election in 1998 of a single municipal council – the only sensible solution for a registered population of 500.

The crags above the plains hide seven small castles of the Knights of St John, as well as several medieval chapels (all closed). **Éristos** in the west is the largest and (arguably) best beach; inland extends a great **kámbos** (fertile plain) planted with citrus, the whole surveyed by Megálo Horió. In the far west, **Agíou Pandelímona** (daily summer 10am–7pm, winter 10am–4pm) is the main monastery, and venue for the principal festival (25–27 July, annually).

Circular **Nísyros,** between Tílos and Kós, is not merely "volcanic", as often described, but actually is a volcano – a dormant one that last erupted in 1933. Accordingly, what water exists here is sulphur-tainted, but the island is paradoxically green with oak, almond and other plants that thrive on volcanic soil. Once you're away from the harbour, the capital **Mandráki ⓭** is attractive with its close-packed houses overawed by Panagí Spilianí

Nísyros's semi-active volcano.

In Kós's Archaeological Museum.

A quiet backstreet in Mandráki.

monastery, installed in the inevitable Knights' castle, and the even more imposing remains of the 7th-century BC Doric citadel of **Paleókastro** just south. **Pálli ⓮** is the alternative port for fishermen and yachties, just east of the mineral-water spa. You don't come to Nísyros for beach life, but on the east coast, sandy **Liés** and **Pahiá Ámmos** are more than decent.

There are two inland villages: **Emborió,** essentially abandoned and bought up by outsiders, and the more thriving **Nikiá ⓯** in the southwest, at the edge of the volcanic caldera created in 1422 when the (originally much taller) island blew its top. Coachloads of tourists based in Kós descend periodically, but otherwise the lifeless craterfloor, with its hissing steam-vents and sulphurous smell, is deserted.

Kós

The second-largest Dodecanese island in population, **Kós** is also tied for second in size with Kárpathos. It follows the lead of Rhodes in most things: a shared history, give or take a few years; a similar Knights' castle guarding the harbour, plus a skyline of palms and minarets; and an agricultural economy displaced by tourism. However, Kós is much smaller than Rhodes, and much flatter – amazingly so – with only one mountain, Díkeos. The margin of the island is fringed by excellent beaches, many easily reached by motorbike or even pushbike.

A 1933 earthquake devastated most of **Kós Town ⓰** in the north of the island, but gave Italian archaeologists a perfect excuse to comprehensively excavate the ancient city. Hence much of the town centre is an archaeological park, with the ruins of the **Roman agora** (the eastern excavation) extending up to the 18th-century **Loggia Mosque** and the millennial **Plane Tree of Hippocrates,** not really quite old enough to be contemporary with the

DIVING FOR SPONGES

In the old days, divers used to submerge themselves by tying heavy stones to their waists. Holding their breath, they could usually get two or three sponges before they had to resurface. Then the "machine" was introduced, a rubber suit with a bronze helmet connected to a rubber hose and a hand-powered air pump. The diver was given enough air-hose for his final depth, where he could stay a long time owing to the constant air supply. Too long, as it soon turned out – compressed air delivered to divers at the new, greater depths bubbled out of solution in their bloodstream as they rose, invariably too rapidly. The results of this nitrogen embolism – "the bends" – included deafness, incontinence, paralysis and often death. By the 1950s, this had been understood and the carnage halted, but it was too late for hundreds of Kalymniot crewmen.

great ancient healer. The western digs offer covered mosaics and the colonnade of an indoor running-track; just south stand an odeion (always open) and the **Casa Romana** (Tue–Sun 8.30am–3pm; may close for staff shortages), a restored Roman villa with more mosaics and murals.

The Italian-founded **archaeological museum** (closed for renovation until 2014) has a predictable Latin bias in exhibits, although the highlighted statue, purportedly of Hippocrates the father of medicine, is in fact Hellenistic. Hippocrates himself (c.460–370 BC) was born and practised here, but probably died just before the **Asklepeion** ⓱, an ancient medical school 4km (2.5 miles) southwest of town, was established. The site (Tue–Sun summer 8am–6pm, winter 8.30am–2.30pm) impresses more for its position overlooking the straits with Turkey than any structures, for the masonry was thoroughly pilfered by the Knights to build their enormous **Castle** in town (summer Mon 3–8pm, Tue–Sun 8am–7pm, winter Tue–Sun 8.30am–2.30pm), which – unlike the one at Rhodes – was strictly military.

Between the Asklepeion and Kós Town, pause at **Platáni,** roughly halfway, to dine at one of three excellent Turkish-run tavernas – although as on Rhodes, most local Muslims have chosen to emigrate to Turkey since the 1960s. There was a small Jewish community here too, wiped out with the Rhodian one in 1944 when all Jews were taken to concentration camps, leaving behind only the marvellous Art Deco **synagogue** by the town agora.

The road east of town dead-ends at **Brós Thermá,** enjoyable hot springs which run directly into the sea. West of town are the package resorts of **Tingáki** and **Marmári**, with long white beaches, and the less frantic **Mastihári,** with a broader beach and a commuter boat to Kálymnos. In the far southeast, facing Nísyros, are the most scenic and sheltered beaches, with names like "Sunny" and "Magic"; at nearby **Ágios Stéfanos** ⓲, twin 6th-century basilicas (unenclosed) are the best of several early Christian

Kós harbour.

FACT

So many Kalymniots emigrated to Darwin, Australia, in the 1950s and 1960s that the Australian-Greek taxi drivers there now simply call the city "Kálymnos".

monuments on the island. The Kéfalos headland beyond saw the earliest habitation of Kós: Aspri Pétra cave, home to Neolithic man, and Classical Astypalia, birthplace of Hippocrates, with its remaining little theatre.

On the western flank of Mount Díkeos, the Byzantines had their island capital at **Paleó Pýli ⓳**, today a jumble of ruins below a castle at the head of a spring-fed canyon. Closer to the 846-metre (2,776-ft) peak cluster the appealing villages collectively known as **Asfendioú,** on the forested north-facing slopes looking to Anatolia. At Ziá, tavernas are more numerous than permanent inhabitants. Asómati's vernacular houses are slowly being bought up and restored by foreigners.

Kálymnos

First impressions of **Kálymnos,** north of Kós, are of an arid, mountainous landmass, and a decidedly masculine energy to the main port town of **Póthia ⓴**, whose biggest attraction is a 2009-opened **archaeological museum** (Tue–Sun summer 8.30am–2.40pm, winter 9.30am–12.30pm),

with excellent Roman-era finds, including a life-size female bronze statue. The now almost-vanished sponge industry has left many reminders: Kálymniot *salónia* crowded with huge sponges and shell-encrusted amphoras, souvenir shops overflowing with smaller sponges, and, more ominously, various crippled old men.

To the northwest loom two castles: Hrysoherías (unenclosed), the Knight's stronghold, and the originally Byzantine fort of Péra Kástro (Mon–Fri 9am–1pm; free), above the medieval capital of **Horió ㉑**, still the island's second town. Most visitors stay at the beach resorts on the gentler west coast between Kandoúni and Massoúri, with **Myrtiés** the most developed of these, or at the port for the idyllic, car-free islet of **Télendos ㉒**. The east coast is harsh and uninhabited except for the green, citrus-planted valley extending inland from the fjord of Vathýs.

Astypálea

Lonely, butterfly-shaped **Astypálea,** stuck out on a subsidised ferry line

Taking in the view at the Asklepeion.

between the Dodecanese and the Cyclades, would be probably more at home among the latter archipelago. The Knights did not make it this far; a Venetian clan is responsible for the fine castle at the summit of **Hóra ㉓**, the most dazzling Dodecanese hill-village aside from the Hóra of Pátmos. Houses with colourful wooden *poúndia* (balconies with privies) adorn the steep streets, and until the 1950s there was also a separate hamlet inside the upper castle. Hóra aside, however, Astypálea is rather bleak, with only a few good beaches to the southwest (**Tzanáki, Ágios Konstandínos** and **Vátses**) plus a few more like those at Marmári and Stenó along the island's narrow middle. Most travellers stay at the uninspiring port of Skála, at more congenial **Livádi** each west of Hóra, or at Análipsi (Maltezána) by the airport.

Léros

Léros, with its half-dozen deeply indented bays, looks like a jigsaw-puzzle piece gone astray. The deepest inlet, Lakkí, sheltered an important Italian naval base from 1935 onward, and from here was launched the submarine that torpedoed the Greek battleship *Elli* in Tínos harbour on 15 August 1940.

Today, the main ferry port, **Lakkí ㉔** seems incongruous, an Internationalist-Rationalist-style planned town far too grand for the present token population. Its institutional buildings, long neglected as reminders of colonial subjugation, have mostly been restored. The local atmosphere was for years dampened by the presence of three hospitals for handicapped children and mentally ill adults. Substandard conditions in all of these prompted uproar when exposed by the international press; all but one of the institutions has since closed, with a nursing school now operating in their stead.

The rest of Léros is more inviting, particularly **Pandéli** with its waterfront tavernas, just downhill from the capital of **Plátanos ㉕**, draped over a saddle culminating in a well-preserved Knights' castle. South of both, **Vromólithos** has the best, easily accessible car-free beach on

Plátanos and its Knights' castle, Léros.

an island not known for soft sand. **Ágia Marína**, beyond Plátanos, is the hydrofoil and occasionally catamaran harbour; like Pandéli, it offers good tavernas. **Álinda** , to the north around the same bay, is the oldest established resort and has a long coarse-sand and gravel beach – plus a poignant Allied cemetery for casualties of the 1943 Battle of Léros.

Lipsí and baby islets

Lipsí ㉗, the small island just north of Léros, has like Tílos awakened to tourism in recent years. It also awoke to unwanted notoriety as the "Island of Terrorism" when Alexandros Giotopoulos, supremo of the notorious November 17 group, was arrested here in 2002 prior to conviction on terrorism charges. The island's fertile appearance is deceptive – there is only one spring, and up to four times the current local community have emigrated (mostly to Tasmania) since the 1950s. All facilities are in the single port town, built around the best natural harbour; smaller bays, with beaches, are at **Katsadiá** in the south,

The monastery walls.

Platýs Gialós in the northwest and Monodéndri on the east coast.

Beyond Lipsí, other tiny islets see few visitors outside of high summer. **Arkí** ㉘ (pop. 35) clings gamely to life, its scattered houses dependent on solar panels and visits from yachts to the sheltered Port Augusta, with all tourist facilities. Across the way sprawls **Maráthi**, with a long sandy beach and three taverna-rooms. **Agathonísi**, halfway to Sámos, is a metropolis in comparison, with 90 year-round inhabitants scattered in three hamlets. Goats graze the mastic-and-carob-covered hills sloping down to pebble beaches.

Pátmos

Pátmos (www.patmos-island.com) has been indelibly linked to the Bible's Book of Revelations (Apocalypse) ever since tradition placed its authorship here, in AD 95, by John the Evangelist. The volcanic landscape, with its eerie rock formations and sweeping views, seems suitably apocalyptic. **Skála** ㉙ is the port and largest village, best appreciated late at night when crickets serenade and yacht-masts glimmer against a dark sky. By day, Skála sacrifices any charm to stampeding cruise-ship patrons; all island commerce, whether shops, banks or travel agencies, is here. Buses leave regularly from the quay for the hilltop **Hóra ㉚**, but a 40-minute walk along a cobbled path – a short-cut avoiding the road – is preferable.

Just over halfway stands the **Monastery of the Apocalypse** (daily 8am–1.30pm, Tue, Thur, Sun 4–6pm), built on the grotto where John had his Revelation. A silver band on the wall marks the spot where John laid his head to sleep; in the ceiling yawns a great cleft through which the divine voice spoke.

Hóra's core, protected by a huge, pirate-proof fortress and visible from a great distance, is the **Monastery of Agíou Ioánnou Theológou** (same hours as Apocalypse), founded in 1088 by the monk Hristodoulos. A photogenic maze of interlinked courtyards, stairways, chapels and passageways, it occupies the site of an ancient temple to Artemis. The Treasury (entrance fee) houses Greece's most impressive monastic collection outside of Mount Áthos: priceless icons and jewellery are on display, although the prize exhibit is the edict of Emperor Alexios Komnenos granting the island to Hristodoulos. The library, open only to ecclesiastical scholars, contains over 4,000 books and manuscripts.

Away from the tourist-beaten track, Hóra is filled with a pregnant silence, its thick-walled mansions with their pebble courtyards and arcades the preserve of wealthy foreigners. From Platía Lótzia on the north side, one of the finest views in the Aegean takes in at least six islands on clear days.

The rest of the island is inevitably anticlimactic, but the beaches are good. The biggest sandy one is **Psilí Ámmos** in the far south, accessible by boat trip or a 20-minute walk from the road's end, and favoured by naturists. Beaches north of Skála include Melóï, with a good taverna; Agriolivádi; Kámbos, popular with Greek families; isolated Livádi Geranoú, with an islet to swim to; and finally Lámbi, sprinkled with colourful volcanic pebbles, and an excellent taverna.

FACT

The Monastery of St John was built as a fortress to protect its treasures from pirates: there are even slits in the walls for pouring boiling oil over attackers.

Monks in the monastery of Agíou Ioánni Theológou.

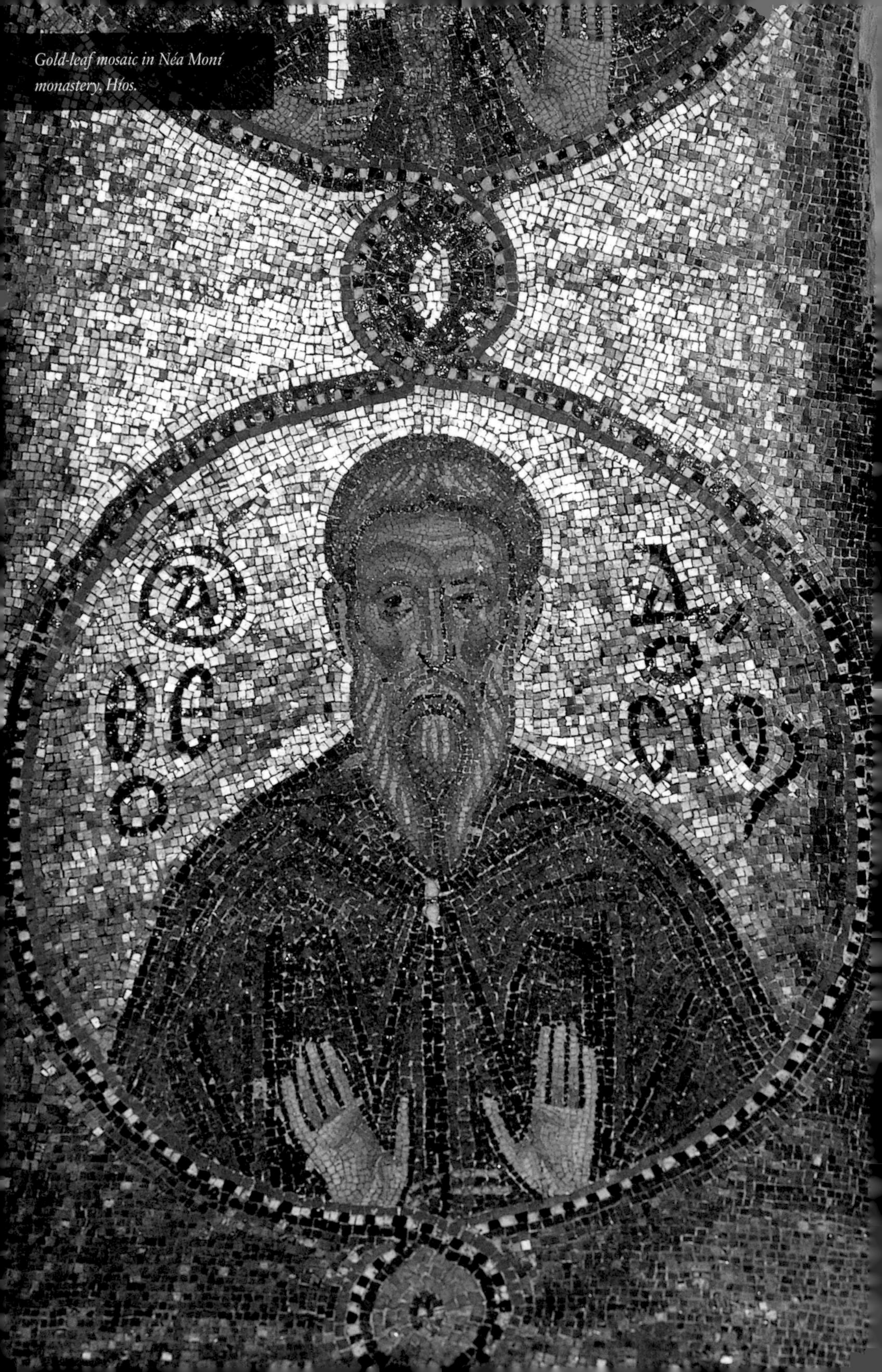

Gold-leaf mosaic in Néa Moní monastery, Híos.

THE NORTHEAST AEGEAN

While the cosmopolitan eastern islands of Sámos, Híos and Lésvos once played a leading role on the world's stage, the scattered isles of the northeast are still relatively untouched by tourism.

The islands of the northeast Aegean have little in common other than a history of medieval Genoese rule. The northerly group, comprising Thásos, Samothráki and Límnos, has few connections with the south Aegean; indeed Thásos belongs to the Macedonian province of Kavála, and Samothráki to Thracian Évros. These islands, so conveniently close to the mainland, with a short summer season, inevitably attract Greek (and Bulgarian) vacationers more than tourists from further overseas, although Germans are plentiful.

Lésvos, Híos and Sámos to the southeast once played leading roles in antiquity, establishing colonies across the Mediterranean and promoting the arts and sciences, though little tangible evidence of ancient glory remains. All three islands served as bridges between Asia Minor and the rest of the Hellenic world and were, in fact, once joined to the coast of Asia Minor until Ice Age cataclysms isolated them. Turkey is still omnipresent on the horizon, a mere 2km (1.25 miles) across the Mykale straits at Sámos. Historically, relations between the countries have been strained, although recent rapprochement has led to better, cheaper boat connections and more visits by upwardly mobile Turks.

Sunbathing in Lésvos.

Thásos

Just seven nautical miles from mainland Macedonia, mountainous and almost circular **Thásos** is essentially a giant lump of marble, mixed with granite and schist, crumbling into white beach sand at the island's margins. Along with numerous illegal ones scarring the landscape, Greece's largest legal marble quarry provides employment; the cut slabs, lying stacked or being trucked about, are a common sight. In antiquity, gold, silver and precious stones were also mined here.

Main Attractions
PANAGÍA, THASOS
SANCTUARY OF THE GREAT GODS, SAMOTHRÁKI
EVGÁTIS, LÍMNOS
SKÁLA ERESSOÚ, LÉSVOS
GIUSTINIANI MUSEUM, HÍOS
MASTIHORHORIÁ, HÍOS
NÉA MONÍ, HÍOS
ARMENISTÍS, IKARÍA
ARCHAEOLOGICAL MUSEUM, SÁMOS
SEÏTÁNI BEACHES, SÁMOS

*Stunning cove near
Alykí.*

Ferries and hydrofoils for Thásos leave regularly from Kavála; there are even more RO-RO services for drivers from Keramotí further east. Bus services around the coastal ring road are adequate, though most visitors hire motorbikes – Thásos is small enough for a long day tour – or cars. The east and south coasts have the better beaches; the west coast has access to most inland villages. Honey, preserved walnuts and *tsípouro*, the northern Greek firewater, are favourite souvenirs.

Thásos's past glory as a wealthy mining island and regional seafaring power is most evident at the harbour capital of **Liménas** (or **Thásos Town**) ❶, where substantial remnants of the ancient town have been excavated by the French School; choice bits of the ancient acropolis overhead are nocturnally illuminated. The biggest area, behind the picturesque fishing harbour, is the agora; the nearby **archaeological museum** (Tue–Sun 8.30am–3pm) displays a 4-metre (13-ft) kouros (standing statue of a man) carrying a ram.

Beginning at the **Temple of Dionysos**, a good path allows you to explore the ancient acropolis. First stop is the Hellenistic **theatre** (only open for occasional summer festival performances); continue to the medieval **fortress,** built by a succession of occupiers from the masonry of an Apollo temple. Tracing the course of massive 5th-century BC walls brings you next to the foundations of an **Athena temple,** beyond which a rock outcrop bears a shrine of Pan, visible in badly-eroded relief. From here, a vertiginous "secret" stairway plunges to the **Gate of Parmenon** – the only ancient entry still intact – at the southern extreme of town.

The first village south from Liménas, slate-roofed **Panagía** ❷ is a busy place whose life revolves around the plane-tree-filled square with its four-spouted fountain. **Potamiá**, further down the valley, is less architecturally distinguished. Visitors come mainly for the **Polygnotos Vagis Museum** (summer only daily 10am–1pm, 6–8pm), featuring the work of this locally born

sculptor. Beyond, the road plunges to the coast at Potamiá Bay. **Skála Potamiás,** at its south end, is purely lodging and tavernas, with more of that just north at Hryssí Ammoudiá; in between stretches a fine, blonde-sand beach. There are even better strands at **Kínyra,** 24km (15 miles) from Liménas, but most one-day tourists schedule a lunch stop at the several beach front tavernas in the hamlet of **Alykí ❸,** architecturally preserved thanks to adjacent ruins: an ancient temple and two atmospheric Byzantine basilicas.

Rounding the southern tip of Thásos, you pass three beach resorts at Astrída, Potós and Pefkári. Only **Astrída** remains attractive, Potós in particular being an overbuilt package dormitory. At **Limenária ❹,** now the island's second town, mansions of the departed German mining executives who used to work here survive. More intriguingly perhaps, it's the starting point for a safari up to hilltop Kástro, the most naturally pirate-proof of the inland villages. Beyond Limenária, there's little to compel a stop on the coast.

Theológos ❺, actually reached from Potós, was the island's Ottoman capital, a linear place where most houses have walled gardens. **Mariés** sits piled up at the top of a wooded valley, just glimpsing the sea. By contrast, **Sotíros** enjoys phenomenal sunsets, best enjoyed from its central taverna shaded by enormous plane trees. Of all the inland settlements, **Megálo Kazavíti ❻** (officially Megálo Prínos) has the grandest **platía** and the most numerous traditional houses, snapped up and restored in variable taste by outsiders.

Samothráki (Samothrace)

Samothráki raises forbidding granite heights above stony shores and storm-lashed waters, both offering poor natural anchorage. Homer had Poseidon perched on top of 1,611-metre (5,285-ft) **Mount Fengári,** the

Aegean's highest summit, to watch the action of the Trojan War to the east. Over time, the forest cover has receded from the now-barren peak, where modern climbers – on rare occasions – still have the same view, extending from northwestern Turkey to Mount Áthos.

Fengári (Mount Moon) and its foothills occupy much of the island, with little level terrain except in the far west. Tourism is barely developed, and the remaining islanders prefer it that way; in its absence, the permanent population has dipped below 3,000, as farming can support only so many. Certainly an overpriced carferry from Alexandroúpoli on the Thracian mainland does not help matters. Boats dock at **Kamariótissa,** the functional port where hire vehicles are in short supply, and although most roads are now paved, only the west of the island has a rudimentary bus service. **Samothráki (Hóra) ❼,** 5km (3 miles) east, is more rewarding, nestled almost invisibly in a circular hollow. A cobbled commercial street serpentines past sturdy, basalt-built

The Sanctuary of the Great Gods, Samothráki.

Lésvos claims to produce the finest olive oil in all Greece. The olives are harvested in November and December, and pressed within 24 hours of being picked..

houses. From outdoor tables at the two tavernas on Hóra's large platía, you glimpse the sea beyond a crumbled Byzantine-Genoese fort at the edge of town.

Samothráki's other great sight is the **Sanctuary of the Great Gods** **8**, tucked into a ravine some 6km (4 miles) from Kamariótissa along the north-coast road. From the late Bronze Age until the coming of Christianity, this was the major religious centre of the Aegean. Local deities of the original Thracian settlers were easily syncretised with the Olympian gods of the later Aeolian colonists, in particular the Kabiri, or divine twins Castor and Pollux, patrons of seafarers – who needed all the help they could get in the rough seas hereabouts.

The sanctuary ruins (daily 8.30am–3pm; museum closed Mon) visible today are mostly late Hellenistic, and still eerily impressive if overgrown. Obvious monuments include a partly re-erected temple of the second initiation; the odd, round **Arsinoeion**, used for sacrifices; a round theatre area for performances during the summer festival; and the fountain niche where the celebrated Winged Victory of Samothrace (now in the Louvre) was discovered.

About 6km (4 miles) further east, hot springs, cool cascades and a dense canopy of plane trees make the spa hamlet of **Thermá** **9**, the most popular base on the island, patronised by an unlikely mix of the elderly infirm and young bohemian types from several

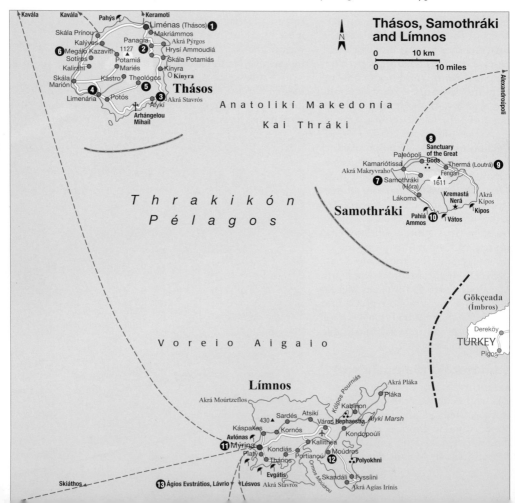

Thásos, Samothráki and Límnos

nations. Hot baths come in three temperatures and styles – including outdoor pools under a wooden shelter – while cold-plunge fanatics make for **Gría Váthra** canyon to the east. Thermá is also the base camp for the climb of Mount Fengári, a six-hour round trip.

Villages south of Hóra see few visitors, though they lie astride the route to **Pahiá Ámmos** ⑩, the island's only sandy beach. From **Lákoma** village, it's about 8km (5 miles) by unpaved road to the beach, where a single seasonal taverna operates. Beyond Pahiá Ámmos, you can walk to smaller **Vátos** nudist beach, but you'll need a boat – or to drive clockwise around Samothráki – to reach the gravel beach of **Kípos** in the far southeast.

Límnos

Nowhere in the Aegean does legend match landscape so closely as here. In mythology, Zeus cast hapless Hephaestos from Mount Olympos (Ólymbos) onto Límnos with such force that the fall lamed him permanently. The islanders rescued the god, revering him as a fire deity and patron of metallurgy, an understandable allegiance given the overtly volcanic terrain of Límnos. Hephaestos re-established his forge here; now-solidified lava crags in the west oozed forth as late as the Classical period, reassuring Limnians that Hephaestos was at work.

Dominating the sea approaches to the Dardanelles, Límnos has been occupied since Neolithic times, and has always prospered as a trading station and military outpost, rather than a major political power. The Greek military still controls much of the island's extent, including half of the huge airport, belying an otherwise peaceful atmosphere. The volcanic soil crumbles to form excellent sandy beaches, and produces excellent wine and a variety of other farm products; the surrounding seas yield plenty of fish, thanks to periodic migrations through the Dardanelles.

Most things of interest are found in the port-capital, **Mýrina** ⑪, or a short distance to either side – luckily, since the bus service is appalling.

View of Mýrina from the ruined kastró.

Volcanic stone has been put to good use in the older houses and street cobbles of Mýrina, while elaborate Ottoman mansions face the northerly town beach of Romeïkós Gialós with its cafés; the southerly beach of Néa Máditos abuts the fishing port and seafood tavernas. Public evidence of the Ottoman period is limited to an inscribed fountain and a dilapidated octagonal structure – probably a dervish tekke (lodge) – behind a supermarket, both near the harbour end of the long market street. Festooned engagingly over the headland above town, the ruined **kástro** (always open) is worth the climb for sunset views. Mýrina's admirably presented **archaeological museum** (Tue–Sun 8.30am–3pm) holds finds from the island's major ancient sites: Kabeirio (Kavírio), Hephaestia (Ifestía) and Polyokhni (Polyóhni). These are all a long trip away in the far east of Límnos, and of essentially specialist interest.

Sadder relics of more recent history flank the drab port town of **Moúdros** 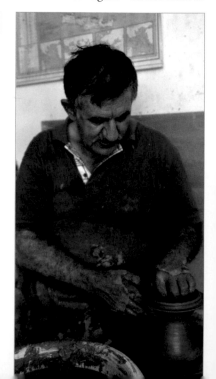 – two Allied cemeteries maintained by the Commonwealth War Graves Commission. During World War I, Moúdros was the principal base for the disastrous Gallipoli campaign; hundreds of war casualties are interred outside Moúdros on the way to Roussopoúli, and behind the village church at **Portianoú**, across the bay.

The road north from Mýrina passes the Italian-dominated Aktí Mýrina resort en route to good beaches at **Avlónas** and **Ágios Ioánnis.** Further north lie the spectacular **dunes of Gomáti**, a protected natural environment beyond a bird-rich marshy area.

In the opposite direction lie even better ones at **Platý** and **Thános,** with tiered namesake villages on the hillsides just above; continuing southeast from Thános brings you to **Evgátis,** justifiably acclaimed as the island's best beach.

Ágios Evstrátios (Aï Strátis)

A tiny wedge of land south of Límnos, **Ágios Evstrátios** (Aï Strátis; off map) is doubtless the most desolate spot in the northeast Aegean – all the more so

Pottery shop on Lésvos.

THE GARDEN OF THE AEGEAN

Early inhabitants of **Lésvos** were related to the Trojans; in Homer's *The Iliad*, the Achaeans punished Lesbos for siding with Troy. Natives were later supplemented by Aeolian colonists, who – in a convoluted topography created by two penetrating gulfs – founded six city-states, the most important being Eressos, Mithymna, Antissa and Mytilene. Although they vied for political supremacy, Lesbos developed a uniform culture, nurturing such bards as Terpander and Arion well before Alkeos and Sappho in the 6th century pushed lyric poetry to new heights, while their contemporary Pittakos (no friend of aristocrats like Alkeos or Sappho) initiated democratic reforms.

With its thick southern forests and idyllic orchards, Lésvos was a preferred Roman holiday spot; the Byzantines considered it a humane exile for deposed nobility, while the Genoese Gattilusi clan kept a thriving court here for a century. To the Ottomans it was "The Garden of the Aegean", their most productive, strictly governed and heavily colonised Aegean island. Following 18th-century reforms within the empire, a Christian land-owning aristocracy developed, served by a large population of labouring peasants. This quasi-feudal system made Lésvos fertile ground for post-1912 Leftist movements, and its habit of returning left wing MPs since the junta fell has earned it the epithet of "Red Island" among fellow Greeks.

since a 1968 earthquake devastated the single village. Thanks to junta-era corruption, reparable dwellings were bulldozed and the surviving inhabitants (22 were killed) provided with ugly, pre-fab replacement housing laid out on a grid plan. This, plus two dozen surviving older buildings, is all you see as you disembark the regular ferries stopping here on the Lávrio–Límnos–Kavála route, or (in summer) the small Límnos-based ferry. Despite all this, the island has grown in popularity as a summer retreat, and you may just have company at the several beaches; the remotest are a tough 90 minutes' walk north or south of "town".

Lésvos (Mytilíni)

Greece's third-largest island, measuring 70 by 40km (44 by 24 miles) at its extremities, distant, fertile **Lésvos** is the antithesis of the *nisáki*, or quaint little islet. Between its far-flung villages lie 11 million olive trees producing 45,000 liquid tonnes of oil a year. Shipbuilding, carpentry, *oúzo*-distilling and pottery remain important, but none rivals the olive, especially since

it complements the second industry, tourism. Nets to catch the "black gold" are spread in autumn, once most of the tourists have packed up and left.

Lésvos has a rich and fascinating history, with familiar names like Homer and Sappho featuring. More recently, the years after 1912 also saw a vital local intelligentsia emerge, among them novelists Stratis Myribilis and Argyris Eftaliotis. Since World War II, however, Lésvos's socioeconomic fabric has shrunk considerably with emigration to Athens, Australia and America. However, the operation here since 1987 of the University of the Aegean has stabilised cultural matters.

Mytilíni ❶, the capital (its name is a popular alias for the entire island), has a revved-up, slightly gritty atmosphere, as befits a port town of 30,000 – interesting to stroll around, though few outsiders stay. Behind the waterfront, assorted church domes and spires enliven the skyline, while **Odós Ermoú,** one street inland, threads the entire bazaar, passing a mosque (ruined) and Turkish baths

The harbour at Mytilíni.

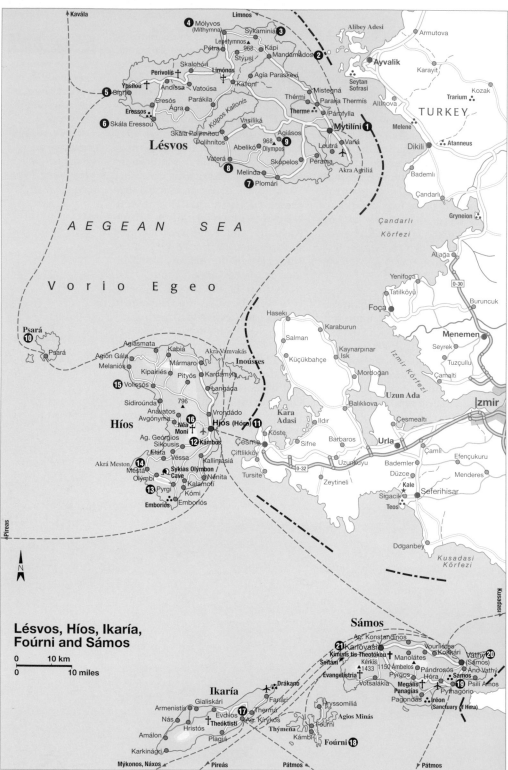

Kavála

Mólyvos **4**
(Mithýmna)
Límnos
Sykaminiá **3**
Lepétymnos
Pétra
968
Skalohóri
Kápi
Stýpsi
Mandamádos **2**
Perivolís
Limónos
Agía Paraskeví
Ayvalik
Alibey Adesi
Armutova
Karayit
Kozak
Seytan
Sofrasi
Trarium
Altínova
Ypsiloú
Sígri **5**
Andíssa
Vatoúsa
Parákila
Kalloní
Mistegná
Thérmi
Paralía Thermís
Therme
Pámfylla
Melene
TURKEY
Eresós
Ágra
Skála Eressoú **6**
Kólpos Kallonís
Vasiliká
Mytilíni **1**
Leutrá
Vaná
Dikili
Bademli
Lésvos
Skála Polihnítou
Polihnítos
Abelikó
Olympos
968
Agiásos **9**
Skópelos
Pérama
Vaterá
Melinda **8**
Plomári **7**
Akra Agriliá
Çandarlı
Çandarlı
Körfezi
Gryneion
Atanneus

A E G E A N   S E A

V o r i o   E g e o

Aliağa
Yenifoça
0-30
Tatilköyü
Buruncuk
Foça
Menemen
Seyrek
Tuzçullu
Çamalti

Psará **10**
Psará

Agiásmata
Kabiá
Akrá Vamvakás
Inoússes
Hasekı
Salman
Karaburun
Küçükbahçe
Kaynarpınar
Isk
Mordoğan
İzmir Körfezi
Uzun Ada
İzmir
Agión Gála
Melaniós
Kipariés
Pityós
Mármaro
Kardámyla
Langáda
Balıklıova
Çeşmealtı
Ildir
Volissós **15**
Sidiroúnda
796
Vrondádo
Kara
Adası
Urla
Anávatos
Avgónyma
Híos
Néa **16**
Moní
Ag. Geórgios
Sikousís
Kámbos **12**
Eláta
Véssa
Híos (Hóra) **11**
Çeşme
Köste
Sifne
Barbaros
Çamlı
Efençukuru
Uzunkuyu
Bademler
Düzce
Menderes
Akrá Meston
Méstá **14**
Olýmbi
Pyrgi **13**
Sykiás Olýmbon /
Cave
Nénita
Kalamotí
Kómi
Kallimasiá
Çiftlikköy
Tursite
Zeytineli
0-32
Kale
Sigacik
Teos
Seferihisar
Emborios
Emboriós

Pireas

N

Doğanbey
Kuşadası
Körfezi

Lésvos, Híos, Ikaría,
Foúrni and Sámos

0   10 km
0   10 miles

Sámos
Ag. Konstandínos
Karlóvasi **21**
Kímisis tis Theotókou
Soutári
Evangelístria
Kérkis
1433
Manolátes
Pýrgos
1150
Ámbelos
Votsalákia
Vourliótes
Kokkári
Pándrosos
Hóra
Vathý **20**
(Sámos)
Áno Vathý
Sámos **19**
Psilí Ámos
Pythagório
Megális
Panagías
Pagóndas
Iréon
(Sanctuary of Hera)

Ikaría
Gialiskári
Armenistís
Nás
Amálon
Karkinágri
Plagiá
Hristós
Evdílos
Theóktisti **17**
Drákano
Fanári
Thermá
Ag. Kírykos
Thýmena
Kámbi
Foúrni
Foúrni **18**
Chryssomiliá
Agios Minás

Mýkonos, Náxos
Pireás
Pátmos
Pátmos

(well restored) en route. Behind the ferry dock stands the **archaeological museum** (Tue–Sun 8.30am–3pm), spread over two premises; the new, uphill annexe features superb mosaics rescued from local Roman villas. Not far away, the Byzantine Museum (Mon–Sat 9am–1pm) is newly renovated, with a number of attractive exhibits.

Also noteworthy are a pair of museums in **Variá**, 5km (3 miles) south of town. The **Theophilos Museum** (Tue–Sun 10am–4pm) contains over 60 paintings by locally born Theophilos Hazimihaïl, Greece's most celebrated naive painter. The nearby **Theriade Museum** (Tue–Sun summer 9am–2pm, 5–8pm, winter 9am–5pm) was founded by another native son who, while an avant-garde art publisher in Paris, assembled this collection, with work by Chagall, Picasso, Rouault, Giacometti, Matisse and Léger.

The road running northwest from Mytilíni follows the coast facing Turkey. **Mandamádos** ❷, 37km (23 miles) from Mytilíni, has on its outskirts the enormous **Taxiárhis Monastery** (daily, all day) with its much-revered black icon. At Kápi, the road divides; the northerly fork is wider, better paved and more scenic as it curls across the flanks of Mount Lepétymnos, passing by the handsome village of **Sykaminiá** ❸ and its photogenic, taverna-studded fishing port.

You descend to sea level at **Mólyvos** ❹, linchpin of Lésvos tourism and understandably so: the ranks of sturdy tiled houses climbing to the medieval castle are an appealing sight, as is the stone-paved fishing harbour. Its days as a colony for bohemian artists and alternative types are over, however, with package tourism now dominant.

Pétra, 5km (3 miles) south, accommodates the overflow on its long beach, while inland at the village centre looms a rock plug crowned with the Panagía Glykofiloússa church. At its foot, the 18th-century **Vareltzídena**

Mansion (Tue–Sun 8am–2.40pm; free) is worth a look, as is the 16th-century frescoed church of **Ágios Nikólaos** (daily 9am–7pm).

From Pétra, head 17km (10 miles) south to the turning for **Límonos Monastery**, home to an ecclesiastical museum (daily 9.30am–6.30pm; charge), before continuing west towards the more rugged half of the island, with its lunar volcanic terrain. Stream valleys foster little oases, such as the one around **Perivolís Monastery** (daily 10am–1pm, 5–6pm; donation welcome), 30km (19 miles) from Limónos, decorated with wonderful frescoes. Some 10km (6 miles) beyond, atop an extinct volcano, the **Monastery of Ypsiloú** (museum inside open 8.30am–3pm) contemplates the abomination of desolation – complete with scattered trunks of the "petrified forest", a few prehistoric sequoias mineralised by volcanic ash.

Roadside shrine on Lésvos.

Lésvos mansion.

Hiking up to the Panagía Glykofiloússa, an 18th-century church in Pétra, Lésvos.

View towards the gulf, southern Lésvos.

Ólympos. **Plomári** ❼ on the coast is Lésvos's second town, famous for its oúzo industry; most tourists stay at pebble-beach **Ágios Isídoros** 3km (2 miles) east, though **Melínda**, 6km (4 miles) to the west, is more scenic. **Vaterá** ❽, whose 7-km (4-mile) sand beach is reckoned the best on the island, lies still further west; en route, you can stop for a soak at restored medieval spas outside Lisvóri and Polyhnítos, 45km (28 miles) from Mytilíni.

Inland from Plomári, the remarkable hill village of **Agiásos** ❾ nestles in a wooded valley under Ólympos. Its heart is the major pilgrimage church of Panagía Vrefokratoússa, which comes alive for the 15 August festival, Lésvos's biggest.

Psará

Scarcely 450 inhabitants remain on melancholy **Psará** ❿, its bleakness relieved only by occasional fig trees and the odd cultivated field. Besides the lone port village, there's just one deserted monastery in the far north. Six beaches lie northeast of the port, each better than the preceding, though all catch tide-wrack on this exposed coast. Indeed, the island's main claims to fame are as the site of a massive 1824 massacre by the Ottomans, and being the birthplace of Ioannis Varvakis, hero of the 2012 film *God Loves Caviar*. A few tourists trickle over from Híos, on regular local ferries from Híos Town or Limáni Mestón; big ferries call weekly from Lávrio and Kavála.

Híos (Chíos)

Although the island had been important and prosperous since antiquity, the Middle Ages made the **Híos** (www.chios.com) of today. The Genoese seized control here in 1346; the Giustiniani clan established a cartel, the *maona*, which controlled the highly profitable trade in gum mastic. During their rule, which also saw the introduction of mandarin fruit, Híos became one

Sígri ❺ (90km/56 miles from Mytilíni), a sleepy place flanked by good beaches, is very much the end of the line, guarded by a Turkish-built fort. Most prefer **Skála Eressoú** ❻, 14km (9 miles) south of Ypsiloú, for its beach; in particular, numerous lesbians come to honour Sappho, who was born here.

Southern Lésvos, between the two gulfs, is home to olive groves rolling up to 968-metre (3,175-ft) Mount

of the wealthiest and most cultured islands in the Mediterranean. Local prowess in navigation was exploited by 150 ships calling here annually and Christopher Columbus apocryphally came to study with Hiot captains prior to his voyages.

In 1566, the Ottomans expelled the Genoese, but granted the islanders numerous privileges, so that Híos continued to flourish until March 1822, when poorly armed agitators from Sámos convinced the reluctant Hiots to participate in the independence uprising. Sultan Mahmut II, enraged at this ingratitude, exacted a terrible revenge: a two-month rampage commanded by Admiral Kara Ali killed 30,000 islanders, enslaved 45,000 more, and saw all settlements except the mastic-producing villages razed. Híos had only partly recovered when a strong earthquake in March 1881 destroyed much of what remained and killed 4,000. Today, Híos and its satellite islet Inoússes are home to some of Greece's wealthiest shipping families.

Its catastrophic 19th-century history ensures that **Híos Town** or **Hóra** ⑪ (pop. 25,000) seems at first off-puttingly modern. Scratch the ferro-concrete surface, however, and you'll find traces of the Genoese and Ottoman years. The most obvious medieval feature is the **kástro** (Venetian style of town planning with all the houses directed inwards). Moated on the landward side, it lacks a seaward rampart, destroyed after the 1881 quake. Just inside the imposing Porta Maggiora stands the outstanding **Giustiniani Museum** (Tue–Sun 9am–2.30pm), a continually changing collection of religious art rescued from rural churches.

Off a small nearby square is a Muslim cemetery with the tomb of Kara Ali – he of the massacres, blown up along with his flagship by one of Admiral Kanaris's fireboats in June 1822. The square itself is lively with the tables of a popular, trendy bar-ouzerí. Further in lies the old Muslim and Jewish quarter with its derelict mosque and overhanging houses; Christians had to settle outside the walls. A hammam at the far end has been carefully

Plomári elders.

A STICKY BUSINESS

The mastic bushes of southern Híos are the unique source of gum mastic, the basis for many products before petroleum was refined. It was popular in Constantinople as chewing-gum, allegedly freshening the breath of the sultan's concubines. The Romans made mastic toothpicks to keep their teeth white and prevent cavities; Hippocrates praised its therapeutic value for coughs and colds; and lately practitioners of alternative medicine make even more ambitious claims on its behalf.

During the 14th and 15th centuries, the Genoese set up a monopoly in the substance. At its peak, the trade generated enough wealth to support a score of *mastihohoriá* (mastic villages). However, the coming of the Industrial Revolution and the demise of the Ottoman Empire was the end of large-scale mastic production.

Today, smaller amounts are generated in a process which has not really changed since ancient times. In late summer, incisions made in the bark weep resin "tears", which are scraped off and cleaned. Finally, the raw gum is sent to a central processing-plant where it is washed, baked and formed into lozenges of gum. Some 150 tons are produced annually, most of it exported to France, Bulgaria and Saudi Arabia for prices of up to $35 a kilo. However, the severe fire of summer 2012 destroyed nearly 40 percent of the mature mastic bushes, which take 30 years to reach a productive age.

The streets in Mestá can feel a little claustrophobic.

Mólyvos surmounted by its medieval castle.

restored for use as an exhibition venue.

South of Hóra you pass through **Kámbos** ⑫, a broad plain of high-walled citrus groves dotted with the imposing sandstone mansions of the medieval aristocracy, standing along narrow, unmarked lanes. Many were destroyed by the earthquake, while a few have been restored as accommodation or restaurants. Irrigation water was originally drawn up by *manganós* or waterwheel; a few survive in ornately paved courtyards.

The onward road heads southwest towards southern Híos, with its 20 **mastihohoriá**, built as pirate-proof strongholds by the Genoese during the 14th and 15th centuries. Laid out on a dense, rectangular plan, their narrow passages are overarched by earthquake buttresses, with the backs of the outer houses doubling as the perimeter wall. Sadly, an August 2012 fire devastated both the local pines and mastic bushes.

Pyrgí ⑬, 21km (13 miles) from Hóra, is one of the best-preserved *mastihohoriá*, most of its facades adorned with black-and-white geometric patterns called *xystá*. A passageway off the central square leads to the Byzantine Ágii Apóstoli church (rarely open) decorated with later frescoes. In the back alleys, tomatoes are laboriously strung for drying in September by local women.

Some 11km (7 miles) west, **Mestá** ⑭ forms a more sombre, monochrome labyrinth, which retains defensive towers at its corners – several three-storeyed houses have been restored as accommodation. Such quarters are typically claustrophobic, so guests will appreciate the nearby beach resorts of **Kómi** (sand) and **Emboriós** (volcanic pebbles).

With your own car, the beautiful, deserted west coast with its many coves is accessible via attractive **Véssa** and **Sidiroúnda**, the paved road eventually taking you to castle-crowned **Volissós** ⑮ in the far northwest. Around this

half-empty village are the island's fin-est beaches – and scars from a series of recent fires which burnt two-thirds of Híos's forests. The best excursion north of Volissós is to **Ágion Gála** vil-lage, with its mysterious cave-church (Tue–Sun 11am–7pm; escorted tour only) at the outskirts.

Between Kastélla and Elínda bays, a good road snakes east uphill to **Avgónyma**, a clustered village well restored by returned Greek-Americans. Just 4km (2.5 miles) north perches almost-deserted, crumbling **Anávatos**, well camouflaged against its cliff; from this in 1822, 400 Hiots leapt to their deaths rather than be captured.

Some 5km (3 miles) east, the monas-tery of **Néa Moní ⑯** (daily 8am–1pm, 4–8pm; 5–8pm in summer) forms one of the finest surviving examples of mid-Byzantine architecture, founded in 1049 by Emperor Constantine Monomachus IX on a spot where a miraculous icon of the Virgin had appeared. It suffered heavily in 1822 and 1881, first with the murder of its monks and the pillage of its treasures, and then with the collapse of its dome.

Despite the damage, its mosaics of scenes from the life of Christ are outstand-ing and numerous.

Ikaría and Foúrni

The narrow, wing-shaped island of **Ikaría** (www.island-ikaria.com) is named after mythical Icarus, who supposedly fell into the sea nearby when his wax wings melted (the Greek Air Force has adopted him as patron, apparently impervious to the irony). One of the least developed large islands in the Aegean, Ikaría has little to offer anyone intent on tick-ing off four-star sights, but appeals to those disposed to a decidedly eccentric environment. For three brief months after 17 July 1912, when a certain Dr Malahias declared the island liberated, it was an independent republic, with its own money and stamps. In later decades, Ikaría served as a place of exile for hundreds of Communists; the

Harvesting resin from the mastic trees, Híos.

An exquisite example of xystá decorations in Pyrgí.

Fishing on Ikaría.

locals with whom they were billeted thought they were the most noble, humanitarian folk they'd ever met and still vote Communist in droves – not quite what Athens intended.

Ágios Kírykos ⓱ is the capital and main southerly port, its tourist facilities geared to the clientele at the neighbouring spa of Thermá. Taxis are more reliable than the bus for the 41-km (25-mile) drive over the 1,000-metre (3,300-ft) Atherás ridge to **Évdilos**, the north-facing second port. Another 16km (10 miles) takes you past **Kámbos,** with its sandy beach and ruined Byzantine palace, to the tiny port-resort of **Armenistís**. Here only do foreigners congregate, for the sake of excellent beaches – Livádi and Mesakhtí – just east, though the surf can be deadly. **Nás,** 4km (2.5 miles) west, is named for the **naos** or temple of Artemis Tavropolio on the banks of the river draining to a popular pebble cove. **Gialiskári,** a fishing port 4km (2.5 miles) east, is distinguished by its photogenic jetty chapel.

There are few bona fide inland villages, as the proud Ikarians hate to live on top of each other, keeping plenty of room for orchards between their houses. Above Armenistís are four hamlets lost in pine forest, collectively known as **Ráhes;** at Hristós, the largest, people cram the café-bars all night, sleep until noon and carry belongings (or store potent wine) in hairy goatskin bags. The surrounding countryside completes the hobbit-like image, with vertical natural monoliths and troglodytic cottages for livestock made entirely of gigantic granite slabs. One of these, 4km (2.5 miles) above Kámbos, gives dramatic shelter to **Theoskepastí** chapel below which stands **Theóktisti monastery** (usually open) with engaging 17th-century frescoes.

Foúrni ⓲, one of several islets southeast of Ikaría, lives from its thriving fishing fleet and boatyards; (expensive) seafood dinners figure high in the ambitions of arriving tourists, who mostly stay in the surprisingly large port town. A road links this with Ágios Ioánnis Hrysóstomos in the south and remote Hryssomiliá in the far north, the only other villages,

but path-walking (where possible) and boat-riding are more relaxing ways of getting around – there's no bus, and only seasonal scooter hire. Best of many beaches are at **Kámbi,** one ridge south of port, or at naturist **Áspa,** a tough trail walk beyond.

Sámos

Almost subtropical **Sámos,** with vine terraces, cypress and olive groves, surviving stands of black and Calabrian pine, hillside villages and beaches of every size and consistency, appeals to numerous package tourists. Forest fires – the worst of these in July 2000 – and development have blighted much of the island, but impassable gorges, the Aegean's second-highest mountain, and beaches accessible only on foot hold sway in the far west.

From the immense harbour mole at heavily commercialised **Pythagório** ⑲, constructed by ancient slaves and scarcely changed, you can watch majestic Mount Mykale in Turkey change colour at dusk. The port's shape suggested a frying-pan, hence Tigáni, the town's former name – perhaps too

prophetic of what it's become: a casserole of lobster-red Scandinavians fried in suntan-oil. The authorities changed the name in 1955 in honour of native son Pythagoras. The main attraction in town is the 2010-opened **archaeological museum** (Tue–Sun 8.30am–2.40pm, may open later summer), where highlights include a huge hoard of Byzantine gold coins found in 1984, and monumental Roman statuary.

The 1,040-metre (3,410-ft) **Evpalínio Órygma** (Eupalinos's Tunnel; Tues–Sun summer 8am–7pm, winter 8.30am–2.40pm), an aqueduct built during the rule of the brilliant but unscrupulous tyrant Polykrates (538–522 BC), cuts through the hillside northwest of town. It is one of the technological marvels of the ancient world: surveying was so good that

The Ottoman viper, Vipera xanthina, a medium-sized viper species, can be found on the Aegean islands. It is by far the most venomous snake of Europe.

Sámos beach resort.

two work crews beginning from each end met with no vertical error, and a horizontal one of less than 1 percent. You can visit the first 200m, along the catwalk used to remove spoil from the water channel far below. One re-erected column and sundry foundations – the ruins of what was once a vast **Sanctuary of Hera** (ancient Heraion, Iréon in modern Greek; Tue–Sun summer 8am–8pm; winter 8.30am–3pm) – lie 8km (5 miles) to the west of Pythagório, past coastal Roman baths and the airport.

Vathý or **Sámos Town** ⓴, built along an inlet on the north coast, is the main port, founded in 1832. Tourism is less pervasive here; the principal attraction is the excellent, two-wing **archaeological museum** (Tue–Sun 8.30am–2.40pm), with a rich trove of finds from the Sanctuary of Hera. Star exhibit is a 5-metre (16-ft) high, nearly intact kouros (male votive statue), the largest ever found. The small-objects collection confirms the temple's Middle Eastern slant of worship and clientele: orientalised ivories and locally cast griffin's heads.

Fishing boats in Pythagório harbour.

Áno Vathý, the large hillside village 1.5km (1 mile) southeast, existed for almost two centuries before the harbour settlement; a stroll will take you through steep cobbled streets separating 200-year-old houses, their overhanging second stories and plaster-lath construction akin to those of northern Greece and Anatolia, though many are senselessly destroyed annually.

First stop of note on the north-coast road (12km/7 miles) is **Kokkári**, a former fishing village now devoted to tourism. The original centre is cradled between twin headlands, while windsurfers launch themselves from a school one cove west of town, the first of several pebble beaches on this coast. Overhead loom the scorched crags of Mount Ámbelos (1,150 metres/3,800 ft), while just past Avlákia a road climbs to the attractive and thriving little village of **Vourliótes**, named after its first inhabitants (who came from Vourla in Asia Minor), and justly famous for its wine production.

The coastal highway continues west, sometimes as a sea-level corniche route, to **Karlóvasi** ㉑, 29km

(18 miles) from Vathý. It's a sprawling, somewhat dishevelled place, little visited and lumped into five neighbourhoods. Néo, the biggest, houses post-1923 refugees and the university; cavernous, derelict warehouses dominate waterside Ríva district, vestiges of a leather-tanning trade which thrived here before 1970. In one such former warehouse, the excellent **Mousío Vyrsodepsías/Tanning Museum** (Tue–Sat 9am–2pm, summer also 6–9pm; free) gives a fascinating overview of the vanished industry, including massive machinery in situ.c Meséo is more village-y, as is Paleó, lining a green valley behind the sentinel church of Ágia Triáda. Limín, below Áno, has most local tourist facilities, including the ferry port. The shore west of here has some of Sámos's best beaches, including sand-and-pebble **Potámi,** visited by most of Karlóvasi at weekends. Beyond here, you must walk to a pair of remote, scenic beaches at **Seïtáni**, now a nature reserve to protect its resident monk seals.

Karlóvasi lies roughly halfway around an anticlockwise loop of the island; head south, then east through an interior dotted with small villages of tiled, shuttered houses and stripey-domed churches. At **Ágii Theodóri** junction, choose southwest or east.

Going southwest takes you past Marathókambos and its sleepy, atmospheric port, Órmos, to **Votsalákia**, Sámos's biggest beach resort. Less busy beaches like Psilí Ámmos and Limniónas can be found further west along the road curling around the base of Mount Kérkis (1,437 metres/4,725ft), which forms the west end of the island. The mountain is usually climbed from the uninhabited **Evangelístria convent** on the south or Kosmadéï on the north – either way it is a full day's outing. Returning to Pythagório, schedule stops at the roadside stalls before **Pýrgos** for a jar of local honey, and just below Koumaradéï, at the monastery of **Megális Panagías** (Mon–Sat 10am–1pm, 5.30–8pm), with smudged frescoes dating from after 1586 (there are older, better ones at **Petaloúda** church – always open – near Karlovássi).

Olive grove in Sámos.

GREECE IN BLOOM

The Greek landscape is at its most bountiful in spring and early summer, when every hillside and valley is decorated with glorious colour.

Greece in spring is a botanist's dream and a gardener's despair. Some 6,000 species of wild plant grow in Greece and the islands, and in the spring (March to May), visitors may enjoy a magnificent cornucopia of flowers and fragrances.

Hillsides resemble giant rock gardens, while brilliant patches of untended waste-ground outdo Northern Europe's carefully tended herbaceous borders with ease. Winter rains, followed by a bright, hot, frost-free spring, produce a season's blooming compressed into a few, spectacular weeks before the summer's heat and drought become too much. By late May or early June, the flowers are finished, the seeds for next year's show are ripening, and greens are fading to brown to match the tourists on the beaches.

Summer survival

Except in the cooler, higher mountains, most plants go into semi-dormancy to survive the arid summer. The first rains of autumn, which can come any time between mid-September and late October, tempt a few autumn bulbs into flower, but also initiate the germination of seeds for plants that will grow and build up strength during the winter in preparation for the following spring, when their flowers will again colour in the waiting canvas of the hills and valleys.

The richness and diversity of the flora are due in part to the islands' location between three continents – Europe, Asia and Africa – partly to the Ice Age survival in southern Greece of pre-glacial species, and partly to the wonderful variety of habitats. Limestone, the foundation of much of Greece, is a favourite home for plants, providing the stability, minerals, water supply and protection they need.

Daisies on the east coast.

Wild artichokes are painfully spiny to prepare for the pot; but their flavour is prized by Greek country folk over the spineless cultivated variety, and accordingly they command a price premium.

The hills are alive – sunshine, colour and quantity mark the spring flowering on the islands, as here in the mountains of Crete in mid-April.

Butterflies abound from spring to autumn.

BEETLES, BEES AND BUTTERFLIES

The profusion of flowers and plants provides food for an equal profusion of insects. Butterflies are conspicuous from spring to autumn, including the lovely swallowtail whose colourful caterpillars feed on the leaves of common fennel. Its larger, paler and more angular relative, the scarce swallowtail, despite its name, is actually more abundant.

Look for clouded yellows and paler cleopatras, reddish-brown painted ladies and southern commas, white admirals, and a myriad of smaller blue butterflies.

Butterflies, bees and day-flying hawk moths tend to go for flowers with nectar, while beetles and flies go for the pollen. Some insects even use the heat accumulated in the solar cup of many flowers in order to warm up their sex lives.

The leaves of plants feed armies of insect herbivores, which themselves are eaten by more aggressive insects. Some of the omnivorous Greek grasshoppers and crickets are as happy munching through a caterpillar, or even another grasshopper, as the grass it was sitting on.

The robustness of the native oleander makes it popular as an ornamental roadside hedge; it also colonises stream beds.

According to legend, fire was brought to earth by Prometheus hidden in the smouldering stem of a giant fennel (Ferula communis).

A lovely little chapel awash with colour on Mýkonos.

A lick of fresh paint, Skiáthos Town.

THE SPORADES AND ÉVVIA

The four "scattered islands" (Sporádes) are all different – Skiáthos lively and busy, Skópelos quieter and beautiful, Alónisos the least developed, and Skýros with its own unique culture.

Main Attractions
KÁSTRO, SKIÁTHOS
SKIÁTHOS BEACHES
SKÓPELOS TOWN
VELANIÓ BEACH, SKÓPELOS
HÓRA, SKÝROS
FALTAÏTS MUSEUM, SKÝROS
STENÍ "HILL STATION", ÉVVIA
DIMOSÁRI GORGE HIKE, ÉVVIA
LÍMNI, ÉVVIA

The three northernmost Sporades, set in one of the more blue-green reaches of the Aegean, are, with their lush vegetation and excellent beaches, a quintessential holiday destination; there's little trace of the ancient past here, so ruin-spotters may be disappointed. Culturally and administratively, Skýros and Évvia off to the southeast have had little to do with their neighbours; Évvia in particular often feels like part of the mainland.

Skiáthos

The sandy scythe of **Koukounariés** ❶ on Skiáthos is used as evidence on thousands of postcards that the Aegean can produce the kind of beach normally associated with the Caribbean. Propriety would prevent as many postcards from featuring **Mikrós Krassás** (colloquially "Little Banana Beach"), because it caters for gay nudists. The fact that no one cares whether bathers at Banana Beach strip off or not is typical of the easy-going nature of the people of Skiáthos as a whole. The island has beaches for all occasions: some among the supposed 60 will always be sheltered whichever direction the wind is coming from.

Koukounariés and Banana Big (straight) and Little are near-neighbours at the end of the twisting, busy 18-km (11-mile) road that runs along

Lalária beach, Skiáthos.

the south coast of Skiáthos. There are dozens of beaches along it, many with a taverna or at least a kiosk selling drinks and sandwiches, and many even with luxury hotels – Vromólimnos has the best daytime bar scene. North-coast beaches like **Mandráki** and **Eliá** are more pristine. Round-the-island boat trips pass the rocky and otherwise inaccessible northern shoreline where the only human construction is the **kástro** ❷, the abandoned 16th-century capital once connected to the rest of the island by a single

Skópelos Town can lay claim to some distinguished houses, which its inhabitants are proud to adorn.

drawbridge. For 300 years, the islanders huddled on this wind-buffeted crag, hoping the pirates would pass them by. In World War II, Allied soldiers hid out here, waiting for evacuation. Today, it is an obligatory stop for the excursion caïques after they have dipped into technicolour grottoes and dropped anchor at **Lalária,** a cove famous for its rock arch, and before proceeding to a beach taverna (usually at Megálos Asélinos) for lunch.

The bluff above under-used **Xánemos** beach at the end of the very busy airport runway has produced fragments suggesting a prehistoric settlement, but neither it nor the rest of the island have ever been properly excavated. German bombing of an Italian ammunition dump in September 1943 severely damaged much of the pretty prewar town, burned again in August 1944. But **Skiáthos Town** ❸ makes up in liveliness what it may lack in architectural merit. In fact, its nightlife is probably the most important consideration

after the beaches for the type of visitor that Skiáthos attracts in intimidating numbers during the summer.

The preferences of the fast-living set change constantly, but it is not difficult to spot which places are in vogue, whether one's preference is for beer and blues, wine and Vivaldi, or tequila and trance. The lights are brightest but also the tackiest along **Papadiamándis,** the paved pedestrian street which bisects the two hills on which the town stands, and along the old harbour. The atmosphere is more Greek-oriented at the designer clubs on the water past the yacht marina, somewhat more international at the old-port bars. Expect restaurants, with international flavours as well as Greek, rather than tavernas, and be prepared to pay accordingly, especially along the seafront.

A scooter or hired car is useful to follow the unpaved roads looping through the mountains. They provide stunning views, as well as the chance to pop into monasteries which, with Kástro, are more or less the only buildings of historic interest.

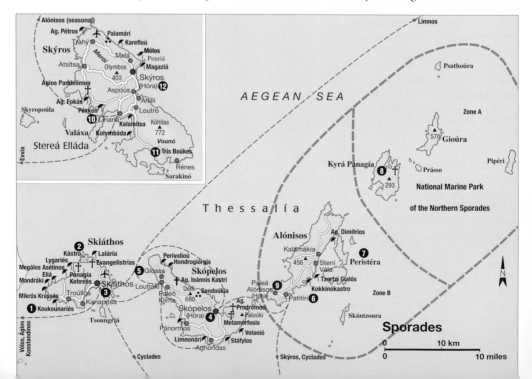

Of these, the grandest and closest to town is **Evangelistrías,** with frescoed **Panagías Kehreás** and **Panagías Kounístras** (all three open daily) also pilgrimage-worthy if the beaches should pall.

Skópelos

Skópelos (www.skopelos.gr) has a distinguished past, which is not so much demonstrated by prominent historical sites as by the exceptionally fine houses in **Skópelos Town ④**; they form a handsome amphitheatre around a harbour lined with cafés and tavernas under mulberry trees.

The island has escaped earthquakes and Nazi vindictiveness and is therefore the most "authentic" and traditional of the three northern Sporádes (Skýros being in a class by itself). Slate roofs, wooden balconies, hand-painted shop signs and flagstone streets give it a serenity and dignity rarely found in Skiáthos in season. On the other hand, beaches are not as sandy or as numerous as on Skiáthos – mostly on the south-facing coast – though north-facing **Glystéri** is the closest to Hóra.

Nudists are welcomed at long, fine-pebble **Velanió** just beyond the family beach of **Stáfylos** (where a gold crown and ornate weapons dating from Minoan times were found; they are now in the National Archaeological Museum in Athens). Local beaches were, in any case, good enough to serve as locations for the 2007 shooting of the film version of **Mamma Mia!,** a fact the islanders have not been slow to exploit.

Further along the southwest coast, **Agnóndas** serves as an alternative harbour when Skópelos Town is storm-shut; there are good tavernas but not much of a beach. For more of those, carry on down the island "trunk road" to **Pánormos**, the biggest resort after Hóra and environs, with a long gravel beach and yacht shelter at Blo inlet. Better, pine-backed beaches lie just around the corner at **Miliá** and **Kastáni**. The road passes the quake-damaged hamlet of **Paleó Klíma** – now bought up and renovated by outsiders – before ending in the northwest at **Glóssa ⑤**, Skópelos' second village whose architecture

FACT

The hugely successful movie Mamma Mia!, starring Meryl Streep and Pierce Brosnan, was filmed largely on Skópelos' Kastáni beach. Boat tours are just one of the ways locals are cashing in on this.

Cape Kástro, north Skiáthos.

Sailing lesson in the Skiáthos waters.

Card-players, Skópelos Town.

(like Paleó Klíma's) betrays the strong Thessalian influence tangible on all the northern Sporades. Far below Glóssa to the south is **Loutráki,** another rather nondescript ferry port; some of the very few north-facing Skópelos beaches lie in the other direction, at **Perivolioú** and **Hondrogiórgis**.

Inland and north from the main road, Skópelos has denser forest than Skiáthos, still mostly unburnt and crisscrossed by a mix of dirt tracks and paved lanes. These pass by a reputed 40 monasteries and hundreds of churches (of these, 123 are scattered around Hóra alone). On the side of the island's summit – Mt Délfi – are three ancient cyst-type tombs: the **Sendoúkia**, with their lids ajar. The 15-minute walk there is prominently signposted.

Alónisos

On a hill above **Patitíri** ❻, the last port on the Vólos/Ágios Konstandínos-based ferry, catamaran and hydrofoil routes, is **Hóra,** the former capital of Alónisos, battered by an earthquake in 1965. This quake compounded the blow the islanders had already suffered when all their grapevines died from phylloxera only a decade earlier. Alónisos seems to have been ever thus: the previous capital, Ikos, also the Classical name for the island, literally disappeared when the ground on which it stood sunk into the sea. The submerged remains of Ikos, off **Kokkinókastro** beach, may be explored with a snorkel but not with scuba tanks (a general rule in the Aegean to prevent pilfering and damage).

Alónisos has adjusted to its unrealised potential and bad luck with considerable good grace, attracting a loyal repeat clientele amongst both Greeks and foreigners. Yet it remains the least architecturally distinguished and least developed of the Sporádes, a quiet island surrounded by an interesting collection of islets. Some of them are off-limits to tourists and fishermen alike, protected areas within the National Marine Park reserved for the endangered monk seal and other rare fauna. **Gioúra,** for example, is home to a unique breed of wild goat and also has a cave that in legend sheltered Homer's Cyclops. It and **Pipéri** may not be visited but caïques leave Patitíri on calm days for excursions to the closer islets of **Peristéra** ❼ and **Kyrá Panagía** ❽, where ancient potshards can be seen by snorkellers on the sea bed and the eponymous medieval monastery on the latter island still has one monk. Passenger numbers and daylight allowing, trips extend to remote **Psathoúra,** with its huge lighthouse and long sandy beach.

Back on Alónisos, a paved but twisty road links the south and north of the island, including a detour to the little yacht anchorage of **Stení Vála**, with its scuba centre and summer-only information post on the monk seal (the main, all-year information centre is in Patitíri). Otherwise, high-season taxi-boats at Patitíri take bathers to the beach of their choice – the best east-coast ones are **Leftós Gialós**, with two good tavernas, and **Ágios Dimítrios**, with a naturist zone.

Walkers are well catered for with a network of 14 routes, waymarked and maintained with EU funding. One of them leads up pleasantly, in 45 minutes, to the earthquake-shattered Hóra **9**, also known as **Paleá Alónisos**. Thanks largely to foreigners who spied a bargain and bought damaged houses to fix up, it is now largely inhabited – though overly manicured and not particularly Greek except for one tiny shop selling local dairy products.

Skýros

Skýros (www.greektravel.com/greekislands/skyros) was possibly two islands originally, the halves joining near where there is now a road linking **Linariá** **10**, the port, with the little village of Aspoús on the way to Skýros Town. The southern part of the island (Vounó) is mountainous and largely barren, and visitors are unlikely to venture below

Kolymbáda beach unless they are heading for Rénes beach or the poet Rupert Brooke's grave in an olive grove at **Trís Boúkes** **11**. Trís Boúkes is about a 30-minute drive from Kolymbáda, and it's another 15 minutes more to the trailhead for Rénes.

The real appeal of Vounó is from the sea, for cliffs along most of the coast from **Rénes** all the way around to Ahílli Bay near Aspoús fall straight down into the sea. These cliffs are inhabited by a few wild goats and seemingly innumerable Eleanora's falcons, which can be seen darting around the heights all the way over to Skýros Town. Boat excursions can be arranged at Linariá.

Hóra (Skýros Town) **12** is on the northern half of the island (Meróí) on the east coast, high above the long sandy beach (better at the south end) that fringes the now-contiguous settlements of **Magaziá** to the south and **Mólos** at the north end. Town life plays out all along the meandering main street, which runs from the main lower square with its nocturnal bars to the elevated plaza at the northern edge

Feline residents, Skópelos Town.

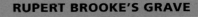

RUPERT BROOKE'S GRAVE

It was quite by chance that Skýros became the burial place of the poet Rupert Brooke. When war broke out in 1914, Brooke first thought of becoming a war correspondent, but soon changed his mind and enlisted as a second lieutenant in the newly formed Royal Naval Division, briefly seeing action at the fall of Antwerp. In the spring of 1915, he arrived on the island of Límnos, where ships and men had begun massing in preparation for the ill-fated assault on Gallipoli.

Moúdros Bay became so crowded that Brooke's detachment was ordered to wait instead off the bay of Trís Boúkes, in the far south of Skýros. Between manoeuvres, he and some fellow officers rested on shore in a small olive grove above the bay which, the others remembered, the poet particularly liked. Several days later, on 23 April, he died on a French hospital ship of blood-poisoning caused by a septic mosquito bite, aged 27; his fellow officers buried him in the olive grove.

Brooke was subsequently beatified in the eyes of a nation mourning its youthful heroes, even though he never lived to see the horrors of trench warfare. Today, the site can be reached by caïque, a long walk from Kolybáda, or by vehicle. There is also a memorial to Brooke in Skýros Town – a highly romanticised bronze statue of "Immortal Poetry".

The Church of Christ, a Skópelos landmark.

of Hóra. Here, the nude statue of Rupert Brooke, which caused a scandal when erected in the 1930s, commands the view beside the excellent, private **Faltaïts Museum** (10am–noon, 5.30–8pm or 6–9pm) of ethnographic displays, including a tobacco press, a mocked-up Skyrian house interior, antique metalware and local pottery. Traditional costume has more or less disappeared with the last generation, but the carving of mulberry furniture and screens is still practised.

Nearby, the worthwhile **archaeological museum** (Tue–Sun 8.30am–2.40pm) has choice island finds like a Geometric rhyton (ornate drinking vessel) in the form of a Skyrian pony and an even older faience necklace. A series of small side streets meander up to the **kástro** (closed for repairs), the old Byzantine/Venetian castle on the heights.

Besides the Magaziá-Mólos beach, there are better if more exposed beaches at **Gyrísmata, Karefloú** and

Ágios Pétros further along the north coast. At **Palamári**, an important Bronze Age town (Mon–Fri 8am–2.30pm; free) is being excavated. Beyond Palamári, and the turning to scenic Ágios Pétros, pine forest appears, compensating for the mediocrity of west-coast beaches either side of **Atsítsa** and **Ágios Fokás** (each with tavernas). The road loops back all the way to Linariá from Atsítsa, via the stunning viewpoint of **Ágios Pandelímon** and the turn-off for the much better sandy beach of **Pévkos**.

Évvia (Euboea)

Évvia, Greece's second-largest island (after Crete) lies just off the coast of mainland Greece, looking on the map like a large jigsaw-puzzle piece just slightly out of position. The capital, **Halkída ❶**, is close enough to the mainland for a small drawbridge and a newer, far larger suspension bridge to make easy connection. Aristotle is supposed to have been so frustrated in trying to understand the swift tides here in the narrow **Évripos channel**, which reverse

direction regularly, that he jumped into the waters.

Halkída is a brash industrial town, but the **kástro** with its mosque and church of **Agía Paraskeví** are worth visiting, as is the archaeological museum (Tue–Sun 8.30am–2.40pm) in the new town. There is also a synagogue, rebuilt after a fire in 1854 and still used by the small (90-member) but active Romaniote Jewish community. **Erétria ❷** to the south is a crowded, grid-plan resort town where the ferries land from **Skála Oropoú** on the mainland. Like Halkída, Erétria is a town to pass through, but the small **archaeological museum** is very good, as are the adjacent remains of excavated ancient Erétria (museum and site Tue–Sun 8.30am–2.40pm).

In general, southern Évvia is drier and less green. The coastal road from Erétria is dotted with villages and summer homes until just before **Alivéri** where it turns inland. At Lépoura, turn south for the prosperous seaside town of **Kárystos ❸**, with beaches to either side, and Mount Óhi – with its eminently scenic and hikable **Dimosári Gorge** – overhead. An old cobbled trail traverses the gorge in about three hours from a start-point on the flank of Óhi, finishing at Kallianós beach hamlet.

From Lépoura, the main road forges eastwards through **Háni Avlonaríou**, with the large and unusual 14th-century church of **Ágios Dimítrios**, before continuing through often beautiful hilly farmland to drop down on the east coast to **Stómio** where a small river reaches the sea. The way then hugs the shore through **Platána** to the harbour at **Paralía Kýmis ❹** and the boat to Skýros.

North of Halkída – or west from Kými on a very scenic road – the small village of **Stení ❺** on the slopes of **Mount Dírfys** is a favourite goal for Athenians seeking clean air and grill restaurants. **Límni ❻** on the west coast is the most atmospheric and

historic port on the island, its neoclassical houses funded by 19th-century shipping wealth. Just south, in the dense forest of Mt Kandíli, **Galatáki convent** (summer 9am–noon, 5–8pm, winter 9am–noon, 2–5pm) is home to several nuns, one of whom will show you 16th-century frescoes in the narthex.

Good pebble beaches begin just north of Límni, appearing intermittently en route to **Loutrá Edipsoú ❼**, with its stunningly refurbished spa-hotel. Beyond, the main road curls around Évvia's northerly Cape Artemísio – where the famous bronze of spear-throwing Poseidon was fished from the sea in 1928. The east coast is mostly mountainous, with rocky shoulders dropping sharply down to the sea, but the road does pass a series of beaches: **Elliniká, Psaropoúli, Paralía Kotsikiás, Angáli**. The first is the smallest and most scenic, the last the most developed. **Agía Ánna ❽**, the hill village inland from Angáli, has an exceptionally well done **Folklore Museum** (Wed–Sun 10am–1pm, 5–7pm).

The bridge to Halkída, Évvia.

Lunch with a view at Boukari
Beach restaurant.

CORFU

Few places have been as exploited and developed for tourism as Corfu. Yet, away from the package-tour resorts, there is much to savour on this beautiful green island.

Strategically poised between the Ionian and Adriatic seas, just off the Greek mainland, Corfu (Kérkyra) has an unsurprisingly turbulent history and a long catalogue of invaders. The Venetians in particular left a rich legacy of olive groves, which still form much of the local vegetation. Despite up to a million visitors a year, tourism has not entirely steamrollered the entire island: 10km (6 miles) from the most brazen fleshpots, you can drive along a one-lane potholed road through sleepy villages whose inhabitants stare or wave at you.

Corfu Town

Corfu Town, also known as Kérkyra ❶, occupies a central east-coast location. "Corfu" is a corruption of *koryfí*, "peak", of which there are two on a Byzantine-fortified outcrop transformed into the Paleó Froúrio Ⓐ (Old Fort; summer Mon–Fri 8.30am–7pm/to 2.40pm, winter, Sat–Sun 8.30am–2.40pm) by the Venetians during the 15th and 16th centuries, when they cut a canal to make the citadel an island. The Old Fort overlooks Mandráki Harbour, originally a Venetian galley port but now a pleasure-craft marina. The more complete Néo Froúrio (New Fort) Ⓑ to the west (daily 8.30am–2.40pm, until 7pm summer) is strictly Venetian and offers wonderful views.

With its tottering, multistoreyed apartments and maze-like lanes ending in quiet plazas, the Old Town constitutes a *flâneur*'s paradise, now listed by Unesco. Vacant bomb sites still yawn near the Néo Froúrio, and many main thoroughfares are brashly commercialised, but the backstreets are surprisingly unspoilt, festooned with washing lines and echoing to pigeon coos. An elegant counterpoint is the Listón Ⓒ, to the east, built by the French as a replica of the Parisian Rue de Rivoli. The name refers to local

The Catholic Cathedral in Corfu Town.

Corfu Town's Listón still buzzes at night.

aristocrats listed in the Venetian Libro d'Oro, who were the only citizens entitled to walk beneath the arcades.

The Listón faces the **Spianáda ⓓ** (Esplanade), a large and grassy open space cleared by the Venetians to deprive attackers of cover. On the southern half of the Esplanade is the plain **Ionian Monument**, which celebrates the island's union with Greece in 1864. It is surrounded by marble reliefs displaying the symbols of the seven Ionian Islands (the *Eptánisa*). Nearby is the Victorian bandstand, where Sunday concerts are held in summer, and the Maitland Rotunda, dedicated to the first, albeit unloved, British High Commissioner. At the far end is the statue of Greece's first president (1827–31) and Corfu's greatest son, Ioannis Kapodistrias. Until the 2008 move to a purpose-built stadium at Gouviá, the Spianáda hosted idiosyncratic cricket matches, an enduring British legacy, as is the enormous Victorian cemetery outside town, and the ginger beer that is still available at some of the Listón's cafés.

Both music and Saint Spyrídon are integral parts of Corfiot life. Until it was destroyed by Nazi bombs, Kérkyra had the world's largest opera house after Milan's La Scala; there are still regular classical or brass-band performances and thriving conservatories. A few blocks back in the streets behind the Listón is the 16th century **Church of Ágios Spyrídon ⓔ** (usually open), with sumptuous ceiling murals by local master Panagiotis Doxaras. Spyrídon, after whom seemingly half the male population is named "Spýros", was a 4th-century Cypriot bishop whose remains were taken to Constantinople in the 7th century and then, in 1456, smuggled to Corfu, where he is credited with miraculously saving the island from several disasters. His casket, prominently displayed in the church, is processed around town four times a year.

Across the north side of the Spianáda stands the imposing **Palace of St Michael and St George ⓕ**, erected in 1819–24 as the residence for the British High Commissioners. When the British left, Greek royalty

Corfu Town

0   200 m
0   200 yds

used it as a summer residence. The bronze toga-clad figure who stands above a lily pond in front of the palace is Sir Frederick Adam, Britain's second High Commissioner. The pool and its water spouts are there to remind people that Adam was the first to ensure Kérkyra Town a reliable water supply, with an aqueduct system still in use today. The palace's state rooms now house the **Museum of Asian Art** (spring/autumn Tue–Sun 8.30am–3pm, summer until 7.30pm). Its collection of almost 11,000 Asian artefacts is one of the most comprehensive collections of its kind in the world, encompassing Buddhist devotional art, Gandhara relief work, Hindu deities and Japanese scrolls.

West of here, the church of Panagía Andivouniótissa accommodates the **Byzantine Museum** Ⓖ (Tue–Sun 8.30am–3pm). The *exonarthex* (vestibule) surrounding the single-aisled church on three sides exhibits an impressive array of icons from the 15th to 19th centuries, many of the so-called 'Cretan School'; after the fall of Crete to the Ottomans, many skilled artists came as refugees to Venetian-held Corfu.

Sadly, the **archaeological museum** Ⓗ, with its superb late Archaic artefacts, is closed for repairs until 2015. Most displays came from excavations in Mon Repos estate, 1km (0.6 miles) to the south, the birthplace of Britain's Prince Philip, which has a more modest museum (summer Mon–Fri 8am–7pm, Sat–Sun, daily winter 8am–3pm) with good temporary exhibits.

Just south of Mon Repos at Kanóni are the photogenic islets of **Vlahérna**, with a little whitewashed monastery (erratic opening times) and causeway to it, and **Pondikonísi**, said to be a local ship petrified by Poseidon in revenge for the ancient Phaecians helping Odysseus.

The north of the island

The coast northwest of town supports busy resorts such as **Kondókali**, **Komméno**, **Dassiá** and **Ýpsos**. Beyond **Barbáti**, the mountains plunge more sharply to the sea and the landscape becomes more stereotypically Mediterranean, mingling cypress

Paleó Froúrio, one of Kérkyra's two Venetian fortresses.

CORFU'S COLONISERS

Habitation dates back 50,000 years, although Corfu enters history as "Corcyra" in the 8th century BC, when it was colonised by ancient Corinth. By the 5th century BC, Corcyra had become a major, independent naval power, siding with Athens against Sparta in the Peloponnesian Wars.

Nearly eight centuries of Byzantine tenure from AD 395 brought a measure of stability and prosperity; but latter years saw incursions by the Norman-Angevin Kingdom of the Two Sicilies, the Despotate of Epirus, and the Venetians. Weary of misrule and piracy, in 1386 the Corfiots submitted voluntarily to Venetian rule, which endured for 411 years despite four Ottoman sieges. Napoleon dissolved what remained of the Venetian Empire in 1797, and the French held the island until 1814 (except for the brief reign of the Ottoman-Russian-controlled "Septinsular Republic). The British were occupiers between 1814 and 1864, when all the Ionian Islands were ceded as a sweetener for George I's ascent of the Greek throne.

During World War I, Corfu was the final destination of the retreating Serbian army and government-in-exile, and memorials and cemeteries from that era remain. World War II saw Kérkyra Town suffer extensive damage under a German bombardment to displace the Italian occupiers, who had surrendered to the Allies. During a brief but brutal occupation, the Nazis deported Corfu's significant Jewish community.

Locally made lace for sale.

The 13th-century Angelókastro.

with olive trees. To escape the bustle of the resorts, wander inland on an uphill journey past quiet villas and olive groves to **Káto Korakiána**. Here, installed in an old, three-storey villa, is the **National Gallery Annexe of Corfu ②** (Mon–Wed 10am–2pm, 6–9pm, Thur, Fri, Sun 10am–3pm, Sat 10am–2pm), displaying 150 works of prominent Greek painters from all eras since 1830, on permanent loan from the Athens parent collection.

The mini-Riviera between **Kalámi ③** and **Ágios Stéfanos Sinión** basks in the nickname of "Kensington-on-Sea" after a posh clientele who stay in villas – there are almost no hotels – and enjoy secluded pebble coves. The adjacent villages of **Kalámi** and **Kouloúra** were beloved of the Durrell family.

Mass tourism resumes at **Kassiópi ④**, once a small fishing village and now a busy resort. The Romans Cicero, Cato and Nero stopped by, but only the crumbled Angevin castle recalls past prominence.

Alternatively, head up the north slopes of 914-metre (2,950-ft) **Mt Pandokrátor** to **Paleá Períthia**, a well-preserved Venetian-era village with several tavernas and innovative lodging. Back on the coast, **Aharávi**, **Róda** and **Sidári ⑤** are three over-developed resorts. From Sidári ply the most reliable boats to two of the small inhabited **Diapóndia** islets, Erikoússa and Othoní (the westernmost point of Greece), popular with Italians. Sidári's finest feature is the series of striking rock formations that rise out of the sea at the western end of the resort.

The west-coast beaches beyond Sidári are calmer, beginning below **Perouládes ⑥**, with its superlative sunsets, continuing through Ágios Stéfanos Avliotón, Arílas and Ágios Geórgios Págon. From Ágios Stéfanos Avliotón, boats go to the third

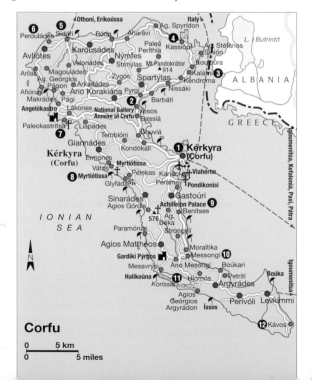

Diapóndia islet, **Mathráki**, with its lovely long, uncrowded beaches.

Beyond Makrádes and **Kríni** looms the shattered but still impressive Byzantine-Angevin **Angelókastro** (Mon–Fri May–Sept 8.30am–3pm) guarding the approach to the beautiful double bay of **Paleokastrítsa** **❼**, once idyllic but now swamped. The best view of Paleokastrítsa is from the village of **Lákones** above it. Sandy beaches resume at diminuitive **Myrtiótissa** **❽** – beloved of naturists – or much bigger **Glyfáda,** while **Ágios Górdis** is both backpackers' paradise and family resort. Inland, **Pélekas** offers island panoramas from the "Kaiser's Throne", a modified rock formation from which Kaiser Wilhelm II used to watch the sunset.

The south of the island

Inland and south of Kérkyra stands the monstrously kitsch **Achilleion Palace** **❾** (daily April–Oct 8am–7pm, Nov–March 8.45am–3.30pm), built in 1890 for Empress Elisabeth of Austria, then acquired after her 1898 assassination by Kaiser Wilhelm II. It has variously served as a military hospital, casino, film location and conference venue, but the ground floor is now a museum, mostly of Elisabeth and Wilhelm's home furnishings.

Benítses is slowly reinventing itself from downmarket party resort to serious yachtie haven, thanks to its new marina, the largest on Corfu. The main street in **Moraïtika** is an uninterrupted line of restaurants/bars/shops, but the beach is good. The older, inland part of Moraïtika has no tourist development, just an attractive taverna or two as antidotes to the hectic resort below. **Mesongí** **❿** is marginally more pleasant, although the long but very narrow pebble beaches are closely hemmed in. Inland, Mesongí has some of Corfu's oldest olive groves, planted by the Venetians more than 500 years ago.

The main road turns inland here and reaches a crossroads at Áno Mesongí. Continue straight on to excellent Halikoúna beach at the northwest end of the **Korissíon lagoon** **⓫**, a protected nature reserve. From the village of **Ágios Matthéos**, you can access long, sandy, scarcely developed **Paramónas** beach.

Turning left instead at Áno Mesongí, then leaving the main road at **Argyrádes** takes you to the coastal hamlet of **Boúkari**, spared exploitation by an utter lack of beaches. On the opposite shore lies **Ágios Geórgios Argyrádon**, a straggling, nondescript resort with only a splendid beach to its credit. The northernmost part of the beach is **Íssos**, which borders the southeast end of the Korissíon Lagoon. The Corfiots have deliberately quarantined the boozing-and-bonking youth element at the far southeast tip of the island, at **Kávos** **⓬**, now fallen on hard times. **Levkímmi**, the underrated second-largest town on Corfu, with a picturesque river, goes about its business just inland, seemingly oblivious to its neighbour.

FACT

Lawrence Durrell wrote *Prospero's Cell* while living in the White House in Kalámi (now a taverna), while Kouloúra gave rise to his brother Gerald's *My Family and Other Animals.*

The crystal-clear water at Barbáti beach.

The two-tone waters of Ásos, on the west coast of Kefaloniá.

THE IONIAN ISLANDS

Lushest of all the Greek island chains, the Ionians
offer superb beaches, great natural beauty and a
distinct culture – including a graceful Venetian
influence in the local architecture.

Throughout the Ionian archipelago, as on Corfu, the long Venetian domination (1386–1797) left an indelible mark. Culturally, these islands look west to Europe rather than north to the Balkans or east to Anatolia; only Levkáda had a brief period of Ottoman rule.

A heavy rainfall makes the Ionians among the greenest of Greek island chains. Olive groves and vineyards are reminders that agriculture, rather than tourism, still claim a part in the economy. However, this same unsettled weather has dampened many a traveller's holiday: from mid-September until mid-May, rains can wash out any beach visit quite without warning. The rest of the year, the northwest wind or *máïstros* substitutes for the *meltémi* blowing elsewhere in Greece.

Paxí (Páxos)

Small, hilly and green, **Paxí** (or **Páxos**) ❶ has a rugged west coast with cliffs and sea caves, and various pebble beaches on the gentler east shore. Paxí figures little in ancient history and mythology, and was systematically populated only during the 15th century. Here too the Venetians left a legacy of olive trees, and Paxiot oil ranks among the best in Greece.

All boats dock at the small capital, **Gáïos**, arrayed around its main square

and sheltered by the two islets of **Ágios Nikólaos** (castle) and **Panagía** (small monastery). Gáïos offers narrow streets and a few 19th-century buildings with Venetian-style balconies and shutters, plus most island shops.

Paxí's single main road meanders northwest through olive groves and tiny hamlets consisting of a few houses and perhaps a *kafenío* at lane junctions. Walking is still the best way to explore the maze of old walled paths, dirt tracks and paved lanes crisscrossing the island. **Longós** on the

Main Attractions

ANDÍPAXI, PAXÍ
LEVKÁDA TOWN, LEVKÁDA
PÓRTO KÁTSÍKI, LEVKÁDA
VATHÝ, ITHÁKI
PETANÍ, KEFALONIÁ
MELISSÁNI CAVE, KEFALONIÁ
ÁSSOS, KEFALONIÁ
GÉRAKAS, ZÁKYNTHOS
NAVÁGIO BAY, ZÁKYNTHOS
BLUE CAVES, ZÁKYNTHOS

Bar sign in Sámi.

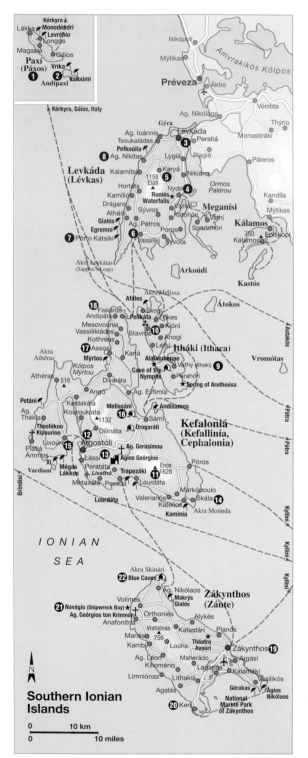

Southern Ionian Islands

0   10 km
0   10 miles

northwest coast is the most exclusive resort, flanked by the popular beaches of Levréhio and Monodéndri. The "motorway" ends at **Lákka**, favoured by yachts and the majority of land-bound tourists, with small beaches like Orkós lying nearby.

The satellite islet of **Andípaxi** (**Andípaxos**) ❷ shelters two excellent beaches mobbed by day-trippers in season, when four tavernas operate. Andípaxi's vineyards produce a heavy red wine favoured for local festivals, and a lighter tawny white.

Levkáda/Levkás

Levkáda is barely an island, joined to the mainland by a floating drawbridge over a canal dredged in ancient times. Yet it feels like one of the Ionians, with predictable Venetian influences on speech and cuisine, plus the imposing fort of Santa Maura by the bridge. Levkáda's rugged landscape has preserved rural lifestyles in the hill villages: older women still wear traditional dress, while local crafts and foodstuffs are avidly promoted.

Levkáda Town ❸ faces the canal and the lagoon enclosed by Gíra sandspit, with safe mooring for numerous yachts on the southeast quay. Much of downtown is off-limits to cars.

There are several ornate Italianate churches dating from the late 17th or early 18th century, their Baroque relief work sitting oddly beside antiseismic belfries modelled on oil derricks. The churches (usually open) contain some admirable artwork from the Ionian School painters such as Doxaras, and beautiful iconostases. Secular architectural responses to the 1953 earthquake could be termed "Caribbean-Tudor"; stone-built ground floors are often preserved, supporting lighter, half-timbered upper stories sheathed in corrugated tin.

Heading down Levkáda's east coast, the little port-resorts of **Lygiá** and **Nikiána,** with pebble coves and fish tavernas, are calmer than **Nydrí** ❹, 20km (12 miles) south of

Levkáda, opposite a mini-archipelago of four islets. Until the 1970s, it was a tiny fishing village, where Aristotle Onassis used to pop over for dinner from Skorpiós, his private island. Now, Nydrí is a busy package resort despite poor beaches. Some 3km (15 miles) inland, the **Roniés Waterfalls** prove surprisingly impressive, revealing abundant water at the heart of Levkáda. Beyond this stretches a fertile upland, studded by churches with Venetian belfries. The main village here is **Karyá ❺**, its vast central *platía* shaded by several giant plane trees.

Beyond Nydrí, Dorpfeld, the German archaeologist, excavated at Stenó and is buried on the far side of sumpy Vlyhó bay. The island ring road curls past **Mikrós Gialós** and **Sývota** bays before descending to **Vassilikí ❻**, 40km (25 miles) from town, one of Europe's premier windsurfing resorts. Beyond Cape Levkátas (Ákra Doukáto) – from where Sappho legendarily leaped to her death – lie spectacular west-coast beaches, accessible by roads of varying steepness. **Pórto Kátsíki ❼** stars on every third postcard of Levkáda; **Egremní** and **Gialós** are less frequented but nearly as good, while panoramic **Athání** village has the closest tourist facilities. Further on, **Drymónas** has the best rural architecture, while **Kalamítsi** has an eponymous beach and "shares" **Káthisma**, Levkáda's longest, with **Ágios Nikítas** (**Aï Nikítas**) ❽. The only port actually on the west coast has become its main resort, worth avoiding in peak season.

Itháki (Ithaca)

Most boats dock at the main town, **Vathý ❾**, at the end of a deeply inset bay. The town was badly damaged by an earthquake in 1953, but much has been restored. The attractive harbour front is known for its huge number of tavernas. To the south of the town are a number of sites supposedly associated with events in Homer's Odyssey. These include the **Arethoúsa Spring**, the **Cave of the Nymphs** and,

near the port of **Píso Aetós**, ancient **Alalkomenes**. Above Píso Aetós is the island's deserted medieval capital of **Perahóri** (only a few derelict buildings to see now). The route across the isthmus and along the west coast to the villages of **Léfki** and **Stavrós** in the northern half of the island is particularly beautiful.

Stavrós ❿ is a pleasant but undistinguished town above the west-coast beach and port at **Pólis**. Remains of the island's oldest settlement are on **Pelikáta hill** here. A road winds up past the little hill-village of **Exogí** to a chapel, from where there are spectacular views over the bay of **Afáles**. Another road from Stavrós leads to **Platrithiás,** which also has Mycenean remains. The two lovely port villages of **Fríkes** and **Kióni** are lovely places to stay, but very popular.

Kefaloniá (Cephalonia)

Kefaloniá is the largest and second most mountainous of the Ionian Islands. It holds the highest peak in the island chain, **Mount Énos ⓫** (1,628 metres/5,340ft), whose summit

Italianate church in Levkáda Town.

FACT

In 1939, Itháki had a population of around 15,000; now it is nearer 3,000, thanks to mass emigration – particularly to Australia and South Africa – following the 1953 earthquake.

is set aside as a national park to preserve the native Cephalonian fir.

Argostóli , the island's capital, is on the west coast on the large Argostóli Gulf. Almost completely destroyed in the huge 1953 earthquake, it has now been rebuilt and is a convenient base from which to explore. The town itself has a few attractions – a small but well-laid-out **archaeological museum** (Tue–Sun 8.30am–3pm), the fascinating **Korgialenios Museum** (Mon–Sat 9am–2pm; www.corgialenios.gr), with its exhibits of bourgeois island life, and the **Fokas-Kosmetatou Foundation** (Mon–Sat 9.30am–12.30pm, also 7–9.30pm in summer), in a beautifully restored neoclassical mansion, displaying mainly antique furniture, paintings and lithographs.

Just south of Argostóli is **Votanókypos Kefaloniás** (Tue–Sat 9am–2.30pm; free), a botanical garden set in an old olive grove which aims to preserve rare species from the island's flora. Further south, across the Livathó plain, are the ruins of the island's Venetian capital, **Ágios Geórgios** (Tue–Sun 8.30am–3pm), perched on a

hill above the village of Peratáta. The views from the citadel's ramparts are fabulous.

To the north of Argostóli are the *katavóthres* ("sea mills"), where seawater runs down holes and under the whole island to Melissáni Cave. Although now just a trickle, before the 1953 earthquake, the flow was strong enough to power flour mills. Heading south from Argostóli, there are more fine beaches, beginning with Makrýs and Platýs Gialós at **Lássi**, Kefaloniá's largest resort, then round the south coast via Trapezáki and Lourdáta all the way to **Kateliós** and **Skála**. Here, some impressive mosaics lie within the foundations of a Roman villa (summer daily 10am–2pm, 5–8pm).

Lixoúri on the Pallíki Peninsula on the western side of the Argostóli Gulf, can be reached by a frequent car ferry from Argostóli. The town itself is rather sleepy, but the **museum and library** (Tue–Sat 9.30am–1pm) are worth a look. South of Lixoúri, across the earthquake-ruptured plain of Katogís, are the wonderful red

Popular Andísamos beach.

sand beaches of **Mégas Lákkos** and **Xí.** Beyond Xí is **Kounopétra,** the huge boulder that used to rock on its base until the 1953 earthquake set it still. The beautiful fine-pebble beach at **Petaní** is in the northwest of the peninsula.

The spectacular road that crosses the island north of Mount Énos brings you to the monastery of Ágios Gerásimou 16 (daily 9am–1pm, 4–8pm), which has an impressive main sanctuary and underground cave where the saint meditated. Next door is the Robola winery, and the road then leads to the port of **Sámi.** The harbour and the wonderful nearby beach of **Andísamos** were used as locations in the filming of *Captain Corelli's Mandolin,* the book of which was set on the island.

Close by Sámi are the caves of **Melissáni** and **Drogaráti.** The **Melissáni Cave** (May–Oct daily 8am–7pm, Nov–Apr Fri–Sun 10am–4pm) is an underground lake with part of the roof open to the sky; when the sun shines down on the water, it becomes a bright translucent blue. The large chamber of **Drogaráti** (summer only daily 9am–8pm) is decorated with hundreds of stalactites and stalagmites. The main road south from Sámi leads to the faded resort of Póros and the excavated Mycenean tholos tomb at **Tzanáta.**

The northern part of Kefaloniá comprises sheer mountains whose cliffs fall precipitously to the sea, as well as pretty villages that largely escaped the 1953 earthquake. The west-coast road is a spectacular, if rather worrying, ride. The famous beach at **Mýrtos** looks impressive from above but consists of coarse pebbles and has a dangerous undertow. Further north is the perfect horseshoe harbour of **Ássos** ⓱. On the isthmus leading to a large hill rising sharply out of the sea is a large 16th-century Venetian fort. However, the island's most upmarket resort is the small port of **Fiskárdo** ⓲, slightly too pretty and popular as

a yachting harbour for its own good. There are many wonderful small pebble beaches, many of them backed by cypress trees, all around this northern part of the island.

Zákynthos (Zante)

Dubbed "Zante, Fior di Levante" by the Venetians, the central plain and eastern hills of Zákynthos still support luxuriant vegetation. The south and east coasts shelter excellent beaches, some almost undeveloped, others

A reminder that Captain Corelli's Mandolin was filmed in Kefaloniá.

Melissáni is an underground lake.

FACT

Kefaloniá is noted for its honey (thyme-scented), quince jelly, rabbit stew and a local speciality called riganáta – féta cheese mixed with bread, oil and oregano.

home to rampant and unsavoury tourism. The once-elegant harbour town of **Zákynthos**  was rebuilt after the 1953 earthquake in the same style, and though not quite convincingly Venetian, the atmosphere is still pleasant. At the southern end of the harbour is the church of **Ágios Dionýsios** (**daily** 8am–1pm, 5–10pm), the island's patron saint, rebuilt after an earthquake in 1893 and again in 1948. It has a very opulent interior with lots of gold and superb colourful murals.

At the harbour's northern end is Platía Solomoú, surrounding which are the town's other main attractions: the church of **Ágios Nikólaos tou Mólou** (no fixed hours), the huge Byzantine **Museum** (Tue–Sun 8.30am–3pm) with its glorious 17th- and 18th-century paintings; and, tucked behind on Platía Márkou, the **Museum of Solomos and Eminent Zakynthians** (daily 9am–2pm), chiefly dedicated to the poet Dionysios Solomos. Above the town is the Venetian fort at **Bóhali** (daily summer 8am–8pm, winter 8.30am–3pm)

with a very attractive pine-filled interior and wonderful views.

At the southeastern tip of the island is the beautiful **Vasilikós Peninsula**, location of some of the better beaches on the island. The best of these is **Gérakas** on its eastern side. However, the beaches on Laganás Bay are some of the last few nesting sites of the Mediterranean loggerhead turtle. As the majority of visitors to the island are flown into the brash and raucous resort of **Laganás**, there is an agglomeration of hotels, restaurants and bars, fast-food joints and clubs along this coast, severely endangering the survival of the turtles. In response, the **National Marine Park of Zákynthos** has been set up, encompassing the whole gulf between capes Gérakas to Kerí. All affected beaches have wardens to protect the nests, dusk-to-dawn curfews, and boating and land access are restricted.

The broad central plain is the most fertile region in the Ionians and is given over to intensive agriculture. One highlight is the **Skaliá Cultural Centre/Théatro Avoúri** (www.zak

Glitzy Fiskárdo port at dusk.

ynthos-net.gr/skalia/) near Tragáki, a series of stone-built auditoria where storytelling events are held. In the village of Maherádo to the west is the pilgrimage church of Agías Mávras (flexible opening), with its ornate gilded Baroque interior. Over on the east coast are the popular, and slightly tacky, resorts of **Tsiliví** and **Alykés**.

The mountainous west coast is much wilder, and sees far fewer tourists. From the cliffs at **Kerí** ⓴, on the southwest peninsula, there are incomparable views of the sea. A string of pretty hill villages runs along the western side of the mountains. The most attractive is **Loúha,** one of the highest settlements on the island, like its neighbours, undamaged by the 1953 tremor. From **Kilioméno,** the road runs north past **Kambí** where a huge cross on a headland commemorates a wartime massacre. Before Kábi, down by the sea is a beautifully situated taverna at **Limniónas** where you can swim off the rocks. Further north, past the monasteries of **Anafonítria** and **Ágios Geórgios ton Krimnón,** is perhaps the Ionians' most iconic tourist sight: the shipwreck at **Navágio Bay** ㉑, surrounded by towering white cliffs. Further on is the mountain village of **Volímes**, noted for its honey and textiles. At the very northern tip of the island (Cape Skinári) are the **Blue Caves** ㉒; sun on the clear water here reflects an iridescent blue on the cave walls (excursions run from the small port of Ágios Nikólaos and Alykés).

Kýthira

The island of **Kýthira** sees at least one ferry boat daily from Gýthion and/or Neápoli, plus occasional sailing from Pireás. Essentially a bleak plateau slashed by well-watered ravines, the island forms part of a sunken landbridge between the Peloponnese and Crete. It shares a history of Venetian and British rule like the other Ionian isles to which it theoretically belongs, although it is now lumped administratively with the Argo-Saronics under

Pireás. Architecturally, it's a hybrid of Cycladic and Venetian styles with an Australian accent, courtesy of remittances from the 60,000-odd locals who headed Down Under in the 1950s.

The island does not put itself out for visitors: accommodation is expensive and oversubscribed, the season short, and good tavernas thin on the ground. Yet Kýthira seems increasingly popular thanks to regular flights from Athens. **Kýthira Town** is also one of the finest island capitals of the Aegean, with medieval mansions and Venetian fortifications. Far below, **Kapsáli** is the yacht berth, though there are better beaches on the east coast, as far as the fishing anchorage of **Avlémonas**. More castles are to be found there and at Venetian **Káto Hóra,** just above **Agía Sofía cavern**, the principal west-coast attraction. In the northeast, the ravine-edge ghost village of **Paleohóra** was the capital from 1248 until 1537, when it failed the pirate-proof test.

The National Marine Park of Zákynthos was set up to protect nesting turtles.

Navágio beach, Zákynthos, is the most photographed in the Ionians.

Herding sheep in Crete.

INSIGHT GUIDES TRAVEL TIPS
GREECE

TRANSPORT

GETTING THERE AND GETTING AROUND

Greek customs.

GETTING THERE

By Air

Greece has good air connections with the rest of the world and is serviced by numerous international airlines. Charter flights generally operate from early May to the end of October, even into November to Rhodes and Crete. Nowadays, unless you're on a multi-stop or round-the-world ticket, e-tickets bought online are the norm. The airlines' own websites can be a good source of discount tickets, matching (or nearly so) the prices offered by general websites like Expedia, Momondo and Fly.com.

The majority of scheduled airline passengers travelling to Greece make Athens' Eleftherios Venizelos Airport their point of entry, though a number of services (from the rest of Europe only) arrive at Thessaloníki's Macedonia Airport, Rhodes, Corfu and Irákli o/Haniá, Crete.

Getting from Athens airport to central Athens and Piraeus

Between Eleftherios Venizelos Airport at Spáta, central Athens and Piraeus, there are various connecting services. Line 3 of the metro takes you – surprisingly slowly, from 6.30am to 11.30pm – into town for €8. Alternatively, take the X95 express bus all the way to central Sýndagma Square (every 15–20 minutes), or the X96 express bus to Pireás port (every 30 minutes). The Piraeus terminus for the X96 bus is all the way anticlockwise around the port, at Aktí Vassiliádi, near gates E1 and E2, however, it does make stops all along the quay in each direction. Tickets for both the X95 and the X96 cost €5 for a single journey; the express buses run around the clock, though with long gaps between midnight and 6am.

A taxi from Venizelos Airport into Athens will cost €30–45 depending on the time of day/night and your final destination, but includes airport supplement and per-bag fee. Even using the Attikí Odós, the toll highway into Athens, the journey time can still amount to over an hour; the same is true for trips to Piraeus via the coastal suburbs.

Getting to Thessaloníki from Macedonia Airport

Macedonia Airport is 15km (9 miles) southeast of Thessaloníki. Regular buses go to the city centre (90 cents, coin-machine-sold tickets, no change given) and take around 35 minutes. Taxis take 15–20 minutes and cost €10–12.

From Rhodes airport to Rhodes Town

From 6.30am to 11.15pm in season, there is a local bus connection (€2.30) into town. The bus stop is outside between the two terminals (turn left out of arrivals). Otherwise, a taxi into town will cost €20–25

Useful Airlines Serving Greece from Anglophone Countries

At the moment, there are only guaranteed direct services to Greece from Great Britain and (seasonally) the US; USAir seems to have abandoned its seasonal route from Philadelphia as of 2012. Services from Eire come and go, and there has not been non-stop service from Australia or South Africa in several years.

Aegean Airlines (www.aegeanair.com). Between Athens and London (Gatwick & Heathrow).

British Airways (www.ba.com). Between Athens–Heathrow and Thessaloníki–Gatwick.

Delta Airlines (www.delta.com). Between New York and Athens, May to October only.

easyJet (www.easyjet.com). Between various UK airports and Athens, Thessaloníki, Rhodes, Corfu, Kos, Zákynthos, Haniá, Iráklio.

Qatar Air (www.qatarairways.com). Between Athens and New York, much of the year.

depending on number of bags and exact destination.

From Corfu airport to Kérkyra Town

There is no bus service linking the airport with Kérkyra Town. Taxis charge a set, inflated €10 for the short run into town. Pre-booked car rental is so advantageously priced that you should forego their blandishments.

From Crete's main airport to Iráklio

A bus service runs the 5km to and from Platía Eleftherías in the centre of town until late at night.

By Sea

Most visitors entering Greece by sea do so from the west, from Italy. You can catch a boat to Greece from Venice, Ancona and Bari, but the most regular service is from Brindisi. Daily ferry lines (less frequent in the low-season) connect Brindisi with the three main western Greek ports: Corfu, Igoumenítsa and Pátras. Corfu is a 6.5-hour trip; Igoumenítsa 8 hours; and Pátras 11–14 hours, depending on whether you take a direct boat or one that makes stops in Corfu and Igoumenítsa. The "Superfast" ferries between Ancona and Pátras offer an efficient 22-hour crossing.

Igoumenítsa is the ideal port of call for those setting off to see central-western Greece. Pátras is best if you want to head directly to Athens or into the Peloponnese. Regular buses and trains connect Pátras and Athens (4 hours by train, a bit less by bus). If you plan to take your car with you on the boat, you should make reservations well in advance. Otherwise, arriving a few hours before the departure time should suffice, except during peak seasons when booking in advance is essential for seats or berths.

By Land

From Europe It is no longer possible to buy a through train ticket from the UK to Greece, and economically it never made much sense. If, as a railpass holder, you're intent on the journey, consult the ultra-useful rail-

Landing at Corfu airport.

travel planning site www.seat61.com.

From Asia via Turkey If you are travelling strictly overland to Greece from Asia you will pass through Istanbul and cross into Greece at the Évros River. The best way to do this is by car or bus. The road is good and the journey from Istanbul to Thessaloníki takes approximately 15 hours; several bus companies serve the route.

The train has the appeal of following the route of the old Orient Express, with better scenery than the road. But, unless you're a great rail fan, the travel time can be off-putting: 17 hours by the timetables, up to 19 hours in practice, including long halts at the border. However, Greek trains currently do not provide international service from neighbouring countries and are unlikely to in future. You will have to get from Turkey to Kastaniés or Kípi, the first stations on the Greek side of the frontier that still have domestic service towards Thessaloníki, though usually with long layovers at Alexandroúpoli.

Another popular option is to take one of the small boats between western Turkish ports and select Greek islands just opposite. Fares are overpriced for the distance involved, but it is undeniably convenient. The most reliable links are from Çeşme to Híos (runs all year), Bodrum to Kos (the cheapest crossing) and Kuşadasi to Sámos (no cars carried).

GETTING AROUND

Public Transport

By air

Flying is considerably more expensive than travelling by boat, bus or train, though still reasonable when compared to the price of domestic flights in other countries. For example, the 50-minute propeller-plane flight between Athens and Sámos costs anywhere from €55 to €130 one way – fares are deregulated, and pitched on a demand basis.

There are currently too many airlines in the Greek skies for the size of the market and health of the local economy. In principle, Aegean bought up Olympic late in 2012, but this is subject to approval by the EU Commission on Competition (the last attempt at same was disallowed). The best, most current sources of discount tickets on extant Greek airlines are the local travel sites www. airtickets.gr, www.travelplanet24. com and www.viva.gr. Foreign credit or debit cards may be viewed with some suspicion, so keep your mobile switched on when booking in case somebody wants to ring you to confirm your identity. Leave plenty of leeway in your domestic flight arrangements if you have to be back in Athens for an international flight. Island flights are often fully booked over the summer, so book these at least a month in advance. Seats bought from a travel agency or one of the very few walk-in offices for any of the airlines listed below are subject to extra surcharges.

Italy–Greece Ferry Companies

Agoudimos – www.aferry.co.uk
ANEK – www.anek.gr
Endeavor Lines – no English website
Minoan Lines – www.minoan.gr

Superfast/Blue Star – www.superfast.gr
Ventouris – www.ventouris.gr
www.goferry.gr – a good consolidator/overview site

TRANSPORT
ACCOMMODATION
EATING OUT
ACTIVITIES
A – Z
LANGUAGE

By bus

A vast network of bus routes spreads across Greece: the KTEL is a syndicate of bus companies whose buses are cheap and generally punctual, though rural depopulation has meant that schedules on many routes have been thinned or axed completely. KTEL buses on the more idiosyncratic rural routes often have a distinct personal touch, their drivers decorating and treating the bus with great respect. Bus tickets should be secured in advance at the stations for major routes, where seats often sell out. On minor village routes, tickets are dispensed on the bus by the conductor.

In the larger cities, there may be different KTEL stations for different destinations. Travelling from Thessaloníki to Halkidikí, for example, you will leave from a remote eastern station, though all other destinations are served by the more modern unitary terminal. Athens has two terminals, while Iráklio in Crete has three.

City buses

Most of the regular Athens blue-and-white buses are now modern, air-conditioned vehicles, and using them is much less of an ordeal than it used to be. They are still usually overcrowded, and the routes are a mystery even to residents. Trolley buses, with an overhead pantograph, are marginally faster and more frequent. Most services run until nearly midnight. Ticketing can be a trap for the unwary. Plain clothes ticket inspectors will levy fines of 60 times the basic fare for travelling with the wrong ticket, a ticket that hasn't been validated, or no ticket.

There are several kinds of tickets: a single journey ticket (costing €1.20); a 90-minute ticket (€1.40) allowing transfers, which must be validated

Island-hopping by ferry is a popular choice.

again before your last journey; a day pass valid for all urban transport methods (currently €4, valid 24hr from validation) and a one-week ticket good for seven days from validation. Tickets are only obtainable from a seemingly dwindling network of newsagent kiosks – most can no longer be bothered to sell them – or at booths run by the bus company itself.

The most useful suburban services for tourists are the orange-and-white KTEL Attica buses going from 14 Mavromatéon Street, Pédio tou Áreos Park, to Rafína (an alternative ferry port for the Cyclades and northeast Aegean), Lávrio (the port for Kéa) and Soúnio (for the famous Poseidon temple there).

Rural buses

In the countryside and on islands, buses can be converted school buses or modern coaches, or even pick-up trucks with seats installed in the payload space to transport tourists. Some drivers ricochet through mountain roads at death-defying

speeds; bus accidents, however, appear to be rare. Just stow your luggage carefully to be on the safe side.

On islands, a bus of some description will usually meet arriving ferries (even if a boat is delayed) to transport passengers up the hill to the island's *hóra*, or capital. Bus stops are usually in main squares or by the waterfront in harbours, and vehicles may or may not run to schedule.

A conductor dispenses tickets on the bus itself; often the fare required and the ticket will not show the same price, with the lower old price over-stamped. This isn't a con, but merely a practice – bus companies use pre-printed tickets until the supply is gone, which may take several years.

By metro, tram and suburban trains

The Athens metro system has halved travel times around the city and made a visible reduction in surface traffic. It runs from 5.30am to 12.20am Sun–Thur, 5.30am–2.20am Fri–Sat, subject to strikes and staff availability. The stations themselves are palatial and squeaky-clean, with advertising placards kept to a minimum. The old ISAP electric line, in existence since the 1930s, has been refurbished and designated Line 1 (green on maps); it links Piraeus with Kifisiá via the city centre. Line 2 (red) links Agios Dimítrios in the south with Agios Andónios in the northwest of town, with extensions works underway down to Glyfáda and up to Thívon. Line 3 (blue) joins Egáleo with the airport at Spáta, via Monastiráki. The main junction stations are Omónia, Sýndagma and Monastiráki.

A single journey on the metro is €1.40 – though it does entitle you to a transfer or two onto above-ground transport within 90 minutes. Alternatively, get a day or week pass from the attended ticket windows (you're encouraged to use the coin-op machines for simple tickets). As on the buses, plain clothes inspectors do a roaring trade in fines levied against fare dodgers.

There are also three tram lines: Néos Kósmos metro station to Agios Kosmás, Glyfáda to Néo Fáliro, and Sýndagma to Glyfáda. Single tickets on this cost €1.20, €1.40 if you want a transfer facility. Daily and weekly cards are valid on these too.

Thessaloníki has begun construction of its own metro/light rail system, but inauguration is several years away.

Around Athens, there is a network of suburban or proastyakó trains, which most usefully gets you from the town centre to Kláto in the Peloponnese, where you change platforms for the "real" onward train to Pátra.

By train

We hesitate to write much about Greek trains under present circumstances. Grossly overstaffed, the state railway organisation – OSE in Greek – has been awash in red ink for years, and the troïka of aid lenders would like nothing better than to compel closure of the whole network. Up to now, most Peloponnesian lines (except for Athens–Pátra, with a change at Kiáto, and the rack-and-pinion railway between Diakoftó and Kalávryta) have been axed, as have all mainland peripheral services and international departures to Turkey, FYROM and Bulgaria. Main lines currently running, and likely to survive albeit at reduced frequencies, are those from Athens to Kalambáka (for

the Metéora), Athens to Halkída, and Athens to Thessaloníki, as well as Thessaloníki to Alexandroúpoli.

Train travel is cheaper than the bus, and more comfortable, especially if you get an overnight sleeper to/ from Thessaloníki. In Pátra, the station is conveniently opposite the ferry docks. Trains are usually slower than the equivalent bus route. However, you can speed things up by taking an Intercity express train if you're willing to pay a considerable surcharge. Austerity or no, there should still be a significant discount for round-trip tickets. Students and people under 26 are usually eligible for more discounts. All the common railpasses are honoured in Greece, though you may still have to pay certain supplements and queue for seat reservations.

OSE has a schedule and purchase website – http://tickets.trainose. gr/dromologia/ – though even the English option has plenty of Greek script strewn about it; if you can't find a Greek person to help you, you're best off heading down to the station to buy in person.

By sea

Ferries

Piraeus is the nerve centre of the Greek ferry network, and chances are you will pass through it at least once; in roughly diminishing order of importance, Rafina, Thessaloníki, Lávrio, Vólos, Ágios Konstandínos, Igoumenítsa, Pátra, Kyllíni, Kavála, Kalamáta and Gýthio are also mainland ferry ports. In high season, routes vary from "milk runs" stopping at five islands en route to your destination, to "express" (semi-)direct ones, so it is worth shopping around

before purchasing your ticket. It is also advisable not to purchase your ticket too far in advance: very rarely do tickets for the boat ride actually sell out – this does, however, happen around Easter, from mid-August to early September, and around election times – but there are frequent changes to schedules which may leave you trying to get a refund.

Personalised ticketing for all boats has long been the rule; it is no longer possible to purchase tickets on board, though you can upgrade your class of travel. The only exceptions are a few of the RO-RO short-haul ferries (eg Igoumenítsa-Levkímmi, Páros–Andíparos).

When you buy your ticket, get detailed instructions on how to find its berth – the Piraeus quays are long and convoluted. The staff who take your ticket should make sure you are on the right boat.

Above all, be flexible when travelling the Greek seas. Apart from schedule changes, a bad stretch of weather can keep you island-bound for as long as the wind blows. Strikes, too, are often called during the summer, and usually last for a few days. Out on the islands in particular, the best way to secure accurate, up-to-the-minute information on the erratic ways of ferries is to contact the Port Authority *(limenarhío)*, which monitors the movements of individual boats. Port Authority offices are usually located on the waterfront of each island's principal harbour, away from the cafés. Boats are often very late arriving – to avoid wasting time around the dock, track the real-time progress of your ferry on the live shipping map at www. marinetraffic.com.

If you are travelling by car, especially during the high season, you will have to plan much further ahead because during the peak season, car space is sometimes booked many weeks in advance. The same applies to booking a cabin for an overnight trip during summer.

Gamma class – also known as deck, tourist or third – is the classic, cheap way to voyage the Greek seas. There is usually a seat of one sort or another (you may have to pay a bit extra for a numbered seat) – though in the newer generations of boats, very limited deck space. If the weather turns bad, you can always go inside to the "low-class" lounge or the snack bar.

Catamarans/"high speeds"

Fleets of sleek new "high speed" ferries or true catamarans, made

Entering Ermoúpli harbour.

TRANSPORT
ACCOMMODATION
EATING OUT
ACTIVITIES
A – Z
LANGUAGE

in France or Scandanavia, are steadily edging out most ordinary craft (as a stroll around the quays at Piraeus will confirm). They have some advantages over hydrofoils – they can be even faster, most of them carry lots of cars, and they're permitted to sail in wind conditions of up to Force 7, whereas "dolphins" are confined to port at 6.

The bad news: there are usually no cabins (because they mostly finish their runs before midnight), food service is even worse than on the old ferries and there are no exterior decks. The aeroplane-seating salons are ruthlessly air-conditioned and subject to a steady, unavoidable barrage of banal Greek TV on overhead monitors (even in *diakikriméni* or "distinguished" class). Cars cost roughly the same to convey as on the old-style boats, but seats are priced at hydrofoil levels. Fuel consumption on such craft is

Ferry/Catamaran/Hydrofoil Timetables

The best schedule resource is the website of the GTP (Greek Travel Pages), www.gtp.gr, which is fairly accurate, with updates at least every few weeks.

Alternatively, major tourist information offices (Rhodes, Iráklio, etc) supply a weekly schedule, and most offices hang a timetable in a conspicuous place so you can look up times even if the branch is closed. This should, however, not

be relied on implicitly – you may miss your boat. In general, for the most complete and up-to-date information on each port's sailings the best source is the Port Police (in Piraeus and most other ports), known as the *limenarhío*.

Be aware that when you enquire about ferries at a travel agent, they will sometimes inform you only of the lines for which they sell tickets.

horrendous; they only turn a profit when at least three-quarters full, and seem to spend much of their time at half-throttle.

Catamarans come in all shapes and sizes, from the 300-car-carrying behemoths of nel Lines in the northeast Aegean, Cyclades and central Dodecanese, to the tiny Sea

Star in the Dodecanese. The far more useful *Dodekanisos Express* and *Dodekanisos Pride* serve more of the Dodecanese, and can take five cars each.

Hydrofoils

Like catamarans, hydrofoils are more than twice as fast as the ferries and about twice as expensive but, as ex-Polish or ex-Russian river craft, are not really designed for the Aegean, and prone to cancellation in bad weather conditions.

Hydrofoils (nicknamed *delfínia* or "dolphins" in Greek) connect Piraeus with most of the Argo-Saronic region (Égina, Angístri, Póros, Ýdra and Spétses), as well as Vólos and the three northerly Sporades (Alónisos, Skiáthos, Skópelos). In the northeast Aegean, there are local, peak-season services between Thásos and the mainland, while in the Dodecanese all the islands between Sámos and Kos, inclusive, are served between May and October only.

Phone numbers for the few surviving hydrofoil companies are constantly engaged, or spew out only pre-recorded information in rapid-fire Greek, so the best strategy is to approach the embarkation booths in person. In Piraeus, these are on Aktí Miaoúli quay, in Kavála right at the kink in the quay. At Vólos, apply to the gatehouse for the harbour precinct; elsewhere, tickets are best obtained from travel agents in towns.

How to Get a Taxi in Greece

Taxis in Greece, especially in Athens, merit a guidebook to themselves. There are three stages to the experience.

First: getting a taxi. It's almost impossible at certain times of the day in Athens, and probably worst before the early afternoon meal. When you hail a taxi, try to get in before stating your destination. The drivers are very picky and often won't let you in unless you're going in their direction. If you see an empty taxi, run for it, be aggressive – otherwise you'll find that some quick Athenian has beaten you to it. Alternatively, you can ask your hotel to book a cab for you.

Second: the ride. Make sure the taxi meter is on "1" when you start out, and not on "2" – that's the double rate, which is only permitted from midnight to 5am, or outside designated city limits. Once inside, you may find yourself with company. Don't be alarmed. It is traditional practice for drivers to pick up two, three, even four individual riders, provided they're going roughly in the same direction. In these cases, make a note of the meter count when you get in. In fact, because taxis are relatively affordable, they can end up functioning as minibus services.

Third: paying up. If you've travelled with other passengers, make sure you aren't paying for the part of the trip that happened

before you got in. You should pay the difference in meter reading between embarking and alighting, subject to a minimum fare of €3.20. Otherwise, the meter will run from €1.20 (not zero) and tell you the straight price, which may be adjusted according to the tariff that should be on a laminated placard clipped to the dashboard. There are extra charges for each piece of luggage in the boot, for leaving or entering an airport or seaport, plus bonuses around Christmas and Easter.

Some drivers will quote you the correct price, but many others will try to rip you off, especially if it seems that you're a novice. If the fare you're charged is clearly above the correct price, don't hesitate to argue your way, in whichever language, back down to a normal price. Coming out of an airport or seaport waving 50- or 100-euro notes is asking for trouble – always keep small bills and coins handy.

These rules apply more to Athens than to the islands, although it's still necessary to be pretty assertive in Thessaloníki or on Crete and Rhodes.

Various radio taxi services exist in Athens and most other larger towns. They can pick you up within a short time of your call to a central booking number, though there are chunky surcharges for this (at least €2).

Private Transport

Cars

Having a car in rural Greece enables you to reach a lot of otherwise inaccessible corners of the country; however, driving a car in Athens or Thessaloníki is unpleasant and confusing. Tempers run short, while road signs, or warnings of mandatory turning lanes, are practically non-

Athens' Rush Hour

Drive at your peril in Athens during its multiple rush hours (7–9.30am, 2–3pm, 4.30–5.30pm, 8–10pm).

existent or obscured by trees.

EU-registered cars are no longer stamped into your passport on entry to the country, can circulate freely for up to six months, and are exempt from road tax as long as this has been paid in the home country – however, you are not allowed to sell the vehicle. Non-EU/EEA nationals will find that a bizarre litany of rules apply to importing cars, chief among them that you must re-export the car when you depart, or have it sealed by Customs in an off-road facility of your choosing.

Car Hire (Rental)

Hiring a car in Greece is not cheap owing to high insurance premiums and import duties. Prices vary with the type of car, season and length of rental and should include CDW (collision damage waiver) and VAT at 23 percent. Payment can, and often must, be made with a major credit card. You must be at least 21 years old and have a full driving licence (EU/EEA residents) or an international driving permit (all others).

From overseas, you can book a car in advance through websites such as www.comparecarrentals.co.uk, www.skycars.co.uk, www.autoeurope.com, www.auto-europe.co.uk and www.rentalcargroup.com. Only if you're a member of some corporate or other affinity group are you likely to get as good a deal (or better) directly through the websites of major rental chains like Hertz, Avis or Budget.

For a walk-in rental in Athens, many small local agencies are along or near Syngroú Avenue in the Makrygiánni district.

Autorent
Syngroú 11, tel: 210 92 15 430, www.autorent.gr

Avance
Syngroú 40, tel: 210 92 00 100, www.avance.gr

Avanti
Syngroú 50, tel: 210 92 33 919, www.avanti.com.gr

Kosmos
Syngroú 9, tel: 210 92 34 696, www.kosmos-carrental.com

Driving in Greece

All EU/EEA licences, and licences held by returning diaspora Greeks irrespective of issuing country, are honoured in Greece. Conversely, all other licences – this includes North American and Australian ones – are invalid, as many tourists from those nations attempting to hire cars have discovered to their cost. These motorists must obtain an international driving permit before departure (issued by the AAA or CAA in North America on the spot for a nominal cost); the Greek Automobile and Touring Club (ELPA) no longer issues them to foreign nationals in Greece. Similarly, with the advent of the single European market, insurance Green Cards are no longer required, though you should check with your home insurer about the need for any supplementary premiums – many policies now include pan-European cover anyway.

Greek traffic control and signals are basically the same as in the rest of continental Europe, though roundabouts are handled bizarrely by French or English standards – in many cases, the traffic entering from the slip road, not that already in the circle, has the right of way – watch for "stop" or "yield" signs or invariably faded pavement markings.

Motorways speeds are routinely in excess of the nominal 100–120 kph (62–75 mph) limits, and drivers overtake with abandon. A red light is often considered not so much an obligation as a suggestion, and oncoming drivers flashing lights at you on one-lane roads means the opposite of what it does in the UK. Here, it means: "I'm coming through" (although sometimes it can mean "Beware! Police checkpoint ahead"). Greece has the highest accident rate in the pre-2004 EU after Portugal, so drive defensively.

Greece has a mandatory seatbelt law (stiff fine for violators), and children under 10 are not allowed to sit in the front seat. It is an offence to drive without your licence on your person (this incurs a stiff fine). Every car must also carry a first-aid kit in the boot (though hire companies tend to skimp on this). Police checkpoints at major (and minor) junctions are frequent, and in addition to the above offences, you can be done for not having evidence of insurance, paid road tax or registration papers in/on the vehicle. If it's clear you've no fixed residence in Greece, your licence may be confiscated and held to ransom at the nearest police station pending payment of the fine (within 10 working days).

Super and normal unleaded petrol, as well as lead-substitute super and diesel, are readily available throughout Greece, though filling up after dark can be difficult off the main intercity highways. Most filling stations close around 8pm and, although a rota system operates in larger towns, it is often difficult to determine which station is open. Credit cards are widely accepted, but always ask first – card-swiping machines can be mysteriously "broken".

Road maps

Gone are the days when visitors had to suffer with mendacious or comical maps which seemed based more on wishful thinking (especially projected but unbuilt roads) than facts on the ground. There are now three commercial Greek companies producing largely accurate maps to the Greek mainland, mountain areas and islands: Terrain (www.terrainmaps.gr), Emvelia (www.emvelia.gr) and Anavasi (www.anavasi.gr). They can be found country-wide, in tourist-shop racks and better bookshop chains like Newsstand or Papasotiriou. Anavasi has its own convenient shop in central Athens at Voulís 32, selling some of the other two companies' products as well.

Motorcycles, quad-bikes and bicycles

On most Greek islands and in many mainland tourist areas, you'll find agencies that hire small motorcycles, various types of scooters of 50cc to 100cc displacement, and even mountain bikes. These give you the freedom to wander where you will, and weekly rates are reasonable.

For any scooter, even just 50cc, helmets and a motorcycle driving licence are both theoretically required, and increasingly these rules are enforced. The ill-fitting helmets

Breakdowns

The Greek Automobile Association (ELPA) offers a breakdown service for motorists, which is free to AA/RAC members (on production of their membership cards).

Phone 10400 for assistance nationwide. Some car-hire companies have agreements instead with competitors Hellas Service (tel: 1057), Interamerican (tel: 1168) or Express Service (tel: 1154), but these national call centres can be slow to dispatch aid. Always ring a local garage number if this is what the hire company instructs you to do.

offered are a bit of a joke, but if you refuse them you may have to sign a waiver absolving the dealer of criminal/civil liability – and police checkpoints can be zealous, levying stiff fines (nearly **€200**) on locals and visitors alike. Having only a car licence while driving a scooter will get you another, steeper fine. Many rental agencies now refuse to give out scooters to folk without the requisite licence, steering them to quad bikes instead – which accounts for their sudden popularity. They are unstable on turns (thus helmets are handed out for riding them too) and arguably the stupidest looking road conveyance ever devised – they're basically modified tractors – but given the two-wheeler licence law, you may not have another choice.

Before you set off, make sure the bike of whichever sort works by taking it for a test spin down the street. Brakes in particular are sometimes badly set (too loose), lights may need new fuses or bulbs, and spark-plugs get fouled. Otherwise, you may get stuck with a lemon, with the added insult of being held responsible for its malfunctioning when you return it.

Reputable agencies now often furnish you with a phone number for a breakdown pick-up service, or will come and fetch you themselves.

Above all, don't take unnecessary chances, like riding two on a bike designed for one. More than one holiday in Greece has been ruined by a serious scooter accident – hospital casualty wards are wearily familiar with "road rash". It is strongly suggested that, where possible, you stick with the traditional, manual-transmission Honda/Yamaha/Suzuki

Hiring a boat can be an option.

Cruises

Apparently, one in six of all visitors to Greece embarks on an Aegean cruise. These cruises can range from simple one-day trips to the Saronic Gulf islands close to Athens and Piraeus, to luxury multi-day journeys taking in part of the Turkish coast, Rhodes and Crete. Many people opt for a seven-day excursion, which offers an opportunity to see a couple of islands in the Cyclades, a few of the Dodecanese islands, and a foray over to Istanbul or Ephesus for good measure.

One company that offers a fine alternative to the mega-gin-

scooters of 50–100cc, with skinny, large-radius, well-treaded tyres. The new generation of automatic, button-start *mihanákia/papákia* (as they're called in Greek slang), with their sexy fairings and tiny, fat, no-tread tyres, look the business but are unstable and unsafe once off level asphalt. In particular, if you hit a gravel-strewn curve on one of these, you will go for a spill, and at the very least lose most of the skin on your hands and knees.

Balloon-tire pedal-bike hire is widely practised on flat Kos, with its extensive network of cycle paths. It's also known around Rhodes Town, but not especially recommendable anywhere else. On the more mountainous islands and parts of the mainland, mountain bikes are often hired as part of organised 'safaris'.

Yacht charter

Chartering a yacht is one of the more glamorous ways of island-hopping

palaces that ply the Aegean is Seafarer (UK tel: 020 83243117, www.seafarercruises.com), with five thoughtful itineraries, some on 8-passengers yachts, in the Ionian Sea, around the Cyclades, through the Dodecanese, and touching on Turkey. UK-based **Swan Hellenic Cruises** (UK tel: 01444 462 180; www.swan hellenic.com) offer upmarket, all-inclusive holidays on large luxury liners, with guest speakers instructing passengers on anything from archaeology to marine biology.

in Greece. It is by no means cheap, although hiring a boat with a group of friends may not far exceed the price of renting rooms every night for the same number of people.

Depending on your nautical qualifications and your taste for autonomy, you can either take the helm yourself or let a hired crew do so for you. There are over a thousand yachts available for charter in Greece, all of which are registered and inspected by the Ministry of the Merchant Marine. Charter is best done in advance from overseas, through the aegis of agencies like Nautilus (www.neilson.co.uk) and Sunsail (www.sunsail.com).

Kaïkia and taxi boats

Apart from conventional ferries, most of which carry cars, there are swarms of small *kaïkia* (caïques) which, in season, offer inter-island excursions pitched mostly at day-trippers. Since they are chartered by travel agencies, they are exempt from Ministry of Transport fare controls – as well as the rule that vessels over 35 years old should be scrapped, which is (haphazardly) enforced in Greece for scheduled ferries – and can be very pricey if used as a one-way ticket from, say, Sámos to Pátmos. The stereotypical emergency transfer by friendly fisherman is, alas, largely a thing of the past; never comfortable at the best of times, it is now highly illegal. Knowing this, skippers quote exorbitant prices if approached, and must undertake the journey when the port policeman's gaze is averted.

On many islands where there are remote beaches with poor overland access – most notably Sými, Itháki, Alónisos, Skiáthos, Hálki – local taxi boats provide a fairly pricey shuttle service.

ACCOMMODATION

HOTELS, YOUTH HOSTELS, BED AND BREAKFAST

How to Choose

There is a broad range of accommodation in Greece, from de luxe hotels to backpacker hostels. Listed are a sample of different categories across the country.

On the islands and in many parts of the mainland, the main type of affordable lodging is private rented rooms (*domátia*) and, increasingly common these days, self-catering studios or apartments (*diamerísmata*). These are classified separately from hotels, but also subject to official regulation.

In general, when looking for any kind of accommodation, local tourist offices or the Tourist Police can be of help if you're in a fix – most obviously if no rooms are on offer when you disembark at the dock. "Tourist offices", however, are rarely official and rarely disinterested. The best system, really, is booking a room yourself a few days (or weeks, or months) in advance on the internet.

In popular mass-market resorts like the north coast of Crete, Kos, Corfu, Skiáthos and Zákynthos, many beach side hotels have commitment contracts with overseas package-holiday operators and are barely (if at all) interested in walk-in custom. However, with the demise of many northern European travel companies and the rise of no-frills airlines, smart accommodation proprietors are going back to courting on-spec individual bookings.

Hotel Categories

The Greek authorities have six categories for hotels; this is currently expressed through a star system (no star = basic; five-star = de luxe). This has supposedly replaced an older letter-based categorisation (E to A, plus de luxe), though there are still some hoteliers resisting the change. Although the number of stars is supposed to reflect a hotel's quality, a conference hall, swimming pool or tennis court could place an establishment in the three-star or four-star bracket even though in every other respect – specifically room appointments – it has indifferent facilities. Also, the number of rooms can limit the maximum rating, so you commonly encounter 20-room three-star hotels which are superior in every respect to a nearby 50-room four-star hotel.

Monastery Stays

Monasteries and convents can occasionally provide lodging for travellers of the appropriate gender, though their xenónes (guest lodges) are multi-bedded rooms intended primarily for Orthodox pilgrims. Mt Áthos, of course, has a long tradition of this hospitality – for men only; see page 221 for details on how to obtain a permit to go there. You will have to dress and behave appropriately. The doors may close as early as sunset and some kind of donation may be expected.

Youth Hostels

Greece has a very limited number of official, YHA-affiliated youth hostels for which you theoretically need a youth hostel card. However, you can often buy a YHA card on the spot or just pay an additional charge for the night. There are surviving hostels in Athens, Olymbía and Thessaloníki, and on Santoríni plus Crete at Iráklio, Réthymno, and Plakiás. There is also private, unaffiliated backpacker accommodation of varying quality

Santoríni hotel with a sea view to die for.

and repute in Athens, Pátra and on Rhodes and Corfu.

Traditional Settlements

Traditional settlements (**paradosiakí ikismí**) are villages that have been recognised by the Greek government as forming an important part of the national heritage and have been protected from modern intrusions and constructions by law. Almost all of these inns are now in private hands.

Camping

Those who want to stay at organised campsites will find them all over Greece; these are all privately owned. The most beautiful campsites in Greece, however, are usually ones you find on your own. While in most places it is officially illegal just to lay out your sleeping bag or pitch a tent, if you're discreet you will rarely be bothered. That always means asking permission from the owners if you seem to be on private property, patronising nearby businesses and leaving the place looking better than it did when you arrived.

In the mountains, camping is the rule as few alpine refuges are staffed, but even here you should get the local shepherds' consent if they're around.

TRANSPORT

ACCOMMODATION

EATING OUT

ACTIVITIES

A – Z

LANGUAGE

ATHENS

Acropolis House
Kódrou 6–8, metro Sýndagma
Tel: 210-322 2344
www.acropolishouse.gr
This was the first neoclassical mansion in Athens to be converted into a pension. The building's listed status means some rooms are not en suite, though for the academic clientele that's part of the charm, and it is well kept. All rooms have solid wood floors, most have high ceilings (some with murals). Communal fridge and two breakfast rooms. €–€€

Attalos
Athinás 29, metro Monastiráki
Tel: 210-321 2801
www.attalos.gr
This friendly hotel is good value and retains many of its period features, but medium-sized rooms – about half with balconies, costing a tad more – have modern furnishings, double glazing against street noise, parquet floors and pastel/earth tones. Facilities include free wi-fi and a very popular if somewhat cramped roof-terrace bar operating from 6.30pm onwards. €€

Ava
Lysikrátous 9–11, metro Acropolis
Tel: 210-325 9000
www.avahotel.gr
Suite-format hotel, thoroughly overhauled to the highest standards in 2010. Upper units have balconies with courtyard, or oblique Acropolis views. Excellent for families, as the roomier options (up to 55 sq metres), effectively one-bedroom apartments, comfortably fit four. There are also smaller suites suitable for couples. Breakfast included, wi-fi throughout, assiduous service. €€€€

Cecil
Athinás 39
Tel: 210-321 7079
www.cecil.gr
A well-restored 1850s vintage mansion has become a characterful small hotel, right down to its interwar "cage" lift. The rooms only have ornamental balconies but do offer parquet floors, iron bedsteads, double glazing, free wi-fi and designer-tiled bathrooms. Common areas are limited to a breakfast room with its original wooden floor and painted ceiling, and a street-level café. €€

Fresh
Sofokléous 26, corner Klisthénous, metro Omónia
Tel: 210-524 8511
www.freshhotel.gr
You will either love or hate this

The rooftop restaurant at the Grande Bretagne, Athens.

startling 'design' hotel, with its lollipop colour scheme of panels everywhere from reception to the balconies. Chrome, leather and glass abound, but there is also plenty of oak and walnut. Modern room features include bedside remote control of windows and plasma TV. The rooftop pool-and-bar is a big hit and executive rooms or suites have private Zen rock gardens. €€€

Grande Bretagne
Platía Syndágmatos, metro Sýndagma
Tel: 210-333 0000
www.grandebretagne.gr
Perhaps the most famous hotel in Athens, the Grande Bretagne on Sýndagma Square dates from 1846. A 2004 renovation restored every period detail to its Belle Epoque glory, with 'de luxe' doubles comparable to junior suites elsewhere. Sumptuous common areas include a landscaped pool garden, a ballroom, plus a basement spa with a palm court, and large pool, hammam and sauna. The rooftop restaurant is a pole of attraction. €€€€

Hera
Falírou 9, metro Acropolis
Tel: 210-923 6682
www.herahotel.gr
The Hera has perhaps the best roof garden in the area, with a heated bar-restaurant for all-year operation. Rooms are on the small side, so it's worth paying extra for three fifth-floor suites with bigger balconies (some fourth-floor rooms also have Acropolis views). The dome-lit atrium-breakfast room, and friendly staff, are further assets. €€€

Hermes
Apóllonos 19, metro Sýndagma

Tel: 210-323 5514
www.hermeshotel.gr
The Hermes has all-marble-clad bathrooms, variable in size, and oak-effect-floored rooms. Front-facing ones are smaller but benefit from a terrace; rear rooms are larger, some with sofas. The breakfast room is decorated with manager Dorina Stathopoulou's professional photographs. If they're full, you'll be offered space in one of their two affiliated hotels nearby. €€€

Herodion
Rovértou Gálli 4, metro Acropolis
Tel: 210-923 6832
www.herodion.gr
The Herodion scores most points for its common areas: the café-restaurant with conservatory seating shaded by wild pistachios, a small business/computer corner, and the roof garden with two jacuzzi tubs and eyefuls of the Acropolis. Functional but fair-sized rooms, some with Acropolis views. Overflow is referred to the affiliated, nearby, more modest Philippos Hotel. €€€€

Marble House
Alley off Anastasíou Zínni 35, metro Syngroú-Fix
Tel: 210-922 8294
www.marblehouse.gr
This welcoming, family-run pension has an enviably quiet, yet convenient location. All rooms were renovated in 2010, with balconies, mostly en suite bathrooms, fridges, air con and free wi-fi. Great value – book well in advance. €

Orion/Dryades
Emmanouíl Benáki 105/Dryádon 4
Tel: 210-330 2387

www.orion-dryades.com
These co-managed, almost adjacent hotels (joint reception in the Orion) serve a youngish crowd who've outgrown hostels but still take advantage of the self-catering kitchens in each well-maintained building (the Orion's has a particularly stunning city view). Both are now fully en suite, though the Dryades tends to have more balconies, LCD televisions, and better views. €–€€

Periscope
Háritos 22
Tel: 210-729 7200
www.periscope.gr
Unlike many Athens hotels, the lounge and common areas here are minimal as well as minimalist: the focus is instead on the black-, white- and grey-toned rooms. Aerial photos of the city comprise the wall and ceiling art, along with

real-time projections of the skyline relayed by... a periscope down to the handy ground-floor bistro. The higher in the building you go, the better, culminating in airy suites with balconies and a rooftop jacuzzi. All units have wood floors, LCD TVs, CD/DVD players and a choice of pillows. €€€€

Radisson Blu Park
Alexándras 10, metro Viktória
Tel: 210-889 4500
www.rbathenspark.com
The former *Athens Park*, dating from 1976, had a remarkable makeover (and rebranding) in 2011 – the Pédion Áreos park opposite has come indoors, as it were, with tree trunks in the foyer, turf-like carpets in three grades of rooms, bicycle decor (and rental), plus light green and russet colours for the soft furnishings. The rooftop, poolside

St'Astra restaurant was always a worthy destination in its own right, now joined by the ground-floor all-day bistro. Free parking (and interconnecting family rooms) are big pluses, as is an indoor gym/sauna and walking distance to the National Archaeological Museum. €€€€

St George Lycabettus
Kleoménous 2, Kolonáki, metro Evangelismós
Tel: 210-729 0711
www.sgl.gr
Located at the foot of Mount Lykavittós (Lycabettus), the decor here varies from luridly plush to minimalist; all rooms have wi-fi access (charged extra); the most covetable (and pricier) rooms look over the city. Facilities include jacuzzi, sauna, massage studio, gym and roof pool, as well as an in-house art gallery. €€€–€€€€

PELOPONNESE

Areópoli

Pyrgos Kapetanakou
Tel: 27330 51233
This three-storey tower is one of the better executed restoration projects. It is set in a pleasant walled garden, and comprises rooms of various sizes. There are communal balconies, and also a ground-floor refectory. Open all year. €€

Diakoftó

Chris-Paul
Tel: 26910 41715
www.chrispaul-hotel.gr
Named after the family's two children, this small, friendly and spotlessly clean hotel is conveniently situated for the start of the journey up through the Vouraïkós Gorge. Open all year. €€

Dimitsána

Velissaropoulos Rooms
Village centre, under a church
Tel: 27950 31617
Just four good-standard heated rooms with balconies or verandas, in some cases fireplaces, and small self-catering corners. Tiny lounge but no other common areas. Open all year. €€

Xenonas Kazakou
Tel: 27950 31660
www.xenonaskazakou.gr
Externally austere, this stone-and-wood mansion from 1851 is discreetly comfortable inside – with central heating for the five rooms of varying sizes. Situated near the top

Helmos is Kalávryta's only four-star hotel.

of the village, it's very quiet, apart from church bells on Sunday. A rich traditional breakfast is served in the cellar. Limited parking (an issue in Dimitsána). Open all year. €€€

Gýthio

Gythion
Vassiléos Pávlou 33
Tel: 27330 23452
www.gythionhotel.gr
Small, period (1864 vintage) hotel with well-kept, large, air conditioned rooms with balconies facing the sunrise. Decor is not cutting edge, but for the price, you can't complain. Free use of facilities at affiliated Gythion Bay Camping. €

Kalamáta

Haïkos
Navarínou 115

Tel: 27210 88902
www.haikos.gr
Friendly staff and good-sized rooms in this modern hotel on the seafront. Some street noise, but not really a major boulevard. €€

Kalávryta

Helmos
Platía Eleftherías 1
Tel: 26920 29222
www.hotelhelmos.gr

PRICE CATEGORIES

Price categories are based on the cost of a double room for one night in high season:
€ = under €50
€€ = €50–100
€€€ = €100–150
€€€€ = over €150

TRANSPORT
ACCOMMODATION
EATING OUT
ACTIVITIES
A – Z
LANGUAGE

Neoclassical building which partially survived the Nazi arson of 1943, reopening fully renovated in 2005 as the town's only four-star hotel. The plush rooms have soothing earth tones and orthopaedic mattresses; common areas include a huge outdoor pool. Open all year. €€€€

Karýtena
Vrenthi
Tel: 27910 31650
Unbelievably good value rooms in a prominent stone-clad building, two with balconies and all with effective central heating (though no hair dryers supplied). The affiliated bar, in an adjacent premises, will do breakfast and is the hub of Karýtena's admittedly modest nightlife. Open all year. €–€€

Kastaniá
Kastania
Tel: 27470 61289
www.kastania-rooms.gr
Not the most imaginative name, but the top choice for overnighting in the Stymfalía and Feneós area. This welcoming inn has a top standard of furnishings (including stall showers, mini-fridges, big-screen TVs), central heating for winter and great village or mountain views. There's also an attached taverna for meals including breakfast. Open all year. €€

Koróni
Auberge de la Plage
Zánga Beach
Tel: 27250 22401
www.delaplage.gr
No prizes for its 1970s exterior, but the gardens and (most) rooms overlooking sand and sea are incomparable, and the interior has contemporary decor. €€

Kosmás
Xenonas Maleatis Apollo
Tel: 27570 31494
Another place to escape some of the summer's heat, this traditional guesthouse is 1,150 metres (3,775ft) up on the central square of this delightful village on Mt Párnon. A great base for touring this remote part of Arkadía. Simple rooms; some kitchen facilities. €€

Kyparíssi
Kyfanta
Paralía district
Tel: 27320 55356
Well-appointed studio-hotel set in an olive grove, run by Esther (Catalan) and Giannis (Greek). Two apartments will accommodate families or groups.

There is a common area with plaza-bar and trading library. Open all year. €€

Loutráki
Petit Palais
Georgíou Lékka 48
Tel: 27440 61977
http://petitpalais.gr
Loutráki resort makes the best base for touring the Korinthía district, and Petit Palais, with sea views, at the north end of town, is a good-value, all-year choice. Rooms are large and updated, with split-level heating/air con; the panoramic breakfast room is on the top floor. €€

Mavromáti
Arhea Messini
Tel: 27240 51297
The better of just two places to stay at ancient Messene, comprising four large, 1980s-style self-catering units on the through road. Not bargain basement for the location, but owner Victoria is a big asset. Open all year. €

Methóni
Aris
Platía Syngroú
Tel: 27230 31125
Basic but clean and well-kept hotel, in a quiet corner of town with easy parking. Open all year, with central heating. €€

Monemvasiá
Kinsterna
Ágios Stéfanos district
Tel: 27320 66300
If you have the funds, this is the top choice in the area: an 800-year-old mansion renovated in 2010 as a five-star resort. The name refers to the old Byzantine cistern, core of the place and now a decorative pond, which originally watered the burgeoning orchards all around; the same spring that fills the cistern now fills the river-like swimming pool. Just 27 suites and rooms, plus a full-service spa and good (if pricey) on-site restaurant. Unsurprisingly, weddings and honeymoons a speciality. Distant views of Monemvasiá. €€€€
Malvasia
Tel: 27320 63007
www.malvasia-hotel.gr
The scattered units of this complex are some of the best in town. Each room, well appointed in wood, local stone and marble, is unique, with features such as fireplaces and balconies. Unit size varies from simple doubles to an apartment. Open Apr–Oct plus winter holiday weekends. €€€€

Návplio
Byron
Plátonos 2, Platía Agíou Spyridóna
Tel: 27520 22351
www.byronhotel.gr
This was Návplio's first boutique hotel, installed in a restored old mansion back in the 1980s, and, after recent renovation and expansion, is again among the best. Many units overlook the domes of a medieval hammam, and some have balconies. There are a range of rooms scattered over two buildings – our favourite is the mid-priced one with solid-wood floor and pitched roof beams – for every taste and budget. Open all year. €–€€
Marianna
Potamaníou 9
Tel: 27520 24256
www.hotelmarianna.gr
Another beautiful mansion-conversion hotel, with a rather bright colour scheme, tucked in under the walls of the Akronavplía fortress. Breakfast terrace (organic breakfast €5 extra) has wonderful views; some rooms have balconies. €€

Néos Mystrás
Byzantion
Tel: 27310 83309
www.byzantionhotel.gr
Most rooms at this hotel, renovated in the mid-Oughties, offer an unbeatable view of the Byzantine ruins. Small pool in lawn-garden. Open Apr–Oct. €€

Olympía (Olympia)
Hercules
Tel: 26240 22696
www.hotelhercules.gr
An excellent budget choice with friendly management, easy street parking, and central yet quiet location near the school. Rooms (and their baths) are resolutely 1980s in decor, but all have balconies, air con and televisions. Pleasant breakfast lounge plus wi-fi. Open all year. €€
Pelops
Varelá 2
Tel: 26240 22543
www.hotelpelops.gr
A relatively plush option with veneer floors and quality furnishings for the rooms, which do vary – some have bathtubs, others only stall-showers, and some without balconies. €€

Pátra
Byzantino
Ríga Feréou 106
Tel: 26102 43000
www.byzantino-hotel.gr

A beautifully decorated, high-class hotel, near the centre of town in a neoclassical refurbishment; just 25 somewhat quirky rooms. Conference facilities. Open all year. €€€

Pýlos

Romanos Costa Navarino
Navaríno Dunes, Romanós village, north of Pýlos
Tel: 27230 96000
www.romanoscostanavarino.com
Five-star golf, beach and spa resort, funded by a ship-owning family, that's caused a sensation since opening in 2009. Choose from among seven grades of impeccably done-up rooms, suites and villas – the higher six

of which have private infinity pools ranging from just plungeable to serious lap-swimming. Standard rooms start from around €300, and if you have to ask what the suites cost, you can't afford them. There are five on-site restaurants – which get mixed reviews – plus a complete water sports programme off the gorgeous one-kilometre-long beach. €€€€

Stemnítsa

Xenonas Stemnitsa
Off main platía
Tel: 27950 81349
www.xenonas-stemnitsa.gr
Best value amongst the comfortable

local inns, with beamed ceilings, exposed stonework, plush furnishings and all other mod cons in the four rooms and single studio. Open all year. €€€

Stoúpa

Lefktron
Tel: 27210 77322
www.lefktron-hotel.gr
Well-sited hotel in the centre of the resort, five minutes' walk from the beach. Popular with packages, but welcomes walk-ins. Comfortable rooms with renovated bathroom including proper shower stalls, decent buffet breakfast, friendly management, small pool. €€

CENTRAL GREECE

Ágios Ioánnis

Theodorides Estate
Hillside above resort, 15-min walk to Pláka beach
Tel: 24260 31872
www.pelioncountryvillas.com
Purpose-built, traditional Pílio-style villas with sweeping views, divided into maisonettes fitting two to four persons, completely self-catering and ideal for families. Unusually for such accommodation, there is wi-fi. Pool to hand, and fireplaces (though the villas are generally not open in winter) – notional season April–Oct. €€€

Aráhova

Lykoria
West edge of town
Tel: 22670 32132
www.likoria.gr
Huge standard balconied doubles, plus suites and designer bathrooms. Common amenities include a terrace garden, pool, gym/sauna. Buffet breakfast served in a somewhat dark salon; easy (for Aráhova) parking. €€€

Xenonas Generali
Eastern outskirts, below the primary school and clock tower
Tel: 22670 31529
www.generalis.gr
A restored inn offering the best standard in town: Nine rooms, all different (most with fireplace), the decor of which can be a bit garish, but the welcome is warm and the breakfasts are calorie-"enhanced" during ski season, when a pool, spa, hammam and sauna also operate. €€€

Argalastí

Agamemnon
Village centre

Tel: 24230 54557
Another restored mansion, with exposed stonework and fireplaces in the rooms, antiques in the common areas and a large pool outside – a good base in the south of the peninsula. €€

Aspropótamos

Pyrgos Mantania (Mantania Tower)
Near Kalliroe village
Tel: 24320 87351
www.mantania.gr
A superb stone-built inn, poised to take advantage of river-kayaking and forest-walking aficionados who visit this area. Families are catered for in the upstairs four-bedded suites with fireplaces, plus the five newer units by the pool; cheaper but still large standard rooms on the lower floors. Well-regarded, if somewhat impersonal, restaurant-bar in a separate building. €€

Damoúhari

Damouhari Hotel
Centre bay
Tel: 24260 49840
www.damouchari.gr
Part of this mock-traditional, stone-built studio complex can be monopolised by package companies, but the bay-side annexe, with five state-of-the-art rooms over the restaurant, is kept back for walk-ins. You still have access to the hillside pool, and the eclectically decorated bar. €€

Delfí (Delphi)

Pan
Vassiléon Pávlou and Frederíkis 53
Tel: 22650 82294
An excellent mid-range hotel, with

plain doubles but excellent family suites with large bathtubs. Their annexe across the road, Artemis, has a higher standard – most of the bathrooms have mini-tubs – but you sacrifice the view. €

Sun View
Apóllonos 84
Tel: 22650 82349
Very quietly located pension on the uppermost street; rooms are decorated in pastel shades, with art on the walls. There's a breakfast salon downstairs, and fairly easy parking outside. €

Galaxídi

Galaxa
Hillside above Hirólakas bay
Tel: 22650 41620
Rooms at this restored-house hotel are somewhat casually maintained, but the views are superb and the welcome friendly. The best bit is the garden bar, under the vines across the way, where breakfast and drinks are served. €€

Ganimede
Nikólaou Gourgoúri 20 (southwesterly commercial street)
Tel: 22650 41328
www.ganimede.gr
Under the energetic management of Kósta and Hrysoúla Papaléxis

PRICE CATEGORIES

Price categories are based on the cost of a double room for one night in high season:
€ = under €50
€€ = €50–100
€€€ = €100–150
€€€€ = over €150

since 2004, this is the clear winner amongst local lodging, despite the lack of sea views. Four refurbished doubles in the old house (best is No. 1), with fridges and satellite TV, and a family suite with loft and fireplace. The copious breakfast still features founder Bruno's recipes for pâtés and jams, plus novelty breads from the family bakery. €€

Kalambáka

Alsos House
Kanári 5
Tel: 24320 24097
www.alsoshouse.gr
This inn at the top of the old town, near the path up to Agías Triádos monastery, has units of doubles, triples and a quad suite, plus a well-equipped communal kitchen. The helpful owner speaks good English. €

Karpenisiótis Valley

Agrambeli
Gávros
Tel: 22370 41148
A riverside pension with cool, cavernous rooms redone in 2006; there's a breakfast bar and large swimming pool in the middle of the lawn. €
Helidona
Old Mikró Horió
Tel: 22370 41221
www.ihelidona.gr
In a region known for very pricey lodging, this 2001-reburbished hotel remains affordable. Superbly set on the old platía, with a ground floor restaurant; great views from the rear rooms. €€

Karýtsa

Dohos
Between Karýtsa and Stómio
Tel: 24950 92001
www.dohos.gr
On the slopes of Mt Kíssavos, this 2002-built hotel nestles in the forest above some of the best and least visited beaches in Greece. Huge wood-floored rooms or suites; all have sea-facing balconies and full bathtubs, while some have cooking facilities. The stone-floored common areas include a pool, outdoor theatre and conference hall, the latter two hosting special events in the summer. Often closed Nov–Dec. €€

Kastráki Meteóron

Doupiani House
West edge of village, well-signed above road to monasteries
Tel: 24320 77555
www.doupiani-house.com
This much-loved domátia was

converted into a comfortable three-star hotel in 2008 without shedding Thanássis' and Toúla's warm welcome which had won them many fans over the years. The in-your-face views of the rock formations and lovely grounds (including jacuzzi and ample parking) mean you always have to pre-book here in season. Open all year. €€
Xenonas Sotiriou
Mesohóri Plaza
Tel: 24320 78104
www.guesthouse-sotiriou.gr
Stone-built mansion from 1845 – one of the few buildings that escaped the Nazis' 1944 reprisal burning here – restored as a quality inn. Some of the five rooms have a fireplace; all have wood floors and ceilings and mock-antique furniture. €€

Makrynítsa

Arhondiko Pandora
300 metres below centre
Tel: 24280 99404
www.pandoramansion.gr
Much the best of various restored mansion-inns here, redone by an architect/designer owner of international repute. Very private, gated courtyard with a café-restaurant precedes two upper floors of standards and suites. €€€

Moúressi

The Old Silk Store
Curve in access road by bakery
Tel: 24260 49086
www.pelionet.gr/oldsilkstore
Nineteenth-century silk-merchant's mansion lovingly converted into a B&B by Cornishwoman Jill Sleeman, who also leads walks in the area. Excellent breakfasts (own-made jams and wholemeal breads) served in the idyllic garden. There's also a self-catering studio adjacent. Open April–early Oct. €€

Návpaktos

Akti
Grímbovo, by the fountain-stream
Tel: 26340 28464
www.akti.gr
This hotel is the town's clear winner, set behind the easterly beach: it's the little touches like insect screens and oblique sea views from about half the rooms that make the difference. Good standard of breakfast; palatial top-floor suites. €€
Ilion
Inland at the base of the kástro
Tel: 26340 21222
For a stay in the old town, try this quiet little 10-room inn – though it's best to be travelling light, as you're

some way distant (and uphill) from the nearest parking. €€

Portariá

Kritsa
Central platía
Tel: 24280 99121
www.hotel-kritsa.gr
Taste is the keyword here, transforming an indifferent, interwar hotel building into something worth going out of your way for. It has just eight rooms (some of them suites), four with balconies and views over the square. The massive breakfast puts to shame bog-standard continentals offered at the same price elsewhere. €€

Pórto Germenó

Maria Meïntani Rooms
Tel: 22630 41552
Easily reachable even with a late start out of Athens, these very friendly self-catering rooms, set slightly inland, are an ideal solution for a quick overnight or two in this idyllic corner of the Corinth Gulf. Open all year. €

Potistiká

Elytis
On slope above the beach
Tel: 24230 55095
www.elitis-hotel.com
If you just want a seaside holiday without cultural distractions, this is probably the best place on Pílio to do it: a pristine, undeveloped bay, and this welcoming (if bland) hotel just inland, with an attached full-service restaurant. €

Tsangaráda

The Lost Unicorn
Agía Paraskeví district, off main platía
Tel: 24260 49930
www.lostunicorn.com
Under the sympathetic management of Clare and Christos Martzos, this boutique hotel scores as much for its common areas – kitted out like a British gentlemen's club – and champagne breakfasts as for the eight antique-furnished, mosaic-floored rooms in the 1890s building. A pricey "continental cuisine" restaurant operates two to seven nights weekly May to October, as well as winter holiday weekends. Open all year except one month mid-winter. €€€

Vólos

Domotel Xenia Volou
Plastíra 1
Tel: 24210 92700
www.xeniavolou.gr

A 1960s ugly duckling transformed into a swan in 2006. Great position in secluded seafront gardens (half the rooms do face inland). Pool, spa, fitness centre and abundant breakfasts. €€€€

Roussas
Iatroú Tzánou 11
Tel: 24210 21732
At the east end of the seafront, this is the city's best budget hotel, underrated at E-class/no-star – a bargain. Well kept en suite rooms, and free parking nearby, though no breakfast. €

Vyzítsa

Kontou
Up the slope from the car park
Tel: 24230 86793
A good standard of restored accommodation (originally dating from 1792) on two floors, at an affordable price; mind your head on the low door frames. €€

Thetis
By the church and central car park
Tel: 24230 86111
May not be the grandest restored arhondikó here, but popular, thanks to its kafenío (serving breakfast)

and excellent value. A mix of wood-trimmed rooms, both en suite and not. €

Zagorá

Villa Gayannis
Tel: 24260 23391
www.villagayannis.gr
One of the few surviving 18th-century mansions in the north of Pílio. Well-converted rooms, spacious common areas (including the courtyard) and a good buffet breakfast. Only let by the week in peak season. €€€€

EPIRUS

Ano Pediná

Porfyron
Tel: 26530 71579
www.porfyron.com
Lovely antique-furnished rooms in a restored mansion with painted/carved ceilings, plus a big terrace-garden with arbour and parasols. The taverna, showcasing organic fare, is open to all, and cooking courses are offered by the Dutch/Greek proprietors. The inn is frequently booked by walking groups; your best chance on-spec is high summer. Open most of the year. €€€

Dílofo

Arhondiko Dilofo
Village centre
Tel: 26530 22455
www.dilofo.com
Another superbly executed mansion-restored inn in one of the less touristy Zagori villages, but still convenient for the best hikes. Wood flooring, exposed stone pointing, quality textiles, fireplaces in many rooms. Parking is at the edge of the village, within easy walking distance. No full-service restaurant on site, but there is a good one nearby on the platía. €€

Ioánnina

Kastro
Androníkou Paleológou 57
Tel: 26510 22866
www.hotelkastro.gr
Small, cosy restored inn on the way to the inner citadel, with seven varied rooms (ground-floor ones, with fans but no air-con, are a tad cheaper). Decent breakfast with special requests accommodated; limited street parking. Open all year. €€

Orizon/Horizon

Lyngiádes village, 12km out of town
Tel: 26510 86180

www.hotel-horizon.gr
Stunning views over the entire lake valley from this well-designed hotel run by the Pappas family, refurbished in 2007. The seven rooms vary but are all huge with wood floors, four of them with fireplaces. Very popular with Greek weekenders, so mandatory to reserve then. The approach to the parking is steep, and only suitable for confident drivers. Open all year. €€

Politeia
Anexartisías 109A
Tel: 26510 22235
www.etip.gr
Studio-hotel on the site of an old tradesmen's hall. Though units, including big upstairs suites, are self-catering, breakfast is offered in the courtyard. Pretty quiet, despite the bazaar location; limited off-street parking. Open all year. €€

Karavostási

Karavostasi Beach
Back from middle of the beach
Tel: 26650 91104
www.hotel-karavostasi.gr
Well-designed beach hotel with large pool, well-kept gardens and decent breakfasts as well as other meals. Rooms, in particular the bathrooms, were renovated in 2011 to be more comfortable and colourful. A good family base. Open end May–early Oct. €€€

Kónitsa

Grand Hotel Dentro
On town access road from main highway
Tel: 26550 29365
www.grandhoteldentro.gr
The best facilities offered within town limits; standard doubles have good bathrooms, and sometimes balconies, while top floor suites offer fireplaces and hydromassage tubs. On-site restaurant. €€€

Métsovo

Bitouni
Main street
Tel: 26560 41217
www.hotelbitouni.com
Luxurious digs, redone in 2010, managed by English-speaking brothers who spent many years in London. Most rooms have balconies, plus there are attic family suites and a sauna for the ski season. €€

Filoxenia
Near the central plaza
Tel: 26560 41332
An excellent-value inn on the side of the square. Comfortable rooms in two grades; the rear ones have stunning views. €

Pápingo (Megálo)

Nikos Tsoumanis
Village centre
Tel: 26530 42237
www.tsoumanisnikos.gr
Attached to the namesake restaurant, these 10 units built in traditional style are comfortable if a bit dark in some seasons, but you're unlikely to be indoors by day around here. Beds with down duvets are a big plus. €€

Papaevangelou
North end of the village
Tel: 26530 41135
www.papaevangelou.gr
The best traditional-style inn here, with enormous rooms (some self-catering), and equally spacious bar, where the better-than-average

PRICE CATEGORIES

Price categories are based on the cost of a double room for one night in high season:
€ = under €50
€€ = €50–100
€€€ = €100–150
€€€€ = over €150

breakfast is served. Friendly, helpful management. €€€
Pension Koulis
Behind central kafenío
Tel: 26530 41115, www.papigo-koulis.gr
The original village inn, converted in 1993 to six en-suite rooms (three with fireplace) and renovated in 2009; Koulis himself has retired and sons Nikos and Dimitris are now at the helm. €

Pápingo (Mikró)
Dias
Tel: 26530 41257, www.diaspapigo.gr
An excellent renovation inn spread over two traditional buildings, bracketing an often lively terrace restaurant and a bar. The proprietor is particularly trekker-friendly and

helpful, as mountaineering is the main enterprise hereabouts. €€

Párga
Golfo Beach
Kryonéri beach
Tel: 26840 32336
The diametric opposite of Magda's; a slice of 1970s Greece, the oldest inn at Párga. Rooms are basic, about half en suite. Half of them face the sea, the others a pleasant garden. Good restaurant downstairs. Open May–Oct. €
Magda's Apartments
Below road to Agiá
Tel: 26840 31728
www.magdas-hotel.com
The best standard within the town:

several ranks of self-catering studios and superior apartments in an olive grove, with a bar, spa and pool terrace. There is some package allotment, so book early. Open Greek Easter–late Oct. €€

Tsepélovo
Anthoula Gouri
East side of village
Tel: 26530 81214/81288
Mobile: 6947 561463 for English
Run by Anthoúla and daughter María, this welcoming en suite inn has long been popular with walkers in the region, thanks to the late Alékos Goúris' efforts to promote local trekking. If you're offered half board, it is advisable to accept it, as the platía tavernas are very average. €

THESSALONIKI

Augustos Hotel
Ptolemaon 1
Tel: 2310 522550
www.augustos.gr
In a quiet location off Egnatía, this old style hotel has a variety of simple rooms with high ceilings and slightly antiquated furniture but is one of the best budget options. €
Bristol Hotel
Oplopioú 2
Tel: 2310 506500
www.bristol.gr
Perhaps Thessaloníki's most sumptuous boutique hotel. Sixteen individually named rooms, each immaculately restored, in the shell of the former Bristol Hotel. €€€
Capsis Hotel
Monastiríou 18
Tel: 2310 596800
www.capsishotel.gr
This modern city-centre hotel offers all the expected luxury facilities including a roof garden, gym, swimming pool and sauna. €€€€
Electra Palace
Plateía Aristotélous 9
Tel: 2310 294011
www.electrahotels.gr
Another central hotel, overlooking the broad Platía Aristotélous. Neoclassical facade, very imposing and very comfortable. €€€€
Kinissi Palace
Egnatías 41
Tel: 2310 508082
www.kinissipalace.gr
A renovated city-centre hotel retaining its original style and atmosphere. Rooms are large and airy with double glazing; there's also a small sauna and massage centre. €€

Hotel Luxembourg in Thessaloniki.

Le Palace
Tsimiskí 12
Tel: 2310 257400
www.lepalace.gr
Another central hotel in an old (1926) building. Fully renovated, Le Palace has a style reminiscent of Paris in the 1930s. There's a relaxing in-house café called the Deli Deli. €€
Luxembourg
Komninón 6
Tel: 2310 252600
www.hotelluxembourg.gr
In the heart of the commercial district, this hotel is vaguely Art Deco in style. Rooms are standard but comfortable enough. €€€
Mediterranean Palace
Salamínos 3 and Karatásou

Tel: 2310 552554
www.mediterranean-palace.gr
You can't get closer to the port or the Ladádika district than with this imposing Belle Epoque hotel. Large, lavishly furnished rooms and airy public areas. €€€€
Minerva Premier
Egnatías 44 and Syngroú 12
Tel: 2310 566440
www.minervapremier.gr
Built within a 1929 neoclassical building, the hotel's standard rooms are comfortable, its business rooms mini-offices. Lots of marble, crystal, wood. Good online deals. €€
Orestias Kastoria
Agnóstou Stratiótou 14
Tel: 2310 276517
www.okhotel.gr
Of all the budget choices, this one stands out from the others. Away from the noise of Egnatía, in a neoclassical building, it has light, clean and airy rooms that are very presentable. €€
Tourist Hotel
Mitropóleos 21
Tel: 2310 270501
www.touristhotel.gr
A comfortable budget hotel with standard-sized and reasonably well-appointed rooms, nicely decorated. Very central. €
The Tobacco Hotel
25 Agiou Dimitriou
Tel: 2310 515002
www.davitel.gr
A fairly central, modern hotel in one of the city's oldest tobacco houses, the 57 rooms are furnished in smoky brown tobacco tones. Modern facilities, including a business centre. €€

Panórama

Hotel Panorama
Analípseos 26
Tel: 2310 344871
www.hotelpanorama.gr
A 1970s renovated hotel in the hills

above Thessaloníki, the Panorama is good for travellers with transport. Comfortable rooms and panoramic views. **€€€**

Nepheli
Komninón 1

Tel: 2310 342002
www.nepheli.gr
Another good, out-of-town choice. Pretty roof garden, splendid views. comfortable rooms and good restaurant. **€€**

MACEDONIA AND THRACE

Alexandroúpoli

Thraki Palace
4km (25 miles) along Alexandroúpoli-Thessaloníki road
Tel: 25510 89100
www.thrakipalace.gr
One of several upmarket hotels that have blossomed recently around Alexandroúpoli. A little out of the city centre for travellers without transport, but self-contained and with its own private beach. A nicely designed place with well thought-out public areas, restaurant and bar. **€€€**

Amouliani

Agioníssi Resort
1.5km (1 mile) from the port
Tel: 23770 51102
www.agionissiresort.com
Top-class accommodation in this low-key bungalow-style island resort. Built amphitheatrically close to a sandy beach, the individual bungalows are spacious and well-appointed, with local furnishing touches from Halkidikí. There's a pool and manicured garden, and a private ferry service to and from the Áthos coastline opposite. **€€**

Arnéa

Oikia Alexandrou
Platía Patriárhou Vartholoméou 1st
Tel: 23720 23210
www.oikia-alexandrou.gr
A family home turned into a boutique *pension*. The immaculately decorated interior features cosy, wood-floored rooms with all modern conveniences. The bar-cum-restaurant downstairs serves up wholesome Macedonian dishes and in winter there is a welcoming log fire. **€€**

Dadiá

Ecotourism Hostel
1km (0.5 miles) beyond Dadiá village
Tel: 22540 32263
www.ecoclub.com/dadia
Run by the Visitors' Centre for WWF's Dadiá Wildlife Refuge, each of the simply furnished en suite rooms has been named after birds that frequent the Dadiá Forest. This is the best place to stay if you want to get up

early to see the raptors soaring and feeding in the Refuge, an hour's brisk uphill hike deep into the forest. There are a couple of decent tavernas in the village. **€**

Édessa

Varósi
Arhieréos Meletíou 45–47
Tel: 23810 21865
www.varosi.gr
Tucked away in the backstreets of the town's Ottoman quarter, this faithfully refurbished old home is now an inexpensive, cosy boutique pension. The modern yet traditional-styled rooms are wooden-floored and stone-walled. Enormous optional breakfast in the fireplace-equipped dining/sitting area. **€€**

Kastoriá

Allahou Guesthouse
Panayias Faneroménis 18
Tel: 24670 27058
www.kastoria.allahou.gr
Tucked down a quiet alley, this lovingly converted mansion has five gaily painted rooms and a bright conservatory, where you can enjoy the complementary gourmet breakfast. **€€**

Arhondikó tou Vérgoula
Aidístras 14
Tel: 24670 23415
www.vergoulas.gr
A converted old mansion on the quiet side of town. Ideal for a weekend getaway, the old-fashioned rooms in this mansion simply ooze old-world style. There is a large yet homely breakfast room and wine bar downstairs. **€€**

Kavála

Hotel Nefeli
Erythroú Stavroú 50
Tel: 2510 227441
www.nefeli.com.gr
Renovated thoroughly in 2002, the Nefeli manages to combine the convenience of its central location with sufficient comfort. As a business hotel, it provides all the expected amenities. For travellers, it's as close as you can get to bus and ferry links onwards. **€€**

Imaret
Poulídou 6
Tel: 2510 620151
www.imaret.gr
One of the most outstanding hotels in Greece, occupying an old Ottoman medrese (Islamic school). The rooms and suites are beautifully converted so as not to lose the building's original character. Hammam, massage parlour, pool and fine restaurant all on the premises. **€€€€**

Kerkíni

Oikoperiigitis
Near the village centre
Tel: 23270 41450
www.oikoperiigitis.gr
The best place to stay near the lake. Rustic but comfortable, with a lot of appealing alpine-style wooden fittings, plus a good restaurant and staff who are very knowledgeable about the local birdlife. **€€**

Komotiní

Olympos Hotel
Orféos 37
Tel: 23510 37690
www.hotel-olympos.gr
Most of Komotiní's hotels are business-oriented and impersonal. The Olympos is an exception – friendly and welcoming, but modern and up-to-date after recent renovation. It's very handy for the centre of town and a clutch of good-quality local restaurants. **€€**

Litóhoro

Xenonas Papanikolaou
N E Kítrous 1, 100m from square
Tel: 23520 81236
www.xenonas-papanikolaou.gr
In a central but quiet location, this nicely modernised yet traditional looking house offers very cosy rooms

PRICE CATEGORIES

Price categories are based on the cost of a double room for one night in high season:
€ = under €50
€€ = €50–100
€€€ = €100–150
€€€€ = over €150

with central heating and cable TV. The welcoming owners can advise about climbing Olympos too. €

Pórto Koufó

Porto Koufo
Right on the beach
Tel: 23750 51207
www.portokoufohotel.gr
Bright white and marine blue set of sparkling self-contained units, individually decorated, with big bathtubs and balconies looking across the bay. €€

Préspa

Ágios Germanós Hostel

Centre of Ágios Germanós village
Tel: 23850 51357
www.prespa.com.gr
In two buildings converted from a stone and wood farmhouse, opposite the main church, are these 10 well-equipped and very comfortable rooms, all centrally heated, and two with working open fireplaces. €€

Stavroúpoli

Nemesis
2km south of Stavroúpoli
Tel: 25420 21005
www.hotelnemesis.gr

A rambling complex of castle-like buildings set in lush countryside, with a variety of comfortable rooms and suites, some with working fireplaces. Breakfast included. €€

Xánthi

Orfeas
Mihaíl Karaóli 40
Tel: 25410 20121
Simple but good value hotel that extends a warm welcome to business guests and travellers alike. All rooms have fridges and TVs. Very close to the central square. €€

SARONIC GULF

Aegina

Hotel Brown
Aktí Hatzí 3–4, Égina Town
Tel: 22970 22271
www.hotelbrown.gr
Right on the southern waterfront a 5-minute walk from the ferry quay is this converted sponge factory, now a three-star hotel still owned by the original family whose ancestry was partly English (hence the name). Rooms, redone in 2008, are spacious and tidy and there's a large, leafy garden with bungalow units. €€
To Petrino Spiti
Petrítou 5, Égina Town
Tel: 22970 23837
A distinctive three-floored stone house (pétrino spíti) a 10-minute walk from the harbour. There are nine comfortable studios all done out in different styles – a couple of them in antique style. €

Angístri

Alkyoni
South end of Skála, at clifftop
Tel: 22970 91377
www.alkyoni-agistri.com
Peacefully set hotel with simple but pleasant, flagstone-floored standard doubles on the ground floor and somewhat higher standard family rooms upstairs – just 15 units in total. The terrace restaurant, like the hotel going for over three decades now, is the island's most accomplished eatery, blending traditional Greek dishes with more "oriental" influences. Open all year by arrangement. €

Póros

Saronis
Galatás Trizinías
Tel: 22980 42356
A good solution for avoiding some

overpriced lodging on Póros itself – stay here, looking across the narrow strait to the clock tower hill, just a few paces from the foot-passenger ferry. This hotel is basic but cheerful and well-maintained, with a ground-floor cafeteria. Open all year. €

Pavlou

Póros Town
Tel: 22980 22734
www.pavlouhotel.gr
Good, family-friendly choice right behind one of the island's better beaches, this hotel has big-balconied rooms renovated in 2008, a decent on-site restaurant, pool and tennis court. Open Apr–Oct. €€

Spétses

Armata Boutique Hotel
Inland from Dápia on pedestrian lane
Tel: 22980 72683
www.armatahotel.gr
A converted-mansion hotel, opened in 2004, with 20 very plush rooms, copious breakfast, willing service and (unusually for the island) a pool. Open March–Oct. €€€€
Economou Mansion
Kounoupítsa shore
Tel: 22980 73400
www.spetsesyc.gr/economoumansion.htm
Another restored inn, occupying part of a vintage (1851) property. The ground floor of the main house has six well converted rooms retaining ample period features; an outbuilding hosts two luxury sea-view suites. Breakfast is served by the fair-sized pool. Open all year. €€€€
Poseidonion
West of Dápia, on shore
Tel: 22980 74553
www.poseidonion.com
Landmark Edwardian (1914) building which, after years of neglect,

reopened in 2009 as the island's top hotel. Rooms are divided between traditional ones in the original building and less characterful bungalows out back around the pool. Restaurant serves dinner only in summer, though the "Library Bar Brasserie" works all day. €€€€

Ydra

Bratsera
200 metres in from centre quay
Tel: 22980 53971
www.bratserahotel.com
The island's top choice for comfort and room size (seven grades to choose from here) at this A-class/four-star hotel occupying a former sponge factory. Vast common areas (bar, restaurant, conference room and pool) serve as a de facto museum of the sponge industry, with photos and artefacts. Open April–Oct. €€€€
Miranda
Tel: 22980 52230
www.mirandahotel.gr
Set in a mansion built in 1810, Miranda is another traditional restoration hotel with 14 differently decorated rooms, some traditional, others Art Deco. The classy atmosphere is enhanced by the in-house art gallery. Breakfast is served in the garden. Open April–Oct. €€€
Orloff
Tel: 22980 52564
www.orloff.gr
A very comfortable mansion turned hotel with all creature comforts. All rooms (renovated in 2012–13) are individual, in different shapes and sizes. Some look out over the town, others onto the flower-filled courtyard, where a large buffet breakfast is served. Open Apr–Oct. €€€€

CYCLADES

Amorgós

Aigialis
Órmos Egiális
Tel: 22850 73393
www.amorgos-acgialis.com
Modern, comfortable hotel built in tiers on the north hillside beyond the bay, with stunning views. Most rooms (in two grades) have been refurbished since 2006, there's a large outdoor pool and decent restaurant, plus a stunning indoor spa and pool used year-round by the locals – a telling accolade. Open all year. €€€€

Pagali Hotel
Langáda
Tel: 22850 73310
www.pagalihotel-amorgos.com
Assorted, large, white-decor rooms and studios (fitted with award-winning beds) in one of the more attractive villages on the island, often booked by special-interest groups. A main advantage is an excellent affiliated restaurant next door. Open all year. €€

Panorama Studios and Pension
Hóra
Tel: 22850 74016
http://panorama-studios.amorgos.net
A mix of ordinary doubles and self-catering studios in a commanding position, of a standard one notch up from the normal island decor of Swedish pine furniture and white tiles. €€

Anáfi
Maroulia Rooms
Hóra
Tel: 22860 61307
Just four simple but well-kept units (two self-catering), with abundant hot water, unobstructed sea views, and a friendly managing family. €

Apollon Village
Hillside above Klisídi beach
Tel: 22860 28739
www.apollonvillage.com
Top of the heap in all senses for Anáfi, the tiered maisonettes of this small (12-unit) complex are arrayed with a good eye for privacy. Typically Cycladic-style studios have full kitchens, though the restaurants of Klisídi and Ágios Nikólaos are just a short walk away. Open May–Sept. €€

Andíparos

Kouros Village
West end of waterfront, main village
Tel: 22840 61084
www.kouros-village.gr
Family-friendly complex of studios and apartments (up to two-bedroom), plus pool and on-site restaurant, with

fine views east. High service level from Greek/Swedish proprietors. Open mid-April to mid-Oct. €€

Ándros

Andros Holiday Hotel
Gávrio
Tel: 22820 71384
www.androsholidayhotel.com
Mainstream resort hotel, overlooking a small private beach just outside town. Attractive, great-value rooms with sea-view terraces, swimming pool, tennis courts and competent restaurant. Open Apr–Oct. €€

Mare e Vista Epaminondas
Batsí
Tel: 22820 41177
www.mmyandroshotel.com
The island's best hotel, with a range of rooms, apartments and suites, a large pool, gardens and a garage; 15 minutes' walk from the town, even nearer to the beach. €€€

Niki
Ándros Hóra
Tel: 22820 29155
Opened in 2002, this redone main-street mansion is convenient, elegant and inexpensive. All six rooms have balconies, some facing the main street, some the sea. Open all year. €€

Paradisos
Ándros Hóra
Tel: 22820 22187
www.paradiseandros.gr
Another, much larger but still elegant neoclassical mansion near the centre of town, incorporating a walled tennis court and pool. Airy rooms with superb views from the balconies. €€€€

Folégandros

Anemomylos
Hóra
Tel: 22860 41309
www.anemomilosapartments.com
A fully equipped apartment complex built in traditional Cycladic style around a courtyard and pool. Stunning views from the balconies overhanging the cliff edge. Some have only partial views, and thus are cheaper. Open May–Sept. €€€€

Castro
Hóra
Tel: 22860 41230
www.hotel-castro.com
A 500-year-old traditional house that is actually part of the ancient Kástro walls. Quaint rooms – set for renovation in the near future – have pebble mosaic floors, barrel ceilings

and spectacular views down sheer cliffs to the sea. €€

Polikandia
Hóra, near Poúnda Platía
Tel: 22860 41322, www.polikandia-folegandros.gr
Newish boutique hotel, around a large pool, with four grades of rooms and suites, plush and rather brightly hued. Other facilities include a communal jacuzzi and a roof terrace. €€€€

Íos

Íos Palace
Mylopótas
Tel: 22860 92000
www.iospalacehotel.com
Modern hotel near the beach; though notionally four-star, there's a range of rooms and suites for all budgets, with the top grades having unobstructed sea views. On-site spa with a full range of treatments. Open May–Oct. €€ and €€€€

Kéa

Koufonísi
Gitonia tis Irinis
East edge of Hóra
Tel: 22850 71674
www.koufonisia-diakopes.gr
Very charming, traditionally Cycladic bungalow complex, designed by artist-owner Andonis Mavros, with 15 cave-like self-catering units ranging from singles to family quads. €€€

Porto Kea Suites
Livádi district, Korissía
Tel: 22880 22870
www.portokea-suites.com
Well executed bungalow hotel, a mix of standard doubles and (large) suites, mimicking local architectural elements with its stone cladding, fronting a pool and its own beach. The top standard on the island. €€€€

Mílos

Kapetan Tassos
Pollónia
Tel: 22870 41287
www.kapetantasos.gr
Designer suites in traditional blue-and-white island architecture, with good sea views and nice touches like

PRICE CATEGORIES

Price categories are based on the cost of a double room for one night in high season:
€ = under €50
€€ = €50–100
€€€ = €100–150
€€€€ = over €150

wi-fi (often absent in apartments) and complimentary Korres sundries (the Greek answer to Clarins). 11km (7 miles) from Adamás, so you need transport. €€€€

Panorama

Klíma

Tel: 22870 21623, www.panorama-milos.com

Small seafront hotel, family-run with friendly service. Simple but perfectly adequate rooms with, of course, views. The owner sometimes takes guests fishing. €€

Popi's Windmill

Trypití

Tel: 22870 22286

A luxuriously converted windmill with all the amenities for an elegant self-catered stay, plus beautiful views towards Adamás port. Actually two windmills, each with two bedrooms. €€€

Cavo Tagoo

500m north of Hóra

Tel: 22890 23692

www.cavotagoo.gr

Beautiful furnishings, prize-winning Cycladic architecture, impeccable service and friendly atmosphere, plus good views and infinity seawater pool. About half the 80 units are "superior" rooms, suites or villas, worth the extra expense for the enhanced views alone. Open May–Sept. €€€€

Harmony

North end of Hóra, overlooking old port

Tel: 22890 28980

www.harmonyhotel.gr

Just 22 variable units at this self-described boutique hotel in bungalow format, priced by their view; some have bathtubs, others showers,

the suites jacuzzis. All have small balconies or terrace space, and there are some disabled-compatible rooms. Common facilities include a medium-sized pool, gym and sauna. A bit bland in decor, but a great position and one of the very few lodgings open all year. €€€€

Matogianni

Matogiánni Street

Tel: 22890 22217

www.matogianni.gr

An excellent mid-range choice, with designer-minimalist rooms on three floors redone comfortably in 2007 in bright but not outré colours. All have either balconies or a terrace, facing a tiny rear garden or the front terrace where breakfast can be taken – alternatively, it's served in the rather zany bar. Open all year. €€€–€€€€

Philippi

Kalogéra 23, Hóra

Tel: 22890 22294

E-mail: chriko@otenet.gr

The best budget option – by Mýkonos standards, anyway – in town, with good-sized rooms (mostly twin-bedded) sporting white tiles and dark furniture, many looking onto a lovely garden with gourds, citrus trees and ceramic urns. Open Apr–Oct. €€€

Semeli

Róhari district, Hóra

Tel: 22890 27466

www.semelihotel.gr

Understated designer hotel with mostly earth-tone palette in soft furnishings, exposed stonework and ceiling beams, plus distant sea views for the better rooms. Five of these are near the reception, the rest – standard, superior or suites – surround the exceptionally large

pool. Bathrooms, with butler sinks and rain-showers, are naturally lit via translucent panels. The buffet breakfast offers plenty of choice, and the subterranean spa features surprisingly normal prices. Occasional noise from a sports ground just below. Open Feb–Nov. €€€€

Chateau Zevgoli

Kástro, Boúrgos district

Tel: 22850 26123

www.naxostownhotels.com

Just six standard doubles (half with sea view) and two suites, with marble floors throughout in this converted old mansion. The suites, one with private veranda, are the best. Common areas comprise a shady front patio and lounge-breakfast area. There are also two self-catering apartments nearby. Open all year by arrangement. €€

Glaros

Ágios Geórgios beach, Hóra

Tel: 22850 23101

www.hotelglaros.com.

A 2010 renovation made this boutique hotel a top choice amongst several hereabouts. Overwhelmingly white rooms, most with sea view, score highly for the bathrooms with butler sinks and proper stall showers; size varies, with the biggest suites at the "penthouse" level. €€–€€€

Grotta

Iakóvou Kambanéli 7, Hóra

Tel: 22850 22215

www.hotelgrotta.gr

For many, the best – and best-value – in-town hotel, bar none. Rooms are of boutique standard, done up in light pastel tones, the managing family (especially Nikoletta) is assiduously welcoming, the buffet breakfast rich and copious, the views – towards the Kástro, or towards sunsets beyond the Apollo temple and Páros island – unimprovable. Easy path-walk down to town centre, feasible parking nearby. Open all year. €€

Kavos

Stelída peninsula hillside, Ágios Prokópios

Tel: 22850 23355

www.kavos-naxos.com

Hillside oasis of stone-clad cottages in four grades, from studio suites ideal for honeymooners to multi-bedroom bungalows fit for families. Appointment is comfortable rather than luxurious, but pays ample homage to local architectural features. Assiduous service, and a restaurant that's worth dining at (unlike at many multi-star hotels) adds up to a superlatively good-value package. Open early May to mid-Oct. €€€€

The stunning pool at Cavo Tagoo, Mýkonos.

Páros

Captain Manolis
Behind National Bank square, Parikiá
Tel: 22840 21244
www.paroswelcome.com
Cheerful rooms here in pastel shades, fitted with laminate flooring plus small balconies, were refurbished in 2012. About the best budget option in the town centre, especially for those planning to hit the local nightlife. Breakfast is offered in the large courtyard; all-year operation is another benefit. €€

Golden Beach
Hrysí Aktí beach
Tel: 22840 41366
www.goldenbeach.gr
The hotel's lush lawn-garden, fronting the restaurant and bar, extends down to the south end of Páros' longest sandy beach, with windsurf equipment for hire. The rooms are simple but tastefully done, with marble flooring and some interconnecting units for families. Only some rooms, however, have sea views. It's understandably a popular wedding venue. Open Easter–mid-Oct. €€€

Paros Bay
Delfíni cove, 2km southwest of Parikiá
Tel: 22840 21140
www.parosbay.com
The closest "resort" hotel to the port, this low-rise, French-run bungalow hotel has 63 quality rooms (redone 2008) with LCD televisions and proper shower stalls, a huge salt-water pool, a small spa-and-massage area, an amphitheatre and the ability to organise events including weddings. Open May to mid-Oct. €€€

Petres
Ágios Andréas district, 1km before Náoussa
Tel: 22840 524567
www.petres.gr
Sotiris and Clea, as welcoming hosts as you could hope for, have created an enduringly popular retreat-hotel on this hillside. The 16 rooms plus one suite spread over two wings all have distant sea views – even the ground-floor units; furnishings vary but all share red tile floors and beam-plus-reed ceilings. Common facilities comprise a big pool with adjacent fireplace lounge for spring nights, a tennis court, and a small glassed-in gym with sauna and jacuzzi. Open Easter/May–early Oct. €€€

Sofia
Livádia district, Parikiá
Tel: 22840 22085
www.sofiapension-paros.com
The USP of this friendly family-run pension is a lush garden-orchard setting, with water features and gazebos where breakfast or a drink may be taken. The 12 rooms, distributed over two wings, punch above their weight with hotel features -like make-up mirrors and hair dryers. Breakfast, with fruit, yogurt, omelette and cafetière coffee options, is well worth the extra charge. You must like cats – there are lots about. Open all year. €

Santoríni

Afroessa
Imerovígli
Tel: 22860 25362
www.afroessa.com
Most accommodation in Imerovígli glories in stunning views over the caldera to the islets and the sunset, but this 10-unit boutique hotel offers a little bit extra. The obligatory pool next to the bar is the biggest around, swimmable rather than just for a plunge; there are handmade tiles underfoot in the bathrooms. The upper units were old skaftá (dug-out) houses, and one still preserves its original linós (wine press), now glassed over. Helpful, clued-up management a bonus. Open Easter–early Oct.

Chez Sophie
Kamári, south end of resort, behind beach
Tel: 22860 32912
www.chezsophie.gr
Much better than average hotel complex around a small pool – probably not needed given the excellent beach – with willing service and near-boutique standard of appointments in the rooms. Opened in 2008, so minimal wear and tear on facilities. €€

Fanari Villas
Ía, near west end of village
Tel: 22860 71008
www.fanarivillas.gr
Traditional skaftá cave-houses converted into luxury suite accommodation for up to four people. Pool, breakfast terrace, bar-restaurant, spa and 240 steps down to Ammoudiá Bay. Attentive, friendly service. €€€€

Ikies Traditional Houses
Ía, Perivolás district
Tel: 22860 71311
www.ikies.com
Arguably the best (and most expensive) of several similar complexes in the village, with keen multi-national management and mostly Anglophone clientele. Some of the 11 tiered units – for example the stunning no. 14, for which the rack rate is nearly €1000 – take four people, but really only as two couples rather than a family. Open Easter–late Oct. €€€€

Ilioperato
Imerovígli
Tel: 22860 24142
www.ilioperato.com
Right next door to Afroessa near the north end of the village, the Ilioperato is a very honourable fall-back choice. The 11 tiered units vary from doubles with a small kitchen area to proper two-bedroom apartments, all furnished in mock-antique style. Bathrooms are spacious, with stall showers. Breakfast is "enhanced" continental, served in the shaded bar. Open 1 Apr–31 Oct. €€

Sérifos

Indigo Studios
Livádi
Tel: 22810 52538
www.indigostudios.gr
High-standard self-catering units and standard rooms set inland; kitchens aren't really for whipping up full meals, but bathrooms are fine, with butler sinks and stall showers, and breakfast is offered at an affiliated café. €€

Maïstrali
Livádi
Tel: 22810 51220
www.hotelmaistrali.com
Tall, 1970s-vintage hotel, where typically equipped rooms have either sea or Hóra views from their balconies, but what makes the place is the enthusiasm of the proprietor Babis, who will steer you right on your forays around the island. €€

Vaso Stamataki
Livadáki
Tel: 22810 51346
Rambling complex of rooms by the roadside, but most with distant views of the beach, and garden settings. Big balconies, self-catering facilities. Basic, but friendly and walkable to and from the ferry jetty. €

Sífnos

Petali Village
Apollonía, Áno Petáli district
Tel: 22840 33024
www.sifnoshotelpetali.com
Top of the pile, in all senses, for this island: three-star standards in a

PRICE CATEGORIES
Price categories are based on the cost of a double room for one night in high season:
€ = under €50
€€ = €50–100
€€€ = €100–150
€€€€ = over €150

commanding position overlooking all of eastern Sífnos. Five grades of tasteful, earth-toned accommodation, from standard doubles to an apartment hosting four. Pool terrace and roof garden for breakfast. Open all year; four-day minimum stay in high season. €€€

Artemon
Artemónas
Tel: 22840 31303
www.hotel-artemon.gcom
Not much to look at from the outside – a 1970s concrete block, in fact – but the rooms, redone in 2004, are perfectly adequate with designer touches, and keenly priced for this island. Rear units overlook fields rolling towards the sea. €€

Alexandros
Platýs Gialós
Tel: 22840 71300
Offering the best value in its class at this beach resort, this hotel – arrayed around a huge pool – comprises unusually large, mock-antique-furnished units ranging from standard doubles to independent cottages that accommodate families. €€€€

Síkinos

Lucas
Aloprónia
Tel: 22860 51076
www.sikinoslucas.gr
A complex of studios and larger apartments on the quieter side of the bay, just back from the beach; also with an affiliated restaurant that's your only local eating option in low

season. Open Apr–Oct. €€

Porto Sikinos
Aloprónia
Tel: 22860 51220
www.portosikinos.gr
The best accommodation on the island: a complex of 18 Cycladic-style buildings right on the beach. Good, if unvarying, breakfast and strong wi-fi signal. Open May–Sept. €€€

Sýros

Dolphin Bay Hotel
Galissás
Tel: 22810 42924
www.dolphin-bay.gr
The largest resort-hotel on the island, four-star and family-friendly with units ranging up to two-bedroom apartments; large swimming pool, restaurant and beautiful views over the bay. €€–€€€

Sea Colours
Vapória District, Ermoúpoli
Tel: 22810 83400
www.teamwork.gr
Ten variably sized studios and apartments for up to six, right above some swimming lidos; one of the quietest spots in town. Open all year. €€–€€€

Omiros
Omírou 43, Ermoúpoli
Tel: 22810 24910
www.hotel-omiros.gr
This 150-year-old neoclassical mansion has been restored to a high standard. Rooms furnished in traditional style with views of the lively harbour. €€

Palladion
Stamatíou Proïou 60, Ermoúpoli
Tel: 22810 86400
www.palladion-hotel.com
Very convenient yet quiet hotel, especially if you get a room (some balconied) overlooking the interior courtyard. Rooms were renovated in 2009 with laminate flooring, built-in shelving and modernised baths. Breakfast (included) can be disappointing, though in summer you can choose extra dishes to order. Open all year. €€

Tínos

Porto Raphael
Ágios Ióannis district, Pórto
Tel: 22830 23913
www.portoraphael.com
Superbly designed and meticulously managed beachside complex of studios and apartments housing up to six people; the buildings flank a lawn garden rolling down to the sea. No pool, and if it's windy (often the case) you can't really use the adjacent beach. Good breakfast, and on-site restaurant for other meals; staff are helpful about arranging car hire and/or port transfers, as you are slightly isolated. €€€

Tinion
Hóra
Tel: 22830 22261
www.tinionhotel.gr
Charming old-world hotel in the centre of town, with tiled floors, lace curtains and a large veranda cafe where breakfast is served. €€

CRETE

Agía Roúmeli

Tarra
Tel: 28250 91231
www.agiaroumeli.gr/tarra/index.html
Having hiked the Samarian Gorge, reward yourself with a beachside stay at this hotel rather than pelting off immediately to Hóra Sfakíon. Closed when the gorge is (typically Nov–early Apr). €

Ágios Nikólaos

Du Lac
Ikostiogdóis Oktovríou 17
Tel: 28410 22711
www.dulachotel.gr
Right beside Lake Voulisméni in the heart of the action, the excellent-value Du Lac offers a mix of designer-decor rooms and studios (the latter effectively one-bed apartments), half of which overlook the water. Convenient ground-floor restaurant

The Minos Beach Art Hotel, Crete.

and café. €€

Minos Beach Art Hotel
Aktí Ilía Sotírhou, Ammoúdi
Tel: 28410 22345
www.bluegr.com
De luxe coastal resort: mostly
bungalows plus a few suites amidst
mature gardens, set on a small
peninsula studded with specially
commissioned contemporary
sculpture. A five-star outfit – rack
rates for sea view bungalows run
from €400–600 for a double – with
service standards to match, and a
clutch of on-site restaurants. €€€€

**St Nicolas Bay Resort Hotel and
Villas**
Tel: 28410 25041
www.stnicolasbay.gr
On the Nisí peninsula overlooking
Mirabéllo Bay 1.5km (about a mile)
north of town, the stone-clad St
Nicolas Bay offers discreet luxury
with an admirable degree of privacy
for its suite-sized standard rooms,
superior suites with private infinity
pools, and a cluster of three- or-four-
bedroom villas with a private lido.
Sandy coastline is limited to one
small cove, but there's a full water
sports programme and 34-foot sailing
boat to charter. A spa, kid's club and
several (pricey) à la carte restaurants
complete the profile. Open Apr–Oct.
€€€€

Eloúnda

Elounda Beach
Tel: 28410 63000
www.eloundabeach.gr
One of the most luxurious resorts in
Greece, overlooking Mirabello Bay;
many of the villas have a private pool
and gym, and main-wing rooms are of
generous size. Private beach, spa, the
usual complement of on-site bars/
restaurants, and a high repeat-visit
rate amongst the jet-set clientele.
€€€€

Elounda Mare
Tel: 28410 68200
www.eloundamare.gr
Stablemate of the co-managed Porto
Elounda complex (many facilities
are shared), the Elounda Mare
strikes a warmer, more intimate
note, especially in its bungalows
and bungalow-suites with their
fireplaces, wood floors and private
sea-water pools. Superior suites in
the main wing clock a whopping 42
to 70 square metres. The lounge
and common areas continue outside
as lovely terraced grounds leading
down to stone lidos – there's little
real beach. Open late April–late Oct.
€€€€

Falásarna

Anastasia Stathis
Approach road, 5km down from Plátanos
village
Tel: 28220 41480
www.stathisanastasia.com
Closest (300m distant) quality lodging
to the legendary beach here; big,
simply decorated pension rooms and
self-catering studios. Breakfast on
request in the stone-clad salon. €

Georgioúpoli

Anna's House
300 metres across the river bridge,
towards Vámos
Tel: 28250 61556
www.annashouse.gr
More accurately Anna's houses,
comprising four grades of rooms,
apartments and villas, in landscaped
grounds around a large pool.
Beige-and-brown-accented luxury
apartments measure a spacious 60
square metres, with butler sinks and
properly screened bathtubs. Open 15
March–15 Nov. €€€–€€€€

Haniá

Casa Delfino
Theofánous 7, Tophanás area
Tel: 28210 93098
www.casadelfino.com
Honeymoon-calibre suite-format
hotel, where designer fittings are
juxtaposed with recycled timber.
The premises have been renovated
by a descendent of the Genoese
Delfino family which originally built
this mansion. Differing units all
have handmade Italian furniture
and marble or solid wood flooring.
Newer are three suites in an adjacent
building, a spa and roof-terrace bar;
still the same excellent service. Open
all year. €€€€

Doma
Venizélou 124, Halépa district
Tel: 28210 51772
www.hotel-doma.gr
This converted neoclassical mansion
was once the Austro-Hungarian,
then the British Consulate. Now it's
one of the gems of Crete, neither
stuffy nor luxurious but appealing
to those who want a low-key yet
personal stay recalling the genteel
old days. The owner has a prized hat
collection and has filled the public
areas with antiques. The top-floor
suite is unbeatable, but standard
rooms are elegant enough. The dining
room serves Cretan specialities for
breakfast and pre-booked dinner.
Open Apr–Oct. €€–€€€

Porto del Colombo
Theofánous 7, Tophanás
Tel: 28210 70945
www.portodelcolombo.gr

This Venetian mansion had previously
served – in the following order – as
the Ottoman military command, the
French consulate and Eleftherios
Venizelos' offices before being
restored as a 10-unit boutique hotel,
most recently in 2010. Rooms,
especially the galleried maisonettes,
are large, with carved-wood furniture
and coloured tiles plus proper shower
stalls in the bathrooms. There are
also two-bedroom apartments
adjacent. Open all year. €€–€€€

Theresa
Angélou 8, west side of old port
Tel: 28210 92798
www.pensiontheresa.gr
This characterful, budget pension
occupies another old mansion in
the Tophanás area. En suite, often
galleried rooms are accessed by
the town's most serpentine wooden
staircase; the best are on the first
floor. If you arrive and reception is
unattended, simply book yourself
in. There's a small kitchen, and
roof terrace for great views over the
harbour. Breakfast is available next
door at Café Meltemi, where the
Theresa's owner Giorgos Nikitas often
sits. Advance booking essential in
season. Open all year. €–€€

Ierápetra

Cretan Villa
Lakerdá 16
Tel: 28420 28522
www.cretan-villa.com
An 18th-century mansion restored as
a hotel, the best in the town centre;
rooms, arrayed around a pleasant
courtyard, are simple but with nice
touches like exposed stone pointing.
Friendly owner full of helpful local
advice. Street parking possible
nearby. €

Kakkos Bay
Koutsounári, 9km east of town T
Tel: 28420 61241
www.kakkosbay.com
1980s-vintage but very pleasant little
resort scattered amidst well-tended
gardens, pines and olive trees.
Spacious bungalows (preferable to
standard rooms) resembling Cretan
country chapels from outside, with
blue-and-white trim and travertine
floors inside, fit two to three. A

PRICE CATEGORIES

Price categories are based on the
cost of a double room for one night
in high season:
€ = under €50
€€ = €50–100
€€€ = €100–150
€€€€ = over €150

pool with all-day restaurant seems superfluous, since the complex brackets one of the calmest sandy coves in the region, sheltered from prevailing winds. Open May–Oct. €€

Galaxy Hotel
Dimokratías 75, south of Platía Eleftherías
Tel: 28102 38812
www.galaxy-hotel.com.gr
The city's top-drawer hotel, with 2008-redone rooms and suites (all the expected comforts), grand public spaces and willing service. Interior-facing units are quieter, and you lose nothing as regards the view. Facilities include a large pool, gym, restaurant and two bars (one at poolside). €€€€

Lato Hotel
Epimenídou 15
Tel: 2810 228103
www.lato.gr
Iráklio's first self-styled boutique hotel, with the best, balconied rooms or suites facing the Venetian harbour (singles are very small). Walkable to all attractions yet reasonably quiet at night; summer roof-garden restaurant. Features suites (worth the extra money), a sauna and "mini-gym" plus unbeatable views over the old Venetian harbour. €€€

Marin Dream
Doukós Bofór 12
Tel: 2810 300018
wwwmarinhotel.gr
Another boutique hotel with sweeping port views from the spacious front rooms – again, singles are tiny. A good breakfast is provided at the roof restaurant (not otherwise recommended). €€€

Stella's Traditional Apartments
Tel: 28430 23739
www.stelapts.com
Looking down over the local oasis

The Galaxy Hotel in Iráklio.

to the eastern edge of Crete, these comfortable apartments are set in lush terrace-gardens with hammocks. There's spring water on tap and a sense of complete peace. The same family also keep five studios and a villa nearby, and have admirably helped signpost local paths. €€–€€€

Selini Suites
Rapanianá district
Tel: 28240 83033
www.selinisuites.com
A mix of large studios and one-bed apartments in this beachfront holiday complex pitched at families, with plenty of children's amenities. Despite self-catering facilities, the decent restaurant offers breakfast as well as other meals. €€

Blue House
Tel: 28250 91337
www.bluehouse.loutro.gr
A mix of seafront, en-suite rooms and slightly more expensive upstairs units at this informal pension, as well as a very creditable on-site taverna. €

Porto Loutro
Tel: 28250 91433
www.hotelportoloutro.com
Vehicle-free Loutró is accessible only by boat or on foot, so is wonderfully peaceful at night. This is the best hotel here, though still zen-minimalist. Two white-painted wings shelter standard rooms and studios with beamed ceilings and slate or marble flooring. The big attraction is taking in the sea view and slowing down to local pace from your balcony. Open mid-March–end Oct. €€

Eva Marina Hotel
Tel: 28290 45125
www.evamarina.com

Small 1980s-vintage hotel with pale pine furniture and white-tile decor set in lush gardens just 100 metres back from the sea. €

Big Blue
West edge of town, by Roman cistern
Tel: 28420 51094
www.big-blue.gr
Choose from three grades of lodging at this ecologically run complex with the best views in the resort. Just 10 steps to the beach, with a small terrace garden for breakfast; extremely knowledgeable proprietor. €–€€

Exari Hotel
Tel: 28210 67180
www.exari.gr
Best of three hotels in this hamlet, aimed at walkers wanting an early start down the Gorge of Samariá. The in-house restaurant relies in part on products from the managing family's cheese factory. The name comes from a famous six-man (exári in Greek) local raiding party during one of the 19th-century rebellions against the Ottomans. €

Palékastro (near Váï)
Marina Village
Behind Koureménos beach
Tel: 28430 61284
www.palaikastro.com/marinavillage
The three small wings of this 1980s-built hotel are idyllically set in olive groves and orchards, if a bit hard to find (follow the signs). Rooms are fair-sized and Oughties-renovated, if a bit nondescript; common areas include a pool, tennis court and shady breakfast gazebo. Snack bar, but no full-service restaurant. Open 15 April–31 Oct. €€

Sandy Beach
Tel: 28230 42138
www.sandy-beach.gr
Cosy (12-room) hotel sited, as the name suggests, behind the town's main beach, near the castle; with balconied, spacious sea-view rooms done up in predominantly dark green and ochre tones, and a cheerful ground-floor breakfast salon. €€

Zafiri 2
100m back from Pahiá Ammos (west) beach
Tel: 28230 41811
www.zafiri-studios.com
Studios and apartments on a quiet lane, with spacious, pleasant bedsit areas and long, narrow balconies affording limited sea views, though

bathrooms are dated. The USP is the vast front lawn-garden where guests take their breakfast. €€

Plakiás

Just about every rented room, studio or apartment near the beach or in surrounding hamlets – some 150 of them – are found, complete with photos and contact details, on the community website www.plakias-filoxenia.gr

Réthymno

Fortezza Hotel
Melissinoú 16
Tel: 28310 55551
www.fortezza.gr
This modern yet stylish hotel on the north side of the old quarter, just below the Venetian fortress, is handy for the town centre and waterfront, yet quiet. Comfortable, air-conditioned rooms, renovated in 2011, represent great value; medium-sized pool in the courtyard. Parking a few blocks away. €€
Palazzo Vecchio
Melissinoú corner Iróön Polytekhníou
Tel: 28310 35351
www.palazzovecchio.gr
A 15th-century Venetian building converted into a complex of self-catering studios, apartments and maisonettes with warm-toned soft furnishings. Patio plunge-pool with adjoining bar, but no restaurant. €€€€
Sea Front
Arkadíou 159
Tel: 28310 51981
www.rethymnoatcrete.com
If you have to be on the town beach, this – an old mansion converted into a pension with 10 well-equipped, wood-floored, en suite rooms – is the closest spot, while still convenient for the

centre. The same owners manage the modern Sea View Apartments nearby, comprising four studios and two larger family units (these last don't, however, have the eponymous views). €€
Veneto
Epimenídou 4
Tel: 28310 56634
www.veneto.gr
One of the better inns, occupying a 14th-century Venetian building in the old quarter, with an acclaimed in-house restaurant (half-board rates given). Public areas – including a large, arcaded courtyard with three potable springs, where breakfast is served – somewhat overshadow the rooms; upper-storey ones are airier and balconied. €€€

Sitía

El Greco
Arkadíou 13
Tel: 28430 23133
www.elgreco-sitia.gr
Best-value and friendliest hotel in the town centre, with 2007-redone rooms, good views from the higher ones and a pleasant lobby. Only down side: tricky street parking. €

Soúgia

Syia
Approach road
Tel: 28230 51174
www.syiahotel.gr
The top-standard lodging in this little resort, furnishings-wise, making up for an uninspiring inland position (though some parts of the hotel have distant sea views). Most rooms are quads suitable for families. €€€

Spíli

Heracles
Below through road

Tel: 28320 22111
e-mail heraclespapadakis@hotmail.com
The quietest and best-run of three extant lodgings in this mountain town, Heracles has well-kept balconied rooms with bug-screens; the owner is a mine of information about the area. Breakfast included in rates; bicycles rented. €

Vámos

Vamos
Tel: 28250 22190
www.vamosvillage.gr
Restored, stone-built houses scattered through Vámos old town, just 20 minutes from the sea. Most are maisonettes, with bedroom and bath upstairs, fireplace-lounges downstairs. Accommodation ranges from two-person apartments to houses suitable for up to eight, with private or shared pool. There's an affiliated taverna, self-guiding walks and cooking courses held in an abandoned olive mill. €€–€€€

Vlátos

Milia Mountain Retreat
Tel: 28210 46774
www.milia.gr
This 'eco-lodge' has rescued a 1945-abandoned village in the hills of western Crete, off a secondary road between Kíssamos and Paleóhora. Old stone cottages of different sizes (two–four persons) have fireplaces for cool nights. An excellent affiliated taverna serves up three meals daily, based on local produce. By day, you can hike through nearby gorges or take painting courses; nights are spent gazing at the stars. €€–€€€

RHODES

Andreas
Omírou 28D, Rhodes Old Town
Tel: 22410 34156
www.hotelandreas.com
At the highest point of the Old Town stands this exquisite little pension with comfortable rooms in a variety of formats, from tiny singles and galleried family quads to a spectacular tower suite in what was a Turkish mansion. All units are air-conditioned, but some bathrooms are down the hall. New for 2013 is an enormous front patio-garden, the venue for breakfast or drinks; what remains of the old terrace bar has arguably the best view in the old

town. Two-night minimum stay. Open Mar–Nov. €€
Elafos
Profítis Ilías
Tel: 22460 22402
After languishing neglected for decades, this Italian-built period piece from 1929 reopened in 2006 as a rustic hotel popular with walking groups. The high-ceilinged units (three suites are worth the extra charge) have considerable retro charm, and there are great views of the forest from the balconies. The à la carte ground-floor café makes a good rest stop if touring – try their homemade carrot-nut cake (evening

meals only by arrangement). Open all year. €–€€
Lindian Village
Near Glýstra cove, east coast
Tel: 22440 35900
www.lindianvillage.gr
This ingeniously designed bungalow

PRICE CATEGORIES

Price categories are based on the cost of a double room for one night in high season:
€ = under €50
€€ = €50–100
€€€ = €100–150
€€€€ = over €150

TRANSPORT

ACCOMMODATION

EATING OUT

ACTIVITIES

A–Z

LANGUAGE

complex has its own private beach, a small spa/gym, a central "lazy river" bubbling through, several gourmet restaurants and three grades of units (the suites have their own secluded plunge-pools). Although children are accommodated, it is really more of a romantic adults' resort. Open May–Oct. €€€€

Lindos Mare Hotel
Vlýha, east coast
Tel: 22440 31130
www.lindosmare.gr
Situated on a hillside just 2km (1 mile) northwest of Líndos, this tiered hotel manages to feel low-key and intimate despite comprising 142 designer units (one-third of them suites). A funicular (or shady walkway) brings you down through lush grounds from the larger of two pools to the beach. There are also two full-service restaurants and a fully equipped spa. Immediately adjacent, the ultra-sleek adults-only Lindos Blu €€€€ (tel: 22440 32110, www.lindosblu.gr) is a five-star annexe, a bit forbidding by comparison, with only water features for relief. Unlike its neighbour, its units – in several grades, many with private pools – are often full, thanks in part to exceptional levels of staff service and a repeat clientele. Both open May–Oct. €€€€

Marco Polo Mansion
Agíou Fanouríou 42, Rhodes Old Town
Tel: 22410 25562
www.marcopolomansion.gr

Hardly noticeable off the cobbled thoroughfare, this discreet inn, converted from a rambling old Ottoman mansion, is stunning once inside. All rooms are furnished with antiques from the nearby eponymous gallery, plus natural-fibre, handmade bedding; the garden-side rooms are a bit cheaper (but also less airy). Buffet breakfasts (enhanced continental style, with fruit and muesli) are served in the courtyard with its well, which becomes one of Rhodes' best restaurants after dark. Open Easter–mid-Oct. €€€

Melenos
Líndos, second lane above the north beach, by the school
Tel: 22440 32222
www.melenoslindos.com
Constructed in traditional style, this boutique hotel has taken advantage of the best location in the village. The 12 cedar-wood-trimmed units vary in plan, but all have wooden bed-platforms, big designer baths with glazed tiles, and semi-private sea-view patios with pebble mosaics underfoot. Whether it is worth the price tag of up to €800 a night is a personal decision. There is an equally pricey bar-restaurant sheltering under a fabric marquee with stunning views. €€€€

Rodos Park Suites
Ríga Fereoú 12, New Town
Tel: 22410 24612
www.rodospark.gr

Arguably the best-quality accommodation in the New Town (yet very convenient for the walled city), this boutique hotel offers three grades of rooms or suites with tasteful soft furnishings and sleek modern fittings. Rear units face a quiet hillside and archaeological dig, front ones overlook the fair-sized pool. A highlight is the wood-decked summer roof-bar, with unrivalled views. The basement spa, free gym/sauna/hammam and two competent on-site restaurants (one poolside) complete the picture. Open all year. €€€€

Spirit of the Knights
Alexandrídou 14 by Hamza Bey Mosque, Old Town
Tel: 22410 39765
www.rhodesluxuryhotel.com
'Medieval chic' sums up this six-suite, eco-friendly hotel in a painstakingly restored 15th-century manor house on a quiet cul-de-sac. One of the loveliest gardens in the old quarter comes complete with fountain, breakfast tables and jacuzzi. The upstairs suites, many galleried and one with a hammam, all lead off an oriental-style salon with well-stocked library. Pleasant, arcaded bar-lounge downstairs. Felicity and her extended family are keen to please, meeting guests at the designated taxi-dropoff point at the D'Amboise Gate. Open all year. €€€€

DODECANESE

Astypálea

Australia
Skála
Tel: 22430 61067
Basic but adequate rooms and studios – a rare budget option for this island – in two separate blocks, with phones, fans, air conditioning; good affiliated restaurant. €€

Kilindra Studios
West slope of Hóra
Tel: 22430 61966
www.astipalea.com.gr
Mock-traditional units fitting up to three persons, built in 2000 in the shadow of the castle, offering all luxury amenities including a swimming pool. Open Apr–Dec. €€€

Venetos Studios
Base of west hillside, Livádia
Tel: 22430 61490
www.venetosstudios.gr
Units in several buildings scattered across an orchard; facilities range

from basic studios to four-person cottages. Open May–Sep. €€

Hálki

Most accommodation is block-booked by package companies from April to October; here are two exceptions.

Captain's House
North of the church and inland
Tel: 22460 45201
Four-room, en suite pension in a converted mansion with garden bar and helpful management. €

Art Hotel Halki
Emborió South Quay
Tel: 22460 45244
www.arthotelhalki.gr
After a decidedly chequered career, the municipally run hotel housed in an old sponge factory emerged from a total overhaul in 2008 as boutique lodging with its own lido, gym and conference facilities. The suite is a generous 50 square metres. Reserve

well in advance, as special-interest groups often book it out. €€€

Kálymnos

Akrogiali
Massouri
Tel: 22430 47521 or 6938 913210
Exceptionally tastefully appointed beach side apartments below the road, sleeping two adults and two children. Unsurprisingly, they require booking long in advance. €€

Villa Melina
Evangelístria district, Póthia
Tel: 22430 22682
www.villa-melina.com
The town's top choice: en suite rooms in a 19th-century mansion, plus an annexe of modern studios behind the large pool and gardens. Main house refurbished 2006; very good breakfasts served on the patio; a warm welcome assured from Andonis, Themelina and family. Open all year. €–€€

Kárpathos

Akrogiali Studios
Potáli bay, Paralía Lefkoú
Tel: 22450 71104
Just eight, spacious units, all with views towards the pebble beach; friendly management, minimarket downstairs for restocking. €

Astro
Ólymbos
Tel: 22450 51421
A good, relatively comfortable en suite guesthouse in this traditional village, kept by two sisters, who manage the Café Restaurant Zefiros where breakfast is served. €

Blue Bay
Vróndi Beach Road, Pigádia
Tel: 22450 22479
www.bluebayhotel.gr
One of the few hotels along the beach strip that's not totally monopolised by packages, and an excellent choice if you've rented a car – leave it here and walk into town, or to the water. The rooms are island-standard but very good value; the lobby bar is a work of art; and co-manager Manos Kritsiotis is very clued up. Open Apr–Oct. €€

Glaros
Diafáni
Tel: 22450 51501
www.hotel-glaros.gr
The most comfortable and well-placed lodgings in the area, with 16 studios on the south hillside, some accommodating families. Breakfast available by arrangement; George and Anna are wonderful hosts. €

Vardes Studios
Amopí beach
Tel: 22450 811111/6972 152901
www.hotelvardes.gr
The best standard here among outfits accepting walk-in trade, with huge units overlooking well-tended gardens some way inland. Family environment, good breakfasts available. €

Kastellórizo

Karnayo
Platía at west end of the south quay
Tel: 22460 49225
www.karnayo.gr
The best, architect-designed restora-tion accommodation on the island. Rooms, studios and a four-bed apart-ment occupy two separate buildings, with wood-and-stone interiors. €€

Kastellorizo
West quay
Tel: 22460 49044
www.kastellorizohotel.gr
These air-conditioned, quality-fitted studios or galleried maisonettes, some with sea view, offer the best facilities on the island. Tiny plunge pool, and its own lido in the bay. Open

March–Nov. €€€

Mediterraneo Pension
North end of the west quay
Tel: 22460 49007
www.mediterraneo-kastelorizo.com
Another architect-executed refurbishment, this offers simple but well-appointed rooms with mosquito nets and wall art, half with sea views, plus an arcaded ground-floor suite from which you can literally roll onto the waterside lido, and optional breakfast with owner Marie's homemade marmalade. Unusually, open all year. €€

Kós

Afendoulis
Evrypýlou 1, Kós Town
Tel: 22420 25321
www.afendoulishotel.com
Welcoming, family-run C-class/two-star hotel: cheerful en suite rooms with air con and fridges, most with balconies, plus some cooler basement "caves" much sought after in summer. Proprietors Alexis, Dionysia and Ippokratis are as helpful hosts as you could hope for – including port transfers with prior arrangement – and Dionysia's breakfasts are well worth ordering, up to noon. Open Apr–late Oct. €

Fenareti
Mastihári
Tel: 22420 59002
fenareti.kosweb.com
Hillside hotel in the least packaged of Kós's coastal settlements, overlooking the widest part of the beach; rooms and studios in a peaceful garden environment, with kitchen corners and mosquito nets. €

Kos Imperial Thalasso
Psalídi
Tel: 22420 58000
www.grecotel.gr
One of the premier members of the Grecotel chain, this standard-wing and bungalow hotel with stunning common areas abuts a good beach in landscaped tiers. Individual units are spacious and well-appointed, though not cutting edge in decor. The thalasso-spa is, of course, the heart of the establishment. Unfortunately, when the wind blows in a certain direction, there are whiffs from the nearby sewage plant. €€€

Sonia
Irodótou 9, Kós Town
Tel: 22420 25594
A 2009-renovated small hotel, long a backpackers' haven, overlooking the Hellenistic baths. Rooms large, wood-floored and en suite. Self-catering kitchen and terrace. Open late Mar–early Nov. €

Léros

Alinda (aka Mavrakis)
Álinda beach
Tel: 22470 23266
www.alindahotel-leros.gr
The first hotel established here, the Alinda has well-kept, thoroughly refurbished (originally 1970s) rooms with a mix of sea and mountain views and a respected restaurant with garden seating. €€

Archontiko Angelou
Álynda, signposted well inland
Tel: 22470 22749
www.hotel-angelou-leros.com
Marvellously atmospheric converted Belle Epoque mansion hiding amidst orchards with the feel of a French country hotel. Victorian taps in the baths, beamed ceilings, old tile or wood floors and antique furnishings. €€€

Crithoni's Paradise
Krithóni
Tel: 22470 25120
www.crithonisparadisehotel.gr
Léros' most starred accommodation, a low-rise complex with a smallish pool (whose bar can generate some nocturnal noise), disabled access and large, well-appointed rooms. Buffet breakfast. Open all year. €€€

Rodon
Between Pandéli and Vromólithos in Spiliá district
Tel: 22470 23524/22075
Small but well-kept, mostly balconied rooms better than the official E-class/no-star rating; also ground-floor three-person studios, with less of a sea view. €

Lipsí

Galini Apartments
By the ferry jetty
Tel: 22470 41212
Well-appointed rooms with balconies and fridges, and a very welcoming family. €

Nefeli
Above Kámbos beach
Tel: 22470 41120
www.nefelihotels.com
2005-built bungalow hotel offering ground-floor studios and airier one- and two-bedroom apartments on upper floors. Open May–Oct. €€€

PRICE CATEGORIES

Price categories are based on the cost of a double room for one night in high season:
€ = under €50
€€ = €50–100
€€€ = €100–150
€€€€ = over €150

Nísyros

Porfyris
Mandráki centre
Tel: 22420 31376
www.porfyris-nisyros.com
By default, the best conventional
hotel on the island, with balconied
rooms partly redone in 2008. These
overlook either orchards and the sea,
or the large saltwater pool. €€

Ta Liotridia
On the shore lane near the windmill
Tel: 22420 31580
Email: liotridia@nisyrosnet.gr
Two comfortable four-person suites
in a restored house – one of the few
such projects on Nísyros – arguably
worth the premium price for the sea
views and volcanic-stone-and-wood
decor. Lively bar downstairs, but
apparently noise not a problem.
€€€

Pátmos

Blue Bay
Skála, Konsoláto district
Tel: 22470 31165
www.bluebay.50g.com
The last building on the way out of
town towards Gríkou, and spared the
late-night ferry noise that plagues
most hotels here. Friendly Australian-
Greek management, and on-site
internet café. €€

Effie
Skála, Kastélli hillside
Tel: 22470 32500
Bland, blonde-pine-and-tile rooms
spread over two hotel wings, but with
balconies and air conditioning they're
good value and in a quiet setting.
Open all year. €€

Porto Scoutari Romantic
Hillside above Melói beach
Tel: 22470 33123
www.portoscoutari.com
The island's top digs, renovated in
2007 with a spa added. Enormous
self-catering suites, arrayed around
the pool area, have sea views and
air-con/ heating, as well as mock-
antique furnishings and original wall
art. Elina, who runs the place, is a
font of island knowledge. Wedding
packages a speciality. €€–€€€

Studios Mathios
Sápsila cove

Tel: 22470 32583
www.mathiosapartments.gr
If you've a car or bike, these rural,
superior self-catering units make an
idyllic base thanks to their creative
furnishing, extensive gardens and
a welcoming managing family. The
coarse-pebble cove, however, is not
great for swimming. €€

Sými

Albatros
Gialós marketplace
Tel: 22460 71707
www.albatrossymi.gr
Partial sea views from this
exquisite, small hotel with French
co-management; pleasant second-
floor breakfast salon, and air-con. The
website also gives booking access to
co-managed apartments suitable for
families in various restored houses
around town. €€

Iapetos Village
Gialós, inland from platía
Tel: 22460 72777
www.iapetos-village.gr
The best of several fair-sized
bungalow complexes in Gialós. It
comprises maisonettes fitting up to
six and self-catering studios, arrayed
(rather extravagantly for dry Sými)
around a covered pool and luxuriantly
landscaped grounds. Actual room
decor is simple – exposed roof
beams, pale tiles – but adequate. A
generous breakfast is offered by the
pool bar, or you can prepare your own
in the well-equipped kitchens. Open
Apr–Nov. €€€

Les Catherinettes
North quay, Gialós
Tel: 22460 72698
Email: marina-epe@rho.forthnet.gr
Creaky but spotless en suite pension
above the restaurant of the same
name, in a historic building with
painted ceilings and sea-view
balconies for most rooms. €€

Symi Visitor Accommodation
Head of Gialós Bay
Tel: 22460 71785
www.symivisitor-accommodation.com
Wendy and Adriana offer a wide range
of restored properties, ranging from
simple studios to mansions suitable
for large families. All are serviced

second homes let in their owners'
absence, so they come with fully
equipped kitchens, libraries, music
systems – and unpredictable quirks.
Available April–Nov. €€–€€€

Télendos

On the Rocks
Tel: 22430 48260
www.otr.telendos.com
Four smartly appointed rooms with
double glazing, mosquito nets etc,
above amiable Greek-Australian-run
bar of the same name, plus remote
studios overlooking Hókhlakas
Beach. Open Apr–Nov. €€

Porto Potha
Tel: 22430 47321
www.telendoshotel.gr
At the very edge of things, but this
hotel, a mix of plainly decorated
standard doubles and studios, has
a large pool and a friendly managing
family. Open Apr–Oct. €

Tílos

Blue Sky Apartments
Ferry dock, above Blue Sky taverna
Tel: 22460 44294
www.tilostravel.co.uk
Nine well-appointed, galleried two-to-
three person units with unbeatable
sea views, built in 2002. €€

Eleni Beach
About halfway around the bay
Tel: 22460 44062
www.elenihoteltilos.gr
Willing management for large, airy,
white-decor hotel rooms with bug
screens, proper shower stalls and
wi-fi, requiring advance booking.
Rooms distributed over several wings,
some added since 2007. €€

Irini
200m inland from mid-beach
Tel: 22460 44293
www.tilosholidays.gr
Long the top hotel on Tílos, Irini still
wins points for its beautiful grounds
and common areas, including large
pool. The same management keeps
the hillside Ilidi Rock Aparthotel,
which has outstripped its stable-mate
with a conference hall, gym (but no
spa), private beach and one wing
with disabled access. Ilidi Rock €€€
Irina €€

NORTHEASTERN AEGEAN

Fourni

Archipelagos
Overlooking fishing port
Tel: 22750 51250
www.archipelagos.gr
A 2007-built hotel with high-quality

fittings for its 18 doubles and suites,
a very keen proprietor, and an on-site
restaurant operating during summer.
Open all year. €€

Patra's Rooms
Immediately left of the kaïki quay

Tel: 22750 51268
www.fourni-patrasrooms.gr
Choose between wood-floored,
antique-furnished bedrooms, some
with balconies, just above the
family sweet shop, or 14 superb

apartments, some sleeping up to four, in a tiered hillside complex with views as expected. €

Chios Rooms
Egéou 110, Híos Town
Tel: 22710 20198
www.chios rooms.gr
Upstairs rooms with high ceilings and tile-and-wood floors, some en suite, in lovingly restored 19th-century building managed by a New Zealand/Greek couple. Best is the "penthouse", with a private terrace; others have small balconies, some are en suite. €

Kyma
East end of Evgenías Handrí
Tel: 22710 44500
Email: kyma@ehi.forthnet.gr, kkk@otenet.gr
B-class hotel inside a converted neoclassical mansion (plus less attractive modern extension). Very helpful management, good breakfasts in the original salon with painted ceiling. €€

Markos' Place
South hillside, Karfás beach
Tel: 22710 31990/697 32 39 706
www.marcos-place.gr
Inside a disused monastery, Markos Kostalas has created a uniquely peaceful, leafy environment. Guests are lodged in the former pilgrims' cells; individuals are welcome (several single "cells" available), as are families (two "tower" rooms sleep four). Minimum stay four days. Open Apr–Nov. €

Medieval Castle Suites
Mestá village
Tel: 22710 76345
www.mcsuites.com
No expense has been spared in these high-end apartments located in a central mansion in this protected village. All units have sumptuous baths, mini-kitchens and either a ground-floor patio or roof terrace – the latter a necessity in what can be a claustrophobic environment. Open Easter–Oct. €€

Volissos Travel
Tel: 22740 21413
www.volissostravel.gr
Six apartments spread over several old village houses restored in the late 1990s. Units, all with period features, accommodate two people or a family of four. €–€€

Ikaría
Akti
On a knoll east of the hydrofoil and kaïki quay, Ágios Kírykos
Tel: 22750 22694
www.pensionakti.gr
Not a place for a long stay, but ideal if waiting for an early ferry. Friendly and

spotless; all rooms en-suite, with a big rear terrace for coffee. €

Daidalos
Armenistís
Tel: 22750 71390
www.daidaloshotel.gr
One of the less "packaged"-feeling hotels in this resort, with decent breakfasts on a shady terrace, rooms appointed with quirky artistic touches, and an eyrie-pool above the sea. €€

Erofili Beach
Right at the entrance to Armenistís
Tel: 22750 71058
www.erofili.gr
Considered the best hotel on the island, though the ample common areas are more impressive than the sea-view rooms. A small saltwater pool perches dramatically over Livádi beach. €€

Aphrodite Beach
Eastern end of Vaterá beach
Tel: 22520 61212
www.aphroditehotel.gr
Owned by an extremely friendly Greek-Canadian family, the blue and white painted units are kept spick and span and have little balconies with sea views. Great food in the attached taverna too. €

Clara
Avláki, 2km/1.5 miles south of Pétra
Tel: 22530 41532
www.clarahotel.gr
The large, designer-furnished rooms (in grades up to one- and two-bedroom suites) of this bungalow complex look north to Pétra and Mólyvos. Particularly renowned for its ample buffet breakfasts relying on local products. Tennis courts and pool. €€€

Molyvos
Mólyvos beach lane
Tel: 22530 71496
www.molyvos-hotels.com
Nominally B-class outfit on the pebble shore, behind the tamarisks and a stone-paved terrace where breakfast is served. Large, tile-floored, 1980s rooms; reasonable buffet breakfast. You get the use of (and shuttle to) the pool and sports facilities at sister-hotel Molyvos II at Eftaloú, though there is a "private" beach area here. €€

Pyrgos
Eleftheríou Venizélou 49, Mytilíni
Tel: 22510 25 069
www.pyrgoshotel.gr
The town's premier restoration accommodation, a 1916 mansion with over-the-top kitsch decor in the common areas. Rooms, most with balcony, are perfectly acceptable, and there are three round units in the tower. €€€

Evgatis Hotel
Opposite (N)evgátis beach
Tel: 22540 51700
www.hotel-evgatis.gr
Small, modern hotel expanded in 2008, overlooking the best beach on the island (100 metres across the road) and with a decent attached taverna. You'll need a car though, as the Límnos bus service is almost non-existent. €

Ifestos
Andróni district, Mýrina
Tel: 22540 24960
Attractive small hotel whose rooms have a mix of seaward and hillside views. Balconies, fridges, air conditioning. €€

Porto Myrina Palace
Ávlonas beach, 2km/1.5 miles north of Mýrina
Tel: 22540 24805
Considered the best luxury hotel on the island, with grounds incorporating a small Artemis temple. Many rooms are taken by the UK-based Neilson active holidays company. €€€

Villa Afroditi
Platý beach
Tel: 22540 23141
www.afroditi-villa.gr
Run by returned South African Greeks, this comfortable small hotel has a poolside bar and sumptuous buffet breakfasts. €€

Athena
West beach road, Kokkári
Tel: 22730 92030
Email: h-athena@otenet.gr
The best accommodation available on a walk-in basis at this north-coast resort, with contemporarily appointed rooms distributed over three buildings in carefully tended grounds (including a large pool) right across from the beach. Very clued-up Greek-Canadian proprietor. Open Apr–Oct. €€

Daphne
Platanákia, 1km inland from Ágios Konstandínos
Tel: 22730 83200
www.daphne-hotel.gr
Modern, airy hotel with flagstones underfoot throughout, bathrooms with tubs and marble trim, knockout views

PRICE CATEGORIES
Price categories are based on the cost of a double room for one night in high season:
€ = under €50
€€ = €50–100
€€€ = €100–150
€€€€ = over €150

(especially from the pool terrace) and fridges in the white-tiled, pastel-tinted rooms. Some package-company allocation, but usually walk-in vacancies. The affiliated restaurant on the shore is Fawlty Towers resurrected – you have been warned. Open early May to late Oct. €€

Doryssa Seaside Resort
Potokáki, near airport
Tel: 22730 88300
www.doryssa.gr
One of the few actual beach front resorts on Sámos, with a saltwater pool just in from the best local patch of sand if the sea's too cold. Choose between the designer-refitted hotel wing or the meticulously constructed fake bungalow "village", no two of these alike and incorporating all the vernacular styles of Greece. €€€€

Kerveli Village
Approach to Kérveli beach
Tel: 22730 23631
www.kerveli.pro.samos.com
This well-executed, smallish bungalow hotel set among olive trees and cypresses has superb views

across to Turkey and over Kérveli Bay. Dynamic new young management in place since 2010. A good selection of beaches (including its own private one) and tavernas are within walking distance, or take advantage of in-house car rental. €€

Aiolos
Kamariótissa
Tel: 25510 41595
www.hotelaiolos.gr
Samothráki's port and capital is home to a few hotels including this decent mid-range choice. Rooms are simple but clean and welcoming. Some have views overlooking the hills, others towards the sea. Continental breakfast is included. €

Mariva Bungalows
Loutrá Thermá
Tel: 25510 98230
www.mariva.gr
Situated in the island's resort centre, these lovely flower-shrouded bungalows are built on a gentle hillside. All units are self-contained,

comfortable, with colourful or mock-antique furniture, and reasonably spacious. Ideal for a longer stay. €€

Alkyon
Liménas
Tel: 25930 22148
Spacious rooms, with harbour or garden view, plus gregarious Anglo-Greek management and afternoon tea, make this a firm favourite with English-speaking travellers. €

Kipos Studios
Liménas
Tel: 25930 22469
With a nice flowery garden surrounding its small pool, this place has ground floor doubles and larger apartments on the upper floor. €

Thassos Inn
Panagía village
Tel: 25930 61612
www.thassosinn.gr
Quiet except for the sound of water in runnels all around, this modern building in traditional style has most rooms facing the sea from on high. €

SPORADES AND ÉVVIA

Konstantina's Studios
Hóra (Old Alónisos)
Tel: 24240 66165
www.konstantinastudios.gr
High up in the old renovated village, this small, traditional building houses eight tastefully decorated studios and one apartment. All have exceptional sea views and wooden balconies with canvas deck-loungers. €€

Liadromia
Patitíri
Tel: 24240 65160
www.liadromia.gr
One of the first hotels to open in Alónisos, this has an old-world charm with a dash of modernity. Rooms and studios have stucco walls, terracotta-tile floors and a slightly "hot" colour scheme. Overlooking the harbour at the north side of Patitíri Bay, handy for island facilities. Open all year. €€

Milia Bay
Miliá
Tel: 24240 66032
www.milia-bay.gr
Tucked away overlooking tiny Miliá Bay, this quiet retreat consists of 12 ecologically constructed self-catering apartments, from studios to family-friendly two-bedrooms, all very spacious and tastefully decorated. If you don't fancy the short walk to the part-sand beach, there's a pool, as

well as the in-house restaurant. Open April–Oct. €€€

Karystion
Kriezótou 2, Kárystos
Tel: 22240 22391
www.karystion.gr
A busy foreigner-friendly hotel in the far south of Évvia, close to the fortress on the south side of town. Neat, air-conditioned rooms, partly redone in 2005. The town's best bathing spots are a few minutes' walk way. €€

Mousiko Pandohio
Stení, west entrance to village
Tel: 22280 51202
www.mousikopandoxeio.gr
This is the brainchild of a Greek composer-musician Tassos Ioannides, long resident in Australia. The name means "Musical Lodge", and musical decorative motifs – plus regular weekend acoustic concerts in the lounge – predominate. The rooms vary from standard doubles, some with fireplaces, to quads and suites suitable for families. The attention to detail throughout – with the entire family having participated in the design – is admirable. A one-of-a-kind hotel for the island. €€€

Thermai Sylla Spa Wellness Hotel
Loutrá Edipsoú

Tel: 22260 60100
www.thermaesylla.gr
Perhaps Greece's only official anti-stress hotel, this magnificent Belle Epoque edifice at the northern end of the promenade is an old-world experience brought up-to-date with beauty and therapy treatments based on the waters of the ancient spa. Non-guests can use spa on a day basis. €€€€

Aegean Suites
Megáli Ámmos, 1.5km (1 mile) west of town
Tel: 24270 24069
www.aegeansuites.com
A suite hotel redone in 2007, the adults-only sister to its Santikos Hotels chain-mate the Skiathos Princess. Not a beach front position, but high enough to avoid road noise. There are only 21 units – which adds to the exclusive feeling – all of them big (55–60 sq

---

PRICE CATEGORIES

Price categories are based on the cost of a double room for one night in high season:
€ = under €50
€€ = €50–100
€€€ = €100–150
€€€€ = over €150

The stunning entrance to the Aegean Suites on Skiáthos.

metres), with bug screens, wi-fi and sound systems, "de luxe" ones only differing in having an unobstructed sea view. Large pool, small but pleasant gym, parking and a "live cooking" poolside restaurant. €€€

Atrium
Plataniás
Tel: 24270 49345
www.atriumhotel.gr
The Atrium Hotel is chic, beautiful and enjoys a splendid view south over the sea. Rooms, suites and maisonettes feature wood flooring, white soft furnishings and private balconies or patios. There's a pool – a necessity given the distance to the beach – and a poolside restaurant. €€€€

Mandraki Village
Koukounariés, Bus Stop 23
Tel: 24270 49670

www.mandraki-skiathos.gr
A 2007-built complex with tasteful, pastel-hued family quads and junior suites with bigger bathrooms (worth the small price difference), a small pool, lushly landscaped grounds and a competent (if garishly coloured) on-site restaurant. €€€€

Skópelos

Adrina Beach
Pánormos
Tel: 24240 23373
www.adrina.gr
This expansive hotel complex (42 standard rooms and 10 bungalows) occupies a large tract of hillside just to the north of Pánormos Bay, looking out onto a virtually private beach (there is also a large seawater pool). Since 2011, a higher-standard sister

property is nearby, the Adrina Resort and Spa, open only late June to early September. €€€€

Kyr Sotos
Hóra, just in from mid-quay
Tel: 24240 22549
www.skopelos.net/sotos/
Rambling, old-house pension with wood-floored, en suite rooms that's justifiably a favourite budget option. Rear units (all en suite with air-con) facing the courtyard are quieter; best is No. 4, with a fireplace. Open all year. €

Skópelos Village
Hóra, far east side bay
Tel: 24240 22517
www.skopelosvillage.gr
The top digs in the town, redone in 2007 – when some of the Mamma Mia! film parties took place here. Units range from studios up to large family apartments; all with touches like Victorian taps. Two outdoor pools, superior restaurant terrace, lovely breakfast salon. €€€

Skýros

Linaria Bay
Linariá, south hillside
Tel: 22220 93274
Very friendly, well-kept rooms, with individual balconies and a common terrace ideal for catching the sunset. A good choice for out-of-season visits when there's little advantage to staying near the beaches. Open all year. €€

Nefeli – Skyriana Spitia
Hóra
Tel: 22220 91964
www.skyros-nefeli.gr
Combining standard hotel rooms and a stand-alone group of Skyrian houses (in practice two–three person studios), this is a tidy complex around a salt-water pool at the entrance to Hóra. The studios are very cosy with their fireplaces. Good low-season deals. €€€

Perigiali
Magaziá
Tel: 22220 92075
www.perigiali.com
Very welcoming, secluded mix of studios and well furnished rooms with phone, overlooking a pool and a large garden where breakfast is offered. Open all year; heated. €€

CORFU

Kérkyra Town and around

Bella Venezia
Napoleóntos Zambéli 4, Pórta Remoúnda district
Tel: 26610 46500/20708
www.bellaveneziahotel.com

Kérkyra Town's worst-kept secret, and enduringly popular, this 2008-renovated hotel occupies a converted neoclassical former girls' school. The best rooms, with high ceilings and sometimes balconies, are

on the first two storeys, though the third-floor suites can accommodate families of four. An adequate breakfast is offered in the back-garden conservatory. Stylish lobby bar and helpful staff complete the profile. €€€

TRANSPORT

ACCOMMODATION

EATING OUT

ACTIVITIES

A – Z

LANGUAGE

Corfu Palace
Dimokratías 2, north end of Garítsa Bay
Tel: 26610 39485
www.corfupalace.com
The dowager empress of town hotels, a favourite with conference and business folk as well as holiday-makers, this five-star outfit scores for an unbeatable position just 10 minutes' walk from the Listón, and willing staff, as much for its accommodation. Standard rooms are large, with recent soft furnishings and veneer floors, while superior units have double sinks in the bathrooms; all have sea views over Garítsa Bay. Breakfast is taken indoors or out on the lawn-garden by the salt-water pool. There's also an indoor pool by the small spa, and the island's only casino. Open all year. €€€€

Grecotel Corfu Imperial
Komméno
Tel: 26610 88400
www.grecotel.gr
Set at the tip of a private peninsula with man-made sandy-cove beaches on the sheltered inland side, this luxurious self-contained resort is considered one of the two or three top lodgings on the island – and thus often booked out. There's a huge seawater swimming pool, shoreline water sports, a choice of restaurants and bars, a tennis club, spa and gym. Rooms are luxuriously furnished and are either in the main block or in bungalows dotted around the pretty grounds with Italianate gardens and olive trees. Open April–Oct. €€€€

Konstantinoupolis
Zavitsiánou 11, Old Port
Tel: 26610 48716
www.konstantinoupolis.com.gr
Renovated building dating from 1862, but still pleasantly old-fashioned, this two-star hotel has both sea and mountain views from the front balconied rooms, which are large – though bathrooms are small and basic, if brightly tiled. Rooms are reached either by a spiral wooden staircase or antique lift, past the more modern mezzanine breakfast area and lounge. €€

Kontokali Bay
Tel: 26610 90000
www.kontokalibay.com
This low-rise bungalow-style resort has most units scattered in clusters through beautiful gardens next to a private sandy beach. Superior standard rooms (redone 2007–08) are like junior suites with their sofas and big balconies, while the garden-view family bungalows were renovated in 2010. Bathrooms have butler sinks and proper shower screens. Facilities

are commensurate with a five-star rating, and include an elevated infinity pool, beachside restaurant, state-of-the-art freestanding spa, tennis courts, water sports at the private port and an imaginative children's club. Open late April–Oct. €€€€

Centre-west of Corfu

Casa Lucia
Sgómbou hamlet, at Km 12 of Kérkyra–Paleokastrítsa road
Tel: 26610 91419
www.casa-lucia-corfu.com
A restored olive-mill complex set among lovingly tended gardens with a large pool. Just eight self-catering units ranging from studios to family cottages; all share simple (read, 1980s vintage) if adequate furnishings, and are often occupied by patrons attending the yoga, t'ai chi or massage workshops held here. Peaceful setting at the very centre of the island makes this an excellent touring base. No on-site restaurant per se, but the affiliated Bio-Bistro Lucciola (often with entertainment) is just a few steps away on the main road. Open year round, but Nov–March on weekly or monthly basis. €€–€€€ depending on cottage.

Fundana Villas
Turn onto side road, Km 17 of Kérkyra–Paleokastrítsa highway
Tel: 26630 22532
www.fundanavillas.com
Another 1980s restored inn, this time converted from an 18th-century manor, with a commanding ridgetop position in the middle of a gorgeous landscape. Units, from double studios to family-sized bungalows or suites, are all different, some with brick-and-flagstone floors or timber beams, and refreshed in the mid-Oughties. Large pool, bar and grill, olive-press museum on site. Active types can follow part of the Corfu Trail, which passes right by. Open Easter–Oct. €€

Levant Hotel
Above Pélekas (fork right at the church) beside "Kaiser's Throne"
Tel: 26610 94230
www.levanthotel.com
Hotel in mock-traditional style, with superb panoramic views both east and west over the island. Rooms are wood-floored, baths marble-trimmed. There's a medium-sized pool and spa tub on a grassy terrace, but with some of the island's best beaches a few kilometres away, you may not use them. Ground-floor faux-rustic common areas comprise wood/marble-floored bar and restaurant, with the breakfast area outside taking advantage of the view. A popular wedding venue. Open Apr–Oct. €€

The north of the island

Delfino Blu
Ágios Stéfanos Gýrou
Tel: 26630 51629
www.delfinoblu.gr
This small boutique hotel has a gorgeous setting overlooking one of the best sandy beaches in the area, and is often full, even in spring or autumn. The self-catering apartments and suites, done up in pastel hues, all have sea views, balconies and mod cons. Gourmet restaurant downstairs and excellent pool and beach bars. On-site motor-yacht rental, plus small gym and sauna. Open May–October. €€€–€€€€

Villa de Loulia
Perouládes, 500m from beach
Tel: 26630 95394
www.villadeloulia.gr
One of Corfu's few rural restored inns, this mansion dating from 1803 has been refurbished to provide nine varying rooms, with high-standard furnishings and fittings in excellent taste. The bar, lounge and gourmet restaurant occupy a separate purpose-built structure flanking the large pool. Heating but only fans, no air conditioning. You're paying for the exclusivity – better value out of peak season. Open May–Oct. €€€€

The south of the island

Boukari Beach
Boúkari, 4km/2.5 miles beyond Messongí
Tel: 26620 51791
www.boukaribeach.com
Some 700m from the excellent, eponymous waterside restaurant (see page 389) are two peaceful, secluded units (inside Villa Lucia) sleeping up to four in each, as well as studios and double rooms in the larger Hotel Penelope, with all amenities including coffee machines. Villa Alexandra, next to the restaurant, is similar to Villa Lucia inside but with a hillside position has even more fantastic views. Open April–Oct. €€€

Kerkyra
Benítses, in new village, 400m south of square, 50m inland
Tel: 26610 71111
www.kerkyrarooms.com
Andy and Sarah-Jane Monro, formerly of the now-closed Avra Hotel, have moved next door to take over this place, with their past high level of service and decorative fillips to 1980s Greek architecture. Likely to remain a firm favourite for those traversing the Corfu Trail, with the added bonus of Sarah-Jane's new bakery across the way. Open April–Oct. €

THE IONIANS

Itháki

Captain's Apartments
Kióni
Tel: 26740 31481
www.captains-apartments.gr
Set up on the hill towards Rahí, with commanding views of Kióni's bay, each spacious air-conditioned studio has cooking facilities, cable TV and a veranda. There is also a communal garden to relax in. €

Captain Yiannis
On east quay, Vathý
Tel: 26740 33311
www.captainyiannis.com
The closest thing to an exclusive "resort" on the island, with just 11 self-catering units set in ample walled grounds with a pool and tennis court. €€

Nostos
About 200 metres inland from the quay, Fríkes
Tel: 26740 31644
www.hotelnostos-ithaki.gr
Smallish but upmarket three-star hotel where all rooms look over a field towards the sunrise. €€

Perantzatha 1811 Art Hotel
Odysséa Androútsou, Vathý
Tel: 26740 33496
www.perantzadahotel.com
Chic and fairly pricey, but by far the loveliest hotel in Vathý. The 12 understated and tasteful rooms have been individually designed and are very comfortable. Not on the harbour front itself (and so quieter than some other places), the rooms look out over Vathý's pretty rooftops to the sea. The breakfasts are excellent. €€€
For rooms or villas across the island, contact one of these two

The chic Perantzatha 1811 Art Hotel.

travel agencies:
Delas
Tel: 26740 32104
www.ithaca.com.gr
Polyctor
Tel: 26740 33120
www.lthakiholidays.com

Kefaloniá

Emelisse Art Hotel
Émblisi, near Fiskárdo
Tel: 26740 41200
www.arthotel.gr
Chic "boutique" hotel (one of the small local Tsimaras Hotels chain) set in a traditional building. The well designed rooms have luxurious bathrooms and, inevitably, the hotel's infinity pool has a lovely view. For this sort of money, you should expect to be pampered and the service lives up to expectations. €€€€

Hotel Ionian Plaza
Platía Vallianoú, Argostóli
Tel: 26710 25581
www.ionianplaza.gr
Excellent value three-star designer hotel, with modern bathrooms and balconies overlooking the palm-studded square; the rooms are on the small side, but the staff are friendly. Open all year. €€

Kanakis Apartments
Ássos
Tel: 26740 51631
www.kanakisapartments.gr
Among the limited accommodation options in picturesque Ássos, these comfortable purpose built studios and maisonettes stand out for their amenities, including a pool. €€

Kastro Hotel
Sámi
Tel: 26740 22656/22282
A little way out of the centre, but close to the sea is this medium-sized, good value one-star hotel. The good, if smallish, rooms either look out over the pool and sea or to the mountains. Breakfast is provided and there is also a restaurant. €

La Cité
Lixoúri
Tel: 26710 92701
www.lacitehotellixouri.gr
This compact hotel four blocks up from the seafront has been completely renovated with air conditioning and stylish furnishings to add a touch of the French ambience its name suggests. Competitively priced and by far the best option in town. €€

Moustakis Hotel
Agía Evfimía
Tel: 26740 61060/61030
www.moustakishotel.com
Smallish and tucked away behind the harbour front, this is one of the most pleasant hotels in town. All the rooms have air-con and balconies. Breakfast is available for an extra charge. Discounts are available for long stays. €

Odysseus Palace
Póros
Tel: 26740 72036
www.odysseuspalace.eu
This modern hotel is a comfortable place to stay in town. Good discounts may be available for the large and airy rooms (studios and apartments). Being away from the seafront, the hotel is quieter than most. Open all year. €€

Regina's
Fiskardo
Tel: 26740 41125
Most of the smallish but well-maintained rooms in this lovely family guesthouse at the back of the village have balconies that look towards the harbour or across the pleasant courtyard. Better value and less cliquey than many Fiskardo establishments. €

Tara Beach
Skála
Tel: 26710 83341/83250
www.tarabeach.gr
A large but unobtrusive hotel right on the excellent beach. The rooms are decent and, if you can't be bothered to waddle the few metres to the sea, there is a good pool in the pleasant gardens, beside which is a handy bar. €€

Trapezaki Bay Hotel
Trapezaki
Tel: 26710 31501-2
www.trapezakibayhotel.com
Perched on the hillside just over five minutes' walk from delightful Trapezaki beach, this large modern hotel offers all amenities in its rooms, each of which has a private parking slot. There is also a large pool, restaurant and bar complex. Better value in high summer because prices are fixed for the whole season. €€€

PRICE CATEGORIES

Price categories are based on the cost of a double room for one night in high season:
€ = under €50
€€ = €50–100
€€€ = €100–150
€€€€ = over €150

Kýthira

Kýthira has a short season, with most accommodation only open May–Oct; advance booking is recommended.

Castello Apts
Hóra
Tel: 27360 31869
www.castelloapts-kythera.gr
Lovely tiered group of bright blue and white self-catering studios, with a relaxing garden and great views down to the sea. €

Porto Delfino
Kapsáli
Tel: 27360 31940
www.portodelfino.gr
A pleasant bungalow complex with spacious terraces affording views over the bay and Hóra. €€

Venardos
Agía Pelagía
Tel: 27360 34100
www.venardos-hotels.gr
Large hotel complex with stylishly furnished rooms boasting warm coloured fittings. Facilities include a pool, gym, sauna and spa. €€

Levkáda

Grand Nefeli
Póndi Beach
Tel: 26450 31378
www.grandnefeli.com
This smart beach front hotel makes a good alternative to staying in nearby, congested Vasilikí; its popular outdoor bar and windsurfing facilities on site are pluses. €€

Ionion Star
Panágou 2, Levkáda Town
Tel: 26450 24672
www.ionion-star.com
Levkáda Town's top hotel is more functional than intimate but most rooms have a sea view, plus there's a pool and a games room. €€€

Olive Tree/Liodendro
North approach road, Ágios Nikítas
Tel: 26450 97453
www.olivetreelefkada.gr
Halfway up the hill, with oblique sea views from most rooms. Rooms are typical pine-and-white-tile decor. Friendly Greek-Canadian proprietors. €€

Ostria
North approach road, Ágios Nikítas
Tel: 26450 97483
Email: agnikitasostria@e-lefkas.gr
The 1970s-built rooms of this pension can be cell-like, but are enlivened by terracotta floor tiles, dried flowers and wall art. It's the balcony views of the Ionian (save for four rooms) and the cool, trendy common areas (including a terrace bar open to all) that make the place a delight. €€

Panorama
Atháni
Tel: 26450 33291
One of the island's true getaways. The rooms are simple but clean, above an excellent restaurant. There are superb views and you are as close as you can stay to the stunning beaches of Gialós, Egremní and Pórto Katsíki – although you still need your own transport to reach them. €

Rouda Bay
Mikrós Gialós (Póros)
Tel: 26450 95634
www.roudabay.gr
Spacious apartments, arranged around a well-tended garden, back on to a fine restaurant where the buffet breakfasts are served, just a few metres from the smooth pebble beach. €€

Serenity
500m above Atháni
Tel: 69818 53064
www.serenity-th.com
Unusual for Greece, this Israeli-run retreat offers artistically designed rooms, a chill-out room, a stunning infinity pool, plus yoga and beauty therapies. €€€

Paxí

Paxos Beach Hotel
Gáïos
Tel: 26620 31211
www.paxosbeachhotel.gr
Hillside bungalow complex leading down through trees to its own small pebble beach about 2km (1 mile) east of town. Sports facilities and pool on site. €€€

Planos Tours
Lákka
Tel: 26620 31744
www.planos.co.uk
One of two agencies in this little port, efficiently handling everything from basic rooms to luxury villas island-wide.

Zákynthos

Hotel Palatino
Kolokotróni 10 and Kolivá, Zákynthos Town
Tel: 26950 27780
www.palatinohotel.gr
One of Zákynthos Town's best-value options, stylish and well run. The rooms, designed for business travellers, are decent, with all the trimmings, and the hotel as a whole has been well cared for. A buffet breakfast is provided and there is also a restaurant. €€

Ionian Star Hotel
Alykés
Tel: 26950 83416/83658
www.ionian-star.gr
A smallish and very well kept hotel. The spotless rooms are excellent value (breakfast is included) and there is a restaurant which concentrates on Greek food. €

Levantino Studio Apartments
Kamínia beach, Vasilikós
Tel: 26950 35366
www.levantino.gr
Ten quiet and attractive apartments close to the sea at the Argási end of the Vasilikós Peninsula. All are equipped with a kitchen and some look out over the gardens and sea. Discounts available out of high season. €€

Nobelos Apartments
Ágios Nikólaos
Tel: 26950 27632/31400
www.nobelos.gr
These luxury apartments in the north of the island are expensive but lovely. The four tastefully decorated suites are in a traditional stone-built house, each with an individual character. Along with excellent service, breakfast is provided and a secluded bay is close by. €€€€

Pansion Limni
Límni Kerioú
Tel: 26950 48716
www.pansionlimni.com
Friendly place at the quieter end of Laganás Bay, where guests are presented with home-made wine and olive oil. All rooms have fridges and cooking rings. There are two smart new blocks, one with huge family apartments, further behind the beach from the original pension. €

Sirocco Hotel
Kalamáki
Tel: 26950 26083–6
www.siroccohotel.gr
This is a good and reasonable quiet option for Kalamáki, the renovated and stylish standard rooms a bargain out of season. There is a large pool set in a garden, though the beach is not too far away. €€

Windmills
Korithí, Cape Skinári
Tel: 26950 31132
www.potamitisbros.gr
Two converted windmills and four spacious rooms in a stone house at the north end of the island, close to the Blue Caves. If you want to get away from it all, this is a good option. €€

Zante Palace
Tsiliví
Tel: 26950 490490
www.zantepalace.com
This huge hotel is on the bluff overlooking Tsiliví bay, giving great views across to Kefalloniá. The rooms (which look out over the bay) are good value and if you can't be bothered to walk down to the beach, there is a nicely sited pool. €€

PRICE CATEGORIES

Price categories are based on the cost of a double room for one night in high season:
€ = under €50
€€ = €50–100
€€€ = €100–150
€€€€ = over €150

EATING OUT

RECOMMENDED RESTAURANTS, CAFES, AND BARS

What to Eat

There is considerable regional variety in Greek cuisine and you should keep an eye out for specialities of the house you haven't seen before. Another thing you'll quickly learn is how strikingly different the same dish can be when it is prepared well or badly. It is therefore worthwhile shopping around for your taverna (especially in heavily visited areas), asking the locals what they suggest. For experienced travellers, the term "tourist mousakás" is shorthand for an exploitative version of this standard dish, slathered with potatoes and poorly executed béchamel sauce, with nary a slice of aubergine or a crumb of mince.

Some tavernas, especially in rural areas or on non-touristy islands, may not have menus, in which case it is essential to establish the price of at least the most expensive main courses, particularly seafood.

Vegetarians are not well catered for in Greece: most main courses include

Most meals start with a Greek salad.

fish or meat. Your best bet is to choose a selection of mezédes, many of which are vegetarian.

Many Greek specialities are cooked in the morning and left to stand, so food can be lukewarm (occasionally stone cold), but the Greeks believe this is better for the digestion and steeping of the flavours. For some vegetarian dishes, they are right; for dishes containing meat, this is a rather dubious practice.

Eating out in Greece is above all a social affair, although the ritual of families and friends patronising tavernas twice a week is not observed now thanks to hard economic times. Greeks have had to learn to be careful with money – it is still considered an honour to snaffle the bill but this tends to be a less extravagant gesture these days.

Where to Eat

The more casual eating establishments have essentially the same style and setup across Greece, and menus are similar in design and sequence (indeed, often pre-printed by drinks companies in return for featuring their logo).

However, the classical taverna is by no means the only kind of establishment. You will also encounter the estiatório, the traditional urban restaurant, which ranges from an (ino)magirío, tradesman's lunch-hour hangout, with ready-cooked (magirevtá) food and bulk wine, up to pricey linen-tablecloth places with bow-tied staff.

The psistariá is a barbecue-style restaurant specialising in lamb, pork or chicken on a spit; the psarotavérna specialises in fish and shellfish; while the gyrádiko (gýros stall) and

souvlatzídiko purvey gýros and souvláki respectively, sometimes to a sit-down trade, garnished with salads. Although the best souvlákia are made from lamb, most are of pork nowadays.

Popular among the urban intelligentsia are koultouriárika restaurants, which serve nouvelle Greek cuisine based on updated traditional recipes, and ouzerí or mezedopolío (alternatively called tsipourádika), where the local tipple serves as accompaniment to mezédes or small plates of speciality dishes.

When to Eat

For Greeks, the midday meal is eaten between 2pm and 3.30pm and, even in the cities, is usually followed by a siesta break lasting until 5.30pm.

The evening meal can either be another full meal, or an assortment of mezédes. This is usually taken between 9pm and 11pm.

Breakfast in Greece is traditionally small, usually bread and coffee. There are, however, wonderful píttes (pies and turnovers) available from bakeries, for snacking on the hoof.

Eating Out With Kids

Children regularly dine out with their parents until late at night, and (within their abilities) are expected to converse with the adults. There's no formality about this – kids are as likely to be racing round the taverna playing tag or under the table teasing the stray cats as sitting up at the table. The Greeks are extremely indulgent of their children, so don't be embarrassed to make any special food request for your own.

ATHENS AND ATTIKÍ

Askimopapo
Iónon 61, Petrálona
tel 210 346 3282
Founded in 1968 by leftist actor
Andonis Voulgaris, the bohemian
'Ugly Duckling' is now run alternate
days by his daughters. The inside is
festooned with old theatre photos
and pen-and-ink or charcoal sketches
donated by admirers (many foreign).
The food – a mix of meat-based
magirevtá (ready-cooked meals)
and vegetarian starters – is plainly
presented but well-priced and
wholesome; Límnos white wine or
Neméa bulk red to drink. Open Tue–
Sun dinner, also weekend lunches,
Oct 1 to mid-June. €€

Avli
Methónis 43, Exárhia
Tel: 210 383 8167
There is indeed a small avlí
(courtyard) here, but most seating
is inside this engaging old-house
taverna doing all the standard oven
dishes and appetizers (plus some
creative recipes like chicken-and-
spinach soufflé) with a deft touch.
Open Mon–Sat lunch and dinner,
closed Sun and Aug. €

Diporto
Sokrátous 9, corner Theátrou, central
market district
Tel: 210 321 1463
Diporto ("double entrance") is a
completely anonymous basement
inomagerío tucked under derelict
commercial premises. A diverse
clientele, from "suits" to nearby
market-stall holders, flock here for
the no-nonsense nosh: spicy beef
on kritharáki pasta, chickpeas, little
fried fishes. Bulk retsína is served on
a block of ice in warm weather; the
marble sink for glass-washing and
filling the retsína tins is a work of art.
Just 24 seats, so diners are expected
to share the six tables with strangers.
Open Mon–Sat noon–6pm. €

Fasoli
Emmanouíl Benáki 45, Exárhia
Tel: 210 330 0010
Ippokrátous 22, corner Navarínou,
midtown
Tel: 210 360 3626
The food at both branches is
appetising generic nouvelle-
Mediterranean: pasta, risottos,
salads, sole with potatoes and
squash, salmon in limoncello sauce,
some grills. The cheaper daily-
specials chalk-board is well worth
consulting. Closed Sun. Cash only. €€

Kioupi
Platía Kolonakíou 4

Tel: 210 361 4033
This basement magerío, going since
the 1920s but revamped, is the ideal
solution for lunch after visiting nearby
museums. Going for the chef's daily
specials – which might be keftédes
or fasoláda (bean soup) – keeps the
bill down in the lower category. Good
bulk wine. Open Mon–Sat lunch and
dinner. €€

Ikonomou
Tröon 41, corner Kydantidón, Petrálona
Tel: 210 346 7555.
Crowded pavement tables rather
than a sign announce you've come
to this inomagerío which does just
a handful of dishes per day: laderá,
cabbage dolmádes, roast meat, a
limited repertoire of appetisers in big
portions. There's red wine or good
retsína from the barrel. Inside, enjoy
the old engravings of Attica and
caricatures of wine-drinkers. Open
Mon–Sat dinner only. Cash only. €€

Kapnikarea
Hristopoúlou 2, corner Ermoú, Monastiráki
Tel: 210 322 7394
Platters at this ouzerí – sausages,
saganáki, eggplant dishes, good
salads – are only slightly bumped
up in price thanks to the acoustic
rebétika musicians who play here
every afternoon. Seating is outdoors
in this pedestrianised lane, with
awnings and heaters for winter. Open
daily lunch only, may open Fri/Sat
eves too, closed summer. €€

Klimataria
Platía Theátrou 2, central market district
Tel: 210 321 6629
www.klimataria.gr
An excellent source of hearty, meat-
based cooking like stir-fry with leeks
or mature lamb with stamnagáthi
greens – as the row of gástres, the
traditional backcountry stewing
apparatus, tips you off as you enter.
There are vegetarian and fish choices
(like stuffed thrápsalo) too, and live
acoustic music Thur–Sun lunch.
Open daily except Sun night. €€

Karavitis
Arktínou 33 and Pafsaníou 4
Tel: 210 721 5155
Pangráti's last surviving 1920s
taverna, purveying baked casseroles,
a few mezédes or grills, and
inexpensive Mesógia bulk wine.
Large portions somewhat offset high
mains prices. Traditional desserts like
quince or semolina helva; outdoor
seating in a lovely garden across the
street, indoors with the now-empty
wine barrels. Supper only. €€€

Kriti (Takis)

Stoa at Veranzérou 5, off Platía Kánningos
Tel: 210 382 6998
Popular little Cretan stéki (hangout)
serving regional dishes such as
apáki (cured pork), two kinds of
island sausage (prefer the Sfakian),
stamnagáthi greens and marathópita
(fennel pie), along with more usual
titbits like dákos salad and of course
Cretan rakí. A bit pricey for the area,
but portions are large. Open Mon–Sat
for lunch (when its popularity can
cause lags in service) and supper. €€

Mani-Mani
Falírou 10, Makrygiánni
Tel: 210 921 8180
www.manimani.com.gr
Installed on the top floor of a graceful
interwar house, this established
nouvelle-Greek-cuisine restaurant
does (as the name implies) have a
marked Peloponnesian tendency,
what with sýnglino (streaky pork) and
talagáni cheese from Messinía on
the menu, but there's a wide variety
of mezédes, salads, pasta dishes
and even some seafood, as well
as creative desserts. Open Tue–Fri
3pm–midnight, Sat 1pm–midnight,
Sun 1–5.30pm. €€€€

Nikitas
Agíon Anargýron 19, Psyrrí
Tel 210 325 2591
Probably the oldest (1967-founded)
taverna hereabouts, Nikítas purveys
a short but sweet menu, as well as
daily specials like oven-baked cheese
pie. Drink is confined to beer or oúzo,
and there are no sweets. But for good
value, you can't beat it, especially
if seated outdoors under the trees
beside Ágii Anárgýri church. Open
Mon–Sat noon–6pm. €

Rakoumel
Emmanouíl Benaki 71, Exárhia
Tel: 210 380 0506
Another favourite Cretan-cuisine
spot in Athens, now expanded into
an adjacent annexe, with delicacies
like fennel pie, Sfakian sausages and
seasonal greens imported from Crete.
And of course paximádia (rusks)
instead of bread, and Cretan rakí by
the carafe. Seating on the sidewalk or
inside. May close Sun. €€

Rififi
Valtetsíou 54, corner Benáki 69, Exárhia,
Tel: 210 330 0237
www.rififi-restaurant.gr.
Creative generic Middle Eastern/
Mediterranean dishes are the order of
the day here. Their gávros marinatos
(marinated anchovies) are some of
the best we've sampled, the "winter"
salad feeds three, and the Armenian-

style kebab is succulent and spicy. They seem to make most of their money off their drink, for example their perfumed bulk white wine. Cheerful pale-green environment with changing art exhibits; the bathrooms are a permanent installation masterpiece. Open daily 12.30pm–late. €€

Santorinios
Doriéon 8, Petrálona
Tel: 210 345 1629
Cult taverna installed in an old refugee compound and barrel-making workshop from 1926; seating is in small rooms or the lovely courtyard. There's a limited menu of Santoríni specialties, accompanied by decent island bulk wine (prefer the red). If some dishes rate only three-and-a-half stars, the atmosphere, service and low prices merit four to five. Dinner only Mon–Sat Sept–June, also Sun lunch in summer. €

Steki tou Ilia
Eptahálkou 5, tel 210 345 8052, and Thessaloníkis 7, tel 210 342 2407, Thissío. The two branches (open alternately) of this enterprise fill with locals here for the house speciality: a big platter of grilled succulent lamb chops (or lamb's liver for the daring). Starters

like fáva, tzatzíki and hórta are more than competent, service is quick, and barrelled wine is reasonable. Take a table in no. 5's garden, or sit indoors under the wine barrels. Open Tue–Sat supper only, Sun lunch, closed Mon. €€

Thanassis
Mitropóleos 69, Monastiráki
Tel: 210 324 4705
Three hotly competing *souvláki* grills cluster here where Mitropóleos meets Platía Monastirakíou, but this is the best. Thanassis' speciality is Egyptian-style kebab, mincemeat blended with onion and spices. The side dish of chilli peppers will blow your head off. Open daily noon–midnight except major holidays. €

Zahari kai Alati
Valtetsíou 47, Exárhia
Tel: 210 380 1253
Self-described 'bistrot bar' that delivers on both fronts: superb, rich mezédes platters served in a high, glass-ceilinged atrium, plus a loft bar with cosy rooms up the long stairways. Friendly and buzzing, and worth the slightly higher-than-average prices for the area. €€€

Attikí Peninsula
Galaria
Technological Park

North end Lávrio, en route Keratéa
Tel: 22920 28180
A stunningly converted premises on two levels, installed in the former machine shops of the French mining company. Hearty meals, though it's worth it just to stop in for a drink. Open daily noon until late. €€

Panousis
Ermoú 24, Lávrio
Tel: 22920 60052
Sympathetic little taverna on the central pedestrian zone, about the oldest one of several here – opened by the present owner's grandfather. Decent seafood and starters, bulk wine. Ermoú in general is an ideal meal solution before or after a ferry boat, as only about 500m to the port. Open daily summer, weekends only off-season. €

Remvi
Souníou 14, Paleá Fókea
Tel: 22910 36236
The last in a line of several shoreline tavernas in this little resort just before Cape Soúnio, and the only one not to tout. No need to – reasonable prices for large portions of seafood, meat and unusual starters like domatokeftédes and round Skópelos spinach pie. €€

PELOPONNESE

Ágios Andréas Kynourías

Andrítsena
Ta Pevka
Tel: 26260 22333
The best, most reliably open option for lunch (or dinner) in this gateway for the Néda river gorge and Apollo temple at Bassae, with sustaining dishes like mutton stew, sausages, cabbage salad, decent chips and palatable bulk wine. €

Áno Tríkala
To Hani tou Hania
Tel: 27430 91140
The least pretentious taverna in this long-established "hill station", with hearty dishes like arní lemonáto and spicy sausages, and good bulk rosé wine. Outdoor seating overlooks adjacent Mánna village, and the natal house of St Gerasimos, later patron saint of Kefaloniá. Fireplace interior. Open all year. €

Dimitsána
Drymonas
Tel: 27950 31116
At the south edge of town en route to Stemnítsa, the best of several tavernas here features local dishes like kounéli (rabbit), ladorígani (beets

with their greens), baked eggplant and correspondingly good house wine. Open all year. €

Ellinikó
Georganda, through road
Tel: 27931 31009
It's worth driving here from any of the more touristy surrounding villages to tuck into meat platters, but also cheese-based dishes, trahanás and kolokythokeftédes (courgette patties), accompanied by rather strong rosé. Tasteful wood-and-stone interior, high-efficiency wood stove for winter. €

Paralia
Tel: 27550 31424
Perched high above this little port, amidst ancient walls, this taverna has sweeping sea views and great-value fresh fish. The building dates from 1826, thus it's allowed to operate within an archaeological zone. Open most of the year. €€

Giálova

Spitiko
Shore road
Tel: 27230 22138
As the name implies, good home-style

fare with a Cypriot twist, as well as some seafood. Good white bulk wine based on Chardonnay, not a popular variety in Greece. Open all year. €

Gýthion

Navtilia
Main quay, near central platía
Tel: 27330 22137
Ouzerí offering top-notch seafood like sardines or fried mussels at harbour-front tables served from a small kitchen across the road by traffic-dodging waiters. Service can be a bit distracted, so allow for a leisurely meal. €€

Kalamáta

Spanomihos
Spetsón 130, corner Posidónos, marina

PRICE CATEGORIES

Prices indicated are for a meal per person with modest intake of wine, beer, rakí or tsípouro.
€€€€ = over €35
€€€ = €25–35
€€ = €15–25
€ = under €15

waterfront
Tel: 27210 98305
A real find in a potentially overpriced environment: a friendly, good-value seafood taverna dishing up patently fresh squid, bakaliáros (hake), mavromátika (beans complete with their greens), and good bulk wine. Open all year. €

Karýtena

Kastro
Tel: 27910 31113
Effectively the only taverna in this village, but a goodie, with country fare like wild (not cultivated) hórta, chunky tyrokafterí, lamb chops and pansétta (pork spare ribs), plus creditable bulk wine. €

Katákolo

Karousos
Quay, near parking lot
Tel: 26210 41209
Despite catering to shore-excursion groups from the numerous cruise ships here, quality food and service are maintained; their late summer/ early autumn sardines and atherína platters are excellent. €€

Kiáto

To Mouragio
Kalogeropoúlou 36, Tel: 27420 21433
Behind the marina, this always-crowded premises is the area's top purveyor of seafood and scaly fish, with views of the gulf as a bonus. The best solution for lunch after visiting ancient Sikyon. Open all year. €€

Kosmás

Navarhos
Tel: 27570 31489
The least conspicuous establishment on this mountain village's shady square is much the best; sausages, goat stew, tzatzíki, hórta and bulk wine are the reliable stock in trade. €

Kyllíni

Anna
Shore promenade, westernmost taverna
Tel: 26230 92416
It's worth scheduling time, before or after a Zákynthos ferry or a visit to Hlemoútsi castle, to eat at this seafood-strong taverna in a lovely bucolic setting. It's ace for baby squid, mussels in mustard sauce, sardines and gávros, garnished with krítamo (rock samphire) and hand-cut medallion chips, with easy-drinking bulk wine. Open all year. €

Kyparissía

Apovathra
Old Port

Tel: 27610 24447
The best, and most popular, of three seafood tavernas on the shore here, with good, fair-priced fish, straightforward billing and excellent bulk wine. €€

Léheo

O Faros
Minor coast road, tel: 27410 88841
Skip the tourist tavernas in nearby Arhéa Kórinthos village in favour of the own-baked bread, hand-cut chips, squirmingly fresh seafood and palatable house wine served on the seaside terrace here. Open all year. €€

Loutráki

O Giannis
Poseidónos 3 (seafront esplanade), tel: 27440 62330
Always packed in season or on winter nights, and easy to see why: dynamite fresh beets with their greens, addictive fried mussels, and a large selection of well-priced oúzo and tsípouro by the karafáki. Open all year. €

Loutrá Oréas Elénis

To Pevko
Tel: 27410 33801
Leaving Athens for the Peloponnese in the morning, you're well advised to stop here for lunch, with tables on the pebble beach. Mid-summer squid and atherína are top-drawer, lamb chops excellent, though their imám baíldi eggplant is idiosyncratic. Cheap tipple and the chance to have a quick dip – beaches further along are no better – are extra pluses. Open all year. €

Mavromáti

Ithomi
Tel: 27240 51298
A solid choice in conjunction with visiting the adjacent ruins of ancient Messene, with good renditions of saganáki (an easy dish to make disgustingly greasy) and biftéki, plus palatable bulk wine. Open all year. €

Méthana

Oinotherapevterio Ifaisteio
Kaméni Hóra hamlet
Tel: 22980 92093 or 6977 715676
In 1993, your host Thodoris converted this basalt-built stable/ farmstead into a welcoming taverna that's a prime stop for walkers visiting the nearby volcano. Feast on superb sausages, stuffed peppers, onion croquettes, fava, and non-gamey provatína (mutton). Roaring fire in winter; guided walks offered for groups. Open all year. €

Methóni

Alektor
Central Agorá
Tel: 27230 31838
Magirevtá taverna that prides itself on sourcing most raw materials from its own farm; go early, as they can run out of food, especially during low season. Open all year. €

Nikos

Miaoúli Street
Tel: 27230 31282
Competent, well-priced grills, magirevtá and starters in a salubrious environment with a fire going during the cooler months. Open all year. €

Monemvasiá

Akrogiali
Géfyra seafront
Tel: 27230 61056
As tempting as it is to eat in the heart of Monemvasiá's medieval quarter, you'll find that a premium is charged there for mediocre fare. This, the midmost of three seafood tavernas across the way at Géfyra, is the best value and most Greek-feeling, without picture menus and the like. €€

Návplio

Avoid Staïkopoulou Street, which is one solid tourist trap. There are much better choices closer to the waterfront.

Aiolos
Vassilísis Ólgas 30
Tel: 27520 26828
If you can't get into Omorfo Tavernaki, fear not, this is a very acceptable substitute – some like it better. There's a similarly meat-plus-mezédes menu, cheap bulk wine or tsípouro, objet trouvé decor and probably rebétika music on the sound system. €

Omorfo Tavernaki
Vassilísis Ólgas 1, corner Kotsonopoúlou
Tel: 27520 25944
Sympathetic, busy taverna with all the standard dishes, though having a meat bias. Always busy weekend nights year-round – especially during Epidauros festival time – when you need to book. €

Olympia

Paleá Epídavros
Akrogiali
Tel: 27530 41060
Considered the most accomplished quayside taverna here, with more involved dishes like eggplant in wine sauce, gávros marinatos and cuttlefish with rice. Both artists and audience flock here after summer performances at the nearby Little

Epidauros Theatre, which has bumped prices up – and means you must book then. €€
Parálio Ástros
Rebetiko
Tel: 27550 51691
Most tavernas in this busy resort are mediocre and overpriced; this exception, run by a fisher family, has fair-priced seafood (the loútsos or barracuda is excellent), the usual starters, good rosé in bulk, and rather rough Cretan tsikoudiá. €
Thea
Flokós village, 1.5km south towards Kréstena
Tel: 26240 23264
A superior psistariá (grill taverna) just about within walking distance of modern Olympía, much the best value

in the area – locals go too. And yes, there is a sweeping view as the name suggests. Open all year for dinner, lunch only in summer. €

Pátra
For seafood, there are two local favourites: **Ankyra** €€, by a beached boat at the fishing port (tel: 2610 333 778), with mostly outdoor seating, and **Kylikio Istioploïkos Omilos** (Sailing Club Canteen), €€ Iróon Polytehníou 8, corner Terpsithéas (tel: 2610 435 905), a bit more formal with tables inside.
Stemnítsa
1821 (Giannis)
Main road, north of central square
Tel: 27950 81438
Bean soup, tsoutsoukákia and other

magirevtá are the stock in trade at this popular successor to Giannis' father's much-loved Klinitsa taverna. An all-glass storefront allows views of the world going by. €€

Stoúpa
To Palio Bostani
Kalógria beach, tel: 27210 78282
An unusually good hotel-restaurant that does a particularly good job with mezédes and stews. €€
Vivári Argolídas
Ioannis Diamandopoulos
Tel: 27520 92131
The most down-to-earth of several fish tavernas along the lagoon shore here, with fresh seafood, generous mezédes platters and bulk wine from Neméa. €

CENTRAL GREECE

Ágios Ioánnis
Poseidonas
Central waterfront
Tel: 24260 31222
One of the best and cheapest fish tavernas here; a medium-sized fish, two starters and local wine will leave you change from €20. It is open most of the year. €€

Damoúhari
Barba Stergios
South side of Venetian port
Tel: 24260 49845 or 49207
A reliable, fairly inexpensive venue for non-farmed fish, as well as meat grills and a few magirevtá dishes. There is a lovely seaside terrace for eating during the summer, also a tasteful indoor salon for cooler months. €

Galaxídi
Albatross
Inland street between two churches
Tel: 22650 42233
Lovely magirío with a handful of tables, a limited quantity of home-style food encompassing octopus, spinach/cheese pie, rabbit stew, pale taramosaláta and the house speciality samári (pancetta in savoury sauce). Open daily. €

Gávros
To Spiti tou Psara
Main valley, bottom road
Tel: 22370 41202
Despite the name, lots else besides trout: excellent hortópitta, kafterí dip, own-made wine at reasonable prices. €

Kalambáka
O Skaros (Papalexis)
Tel: 24320 24152
Trikálon highway, 150 metres past the Divani Hotel on the west edge of town
Not many tourists find this spot, but locals certainly know about its meaty platters – particularly excellent kebáb (called kondosoúvli elsewhere), splinándro (offal) and chops – plus home-grown vegetables or wild greens. Open all year. €

Kastráki Meteóron
Paradisos
Through road
Tel: 24320 22723
The best all-rounder of a dozen local tavernas. Besides excellent kokorétsi and biftéki from the grill, there's moussakás, starters and ravaní for dessert; Koula, the owner-cook, has years of experience in Canada and Thessaloníki. €

Katigiórgis
Flisvos (Voulgaris)
Fishing port
Tel: 24230 71071
Folk from Vólos reckon the long trip out here worth it for the fresh fish and honest magirevtá, and you'll probably agree. Tables in the sand, weather and waves permitting. €€

Kissós
Makis
Just off the platía
Tel: 24260 31266
One of the oldest tavernas in Pílio: stress on magirevtá like rabbit stew, gígandes; bulk wine. Open all year. €

Lamía
Ouzo Melathron
Aristotélous 3, up some steps from Platía Laoú
Tel: 22310 31502
Reasonably priced portions of Middle Eastern and Macedonian recipes are washed down by Límnos bulk wine; tables in a courtyard or the stunning interior of an old house. €

Mesolóngi
Filoxenos
Razikótsika 7
Tel: 26310 51660
The local speciality is smoked or grilled eel (héli), hunted with tridents in the lagoon. This is the priciest outlet on this pedestrian lane but worth it for the service and ambience. €€

Mikró Horió
Iy Kyra Maria
Ground floor of Helidona Hotel
Tel: 22370 41221
Atmospheric seating under the plane tree in the centre of the old village, with reasonable food. €

Milína
O Sakis
South end of waterfront

PRICE CATEGORIES

Prices indicated are for a meal per person with modest intake of wine, beer, rakí or tsípouro.
€€€€ = over €35
€€€ = €25–35
€€ = €15–25
€ = under €15

Tel: 24230 66078
This is one of the best tavernas in the south Pelion. A five-platter meal, including *gávros* (fresh anchovy), *hórta* and other *mezédes*, will leave little room for dessert. €€

Mylopótamos

Angelika
Near end of the road into town
Tel: 24260 49588
The fish is a bit pricey, but various *magirevtá* plates are reasonable and service is kind and efficient. Open daily Easter to Oct; Nov–Easter weekends and holidays. €€

Mýtikas

Glaros
Northwest end of quay
Tel: 26460 81240
www.mk-glaros.com
Busy fish taverna with fresh fare and terrace looking out to Kálamos island. They also have refurbished rooms to rent upstairs with superb views. €€

Návpaktos

Papoulis
Sismáni, corner Formíonos, Návpaktos
Tel: 26340 21578
The town's most accomplished

eatery, comprising two premises – a *mezedopolío* and a standard taverna – the former more popular in summer. Big portions of well-executed ouzerí dishes and willing service. €

Pinakátes

Drosia (Taverna tou Papa)
West end of village
Tel: 24230 86772
Excellent leafy dolmádes and goat and lemon sauce as well as off-menu *mezédes*. May close random days Oct–May. €€

Portariá

Kritsa
Central platía
Tel: 22428 99121
Restaurant with tasteful environment, professional service and biggish portions. Specialities include *tyropitákia*, *maïdanosaláta* (parsley dip) and of course Piliot *spétzofaï*. €€

Pórto Germenó

Akrotiri
Tel: 22630 41234 or 6984 173091
The best, friendliest and most consistently open of the tavernas on

the esplanade. A good balance of meat and fish dishes, well priced by the kilo. Good bulk wine, especially the rosé. Open most of the year. €€

Tríkala

Palia Istoria
Ypsilándou 3
Tel: 24310 77627
There are literally dozens of ouzerí in the old market district of Manávika. This one is open for lunch too, and has a light touch with potentially over-rich platters, consistent quality and attractive prices. €

Vólos

Halambalias (Zafiris)
Orféos 8, corner Skýrou
Tel: 24210 20234
A shrine of *magirevtá* that attracts crowds to an uninspiring inland location; good bulk wine, baked seafood and meat dishes. Closed Sunday. €
Monosandalos
Tsopótou 1, east waterfront by Ágios Konstandínos church
Tel: 24210 37525
The doyen of several ouzerí with good prices. Shrimp croquettes a speciality. €€

EPIRUS

Amvrakikós Gulf

Myrtaria (Patendas)
Koronisía
Tel: 26810 24021
This end-of-the-line village on a sandspit has about half a dozen seafood tavernas; Myrtaria is last in line, most notable for its high-quality seafood from an admittedly limited menu. €€€

Eláti

Sta Riza
Centre of Eláti village
Tel: 69370 37544 or 26530 71550
This features Epirot turnovers, vegetarian and dairy starters plus a few cooked dishes of the day at moderate prices, accompanied by bulk wine. If it's not too cold or breezy, eat out on the balcony with an eyeful of Mt Gamíla. Closed Tue, also Thur in low season. €

Ioánnina

Fysa Roufa
Averoff 55
Tel: 26510 70705
A supposedly 24-hour *magirío* whose slightly elevated prices for dishes like *magirevtá* patsás, suckling pig and

spétzofaï are justified by the careful cooking, polite service, big portions and a pleasant environment. €€
Stin Ithaki
Stratigoú Papágou 20A
Tel: 26510 73012
The most consistently good of a half-dozen eateries on the lakefront avenue. The ambitious menu includes Cypriot specialities and Asia Minor recipes as well as Epirot staples like trout, turnovers, cheeses and mushrooms. Starter portions are big, and often better value than the main dishes. €€

Koukoúli

To Tritoxo
Koukoúli, Zagóri
Tel: 26530 71760
Named after the nearby three-arched bridge, this café-restaurant run by village priest Papa-Kosta and his wife serves up hearty, reasonably priced meat dishes plus Epirot *píttes*, accompanied by good local bulk wine. €

Limáni Lygiás

Skaloma (O Gios tou Foti)
Tel: 26820 56240

There's no sign, but it's the only eatery at this little fishing anchorage, and everybody for kilometres around comes here. Big portions of patently fresh seafood and appetisers, small prices. €€

Menídi

Vouliagmeni (Pandioras)
Between Árta and Amfilohía Vouliagmeni, first place on left from main highway
Tel: 26810 88216
Where folk from Árta come for a big plate of the famous Amvrakian *garídes* (prawns, shrimp), as well as scaly fish. €€€

Pápingo, Megálo

Kalliopi
South part of village
Tel: 26530 41081
Home-style cooking, good bulk wine, year-round operation and good music attract a lively crowd. €€
Nikos Tsoumanis
North part of village
Tel: 26530 41893
Huge salads, tasty lamb, regional dishes and assorted offal for the bold, plus unimpeded views of the famous *pýrgi* (rock towers) of Astráka

Tempting dish in a Santoríni restaurant.

from the terrace. €€

Párga

Golfo Beach
Southeast end of town, Mikró Kryonéri cove
Tel: 26840 32336
One of the oldest tavernas in Párga, this has acquired a cult following for its seaside terrace and good-value oven-casserole food. €

Taverna tou Khristou
Sarakíniko beach, 7km (4 miles) northwest
Tel: 26840 35207 or 69779 82207
www.sarakiniko.info
This old favourite features well-executed vegetable dishes, fresh seafood, a few select meat items, and limited bottlings from quality wineries in northern Greece. €€

Préveza

To Kohyli
Parthenagogeio 9, old bazaar
Tel: 6932 416563
Excellent seafood-strong meals here, with tables out in the little alley or indoors; open reliably low season and/or at lunch, not always the case for old-bazaar eateries. €

Thessaloníki

Amanitis
D. Poliorkitoú 44
Tel: 2310 233513

A non-touristy eatery in the Kástra district that will appeal to vegetarians and carnivores alike. €€

Apo Dyo Horia
Výronos 7, Platía Navarínou
Tel: 2310 269204
Top quality yet inexpensive little restaurant where you can enjoy unusual dishes from Crete and the Pontus, such as pickled vegetables and highly spicy sausages. €€

Aristotelous
Aristotélous 8
Tel: 2310 230762
One of the older ouzerís in the city centre, Aristotelous serves classic northern Greece cuisine with a twist alongside ouzerí standards. Excellent wine list. €€

The Barrister
Tsimiskí 103 and Výronos 2
Tel: 2310 253033
This smart, top-of-the-range restaurant presents its European dishes with considerable flair. This is one of Thessaloníki's most sophisticated dining locales. €€€€

Ouzou Melathron
Karýpi 21
Tel: 2310 240043
www.ouzoumelathron.gr
Search for the small Greek sign for this cosy and popular ouzerí tucked away down an alleyway. For your efforts you'll enjoy a wide range of

moderately priced mezédes. €€

Pyrgos
Venizélou 13
Tel: 2310 207769
Pyrgos is one of those quietly successful places that rely on its repeat clientele and its consistently quality fare. Up in the Kástra, this place dishes up a mixed Greek international cuisine with particular emphasis on its fine wine list. The food is well presented and the service friendly. €€€

Ta Adelfia tis Pyxarias
Platía Navarínou 7
Tel: 2310 266432
This is one of the best among several tavernas operating around a pedestrianised square to the east of the city centre. Dine outside or inside among photos on the wall of an old Macedonian home. Succulent kebabs as well as a range of ready-made oven-cooked dishes. €€

Ta Bakaliarakia tou Aristou

PRICE CATEGORIES

Prices indicated are for a meal per person with modest intake of wine, beer, rakí or tsipouro.
€€€€ = over €35
€€€ = €25–35
€€ = €15–25
€ = under €15

Ta Bakaliarakia tou Aristou
Katoúni 3
Tel: 2310 542906
www.mpakaliarakia-aristou.gr
Thessaloníki's answer to a British
chippy, where you can feast on huge
helpings of cod and chips, served on
greaseproof paper, for little cash at
this popular Ladádika joint. €
To Makedoniko
G Papadopoulou, Sykiés
Tel: 2310 627438
Neatly hidden just inside the western
gate of the old town, this very
traditional taverna draws a mixture
of students and locals by virtue of its
tasty grills, salads and good barrelled
retsína. €
To Meteoro Vima Tis Garidas

(Angelopoulos)
Modiáno Market
Tel: 2310 274170
Its name means "the huge step of
the shrimp", but it's better known by
the name of the owner, Angelopoulos.
Either way, it's one of the best ouzería
in the area, with inexpensive portions
of seafood and other mezédes. €€
Toumbourlika
Kalapotháki 11
Tel: 2310 282174
Yet another of the city's famous
ouzería, hidden away in a narrow
street off Platía Dimokratías, this
consists of a couple of small cosy
rooms with a few outside tables. It
specialises in fish mezédes. Some
live music on weekends. €€€

To Yedi
I. Paparéska 13, Kastra
Tel: 2310 246495
www.yenti.gr
High up next to the Eptapýrgio
fortress, this laid-back and friendly
ouzerí serves up no-nonsense high-
quality mezédes. €€
Zythos
Katoúni 5, Ladádika
Tel: 2310 540284
www.zithos.gr
This is a great spot for people-
watching while you dine on a variety
of dishes featuring Greek, Asian and
Western European elements. Zythos
is a restaurant-cum-pub, and apart
from its inventive cuisine, serves up
draft Irish and German beers. €€

MACEDONIA AND THRACE

Alexandroúpoli

To Nisiotiko
Zarífi 1
Tel: 2551 020990
www.nisiotiko.gr
To Nisiotiko stands out for its well
prepared and not overly expensive
food. Fish predominate though
there's a range of grills and
imaginative mezédes. €€€

Flórina

To Petrino
Pávlou Melá 2
Tel: 23850 22560
A local favourite near the railway
station, with fine oven-baked dishes
and a few grills. Popular for lunch. €€

Kastoriá

Doltso
Tsakáli 2
Tel: 24670 24670
This classy dining venue on Doltso
Square is a local favourite, set in a
lovely restored mansion. The top-
class food includes many traditional
Macedonian dishes. €€
Faros
Leofóros Níkis 6
Tel: 24670 23510
Predominantly seafood taverna set in
a partially covered courtyard. Items
include very inexpensive sardines
and mussels, as well as some meat
dishes such as diced and fried pork.
€€

Kavála

O Kanados
Poulídou 27
Tel: 2510 835172
As the name suggests, this friendly
taverna is run by a returnee Greek

Canadian. The speciality is grilled
meat, with a selection of salads and
decent bulk wine. €
Tembelhanio
Poulídou 33b
Tel: 2510 232501
A Macedonian-style ouzerí: the
mezédes are mainly fish, with
shellfish taking pride of place, and
you wash it all down with small
carafes of tsípouro – the fiery grape
spirit that is drunk throughout
Macedonia. Dine in the company
of knowledgeable and appreciative
locals. €€

Komotiní

Ta Adelfia
Orféos 25
Tel: 25310 20201
The food here is simple staples,
cooked in the old-fashioned way.
Go for the daily specials listed on a
blackboard outside. €€

Litóhoro

Gastrodromio "En Olymbo"
On the central square
Tel: 23520 21300
www.gastrodromio.gr
Surprisingly sophisticated
establishment for such a rural
location. Main courses include tender
suckling pig and there are creative
salads such as potato with herring
and apple in mustard. €€€€

Nikiti

Kazanis
Tel: 23750 23333
Typical seashore restaurant in this
attractive resort. Kazanis has been in
the family since 1952 and the fish is
always fresh. Open year-round. €€

Préspa

Akrolimnia
The lakefront, Psarádes village
Tel: 23850 46260
If you eat in the Préspa Lake region,
you should sample famous local
produce – namely fasoláda, a rich
bean soup, or the local lake trout,
péstrofa. This busy lakefront taverna
is one of the best places to enjoy
them. €€

Véria

To Katafygi
Kondogeorgáki 18
Tel: 2331 027227
The impressive and cosy Katafygi
(the name means "refuge", as in
mountain shelter) dishes up a wide
range of game from quail to wild
boar. Vegetarians are well catered for
too. €€

Xánthi

Myrovolos
Platía Hristídi
Tel: 25410 72720
The atmospheric streets of Xánthi's
old town is home to a rash of similar
tavernas. Myrovolos is one of the
better ones and specialises in
tsipouro mezédes. On weekends you
may catch live rebétika music. €€
Erkolos
Bahtetzí 18A
Tel: 25410 67735
A great little spot tucked in a
pedestrian alley not far from the main
square, where you can enjoy tender
fried calves liver and wash it down
with fine local wine or tsípouro. €

SARONIC GULF

Égina

Agora (Geladakis)
Behind fish market
Tel: 22970 27308
One of the oldest (founded c.1960) seafood outfits in town, offering good value without airs and graces – you'll likely have to wait for a table. Summer seating on the cobbles outside, winter tables inside. Bulk wine or oúzo for refreshment. €€

Lekkas
Kazantzáki 4, northerly waterfront
Tel: 22970 22527
Renowned for its good vegetable platters and hygienic meat grills, washed down by excellent bulk wine. Very inexpensive for Égina. €

Póros

Karavolos
Póros Town
Tel: 22980 26158
Meaning a type of snail in Greek, Karavolos is a very popular back-street taverna. Yes, the restaurant does serve snails, served with a rich sauce. There's a selection of ready made *magirevtá* (home cooked) dishes as well as grills. Dine indoors or on a leafy patio. Reservations recommended. €€

Mezedokamomata
Galatás quay
Tel: 22980 43085
It's well worth taking the passenger shuttle across from

Póros, then walking 150m north, for the accurately described mezedokamómata (mezédes feasts) served here: stamnagáthi greens, beets, tyrokafterí, grills and bulk wine. A very sweet managing family and frontal view of Póros are extra bonuses. Open all year. €

Platanos
Póros Town
Tel: 22980 24249
High up in the back streets of Póros town under a plane tree (plátanos), the speciality here is grills ranging from regular steaks to kokorétsi, mixed offal grilled on a long skewer. The atmosphere is relaxed and laid-back; evening dining is the best time to enjoy this place. €

Spétses

Exedra
Old Harbour
Tel: 22980 73497
One of several classy fish tavernas in the Old Harbour; the house speciality is fish cooked in garlic and tomato and baked in the oven. You'll also find prawns and lobster, prepared with cheese or with spaghetti. €€€

Liotrivi
Old Harbour
Tel: 22980 72269
Another fish tavern inside an old olive press (liotrívi), with a very attractive location near the old boatyards. Mainly Greek clientele enjoy all

kinds of variations on fish and other seafood. Best for evening dining. €€€

Patralis
Kounoupítsa waterfront
The most upmarket, white-tablecloth venue away from the Dápia, with excellent service. Their psári ala Spetsióta (fish in ratatouille sauce) is made with fresh, not frozen, fish, as in many other places. The bulk wine is satisfactory, and baked-apple dessert rounds off the experience. Open all year. €€€

Ýdra

Gitoniko (Manolis & Kristina's)
Ýdra Town
Tel: 22980 53615
Popular with locals and foreigners alike, the Taverna Gitoniko offers discreet rooftop dining as well as indoor tables downstairs. Good-value dishes range from simple island vegetarian fare to hearty grilled meats and fish. Veal in quince or red wine sauce is a house speciality. Excellent hýma wine. €€

Kondylenia
Kamíni
Tel: 22980 53520
The poshest tavern, with the best view, at this Hydriot suburb; select magirevtá and seafood (including good grilled cuttlefish on occasion) is the bill of fare. €€€

CYCLADES

Amorgós

Hyma
Hóra, main commercial street
Tel: 22970 86376
Excellent, genuine ouzerí in an ex-grocery store. Strong points are salads and seafood dishes, plus a few meat casseroles. Hýma (in bulk) is your wine. Open all year, off-season by arrangement. €

Limani tis Kyra Katinas
Órmos Egiális
Tel: 22850 73269
Strong contender for best all-round eatery on the island; strengths are seafood, pulses, vegetable casseroles and local cheese. Very reasonably priced for the quality. Open from just before Easter–mid-Oct. €

Nikos
Langáda
Tel: 22850 73310
Polished taverna specialising in

platters like beets with greens, dips, goat-based dishes, fish and some magirevtá. Not cheap for Amorgós but the quality is high, with seating on perhaps the island's loveliest vine-shaded terrace. €€

Anáfi

Liotrivi
Hóra
Tel: 22860 61209
Best in show up here, especially for fish; a few vegetable dishes and dips as well, along with Santoríni bulk wine. Sit on the small, popular terrace or in the vaulted interior. Open May–Oct, the longest of any taverna in the village. €

Roukounas (Tis Papadias)
Just in from Roúkounas beach
Tel: 22860 61206
Going since 1990, and a reliable source of magirevtá like briám – a

more elaborate dish than you'll generally get at a beachside taverna. €

Andíparos

Anargyros
Harbourfront
Tel: 22840 61204
The islet's most venerable taverna – it starred in the 1960 movie Mantalena – is also a dab hand at traditional dishes like pastítsio (a succulent brick laden with béchamel

---

PRICE CATEGORIES

Prices indicated are for a meal per person with modest intake of wine, beer, rakí or tsípouro.
€€€€ = over €35
€€€ = €25–35
€€ = €15–25
€ = under €15

sauce) and thick fáva served with onions and lemon. Open April–Oct. €€

Koufonísi

Karnagio
Loutró cove
Tel: 22850 71694
Exceedingly popular quayside ouzerí, so reservations mandatory in season; the menu offers a full line of píttes, flashed-fried fish, grilled meat and rakí from Náxos; pity about the supermarket bulk wine. €€

Melissa
Hóra centre
Tel: 22850 71678
The best taverna in the village, open (unusually) for lunch too, good for magirevtá and fish; psychedelic chair-colour scheme offsets somewhat glum service. €

Mýkonos

Fisherman (Giorgos & Marina)
Áno Méra square
Tel: 22890 71405
www.giorgosmarina.com
The platía of Mýkonos' second village is ringed by tavernas, some surprisingly expensive; this is one of the cheaper and friendlier, open all year as well. They do móstra (the local version of Cretan dákos) and a preponderance of meat dishes despite the name. €€

Madoupas
Harbourfront, Hóra
Tel: 22890 22224
This combination bar, café and magirío accomplishes the miracle of hearty Greek fare at almost normal prices – their revytháda is excellent,

made with split rather than whole chickpeas, the bread wholegrain, the gávros crisp and fresh, all in generous portions. A local institution, open all year. €€

Ma'ereio
Kalogéra 16, Hóra
Tel: 22890 28825
'Mykonian/homestyle tastes' is the motto of this hole-in-the-wall, very popular with locals who come to scoff on loúza (Cycladic ham), mushrooms, fluffy keftédes and wholemeal bread; a bit more outlay nets you psaronéfri (pork medallions) and the like. The bulk white wine will be a bit too fruity/sweet for some. Open all year, with winter premises out at Ágios Stéfanos. €€€€

Tasos
Paránga beach
Tel: 22890 23002
www.tasostavernamykonos.gr
A superior beach taverna with a deserved cult following. The bread comes with little mini-dip ramekins, "roast eggplant" is more like baba ghanouj on the half-shell with tomato, parsley and garlic, the fried shrimps palpably fresh, the bulk wine decent (though the bottled list is reasonable for Mýkonos). Portions are generous, service efficient and friendly. Open April–late Oct. €€€

Náxos

Axiotissa
18th km of road Hóra–Alykó, approaching Glyfáda
Tel: 22850 75107
Arguably the top organic/vegetarian eatery on the island, with locally sourced ingredients. Dishes run the

gamut from rocket and xinomyzíthra salad, chilli-and-onion sauteed Portobello mushrooms, eggplant with almonds, Armenian sausage and goat or rabbit dishes, accompanied by rosé bulk wine from Moní or a select Greek wine list. Booking mandatory in season. Open weekends only spring/fall. €€

Metaxy Mas
Hóra, Paleá Agorá
Tel: 22850 26425
www.metaximas-naxos.gr
The best-value eatery in the old town, popular with both locals and visitors for its huge portions of local cheese, hórta, some seafood and several dishes of the day. Open daily 1pm–late, all year; summer seating in the lane. €

Platsa
Kóronos centre
Tel: 22850 51243
The ebullient Matina is heart and soul of one of the best tavernas in Náxos' inland villages, with dishes of the day for lunch and strong rakí and candied, organic quince to finish off. Seating is on multiple, arcaded mini-courtyards (plátses in local dialect) festooned with plants. Open most of the year. €

Sto Ladoharto
Quay, Hóra
Tel: 22850 22178
Carnivores repair to these upstairs premises, with great views of the harbour, for strictly grilled-meat platters plus a few salads and starters. The decor is mock-1950s grocery-shop: legacy canned goods, strung-up peppers, bagged dry goods. Open all year. €€

CRETE

Ágios Nikólaos

Avli
Príngipa Georgíou 12
Tel: 28410 82479
All the usual ouzerí standards, as well as desserts like lemon mousse. Polite service and a vine-shaded courtyard (avlí in Greek) setting are big pluses, as is wine from their own vineyard in the Sitía mountains. Open daily April–Oct lunch and dinner. €€

Chrisofyllis
Aktí Papá Pangálou, Kitroplatía cove
Tel: 28410 22705
Creative ouzerí with platters like sfoungáta (onion-sausage soufflé), eggplant with graviéra cheese and beets in yogurt-walnut sauce. A minimalist interior sports old photos (some are for sale). Open all year,

noon until late. €€€

Angouseli005
10km from Spíli or Plakiás
Ifigeneia, West outskirts
Tel: 28320 51362
A shrine of traditional Cretan delicacies like volví skordaláta (pickled wild hyacinth bulbs), stamnagáthi, apáki and boiled goat with gamopílafo (white sticky rice). Open nightly all year; booking suggested. €

Frangokástello

Kali Kardia
Tel: 28250 92123
Old-fashioned taverna where the best tack is to eat what the proprietors are eating: perhaps a fry-up of the very fresh local fish. good hýma wine. €

Haniá

Halkina
Aktí Tombazi 29–30, old harbour
Tel: 28210 41570
Tucked inconspicuously between the tourist traps of the two Venetian ports is this rakádiko, well attended for titbits like eggplant roulade, marathópita (fennel pie) and apáki. Oddly, their bulk wine is preferable to their rakí. Open daily, 1pm until late. €€

Ierápetra
Levante
Stratigoú Samaíl 38
Tel: 28420 80585
The most reliable of the tavernas behind the seafront, with castle views and going since the 1930s. Homestyle dishes like milk-based

xýgalo, stuffed cabbage leaves, papoutsáki and omathiés – rice-and-offal sausage. Open all year. €€

Kalamoti
Venizélou 142, Halépa district
Tel: 28210 59198
A favourite seaside hangout of locals, thanks to sizeable casserole dishes (these can sell out at lunch), vegetarian platters and seafood. Try dolmádes, myzíthra cheese or grilled soupiá (cutttlefish), accompanied by the decent local retsína (pine-resin-flavoured wine). Open all year. €€

Ouzythino
Aktí Papanikolí 6, Neahóra
Tel: 28210 73315
www.ouzythino.com
Ask locals where they go for seaside dining when they tire of the Venetian harbours, and they'll direct you to Neahóra, just west of the old town. With summer tables set out on the fishing-port jetty, this is a popular taverna here, thanks to heaping helpings of marinated anchovies, Sfakian sausages, courgette patties and cheese-stuffed peppers. The name means 'ouzo-beer-wine' – all present and correct, as well as rakí. Open all year for lunch and dinner. €€

Tamam
Zambeliou 49, Evraïkí district
Tel: 28210 96080
www.tamamrestaurant.com.
This former hamam (Turkish bath) built in 1645 contains one of the best, most atmospheric restaurants in town. It's predictably stuffy inside in summer, with outside tables at a premium (bookings taken). The fare is Cretan, plus Mediterranean/Middle Eastern specialities like Iranian pilaf and lots else for vegetarians. Success has prompted the opening of an annexe opposite, with modern decor. Open daily all year for lunch and dinner. €€–€€€

Iráklio

Giakoumis
Fotíou Theodosáki 8, off Evans
Tel: 2810 280277
Classic marketplace taverna, in several contiguous premises in this alley. It specialises in succulent lamb chops, crispy potatoes, seasonal salads and equally good rosé or white bulk wine; service can be distracted, however. Open Mon–Sat lunch and dinner, all year. €

Ippokambos
Sofoklí Venizélou 3
Tel: 2810 280240
Highly regarded ouzerí by the Venetian harbour. Excellent mezédes (including snails), reasonably priced

seafood and winning service. It gets busy, so go early; no reservations. Open April–Nov Mon–Sat for lunch and dinner. €€

Karnagio
Mínoös 3, corner shore road, Tálos district
Tel: 2810 280090
A local favourite, tops for seafood like grilled cuttlefish or octopus, and rich risotto. Both scaly fish and shellfish are affordable, and squirmingly fresh; the house-label bottled wine is also excellent. Daily all year, lunch and dinner. €€€

Paradosiako
Vourváhon 9
Tel: 2810 342927
Secluded, no-nonsense taverna with courtyard seating and intriguing objet trouvé interior, reached by a pedestrian passage; grills, mezédes and a few dishes of the day are the stock in trade. Open Mon–Sat 2pm–midnight, €€

Kourná (Lake)

Lygaria
Shoreline
Tel: 28250 61695
At the far end of the 'strip' here, Lygaria eschews (for the most part) picture-menus, relying instead on its excellent apáki, stífno greens, stuffed squash blossoms and chunky house melitsanosaláta to draw customers. Open all year (weekends only winter). €€

Móhlos
Kohylia
East quay
Tel: 28430 94432
A reliable choice amongst several establishments here, also the oldest (founded 1902). Expect fresh artichokes in spring, little fishes, stews, and daily casseroles like stuffed vegetables or moussakás. A pleasant interior allows cool-season operation. Respectful, non-pushy service. Open Feb–Nov, lunch and dinner. €€

Palékastro

Angistri (Nikolas O Psaras)
Village centre, Angathiás
Tel: 28430 61598
Some of the cheapest, and freshest, fish in the region here, straight from Nikolas' boat. His son and daughter grill and serve respectively. A few cooked dishes as well, plus superb views from the terrace by day. Open all year. €€€

Paleohóra

The Third Eye
Some 50m inland from west beach, south end

Tel: 28230 42223
A remarkable vegetarian restaurant, with an extensive Asian/Indian menu plus a range of desserts. Breakfast also offered; occasional concerts by night. Open all day from before Easter to end Oct. €€

Pláka (opposite Spinalónga)
Haroupia
Tel: 28410 42510
Something of an oddity in a seafood-mad resort, this very competent, Greek-patronised ouzerí straddling the through road does simpler, sustaining fare – apáki, mushrooms, dolmádes and rakí. €€

Réthymno

Dyo Rou
Pánou Koronéou 28t
Tel: 6936 500892
This self-proclaimed inomagiríon (wine-and-cook-shop) in a quiet part of the old quarter proves a winner for stamnagáthi, keftédes and imám-style eggplant, served with bulk wine or the locally brewed organic beer. Portions aren't huge – the emphasis is on quality. The interior constitutes a quasi-museum displaying black-and-whites of old Réthymno and shadow-puppet figures. Open all year, lunch and dinner. €

Rakodikeio
Vernádou 7, opposite Nerantzés Mosque
Tel: 6945 774407
This exquisite little ouzerí, a big hit with Réthymno's student contingent, offers creatively tweaked dishes like pork fried with saffron and oúzo, Hánia-style píta, or beet salad with yogurt and walnuts. Tables on the pedestrian alley or inside by season. Open mid-summer for dinner only, otherwise 2pm until very late. €€

Sitía

Balkoni/Balcony
Foundalídou 19
Tel: 28430 25084
www.balcony-restaurant.com
Widely travelled owner-chef Tonya Karandinou's menu juxtaposes nouvelle Cretan fare (rabbit with walnuts and rosemary, snails in goat-cheese sauce) with creative salads, and Mexican or Asian dishes, legacy of her time running restaurants in

Laguna Beach and London. Pricey wine list. Open dinner only April–Oct. €€€€

Sergiani
Karamanlí 38 (beachfront)
Tel: 28430 24092
Properly flash-fried atherína (sand smelt), vegetarian turnovers and copious salads constitute some of the staples at this unusually good beachside taverna. €€

Anchorage
Main access road
(Papadérou Street)
Tel: 28230 51487
www.taverna-anchorage.com
Forego sea views in favour of a vine-shaded courtyard and decent renditions of angináres me koukiá (artichoke hearts with broad beans), wild hórta, stewed rabbit, and tsigaristó. Open daily Easter–Oct, noon–11pm. €€

Kyma (Paterakis)
On the seafront
Tel: 28230 51688
Kyma's gravel-terrace tables are usually packed, for good reason – big portions of good-value fare like own-made taramosaláta and marathópita, with friendly service. Sadly, the seafood is often frozen, but there's a quaffable bulk wine. Open daily late Apr–late Oct noon–11pm. €€

Stavrós, Akrotíri Peninsula
Zorbas
Behind the giant eucalyptus, near bus stop
Tel: 28210 39402
Generally, we run a mile from tavernas so named, but this one's the real deal – the most locally attended of several on this sandy cove, where the disastrous log-transport scene of Zorba the Greek was filmed. There's a good range of seafood, cheeses, lamb dishes and vegetable casseroles in big portions. Open all year. €

Vóri
Alekos
Behind Agía Pelagía church
Tel: 28920 91094
After visiting nearby Phaistos and Agía Triáda, head for this secluded village taverna. The setting – a courtyard with clothed tables and cushioned bench seating, an interior with fireplace – is matched by the food: hearty portions of deftly executed recipes. A wood-burning oven bakes goat or kid dishes (ordered in advance). Open daily lunch and dinner, all year. €€

Zákros
Kato Zakros Bay (Platanakis), Waterfront, Káto Zákros
Tel: 28430 26887
Tellingly, this taverna at one of eastern Crete's remotest bays gets the most local clientele, for the sake of the homegrown vegetables and home-bred poultry, fair prices and decent quality. Open all day, April–Oct. €€

RHODES

Hatzikelis
Solomoú Alhadéf 9, Old Town
Tel: 22410 27215
www.hatzikelis.gr
Seafood-strong taverna installed in a former Jewish girls' school, from whose vast, professional kitchen issue fair portions of such delicacies as smoked eel and mullet botárgo from Mesolóngi, crayfish nuggets, delicate rozéttia fish, lakérda (cured bonito), mermizéli (Kalymnian-style salad) and – for those with the funds – Beluga caviar. Hórta syvrási makes a nice, tart and oniony change from plain boiled greens, while their soupiórizo (cuttlefish risotto) with pine nuts is excellent. A conservatory and fireplace permit year-round operation. Open daily, lunch and dinner. €€€

Koukos
Nikifórou Mandilará 20–26, Neohóri
Tel: 22410 73022
From beginnings as a young peoples' coffee-bar and takeaway bakery, Koukos has evolved into one of the few genuine, and most popular, mezedopolía in the new town. It's worth showing up just for the multilevel, Tardis-like interior, effectively a private folklore museum, though on fine days everyone is out on the terraces. The fare – seafood probably a better bet than meat – is decent. Open daily most of the day into the evening. €

Marco Polo Café
Ayíou Fanouríou 42, Old Town

Tel: 22410 25562
The courtyard of the Marco Polo Mansion hosts the town's most creative cooking. Platters change seasonally but might include cuttlefish on a bed of courgette mousse and mylokópi (sea perch) fillet in caper sauce, subtly flavoured pilaf with lamb and raisins, and pork medallions with soft manoúri cheese, fig and red peppercorn sauce. Save room for decadent desserts like chocolate frozen with strawberries, white-chocolate mousse or kaltsoúnia (sweet-cheese turnovers). Co-proprietor Spyros is a wine fanatic, so sample his cellar if the bulk wine fails to appeal. Open mid-May to mid-October supper only; last orders 11pm. €€€€

Meltemi
Platía Koundourióti 8, Élli beach
Tel: 22410 30480
Classy and surprisingly well-priced-for-the-location ouzerí offering such delights as crayfish nuggets, octopus croquettes, grilled red peppers in balsamic vinegar, chunky hummus and superb roast aubergine with beans and onions. There is a pleasant winter salon with old engravings inside. Open all day, all year. €€

Mezes
Aktí Kanári 9, Psaropoúla
Tel: 22410 27962
The interior, with rust-coloured paint trim and solid wood surfaces throughout, may not have the quirky charm of Koukos, but the food here is arguably better and more generously

served. Tuck into starters like superior chickpea stew, breaded mastéllo cheese from Híos, oyster mushrooms or lahmatzoún (Armenian pizza); meat and seafood mains are even bigger. Live music some Saturdays. Open daily noon–12.30am. €€

Paragadi
Klavdíou Pépper corner Avstralías, Zéfyros district
Tel: 22410 37775
Seafood, sea-view restaurant where reasonable prices for wine and a limited range of vegetarian starters is offset by somewhat bumped-up fish prices; their seafood risotto is excellent, though it won't satisfy purists. Large parties must book weekend nights. Closed Sun evening and (usually) Mon noon.
€€€–€€€€

Sea Star
Sofokléous 24, Old Town
Tel: 22410 22117
This relatively inexpensive yet quality seafood outlet offers a limited menu of scaly fish (the seared June tuna is ace), shellfish and starters like kápari (pickled caper shoots), chunky grilled eggplant salad and koliós pastós (salt-cured mackerel). Seating is indoors during the cooler months (not open midwinter), otherwise outside on the little square. €€

Mavrikos
Main taxi square, Líndos

Tel: 22440 31232
This family-run restaurant, going since 1933, is rated among Rhodes' best for its extensive menu of creative oven-cooked dishes and seafood (with less prominent meat dishes). *Gígandes* in carob syrup, sweet marinated sardines, or beetroot in goat-cheese sauce precede mains like cured tuna with grilled fennel, lamb-liver chunks sautéed with chillis, or pork belly slabs in grape molasses. Excellent (and expensive) Greek wine list. Open Apr–Nov. €€€€

Perigiali
By fishing anchorage, Stegná
Tel: 22440 23444
Locals come to eat on a raised, tree-studded patio for the excellent seafood like *soupiá* in its own ink, savoury, hand-cut round chips, homemade *yaprákia* (stuffed vine leaves) and ample salads sufficient for two (the 'Perigiali' one has caper greens and grilled aubergine) washed down by good bulk wine. The travertine-clad loos are certainly unique on Rhodes. Open all year. €€

Pigi Fasouli
Psínthos outskirts
Tel: 22410 50071
Vegetable starters here include chunky aubergine salad and beets with their greens, or expertly fried vegetable slices with skordaliá; mains comprise goat in various guises, a few meat-based casserole dishes, or simply grilled lamb chops. You have to ask if you want to try the owner's own, off-menu bulk wine. The outside terrace overlooks the shady oasis and spring (pigí) here. Open Apr–Oct 9am–10pm, Nov–Mar weekends only. €€

Platanos
Lower platía, Lahaniá village
Tel: 22440 46027
The most attractive village-centre setting on Rhodes, under the plane trees after which the restaurant is named, beside two gushing Ottoman fountains. The *mezédes* (*dolmádes*, *húmmus*, *kopanistí*) are top-notch, as are the mains, though fish here is as pricey as elsewhere. Open all year (weekends only winter). €€

Plimiri Beach
Beside Zöodóhou Pigís church, Plimýri Bay
Tel: 22440 46003
This ever popular, very welcoming fish taverna is well placed for lunch on a tour around the island. Presentation (and to some extent prices) are 1980s-style, with excellent chips and a few starters accompanying a wide selection of fresh fish – pick yours from the display. They do wonders with ordinarily disdained species like

kéfalos (grey mullet) and *drákena* (weever). Open Apr–Oct noon until late. €€

Paros

Anna
Dryós, through road
Tel: 22840 41015
It's well worth tearing yourself away from nearby beaches to lunch at this beacon of *magirevtá*, with dishes including *anginátes* a la *políta* (artichoke hearts with carrots and dill), stuffed squash and *katsíki lemonáto*, complemented by their own bulk wine. Secluded upstairs patio seating, or inside a cheery salon at street level. Open late March to early November. €€€

Apoplous
South quay, Alykí
Tel: 22840 91935
www.apoplous.gr
Reckoned the best of several in a line here at Páros' most authentic fishing port, Apoplous features Sífnos-style lamb-in-clay-pot, *goúna* (sun-dried mackerel), *paximadokoúloura* (the Parian versian of *dákos*) and lots of fresh seafood. Tipple is either decent bulk wine or a reasonable bottled list. Open Feb–15 Dec. €€€

Koukoutsi
Back of National Bank square, Parikiá
Tel: 6978 408504
Equal parts café, bar and *ouzerí*, this bohemian joint is always packed for the sake of reasonable tipple – especially strong bulk *rakí* – excellent platters, and the buzz. Just two or three tables inside, eight or nine more popular ones outside. Open 9am until whenever, all year. €€

Lemoni
Seafront, about 200m beyond windmill, Parikiá
Tel: 6984 474111
Only opened in 2012, but already causing a sensation for its creative cooking at decidedly normal prices. Some of the fusions – *revytháda* with *taramosaláta*, beets with pear-and-yogurt sauce – are a bit outré, but a salad of spinach, rocket, pomegranate seeds, walnuts, raisins, soft cheese and tomatini hits the spot. Mains – mostly meat and poultry, but also such as *atherína* in sesame crust – are solid, as are desserts like mousse, cheesecake or carrot cake. Strictly Greek wine list. Service is jolly and efficient. A plank-floored conservatory and artistic interior permit all-year operation. €€

Moskhonas
Old port quay, Náoussa
Tel: 22840 51623
The least expensive, most down-to-

earth of several waterfront options in a rather twee setting. Presentation and fare is basic and sustaining rather than elegant, but the family has their own boat and it is popular. Fare might include *frýssa*, giant autumn sardines of breeding size. Open most of the year. €€

Santoríni

Anemomylos
Ía,Perivolás district
Tel: 22860 71410
Forego the crowds, the caldera view and the expense along Ía's main pedestrian street and head here instead for honest magirevtá (like the best local moussakás) prepared by a chef with years of experience cooking on ships. And yes, there is a partial view north toward Baxédes beach. Open Apr–Oct. €€

Anogi
Imerovígli, central square
Tel: 22860 21285
Again, diners are rewarded for passing on a caldera view at this ever-popular taverna (reservations mandatory in season) with creative Greek recipes like shrimp *moussakás*, *bekrí mezé* mixing two meats, stuffed *biftéki* and a full range of desserts. The wine list highlights microwineries from across Greece. Service is necessarily brisk, given the wait for tables, but friendly. Open daily 2pm–midnight. €€€

Metaxy Mas
Éxo Goniá, 100m down steps from top church
Tel: 22860 31323
www.santorini-metaximas.gr
The proprietor hails from Haniá, so there's a Cretan flair to the menu here: Sfakian *píttes*, *apáki* (lean cured pork), *stamnagáthi* greens, the tumbler of *rakí* that comes with your generous bread basket stocked with local soft cheese. There are also local dishes like *fáva* and white eggplant, and the bulgur wheat topped with lamb in yogurt sauce is stellar. Seating is either on outdoor terraces looking to Anáfi, or inside the vaulted old converted house. Open 1pm until late, all year. €€

Psaraki
Vlyháda

PRICE CATEGORIES

Prices indicated are for a meal per person with modest intake of wine, beer, raki or tsípouro.
€€€€ = over €35
€€€ = €25–35
€€ = €15–25
€ = under €15

TRANSPORT

ACCOMMODATION

EATING OUT

ACTIVITIES

A – Z

LANGUAGE

Tel: 22860 82783
Quite possibly the best seafood/
mezédes taverna for the money
on Santoríni, with views over the
island's main fishing/yacht port to
the Khristiana islets. Savour non-
mushy *gígandes* beans in lemon
sauce, white eggplant salad, grilled
marinated rooster, or *lakérda* (bonito)
done perfectly medium rare – and
save room for desserts like pear
poached in *asýrtiko* wine. Sticking to
mezédes, dishes of the day and the
Karamelengos bulk wine will land you
in the lower price category. Open daily
Apr–Oct. €€€€

Selene
Pýrgos Village
Tel: 22860 22249
www.selene.gr
The upstairs restaurant, run by a chef
famous for his revival of local cuisine
(and cooking courses), represents
a major outlay. The downstairs
"Café-Winebar-Delicatessen", with
similar sweeping views, will do for
most people, having an equally wide-
ranging menu encompassing "local"
salad with cheese, squid sautéed
with greens, eggplant salad with
octopus carpaccio, and a battery of
desserts including chocolate mousse
doused in rose-geranium sauce or
cappuccino pudding. Bulk wine is
"easy drinking"; staff could stand to
be a bit jollier. Café open daily noon–
11pm. €€€€

Sérifos

Fagopoti (Nikoulias)
Avlomónas beach
Tel: 22810 52595

Much the best taverna for the
money in the Livádi area, with
generously proportioned *biftóki*,
expertly butterflied sardines, chunky
tyrokafterí or eggplant salad, and
island wine by the kilo, served with a
smile. Open all year. €

Petros
Hóra
Tel: 22810 51302
Of the handful of tavernas up here,
this works the longest season, and
is open at lunch. Stresses *magirevtá*,
including bean dishes, eggplant in
the oven and stews, plus island bulk
wine. €

Sífnos

Leonidas
Kástro
Tel: 22840 31153
Basic-appearing but very
accomplished shrine of *magirevtá*
such as *revytháda*, *moussakás*, rabbit
stew and grilled *mastéllo* cheese, with
views to match. €

Tou Apostoli to Koutouki
Apollonía, Stenó district
Tel: 22840 33186
Upscale eatery that's a good place
to try the clay-pot, meat-based
casseroles that the island is known
for. €€

Sýros

Apano Hora
Áno Sýros
Tel: 22810 80565
By day a popular *kafenío* thanks to its
terrace view, after dark this becomes
an *ouzerí*, often with live acoustic
music at weekends. Titbits may

include carrot-and-cheese turnovers,
local sausages and a dish of the day
or two. Again, very popular terrace.
€€

Iliovassilema
Galissás beach
Tel: 22810 43325
Much the best taverna in this
resort, with creative renditions of
local dishes, like fennel pie and
crunchy *atherína*. Open May–early
Oct. €€

Kyma
Fínikas, mid-beach
Tel: 22801 43526
One of several tavernas here, Kyma
stands out for good value in a
resort and a long operating season.
Signature dishes include thick, fiery
kopanistí, *hórta*, and of course the
local sausages. €€

Lilis
Áno Sýros
Tel: 22810 88087
Huge place, with a very popular
outdoor terrace, where the food
emphasises meat dishes and salads.
There's often live *rebétika* music at
weekends; *rebétika* great, Markos
Vamvakaris, was born in this village
and played in the basement annexe
in 1955. €€

Oinopnevmata
Emmanouíl Roïdi 9, Ermoúpoli
Tel: 22810 82616
The most low-key and reasonable
of the places along "Taverna Row"
east of Platía Miaoúli, with local
sausages, coiled cheese pie, a
version of fennel pie, and probably
panna cotta dessert on the house.
Open all year. €€

DODECANESE

Astypálea

Australia
Just inland from the head of the bay, Skála
Tel: 22430 61275
Kyria Maria presides over the oldest
and most wholesome taverna here,
with fresh seafood and island wine.
Open Apr–Nov. €€

Maïstrali (Tou Penindara)
Head of the harbour, Skála
Tel: 22430 61691
The best spot for a local lobster
banquet, or less extravagantly, a
scaly-fish meal or *magirevtá* from a
broad menu. Open all year for dinner,
lunch as per demand. €€€

To Yerani
In the streambed just behind Livádia
beach
Tel: 22430 61484
The most consistently good taverna

here, renowned for its excellent
magirevtá . Open May–Oct. €

Hálki
Paradosiako Piato tis Lefkosias, Emborió
quay
Tel: 6946 978151
For years, wherever Lefkosia Peraki
was cooking was the top eatery on
Hálki, and her recipes have even
been featured on the BBC. Since
2009, she's had her own restaurant,
featuring elaborate baked dishes,
grills, laboriously concocted *orektiká*
and own-sourced ingredients – which
means everything from her own
livestock and olive oil to home-baked
bread. Open Apr–Oct. €€

Kálymnos

Kafenes
Platía Hristoú, opposite municipal

"palace", Póthia
Tel: 22430 28727
Going since 1950, this hole-in-the-
wall purveys seafood *mezédes*,
great local cheese and salads,
with *laïká* music cranked up loud.
Throw in very low prices, and it's
easy to see why you always wait for
a table. €

Pandelis
Behind Olympic Hotel, Ágios Nikólaos
district
Tel: 22430 51508
The menu only mentions the
ubiquitous Kalymnian *mermizéli* salad
(like Cretan *dákos*) and a few grills
or *magirevtá*; you have to ask after
scaly fish, and fresh shellfish such
as *kalógnomes* (like big mussels),
strídia (round oysters) and *foúskes*
(indescribable). €€

Kárpathos

Gorgona
South end of quay, Diafáni
Tel: 22450 51509
A versatile café-restaurant with offerings blending Greek-style salads and seafood with real Italian-standard coffees, lovely desserts and limoncello liqueur. Does breakfast too. Open all day April–Oct. €€

Dramoundana
Mesohóri, near chuch of Panagía Vryssianí
Tel: 22450 71373
Remarkably reasonably priced, this features local caper greens, village sausages and marinated *ménoules* (a sort of large sardine). €

Iy Orea Karpathos
Southeast end of main quay, Pigádia
Tel: 22450 22501
The best all-round taverna in the port, with palatable local bulk wine, *trahanádes* soup and great spinach pie. The locals treat it as an ouzerí, so it's fine to order just a few *orektiká* to accompany a *karafáki* (small pitcher) or a katroútso of Óthos wine. €

Pine Tree
Ádia, 7km (4 miles) north of Finíki
Tel: 6977 369948
Sustaining, reasonable rural taverna with country fare like lentils and *htapodomakaronáda* (octopus in pasta), washed down by sweet Óthos wine. Sea-view terrace under the trees of the name. €

Kastellórizo

Akrothalassi
Southwest corner of quay
Tel: 22460 49052
The most consistently salubrious fish and meat grills, reliably open at lunch too (unusual here), owing to shade from its arbour. €€

Ypomoni
Mid-quay, Megísti
Tel: 22460 49224
Supper-only seafood specialists (plus a few meat grills) with minimalist presentation, minimalist prices, minimal seating and maximum freshness – so expect to wait for a table. €

Kós

Ambavris
Ambávris hamlet, 800 metres (1/2 mile) south of Kós Town
Tel: 22420 25696
Ignore the perfunctory English-language menu in favour of the constantly changing *mezédes pikilía* or house medley – six platters for about €25 can encompass such delights as *pihtí* (brawn), stuffed squash blossoms, *fáva* dip, *loukánika*. Courtyard

seating. Open for supper May–Oct. €€

Makis
One lane in from front, Mastihári
Tel: 22420 51592
Currently the best – and best-priced – fish on the island outside of Kós Town, and an excellent spot to wait for the ro-ro ferry to Kálymnos. No magirevtá, just a few salads and dips, and oblique sea views at best mean relatively few tourists. €€€

Oromedon
Zía approach road
Tel: 22420 69983
One of the few tavernas here that doesn't need to rely on picture-menus and other gimmicks, thanks to the prime view from its roof terrace, and the good, local food. Open all year. €€

Platáni village
Central junction
Ethnic Turkish management at several clustered establishments dish out tasty Anatolian-style *mezédes* and kebabs; best go in a group so that you can pass the little platters around. The most popular, if the most touristy, is **Arap** (tel: 22420 28442, €€); if you can't get in, head across the way to **Asklipios**, which fills with locals later in the evening. Between November and April, these close, leaving **Gin's Place** a few steps further inland (tel: 22420 25166, €€) – where the food is often even better – as the sole option. At any season, finish off with an Anatolian ice cream, best on the island, at **Zaharoplastio Iy Paradosi** opposite the three summer restaurants.

Pote tin Kyriaki
Pissándrou 9, Kós Town
Tel: 22420 48460
Going since 1997, Kos' only genuine *mezedopolío* has signature platters like *marathópita* (fennel pie), *kavourdistí* (pork fry up) and assorted seafood at friendly prices, complemented by proprietress Stamatia's very strong bulk *tsikoudiá* (distilled spirit), and a soundtrack of Greek music for Greeks, not tourists. Open summer Mon–Sat dinner only, winter Fri–Sat. €

Léros

Dimitris O Karaflas
Spiliá district, on road between Pandélli and Vromólithos
Tel: 22470 25626
The heartiest food on the island, hands down, and the best view of Vromólithos. Stars include chunky, herby Lerian sausages, potato salad, *hanoúm bórek* (stuffed with cheese and *pastourmás* or cured meat). Moderate prices and large portions. Open most of the year. €

Mylos
Out by the sea-marooned windmill, Agía Marína
Tel: 22470 24894
The most romantic setting on the island, whether for lunch or supper. Specialities include *garidopílafo* (shrimp-rice), baked four-cheese casserole and *kolokythokeftédes* (courgette patties). Open mid-Mar–late Sept; reservations mandatory July–Aug, when Turkish yachters crowd the place. €€

Psaropoula (Apostolis)
Pandélli beach
Tel: 22470 25200
A good balance of fresh seafood and magirevtá especially popular with locals at weekends. Open and enclosed sea-view terraces, so open most of the year. €€

Lipsí

Dilaila
Katsadiá, left-hand bay
Tel: 22470 41041
Incongruously classy for the rural surroundings, with platters such as fish with rosemary, saffron rice, excellent fáva. Open June–Sept. €€

Giannis
Mid-quay
Tel: 22470 41395
Excellent all-rounder, with meat and seafood grills but plenty of salads and laderá dishes for vegetarians too. The only taverna open for lunch as well as supper all season long. Open early May–early Oct. €€

Marathi

To Marathi
Southeast end of Maráthi beach
Tel: 22470 31580
The more welcoming of two establishments here, with simple fish and free-range goat served up by piratically garbed Mihalis Kavouras, at attractive prices. Open all day, according to Mihalis' whim. €

Nísyros

Apyria (Triandafyllos)
Emborió
Tel: 22420 31377
The former *kafenío* of this all-but-abandoned village has been transformed into the best meat

PRICE CATEGORIES

Prices indicated are for a meal per person with modest intake of wine, beer, rakí or tsípouro.
€€€€ = over €35
€€€ = €25–35
€€ = €15–25
€ = under €15

Marinated anchovies make for an excellent starter.

taverna on the island – *gouronópoulo* on the spit during summer, otherwise just a few *mezédes* and select meat platters daily at very fair prices, with local *halvás* for dessert. Indoor/outdoor seating. Open all year (weekends only winter). €

Limenari
Limenari cove west of Pálli
Tel: 22420 31023
Expect fair prices and portions for salads, fish, a few dishes of the day, and made-to-order *tyrokafterí* (which takes a while to arrive). A lovely spot in a terraced valley above the bay. Islanders and conscript soldiers go all year, always a good sign. €

To Ankyrovoli
Ágios Sávvas cove, Mandráki
Tel: 22420 31552
The reincarnation of the late lamented Fabrika, this ouzerí features pittiá (courgette and chickpea patties), *boukouniés* (fried pork), bulk wine from Attica, taped Greek sounds and big portions at moderate prices. €€

Benetos
Sápsila cove, 2km (1 mile) southeast of Skála
Tel: 22470 33089
www.benetosrestaurant.com
This eatery has a reputation as one

of the best spots on the island for Mediterranean/Pacific Rim fusion cuisine, with a stress on seafood. Open June–late Sept, supper only except Mon; must reserve in summer, for three rigid seating times. €€€€

Ktima Petra
Pétra beach, south of Gríkou
Tel: 22470 33207
www.ktimapetra.gr
Hands down the best beach taverna on the island. Chunky *melitzanosaláta*, lush rocket salad, and pork *giovétsi* are typical of lunchtime offerings, with excellent retsína from Thebes; at sunset, the grill is lit, and still later the place becomes a full-on bar. Open 1 May–7 Oct; lunch only low season. €€

Livadi Geranou
Above eponymous beach
Tel: 6972 497426
Doesn't look like much, but this taverna has a cult following for the sake of its coarse-cut *hórta*, roast goat and seafood dishes – plus views over the entire island. €

Trehandiri
Main lane to Hókhlakas, Skála
Tel: 22470 34080
Opened in 2012 and already a contender for most popular ouzerí in town, overtaking other old favourites like Ostria and Hiliomodi. No sea view

– no view at all, in fact – but honest portions of starters and all manner of seafood. Open most of the year. €

Dimitris
South quay near ferry dock, Gialós
Tel: 22460 72207
Excellent, family-run, seafood-strong ouzerí with exotic items such as *hohlióalo* (sea snails), *foúskes* (mock oysters), *spinóalo* (pinna-shell flesh) and the indigenous miniature shrimps, as well as more usual platters. Lunch and supper. €€

Georgios
Top of Kalí Stráta, Horió
Tel: 22460 71984
An island institution; nouvelle Greek cuisine in large, non-nouvelle portions, served on the pebbled courtyard. Informal live music some nights. €€

Mythos
South quay, Gialós
Tel: 22460 71488
A supper-only ouzerí that is reckoned among the best-value cooking on the island. Ignore the menu and let chef Stavros deliver a Frenchified medley which may well include salad, seafood starters, or meat followed by home-made desserts. Open late May–Oct. €€€

Kastro
Megálo Horió
Tel: 22460 44232
The managing family can be a bit dour, but it's worth putting up with them for their excellent own-raised meat, goat cheese and *dolmádes*, served at the best terrace on the island. €

Omonia (Mihalis')
Just above the harbour square
Tel: 22460 44287
Sit under the trees strung with fairy lights and enjoy the closest thing to an authentic ouzerí on the island by night; filling breakfasts in the morning. €

To Armenon (Nikos')
On the shore road, Livádia
Tel: 22460 44134
Excellent and salubrious beach-taverna-cum-ouzerí; Alfa beer on tap. €€

NORTHEASTERN AEGEAN

Kali Kardia
Top end of high street, Foúrni town
Tel: 22750 51217

When you tire of overpriced seafood on the front, head inland here for a solid meat feed, including *kokorétsi* (innard roulade) and *kondosoúvli*

straight from the spit turning outside. The meat is all from neighbouring Sámos, proudly proclaims the owner. €

Híos

Fabrika
Volissós, lower platía
Tel: 22740 22045
www.chiosfabrika.gr
As the name suggests, this taverna is installed in a former olive/flour mill, with the machinery left in situ. Ingredients for their salads, eggplant-based dishes and beets are all grown by the management, while chops, kondosoúvli and kokorétsi are all locally sourced. Excellent bulk wine from the nearby Ariousios winery. Open most of the year, with seating indoors or out on the flagstone terrace. **€**

Ikhthyoskala
Desperately unromantic setting by the fish plant, but tables are right on the water and the food is to die for: fiery kopanistí, fresh koukiá beans in lemon sauce, fáva, radíkio, koutsomoúra done to perfection, sundried grilled savrídi fish. Open all year, dinner only. **€€**

Kapileio
Central Thymianá
Tel: 22710 32453
Tuck into top-notch seafood like butterflied skorpiós, and all the usual vegetarian mezédes plus every local oúzo, in the lovely walled garden out back. Open all year. **€€**

Mylarakia €€
Tambákika district, by Híos Town Hospital
Tel: 22710 41412
All eight brands of Hiot oúzo available at keen prices to accompany starters, seafood and some meat dishes. Unbeatably romantic setting on a terrace looking to the three mills of the name. Supper all year; lunch on occasion. **€€**

Passas
Langáda harbour
Tel: 22710 74218
Locals come to this east-coast port especially for a seafood meal; this outfit, with seating under eucalypts, is the most professional of several here, with a mix of fishy (and meaty) standards. **€€**

Ikaría

Arodou
Xylosýrtis, 5km west of Ágios Kírykos
Tel: 22750 22700
If you have transport, give all the port eateries a miss and head out to this superb tavern next to the church on the shoreline. So far, mainly Greeks go – it's been featured in a number of national publications. Daily lunch and dinner, closed Mon off-season. **€€**

Mandouvala
Karavóstamo
Tel: 22750 61204

An enchanting setting in this little-visited port, with a terrace almost swamped by the surf, and food nearly as good as the setting: all the usual ouzerí suspects plus Ikarian suspects like soúfiko (the local ratatouille). The name, in case you were wondering, comes from a popular song of the 1960s. May–Oct daily. **€**

Paskhalia
Armenistís
Tel: 22750 71302
Reliable source of fish grills and dishes of the day, as well as full breakfasts, served ideally on the little terrace overlooking the port. The first tavern to open here (May), the last to close (sometime in October). **€€**

Thea
Nás
Tel: 22750 71491
Returned Ohio-Ikarian lady oversees the best magirevtá this end of the island, with lots of vegetarian dishes. Service can suffer a hit during the crush. Daily dinner June–Sept, lunch also mid-summer, Sat–Sun only in winter. **€€**

Lésvos

Anemoessa
Skála Sykaminiás, closest to the harbour chapel
Tel: 22530 55360
Tops for fresh fish, and good mezédes. Open all year (weekends only Nov–Apr). **€€–€€€**

Balouhanas
Géra Gulf seafront, Pérama
Tel: 22510 51948
Seafood ouzerí with wood-kiosk seating overhanging the water; interesting mezédes and home-made desserts too. Open all year. **€€**

Captain's Table
Fishing harbour, Mólyvos
Tel: 22530 71241
As the name suggests, a strong line in seafood but also meat and vegetable specialities such as their "Ukrainian" aubergine dip, as well as good own-label wine. Open May–late Oct. **€€**

Kornárou
2, corner Ermoú, Mytilíni Town
Tel: 22510 26232
The best and most atmospheric ouzerí of a cluster in Páno Skálo district. Special strengths are sardines, sausages and, Smyrna-style meatballs. **€€**

Taverna tou Panaï
Ágios Isídoros, north edge of village
Tel: 22520 31920
Plainly presented but tasty food: vegetarian mezédes, grills, cheese and so on. Mostly Greek clientele; open all year. **€€**

To Petri
Petrí village, in the hills above Pétra/Mólyvos
Tel: 22530 41239
Friendly, family-run taverna serving magirevtá and grills; unbeatable terrace. Open May–mid-Oct. **€€**

Límnos

Iy Glaropoula
Néa Koútali
Tel: 22540 92325
This is the place for a seafood blowout, with bay views from the terrace. **€€**

O Hristos
Platía of Tsimándria
Tel: 22540 51278
Very cheap, very cheerful, with a nice, quiet location. From amongst grills and a few magirevtá, tick your choices off on the menu-bill combo. Open all year. **€**

Man-Tella
Sardés centre
Tel: 22540 61349
Cult taverna doubling as the central kafenío (thus open all year) of this highest hill village on Límnos. Big portions off a meat-strong menu; good service. **€€**

Tzitzifies
Rihá Nerá beach
Tel: 22540 23756
A proper taverna at this town beach, with tables on the sand. Good ímam baildí, dips and baked dishes. **€–€€**

Sámos

Artemis (Kopanas)
Kefalopoúlou 4, near old ferry dock, Vathý
Tel: 22730 23639
For some years now the best taverna in town, with good hórta and fáva, excellent seafood platters like steamed skate-wing with skordaliá, plus standard meat mains. The smooth red bulk wine from Manolátes won't leave you hung over. Open daily lunch and dinner except Sun night. **€€**

Donna Rosa
Avlákia
Tel: 22730 94703
The tables are right at water level at this organic restaurant, giving the best north-coastal view on the island. Aris and Rosanna specialise

PRICE CATEGORIES

Prices indicated are for a meal per person with modest intake of wine, beer, rakí or tsípouro.
€€€€ = over €35
€€€ = €25–35
€€ = €15–25
€ = under €15

in unusual vegetarian dishes, heaping salads, exquisite seafood and homemade desserts, as well as good bulk wine. Open daily in season, weekends only winter. €€

Glaros
Iréon seafront
Tel: 22730 95457
A friendly family originally from nearby Agathoníssi runs this basic, popular terrace taverna with heaping portions of scaly fish or cephalopods and superior starters like *hórta*, *dolmádes* and squash rissoles. Watching the full moon rise over Turkey in August is a favourite activity and you'll wait for a table then. Open all year. €

Kallisti
Manolátes
Tel: 22730 94661
All three central Manolátes tavernas are excellent, but Kallisti is the favourite thanks to the lovely Magda, heart and soul of the place, dishing out hearty stews (lamb-, goat- or pork-based) and starters like non-greasy spinach pie. Very quaffable bulk wine – beware as the road down to the coast is tricky. Daily lunch and dinner in season, weekends only otherwise. €

Kryfi Folia
Platanákia district of Kérveli
Tel: 22730 25905 or 6937 219315
Near the east tip of Sámos in an isolated olive grove, this recently revamped taverna under new ownership has kept the previous menu featuring competent starters and grilled seafood. Open Easter– early Oct. €

Kyma
Ríva district shoreline, Karlóvassi
Tel: 22730 34017
Long-running ouzeri with titbits like lamb tongues and some of the freshest shrimp around, as well as economical oúzo in bulk. Great sunset-watching from the terrace in the right months. Open nightly May to early October. €

Tarsanas
Little lane 100 metres in from west beach
Kokkári
Tel: 22730 92337
The stock-in-trade at this 1970s throwback are thick-crust pizzas and perhaps two casserole dishes of the day – like the best moussakás in town – at bargain prices. Catch the sea breeze at seating in the lane, or at much-sought-after tables down by the beach. Open May–Oct dinner only. €

Samothráki

1900
Hóra
Tel: 25510 41222
With superb views from its vine- shaded terrace, this welcoming spot is the island's best taverna, serving up the likes of stuffed goat and a range of vegetable dishes. €€

To Perivoli T'Ouranou
Near Thermá
Tel: 25510 98313
Boasting a lush green setting on the road to Gría Váthra, this highly seasonal taverna offers a good range of mezédes, tender grills and often hosts live music. €€

Thásos

Iy Pigi
Central platía, Liménas
Tel: 25930 22941
Old standby dishing out dependable magirevtá next to the spring of the name; best at supper. €€

Opos Palia
Under the central tree, Sotíros village
Tel: 69796 35703
It's no accident the owner chose to call this place "Like the old (days)" because he creates wonderful dishes from simple traditional recipes such as bekri meze. €€

Syrtaki
East waterfront, Liménas
Tel: 69553 04897
Plenty of locals as well as tourists flock here for the excellent fresh fish, ample salads and very palatable barrelled wine. €€€

SPORADES AND ÉVVIA

Alónissos

Elaionas
Leftós Gialós beach
Tel: 24240 66066
The better of two decent tavernas here, with unusual platters like *tsitsírava*, *xynógalos*, other chunky dips and daily specials prepared by three generations of family ladies toiling in the kitchen. Outdoor seating in a gravel court under the olives of the name. May–Sept only. €€

Iy Mouria
Harbour end of the access road, Vótsi
Tel: 24240 65273
Friendly, family-run, inexpensive option with big salads, a couple of magirevtá of the day, ace squid, and bulk wine. They rent rooms upstairs too. €

Évvia

Apanemo
Shoreline at Fanári district, Halkída
Tel: 22210 22614
Halkída is famous for its seafood, so there's no excuse for tolerating the hit-and-miss performance of certain midtown outfits. This seafood taverna has one of the best settings, easiest parking and some of the best food – on the pricey side but worth it. €€€

To Pyrofani (Livaditis)
Límni, northwest end of quay
Tel: 22270 31640
Slightly bumped-up prices for average portions at this seafood-strong ouzerí are justified by the quality, with nice touches like sweet-cabbage marinade as a side dish, and big salads. Stick to their oúzo, as the bulk wine is not a strong point. They also rent decent apartments nearby. €€

Skiáthos

Amfiliki
South edge of town by clinic
Tel: 24270 22839
Good smells wafting out the kitchen up front are the clue you've arrived. Out back, limited seating – about 40 places – with unlimited views of Mégas Gialós bay. The food lives up to the setting, especially off-menu seafood specials like *bráska kípo* (monkfish in spicy tomato sauce), and seafood salad. It's open winter too, with the fireplace going. €€

Alexandros
Old Town, 2 blocks in from fishing port
Tel: 24270 22431
Good grills (especially the lamb chops) and oven dishes, home-made crème caramel for dessert – so it's a shame about the poor bulk wine. Greeks in attendance provide singalongs with acoustic bouzouki and guitar. There's winter seating in a small house opposite, otherwise outside under the mulberry bushes. Dinner only. €

Bakaliko
Airport road
Tel: 24270 24024
Probably the most accomplished of several eateries here in a strip more known for nightlife, with mock decor of a traditional Greek grocer's, unusual takes on traditional recipes and unimprovable seating cantilevered over the water. Live acoustic Greek music some nights. Dinner only. €€

Skópelos

In Hóra (the main harbour), the west quay is the place to eat and where locals go.

Englezos
West quay near dimarhío
Tel: 24240 22230
The creative Greek menu varies by the year, but might include aubergine croquettes with mint and cheese, rock samphire, and a variety of lamb dishes, all done with panache. To drink, bulk wine from the Anhíalos co-op, and delicately perfumed brandy. €€

Klimataria
Right next to dimarhío
Tel: 24240 22273
The best place for reasonable (for Skópelos) fish by weight, plus a few cooked dishes and mezédes – locals conspicuously in attendance. €€

Kymata (Angelos)
Far north end of quay, Hóra
Tel: 24240 22381
About the oldest taverna here, run by an engaging family and renowned for its elaborate magirevtá such as lamb and vegetables in phyllo triangles; also, good eggplant salad and real beets with greens attached. €

Pavlos
Agnóndas port
Tel: 24240 22409
Reliable fish specialist with fair prices, also doing unusual mezédes like tsitsírava (wild pistachio sprouts); good bulk wine from Apostolakis, a local Thessalian vintner. The best of three choices here; waterside seating under trees. Open Mar–Oct. €€

Skýros

Istories tou Barba
Magaziá/Mólos beach boundary
Tel: 22220 91453
Excellent, creative cuisine stressing seafood at friendly prices guarantees a crush here much of the time, especially given the loveliest sea-view terrace on the island. Oddly, Cretan music preferred for their soundtrack. Open all year. €€

Maïstros
Linariá
Tel: 22220 93431
Behind a plane tree on what passes for the central square here, this friendly taverna-ouzerí does an excellent job of mezédes, seafood titbits and local meat platters, washed down by bulk Skyros rosé. Not just for lunch before a departing ferry, but good enough to make a detour here for dinner. €

Perasma
Start of airport slip road
Tel: 22220 92911
The airport staff and seemingly half the air force personnel on the island eat here, knowing a good thing: succulent own-raised meat and cheese dishes, at reasonable prices, plus the inevitable island wine. Seating outdoors or in, according to weather. Open all year. €

CORFU

Kérkyra Town

Hryssomallis (Babis)
Nikifórou Theotókou 6, Kérkyra
Tel: 26610 30342
The sign says zythopsitopolío ('beer-hall-grill'), but it's actually the last traditional oven-food place in the Old Town: stews, hórta, mousakás, stuffed cabbage leaves, lentil soup and so forth, accompanied by smooth but potent red wine. From the outside tables on the street you can just see the Listón. The Durrells ate here during their 1930s stay; the restaurant has been around even longer. Open daily noon–10.30pm. €

Mouragia
Arseníou 15, north quay, Kérkyra Town
Tel: 26610 33815
A good mix of seafood such as flash-fried atherína (sand smelt) and Corfiot specialities such as sofríto and pastitsáda, plus competent starters at this seaside ouzerí – though views to the sea, and Vídos islet, are over the road. Open Apr–Nov noon–12.30am. €€

Rex
Kapodistríou 66, behind Listón
Tel: 26610 39649.
Established in 1932, the Rex is something of a Kérkyra Town institution. Signature dishes include fish soup (in winter), orange-fleshed squash turnover, portobello mushrooms with cheese and other generic Mediterranean recipes. Tables outdoors, or inside (dress up a bit for the latter). Open daily all day. €€€

Tsipouradiko
Prosaléndou 8–10, behind the Efetío (Appeals Court), Spiliá
Tel: 26610 82240.
Tsípouro is the distilled grape-mash spirit popular on the mainland (but also many islands), accompanied here by such platters as grilled mushrooms, courgette pie, tiganiá (pork stir-fry), little fishes, and eggplant specialities. There is also decent bulk wine. The place is always packed with students and the bohemian set thanks to the warm atmosphere and friendly prices. Smoking allowed in the upstairs loft, or outside in the summer courtyard. Large groups must reserve, or be prepared for a long wait. Open Mon–Sat 8pm–1am. €

Around the Island

Alonaki Bay
Paralía Alonáki, near Korissíon lagoon
Tel: 26610 75872
Good country recipes, strong on vegetables and seafood at shady tables on a terrace overlooking the sea. Their version of biánko, with kéfalos (grey mullet) hygienically raised in the lake and garnished with marsh samphire (Salicornia europaea), is to die for. Locals, and free-range chickens underfoot, usually outnumber tourists here – a good endorsement. If you can't tear yourself away from this lovely spot, they have inexpensive rooms to rent upstairs as well. Open daily Apr–Oct lunch and dinner. €€

Boukari Beach
Boúkari, 4km (2.5 miles) beyond Mesongí, 600m before the jetty
Tel: 26620 51791
www.boukaribeach.gr
The best of the seafood tavernas at this seashore hamlet, in an idyllic setting with spectacular views up Corfu's east coast. Typical offerings might include mussels as a starter, heaping salads, succulent octopus and a range of patently fresh scaly fish at fair prices. The Vlahopoulos family are accomplished hosts, and also have accommodation (see page 368). Open lunch and dinner, Easter–Oct. €€€

Etrusco
Just outside Káto Korakiána village, on the Dassiá road
Tel: 26610 93342

PRICE CATEGORIES

Prices indicated are for a meal per person with modest intake of wine, beer, rakí or tsípouro.
€€€€ = over €35
€€€ = €25–35
€€ = €15–25
€ = under €15

www.etrusco.gr
Top-calibre nouvelle Italian cooking by father, son and spouses, served in a carefully restored country manor. Specialities like pappardelle with duck and truffles, octopus carpaccio, lamb baked with garlic and kumquat sauce and a 200-label wine list don't come cheap, but this has been ranked as one of the best five Greek tavernas outside of Athens. Advance reservations required. Open Apr–Oct, supper only. €€€€

Foros
Paleá Períthia
Tel: 26955 950459
One of the first tavernas in this once-deserted Venetian village, working out of a former café on the original square, and still one of the best – Rick Stein has called in approvingly. The emphasis here is on grills, but you can have a very enjoyable mezédes-only meal – sausages, kremydópita (onion turnover), stuffed peppers – while downing tsípouro or bulk wine. Save room for their famous karydópita (walnut cake)

with ice cream. Open daily May–Oct, weekends only otherwise. **€**

Fagopotion
Ágios Stéfanos Sinión
Tel: 26630 82020
The most accomplished of the several waterside tavernas here, Fagopotion only opened in 2008 but has already established an enviable reputation for its traditional recipes, fresh (not farmed) fish caught around the Diapóndia islets and fair prices given the posh location. Signature dishes include roast lamb, rabbit stew, chard-based tsigarélli and melt-in-the-mouth octopus (it's blanched prior to grilling). Kosta's rosé bulk wine is interesting. Open daily for lunch and dinner Easter–Oct, Fri/Sat dinner and Sun lunch otherwise. **€€€**

Klimataria tou Bellou
Main square, Benítses
Tel: 26610 71201
www.klimataria-restaurant.gr
Cult seafood taverna known for purveying only fresh items, and for assiduous service from father-and-son team Nikos and Kostas. Fish

is sold by portion or by weight, and includes some innovative dishes like sardine bourdéto; starters like leek salad and steamed mussels are commendable too. Good Neméa bulk white wine. Blink and you'll miss the mere eight tables outside, so reservations are highly advisable. Open Mon–Sat dinner only, Sunday lunch; winter weekends only, but closed 1 Dec–15 Jan. **€€**

Nikolas
Agní cove, south end
Tel: 26630 91243
www.agnibay.com
This taverna is the oldest one here, built as a family home and café in 1892. Today, Perikles and his family serve Corfiot specialities like eggplant-and-cheese bourékia and lamb kapamá, along with their own wines (the bulk red is excellent). Service usually copes well with typical crowds. Tear yourself away from the picturesque view to browse the old photos and maps lining the walls inside. Open daily May–Oct lunch and dinner; may open winter weekends. **€€**

THE IONIANS

Itháki

To Paliocaravo
Around east quay, Vathý
Tel: 26740 32573
This well-established favourite with locals and visitors alike offers a fine range of mezédes, salads, meat and fish dishes, which can all be washed down with their light, refreshing bulk wine. **€€€**

To Kohili
Around east quay, Vathý
Tel: 26740 33565
By far the best of all the harbour-side tavernas in the capital, specialising in traditional oven-baked main courses such as kléftiko and yiouvétsi, as well as some pasta dishes. **€€**

Rementzo
Fríkes
Tel: 26740 31719
Right in the corner of the harbour, this taverna offers a warm welcome as well as grilled meat or fish, some meat dishes and pretty good pizzas. **€€**

Ulysses
Fríkes
Tel: 26740 31733
Dine on reasonably priced fish and succulent meat dishes like rabbit stifádo or lamb kléftiko, whilst watching the gentle activity in the harbour. **€€**

Kefaloniá

Akrogiali
Lixoúri quay, towards south end
Tel: 26710 92613
An enduring, budget-priced institution, with largely local clientele. Tasty food with a stress on oven-casserole food, and fish and grills in the evening, plus excellent bulk wine. **€**

Arhondiko
Rizospastón 5, Argostóli
Tel: 26710 27213
Meatballs in roquefort sauce are an example of the unusual fare that is on offer inside this small but classy restaurant or on the even tinier patio. **€€**

Blue Sea (Spyros')
Káto Katélios
Tel: 26710 81353
The speciality here is superb grilled fish from the little anchorage adjacent. The bill can creep up if you add mezédes and bottled wine. **€€€**

Kyani Akti
A. Tritsi 1, far end of the quay
Tel: 26710 26680
A superb, if expensive, psarotavérna built out over the sea. The speciality is fresh fish and seafood, all of which is sold by weight. There is also a range of mezédes and salads, and some tasty house wine. **€€€**

Nirides
Ásos, the far end of the harbour
Tel: 26740 51467
This little estiatório in a great spot overlooking the harbour has the usual range of salads and a few grilled and oven dishes, as well as fresh fish by the kilo. **€€**

Odisseas
Agía Ierousalím, nr Mánganos
Tel: 69377 14982
A hidden gem, tucked behind a small, little-visited beach. The proprietors serve up delicious home-spun recipes such as lamb stew, made with free range meat and organic vegetables. They also sell preserves and sweets. **€€**

Romantza (Fotis Family)
Póros
Tel: 26740 72294
This estiatório is in a charming position, built into the headland at the end of the town beach. You eat on a first-storey balcony which has views over the sea to Itháki. The focus of the menu is on a large range of fresh fish (priced by weight), but there are also good mezédes and salads. **€€**

To Foki
At the head of Fóki Bay
This is a very pleasant taverna, friendly and just opposite the beach. It serves simple but tasty food which

is much better, and far cheaper, than anything to be found in Fiskárdo. €€

To Pefko
Andipáta Erísou, by the turn for Dafnoúdi beach
Tel: 26740 41360
A serious contender for the best place to eat on the island, with seating outside under a huge pine tree. A mouthwatering selection of mezédes, oven-cooked dishes and some grilled meat and fish. €€€

Xouras
Petaní
Tel: 26710 97128
The location halfway along the best beach on the Lixoúri peninsula is ideal, and the Greek-American lady owner offers a warm welcome and dishes up an good assortment of meat, fish and veggie dishes, which can be washed down with decent bulk wine. €€

Levkáda

Iy Palia Apothiki
Sývota
Tel: 26450 31895
A favourite among yachters, this lovingly converted 1710 storeroom (hence the name) is the place to enjoy imaginative fare such as giant prawns wrapped in bacon. Good bulk wine. €€€

Pantazis
Nikiána
Tel: 26450 71211
Appealingly set at the far end of the yacht harbour, this locally patronised taverna does fresh seafood at very reasonable prices – though salad trimmings could sometimes be fresher. Magirevtá in high-season evenings; open all day. €€

Regantos
Dimárhou Verrióti 17, Levkáda Town
Tel: 26450 22855
Supper-only taverna with a good balance of grills (especially spit-roasted chicken), oven food and fish; inexpensive and colourful. Sometimes hosts live *kandádes* singing. €€

T'Agnantio
West hillside, Ágios Nikítas
Tel: 26450 97383
www.tagnantio.gr
Tucked away up a lane with views to rival Sapfo's, one of the friendliest, least expensive home-style tavernas on the west coast; stress on magirevta and fresh seafood such as *garídes* from the Amvrákikos gulf. Creditable barrel wine; supper only low season. €€

Ta Platania
Central platía, Karyá
Seating under the giant plane trees of

the name, and fresh wholesome grills, salads and beers at budget prices. Tables for two other eateries share the square. €

Paxí

Alexandros
Platía Edward Kennedy, Lákka
Tel: 26620 30045
The most authentic island cooking and most atmospheric setting in town; own-produced grilled meat and chicken, specialities like rabbit *sofríto* and mushroom pie, a few seafood dishes, but avoid the barrel wine. €€

Lilas
Magaziá
Tel: 26620 31102
Inexpensive little meat grill with good bulk wine in an ex-grocery shop at the centre of the island; usually live accordion or stringed music at weekends. €

Vassilis
Longós quay
Tel: 26620 31587
Now often known as Kostakis after the son who's taken it over, this has grown from a grilled fish specialist to an all-round taverna with imaginative recipes for magirevtá, like stuffed mushrooms and peppers, baked meat dishes and various oven pies. €€

Zákynthos

Alitzerini
Kiliómeno
Tel: 26950 48552
Housed in one of the few surviving 17th-century Venetian village houses, this little *inomagerío* offers hearty, meat-based country cooking and its own wine; *kandádes* some evenings. Evenings only: June–Sept daily, Oct–May Fri–Sun. Reservations essential. €€

Kakia Rahi
Pigadakia
Tel: 26950 63670
Set by a tiny stream in a leafy village a few kilometres inland from Alykés, this taverna serves far more authentic island food, both baked and grilled, in its rambling courtyard than you would find in the resort itself. €€

Kalas
Kambí
By far the best taverna in Kambí, Kalas is set in a pretty garden, shaded by large trees, and serves up all the usual favourites (*fáva*, *loukánika*, *horiátiki* and *patátes*), all tasty and freshly cooked. Good bulk wine as well. €

Komis
Bastoúni tou Agíou, Zákynthos Town
Tel: 26950 26915
A lovely *psarotavérna* tucked into a

rather unlikely spot behind the port authority building. The emphasis is on slightly pricey but fresh and inventive fish and seafood dishes, but there is a good list of mezédes, good wine and tempting desserts. €€€

Malanos
Agíou Athanasíou 38, Kípi district of Zákynthos Town
Tel: 26950 45936
Extremely popular with locals for good reason, as the food is excellent and fairly inexpensive. Lots of fine mezédes, meat and seafood dishes, along with fine bulk wine. Often hosts live kantades. €€

Mikrinisi
Kokkínou, 1km (0.5 mile) beyond Makrýs Gialós
Tel: 26950 31566
Standard, but reasonable, taverna food – horiátiki, kalamarákia, souvláki and other such offerings – but the situation is lovely, on the edge of a headland overlooking a tiny harbour. €€

Porto Limnionas
Pórto Limniónas, near Ágios Léon
Tel: 26950 48650
Location can count for a lot. The food here is relatively expensive, standard taverna fare, but it is served on a promontory overlooking an idyllic rocky bay and facing west to the sunset. €€€

Roulis
Kypséli Beach, near Drosiá
Tel: 26950 61628
This is a friendly place overlooking the sea. Popular with islanders, Roulis gets very fresh fish – one of its main attractions – but also does the usual salads and vegetables well. The house wine is drinkable and the freshness of all the ingredients make it worth the detour from the main coast road. €€

To Fanari tou Keriou
1.5 km (1 mile) beyond Kerí village
Tel: 26950 43384
Watch the moon rise over the Myzíthres sea-stacks below the Kerí cliffs. The food's on the expensive side, but portions are fair size and quality is high – try the daily-made *galaktoboúreko* or vegetable-stuffed *pantsétta*, redolent of nutmeg. Reservations essential. €€€

PRICE CATEGORIES

Prices indicated are for a meal per person with modest intake of wine, beer, rakí or tsipouro.
€€€€ = over €35
€€€ = €25–35
€€ = €15–25
€ = under €15

TRANSPORT

ACCOMMODATION

EATING OUT

ACTIVITIES

A – Z

LANGUAGE

ACTIVITIES

FESTIVALS, THE ARTS, NIGHTLIFE, SHOPPING AND SPORTS

THE ARTS

Theatre and Cinema

Athens has an active theatre life but, as most productions are in Greek, options for English-speakers are limited. Most productions in English take place during festivals.

Going to the cinema in Greece during the summer is a special pleasure not to be missed. Nearly all the movie theatres that run in the summer (the others shut down unless they have air conditioning) are open-air, sometimes tucked among apartment buildings (whose tenants watch the film from their balconies); in other areas, they are perched on a seaside promontory under the stars. Tickets, at €6–8, are slightly cheaper than indoor cinemas and soundtracks are in the original language (with Greek subtitles). On smaller islands, there may be only one showing, at around 9.15pm, while elsewhere there will be two screenings, at 9 and 11pm. Tickets are often much cheaper on Monday night.

Cultural Events

The economic crisis has reduced the scope and length (if not the existence) of many events, but there's still a pretty full calendar between late spring and autumn. These are the most likely survivors, with a long track record behind them.

June. Rhodes Rock Festival.

June–July. Athens Festival at the Herodeio (Iródio) Theatre, among many other venues around the city: events include dance, opera, film, and music, plus modern and classical plays performed by world-ranking artists. Current information on www.greekfestival.gr

July. Kalamáta International Dance Festival: performances and workshops. The big dance event of the year in Greece.

July–August. Epídavros (Epidauros) Festival: performances of ancient and contemporary drama in the open-air Epidauros main amphitheatre and at the lovely little theatre in Paleá Epídavros resort. Current information on www.greekfestival.gr; Sáni Festival, Kassándra, Halkidikí: The best provincial festival in Greece, with a mix of local and foreign acts. www. sanifestival.gr; Thassos Philippi Festival: ancient drama and music concerts at Philippi, Kavála and Thásos.

July–September. Iráklio Festival: theatre and music at various city venues.

August. Lefkáda International Folklore Festival: dance and music by overseas groups.

August/September. Réthymnon Renaissance Festival: medieval-themed cultural activities at many venues.

September. Paxos Festival, chamber music on Paxí; Santorini Music Festival: mostly classical events. www.santorinimusicfestival.com

September–October. Pátra International Film Festival.

July–September. Sými Festival: a mix of classical and Greek pop performances.

September. Thessaloníki Dimitria Festival: theatre, music, dance events. www.dimitria.thessaloniki.gr

November. Thessaloníki International Film Festival: Best new films from both Greece and overseas (often other Balkan countries). www.filmfestival.gr

Music and Dance

Most of the best music and dance performances take place during festivals which occur across the country (see Cultural Events). It is also worth looking out for other events in Athens and Thessaloníki; the best resources for these are either posters, or listings websites like www.culturenow.gr and www.clickatlife.gr, but unfortunately most of these do not have English versions.

In Athens, outstanding Greek and foreign musicians often perform at the Lykavittós Theatre on Mt Lykavittós and at the Théatro Vráhon in a converted quarry on Mt Ymittós, not to mention the larger concerts that take place in the soccer stadiums and the Kalimármaro original Olympic Stadium near the Záppio. Opera can be seen at the Olympia Theatre, performed by the Lyrikí Skiní (the National Opera Company), while classical and jazz music, from national and international ensembles, is typically performed at the Mégaron Musikís near the American Embassy. Top Greek performers do shows at the Mousikí Skiní Avléa (www.avlea. gr) in Votanikós, Iy Alli Okhthi in Néos Kósmos(www.a-o.gr) and Stavros tou Notou with three stages (www.stn.gr), also in Néos Kósmos.

In Thessaloníki, summertime

Public Holidays and Religious Festivals

The Greeks like their holidays and celebrate them in style, so most business and shops close during the afternoon before and the morning after a religious holiday, as well as the day itself.

1 January Feast of Ágios Vasílios (St Basil): celebrated all over Greece. Official holiday as Protohroniá, New Year's.

6 January Epiphany/Agía Theofánia – Blessing of the waters: all over Greece. Official public holiday.

8 January Feast of Agía Domníki (St Domenica), patron saint of midwives: men and women switch roles in the villages around Xánthi, Komotiní, Kilkís and Sérres.

February–March Carnival season for three weeks before Lent: all over Greece. Some places with celebrations of special interest are: Náoussa, Kozáni, Zákynthos, Skýros, Thíva, Xánthi, Híos (Mestá, Olýmbi, Thymianá), Messíni, Amfissa, Lésvos (Agiássos), Galaxídi, Lamía,

Agía Ánna (Évvia), Polýgyros, Kefaloniá, Sérres, Kárpathos, Iráklio, Evxinoúpolis (Vólos), Réthymno and (best of all) Pátra, where there's a parade of dozens of floats and thousands of masquers.

Katharí Deftéri/"Clean" Monday Beginning of fast for Lent. Picnics in the countryside and kite-flying: all over Greece. Official holiday.

25 March Feast of Annunciation/Evangelismós/Independence Day: military parades in all main towns, pilgrimage to Tínos. Official holiday. Easter weekend Good Friday, Holy Saturday and Easter Sunday are celebrated throughout Greece.

23 April Feast of St George: celebrated especially in Kaliópi (Límnos), Aráhova, Así Gonía (near Haniá) and Pylí (Kos).

1 May Labour Day: picnics in the countryside all over Greece, leftist marches in towns. Official holiday.

21 May Anastenárides: fire-walking ritual at Agía Eléni (near Sérres) and

Langáda (near Thessaloníki). Moveable date Agíou Pnévmatos/Pentecost Monday (50 days after Easter). Official holiday.

15 August Kímisis Theotókou/Dormition of the Virgin: festivals all over Greece, usually from the night before. Major pilgrimage to Tínos.

28 October Óhi (No) Day: anniversary of Metaxas' supposed one-word response to Italy's 1940 ultimatum. Military parades in major cities.

Christmas season All over Greece. In a dwindling number of places, children sing kálenda (carols) from door to door for a small gratuity. 25 December Hristoúgenna/Christmas Day, and

26 December Sýnaxis tis Theotókou/Gathering of the Virgin's Entourage, are both public holidays.

31 December New Year's Eve: Many Greeks play cards for money on this occasion, and cut the vasilópitta with a lucky coin hidden in it.

venues include the **Théatro Dásous**, on the slopes beyond Kástra, and **Théatro Kípou**, near the archaeological museum; in winter, performances of music, opera, dance and theatre move indoors to the nearly adjacent **State Theatre** and **Royal Theatre**, near the White Tower. More cutting-edge are the events at newer, small venues like Gaia Live at Dóxis 5 (www.gaialive.gr) or Venteta at more central Ethnikís Amýnas 3 (www.venteta.com.gr). The Mylos complex out in Sfagiá district, which set the paradigm for many similar such industrial conversions across Greece, had a devastating fire some years ago, but still survives as the Club Mylos (www.mylos.gr), hosting more unusual acts.

There is an active dance scene in Athens and Thessaloníki, catering to all tastes, with ballet, folk, modern, jazz and experimental dance troupes resident and visiting.

Greek Music

Thanks to Greece's geographical position and the vast number of cultures that have called it home, there is astonishing regional variety in folk music. Crete has one of the more vital traditions, characterised by the *lýra* (three-string spike fiddle) and *laoúto* (mandolin-like lute). In the Dodecanese, these are often joined by either *tsamboúna*, a goatskin bagpipe, *violí* (violin) or *sandoúri*, the

hammer dulcimer popularised in the islands by refugees from Asia Minor.

Nisiótika is the general name for island music; that of the Ionians is the most Italian-influenced and Western in scale. Mainland music is also unmistakable, characterised by the extensive use of the *klaríno* (clarinet) and, in Epirus, an extraordinary, disappearing tradition of polyphonic singing.

Each region (and sometimes island) of Greece has its own particular folk dances. These ranges from the basic *sta tría* – three steps to one side, followed by a kick (growing gradually faster and faster) – to a frenzied combination of complicated footwork, jumps, slaps and kicks. Troupes, dressed in traditional Greek costume, are most likely to be performing on public holidays (you may also see them on TV). Probably the best-known professional group is the Dora Stratou Greek Folk Dancers, who stage regular shows from May to September at the Dora Stratou Theatre, Filopáppou Hill (southwest slope), Athens.

NIGHTLIFE

Metropolitan nightlife in Greece (essentially confined to Athens, Thessaloníki, Iráklio, Haniá, Vólos, Lárissa, Ioánnina, Tríkala, Kérkyra,

Mytilíni Town, Ródos Town and Pátra) can be roughly divided into four categories: bars; live music clubs with jazz, Greek music (most likely *laïki*, or a watered-down version of *rebétika*) or rock; dance clubs, mostly with a techno, trance, house or ambient soundtrack; and musical tavernas where food prices reflect the live entertainment.

For most Greeks, however, ordinary tavernas remain the most popular site for a night out spent eating, drinking and, sometimes, singing and dancing. In general, younger Greeks frequent the bars and dance clubs, while more formal venues for popular Greek music – which can be mightily expensive – are more patronised by the older generations.

In Athens, the weekly *Athinorama*/www.athinorama.gr (both in Greek) has an extensive listing of all the various venues and events. For Thessaloníki, the main resources are www.cityportal.gr and www.aboutthessaloniki.gr (again Greek only; *About* exists as a print edition also, in many hotel lobbies). If you really want to find out what's going on in these cities, ask a Greek friend to help you sort through the listings.

Tickets for many Athens and Thssaloníkí concerts are advance-sold mainly (or only) through the website www.ticketservices.gr (English option available), though after purchase, you must go to their physical premises in

Well-stocked nightclub bar.

the stoa at Panepistimiou 39, or at the event box-office, to retrieve the actual tickets.

During the summer (late June–early September) many clubs and music halls close down, with musicians of all stripes touring the countryside for the summer festival season, or performing in the islands and coastal resorts.

Casinos

For a more sophisticated – and potentially more expensive – night out, there are casinos in numerous Greek cities and resorts, including Néos Marmarás (Halkidikí), Corfu, Rhodes, Ermoúpoli (Sýros), Loutráki, Párnes, Río, Xánthi and Thessaloníki.

SPORT

Participant Sports

Boating

At many seaside resorts, you can hire motorboats by the day to get to isolated fishing and bathing spots. There does not seem to be any rigorous vetting process as for skippering a yacht.

Caving

Greece is honeycombed with caves, though many are locked to protect delicate formations or archaeological artefacts, and are only opened to qualified spelunkers on an expedition. The following, however, have set hours and facilities for public visits: Koutoúki, Peanía, Attica; Pérama, near Ioánnina; Drogaráti and Melissáni, Kefaloniá; Andíparos, in the Cyclades; the Cave of the Lakes, near Kalávryta in the Peloponnese; Glyfáda and Alepótripa at Pýrgos Dyroú, Máni in the Peloponnese; Petrálona, at Kókkines Pétres, Halkidikí; and the cave of Sykiás Olýmbon on Híos.

Hiking and Mountaineering

Greece has long been a magnet for hikers and mountain climbers, with many footpaths in the mainland mountains and on certain islands, threading through forested areas untouched by the tourist masses. See page 204 for hiking in the Píndos. Big-wall climbing is currently growing in popularity, both on the mainland and on islands such as Kálymnos. For information on trails, maps and excursions, consult one of the specialist guides in the booklist, or if you'd prefer an organised excursion, see page 402.

Horse Riding

Many small stables (some foreign owned) across the country offer horse riding. Reputable stables with a commitment to the animals' welfare are known to exist on the islands of Corfu, Kefaloniá, Kos, Rhodes, Páros, Náxos, Skiáthos and on the mainland at Pápingo (Zagóri) and on Mt Pílio (Pelion).

Scuba diving

Diving in Greece was for a long time tightly controlled, with the aim of preserving the nation's heritage of submerged antiquities. However, the laws on it were liberalised in 2007, with a corresponding eruption of new authorised areas. Dive centres of long standing operate on Rhodes, Kálymnos, Léros, Mýkonos, Santoríni, Náxos, Páros/Andíparos, Crete, Skiáthos, Corfu, Alónisos and Halkidikí. For a crowd-sourced but still-useful summary of the best dive sites, see http://www.scubatravel.co.uk/europe/greece-diving.html.

Although there is a lot to see around the coast – caves, walls, wrecks, antiquities – do not expect undersea fauna and flora of Caribbean splendour; snorkelling in Greek waters is often just as rewarding as scuba-diving.

Sailing

Numerous companies offer sailing packages and cruises round the coast of Greece that can be booked from home – an internet search will be very productive. One useful non-commercial website is: www. sailingissues.com.

Much of the sailing is in flotillas helmed by the hire companies, but experienced sailors can charter their own yacht. Alternatively, once you're in Greece, you can hire boats by the day or week at many marinas. The best two websites for weather conditions (especially wind), used by all yachties, are: www.poseidon.hcmr.

gr/weather_forecast.php?area_id=gr and www.meteorologia.gr

The best times to sail are spring and autumn, as winds can be high through the summer months and prices are hiked up to many times that of the cooler seasons.

There are sailing schools, housed in the navtikí ómili (nautical clubs) of the following towns: Athens (Paleó Fáliro); Thessaloníki; Corfu; Vólos; Sámos; Karlóvas; Híos; Páros; Kos; Rhodes; Sýros; Kalamáta; Alexandroúpolis. They are mostly geared to local residents, especially children, but would probably be thrilled to have guests.

kite sports, with gentle breezes blowing around many small coves. Boards or kites can be rented, and lessons are available (at very reasonable rates) at many popular Greek beaches, and at most of the beaches maintained by the gto.

The premier resorts dedicated to the sport, where people come from overseas just to windsurf, are: Prasonísi and Ixiá, Rhodes; southern Kárpathos; Kokkári, Sámos; Mikrí Vígla, Náxos; Poúnda, Páros; Halikoúna and Ísos beaches, Corfu; and Vasilikí, Lefkáda.

Skiing

Most Greek mountains above 2,400 metres (7,800ft) high have good snow cover for skiing from January to April, with some of the higher mountains (Kaïmaktsalán and Parnassós) skiable in a good year until May.

These are the best downhill resorts, having top points of between 1900m and 2300m, with most offering some sort of cross-country/nordic pistes as well: Mt Parnassós (14 lifts, 16 runs); Mt Vérmio near Naoússa (18 lifts, 30 runs); Mt Helmós, near Kalávryta in the Peloponnese (7 lifts, 12 runs); Vórras on Mt Kaïmaktsalán (6 lifts, 13 runs); Mt. Vassilítsa in eastern Zagóri (8 lifts, 17 runs); Mt Falakró, near Dráma in Macedonia (9 lifts, 21 runs); and Veloúhi on Mt Tymfristós near Karpenísi (7 lifts, 11 runs).

There are a dozen or so other tiny, low-altitude centres across Greece, but those cited above are the only ones with any sort of reputation. You can view a list of all of them at www. gtp.gr/skicenters.asp. Hard times have driven the cost of lift passes down a bit, but they're generally viewed as overpriced, so many northern Greeks in particular prefer to cross the border and ski at Bansko in Bulgaria.

Tennis

Although there are tennis clubs in most larger cities, few are open to non-members/non-residents. Public courts are equally rare. But most island hotels and inclusive complexes of thee-star rating and above have tennis facilities, where you may be able to book court space by the hour.

Water-skiing

Water-skiing (and in some places parasailing as well) is far cheaper in Greece than in most Mediterranean

resorts. You will find organised water-skiing facilities at: Vouliagméni (southeast of Athens); Édessa (Lake Vegoritída); Thessaloníki; numerous locations on Corfu; near Haniá, Crete; Eloúnda, Crete; Pórto Héli; Rhodes; Párga (Váltos beach); Skiáthos; Sývota, Límnos; Kalamáta; and Halkidikí.

Windsurfing and Kiteboarding/Kitesurfing

Greece is ideal for windsurfing and

Spectator Sports

Football (soccer) is the main spectator sport, with matches played nearly every Wednesday night and Sunday afternoon during the season. The top teams are aek (Athens), Olympiakós (Piraeus), Panathanaïkós (Athens) and paok (Thessaloníki).

Basketball is the second most popular sport since the national team won the European Championship in 1987, and the national league is followed keenly. Local Greek-language newspapers have details of games.

Sailing is popular all over Greece.

A – Z

A HANDY SUMMARY OF PRACTICAL INFORMATION

A

Admission Charges

Most archaeological sites and museums, public or private, have admission charges varying from €2 for minor affairs up to €12 for stellar attractions. Occasionally (as in Athens and Rhodes) you can get a joint ticket covering several sites and museums at an advantageous price. From November to March, most state-run sites give free admission to EU nationals on Sunday; Monday or Tuesday are the typical days of closure. Students with valid ID get one-third to one-half off entry fees, as do certified teachers, archaeology students and persons 60 or over. On summer full moon evenings, always in August but sometimes July or September too, major archaeological sites like the Parthenon, Lindos or Olympia have free admission for all until about 1.30am – magical. Ask locally, as not all sites have the staff to participate in this programme.

Children are adored in Greece.

Thessaloníki), €15–20 for your half of a sit-down meal, €6–10 each daily for site admissions, and €13–17 for your share of the cheapest small rental car – before petrol costs, which have risen steeply in recent years owing to excise taxes.

Business Travellers

Business travellersare well catered for; most good-standard hotels now have some sort of "business person's corner" with a computer terminal and printer, as well as wi-fi signal for laptops (in the common areas if not in all the rooms). The same hotels tend to have multiple conference/event rooms as well as lounges suitable for semi-formal meetings.

C

Children

Children are adored in Greece, and many families are still highly superstitious about their welfare – don't be surprised to see toddlers with amulets pinned to their clothes to ward off the evil eye. So expect your own kids to be the centre of attention. Children are given quite a bit of leeway in Greece and treated very indulgently. They are allowed to stay up late and are routinely taken out to eat in tavernas. You may have to put your foot down when shop

B

Budgeting for Your Trip

Since the advent of the euro, Greece is no longer by any stretch of the imagination an inexpensive country. Travelling as one of a couple, allow a minimum of €30 for a share of accommodation (budget €40–50 each minimum in Athens or

CLIMATE CHART

Athens

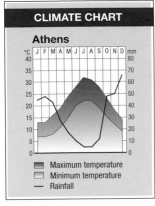

- ■ Maximum temperature
- ☐ Minimum temperature
- — Rainfall

owners offer free sweets, or strangers are over-indulgent towards your own children. There are water parks on several resort islands (Corfu, Rhodes, Crete) but nothing akin to France's Disney World.

Climate

The Greece seen in tourist posters is a perennially warm and sunny place – and it is, by European standards. But this picture does not reflect the considerable climatic variety. The north and inland regions have a modified continental climate, so winters are quite cold and summers extremely hot. In Ioánnina, Trípoli, the Metéora, and Kastoriá, for example, snow and freezing temperatures are not uncommon. In mountainous regions, winters are even more inclement.

The southern islands, the coastal Peloponnese and the Attic Peninsula conform more to the traditional Mediterranean image: a long, warm season of rainless, sunny days extending roughly from late May to mid-October. But here too, the winters can be cool, with rain falling in unpredictable bouts between December and April.

In general, late spring (late April– end June) and autumn (September– October) are the best times to visit. During these periods, you will find mild to warm temperatures, sunny days and fewer tourists. Throughout July and August, Greece is at its most hot and sticky, and most crowded. Still, millions of tourists seem to prefer the heat and the company, choosing this busiest period for their holiday.

Crime and Safety

Sadly, Greece is no longer the crime-free haven of yesteryear.

Locking cars and houses is now the norm everywhere, even in the deep countryside where people until recently used to leave a set of keys dangling from the front door.

Central Athens in particular has become hazardous at times. Cars with valuables exposed (or even not) are routinely broken into in such neighbourhoods as Exárhia, Gázi and Keramikós; the thieves, often apparently drug addicts, will steal almost anything irrespective of value, even old CDs or raggedy items of clothing.

Organised gangs of pickpockets and bag-snatchers frequent the metro lines and stations most popular with tourists, in particular Line 3 from the airport, Line 1 from Piraeus, Monastiráki plus Sýndagma stations, and the X95 bus-stop area at Sýndagma. They usually work in teams, and may be plausibly well dressed. If you are surrounded and pushed up against the carriage wall, or forced to squeeze past them to retrieve your luggage from the rack in the airport-route cars, your wallet, camera or other valuables are about to be (or have been) lifted. Anything in the outside pocket of a daypack or backpack is essentially forfeit. Your cards will be used to obtain cash advances within minutes at exchange booths who are clearly in cahoots with the thieves. Nothing substantive is being done about the problem other than recorded announcements in the metro cars telling you to be aware. If you are new in town, and heavily laden, it's probably worth getting off the metro one station before (Evangelismós) or after (Akrópoli) the central ones and walking back to the centre, or getting an onwards taxi.

Young single females should be alert to the possibility of drugged drinks as a prelude to rape attempts in popular, rowdy beach resorts. Be suspicious of men who offer to bring you cocktails, whose preparation you cannot witness. The perpetrators, it must be said, are as (or more) likely to be other foreigners as Greeks. Use common sense when arranging rides afterwards back to your accommodation.

Because of security considerations, it is unwise to leave luggage unattended anywhere except perhaps in a hotel lobby, under the gaze of the desk staff. Belongings inadvertently left behind in a café will still usually be put aside for you to collect.

Customs Regulations

There are no official restrictions on the movement of goods within the European Union, provided the goods were purchased VAT-paid within the EU. In theory, there are no limitations to the amount of duty-paid goods that can be moved between EU states. However, cigarettes and most spirits are still cheaper in Greece than in Britain and Ireland, so waiting until you reach your destination to buy these goods will save you money.

Duty-paid goods

If you buy goods in Greece for which you pay tax, there are no restrictions on the amounts you can take home. EU law has set "guidance levels", however, on the following:
Tobacco 3,200 cigarettes, or 400 cigarillos, or 200 cigars or 3kg of tobacco.
Spirits 10 litres
Fortified wine/wine 90 litres
Beer 110 litres
If you exceed these amounts, you must be able to prove the goods are for personal use.

Duty-free goods

For travellers arriving from non-EU countries, allowances for duty-free goods brought into Greece are:
Tobacco 200 cigarettes, or 100 cigarillos, or 50 cigars or 250g of tobacco.
Alcohol 1 litre of spirits or liqueurs over 22 percent volume, or 2 litres of fortified, sparkling or still wine.
Perfume 60cc of perfume, plus 250cc of eau de toilette.
Non-EU residents can claim back Value Added Tax (currently between 6 and 23 percent) on any items costing over €120, provided they export the item within 90 days of purchase. Tax-free forms are available at tourist shops and a very few department stores. Keep the receipt and form. Make your claim at the customs area of the airport when departing.

Currency restrictions

There are no limits on the amount of euros visitors can import or export. Cash sums of more than €10,000 or its equivalent should be declared on entry.

Importing cars

Visitors arriving with their own car are allowed to circulate for up to six months without formality; after that the bureaucratic fun begins, and people intending to establish residence will find that it's usually cheaper and easier to buy a Greek-registered car than try to import their overseas motor. Cars detected circulating after the initial six-month period without valid road tax are liable to seizure by customs/tax undercover agents, and are auctioned off if an enormous import duty is not paid.

Disabled Travellers

Despite nudging from the EU, Greece has some way to go before becoming fully compliant with regulations on facilities for disabled people.

Athens, with lifts in the metro, "kneeling" buses on many routes, recorded announcements of upcoming stops on the metro plus some buses, and ramps (when not blocked by illegally parked cars) at kerbside, is furthest ahead.

Elsewhere, amenities can be poor – there are few or no sound pips for the sight-impaired at pedestrian crossings, and it is common to see the wheelchair-bound tooling down the middle of the asphalt rather than risk the obstacle course of a pedestrian pavement.

Few hotels in the provinces are disabled-friendly, though things are improving slowly, and some are setting aside a few rooms with wide doors and safety handles in the bath – ask when booking.

Embassies and Consulates

Foreign Embassies in Athens

All embassies are open from Monday to Friday only, usually from 8am until 2pm, except for their own national holidays (as well as Greek ones).
Australia Corner Kifissías and Alexándras avenues, Level 6, Thon Building, Ambelókipi; tel: 210-870 4000
Canada Gennadíou 4, Kolonáki, (Evangelismós metro); tel: 210-727 3400.

Electricity

220 volts out of double round-pin sockets.

Police officers in Athens.

Ireland Vassiléos Konstandínou 7 (by National Gardens); tel: 210-723 2771.
South Africa Kifissiás 60, Maroússi; tel: 210-610 6645.
UK Ploutárhou 1, Kolonáki (Evangelismós metro); tel: 210-727 2600, http://ukingreece.fco.gov.uk/en
US Vasilísis Sofías 91, Ambelókipi (Mégaro Mousikís metro); tel: 210-721 2951, http://athens.usembassy.gov

Entry Requirements

Citizens of EU nations and Switzerland have unlimited visitation rights to Greece; your passport will not be stamped on entry or exit. With a valid passport, citizens of the USA, Canada, Australia and New Zealand can stay in the country for up to three months (cumulative) within any six-month period, with no visa necessary. Over-stayers are fined very heavily on exit, to the tune of several hundred euros; it may in fact be cost-effective to have the offending passport "disappear" and be replaced. To stay longer, you must obtain a permit from the nearest Aliens' Bureau; however, this is lately proving nearly impossible (and very expensive) to do. Citizens of all non-EU countries should contact the nearest Greek embassy or consulate about visa and permitted length-of-stay requirements, which are liable to change again in future.

Etiquette

The Greeks are at heart a very traditional nation, protective of their families and their customs. So to avoid giving offence, it is essential to follow their codes of conduct.

Locals rarely drink to excess, so drunken and/or lewd behaviour is treated with at best bewilderment, at worse severe distaste (or criminal prosecution, as many young louts on Rhodes, Zákynthos, Corfu and Crete have learned to their cost).

Nude bathing is legal at only a few beaches (such as on the island of Mýkonos), but it is deeply offensive to most Greeks. Even topless sunbathing is sometimes frowned upon, so watch for signs forbidding it on beaches. The main rule of thumb is this: if it is a secluded beach and/or a beach that has become a commonly accepted locale for nude bathing, you probably won't offend anyone.

On Mýkonos, for example, tourists will shock no one by wearing shorts or a swimsuit in most public places. But this same apparel would be severely alienating in a mountain village in Crete. Observe what other people are wearing and dress accordingly.

To enter a church, men must wear long trousers, and women sleeved dresses. Often dresses or wraps will

Emergency Numbers

The following numbers work country-wide:
Police 100
Ambulance 166
Fire brigade, urban 199
Forest fire reporting 191
Tourist police 171 (Athens only; in other parts of Greece, ring 210 171)
Elsewhere, hotel staff will give you details of the nearest hospital or English-speaking doctor.

be provided at the church entrance. Not complying with this code will be taken as insulting irreverence.

Despite assorted scandals and embarrassing espousal of retrograde issues in recent years, the Greek Orthodox Church still commands considerable respect in Greece, so keep any unfavourable comments about the clergy or even Greek civil servants to yourself.

G

Gay and Lesbian Travellers

Overt gay behaviour is not a feature of Greek society. Homosexuality is legal at the age of 17, and bisexual activity fairly common among younger men, but few couples (male or female) are openly gay. Mýkonos is famous as a gay Mecca – Rhodes, Santoríni and Sámos to a lesser degree – while Skála Eressoú on Lésvos (where the poetess Sappho was born) attracts many lesbians. But elsewhere in Greece, single-sex couples are liable to be regarded as odd, although usually as welcome as any other tourists. If discreet, you will attract no attention asking for a double room and will find most people tolerant.

H

Health and Medical Care

Greece has few serious diseases apart from those that you can contract in the US or the rest of Europe. Citizens of the USA, Canada and the EU do not need any immunisations to enter the country.

Drugs and Medicines

Greek pharmacies stock most over-the-counter drugs. The Greeks themselves are enthusiastic hypochondriacs and potion-poppers, and all manner of homeopathic and herbal remedies and premium-ingredient dietary supplements are available – at a price. Many formulas that would be obtainable only on prescription elsewhere, if at all, are freely obtainable in Greece. So you should have no problem obtaining most medicines (except in remote areas and islands).

Essential drugs, made locally under licence, are price-controlled for the moment (though international lenders have their sights trained on this practice), with uniform rates all over the country – eg a tube of 1 percent hydrocortisone cream costs about €4 – but discretional sundries and anything imported can be pricey (eg a packet of four water-resistant French-made bandages for €3.50). If you want to be absolutely sure, pack a supply of your favourite remedies to last out the trip.

Greek authorities take the unauthorised use of drugs very seriously indeed; this is not the country in which to carry cannabis.

Medical Treatment

For minor ailments, your best port of call is a pharmacy. Greek chemists usually speak good English and are well-trained and helpful, and pharmacies stock a good range of medicines (including contraceptives) as well as bandages and dressings for minor wounds.

Certain pharmacies are open outside of normal shop hours and at weekends, on a rotating basis. You can find out which are open either by looking at the bilingual (Greek/ English) card posted in pharmacy windows or by consulting a local newspaper. In big cities, and major tourist resorts such as Crete or Rhodes, one or two pharmacies will be open 24 hours a day.

There are English-speaking GPs in all the bigger towns and resorts, whose rates are usually reasonable. Ask your hotel or the tourist office for details.

Treatment for broken bones and similar mishaps is given free of charge in the state-run Greek hospitals – go straight to the casualty/emergency ward (*epígon peristatiká*). Have on you your European Health Insurance Card, obtainable in the UK online at www.ehic.org. Be aware that holders of such cards are only entitled to free treatment in the casualty ward, and at the few still-functioning agrotiká iatría (remote rural clinics). If you make the mistake of attending a hospital's outpatient clinic, you'll pay full whack for everything at private rates, and charges are eye-watering: eg €130 for a full battery of blood tests.

For more serious problems and unimpeded use of outpatient clinics on a private basis, you should have private medical insurance. If you have a serious injury or illness, you are better off travelling home for treatment if you can. Greek public hospitals lag behind northern Europe and the US in both their hygiene and standard of care; the Greeks bring food and bedding when visiting sick relatives, and must bribe nurses and doctors for anything beyond the bare minimum in care. All these conditions have been severely exacerbated by the ongoing crisis, with health-care provision very hard hit.

Drinking Water

People carrying a large plastic bottle of mineral water is a common sight in Greece, but it is not the best way of keeping hydrated, as sunlight releases toxic chemicals from the plastic into the water, and the spent bottles contribute enormously to Greece's litter problem. Buy a sturdy, porcelain-lined canteen and fill it from the cool-water supply of bars and restaurants you've patronised; nobody will begrudge you this. Although unfiltered tap water is generally safe to drink, it may be brackish, and having a private water supply is much handier. On the mainland and larger islands, certain springs are particularly esteemed by the locals – queues of cars, and people with jerry-cans, tip you off. If you do want bottled water, it can be bought almost anywhere that sells food, even in beach cafés and tavernas, though more conventionally at kiosks and minimarkets. A large bottle should not cost more than about 70 euro-cents, often less.

Animal Hazards

Nearly half the stray dogs in rural

Left Luggage

Airport At the far south end, arrivals concourse, Eleftherios Venizelos airport, Pacific Left Luggage offers service; tel: 210-353 0352. They are, however, hideously expensive for anything more than a few hours.

Hotels Most hotels in Greece are willing to store locked suitcases for a week or two if you want to take any short excursions. This is usually a free service, provided you've stayed a night or two, but the hotel will accept no responsibility in the highly unlikely event of theft.

Commercial offices On the islands, there are left-luggage offices in many harbour towns. For a small charge, space can be hired by the hour, day, week or longer. Although the contents will probably be safe, take small valuables with you.

TRANSPORT

ACCOMMODATION

EATING OUT

ACTIVITIES

A – Z

LANGUAGE

areas carry echinococcosis (treatable by surgery only) or kala-azar disease (leishmaniasis), a potentially fatal protozoan blood disease spread by sandflies. So beware of befriending importunate pooches.

Mosquitoes can be a nuisance in some areas of Greece, but topical repellents are readily available in pharmacies. For safeguarding rooms, accommodation proprietors often supply a plug-in electric pad, which vapourises smokeless, odourless rectangular tablets. If you see them by the bed, it's a good bet they'll be needed; refills can be found in any supermarket.

On the islands, poisonous baby pit vipers and scorpions are a problem in spring and summer. They will not strike you unless disturbed, but do not put your hands or feet in places (such as drystone walls) that you haven't checked first. If you swim in the sea, beware jellyfish whose sting is usually harmless but which can swell and hurt for days. A good over-the-counter remedy for this is called Fenistil.

On beaches, it is worth wearing plastic or trekking sandals to avoid sea urchins (those little black pincushions on rocks that can embed their very sharp and tiny spines into unwary feet). A local Greek remedy is to douse the wound with olive oil and then gently massage the foot until the spines pop out, but this rarely works unless you're willing to perform minor surgery with pen-knife and sewing needle – which should be done, as spine fragments tend to go septic.

Insurance

The benefits of medical insurance coverage for private treatment are noted above. You will have to pay for private treatment up front, so you must keep receipts for any bills or medicines you pay for to make a claim. If you plan to hire a motor scooter in Greece, or engage in any adventure sport, make sure your policy covers such activities.

Internet

Greece has become thoroughly "wired" since the Olympic Games, with bars, cafés, hotels (sometimes only the common areas) and even many tavernas offering a wi-fi signal. Much of the time it is free, or free for

Getting his news fix.

the price of a coffee, drink or meal, but usually password protected. Speeds are apt to be moderate rather than blistering – especially in rural areas. With the prevalence of tablet devices and full-sized laptops, internet cafés per se are heading towards extinction, and always were dismal places full of spotty teenagers playing computer games. Should you have to pay for these, assume a maximum of €4 an hour, with 15- or 30-minute increments usually available. Hotel internet charges can be ruinous – we've heard tales of nearly €20 a day – and should be avoided.

Media

Print

Many kiosks throughout Athens and other major resorts receive British newspapers, plus the International Herald Tribune, either late the same afternoon or, more usually, the next day. The English online edition (www. ekathimerini.com) of centre-right Greek newspaper Kathimerini is the best source of Greek news, albeit heavily abridged from the parent publication. Odyssey (www.odyssey.gr) is a glossy, bi-monthly magazine created by and for the wealthy Greek diaspora, somewhat more interesting than the usual airline in-flight mag.

Radio and TV

Ellinikí Radiofonía is the Greek state-owned radio, divided into three different "programmes". The First and (much better) Second (FM 103.70 near Athens, other frequencies regionally) both have abundant Greek popular music, news and talk shows, some foreign pop and occasional jazz and blues. The Third programme (FM 90.9) features classical music. Private station Kanali 1, out of Piraeus (FM 90.4), is also excellent. Additionally, a plethora of private stations broadcast locally from just about every island or provincial town, no matter how tiny.

The BBC World Service no longer beams directly on short-wave to Greece, but has agreements for rebroadcast of select programmes with the following local stations: Skaï (100.4 FM) and Antenna (102.7 FM).

There are three state-owned and operated television channels (ET1 and NET, out of Athens, ET3 from Thessaloniki) and a half-dozen private television channels (Antenna, Net, Mega, Star, Skaï (no relation to Rupert Murdoch's Sky) and Alpha). Often they transmit foreign movies and programmes with Greek subtitles rather than being dubbed. Several cable and satellite channels, including Sky and CNN, are also available in the better hotels.

Money

For the moment at least, the Greek currency is the euro (evró in Greek), which comes in coins of 1, 2, 5, 10, 20 and 50 cents (leptá), plus 1 and

2 euro, as well as notes of 5, 10, 20, 50, 100, 200 and 500 euro (the latter two denominations rarely seen and viewed with extreme suspicion as likely counterfeits – avoid accepting them at banks).

All banks and most hotels buy foreign currency at the official rate of exchange fixed by the Bank of Greece. Exchange rates go up or down daily. To find the current rate, check displays in bank windows, or the newspapers; you can read the tables even in Greek.

Travellers' cheques are disdained, and very few institutions accept them any longer – or at least not without a 20-minute vetting procedure. It's worth carrying a limited sum of low-denomination banknotes in US dollars or sterling, which are much more rapidly negotiable at travel agencies and exchange bureaux.

Credit/debit cards

Many of the better-established hotels, restaurants and shops accept major credit cards, as do all airline and ferry-company websites, plus the domestic Greek travel websites www.airtickets.gr and www.travelplanet24.com. Many travel agencies and websites, however, will add a surcharge (typically 3 percent) to credit-card purchases of tickets. The average low star hotel or taverna does not, however, take cards, or only accepts details as a booking deposit, so enquire before ordering if that is how you intend to pay. You will find that most brands of card are accepted by the numerous autoteller machines, upon entry of your pin number. However, use debit rather than credit cards in ATMs, as the latter tend to have ruinous surcharges, often amounting to over five percent of the transaction value. This caveat aside, you will find that this is the most convenient and least expensive way of getting funds, and most machines operate around the clock. Prepaid cash cards can be an effective way to push down commission charges.

O

Opening Hours

All banks are open 8am–2.30pm Monday to Thursday, and close at 2pm on Friday. ATMs are now everywhere – even the smaller islands will have at least one – and this is how most travellers obtain cash nowadays, rarely if ever seeing

'Greek Time'

Beware Greek schedules. Although shops and businesses generally operate the hours indicated under Opening Hours, there is no guarantee that when you want to book a ferry or buy a gift, the office or shop will actually be open.

Siesta (*mikró ýpno* in Greek) is observed throughout Greece, and even in Athens the majority of people retire behind closed doors between the hours of 3pm and 6pm. Shops and businesses also close, and it is usually impossible to get anything more done until late-afternoon or early evening. To avoid frustration and disappointment, shop and book things between 9.30am and 1.30pm Monday to Friday.

Since 1994, Athens has experimented with "straight" hours

the inside of a bank.

The schedule for business and shop hours is more complicated, varying according to the type of business and the day of the week. The main thing to remember is that businesses generally open at 8.30 or 9am and close on Monday, Wednesday and Saturday at 2.30pm. On Tuesday, Thursday and Friday, most businesses close at 2pm and reopen in the afternoon from 5pm to 8.30pm (winter), 5.30 or 6pm to 9pm (summer).

Supermarkets, both large and small, are the only shops guaranteed to be open all day (Mon–Fri 8.30am–9pm, Sat 8.30am–8pm). Especially on resort islands, there will be at least one open short hours on Sunday too (typically 10am–4pm).

You'll soon learn that schedules are very flexible in Greece (both in business and personal affairs). To avoid disappointment, allow ample time when shopping and doing business. That way, you may also enter into the Greek spirit of negotiation, in which a good chat can be as important as the matter of business itself.

P

Photography

Although Greece is a photographer's paradise, taking photographs at will is not recommended. Cameras are

during the winter to bring the country more in line with the EU, but this seems to be discretionary rather than obligatory, with some stores observing the hours and others adhering to traditional schedules – which can be rather confusing. So far it has not caught on across the rest of the country.

During summer, the shops in Athens' Pláka district remain open until 10pm or longer to take advantage of browsers, and tourist shops throughout the country usually trade well into the evening. But butchers and fishmongers are not allowed to open on summer evenings (although a few disregard the law), and pharmacies (except for those on rota duty) are never open in the evenings or on Saturday mornings.

permitted in museums, but to be used without tripod or flash. You may have to pay a fee to use your camcorder at archaeological sites. Watch out for signs showing a bellows camera with a red "X" through it, and do not point your camera at anything in or near airports – most of which double as military bases.

Memory chips for most digital cameras are widely available; photo shops will also happily print from chips, or empty their contents onto a CD for a nominal fee (assume €5).

Postal Services

Most local post offices are open weekdays from 7.30am until 2pm. However, the main post offices in central Athens (on Eólou near Omónia Square and on Sýndagma Square at the corner of Mitropóleos Street) are open longer hours on weekdays, as well as for a few hours on Saturday.

Postal rates are subject to fairly frequent change; currently a postcard or light letter costs 78 euro-cents to any overseas destination. Stamps are available from the post office or from many kiosks (*períptera*) and hotels, which may charge a 10–15 percent commission. But many kiosk owners tend not to be up to date with latest international postal rates. Outbound speeds are reasonable – as little as three days to northern Europe, a week or so to North America.

If you want to send a parcel from Greece, do not wrap it until a post office clerk has inspected it, unless it's going to another EU country, in which case you can present it sealed. Major post offices stock various sizes of cardboard boxes for sale in which you can pack your material, as well as twine, but you had best bring your own tape and scissors.

Letters from abroad can be sent post restante to any post office. Take your passport or other ID when you go to pick up mail.

Religious Services

Most major towns and resort areas with significant foreign patronage or a large expat community – most obviously Corfu, Rhodes, Crete, Sámos, Santoríni, Athens and Thessaloníki – have at least one church dedicated to the Catholic, Anglican or other Protestant (eg Swedish Lutheran) rites, or an agreement for part-time use of an Orthodox premises. There are functioning Catholic parishes for locals on Rhodes, Crete, Corfu, Sýros and Tínos, where foreigners are welcome. Placards posted on the churches themselves, or handouts at the nearest tourist office, give current info on schedules (anything from two Sundays a month to two or three times weekly).

Student Travellers

Other than the museum and archaeological site discounts, students and under-26s are eligible for discounted fares and youth passes on ose (the Greek train network) and on some shipping lines, including those operating to and from Italy.

Telecoms

For local calls, including to mobiles, buy an OTE (Greek telecoms) telephone card from a kiosk and use a (usually noisy) street-corner booth. Cards come in 100-unit, 500-unit and 1,000-unit denominations; the Hronokarta

species is slightly better value. Calls from hotel rooms typically have 200–300 percent surcharges on top of the basic rates – to be avoided for anything other than brief local calls. For overseas calls, almost everyone avoids the truly outrageous OTE rates by buying a code-card, whereby you scratch to reveal a 12-digit code, then ring an 807-prefixed number to enter said code, then the number you want. It may all sound a hassle, but savings can amount to about 70 percent. If you have a laptop, bring a Skype headset along to take advantage of wi-fi zones for calling abroad.

Greece has one of the highest per-capita mobile-phone usage rates in the world, and a mobile is an essential fashion accessory for any self-respecting Greek. Foreign mobile owners will find themselves well catered for, with thorough coverage and reciprocal agreements for most UK-based services. North American users will have to bring a tri-band apparatus to get any joy. In the wake of caps on intra-EU call charges, receiving calls within Greece is affordable if you have an foreign-but-EU-based number, but the costs of calling out adds up quickly. If you're staying for any amount of time, you will find it better to buy a pay-as-you-go SIM card from one of the three Greek providers (Vodaphone, Cosmote, Wind). As an anti-terrorism strategy to keep you from using your phone to set off bombs remotely, you will have to register your identity upon purchase.

Time Zone

Greece is two hours ahead of GMT and, like the rest of Europe, observes Daylight Savings from 3am on the last Sunday in March until 3am on the last Sunday in October.

Tipping

Menu prices at most cafés, restaurants and *tavérnes* include a service charge, but it is still customary to leave an extra 5–10 percent on the table for the waiters. Taxi drivers are not tipped per se but may "round up" fares to the nearest half-euro. Hotel porters should be given a euro or so per bag.

Toilets

Public conveniences, often subterranean in parks or plazas, or perched on a harbour jetty, are of variable cleanliness and rarely have any paper. Most people just buy a drink in a café and use their facilities. In busy tourist areas, put-upon cafés may post signs saying "toilets for customers only". Elsewhere, establishments are a bit more lenient about those caught short just popping in.

Tourist Information

Tourist offices

If you would like tourist information about Greece during your trip, visit

Tour Operators

Mass-market bucket-and-spade holidays are easy to find on the web. Otherwise, here are a few suggestions for something unusual:
Quality packages and bespoke itineraries on mainland & islands:
Sunvil, UK; tel: 020 87584758, www.sunvil.co.uk
Hidden Greece, UK; tel: 020 87584707, www.hidden-greece.co.uk
Travel à la Carte, UK; tel: 020 72869055, www.travelalacarte.co.uk
Bicycle tours on Crete, Zákynthos, Peloponnese:
Classic Adventures, USA; tel: 1 800 777-8090, www.classicadventures.com
Wildlife tours across the country:
The Travelling Naturalist, UK; tel: 01305 267994, naturalist.co.uk
Sail-and-trek mixed tours:
Explore!, UK; tel: 0845 013 1537,

www.explore.co.uk
Hellenic Adventures, USA; tel: 1 800 851 6349, www.hellenicadventures.com
Walking holidays, western Crete:
ATG Oxford, UK; tel: 01865 315678, www.atg-oxford.co.uk
Walking and cycling, various parts of Greece:
Exodus London, UK; tel: 020 8675 5550, www.exodus.co.uk
Ramblers Holidays, UK; tel: 01707 331133, www.ramblersholidays.co.uk
Writing workshops/holistic holidays:
Astra, US; tel: 1303 321-5403, www.astragreece.com
Skyros Centre, UK; tel: 01983 865666, www.skyros.com
Yoga Plus, UK; tel: 01273 276175, www.yogaplus.co.uk

the nearest Greek National Tourist Organisation – GNTO, or EOT in Greek. They provide information on public transport, as well as leaflets and details about sites and museums. There are over a dozen regional GNTO offices across the country. The information booth in Athens can be found at the base of Dionysíou Areopagitou, at the edge of the Pláka district.

In some tourist areas, especially on many islands, there are municipal tourist information centres open from June to September. These are usually prominently sited near the centre of the main town, and provide all the local information you might need. Some can even help with finding accommodation.

Tourist Police

The Greek Tourist Police are a branch of the local police, found in most large towns; sometimes, as on Rhodes, they have separate premises. Each tourist policeman should speak at least one foreign language well. They should be your first port of call in the event of a serious incident involving rogue hoteliers or restauranteurs, and should also be consulted if you are the victim of a serious crime such as assault or robbery, if the regular police seem to be dragging their feet.

Greek National Tourist Organisation Offices

Greek National Tourism Organisation, worldwide (www.visitgreece.gr):
Australia: 37–49 Pitt Street, Sydney, NSW; PO Box R203 Royal Exchange, NSW 2000; tel: (2) 9241 1663.
UK and Ireland: 4 Conduit Street, London W1R 0DJ; tel: (020) 7495 9300.
US & Canada: 305 East 47th Street, New York, NY 10017; tel: (212) 421 5777.

Websites

Greek weather forecasts are available at:
www.weather.gr
www.poseidon.hcmr.gr/weather_forecast.php?area_id=gr
Windsurfers in particular should consult the Greece page of:
www.windguru.cz
For local journalism in English, try:
www.ekathimerini.com
www.athensnews.gr

Reviews and sales of books on all aspects of Greece can be found at:
www.hellenicbookservice.com
Everything about Athens buses is at:
www.oasa.gr
Seagoing schedules are available at:
www.gtp.gr
Buying ferry tickets online and don't just want individual company sites?
www.ticket.gr
www.goferry.gr
For general tourist information and links have a look at:
www.greecetravel.com
The Ministry of Culture site has impressive coverage of most of the country's museums, archaeological sites and remote monuments on:
www.culture.gr
Who's on strike in Greece this week/month? Find out at:
www.apergia.gr
Want to buy CDs of Greek music? Go to:
www.xilouris.gr
All the Greek reptiles and amphibians are at:
www.herpetofauna.gr
All the naturist beaches – which usually happen to be the best ones – are on:
http://www.barefoot.info/greekgde.html

Weights and Measures

Greece is completely metric, though land is measured and sold in strémmata (1,000 sq metres/ 10,764 sq ft).

What to Bring

Clothes

Summer visits entail only lightweight, casual clothing. Add a pullover or thin jacket and you will be prepared for the occasional cool night breeze or ferry ride. Lightweight shoes and sandals are ideal in the summer, but you will also need a pair of comfortable walking shoes. If you plan to do any hiking in the mountains or on the islands, bring sturdy, broken-in, over-the-ankle boots with a good tread; leather will be more comfortable in the summer heat than synthetic materials.

In general, both Greeks and tourists dine in casual dress but even in the hottest weather, Athenian men won't wear shorts. Scuffed shoes, ripped jeans, shirt-tails being out or visibly out-of-date clothing are all considered offensive. You will only need formal dress if you plan to go to fancy establishments, casinos

or formal affairs. If you visit Greece during the winter, which can be surprisingly cold, bring the kind of clothes you would wear during spring in the northern US or Central Europe.

Toiletries

Most international brands are widely available, except on the smallest islands. Feminine hygiene products are more likely to be sold in supermarkets than pharmacies.

Sun protection

A hat, sun cream and sunglasses are highly recommended for protection from the intense midday sun (sophisticated sun creams of up to SPF50 are widely available).

Electrical Adaptation

220v AC is the standard electric current throughout Greece. Non-dual-voltage shavers and hair dryers from North America should be left at home in favour of versatile travel models – they can be bought on the spot in Greece. Greek plugs are the standard round, two-pin European continental type, different from those in North America and the UK; plug adaptors for American appliances are easy to find, three-to-two-pin adaptors for UK appliances much less so, so these are best purchased before departure.

Universal plug

Greek basins often aren't equipped with plugs, so if you want water in your sink, a universal plug is essential.

Torch/Flashlight

If you're planning a trip to one of the islands, pack a torch, as walking home from the taverna can be tricky if there's no moon.

Women Travellers

Lone female visitors may still be targeted for attention by predatory Greek males, especially around beach bars and after-hours clubs, but, in general, machismo is no more a problem here than anywhere else in Southern Europe. Greek women have much more sexual freedom than previously, especially in the cities. There is now little controversy in their spending time with their male counterparts, up to and including cohabiting before (or instead of) marriage.

In remote areas, many Greeks are still highly traditional and may find it hard to understand why you are travelling alone. You will not feel comfortable in their all-male cafés.

LANGUAGE

UNDERSTANDING THE LANGUAGE

The Greek Language

Modern Greek is the outcome of gradual evolution undergone by the Greek language since the Classical period (5th–4th centuries BC). The language is still relatively close to Ancient Greek: it uses the same alphabet and much of the same vocabulary, though the grammar – other than the retention of the three genders – is considerably streamlined. Many people speak English, some very well, but even attempting a few words in Greek will always be appreciated.

Pronunciation tips

Most of the sounds of Greek aren't difficult to pronounce for English speakers. There are only six vowel sounds: *a, e, i, o, u,* and *y* are consistently pronounced as shown in the table opposite. The letter s is usually pronounced "s", but "z" before an m or g. The sound represented here as *th* is always pronounced as in "thin", not "that"; the first sound in "that" is represented by *d*. Note that "x" is always pronounced as "ks" at the start of a word, not as "z". The "r" is slightly rolled, as in Scottish.

The only difficult sounds are *h,* which is pronounced like the "ch" in Scottish "loch" (we render this as *kh* after "s" so that you don't generate "sh"), and g before e or i, which has no equivalent in English – it's somewhere between the "y" in "yet" and the "g" in "get".

The position of the stress in words is of critical importance, as homonyms abound, and Greeks will often fail to understand you if you don't stress the right syllable (compare *psýllos*, "flea" with *psilós*, "tall"). In this guide, stress is marked by a simple accent mark (´), except for single-syllable words, which are, however, still stressed.

Greek word order is flexible, so you may often hear phrases in a different order from the one in which they are given here. Like the French, the Greeks use the plural of the second person when addressing someone politely. We have used the polite (formal) form throughout this language section, except where an expression is specified as "informal".

Our Transliteration System

In Greece, all town and village names on road signs, as well as most street names, are written in Greek and the Roman alphabets. There's no universally accepted system of transliteration into Roman, and in any case, the Greek authorities are gradually replacing old signs with new ones that use a slightly different system. This means you will have to get used to seeing different spellings of the same place on maps and signs and in this book.

Below is the transliteration scheme we have used in this book: beside each Greek letter or pair of letters is the Roman letter(s) we have used. Next to that is a rough approximation of the sound in an English word.

NB: the Greek letter have come out wrong here but obviously they have not changed so tell the typesetter to leave them as they are.

A	α	**a**	cat
B	β	**v**	vote
Γ	γ	**g/y**	**g**ot *except before "e" or "i", when it is nearer to* **y**acht, *but rougher*
Δ	δ	**d**	**th**en
E	ε	**e**	egg
Z	ζ	**z**	zoo
H	η	**i**	ski
Θ	θ	**th**	thin
I	ι	**i**	ski
K	κ	**k**	kiss
Λ	λ	**l**	long
M	μ	**m**	man
N	ν	**n**	no
Ξ	ξ	**x**	taxi
O	ο	**o**	road
Π	π	**p**	pen
P	ρ	**r**	room
Σ	σ/ς	**s**	set *or* chari**s**ma
T	τ	**t**	tea
Y	υ	**y**	mildly
Φ	φ	**f**	fish
X	χ	**h**	loch
Ψ	ψ	**ps**	maps
Ω	ω	**o**	road
αι	αι	(ai)	hay
αυ	αυ	(au)	**av/af** have/raffle
ει	ει	(ei)	**i**	ski
ευ	ευ	(eu)	**ev/ef** ever/left
οι	οι	(oi)	**i**	ski
ου	ου	(ou)	**ou** tourist
γγ	γγ	(gg)	**ng** long
γκ	γκ	(gk)	**ng** long
ΓΞ	γξ	(gx)	**nx** anxious
μπ	μπ	(mp)	**b** beg
		or	**mb** limber
NT	ντ	(nt)	**d** dog
		or	**nd** under
TZ	τζ	(tz)	**tz** fads

Emergencies

Help! Voíthia!
Stop! Stamatíste!
I've had an accident Íha éna at'yhima
Call a doctor Fonáxte éna yiatró
Call an ambulance Fonáxte éna asthenofóro
Call the police Fonáxte tin astynomía
Call the fire brigade Fonáxte tous pyrozvéstes
Where's the telephone? Pou íne to tiléfono?
Where's the nearest hospital? Pou íne to pio kondinó nosokomío?
There's been a theft Égine mia klopí

Communication

Good morning kaliméra
Good evening kalispéra
Good night kaliníhta
Hello/Goodbye yiásas (informal: yiásou)
Pleased to meet you hárika
Yes ne
No óhi
Thank you efharistó
You're welcome parakaló
Please parakaló
Okay/All right endáxi
Excuse me (to get attention) me synhoríte
Excuse me (to get past) syngnómi
Please write it down for me Na mou to gráfete parakaló?
How are you? Ti kánete? (informal: Ti kánis?)
Fine, and you? Kalá, esís?(informal: Kalá, esí?)
Cheers/Our health! (when drinking) Yiámas!
Could you help me? Boríte na me voithísete?
Can you show me Boríte na mou díxete...
I want... Thélo...
I don't know Den xéro
I don't understand Den katálava
Do you speak English? Miláte angliká?
Can you please speak more slowly? Parakaló, miláte sigá-sigá?
Please say that again Parakaló, xanapésteto
Here edó
There ekí
What? ti?
When? póte?
Why? yiatí?
Where? pou?
How? pos?

Telephone Calls

the telephone to tiléfono

phonecard tilekárta
May I use the phone, please? Boró na tilefoníso, parakaló?
Hello (on the phone) Embrós/Oríste
My name is... Légome...
Could I speak to... Boró na milíso me...
Wait a moment Periménete mía stigmí
I didn't hear Den ákousa

In the Hotel

Do you have a vacant room? Éhete domátio?
I've booked a room Ého kratísi éna domátio
I'd like... Tha íthela...
a single/double room éna monóklino/díklino
double bed dipló kreváti
a room with a bath/shower éna domátio me bánio/dous
One night éna vrádi
Two nights d'yo vradiá
How much is it? Póso káni?
Do you have a room with a sea-view? Éhete domátio me théa pros ti thálassa?
Is there a balcony? Éhi balkóni?
Is the room heated/air-conditioned? To domátio éhi thérmansi/klimatismó?
Is breakfast included? Mazí me to proinó?
Can I see the room please? Boró na do to domátio, parakaló?
The room is too hot/cold/small To domátio íne polý zestó/krýo/mikró
It's too noisy Éhi polý thóryvo
Could you show me another room, please? Boríte na mou díxete állo domátio, parakaló?
I'll take it Tha to páro
Can I have the bill, please? Na mou kánete to logariasmó, parakaló?
key klidí
towel petséta
sheet sendóni
blanket kouvérta
pillow maxilári
soap sapoúni
hot water zestó neró
toilet paper hartí toualéttas

At a Bar or Café

bar/café bar/kafenío (or kafetéria)
patisserie zaharoplastío
I'd like... Tha íthela...
a (Greek) coffee éna (ellinikó) kafé
filter coffee gallikó kafé/kafé fíltro
instant coffee neskafé (or nes)
cappuccino kapoulsíno
white (with milk) me gála
black (without milk) horís gála
with sugar me záhari
without sugar horís záhari
a cup of tea éna tsái

tea with lemon éna tsái me lemóni
orange/lemon soda mía portokaláda/lemonáda
fresh orange juice éna hymó portokáli
a glass/bottle of water éna potíri/ boukáli neró
with ice me pagáki
an ouzo/brandy éna oúzo/koniák
a beer (draught) mía býra (apó varélli)
an ice-cream éna pagotó
a pastry, cake mía pásta (oriental pastries baklavá/kataïfí)

In a Restaurant

Have you got a table for... Éhete trapézi yiá...
There are (four) of us ímaste (tésseres)
I'm a vegetarian íme hortofágos
Can we see the menu? Boroúme na doúme ton katálogo?
We want to order Théloume na parangíloume
Have you got wine by the carafe? Éhete krasí hýma?
a litre/half-litre éna klló/misó kilo of white/red wine áspro/kókkino krasí
Would you like anything else? Thélete típot' állo?
No, thank you óhi, efharistó
glass potíri
knife/fork/spoon mahéri/piroúni/ koutáli
plate piáto
napkin hartopetséta
Where is the toilet? Pou íne i toualétta?
The bill, please to logariasmó, parakaló

Food

Mezédes/Orektiká

taramosaláta fish-roe dip
tzatzíki yoghurt-garlic cucumber dip
melitzánes aubergines
kafterí tomato and féta dip
kolokythákia courgettes
loukánika sausages
tyrokafterí soft cheese seasoned with hot peppers
tyropitákia small cheese pies
antsoúgies anchovies
eliés olives
dolmádes rice-stuffed vine leaves
saganáki fried cheese
fáva puréed fava beans

Meat Dishes

kréas any meat
arní lamb
hirinó pork
gourounópoulo suckling pig
kotópoulo chicken

Ordering Drinks

býra **beer**
krasí **wine**
áspro **white wine**
kokkinélli **rosé wine**
mávro **red wine**
me to kiló **wine by the kilo**
hýma **bulk, from the barrel**
neró **water**
retsína **resin-flavoured wine**
oúzo **aniseed-flavoured grape-pressing distillate**
rakí **another distilled spirit from vintage crushings**
tsípouro **north-mainland version of rakí**
tsikoudiá **Cretan version of rakí, flavoured with terebinth**
portokaláda **orangeade**
lemonáda **lemonade**

moskhári **veal, beef**
psitó **roast or grilled**
sto foúrno **roast**
sta kárvouna **grilled**
soúvlas **on the spit**
souvláki **meat cubes on skewers**
kokinistó **stewed in tomato sauce**
avgolémono **egg-lemon sauce**
tiganitó **fried**
kapnistó **smoked**
brizóla **(pork or veal) chop**
païdákia **lamb chops**
pantsétta **pork belly**
sykóti **liver**
kymás **mince**
biftéki **burger (without bun)**
keftédes **meat-balls**
kokorétsi **grilled sheep's entrails**
soutzoukákia **rissoles baked in red sauce**
yiouvarlákia **mince-and-rice balls in egg lemon sauce**
makarónia **spaghetti**
mousakás **lamb and aubergine bake**
piláfi **rice**
me kymá **with minced meat**
me sáltsa **with tomato sauce**
kléftiko **baked lamb**
pastitsáda **braised beef (or cockerel) in spiced tomato sauce**
pastítsio **macaroni with minced meat**
sofríto **veal (or rabbit) in white wine**
spétzofäi **sausage, aubergine and green pepper dish**
stifádo **beef (or rabbit) stewed with small onions**
gýros me pítta **doner kebab**
domátes yemistés **stuffed tomatoes**
piperiés yemistés **stuffed peppers**

Seafood

frésko **fresh**
katapsygméno **frozen**
psári **fish**
óstraka **shellfish**
xifías **swordfish**
koliós **mackerel**
barboúnia **red mullet**
sardélles **sardines**
gávros **fresh anchovy**
marídes **picarel**
mýdia **mussels**
strídia **oysters**
kalamarákia **squid**
soupiés **cuttlefish**
htapódi **octopus**
garídes **prawns**
astakós **lobster**

Vegetables

angináres **artichokes**
arakás **peas**
domátes **tomatoes**
fakés **brown lentils**
fasólia/fasoláda **stewed white beans**
fasolákia (fréska) **green beans, in tomato sauce**
yígandes **stewed butter-beans**
hórta **misc. boiled greens**
hortópitta **vegetable pie**
karóto **carrot**
kolokythákia **courgettes**
kounoupídi **cauliflower**
koukiá **broad beans**
kremídi **onion**
láhano **cabbage**
maroúli **lettuce**
pandzária **beetroot**
patátes(tiganités/sto foúrno) **potatoes (chips/roast)**
revýthia **chickpeas**
skórdo **garlic**
spanáki **spinach**
spanakópitta **spinach pie**
vlíta **boiled greens**
saláta **salad**
domatosaláta **tomato salad**
angourodomáta **tomato and cucumber salad**
horiátiki **Greek salad**

Fruit

míla **apples**
ver'ykoka **apricots**
banánes **bananas**
kerásia **cherries**
sýka **figs**
stafýlia **grapes**
lemónia **lemons**
pepónia **melons**
portokália **oranges**
rodákina **peaches**
ahládia **pears**
fráoules **strawberries**
karpoúzi **watermelon**

Basic Foods/Desserts

psomí **bread**
aláti **salt**
pipéri **pepper**
ládi **(olive) oil**
xýdi **vinegar**
moustárda **mustard**
voútyro **butter**
tyrí **cheese**
avgá (tiganitá) **(fried) eggs**
omelétta **omelette**
marmeláda **jam, marmalade**
rýzi **rice**
yiaoúrti **yoghurt**
méli **honey**
záhari **sugar**
galaktoboúreko **custard pastry**
halvás **semolina and walnut pudding**
ravaní **semolina and syrup cake**

Sightseeing

information *plirofories*
open/closed *anihtó/klistó*
Can we see the church/archaeological site? *Boroúme na doúme tin eklisía/ta arhéa?*
Where can I find the custodian/key? *Pou boró na vro to fílaka/klidí?*

At the Shops

shop *magazí/katástima*
What time do you open/close? *ti óra aníyete/klínete?*
What would you like? *Oríste/ti thélete?*
I'm just looking *Aplós kilázo*

Numbers

1 *énas/mía/éna (masc/fem/neut)*
2 *dýo*
3 *tris/tría*
4 *tésseres/téssera*
5 *pénde*
6 *éxi*
7 *eptá*
8 *októ*
9 *ennéa*
10 *déka*
11 *éndeka*
12 *dódeka*
13 *dekatrís/dekatría*
14 *dekatésseres/dekatéssera*
15 *dekapénde*
16 *dekaéxi*
17 *dekaeptá*
18 *dekaoktó*
19 *dekaennéa*
20 *íkosi*
30 *triánda*
40 *saránda*
50 *penínda*
60 *exínda*
70 *evdomínda*
80 *ogdónda*
90 *enenínda*
100 *ekató*
200 *dyakósia*
300 *trakósies/trakósia*
400 *tetrakósies/tetrakósia*
500 *pendakósia*
1,000 *hílies/hília*
2,000 *dýo hiliádes*
1 million *éna ekatom'yrio*

How much is it? *Póso káni?*
Do you take credit cards? *Déheste pistotikés kártes?*
Have you got...? *éhete...?*
size (for clothes) *noúmero*
Can I try it on? *Boró na to dokimáso?*
This is faulty. Can I change it? *Aftó éhi éna elátoma. Boró na to aláxo?*
Can I have a refund? *Boró na páro píso ta leftá?*
a kilo *éna kiló*
half a kilo *misókilo*
a quarter *éna tétarto*
two kilos *d'yo kilá*
100 grams *ekató gramária*
200 grams *dyakósia gramária*
more *perisótero*
less *ligótero*
a little/very little *lígo/polý lígo*
with/without *me/horís*
That's enough *ftáni*
That's all *tipot'állo*

Travelling

airport *aerodrómio*
boarding card *kárta epivívasis*
boat *plío/karávi*
bus *leoforío*
bus station *stathmós leoforíon*
bus stop *stási*
coach *poúlman*
ferry *feribót*
first/second class *próti/défteri thési*
flight *ptísi*
hydrofoil *iptámeno*
motorway *ethnikí odós*

Notices

ΤΟΥΑΛΕΤΕΣ	toilets
ΑΝΔΡΩΝ	gentlemen
ΓΥΝΑΙΚΩΝ	ladies
ΑΝΟΙΚΤΟ	open
ΚΛΕΙΣΤΟ	closed
ΕΙΣΟΔΟΣ	entrance
ΕΞΟΔΟΣ	exit
ΑΠΑΓΟΡΕΥΤΑΙ ΕΙΣΟΔΟΣ	no entry
ΕΙΣΙΤΗΡΙΑ	tickets
ΑΠΑΓΟΡΕΥΤΑΙ ΤΟ ΚΑΠΝΙΣΜΑ	no smoking
ΠΛΗΡΟΦΟΡΙΕΣ	information
ΠΡΟΣΟΧΗ	caution
ΚΙΝΔΥΝΟΣ	danger
ΑΡΓΑ	slow
ΔΗΜΟΣΙΑ ΕΡΓΑ	road works
ΠΑΡΚΙΝΓ	parking
ΧΩΡΟΣ ΣΤΑΘΜΕΥΣΕΩΣ	car park
ΑΠΑΓΟΡΕΥΤΑΙ Η ΣΤΑΘΜΕΥΣΗ	no parking
ΤΑΞΙ	taxi
ΤΡΑΠΕΖΑ	bank
ΤΗΛΕΦΩΝΟ	telephone
ΕΚΤΟΣ ΛΕΙΤΟΥΡΓΙΑΣ	out of order

port *limáni*
return ticket *isitírio me epistrofí*
single ticket *apló isitírio*
station *stathmós*
taxi *taxí*
train *tréno*

Public Transport

Can you help me, please? *Boríte na me voithísete, parakaló?*
Where can I buy tickets? *Pou na kopso isitírio?*
At the counter *sto tamío*
Does it stop at... *Káni stási sto...*
You need to change at... *Tha prépi n'aláxete sto...*
When is the next train/bus/ferry to... *Póte févyi to tréno/leoforío/feribót gia...*
How long does the journey take? *Pósi óra káni to taxídi?*
What time will we arrive? *Ti óra tha ftásoume?*
How much is the fare? *Póso káni to isitírio?*
Next stop please *Epómeni stási parakaló*
Can you tell me where to get off? *Tha mou píte pou na katévo?*
delay *kathysterísi*

Directions

right/left *dexiá/aristerá*
Take the first/second right *Párte ton próto/déftero drómo dexiá*
Turn right/left *strípste dexiá/ aristerá*
Go straight on *Tha páte ísia/cfthía*
after the traffic lights *metá ta fanária*
Is it near/far away? *Íne kondá/makriá?*
How far is it? *Póso makriá íne?*
It's five minutes' walk *Íne pénde leptá me ta pódia*
It's ten minutes by car *Íne déka leptá me to avtokínito*
100 metres *ekató métra*
opposite/next to *apénandi/dípla*
junction *diastávrosi*
Where is/are... *Pou íne...*
Where can I find... *Pou boró na vro...*
a petrol station *éna venzinádiko*
a bank *mia trápeza*
a hotel *éna xenodohío?*
How do I get there? *Pos na páo ekí?*
Can you show me where I am on the map? *Boríte na mou díhete sto hárti pou íme?*
Am I on the right road for... *Yia... kalá páo?*

On the Road

Where can I hire a car? *Pou boró na nikiázo avtokínito?*
What is it insured for? *Ti asfália éhi?*
By what time must I return it? *Méhri ti óra prépi na to epistrépso?*
driving licence *díploma*
petrol *venzíni*

(unleaded *amólyvdi)* NB: Possible deletion – irrelevant as all unleaded now.
oil *ládi*
Fill it up *Yemíste to*
My car has broken down *Hálase to avtokinitó mou*
(I've had an accident *Íha éna at'yhima)* NB: Possible deletion, as it's repeated below in Emergencies.
Can you check... *Boríte na elénhete...*
the brakes *ta fréna*
the clutch *to ambrayáz*
the engine *ti mihaní*
the exhaust *ti exátmisi*
the gearbox *tis tahítites*
the headlights *ta fanária*
the tyre(s) *to lástiho/ta lástiha*

Times and Dates

(in the) morning/afternoon/evening *to proí/to apógevma/to vrádi*
(at) night *(ti) níhta*
yesterday *htes*
today *símera*
tomorrow *ávrio*
now *tóra*
early *norís*
late *argá*
a minute *éna leptó*
minutes *leptá*
an hour *mia óra*
a day *mia méra*
a week *mia evdomáda*
(on) Monday *(ti) deftéra*
(on) Tuesday *(tin) tríti*
(on) Wednesday *(tin) tetárti*
(on) Thursday *(tin) pémpti*
(on) Friday *(tin) paraskeví*
(on) Saturday *(to) sávato*
(on) Sunday *(tin) kyriakí*

Health

Is there a chemist's nearby? *Ypárhi éna farmakío edó kondá?*
Which chemist is open all night? *Pio farmakío dianikterévi?*
I don't feel well *Den esthánome kalá*
I'm ill *Íme árostos (feminine árosti)*
Where does it hurt? *Pou ponái?*
It hurts here *Ponái edó*
I have a... *Éxo...*
headache *ponokéfalo*
sore throat *ponólemo*
stomach ache *kiliópono*
Have you got something for travel sickness? *Éhete lípota gia ti navtía?*
Do I need a prescription? *Hriázete syndagí?*
It bit me (of an animal) *Me dágose*
It stung me *Me kéndrise*
bee *mélissa*
wasp *sfíka*
mosquito *kounoúpi*
sticking plaster *lefkoplástis*
diarrhoea pills *hápia gia ti diária*

TRANSPORT · ACCOMMODATION · EATING OUT · ACTIVITIES · A – Z · LANGUAGE

FURTHER READING

Books go in and out of print, or change imprints, with such rapidity of late that we've elected not to list the publishers, except for obscure Greek publishers with no internet presence, or one-off presses with only internet presence. For most titles, conducting a web search with the author and title should suffice to dredge up its current incarnation (which these days may be a Kindle or print-on-demand edition only, or a used copy for a few pennies).

Ancient History and Culture

Greek Religion: Archaic and Classical, by Walter Burkert. Excellent overview of the gods and goddesses, their attributes, worship and the meaning of major festivals.
The Penguin History of Greece, by A.R Burn. A good, single-volume introduction to ancient Greece.
The Greeks and Greek Love, by James Davidson. This "radical reappraisal of homosexuality in ancient Greece" tries to put queerness back at the centre of the ancient social equation and, despite too many bouts of special pleading, gets some way there.
The World of Odysseus, by M.I. Finley. Reissued 1954 standard on just how well (or not) the Homeric sagas are borne out by archaelogical facts.
Alexander the Great, by Robin Lane Fox. A psychobiography wedded to a conventional history.
Dictionary of Classical Mythology, by Pierre Grimal. Still considered to be tops among a handful of available alphabetical gazetteers.
The Greek World, 479–323 BC, by Simon Hornblower. The eventful period from the end of the Persian Wars to Alexander's demise; the standard university text.

Byzantine History and Culture

The Early Centuries, The Apogee and **The Decline** (3 vols), **by** John Julius Byzantium Norwich. The most readable and masterful popular history, by the noted Byzantinologist; also available as one massive volume, **A Short History of Byantium.**
Psellus, Michael Fourteen Byzantine Rulers. That many changes of rule in a single century (10th–11th), as told by a near-contemporary historian.
Art of the Byzantine Era, by David Talbot Rice. Shows how Byzantine sacred craftsmanship extended from the Caucasus into northern Italy, in a variety of media.
Runciman, Steven **The Fall of Constantinople, 1453.** Still the definitive study of an event which continues to exercise modern Greek minds. His **Byzantine Style and Civilization** covers art, culture and monuments.
The Orthodox Church, by Archbishop Kallistos Ware. Good introduction to what was, until recently, the de facto established religion of modern Greece.

Anthropology and Culture

Honor, family and patronage: A study of institutions and moral values in a Greek mountain community, by John Campbell. Classic study of Sarakatsáni shepherds in the Zagorian Píndos, with much wider application to Greece in general, which got the author banned from the area by touchy officialdom.
The Death Rituals of Rural Greece, by Loring H. Danforth and Alexander Tsiaras. Riveting, annotated photo essay on Greek funeral customs.
Portrait of a Greek Mountain Village, by Juliet Du Boulay. Ambéli, a mountain village in Évvia, as it was in the mid-1960s.
Road to Rembetika: Songs of Love, Sorrow and Hashish (Denise Harvey, Límni, Évvia), by Gail Holst. Introduction to the enduringly popular musical form; with translated lyrics and discographies.
The Modern Greek Language, by Peter Mackridge. In-depth analysis by one of the foremost scholars of the tongue's evolution. His more recent Language and National Identity in Greece, 1766–1976 is a masterful yet easily readable study of the language controversy in all its ramifications, especially the mutually reinforcing dynamic of Greek self-perception and how elites and masses chose to express themselves.
Festive Greece: A Calendar of Tradition, by John L. Tomkinson. Copiously photographed calendar of all the extant rites of the Orthodox Church, their pagan substrata erupting frequently and vividly at popular *panigýria*.

Cuisine

Siren Feasts, by Andrew Dalby. Analysis of Classical and Byzantine texts shows just how little Greek food has changed in three millennia.
Mediterranean Seafood, by Alan Davidson. 1972 classic, redone in 2012, that's still the standard reference, guaranteed to end every argument as to just what that fish is on your tavérna plate. Complete with recipes.
Real Greek Food, by Theodore Kyriakou and Charles Campion. The latest cookery book, part authored by the founder of London's Real Greek and Souvlaki restaurants. Beautifully illustrated.
The Wines of Greece, by Konstantinos Lazarakis. An overview, current to late 2005, of what's happening in Greece's eleven recognized wine-producing regions.

Modern History

Greece, The Hidden Centuries: Turkish Rule from the Fall of Constantinople to Greek Independence, by David Brewer. Refreshingly revisionist, new work on the "Turkokratia", uniformly dismissed in standard (and nationalist) narratives as a new dark ages but here put in proper perspective.
Twice a Stranger: How Mass Expulsion Forged Modern Greece and Turkey, by Bruce Cark. Nearly a century after the compulsory population exchanges, both nations are still engaged in digesting the episode

– with many on both sides recognising it as a mistake,. More thorough on the experience of Orthodox refugees coming to Greece, but still invaluable.
A Concise History of Greece, by Richard Clogg. Clear and lively account of Greece from Byzantine times to 2012, with helpful maps and well-captioned artwork. The best single-volume summary.
Greece: A Jewish History, by K. E. Fleming. The title is carefully chosen; one of the main points here is that local Jews only identified primarily as Greeks after the Nazi deportations – before that, they tended to identify with their hometown and its often indiosyncratic customs.
Greece, the Modern Sequel: From 1831 to the Present, by John Koliopoulos and Thanos Veremis. Thematic and psycho-history of the independent nation, tracing trends, first principles and setbacks.
Salonica: City of Ghosts, by Mark Mazower. A lucid account of this extraordinary city from 1430 to 1950, as Christians, Muslims and Jews came together and prospered, before man and nature tore it apart.
I Was Born Greek, by Melina Mercouri. The tumultuous life and times of Greece's most famous actress, written in 1971 while she was in exile from the junta.
The Greeks: The Land and People Since the War, by James Pettifer. Useful general introduction to politics, family life, food, tourism and other contemporary topics.
Modern Greece: A Short History, by C.M. Woodhouse. Spans the period from early Byzantium to the early 1980s. His classic **The Struggle for Greece, 1941–1949**, reissued by C. Hurst (London), is perhaps the best overview of that turbulent decade.

Modern Greek Literature

An Introduction to Modern Greek, by Roderick Beaton. Readable survey of Greek literature since independence.
An Anthology of Modern Greek Poetry, by **Nanos Valaoritis and Thanasis Maskaleris.** English-only text, but excellent biographical info on the poets and good renditions by two native Greek speakers.
Collected Poems, by C.P. Cavafy. trans. by Edmund Keeley and Philip Sherrard or The Complete Poems of Cavafy, trans. by Rae Dalven. The two "standard" versions available in English; newer 2007 translations by Evangelos Sachperoglou and Stratis Haviaris will also be of interest but

don't break radically new ground.
The Axion Esti, Selected Poems and **The Sovereign Sun, by** Odysseus Elytis. Pretty much the complete works of the Nobel laureate, in translation.
Little Infames, by Panos Karnezis. This collection of short stories is set in his native Peloponnese during the late 1950s and early 1960s; **The Maze** is a darker, more successful novel concerning the Asia Minor Catastrophe. Both display a penchant for old-fashioned plot twists – or excessive whimsical magical realism, depending on point of view. **The Birthday Party** is based on the life of Aristotle Onassis and daughter Christina. Karnezis grew up in Greece, but lives in London, writing in English; however, his concerns remain resolutely Greek.
Zorba the Greek, by Nikos Kazantzakis. This is a surprisingly dark and nihilistic work, worlds away from the crude, two-dimensional character of the film; **The Last Temptation of Christ** provoked riots by Orthodox fanatics in Athens in 1989; **Report to Greco** explores his Cretanness/Greekness; while **Christ Recrucified** (published in the US as The Greek Passion) encompasses the Easter drama within Christian-Muslim dynamics on Crete. Nobel laureate, woolly Marxist fellow traveller and self-imposed exile, Kazantzakis embodies the old maxim that classics are books praised but generally unread. Whether in intricate, untranslatable Greek or wooden English, Kazantzakis can be hard going.
Red Dyed Hair, by Kostas Mourselas. Politically incorrect picaresque saga of urban life from the 1950s to the 1970s among a particularly feckless *paréa*; the Greek original still sells well, and formed the basis of popular TV series.
The Murderess, by Alexandros Papadiamantis; trans. Peter Levi. Landmark novel, set on Skiáthos at the turn of the 19th/20th centuries.
Father Dancing (published as *A Crowded Heart* in the US), by Nick Papandreou. Thinly disguised, page-turning roman-à-clef by the late prime minister's younger son; Papandreou père comes across as an egotistical monster.
Exile and Return, Selected Poems 1967–74, by Yannis Ritsos. The outcome of junta-era internal exile on Sámos for Greece's foremost Communist poet.
Collected Poems 1924–55; Complete Poems, by George Seferis;

trans. Edmund Keeley. The former has Greek-English texts on facing pages and is preferable to the so-called "complete" works of Greece's other Nobel literary laureate.
Farewell Anatolia, by Dido Sotiriou. A best-selling classic since its appearance in 1962, this traces the end of the Greeks in Asia Minor from 1914 to 1922, using a character based on the author's father.
Drifting Cities, by Stratis Tsirkas; trans. Kay Cicellis. Welcome paperback re-issue of this epic novel on wartime leftist intrigue in Alexandria, Cairo and Jerusalem.
An Anthology of Modern Greek Poetry, by Nanos Valaoritis and Thanasis Maskaleris. English-only text, but excellent biographical info on the poets and good renditions by two native Greek speakers.
Z, by Vassilis Vassilikos. Based closely enough on the assassination of leftist MP Grigoris Lambrakis in 1963 by royalist thugs to get the book – and author – banned by the colonels' junta.

Foreign Writers in/on Greece

The Flight of Ikaros, by Kevin Andrews. An educated, sensitive, Anglo-American archaeologist wanders the back-country in surprising freedom as the civil war winds down. Despite the massive changes since, still one of the best books on the country.
A Foreign Wife, A Fair Exchange and **Aphrodite and the Others**, by Gillian Douras. Scottish-Australian marries Greek-Australian, then consents to return to the "mother" country; the resulting trilogy is about the best of many chronicles of the acculturation experience.
Captain Corelli's Mandolin, by Louis De Bernières. Heart-rending tragicomedy set on occupied Kefaloniá during World War II which has acquired cult status and long-term best-seller-list tenancy since its appearance in 1994.
Prospero's Cell and **Reflections on a Marine Venus, by** Lawrence Durrell. Corfu in the 1930s, and Rhodes in 1945–47, now looking rather old-fashioned, alcohol-fogged and patronising of the "natives", but still entertaining enough.
The Magus, by John Fowles. Best-seller, inspired by author's spell teaching on Spétses during the 1950s, of post-adolescent manipulation, conspiracy and cock-teasing (ie, the usual Fowles obsessions).

North of Ithaka, by Eleni Gage. Eleni is the namesake and granddaughter of the Eleni, whose murder her son Nicholas set out to avenge *(see below)*. A New York journalist, she "took leave" for most of 2002 in her grandmother's village in Epirus, rebuilding the family house and more.
Eleni, by Nicholas Gage. Epirus-born American correspondent returns to Greece to avenge the death of his mother at the hands of a Communist firing squad in 1948.
Falconera, by Alexis Ladas. Ripping good yarn, with plenty of Boy's Own action (but some convincingly well-written un-Boy's Own sex), telling in part of a daring raid to interfere with Germany resupply of Crete by the British-supported Greek Raiding Schooner Flotilla, in which the author served.
Travels in Northern Greece and Mani, by Leigh Fermor and Patrick Roumeli. Written during the late 1950s and early 1960s, before the advent of mass tourism, these remain some of the best compendia of the then already-vanishing customs and relict communities of the mainland.
This Way to Paradise: Dancing on the Tables, by Willard Manus. An American expatriate's affectionate summing-up of 40-plus years living in Líndos, from its innocence to its corruption. Wonderful anecdotes of the hippie days, and walk-on parts for the famous and infamous.
The Colossus of Maroussi, by Henry Miller. Miller takes to Corfu, the Argolid, Athens and Crete of 1939 with the enthusiasm of a first-timer in Greece who's found his element; deserted archaelogical sites and larger-than-life personalities.
The Unwritten Places, by Tim Salmon. Veteran Hellenophile describes his love affair with the Greek mountains, and the Vlach pastoral communities of Epirus in particular.
The Summer of my Greek Taverna, by Tom Stone. Set in a thinly disguised Kámbos of early-1980s Pátmos, this is a poignant cautionary tale for all who've ever fantasised about leasing a taverna (or buying a property) in the islands.
Dinner with Persephone, by Patricia Storace. New York poet resident a year in Athens successfully takes the pulse of modern Greece, with all its shibboleths, foundation myths, carefully nurtured self-image and rampant misogyny. Very funny, and spot-on.
Traveller's Greece: Memories of an Enchanted Land, by John Tomkinson. 17th–19th-century traveller's impressions of islands and mainland, ranging from the enraptured to the appalled.

Eurydice Street, by Sofka Zinovieff. An anthropologist and journalist by training, Zinovieff first came to Greece in the early 1980s (contributing to the first Insight Guide Greece), then returned in 2001 with her Greek husband and two daughters to live in Athens. With sharp insights on nationalism, Orthodoxy, politics, 17 November and leisure (among various topics), this is the best single account of life in contemporary urban Greece – tellingly, translated into Greek. Her more recent debut novel, The House on Paradise Street, is a gripping exploration of the lingering effects of the civil war and its aftermath in contemporary Greece, and a good family drama.

Regional and Archaelogical Guides

Anagnosis Guides (www.anagnosis.gr) Several well-illustrated guides to Athens and surroundings that highlight the obscure, unorthodox and overlooked, with directions to cited sites.
The Living Past of Greece, by A.R. and Mary Burn. Worth toting its oversized format around for the sake of lively text and clear plans; covers most major sites from Minoan to medieval.
Byzantine and Medieval Greece, by Paul Hetherington. Erudite and authoritative dissection of the castles

Send Us Your Thoughts

We do our best to ensure the information in our books is as accurate and up-to-date as possible. The books are updated on a regular basis using local contacts, who painstakingly add, amend and correct as required. However, some details (such as telephone numbers and opening times) are liable to change, and we are ultimately reliant on our readers to put us in the picture.

We welcome your feedback, especially your experience of using the book "on the road". Maybe we recommended a hotel that you liked (or another that you didn't), or you came across a great bar or new attraction we missed.

We will acknowledge all contributions, and we'll offer an Insight Guide to the best letters received.

Please write to us at:
Insight Guides
PO Box 7910
London SE1 1WE
Or email us at:
insight@apaguide.co.uk

and churches of the mainland; his *The Greek Islands: Byzantine and Medieval Buildings* is also invaluable, but has some strange omissions.
Various walking guides by Lance Chilton. Short but detailed guide-lets to the best walks around various mainland and island no-frills airline destinations, accompanied by maps. See the full list of 15 titles and order from: www.marengowalks.com
The Mountains of Greece: Trekking in the Pindhos Mountains, by Tim Salmon. The best routes on the northern mainland (including Zagóri, and isolated Mt Ólymbos), with schematic maps and some GPS data.
The High Mountains of Crete: White Mountains, Psiloritis & Lassithi Ranges, by Lorraine Wilson. The best of several guides to the island, with nearly 100 hikes of all levels, described by the most experienced foreign trek leader. Sketch maps are minimal – you'll need an additional commercial product from Anavasi Publications.

Botanical Field Guides

Greek Wildflowers and Plant Lore in Ancient Greece, by Helmut Baumann. As the title says; lots of interesting ethnobotanical trivia, useful photos.
Flowers of Greece and the Aegean, by Anthony Huxley and William Taylor. The only volume dedicated to both islands and mainland, with good photos, though taxonomy is now a bit obsolete.
Flowers of Greece and the Balkans, by Oleg Polunin et al. This book is also showing its age, but again has lots of colour photos to aid identification.
Flowers of the Mediterranean, by Oleg Polunin and Anthony Huxley. Lots of colour plates to aid in identification, and includes flowering shrubs; recent printings have a table of taxonomic changes.

Other Insight Guides

Insight Guides cover nearly 200 destinations, providing information on culture and all the top sights, as well as superb photography and detailed maps. Other Insight Guides to destinations in the region include Greek Islands and Turkey.
Insight **FlexiMaps** and TravelMaps are designed to complement our guidebooks. They provide full mapping of major destinations, and their easy-to-fold, laminated finish gives them ease of use and durability. The range of Greek titles include Athens and Crete.

CREDITS

Insight Guide Credits

Distribution

UK
Dorling Kindersley Ltd
A Penguin Group company
80 Strand, London, WC2R 0RL
customerservice@dk.com

United States
Ingram Publisher Services
1 Ingram Boulevard, PO Box 3006,
La Vergne, TN 37086-1986
ips@ingramcontent.com

Australia
Universal Publishers
PO Box 307
St Leonards NSW 1590
sales@universal
publishers.com.au

New Zealand
Brown Knows Publications
11 Artesia Close, Shamrock Park
Auckland, New Zealand 2016
sales@brownknows.co.nz

Worldwide
Apa Publications GmbH & Co. Verlag
KG (Singapore branch)
7030 Ang Mo Kio Avenue 5
08-65 Northstar @ AMK
Singapore 569880
apasin@singnet.com.sg

Printing
CTPS-China

© 2013 Apa Publications (UK) Ltd
All Rights Reserved

First Edition 1987
Sixth Edition 2013

www.insightguides.com

Project Editor
Carine Tracanelli

Art Editor
Shahid Mahmood

Picture Editor
Tom Smyth

Map Production
Original cartography Berndtson &
Berndtson, updated by Apa
Cartography Department

Production
Tynan Dean and Rebeka Ellam

914.95

INS

MAR 2014

INDEX

Venezia

Durrës
Tiranë

FYROM
(MACEDONIA)

Elbasan
Bitola

1179
Mavrovou

Ancona, Bari

ALBANIA

Límni Mikrá
Préspa

Flórina
Édessa

Vérnon
Óros

Brindisi

Vlorë

ITALY

Kozáni

Véria

Aliakmonas

Katerini

Grevená

Tymfi
2497

Zagori

Vória Pindos

Óros
2917
Olympos
Ólympos

Pinios

Thes

Ha

La

Kérkyra

Ioánnina

Elasóna

Thermekós Kólpos

Kérkyra
(Corfu)

Igoumenítsa

Aranthos

Kalambáka

Tríkala

G

R

Lárisa

Pílion
Pílio Óros

Paxí
(Páxos)
Andípaxi

Árta

Notia Pindos

Kardítsa

Vólos

Preveza

Tehnití Límni
Kremastón

Tymfristós
2315

Fársala

S

Lefkáda

Lefkáda
(Léfkas)

Meganísi

Agrínio

Óri Vardoúsia

Lamía

Ag. Konsta

Kefaloniá
(Cephalonia)

Ithǎki

Aslakós

Náfpaktos

Ámfissa

Livadiá

Argostóli

Póros

Pátra

Korinthiakós Kólpos

Palovouna
1748

Ionian Islands

Kyllíni

2224

Kórinthos

Árgos

IONIAN

Zákynthos
(Zante)

Zákynthos

Pýrgos

Peloponnisos
(Peloponnese)

Náfplio

Argolikós
Kólpos

Spétse

SEA

Trípoli

Spárti

Pláka

(

Taygetos

Párno

Kalamáta

Gýthio

Ar

Lakonikós
Kólpos

Neápoli

MEDITERRANEAN   SEA

Kýthira

Kýthira

N

Andikýthira

La

(Kiss

Pa

Greece: Physical and Main Ferry Routes

0   50 km

0   50 miles